Investigating Economics

Investigating Economics

Brinley Davies

Geoff Hale

Charles Smith

Henry Tiller

MACMILLAN

First published 1996 by
MACMILLAN PRESS LTD
Houndmills, Basingstoke, Hampshire RG21 6XS
and London
Companies and representatives
throughout the world

ISBN 0-333-63808-5

A catalogue record for this book is available
from the British Library.

10	9	8	7	6	5	4	3	2	1
05	04	03	02	01	00	99	98	97	96

Printed in Great Britain by
Butler and Tanner, Frome & London

Dedication

Astrid, Margareta, Henry
Janet, Christopher, Kirsten
Julia, Sally, Matthew
Ead, Amy, Jenny, Lydia

Investigating Economics
Contents

Preface

Welcome to Investigating Economics, a new book specifically designed for a new approach to economics.

For too long, many young people have been turned off economics by the mistaken notion that the study of the subject is purely an exercise in intellectual gymnastics: elegant, but useless. We reject this idea, and our aim is to enable the student to think like an economist, act like an economist, and be an economist.

It is our firm belief that, as an economist, you need to be able to use economics as a tool in carrying out investigations. So rather than attempt to give you a vague acquaintance with esoteric theory, our aim is to give you a thorough knowledge of basic concepts and principles, and to show you how these essentially simple ideas can be used to help analyse complex problems.

The topics cover the syllabuses of all the 'A' Level examining boards, together with equivalent examinations such as the International Baccalaureate. The book should also be useful to students on GNVQ, first year degree, HND, and part-time MBA courses who require an introduction to the basic framework of the subject, together with a practical, issues-based approach to investigating economics.

As companion books, Investigating Economics and Investigating Business together provide the complete solution for entry-level courses in this field. Whether you are a teacher or student, we hope that you will enjoy working with this material; and the authors would be pleased to receive feedback from you, the reader and user.

Each chapter begins with a 'focus' which sets the scene by raising an issue; as the chapter progresses economic principles are introduced to show how economists, as economists, can contribute to debate of the issue in question and related topics. Illustrative material and real-world data are used throughout, together with review questions and examination practice. A Teacher's Guide is available from the publisher.

No previous knowledge of economics is assumed when you pick up this book; and as you work through the chapters a pattern will be discernible, as you view economic issues, problems and decisions at different 'levels': personal, business, national, international and global. We give special attention to current themes of debate, such as the issue of privatisation versus public ownership, the role of the state, and what markets can and cannot be expected to achieve.

Our wide choice of source material is intended to encourage the modern student to develop a critical and informed awareness of such themes and debates.

To students, we say good luck on your economics course. Just like any other subject at this level, the study of economics requires you to do some work; but you will find that work put in is more than matched by the rewards that come out. Investigative economics is more than hard work, it is fun! As teachers and examiners ourselves it is our greatest wish that you should enjoy your economics and do really well in your examinations.

Spring 1996

Acknowledgements

The authors owe thanks to the team of reviewers who have advised on this project from its earliest planning stages and throughout its writing. These experienced teachers and examiners are Nigel Carr, Christopher Dent, Richard Flockhart, Stuart Luker, Clive Pearson and Tilly Watson. Their advice has been invaluable in shaping our ideas and improving each chapter in draft form; but since we have on occasion ignored advice they can take credit for any strengths of the resulting work, while escaping any blame for any weaknesses. We are grateful for the support and guidance of the Macmillan team at Basingstoke, particularly Jane Powell (whose patience has at times been stretched beyond all reasonable limits), Stephen Rutt, Tracy France and their secretarial staff Pearl Jeffery and Gloria Hart together with Keith Povey's editing associates at Bratton Clovelly and various locations. Again we stress that any errors and omissions are the responsibility of the authors alone.

The authors and publishers wish to thank the following for permission to use copyright material:

Philip Allan Publishers for material from S. Ison and G. Hughes, 'Road Transport Congestion', *Economic Review*, Vol.II, 2 (Nov. 1993);

Bank of England for material from various issues of the *Bank of England Quarterly Bulletin* and *Inflation Report* and *Bank Briefing*;

The Body Shop International Plc for their trading charter;

The Booksellers Association for an extract from publicity material;

The British Rail Board for material from an information letter concerning an Aslef rail strike;

British Telecom for an advertisement;

Cartermill International Ltd for adapted material from Patrick Minford, *Economic Affairs*, Oct./Nov. 1988, pp.21-6;

The Cooperative Bank plc for an advertisement concerning Base Rate change;

Comet Group PLC for a sale advertisement;

The Economist for article 'From the boozer to the brand palace?', *The Economist*, 13.5.95;

The European for material from various issues of *The European*;

Roger Fajerfjäll for article 'Economists who are out of touch', *The European*, 13-19 Jan. 1995;

First Choice for material from an Olympic Holidays brochure;

Girobank Plc, 49 Park Lane, London, W1Y 4EQ, UK, for a sample illustration of a Rate Change notice;

Going Places for a holiday advertisement;

Guardian News Service Ltd for articles from various issues of *The Guardian* and *The Observer*;

Haymarket Campaign Publications Ltd for material from various issues of *Campaign Report*;

The Controller of Her Majesty's Copyright Office for Crown copyright material;

Hobsons Publishing PLC for extracts from *Economics and Business for the Future*, 1995;

The Institute of Economic Affairs for William C Mitchell, 'Summary of Hobart Paper 109';

Mary and Bruce Large for their letter to *The Guardian*, 5.9.94;

Lord Lawson for an extract from his Bridge Lecture, 1994;

Leyton Orient Football Club Ltd for an extract from their 1995/96 season ticket form;

Librairie Plon for material from François d'Aubert, 'Main basse sur l'Europe' included in *The European*, 6.1.95;

Macmillan Press Ltd for material from Harrison et al, *Introductory Economics*, 1992, and Charles Smith, *Economic Development, Growth and Welfare*, 1994;

Mirror Syndication International for articles from issues of the *Daily Mirror*;

Morning Star for articles from issues of the *Morning Star*;

New Journal Enterprises Ltd for 'Homeless total tops 420,000', *Camden New Journal*, 14.1.93;

Newspapers Publishing PLC for articles from various issues of *The Independent* and *The Independent on Sunday*;

Organisation for Economic Co-operation and Development for OECD data;

P&O European Ferries Ltd for an advertisement;

Reed Business Publishing Ltd for material from their 'Checkout' magazine;

Safeway PLC for their Bonus Card advertisement;

Sainsbury's for an extract from their publicity material;

Socialist Worker for articles from various issues of *Socialist Worker*;

Solo Syndication Ltd for a headline from the *Evening Standard*;

United Nations Development Programme for material from *Human Development Report*, 1992, 1993;

Wilson Sporting Goods Co Ltd for an extract from David Bates, 'Ball Bearings', *Serve and Volley*, Nov. 1994;

Yorkshire Bank for an advertisement concerning Base Rate change.

Questions throughout the text are reproduced by permission of: The University of Cambridge Local Examinations Syndicate; the Associated Examining Board; the University of London Examinations and Assessment Council; the Welsh Joint Education Committee; the Open University; the International Baccalaureate.

Every effort has been made to trace all the copyright holders, but if any have been inadvertently overlooked the publishers will be pleased to make the necessary arrangement at the first opportunity.

Finally, we record our thanks to our families for their encouragement, and this book is dedicated to them.

The Authors

Brinley Davies retired recently as Head of Economics at Worthing Sixth Form College where he taught both Economics and Business Studies. He is an experienced examiner and Item Writer for A Level Objective tests. He has been a reader and editor in educational publishing, and has contributed reviews for the EBEA's *Journal*. He has delivered economics seminars at Citicorp Bank and been involved in post-graduate teacher training. He is the author of five previous books in the fields of economics and business and is currently engaged in preparing training courses for business. He also runs courses aimed at the International English Language Testing System (IELTS) qualification.

Geoff Hale has a long experience as a teacher of Economics with an interest in curriculum development. He participated in the pioneering work which led to the birth of GCSE Economics and became one of the first chief examiners in the subject at this level. More recently he was Chair of the EBEA's Southern Regional Group contributing to the EBEA's 16-19 Economics Education Project and its resulting book: *Core Economics*. He is also Chair of the Southern Branch of the EBEA. He has great experience as an A Level examiner and is currently a member of the subject panel for Economics and Business Studies for the AEB. He has written *Economics in Focus* and contributed reviews for the *TES* and articles for various economics magazines including the EBEA's *Journal* of which he is now Economics Education Editor. Geoff now lives in Hampshire and is Head of Economics at Havant College.

Charles Smith is currently Senior Lecturer in Economics in the Business School at Swansea Institute of Higher Education, where he teaches to degree and postgraduate level. He taught for many years in comprehensive schools and Further Education, and took part in the planning and implementation of several key developments in economics and business education, including GCSE, A/S and GNVQ. He has written a number of books and articles including, for Macmillan, *Introductory Economics* (as co-author) and *Economic Development, Growth and Welfare* (in the *Economics Today* Series). As Chief Examiner in Economics for the International Baccalaureate Organisation, Geneva, he works with a team responsible for examinations in pre-university economics taken in three languages by students all over the world, and has also contributed to teacher-training workshops and educational conferences in countries on five continents. He also has a long working relationship with the Associated Examining Board, Guildford, and is currently one of their Principal Examiners. He is a committee member of the Wales Branch of the Economics and Business Education Association, and was its chairperson for three years.

Henry Tiller teaches Economics at Newham College of Further Education where he is the Course Manager for the GNVQ Advanced and BTEC National Business programmes. He has gained many years of examining experience with the Associated Examining Board, and was the Chief Examiner in A/S level Economics from 1991 to 1996. He is currently the Assessor for the A and S Level Economics examinations, as well as an Item Writer for the A Level Economics Objective Test paper. He is also an Associate Lecturer for the Open University on the second-level degree course, Economics and Changing Economies, and has recently been appointed as Deputy Chief Examiner in Economics for the International Baccalaureate Organisation.

Comments from Readers

'This book provides a comprehensive coverage of the new subject core for A level Economics and of most of the new A level syllabuses. The essential theories are explained, the various controversies confronted and the authors illustrate well how economic theory can be used to help people to make sense of current economic issues and problems. Students will find the inclusion of a wide variety of past A level questions particularly useful.'

Stuart Luker, Chief Examiner
AEB A level Economics

'Investigating Economics has a number of advantages over the older textbooks. Instead of updating old material the book uses modern examples and contemporary newspaper articles. The tables and charts show the effects of the recession of the early 1990's; and the change to economic rationalism. All students should be able to relate to the material easily and make effective use of it. Economics can be a difficult subject, but this book makes it open to all.'

Richard Flockart, formerly at
Rougement School, Newport, Gwent

'The integration of economic theory and its application is particularly impressive in the way that the framework of analysis is always a real economic problem that the reader can relate to. A wide variety of stimulus materials and assessment tests makes learning economics more enjoyable. More significantly, it enables the reader to maintain concentration and stimulates interest. This is a textbook that is clearly written and well organised in the context of the new Advanced Level syllabus and comparative courses. It is a refreshing and welcome addition to the existing library of economics textbooks.'

Tilly Watson, Wakefield District
College

'A comprehensive textbook, ideally suited to the new syllabuses being introduced; it combines a comprehensive coverage of the subject matter with good, up-to-date questions for the students and is written in a manner which will be appealing and understandable by the average 'A' level student. Theoretical matters and applied topics are linked to enable the reader to appreciate how the study of economics relates to the real world.'

N. J. Carr, Brentwood School

Section 1
Fundamentals

1.1 What is Economics?

FOCUS

Scarcity and choices

The world's resources are scarce. Because of this scarcity we have to make choices; in other words, we have to economise. It is because we cannot have everything we want all the time that we need to study a subject called economics.

The INVESTIGATOR

● I ate a couple of my favourite meals over the last year. One of these featured a wonderfully good tête de veau; the other, more recently, was gravadlax with pickled cucumber, followed by grilled fillet of angus beef with glazed shallots, chips, Bearnaise sauce and a side salad, followed by lemon tart. At £23.50 for three courses, £15.50 for lunch, this restaurant provided very good value...

● Thanks to the Salvation Army, Eddy is wearing clean clothes for the first time in months after two years on the streets. Every day we give homeless people throughout the country the comforts you and I take for granted: a hot bath, clean clothes, a hearty meal. This winter, will you reach out to help someone like Eddy? Just £15 could bring a homeless person in from the cold...

● German wines are the cheapest in Britain. The average price of a bottle of German wine in Britain is a sorry £2.42. The corresponding figures for French and Australian wines are £3.49 and £4.04 respectively. Even for regular drinkers of German wine the country has a faintly tacky image; but if you can persuade people to taste the best German wines, it's easy to convert them. £10 will buy you something from a top estate, which cannot be said of France, California or even Australia. At £15.99 from Oddbins, Mussbacher Eselhaust Rieslaner Auslese is a treat. Soft, ripe, and grapefruity with delicious depth and richness...

● This year, Save the Children is seeking to reduce the number of lives lost from preventable diseases like diarrhoea. More than 8000 children suffering from diarrhoea die every day. Many of these lives could be saved for as little as 10 pence, the cost of a sachet of Oral Rehydration salts. So your £10 could save the lives of 100 children...

Preview

In this chapter we shall investigate the following key areas:

● what economics is about;
● economics and social sciences;
● methods of economics;
● tools of economic analysis.

Scarcity

When economists talk about 'scarcity' they are not only referring to the more obvious situations where things are in short supply, such as famine or drought. Even in countries where people are relatively well off, there is still scarcity, in the sense that not all human wants can be satisfied at once. If you won a jackpot in the National Lottery, then (believe it or not) you would still be faced with scarcity: you might have more money than you actually need, but you would still have to choose how to spend your other precious resources, such as your time; and your spending decisions would still affect the use of world resources, which are, by their very nature, limited in supply.

Why study economics?

Let us say that the average weekly wage is £300. In a class of young economists there might be 20 students. If each of these works for 40 years, then total income is

£300 x 20 x 52 x 40
= £12,480,000.

In other words, if you look around your class, you are facing a combined spending power of over 12 million pounds! And this doesn't even allow for inflation, or the possibility that some of you may be budding rock stars or business whiz-kids.

Advertisers are very well aware of the economic importance of the spending power of young people, as you can tell from the way in which many advertisements attempt to target their message at the young, or use 'youthfulness' as a selling point. Large corporations such as banks and insurance companies are also aware of the importance of income during a 'life cycle', and know that if they can capture customers while they are young, they are likely to be theirs for life. When you open your first pay packet (or when you first receive pocket money) you begin to make economic choices, and so a knowledge of economic principles is a vital piece of your intellectual equipment.

You might be surprised, however, to learn that economics is not essentially to do with money. If money, or the lack of it, were really an economic problem, then there would be nothing to stop a government simply printing more money and distributing it as a Christmas gift. This would, of course, be futile, as creating money does not, in itself, create goods and services. And this is the real economic problem: we are not, as a community, short of money; what we are short of are the things which money can buy. These things, goods and services, are in turn in short supply because in order to produce them we need to use resources. This leads us to a definition of economics:

Economics is the study of ways in which people make the best use of scarce resources.

We can look at the 'best use of scarce resources' on different 'levels', as shown in Box 1.1

Economics is the study of ways in which people make the best use of scarce resources.

| BOX 1.1 | **Ends and means: choices and opportunity costs** |

Ends and means: choices and opportunity costs

(a) *Personal level*	(b) *Business level*
CLOTHES	WAGES
FOOD	ADVERTISING
CAR	DIVIDENDS
ENTERTAINMENT	INVEST IN NEW EQUIPMENT
MORTGAGE	RAW MATERIALS

(c) *National level*	(d) *World level*
LAW AND ORDER	HEALTH
NHS	HOUSING
DEFENCE	EDUCATION
EDUCATION	FOOD
SOCIAL SECURITY	TRANSPORT

Opportunity cost is the cost of a decision measured as the choice forgone.

Diagram (a) in Box 1.1 shows some basic choices at the family and personal levels. It also identifies an important economic principle: the idea of opportunity cost. This is the cost of a choice measured not in terms of money, but in terms of the next best alternative that has been forgone. Buying clothes, for example, has an opportunity cost because fewer resources are left over to buy food. A family's 'scarce resource' might be monetary (the family budget), or non-monetary (limited time, for instance).

Box 1.1(b) moves to the business level and shows some of the allocation decisions made by a firm. Again, the scarce resource might be monetary, with the firm deciding how to dispose of its sales revenue; or non-monetary, involving human resources that are in short supply: work, skills, expertise, and so on.

Box 1.1(c) lists some typical priorities at the national level. Here, decisions are made by the government which, depending on the degree of democracy and consultation, is influenced to a greater or lesser degree by the priorities and wishes of the country's citizens. The principal scarce resource which has to be allocated between competing uses is the government budget, which consists mainly of tax revenue and government borrowing. However, there are other resources which are in many ways more important, since the government can be regarded as the custodian of a country's resources in the widest sense: its people, raw materials, capital stock, and environment.

Box 1.1(d) takes us to the international or global level. When considering levels (a)–(c) we have made some effort to draw attention not only to monetary resources, but also to non-monetary

Factor cost is a measure of the amount of resources used in production.

ones. At the world level less effort is needed to grasp the importance of this distinction. It is perhaps ironic that at this higher level we are forced back to basics; perhaps this is because there is no such thing as a 'world currency'. We have to focus our thoughts clearly on real resources. Since 'green' issues are so prominent nowadays, and since economics is about 'the best use of scarce resources', it is clear that economists should have something interesting to say about some of the most urgent problems facing humanity today.

For example, consider the way in which developed countries choose to use the private car as a main means of transport. We read that the car manufacturers of the world are becoming more and more 'efficient', in a commercial sense. But is our worship of the internal combustion engine efficient in a truly economic sense? Does it make the best use of scarce resources? What are the opportunity costs of car travel,

when we take into account the pollution it causes, and when we allow for the built-in obsolescence which means that cars are actually designed to wear out and need replacing within a short space of time?

Economists use the word 'interdependence' to describe the tendency for economic decisions taken in one part of the world to affect others. If Mexico City is choked with air pollution it is not just a local issue. If exhaust fumes add to global warming, then we all suffer the consequences. Here we see very clearly that the phrase 'the best use of scarce resources' has relevance to us all. The very survival of the human species is threatened by our less-than-best use of the world's resources. It follows that a study of economics is one of the most useful pursuits that a young person can follow.

The way in which economists classify scarce resources is shown in Box 1.2.

BOX 1.2	Scarce resources: the factors of production

Factors of production are resources which are used in the production of goods and services.

Factor	Description	Definition	Factor income
LAND	The natural factor	Useful resources from the earth, sea or atmosphere	RENT
CAPITAL	The man-made factor	Produces goods, which can be used to make consumer goods and services	INTEREST
LABOUR	The human factor	Human time and effort; skills, abilities and work	WAGES

BOX 1.2	ENTERPRISE	The organising factor	The entrepreneur: ownership control, decision-making, risk-taking	PROFIT

Factors of production are resources which are used in the production of goods and services.

For convenience, they can be classified under four headings The production of any good or service is certain to use up at least some of each of these four factors; in other words, there is a 'factor cost'.

Enterprise: a factor of production

TASK 1.1

Consider the following items:
- *a pencil;*
- *a computer.*

Identify the factors of production which have been used in their production.

Is economics a science?

The answer to this question is 'yes and no'. Economics can never be an exact science, and is a different kind of discipline to, say, physics or chemistry. The essence of science is prediction. Physical 'laws' tell us what we believe must happen. If you drop a pencil out of an upstairs window, the known laws of physics predict that it must fall to the ground. If ever a pencil flew vertically upwards, then physicists would have to look again at those laws in order to accommodate this new possibility. One thing that would not enter the discussion would be the possibility that the pencil 'decided' to fly upwards, and here is where the 'laws' of economics are very different from the 'laws' of physics. Economics is a social science, which means that it studies aspects of human behaviour.

Social science *is the systematic study of the behaviour of individuals and societies.*

How the social sciences overlap

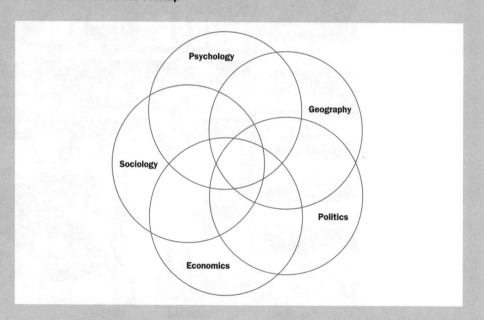

The diagram in Box 1.3 shows some of the social sciences, and suggests that they overlap to some extent. Social sciences study aspects of human behaviour, and human beings can be very unpredictable – indeed, one of the most hurtful or insulting things you can be told is : 'You're so predictable!' If we know that our actions are being predicted, then there is a possibility that we might react against the prediction, as the polling experts who try to forecast the outcomes of elections know only too well. Economic laws have to be hedged around with all sorts of assumptions and qualifications ('ifs' and 'buts') and they attempt only to show general patterns of behaviour.

Large-scale enterprise

Deduction and induction

Box 1.4 explains both of these terms. Study Box 1.4 before reading on.

BOX 1.4	**Deduction and Induction**

Deduction
- Starts from the general and moves to the particular.
- Begins with general assumptions and moves to particular conclusions.
- Develops a theory, and then examines the facts to see if they follow the theory.

Deduction means arriving at particular conclusions from general propositions.

Induction means arriving at general theories from particular observations.

Example:

Let there be 360 degrees in a circle	*(A general assumption)*
There are four right angles in a circle, therefore	*(A logical argument)*
This right angle has 90 degrees	*(A particular conclusion)*

Induction
- Starts from the particular and moves to the general.
- Begins with particular observations and moves to general explanations.
- Collects observations, then develops a theory to fit the facts.

Example:

This apple falls to the ground	*(A particular observation)*
All apples fall to the ground	*(More observations)*
All objects attract each other	*(A general explanation)*

Economics can be a very deductive subject, and economists are used to constructing complicated 'models' of human behaviour which begin with a range of assumptions. However, economics is also an empirical subject, using inductive methods to explain observed facts. Thus the downward sloping demand curve, for example (see Section 2) can be deduced from general assumptions about how people try to maximise their satisfaction from the purchase of goods and services. On the other hand, demand curves can be built up empirically, that is by observing actual customers reacting to actual price changes, and when market researchers, census takers and opinion pollsters collect their information, the data can be used inductively to make economic predictions.

In practice it can be very difficult to say where deduction ends and induction begins. The great economist John Maynard Keynes was known as the 'armchair economist' because it was said that he never had to leave his study in order to formulate his theories. On the other hand, if his theories had been divorced from reality, then they would not have had the success that they did have in improving the conditions of life for millions of individuals. Like Sherlock Holmes, the world's best deducers are also keen observers of human behaviour, and so economists need to use both deduction and induction in their work.

Positive and normative economics

Box 1.5 contains some positive and normative statements and questions. Study these before reading on.

Positive and normative statements and questions

Positive statements and questions

Examples: 'Anthony Hopkins is a Welsh actor'. 'Is this table made of wood?'
These statements/questions...
- deal with objective reality;
- tell us something about the world around us;
- can, in principle, be 'true' or 'false'.

Even if we do not yet have the means to do so (e.g. to prove whether there is intelligent life in space), proof is ultimately possible using methods upon which everyone can agree.

Normative statements and questions

Examples: 'Anthony Hopkins is the best Welsh actor since Richard Burton'.
            'Is this a beautiful table?'
These statements/questions...
- deal with subjective opinions;
- tell us something about people's view of the world, rather than the world itself; they are about values, attitudes or tastes;
- cannot be proved true or false.

They can never be fully resolved because they often depend on moral attitudes (e.g. while most people would agree that Hitler was evil, there are some persons who claim the opposite).

Positive means that which can be tested by objective means.
Normative means that which depends on value judgements.

Positive economics is the study of economic propositions which can be verified, at least in principle, by the observation of real-world events, and without using normative propositions or value judgements. Normative propositions tend to be prescriptive, and tell us what the person making the proposition believes ought to be done. In practice, the distinction between positive and normative economics is blurred. It is possible to put forward economic propositions which appear to be positive, but in fact rest upon value judgements. The propositions of 'perfect competition' (see Section 2) are a case in point. Do they describe how firms and markets actually behave, or do they reflect the views of certain economists of how things ought to be? The use of the word 'perfect' should give us a clue.

TASK 1.2

Discuss whether the following questions can be answered using 'positive' economics, or whether they involve value judgments:

A What is the unemployment rate in the UK?
B Is unemployment in the UK lower than in Germany?
C Is there too much unemployment in the UK?
D Are privatised industries more efficient than state-owned ones?
E Has membership of the European Union (EU) raised UK living standards?

Some tools of economic analysis

To a large extent economics attempts to study things which can be measured. Measurable quantities can be classified as one of two types: constants and variables.

Constants

*A **constant** is a magnitude which does not vary.*

Constants are measurable quantities which never vary. All students are familiar with the constant known as 'pi', roughly equal to 22/7, which is the length of a circle's circumference divided by its diameter. This constant was known to the ancient Egyptians, and used in the construction of their pyramids. Newtonian physics tells us that in a vacuum a feather would fall to the earth in the same time as a grand piano dropped from the same height; both would accelerate according to the gravitational constant at 980 cm per second per second. In economics, however, the existence of constants is very difficult to prove, and some economists would rule them out altogether. In the 1970s and 1980s, for example, monetarists claimed that there was a constant relationship between the rate of growth of the money supply and the rate of inflation (see Section 4). However, this idea has since proved to be very questionable, especially as a guide to government policy. An economic idea known as 'Goodhart's Law' suggests that so-called constant relationships will break down if a government attempts to use them as a means of implementing policy, in the way that monetarist governments have failed to control the money supply as a means of tackling inflation.

Variables

*A **variable** is a magnitude which does change.*

As its name suggests, a variable is a measurable quantity which varies. Variables can be one of three types: stocks, flows or ratios, as shown in Box 1.6.

Stocks, flows and ratios

Stocks
- Have no time dimension
- Are measured at a point in time.

Example from outside economics: the weight of a car.

Examples from inside economics: the working population; the number of people unemployed; wealth, savings, capital.

Flows
- Have a time dimension
- Are measured over a period of time.

Example from outside economics: the speed of a car.

Examples from inside economics: income, saving, consumption, investment, output.

Ratios
- Are neither simple stocks nor flows
- May or may not have a time dimension; might not have any dimensions at all (might just be a number or coefficient).

There are four types:
  - flow/flow
  - flow/stock
  - stock/stock
  - stock/flow.

Example from outside economics: the petrol consumption of a car. (This is a flow divided by a flow: miles travelled per time period/gallons of petrol used per time period = miles per gallon).

Examples from inside economics: price (flow/flow), e.g. Total expenditure on cars per time period/number of cars bought per time period = price per car.
average wages (flow/stock), e.g. Total pay of nurses per time period/number of nurses = pay per nurse per time period.
unemployment rate (stock/stock), e.g. Number of people unemployed at a point in time/number of people of working age at a point in time.
Economic analysis makes use of functional relationships between variables.

Stock is a variable with no time dimension.
Flow is a variable with a time dimension.
Ratios are four types: stock/flow; flow/stock; flow/flow; stock/stock.

Functional relationships occur when one variable depends on another in a specific way.

A functional relationship is said to exist when two or more variables are uniquely related. An example is the demand function. If we write

   Qd = f{P}

then this is a shorthand way of saying 'quantity demanded is a function of the price of a good'. (Demand also depends on other things, such as income, advertising and tastes, but here we are concentrating on one aspect of the demand function.) In the expression above, 'P' is the independent variable while 'Qd' is the dependent variable, meaning that it is thought that quantity demanded depends on price rather than vice versa. Note that the expression does not express the exact relationship between Qd and P. It simply states that we think a relationship exists. If we wish to show a possible form of the demand function, then we have to draw a graph, show a table of figures, or derive a mathematical equation which shows the exact relationship and which would, for instance, tell us exactly what the quantity demanded would be if price were, say, 30 pence.

REVIEW

This chapter has introduced you to some of the basic ideas of economics. As you continue to study this subject the words and phrases used here will gradually begin to take on more meaning and make more sense.

REVIEW

A Explain why the problem of scarcity exists both in countries with high levels and countries with low levels of income.

B Assume that you will spend three years of your life at university. Estimate

    1 the money costs,

    2 the opportunity costs,

    3 the factor costs.

(Consider these costs both from your own viewpoint, and from that of the country as a whole).

1.2 What is an economic system?

Change to a market economy

What happens when a country like Poland becomes a 'market economy'? Why were its old decision-making methods inefficient? Why might higher efficiency increase 'social costs'? Why is 'trade liberalisation' important to a market economy?

The INVESTIGATOR

Tariffs returning to Poland

The way in which Poland's foreign trade policies were decided used to be shrouded in mystery, but according to a report from GATT (the General Agreement on Tariffs and Trade) the return of democratic government in 1989 has made things more transparent.

Economic and political reforms have been accompanied by trade liberalisation, with fewer restrictions on the types of goods and services being traded, and a reorientation of trade from the former Soviet bloc to western markets.

However, there is a possibility that the Polish authorities underestimated the social costs of transition to a market economy, and have recently reintroduced some protection with the use of tariffs and import licensing.

The report says that liberalisation is slowest in sectors such as textiles, clothing, steel and agriculture, traditional industries where Poland seems to have a comparative advantage.

Preview

In this chapter we shall investigate the following key areas:

- the problems of production;
- production possibilities;
- economic systems;
- problems and opportunities of economies in transition.

The problems of production

As we have seen in Chapter 1.1, economics exists because of the scarcity of resources in relation to people's wants. If there were no such thing as scarcity, then there would be no need to economise, and hence no such thing as economics.

The news media give the impression that there are many economic problems: inflation, unemployment, strikes, factory closures, pollution... In fact all economic problems can be viewed as aspects of three basic problems of production. These are the problems of

● WHAT to produce?
● HOW to produce?
● FOR WHOM to produce?

Ultimately, these three basic problems boil down to just ONE fundamental economic problem, that of resource allocation, or 'making the best use of scarce resources'.

What to produce?: the problem of 'product-mix'

Society has to find some way of deciding what mixture of goods and services it wants to produce. This mixture ranges from basic wants, such as food, water, shelter and clothing, to more sophisticated wants such as leisure, education, and transport. In some parts of the world, people live at poverty levels which the citizens of richer countries find difficult or even impossible to imagine. Here, human wants are immediate, and in fact are likely to be better described as 'needs' rather than wants. People facing starvation, homelessness or disease are unlikely to be concerned with more sophisticated wants such as having a dry Martini or a round of golf. Even in the most affluent societies, however, there is no evidence that people's wants are becoming totally satisfied. Even when 'money is no object', there are always opportunity costs, so that priorities have to be decided and choices made; devoting resources to one purpose, such as building a hospital, means that fewer resources are available for another use, such as road building. Look at Box 2.1.

BOX 2.1

*The **production possibility curve** (PPC) shows different combinations of output possible given existing resources.*

The production possibility curve

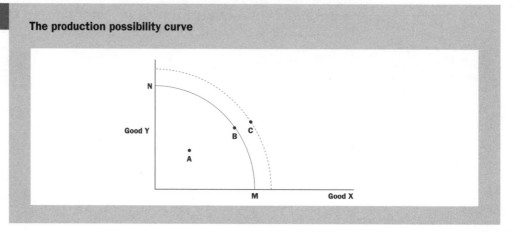

Box 2.1 shows all the possible combinations of two goods which can be produced at any one time, given existing resources. If all resources are devoted to producing good X, then ON can be produced. If, however, all resources are used to produce good Y, then OM units can be produced. If a combination of X and Y is desired, then all possible combinations are shown by the line MN which is drawn with a convex shape when viewed from the origin.

This line MN, the PPC for goods X and Y, shows both factor combination and factor substitution. It shows how a country's factors of production can be combined in different ways in order to produce different patterns of output. It also shows a 'trade off' or opportunity cost. Increasing the use of some factors and reducing the use of others will produce less of one good and more of another. The convex shape reflects the law of diminishing returns, which is further discussed in Section 2.

Essentially, this law operates because factors of production are not perfect substitutes for each other, or in other words, factors of production are not perfectly mobile. To give an example, suppose good Y represents 'tanks' and good X represents 'tractors'. Producing half as many tanks will not necessarily produce twice as many tractors. Tank factories, machines designed for tank production, and people trained to build tanks, cannot be instantly switched to tractor production: factories will need reorganising, machines will need modification or replacing, and workers will need to be retrained. Thus there will be diminishing returns as factors are switched, and the output of tractors rises by a smaller percentage than the output of tanks falls.

The PPC represents a 'frontier' or 'boundary' in the sense that given the current availability of resources and technical knowledge, a country cannot produce at a point to the right of the PPC. The PPC is therefore a 'short-run' diagram: in the long run the productive capacity of a country can be increased, shifting the PPC to the right. A movement from B to C in Box 2.1 illustrates an increase in the productive capacity or potential growth of the economy. A movement from A to B, on the other hand, represents actual growth rather than potential growth. At A, there are unemployed resources: people on the dole, machines lying idle, factories empty, etc. If the degree of utilisation of productive capacity increases, then more resources become unemployed. In Section 2 we shall see that producing on the existing PPC frontier can be regarded as a position of productive efficiency.

TASK 2.1

A The PPC in Box 2.1 shows choices between consumer goods. Explain how such choices affect individual living standards in the short and the long run.

B Draw a convex PPC to show possible combinations of apples and pears that could be produced by a market garden.

C As the amount of pears increases, does the opportunity cost in terms of apples increase or decrease? Suggest a reason for your answer.

D Suppose Robinson Crusoe on a desert island found that it took the same amount of time and effort to net a fish as it took to climb a tree and gather a coconut. Why would his PPC be a straight line? What does this say about the opportunity costs?

How to produce? – the problem of 'factor-combination'

Having decided what goods and services we want, we then have to choose between alternative ways of producing them. If we want electricity, should this be produced by burning coal or gas? If we want transport, should this be achieved via the private car or by investment in railways? Should tuna fish be caught using rod and line or by large drift nets? All of these decisions affect the way in which we combine the factors of production·in order to produce an output.

In a modern society an important issue is the choice between capital-intensive and labour-intensive methods of production.

Individual specialisation is where people concentrate on a narrow range of skills or tasks.

Capital-intensive methods use large amounts of capital relative to labour, in other words they use machinery and tend to be automated; while labour-intensive methods are less mechanised and use human effort instead. In general we find that societies will tend to substitute a cheaper factor for a more expensive one in order to try to minimise the costs of production. This is related to the idea of appropriate technology, which can be broadly described as the technology yielding the greatest rate of return. This rate of return can be narrowly measured, to include only private benefits, or more broadly in terms of social benefits (these terms are considered in depth in Section 3). Thus in Japan, for example, where there is relatively easy access to high grade technology, it might be appropriate to produce state-of-the-art cars using assembly lines and computerised robots. In Sri Lanka, on the other hand, where labour is abundant and relatively cheap, while capital is scarce and so investment in machinery is more costly, it is appropriate to produce less sophisticated cars using labour-intensive methods and local skills and materials.

In a modern economy, both labour and capital tend to become more specialised. In 1776, Adam Smith described human specialisation as the division of labour, and argued that it helped to achieve higher levels of output, because skills can be highly developed in a narrow range of activities. Today, we live in a society where people are highly specialised; and our job-titles (computer programmer, brain surgeon) tend to be highly specific. This specialisation leads to the need for trade. People who spend their lives specialising as office workers do not have time to go out and catch their own fish. They exchange the money they earn for the output of people who specialise in the fishing industry. Since it is no longer possible for people to 'barter', or directly swap goods and services on large scale, the exchange is now done indirectly, using money as a medium of exchange.

BOX 2.2

The tuna wars

During July and August 1994 Spanish fishermen clashed with French and British fishermen in the tuna grounds to the west of the Bay of Biscay.

British fishermen were in the area because their traditional fishing grounds, such as the hake areas between Cornwall and Ireland and the cod areas of the north Atlantic had been 'overfished', so much so that the EU put quotas on the amounts that could be caught, and the UK government attempted to limit the number of days that vessels hunting these fish could put to sea. Cornish and French fishermen learned that tuna was a very profitable fish (commanding some £2000 per ton at the quayside, compared with about £1000 for cod) without any quotas.

The Spanish fishermen objected because they had traditionally caught tuna with rod and line; this method ensured that other creatures such as dolphins were not harmed, and also ensured that tuna were not fished at such a rate that stocks were depleted. However, the French and British obtained permission from the EU to use drift nets, as long as these were less than 2.5 km in length. In answer to the accusation that these nets would kill dolphins, gaps were left in the nets, through which it was claimed the dolphins could escape using their sonic direction-finding ability to sense them. However, these gaps lengthened the nets to beyond 2.5 km, and according to the Spanish the nets were unacceptable anyway, as they would ultimately cause tuna to be overfished. Cornish fishermen invested some £30,000 each in order to equip themselves with drift nets; however, since one boatload of tuna could fetch some £100,000 at the quayside they were not sympathetic to Spanish suggestions that they should not be used.

TASK 2.2

A   Discuss how the tuna wars are linked to the ideas of
   1   scarce resources;
   2   how to produce.
B   Suppose the EU decreed that all tuna fishermen should use rod and line instead of nets. Discuss two reasons why this might benefit all fishermen in the long run.

In Section 2 we consider how different combinations of factors of production, including labour and capital, affect productivity, or the output that can be produced from a given quantity of inputs. Productivity is linked to the idea of efficiency, which is a measure of the extent to which the 'best' use of resources is being made.

For whom to produce? – The problem of 'income distribution'

Once goods and services have been produced how are they going to be shared out? Who is going to benefit from them? This is largely, but not entirely, governed by the way in which incomes are distributed, since it is incomes which give people spending power, and so give them a command over goods and services. Who should have a Ford Escort and who should have a Rolls Royce? Who should be treated in hospital, and when? Who should go to university? Should houses be built for sale by speculators, or provided for rent by local government? Who should be a university professor and who should be a farm labourer?

It is possible to use a variety of 'rationing' methods, such as...

- Prices (the ability to pay) – goods in a supermarket
- The queue (first come first served) – tickets for a free concert
- Merit – university places
- Need – hospital beds
- Lottery – prizes, winnings
- Rota – taking turns.

It is possible to combine some of these methods: for example, people buying fish and chips or going to the cinema might have to both queue and pay a price.

In Section 2 we further consider the principles of income distribution, and in Section 3 we analyse the reasons for allocating certain goods and services in different ways.

Economic systems

In recent times human societies have attempted to use three broad methods of allocating resources; in other words, three kinds of economic systems:

- The planned economy, where a government and its agencies attempt to decide what, how and for whom to produce;
- The market economy, where prices allocate resources, and goods and services are produced by enterprises guided by the profit motive;
- The mixed economy, where price signals are used along with government intervention.

In reality, all economies are 'mixed' to some extent. There is no such thing as a purely planned economy; even the old Soviet Union made some use of markets. Similarly, there is government activity even in those countries such as the USA and Singapore which are prominent examples of free-enterprise market economies. In western economies such as Britain, France and Germany, which have generally been described as 'mixed' economies, there is fierce debate about the degree of government intervention, or planning which is appropriate, and about the extent to which prices and profits should be used as part of the mixture.

Economic systems and ownership

The balance between planning and markets will have an effect on the way in which property is owned in an economy. A planned economy requires a large amount of centralisation, or co-ordination from the central government. Comprehensive planning of the kind that was carried out in the old Soviet Union involves using 'commands' originating from the government to decide not only on the pattern of output, but also on the way in which resources are used in production.

The transformation of the Soviet Union from a backward, agricultural economy to a space-exploring superpower was achieved by the state taking on the ownership of the resources used. Farms were 'collectivised', factories run by committees, and the idea of 'private property' downgraded. In contrast, the industrialisation of the USA took place in a culture in which the idea of private property was almost sacrosanct. During the 1980s and 1990s the transition of planned economies into market economies has been accompanied by privatisation (the selling of state assets to the private sector) on a massive scale; and privatisation has been an often controversial feature of the mixed economies in recent times also.

REVIEW

There have been two strands to this chapter: production possibilities and resource allocation. The debate about what markets can do for us in allocating resources, and what they are less capable of doing, and the issue of 'planning' versus 'prices' as rationing mechanisms, will emerge as important themes in the rest of this book.

REVIEW TASK

THE PEACE DIVIDEND

During the 1980s and 1990s the economic and social changes that occurred during the collapse of the planned economies of Eastern Europe were accompanied by political changes in the form of a relaxation of tension between East and West. These political changes in turn brought about new economic circumstances. Western countries no longer had to maintain armies and tank regiments on the continent of Europe; the former Eastern bloc was able to reduce the amount of resources devoted to developing and maintaining nuclear weapons and delivery systems. Politicians and newspapers began to talk about a 'peace dividend'.

Find a newspaper article giving an example of the 'peace dividend' in practice. Using a production possibility curve, analyse the short-run and long-run implications of the new economic circumstances. You could, for example, link this to new investment in Northern Ireland during the IRA cease-fire of 1995.

Great economists

Milton Friedman (1912–)

Friedman was born in New York, the son of Jewish, immigrant garment workers. He studied economics at Rutgers University, New Jersey, where he developed an interest in empirical work, in particular the use of statistical techniques, in testing the value of economic theories. He later undertook postgraduate studies at the University of Chicago, and was awarded a PhD from Columbia University in 1946. He returned to the University of Chicago to take up a lectureship, and was made a professor in 1948. During his long and illustrious career at Chicago, he became the leading contributor to what became known as the 'Chicago School of Economics'.

Friedman's economics represents a return to the fundamentals of nineteenth-century capitalism – nothing, he believes, should be allowed to interfere with the free interplay of market forces; and to this end the state should withdraw from the lives and pockets of the people. For Friedman, the free operation of markets is the source of economic prosperity, as well as being a precondition for individual liberty; and policies promoting free enterprise should, in his view, take priority over all else. Government provision of unemployment and social security benefits and minimum wage laws are all viewed by Friedman as inherently undesirable on the grounds that they impede the natural workings of the free market; so, too, is the existence of trade unions, which, according to Friedman, actually cause unemployment by making wages 'rigid' in a downwards direction, preventing perfect competition amongst workers.

However, Friedman is probably best known for being the founder of 'monetarism', the belief that the crucial ingredient in

determining short-term fluctuations in the level of economic activity is the amount of money which governments allow to circulate in the economy; more specifically, Friedman believes that the crucial determinant of the rate of inflation is the rate at which the money supply is growing. In 1976, Friedman was awarded the Nobel Prize in economics for his monetary theories.

However, while Friedman's views have been wholeheartedly embraced by those on the political right, his ideas have by no means met with universal acceptance: during the 1970s, he was denounced as a collaborator with fascism for acting as an economic adviser to the murderous military junta of General Pinochet in Chile; in 1983, two eminent econometricians and Oxford dons, Professors David Hendry and Neil Erikson, produced a damning indictment of Friedman's methodology in which they alleged that the statistics used by Friedman in his monetary analysis were highly manipulated, with Hendry claiming that 'we have not been able to find any evidence that money supply creates either income growth or inflation' and Friedmanite policies have been blamed in general by Keynesians and others for the continuing high unemployment and fluctuating economic growth rates, as well as the increased incidence of inequalities, exploitation, poverty and externalities.

Despite these criticisms, Friedman has become the leading conservative economist in the world today. He has been a most prolific writer – *Free to Choose,* written with his wife Rose, and his *Monetary History of the United States*, written with Anna Schwarz, being his most influential works – and has been at the forefront of the counter-Keynesian revolution.

John Maynard Keynes (1883-1946)

Keynes was born in Cambridge. His father was an economist and lecturer at Cambridge University. From a very early age, Keynes excelled at everything he did: he won a scholarship to Eton and was outstanding in mathematics and the classics, and later gained a place at King's College, Cambridge; he was an accomplished mountaineer and bridge player; he made a fortune for himself by speculating on the foreign exchange and commodity markets, undertaking his transactions before emerging from bed each morning, and used part of his gains to found the Cambridge Arts Theatre; he was also an active member of the influential Bloomsbury group of writers and artists whose numbers included Vanessa Bell, E M Forster, Duncan Grant and Virginia Woolfe.

The eminent philosopher Bertrand Russell was in no doubt about Keynes' intellectual capabilities: 'Keynes' intellect was the sharpest and clearest that I have ever known. When I argued with him I felt that I took my life in my hands and I seldom emerged without feeling something of a fool.'

However, it is for his contribution to economics that Keynes is best remembered.

After graduating from Cambridge, Keynes entered the Civil Service in 1907, working in the India Office. His second-place score in the Civil Service examinations prevented him gaining his desired position in the Treasury, and on discovering that his lowest mark was in the economics paper he was moved to conclude that 'the examiners presumably knew less than I did!' Later, during the First World War, he was to join the Treasury, where he worked on ways of financing the war effort, and in 1919 he represented the Treasury at the peace conference at Versailles. His opposition to the terms of reparations imposed on Germany led him to resign from the Treasury, and in *The Economic Consequences of the Peace*, he argued that Germany would never be able to meet the harsh economic conditions imposed, and that this would be a continuing source of instability.

During the 1930s, with the majority of the industrialised world in a state of economic depression, and with millions of workers on the dole, Keynes developed his economic analysis to account for the persistence of large-scale unemployment, culminating in his most famous and influential work, *The General Theory of Employment, Interest and Money*. The novelty of his approach was such that economists came to talk in terms of the 'Keynesian Revolution'. However, the Keynesian revolution, unlike the Bolshevik revolution before it, was one that was designed to *preserve* rather than overthrow the existing order, for Keynes was no revolutionary in the normal sense of the word: a member of the Liberal Party, he was quite clear as to which side of the political fence he stood: 'If we need a religion, how can we find it in the rabid rubbish of the Red bookshop? ... the class war will find me on the side of the educated bourgeoisie.'

For Keynes, capitalism was clearly the best economic system known to man, but he was concerned at the hardship, poverty and suffering caused by the depression of the 1930s. Although his analysis was complex, his basic message was clear: full employment was extremely unlikely to be achieved as a result of unregulated capitalism, and governments must, mainly by increasing their own spending, ensure that the total level of demand in the economy was sufficient to ensure employment of all the nation's resources.

Keynesian ideas were extremely influential throughout the western world in the postwar period up until the mid 1970s, when a new 'ism', known as 'monetarism' came to the fore. Keynes represented the UK at the Bretton Woods Conference in New Hampshire, which was convened to determine the nature of the postwar international financial system, but died in 1946 of a heart attack, without being able to witness the unprecedented growth in the 1950s and 1960s of world trade and living standards for which his policies were at least in part responsible.

Karl Marx (1818-1883)

Marx was born in Trier in Germany. His parents were comfortably off, and although Jewish in origin, they converted to the Lutheran faith so as to make it easier for Marx's father to pursue his career in law. At the age of 17, Marx went to Bonn University to study law, but apparently worked harder at pursuing wine, women and song! To stop this 'wild rampaging', as his father called it, he was transferred to the University of Berlin, where he studied philosophy.

In 1842, Marx became Editor of the *Rheinische Zeitung*, but fled to Paris when the paper was suppressed by the Prussian authorities. There he began what was to become a life-long friendship and working relationship with Friedrich Engels, who stimulated his interest in political economy. On account of his anti-establishment political views, Marx was banished from Germany after a brief return, and in 1849 he took refuge in London where he was to live and write until his death.

Marx was active in socialist political life, and was a prolific writer. His most famous publications were *The Communist Manifesto*, co-written with Engels, and *Das Kapital (Capital),* written in three volumes after painstaking research at the British museum. The first volume appeared in 1867, and the remaining two volumes were edited by Engels and published posthumously in 1885 and 1894.

For many, Marx was one of the greatest thinkers in human history, and his influence not only on economics but also on history, philosophy and sociology has been profound. Indeed, before the collapse of the communist regimes in Eastern Europe in the late 1980s and early 1990s, hundreds of millions of people lived under governments which claimed inspiration from Marx's writings, although Marx himself, were he alive at the time, would almost certainly have been absolutely dismayed to be

associated with such 'Stalinist' regimes! He has also exerted an almost equal opposite influence in the capitalist countries in terms of the hatred and fear that his writings have engendered in those who wield economic power such that the term 'Marxist' is often used as a term of abuse!

So, what is it in Marx's ideas that can stir such controversy, even over 100 years after his death? Although Marx is associated with Socialism and Communism, he actually wrote very little about these types of society, and certainly did not provide any kind of blueprint for the former Communist regimes of Eastern Europe and elsewhere. In fact, Marx devoted his life to the study of capitalism, offering an explanation of how it works, and setting it in the context of the various stages of historical development, with the intention of showing working people how they themselves could bring about a new, more democratic form of society: as Marx noted, 'the philosophers have only interpreted the world in various ways; the point is to change it'.

Marx saw society as being in a constant state of flux, with all human history being one of class struggle between those who own the means of production, i.e. land, factories, offices and mines, and those who do not, and have only their labour power to sell. Marx argued that those who owned society's productive assets derived their wealth and power solely from the labour of the working class, and from nowhere else. Against such injustice, Marx saw resistance, i.e. class struggle, as inevitable.Perhaps his greatest achievement has been to provide a vision to all the oppressed peoples of the world of a superior form of society to capitalism and to offer them the means of understanding and removing their oppression: as Marx and Engels proclaimed in the *Communist Manifesto*, 'The proletarians have nothing to lose but their chains. They have a world to win. Working men of all countries unite!'

What do economists do?

FOCUS

The economist at work

You might be surprised to learn that it is possible to earn a living by being employed as an 'economist'. What is it that economists do, and how does their work differ from that of, say, an accountant or a manager?

Don't shoot the ECONOMIST

Economists undeniably have a bad name. Blamed for the nation's economic ills – as if politicians had nothing to do with policy, managers with business decisions, and economists much to do with both – and accused of inhabiting a fantasy world of their own unrealistic models, they are regarded as reliable only for the capacity to come up with diametrically opposed views on any question put to them. What have they done to deserve this?

Getting into macroeconomic forecasting is maybe one thing. This is a chancy business, to be sure. But forecasting the economy is, for all the publicity it gets, only one small wing of the economists' house. Economists do not spend most of their time in macroeconomics – the aggregates of consumption, investment, public expenditure, national income, inflation, unemployment and the balance of payments – but the microeconomics of individual consumer, producer and market behaviour.

Against the grand-sounding 'macroeconomics', this may seem all rather puny. But the reason that economists worry about such things is to discover how the decisions of a myriad individual consumers and firms affect the performance of the economic system as a whole.

Enter the charge of unworldliness. The microeconomic model of perfect competition – in which there are assumed to be identical firms so numerous that none can individually influence market price; perfectly informed, rational consumers; and tunnel-vision producers concerned only to maximise profits – is not the world that real companies and real managers inhabit. The suspicion is that, unable to deal with the complexity of this real world,

economists have taken refuge in simplified 'abstract' models of their own devising, with which they can cope.

But this is to misunderstand what economists are trying to do. In modelling the behaviour of economic agents and markets, economists are not trying to say what the world is like. As Professor Frank Hahn argued in Cambridge over 20 years ago, they are tackling the question: 'What would the world have to be like for decentralised decision-making by individual consumers and firms, co-ordinated only by market exchange and the workings of the price mechanism, to lead to an ideal state of society?'

The answer is the model of competitive equilibrium with all the assumptions above, plus a lot more concerning such things as: the existence of futures markets in all possible commodities; and the absence of 'externalities' like pollution and traffic congestion and of asymmetries of information between buyers and sellers of goods and services.

If this is unworldly, the conclusion is clear: don't blame the economists for the fact that the real world does not come up to what it would need to be for markets to 'work'. Rather, qualify our faith in the market mechanism, and modify policy accordingly. This, among other things, may mean looking again at privatisation, market-testing, 'quasi-markets' in healthcare delivery, government non-intervention in all markets wherever possible – all of which are predicated on the efficiency of the market in finding the best use of resources to satisfy customer demands.

But this is all heady stuff, far removed from what passes over most managers' desks, or through most consumers' minds at the point of sale. Does economics have anything to offer at this level? The answer is 'yes' – as the inclusion of economics in the core curriculum of any leading business school testifies. Take the idea of demand elasticity. How common is the knee-jerk response to an operating deficit to put up prices! Yet as any first-year economics student knows, if demand is elastic, raising price will lose so many customers that revenue will fall; better, in this case, to reduce prices – cut fares, not trains.

Or consider the fundamental idea of 'opportunity cost' – the alternative forgone when any scarce resource (finance, time, energy) is committed to a particular end. Businesses may have quite a good sense of the trade-offs which due regard for opportunity costs will reveal. But if their capital investment decisions take account of the interest that could have been earned on internally generated funds from elsewhere, thank an economist.

Or take the universally applicable economic decision rule of 'equating at the margin' – ensuring that the last £10 spent on food benefits the family as much as the last £10 spent on holidays; the last £1,000 spent on staff training raises productivity by as much as the last £1,000 of plant or machinery; the last million spent on public health yields as much as the last million spent on maintaining public order. If not, then the welfare of the family, the firm and the nation can be increased within the existing expenditure limits by switching from one head to another, until the equalities hold.

Elasticity, opportunity cost and equating at the margin are all part of the fall-out of economists' inquiry into high-level matters of system-wide resource allocation, and they have direct and immediate relevance to everyday life. These are the simple, practical truths of economics. Others include the distinction (vital in accounting) between fixed and variable costs; the recent idea of 'sunk' – irrecoverable – costs; the principle of knowing when to cut your losses; comparative advantage; the paradox of the 'winner's curse'; and much else.

Then there is game theory – by no means the exclusive preserve of economists, but a field in which John Nash, John Harsanyi and Reinhard Selten were recently named joint Nobel prize-winners in economics. Stripped of its fearsome-looking mathematics, game theory is all about strategic behaviour: what to decide, and how to act; and when what you do – and more importantly what return you get – interacts with the choices of others. As Avinash Dixit and Barry Nalebuff brilliantly demonstrated in their book Thinking Strategically, game theory is bursting with lessons for us all.

Anticipating your rival's response, making strategic moves and credible commitments, brinkmanship, co-operation, co-ordination, bargaining, utilising incentives – it is all there.

Interestingly, empirical research suggests that conscious strategic behaviour is not common in business. So firms anxious to get ahead could do well to see what modern economics has to say. There is, as they say in sporting contexts, everything to play for; and one strategist in a pack of followers has everything to gain.

*Source: **Observer** (15 January 1995).*

Preview

In this chapter we shall investigate the following key areas:

- How economists work;
- How you can begin to think and work as an economist;
- Some hints for tackling assessed coursework in economics;
- Some ideas for assessed or informal economic investigations.

The two profiles in Box 3.1 will give you the flavour of the work of professional economists.

BOX 3.1

A week in the life of a business economist: two profiles
Valerie Burton, BSc (Econ), DPA (London), Group Economist, Bass Plc

Bass Plc is a major UK company in the drinks, hotels and leisure interests fields. It is a major UK brewer, has about 4,500 pubs, and owns the Coral betting shop chain and the Gala bingo clubs. It is a major player on the international hotel scene, owning the Holiday Inn hotel chain, with headquarters in Atlanta, USA.

My function is part of Bass' Strategic Planning Department, which is based at the corporate headquarters in London. I operate from the administrative headquarters in Burton-upon-Trent. Thank goodness we are linked into an office electronic mail system (e-mail) – it has certainly speeded things up in Bass!

Monday

In at 8.00 am to e-mail a note to my Director in London on the strategy Bass has towards the future structure of excise duties and on the stance the Chancellor of the Exchequer might take in forthcoming Budgets.

It is important that the Directors of the company are made aware of the implications for our business of changes in government policy – including legislation emanating from the European Commission in Brussels. Now we operate in a single European market, our beer industry, amongst the most highly taxed in Europe, is vulnerable to the imports of low taxed beer from France for personal consumption. This is a case where the free operation of market forces is skewed by different taxation policies. The more evidence I can provide for our Directors on the economic justification for duty harmonisation, the more chance we have of influencing government policy on this matter.

It's the start of the month: time to put together and send out a one-page fact sheet on the key economic indicators for my Director. Not an economist himself, he needs to understand just what is going on in the financial world. Our hotels are located in the United States and all over Europe and the Far East, so what's happening to the US dollar, the Deutschmark and the yen is important as it affects the conversion of the profit we earn abroad into UK sterling.

BOX 3.1

I need to add a note also on the meaning of the latest changes in UK inflation – now up to 1.9% with further rises anticipated as VAT is imposed on fuel and as the benefits of the 1993 devaluation are eroded. I need to explain how it is that, whilst GDP as measured by output is now on a good recovery path, personal incomes and spending power are under threat. Profit share is being switched from the personal sector to the corporate sector. The implications for Bass' customers are severe and, with less money to spend, the demand for our products could be dampened. It's all part and parcel of that economic theory of income elasticity – sounded boring at college, but I wish now I'd paid more attention! Monday of course is the day when everyone else is setting their programme for the week, so the day is constantly interrupted with phone calls to arrange meetings, asking for information, responding to the reports I sent out last week. Finally I finish the monthly fact sheet and e-mail it to London.

It's long gone 5.00 pm but I need to prepare now for tomorrow's meeting – that's the ITEM Club, in London, where I meet with other economists from the City and other major UK companies to put together a set of economic forecasts – more of that tomorrow.

You might think my day is ended – but it's my evening for a Soroptimist meeting – so a quick dash over to the other end of town. Work and outside interests merge together as far as I'm concerned. Soroptimists are women in all walks of business and professions and our international organisation gives me a welcome chance to network with other women, particularly given the male dominance of the brewing world!

Tuesday

It's an early start today: up at 6.00 am to get the train to London for my 10.00 am meeting. Still, with my portable PC, I can work on the train.

The ITEM meeting always gets my adrenaline going. Some of these City economists are real high fliers – and the interaction between them and us from the 'real world' of business does lead to some interesting new interpretations of academic economic theory! Of course, that's why economics is so challenging – to understand why people are not spending when interest rates come down, you really do need to understand the psychological implications of the fear of unemployment. Of course, subjective judgement and experience do creep into what we like to think of as a science-based discipline. We apply our varied business experience and knowledge of the vagaries of human behaviour to tweaking the model in those areas in which we are unable to establish good econometric equations.

Over lunch the men were discussing the outcome of the annual football match between the City economists and the staff of the *Financial Times* – the FT won hands down!

In the evening, I go over to a Society of Business Economists meeting to hear Professor David Currie of the London Business School. He's one of the seven 'wise men' advising the Chancellor of the Exchequer on economic policy. It's great to meet these stars face to face!

A late train home, but I put work aside and curled up with a favourite book!

BOX 3.1

Wednesday

Back to the drawing board, my economic model in this case. Over the years I've built up on spreadsheet packages a 'model' of the economy so I can generate my own forecasts. In Bass we use these forecasts for our strategic and financial planning. It's important that we have a view of the present and future pattern of consumer spending. The leisure market is an ever changing one, and charting the trends in consumer preferences for beer versus wine, or bingo versus more activity-related pursuits, is a challenging task.

We also need to take a fix on the future path of inflation – how do changes in the relative price of beer impact on demand? This is where the application of pure economic theory can have such a major input into business decisions on pricing and profit margins. Today I need to update the model with the latest indicators published by the Government. One of my skills is knowing where to get these indicators from, and at the least cost to Bass! Running the model through takes all day and into early evening – time-consuming, but I am up against a deadline to get a new set of forecasts out this week. I have to flag up to our marketing people the fact that the latest data indicate the growth in consumer spending might be slowing down. I make a mental note that I shall need to research whether this is evenly spread throughout the country. Bass has a larger market share in the Midlands than elsewhere, so such considerations are important.

Thursday

It's another early start today to write up the report on the forecasts. It's so easy to slip into economists' jargon: GDP (a measure of economic wealth and growth), PDI (personal incomes after tax) are as confusing to financial analysts as their jargon can be to me. And our company is bedevilled by financial analysts! So in layman's language, with as much visual presentation as possible, charts, graphs, and so on, I set about communicating my view of the future path of the economy and its implications for our markets. In Bass we are all charged with measuring our performance, individual and organisational, against 'key performance indicators' – KPIs for short! For me it's getting my forecasts at least as right as those of other economists, so I'm matching my performance against the forecasts of the likes of Bill Martin of UBS or Roger Bootle of Midland! Another of my KPIs is flagging up quickly the implications of the forecasts for the business. So long-winded economic treatises are out; it's all about snappy key punch lines – 'sterling depreciates, imported raw material prices (sugar and barley for our beer) rise, will the consumer cut down consumption if prices rise further?'
In the afternoon I turn back to some outstanding work on overseas markets for hotels and tourism. I need to gather economic data from a variety of sources and turn that data into information. Of course, some awareness of the political scenarios in the relevant countries is vital – hotel investments in the Middle East need to be managed with care to minimise the high risk of operating there, as our experiences in the Gulf War showed.

BOX 3.1

Thursday evening is the monthly meeting of our regional group of the Strategic Planning Society. As an economist working in a strategic planning environment, I need to keep up with the latest thinking on that subject. I chair our local group, and tonight we have a speaker on Strategies for Planning in the Public Sector.

Friday

This morning it's over to a meeting with our Leisure Division. They manage UK-based operations in the three Bs of betting, bingo and bowling, as well as gaming machines. The operations have many features in common, and we are to hear a market research presentation on consumer attitudes to these leisure activities. Statistics was part of a postgraduate diploma I studied years ago. Thank goodness for that knowledge I have of sampling techniques, as I was able to reassure colleagues that the smallness of the sample size did not in this case invalidate the research. The important thing was that the sample properly reflected the socio-economic structure of the population. We also needed to go down below the top-line findings to assess the differences in consumer attitudes between the genders and different age groups. I shall be taking this research further by tying in time-use studies with expenditure patterns amongst consumers. Then it's over to the operations directors to translate these findings into improved marketing plans for their businesses.

Back to the office, and I attempt to uncover all the other papers that have come in during the week in case there are any I've missed that need urgent attention. I spend the afternoon on a myriad of administrative matters, from filing to setting up a meeting next week with the marketing planning managers in our Brewing Division. Then, in the middle of it all, a phone call from the *Financial Times* asking for my view on possible cuts in the Bank Rate. I oblige, and a fifteen minute telephone interview becomes a 'one line' news byte in Saturday's *Financial Times*. Fame at last!

Just as I'm about to call it a day, I uncover a memo asking for my thoughts on what the Chancellor might put into the next Budget – reply required for an important board meeting next Tuesday! How did I miss that one! But I'm out on a date tonight – a dinner at our favourite Italian restaurant with my husband – so it's into the briefcase for attention over the weekend!

Saturday

With my views already well formed on how the Chancellor should play the Budget, though whether he will or not is anyone's guess, it doesn't take long to put a briefing paper together. At least the office is quiet on a Saturday morning! That out of the way, time to unwind and relax, ready for whatever next week has to offer!

Paul Appleby, MA, MPhil (Cantab), Economist with BP

If you had asked me what I wanted to be when I was an A-level student, I would have answered without hesitation 'an economist'. Even at that young age I was sure that being an economist was a worthwhile calling, and a good deal more interesting that being an accountant! Beyond that general wish to be an economist I did not have any clear idea about what being an economist meant, nor where it might lead. One thing was

BOX 3.1

quite certain – I would never consider working for a multinational oil company, the villains of my formative reading as a young economics student.

So here I am, at the age of 33, working as an economist for British Petroleum! I have been with BP for eight years and in that time covered a wide variety of assignments. At present I am a member of a small team of half a dozen economists in BP's head office, providing advice to senior managers on trends in the world economy and in global energy markets. I now consider myself an energy economist, specialising in the analysis of price formation and structural change in oil, gas and electricity markets. To give a recent example of what I do: the announcement of the closure of a large number of UK coal pits since October 1992 has sparked off a rapid review of UK energy policy by the Government, and when BP was asked for its views I was drafted into a small team charged with formulating the corporate response. I provided most of the economic analysis and argument, covering issues such as the costs of electricity generation, the competitive structure of the industry and the outlook for coal, oil and gas prices.
How did I get here? I took A-levels in economics, history and mathematics with statistics and went on to university, where I majored in economics with some politics, philosophy, sociology and history. It was not until very nearly the end of my third year, by which time most of my fellow students had signed up with accountancy firms or merchant banks, that I found what I was looking for. I applied for and obtained a Fellowship of the Overseas Development Institute (ODI), a grand title for a scheme which sends newly graduated economists to all parts of the Commonwealth. I was sent to Malawi – a small and very poor African country – to work as the planning economist in the government department responsible for rural water supplies. After the high theory of university economics, this was a wonderfully down-to-earth experience, and I quickly discovered how few of the sophisticated gadgets in the economist's toolbox can survive testing in the field. However, I also found that, as a way of thinking about problems, economics does have a lot to contribute to real-world decision-making.

After my two-year term as an ODI Fellow ended, I returned to university to take a Master's degree in economics. If anything, I enjoyed my second degree more than my first, largely because I had a clearer idea of what I wanted to do with my economics knowledge and because I was better able to judge which parts of the syllabus were going to be of most use to me as a working economist. I was tempted to stay on in academia, but deep-down I had already decided that what I really wanted to do was apply economic thinking to real decision-making problems.

I attended a BP recruitment fair and something struck a chord in me. Here was an opportunity to work as a professional economist, working in multidisciplinary teams to provide the analysis and advice needed by business decision-makers. I applied, was accepted, and have not looked back since. I started out as a macroeconomic forecaster in BP's London head office and was then posted to BP's office in Melbourne, Australia, to provide economic advice in areas such as macroeconomics, energy markets, and the economics of mining. From Melbourne, I returned to the UK to work in the part of BP that produces and sells natural gas. I arrived just at the time that the UK gas industry was being radically restructured, so there was great demand for an economist's advice on how the market would develop as British Gas's monopoly was dismantled. I moved on from UK gas issues to European gas – another set of markets ripe for change, where BP wanted to know what opportunities might emerge from any restructuring of that industry. Finally, I came back to the London head office to my present job. It is not easy to pursue a career as a professional economist in industry – there is a strong temptation to move into more general commercial management in order to climb the corporate ladder. But I have found it very rewarding, and as long as it continues to provide interesting and varied work, I shall stick at it.

Source: **Economics and Business for the Future** *(Hobsons, 1995).*

The economist as investigator

You might eventually be employed as an economist, but even if you work in some other field, you should find that an economist's investigative skills are useful to you.

As a student of Economics, following a modern syllabus, you are likely to be encouraged to work 'like an economist', probably through the completion of a coursework assignment, or investigation. This investigation might be 'formal' in the sense that it will be assessed and contribute towards your final external grade, or it might be 'informal', set by your teacher as part of your learning process, but not necessarily directly linked to your final grade.

Whether formal or informal, an economics investigation will enable you to demonstrate an ability to:

- recall knowledge of the content of an economics syllabus;
- use this knowledge in verbal, numerical, diagrammatic, pictorial or graphical form;
- gather, select, analyse, interpret and apply economic data;
- distinguish between factual evidence and opinions;
- examine arguments, make reasoned judgements, draw conclusions, and communicate in an accurate and logical manner.

Before beginning an economic investigation there are two things that you must do:
- Choose a topic area
- Take aim.

Choosing a topic area

Sometimes you will be 'prescribed' a topic; sometimes your topic will be 'negotiated'. A prescribed topic is handed down from your examiners and/or teachers, whereas a negotiated topic is agreed between these people and yourself.

Once you have a topic area, then you need to choose a title which lies within it. This should give a clear indication of what your investigation is all about.

Try to draft a title which is not too broad, but which concentrates on a specific issue. It should also be a title which gives you a reasonable chance of gathering information, either through fieldwork (obtaining data from the world about you) or desk research (obtaining data from books and other sources).

Some of your research data will come from primary sources. These might give raw data which you collect yourself, through the use of a questionnaire, or which you can obtain from government statistics or other sources. Other data will come from secondary sources, such as books and journals. Secondary material will already have been sifted and commented on by another person; so if you wish your work to have some originality, it is important to use these carefully. In some cases, a source might be seen as either primary or secondary. Newspapers, for example, are a secondary source if you use them to obtain facts and figures which have been obtained from a primary source by a journalist. If, however, you are investigating how newspapers report economic issues, then clearly the writing of journalists is a primary source.

Topics which are focused, and not too broad are likely to yield better results than wide-ranging topics, which cannot realistically be covered in a reasonably brief report.

Thus:

- 'The factors that determine the demand for a family car' is better than
- 'The economics of the UK car industry'.

What is it that distinguishes an economics investigation from one that is geographical, historical, or to do with business or management? Remember from Chapter 1.1 that economics is about making the best use of scarce resources. It should therefore be possible to relate your topic and title in some way to fundamental questions of what? how? or for whom?

Taking aim

Your investigation needs a target, so that you can concentrate your mind on specific tasks, rather than attempt to cover too much ground. A good plan is to put forward an hypothesis, or theory, to be tested. An hypothesis can be put forward as a simple statement that the evidence you collect will either support or contradict, such as

'Demand for rail travel from my town to the next is price-inelastic'.

This statement might be correct or incorrect, and it doesn't really matter. What is important is that it can be tested by evidence which can be collected and analysed. A well designed hypothesis will give you a sense of direction, and will enable you to design meaningful tasks to collect suitable data. In this example, a useful starting point might be a questionnaire for use with a sample of rail travellers; or it might be possible to approach the rail company for information.

A very useful way of framing an hypothesis is to express it as a research question. This is often a simple matter of re-phrasing, so that the above title would become:

'What is the elasticity of demand for rail travel from my town to the next?'

There are at least two advantages of using a questioning technique of this sort.

1 The research question can be used as a tool, throughout your period of research activity, to help you to cut through the information you collect, and decide what is useful and what is not. Very often, young economists find that they gather more information than they need, and must sort out the relevant from the irrelevant. Simply by asking yourself: 'Does this information help to answer my research question?' you can sift out the information you really need and distinguish it from

what is less useful.

2 The research question can lead on to further questions, or subsidiary questions, which show the usefulness of the work you have carried out. For example, once you have determined the elasticity of local train travel, you could go on to ask:

'Why is this elasticity important?'

In answering this question you could try to show how the railway company's revenue, and hence its profit, will be affected by decisions to increase or reduce the price of train tickets.

Having chosen a topic area and taken aim, there are four further steps in undertaking an investigation:

- planning and preparation;
- gathering information;
- using information;
- writing and presentation.

Planning and preparation

Your investigation will end with the writing of an assignment, probably in the form of a 'report'. It is worth drawing up an outline of the basic structure of this report before you start. This will map out the main section and subject headings, and give some indication of the proposed content of each. This 'synopsis' can be thought of as a battle plan, which gives you a basic structure; around this framework you can build up your final piece of written work. You need not stick to your synopsis rigidly; some of your original ideas might turn out to be irrelevant in practice, while during the process of gathering information, new ideas will occur to you and you might decide to follow up 'leads' in unanticipated directions. You might even find that you need to consider altering the title of your investigation to more accurately reflect the final outcome.

Gathering and using information

There is no shortage of sources of economic information: your local library, and your school or college library are obvious starting points. Government publications such as Economic Trends are often very useful, as are the newspaper and journal articles available on CD ROM. As time goes on, computer-based sources of information such as the World-Wide Web on the 'Internet' will become increasingly accessible and useful. In addition to the mainly 'secondary sources' available through desk research, it is also possible to go to 'primary sources' through field research; in other words, you can generate your own information through the use of questionnaires.

In some ways, it is possible to find that economists are faced with too much information; it is necessary to be selective and sift through it, sorting out the pieces which are of most use.

Writing and presentation

As an economist, you are likely to find it necessary to present findings in the form of a report. Remember that a report is always:

TO someone, FROM someone and ABOUT something.
Using an appropriate format such as the following will help. Look at Box 3.2.

BOX 3.2

Writing reports

Very often in business-related subjects you are asked to write a "report". It is important to use an appropriate business format or layout when writing such a report. Remember...

- A report is always
  FROM someone;
  TO someone;
  ABOUT something.
- A report usually needs to come to conclusions or make recommendations (sometimes both)

An example format is shown below. It may not be completely suitable for all purposes, but you can adapt it.

Sometimes you are asked to write a report as part of a 'scenario'. Then you would sign your report in your role (e.g. Personnel Manager). If the report is not based on a scenario or simulation, then sign in your own name and direct the report to your lecturer.

The report might take up more than one page, in which case you can use continuation sheets. If the report is part of a class assignment, then your lecturer will give instructions as to minimum and maximum word counts. As a very rough guide, one side of A4, closely typed, gives about 500 words.

In a business setting, where people have limited time to absorb information, it is often desirable to provide a summary report or abstract. A recent Prime Minister has stated that anything worth saying can be said on one side of A4, and that it is rarely worth reading any further. The discipline of being able to convey the essentials of a problem as succinctly as this is a skill worth developing.

Any graphs, statistics, supporting information, sources, etc. should be grouped together in an 'appendix', so that it can be referred to without cluttering up the main body of the report.

BOX 3.2

Report

Date _____

From _____ (Name) _____ (Position)*

To _____ (Name) _____ (Position)

Subject/topic/title _____

Background information/outline of the problem _____

_____

_____

Analysis/findings _____

_____

_____

_____

_____

_____

_____

_____

_____

_____

_____

_____

_____

_____

_____

_____

(Use continuation sheets if necessary).

BOX 3.2

Conclusions/recommendations

1.
2.
3.
(Etc.)

Signed

Note: Write in your 'position' (e.g. 'Personnel Manager') if the report is part of a scenario; otherwise just put your own name.

Sections of a report

1 **Title page**
   This signals what the report is about. The title should be clear and concise.

2 **Contents page**
   This lists the sections of the report, and states the page number where each one starts.

3 **Introduction**
   This states the aims of the report, and should therefore contain an hypothesis or pose a question.

4 **The text**
   This is the main content of the report, and contains the research findings. It may be broken down into several sections, and sections may be further divided into sub-sections, with these pieces fitted together in a logical order. When presenting statistics, use a variety of presentation techniques, including pie-charts, bar diagrams and graphs as well as tables of figures. Remember that a picture can paint a thousand words, and that in economics it is usually possible to present information in a variety of ways, as in Box 3.3.

BOX 3.3

Presentation of information
Information in economics can be presented...

● **Verbally** (in words)
   If the price of rail tickets increases by 2%, the quantity demanded falls by 2%.

● **Algebraically** (as an equation)
   Elasticity = P.dQ/Q.dP = 1

● **Diagrammatically** (as a flowchart, for example, or more usually as a graph)

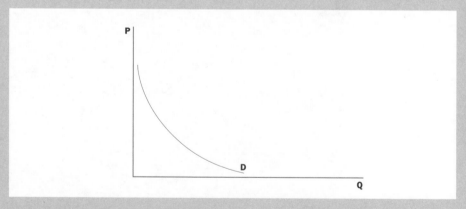

● **Numerically** (as a table)

Price (£)	Quantity (journeys per hour)	Revenue (£)
10	100	1000
5	200	1000
2	500	1000

5 **Conclusions and evaluation**
   A report should end with some conclusions; if, however, the results of research are inconclusive, then recognise this fact and say so. If you have been asked to make recommendations, then these should be listed, with reasons given in support. It is also worth evaluating the whole exercise: state whether the research has achieved its aims, the effectiveness of various research methods used, and comment on any problems encountered.

Investigative skills

As a newcomer to economics, you might find that it is some time before you have to carry out a formal investigation and present a polished report. If you are following an examination syllabus which requires something of this sort, then you will clearly do this sooner than if you are going to be examined in a different way. However, even examination syllabuses without 'coursework' as such nowadays adopt much more of an investigative approach. Data-response questions, for example, require you to apply your knowledge, and use your knowledge of economics as a tool for analysing everyday information sources such as newspaper articles. And even the traditional 'essay' can be used to encourage the use of the 'applied' nature of economics and problem-solving techniques.

Even if you are never going to work as an economist, it is never too soon to develop investigative habits, or to adopt an investigative approach. For example, one of the most useful skills you can acquire is the ability to look critically at what you read in the press or see on the television. If, for instance, the railways are privatised, or if interest rates are increased, your knowledge of economics should equip you to consider whether the reasons being put forward by journalists or politicians actually make sense.

REVIEW

This chapter has introduced you to the type of work that economists do, and some of the methods that can be used in economic investigations.

An old economics teacher used to have a favourite saying: *'You can't do economics until you understand it, and you can't understand economics until you've done it.'*

There is a lot of truth in the second part of this statement, but we don't totally agree with the first part. The first part is true in the sense that economics consists of a chain of related economic topics. As you study the subject, you are gradually making connections between links in the chain. Lose one link and understanding is lost. In this way, you will find that the more economics you know, the more you will understand it; and in this way the subject becomes easier as time goes on, when you begin to see the 'whole picture', and initial effort is rewarded with increasing returns. However, we firmly believe that you can do economics before you know and understand it all; what is important is that you should be constantly active in your study.

REVIEW

To think and work as an economist you need to approach each topic by asking

1 What does economic theory tell me about this topic?
2 How does this theory link up to other topics in the framework of economics?
3 How does this topic relate to examples in the real world?

In other words, as an economist, you can identify linkages and insights. You will see linkages between economic principles and the topics you are studying, and linkages between topics in different parts of the framework of economics. You will also find that economics gives you a special viewpoint; your knowledge of economic principles gives you a special viewpoint on world events, which you would not have if you were not an economist. So even if you are never asked to undertake a full-blown economics investigation culminating in a written report which is graded and assessed, we firmly believe that you should approach every topic in economics, no matter how large or small, with an investigative attitude. If you simply read the press and watch TV news with a more critical eye, you will have started along this road.

REVIEW TASKS

Coursework

As you work through this book, you will find various topics which are particularly useful for investigative work in economics. As a preliminary exercise, you could carry out an investigation into unemployment in your local area. What is the unemployment rate? Is it lower or higher than the average for the UK? What are the costs and benefits of policies aimed at reducing unemployment?

Section 2
What Markets Can Do

2.4 What is a market?

Are you old enough to buy ice cream?

Ice cream used to be just a product for children but the market is changing. The arrival of Häagen-Dazs has turned a cheap, bland, frozen, white blancmange-like substance into an expensive, adult fantasy sex aid. What Häagen-Dazs succeeded in doing (actually it was a company called Grand Metropolitan which created the Häagen-Dazs brand name to sound suitably Scandinavian) was to take a traditional product, upgrade its quality and reposition it to appeal to a different set of consumers. A profitable slice of the market or market niche was created into which Häagen-Dazs was the only supplier.

But Häagen-Dazs has not had it all its own way. The supermarket chains tried out the premium brands in their own stores and spotted the shift in consumer tastes. Their response was to launch their own label rival brands of ice cream to appeal to the same buyers. They climbed in on the back of Häagen-Dazs advertising which had essentially created the market. Losely and New England were early producers of luxury ice cream and, more recently, Ben & Jerry's ice cream (Häagen-Dazs's main competitor in the USA) is now sold in the UK. Walls, the overall market leader in ice cream sales, has now entered the market with its new up-market brand called Ranieri and Sainsbury's now sell their own luxury range of 'Indulgence' ice cream.

*Source: **The Times** (30 November 1994).*

Preview

In this chapter we shall investigate the following key areas:
- markets;
- price;
- the characteristics of markets.

How would an economist comment on Focus 2.4?

Decisions about how scarce resources are to be used in free market economies are determined by the actions of markets. In this Focus we are given some information about what is happening in one particular market. More people, capital, raw materials and land are being used to supply more expensive ice cream which seems to appeal to the adult buyer. So those scarce resources will not now be available to produce other goods or services. There is an opportunity cost: we get more adult ice cream but we get less children's ice cream, sweets or other products those resources might have made.

Resources often change their use. As new products become popular, firms find that they can sell them at higher prices and, consequently, make higher profits. This acts as a signal to other firms to get into that industry to try to earn some of these new profits. For example, as a new clothing fashion takes hold, other firms jump on the bandwagon to try to imitate the successful product. (see Focus) As products such as Levi jeans, Dr Martens footwear and Nike or Reebok trainers have become market leaders, more companies have been attempting to produce similar products. Resources have moved into the growth areas so that consumers are provided with what they want.

Decisions about the use of resources are taken by firms but are strongly influenced by what is often called 'the invisible hand' of the market.

What is a market?

*A **market** is a set of arrangements which brings buyers and sellers together to undertake transactions for their mutual benefit.*

The extract in Focus 2.4 is about the market for a certain type of ice cream. What features are present in this market?

- The product has distinct characteristics which separate it from other, even quite similar, products.
- One or more firms supply this product to the market and make it available for sale.
- The producing firms do not have to get involved in the selling of the product directly to the buyers, although they may choose to do so. They tend to leave the selling to specialist retailers who try to develop knowledge of what the buyers are looking for when making a purchase.
- Buyers need to make choices about which of the range of goods on offer they will purchase. Consumers will broadly be looking for the same kinds of benefits from the product but each consumer will have his or her own individual preferences.
- Before buying decisions are made, consumers need to collect information. This could be very basic such as whether the good is in stock or what is the price. It could be more complex if the consumer is thinking about buying a more technically advanced product such as a CD player.

- The market may be small or large. It may be located in a particular place or widely dispersed. It may be totally separate from other markets or closely integrated with them. It may be dominated by a single large firm or supplied by a large number of small firms.
- In well established markets products may appear to change little whilst in others firms work hard to make their products seem different to all of the others on the market and new designs are constantly being introduced.

In short, a market describes a set of arrangements which bring buyers and sellers together to undertake transactions for their mutual benefit. There is a market for ice cream, a market for newspapers and there are markets for holidays, cars and insurance. Each of these markets may be broken up into smaller market segments appealing to particular kinds of people. So the ice cream market may be divided between adult, take-home and impulse buys; newspapers are divided between the popular tabloids such as the *Sun* and the *Mirror* and the quality broadsheets such as the *Guardian* and *Telegraph*. What are the different segments in the holiday, car and insurance industries?

Linkages between markets

What happens in one market often affects what then happens in other markets. Markets are interdependent or inter-related. In our example of the adult ice cream market, what happens will be strongly affected by what is going on in the general market for ice cream. Some consumers may see more ordinary ice cream as a perfectly acceptable alternative to adult ice cream, so buyers may switch between markets. If consumers are buying ice cream as a dessert they may see yogurts or other puddings as substitutes, and so these markets will be closely linked. Sometimes markets will be linked in a less direct way. If people are spending more on buying ice cream they may be spending less on fruit or even magazines, videos or going out. One of the skills of the economist is to attempt to predict what effects will result from changes in markets.

TASK 4.1

What makes the adult ice cream market a market?

To answer this question we need to ask another set of questions. Answer the following questions using your own knowledge of the ice cream market.

- Is adult ice cream a distinct product? What makes it different from ordinary ice cream?
- Who are the manufacturers of luxury ice cream? Do they only supply this market?
- Who sells the ice cream to the consumers? Where is it sold?
- What are the buyers of luxury ice cream looking for? What are the main factors influencing a consumer's decision to buy luxury ice cream?
- What information would the consumer need to collect before making a decision to buy?
- Is it a large or small market? Is it growing? Will new firms be entering the market?
- Where is the market for luxury ice cream?
- What are the links between the luxury ice cream and other markets?
- Could the resources used to manufacture luxury ice cream be better used to make other products?

Try asking these questions of other markets such as the markets for butter, bicycles, beef or beer.

Buyers and sellers

To take our analysis of the luxury ice cream market further we need to have more information about the buyers and sellers. We need more data about the market. Some additional information is contained in Box 4.1.

BOX 4.1

The ice cream market

	1989	1990	1991	1992	1993
Total sales (£ million)	715	795	792	815	858
% growth	–	–	–	–	–
Adult ice cream sales (£ million)	53.3	69	86	101.5	113
% growth	–	–	–	–	–
% of the total market for adult ice cream					

TASK 4.2

1 Complete the table by filling in the % growth figures.
2 Has anything amazing happened in this market? (Remember that this period covers a time when the UK economy was going through a recession when income levels were either falling or rising slowly.)

In Box 4.1 we can begin to see a picture emerging. It is clear that both the sales of ice cream and adult ice cream have been growing in recent years: the market has been growing. To get a better idea of the changes which have occurred we need to complete Task 4.2. We will then be in a position to compare the growth in the sales in the adult market with the growth in the general market for ice cream to see if anything extraordinary has happened.

Once the changes have been noted, the economist is still not satisfied. Next, we want to know why the changes have occurred. One puzzling feature of this market is that we are dealing with a high priced product which has still managed to increase sales. Why have these manufacturers been able to scoop high profits during a difficult trading period for most companies? Who are the buyers? Häagen Dazs and Sainsbury's probably carried out market research to find out about them before launching their products.

In 1992, 35% of adults were buying ice cream once a month or more but the age profile of the buyers is interesting. Only 27% of the 15–24 age range were buying ice cream regularly whereas nearly half the 25–44 age group were regular buyers. Many of these were in the higher income groups and a manufacturer might well have concluded that, at the time, there was no product specifically geared to the needs of these people. Adult ice cream had not appeared on the scene and there seemed to be a gap in the market.

How did the producers respond?

The sale of ice cream is organised in three ways:

A the take home market with sales largely coming through the big retail chains and independent convenience stores;
B the ready wrapped or impulse buys, e.g. Cornettos or Mars ice creams;
C scoops of ice cream from an ice cream freezer.

The impulse market was sewn up by the large manufacturers with Mars and Walls together responsible for 70% of the market. New producers always find it tough to get a foothold in a market dominated by the large players, especially when companies such as Walls have exclusive arrangements with retailers so that they only sell their products from freezers which they have provided.

The scoop section of the market was small. It only accounted for 11% of the market and the market share was falling.

The take-home market was more open. Häagen-Dazs used heavy advertising to convince the consumer that here was a product of high quality and, to reinforce that image, opened its own shops in prestigious locations. Their marketing approach was so successful that, by 1993, Häagen-Dazs controlled over 30% of the take-home market with strong competition coming from supermarket own brands accounting for 41%.

All of the promotion was aimed at persuading the older, higher income consumer to buy more of their ice cream. Perfectly sensible people began to believe that an evening spent at home could be improved by the addition of a few dollops of very expensive ice cream. The demand for the product was identified and developed by the manufacturers.

Attempts to control the market

Once a number of firms begin to compete in the same market, interest in the product tends to rise. Firms respond to the emergence of new competitors by stepping up their own promotional efforts in order to hang on to their market. Firms attempt to control the market as much as they can but still some factors are uncontrollable. Ice cream sales are greatly affected by the weather: a hot summer sees sales leap, a wet and cold summer hits sales.

Companies cannot control the strategies of competitors. Häagen-Dazs might have thought that it would have control of the market on its own but the decision of Ben & Jerry's to export to the UK and the decision of supermarkets to market their own branded products has changed market conditions.

Critical reports by external bodies can reduce sales. Tobacco companies have long been countering reports which link their product to cancer. One technique they have favoured is to associate their product with suitably exciting sports and individuals, hoping that these positive images will outweigh the negative in the minds of potential consumers.

The state of the economy can affect sales. During the early 1990s the UK was in a recession. The economy was reducing in size, incomes were falling, unemployment was increasing, all of which were causing the sales of many products to fall. Many firms struggled to survive in this economic climate but clung on hoping to benefit from any upturn in the economy.

Changes in government policy also affect markets. Decisions to raise or lower the level of taxation affect the potential level of sales of any product. The motor manufacturing industry is particularly vulnerable. Rises in income tax will reduce people's spending on cars, a rise in the tax on petrol or the road fund licence could affect sales, any rise in VAT will push up prices of cars and any change in interest rates will affect the amount that people are prepared to borrow to finance the purchase of cars. In addition, any change in the exchange rate of the pound will affect sales. A rise in the pound will have the effect of making imported cars cheaper and so increasing the level of competition faced by home producers.

Changes in the law will also have an impact upon markets. Firms have to respond to new laws and these may well have an impact upon the costs and profitability of operating in certain markets.

Who decides price?

At first sight fixing the price of any good appears simple. The manufacturer or provider of the service must decide the price at which that good or service is sold. Häagen-Dazs must decide their price just as Ben and Jerry must decide theirs. But do companies have total control over this decision?

Much depends on the degree of competition existing within the market. If there are no competitors then the firm has a monopoly over the supply of the product and great control over the price charged. The consumer has very little choice other than to pay the price demanded. As soon as new firms enter an industry and some competition develops, firms have to start to take notice of what the other firms are doing. With a lot of competition, firms may find that
they have a very limited control over price and will have to go along with the prices charged by other firms in the market.

Companies may set themselves a complex range of objectives but, for most, making profits comes high on the list. Firms will seek to charge a price to ensure profitability. Many pricing strategies exist:
- competitive pricing, where firms set prices according to price levels established by other firms in the market;
- cost plus pricing, where firms add on a fixed percentage profit to their costs of production;
- predatory pricing, where firms deliberately undercut the competitors to steal market share;
- market skimming, where firms charge a high price initially to cream off the high profit in a market when there are few competitors, as might be the case with Häagen-Dazs;
- price discrimination, where firms might sell the same product to different consumers at different prices. This may sound impossible but just look at the prices charged by rail companies for people to travel at different times of the day, or the variation in the prices of holidays or aircraft travel.

Generally firms find that if they try to charge too high a price, sales will fall, although this can depend on the kinds of messages customers pick up from price. For some products such as perfume, a high price could reassure the customer of high quality. A high price may indicate exclusivity and make the product more attractive and sales could even increase. Pricing decisions are finely balanced and all producers will be concerned about the way in which demand responds to changes in price.

How is the market for luxury ice cream different from other markets?

Ice cream and cars might seem to have little in common but it is still possible for the markets for the two products to have several similarities:

- both markets are dominated by a small number of firms;
- both markets are segmented with a separate luxury market;
- both products are heavily advertised;
- both markets are affected by seasonal demand (most new car sales occur in August when the registration letter changes);
- both markets experience a considerable amount of competition from foreign producers.

However, there are some major differences:

- the decision-making process for the consumer will be very different for each of the products;
- there is a great difference in the size of the two markets;
- it is much easier to enter the ice cream industry than it is to enter the car manufacturing industry;
- changes in the market for cars have important repercussions for the whole econom;, changes in the ice cream industry are important but less significant.

BOX 4.2

Anyone for ICED TEA?

Helen Davidson

Two former window-cleaners and a shopkeeper from Brooklyn, New York, have achieved the rare distinction of provoking a multi-million-pound battle in Britain with PepsiCo and Unilever. The product? Iced tea.

Eight years ago Arnold Greenberg, Hyman Golden and Leonard Marsh set up Snapple, a company selling iced teas and fruit drinks made entirely from "natural" ingredients.

Today the company is worth £937m, has a turnover in excess of £322m, and trades in more than a dozen countries around the world.

A year ago the company launched a handful of its exotically named drinks, among them Lemon Flavoured Iced Tea, Mango Madness and Melonberry Cocktail, in Britain.

Within six months of Snapple's arrival, it had sold around 100,000 cases worth over £2m at shop prices in its launch area within the M25.

Harry Drnec, the man who introduced fashionable Sol lager to Britain, is co-ordinating distribution.

"We are not going to replace colas, and we're not going to supplant hot tea," said Mr Greenberg, the company's chief operating officer.

"But we think there's a big market for iced tea and our other products in Britain." Plans are now afoot to begin an ambitious expansion programme outside London.

Iced tea is the fastest growing soft drinks category in the world, and sales have tripled in the past four years.

In Britain, where four billion litres of soft drinks are sold each year, that represents a significant opportunity.

Within a few months of its launch Snapple quickly gained a foothold in Britain, particularly among 18 to 45-year-olds who are prepared to pay a high premium for a trendy "New Age"

BOX 4.2

beverage which offered a healthy alternative to canned fizzy drinks.

"Iced tea is a growth area that the major companies are now focusing on," said Mark Lynch, an analyst with S G Warburg. "'It was an area ignored by Coca-Cola and Pepsi and that has been exploited by people like Snapple who have done a good job in building up the market."

In March, seven months after Snapple first appeared in London, PepsiCo teamed up with Unilever and Britvic to produce a rival iced tea, called Liptonice, under the collective brand name Lipton.

Cheaper, and more mainstream than Snapple in its appeal, various forms of the Lipton brand have been on sale across the Atlantic since 1992, where according to S G Warburg the iced tea market is now worth more than £125m. Last year Lipton accounted for a quarter of that figure, while Snapple cornered more than a third of it.

In Britain, Lipton backed up its launch with a £6m advertising campaign by Ogilvy & Mather with a voice-over from Angus Deayton, celebrity presenter of television's *Have I Got News for You.*

"We wanted to challenge people's perceptions that iced tea is just cold tea, but in a humorous way," Gill Noble, senior marketing manager at Unilever, explained. "We thought Angus Deayton's humour was bound to appeal to people."

In July, Snapple retaliated with a quirky campaign from Banks, Hoggins O'Shea, at a modest cost of only £1m, which featured real shopkeepers from London in unscripted interviews.

"Our job was to emphasise that Snapple wasn't coming from the big guns like Pepsi or Coke," said John Banks, a partner in the

agency. "So we avoided all the traditional shots like boy-meets-girl to make people think it was their product, a friendly product." The campaign has pushed sales estimates for the year to 600,000 cases worth £14m.

Though the advertising campaigns are targeting the same market, there are significant differences between the products being promoted.

Snapple's drinks cost around £1, are made with still water and sell in large glass bottles. All of them are recognisably transatlantic in origin.

In contrast, Lipton has concentrated on basic iced lemon tea, made with carbonated water, sold in traditional 330ml cans, and costing a third of the price of a Snapple drink. Liptonice has been specially formulated to suit British taste buds.

Gill Noble at Unilever reckons the market in this country for Liptonice this year alone will be more than £20m and she expects that to rise 15-fold to more than £300m over the next five to 10 years.

Other companies are expected to join the fray. In the United States Nestlé and Coca-Cola have a joint venture to make an iced tea product called Nestea, established in 1991, which has a fifth of the American iced tea market, and is already on sale in a score of countries round the world.

"There are no current plans to launch it in this country, but we haven't ruled it out," said a Coca-Cola spokesman.

Industry experts agree that after Sainsbury's aggressive attack on the cola market earlier this year, the makers of "The Real Thing" will be watching Lipton's and Snapple's progress carefully.

*Source: **Sunday Independent,** Business Section (4 September 1994).*

TASK 4.3 How does the market for this part of the soft drinks market compare with the market for adult ice cream?

Factor markets

Derived demand is where the demand for one item is determined by the demand for another.

The changing markets for products such as ice cream and soft drinks have an effect on the quantities of resources employed in each of those industries (see Box 4.2). As the demand for ice cream expands so manufacturers will wish to step up production. To do this they may have to take on more workers, buy some more equipment or expand the factory and this will affect the markets for labour, capital and land. The markets for these factors of production are dependent on what is happening in the product markets. The markets are interdependent. The demand for any factor is a derived demand (see Box 4.3) in that it is determined by the demand for the goods or services that the factors are used to produce. An increase in the demand for portable telephones will require more people to be employed in their manufacture and sale. Most of the manufacturing jobs may well be created abroad but sales staff will be needed in the UK. A fall in the demand for houses will require fewer building workers.

BOX 4.3

A derived DEMAND

B & Q creates 2,000 jobs

Michael Tate, Deputy City Editor

Two thousand new jobs will be created this year by DIY market leader B&Q, which is stepping up its expansion programme in a move that will be seen as a direct response to Sainsbury's £290 million merger of Homebase and the Texas Homecare chain.

B&Q, part of the Kingfisher retail group, where a boardroom reshuffle 10 days ago saw Sir Geoffrey Mulcahay resume the chief executive role, plans to open six more giant warehouses this year, as well as three new ordinary stores, even though the DIY market is still widely considered to be saturated. Bill Whiting, managing director of the B&Q Warehouse division, added that another 20 of 260 smaller, more traditional stores, known as Supercentres, would be revamped under a new format.

'They will concentrate on the more decorative end of the market – what we call home enhancement,' he said. He denied that this was a defensive move in the face of the Homebase

BOX 4.3

challenge. 'It is the culmination of a couple of years' work, but it now looks even more appropriate.'

Together, Homebase and Texas are expected to command 11.5 per cent of the home improvements market, and the combined group represents a considerable threat to B&Q's leadership with just under 14 per cent.

B&Q's expansion at the warehouse end of the market also pre-empts the expected arrival in this country this year of America's biggest

DIY retailer, Atlanta-based Home Depot.

B&Q has already rethought its Warehouse concept, after finding that the bigger it built then, the greater the success. 'From now on,' said Whiting, they will all be 100,000 sq ft – three times bigger than the traditional DIY store, and carrying 40,000 lines, twice the normal figure.'

Source: **Observer,** Business Section
(5 February 1995).

TASK 4.4

Why are B&Q creating 2000 jobs?

Like products, factors also command a price. With labour, the price is the wage paid, with capital it is the interest received, with land it is the rent paid and with enterprise it is the profit earned. If there are shortages of a particular factor such as computer engineers, we would expect the price paid for them to increase and the wages of computer engineers would rise. There is some debate about how similar the product and factor markets are and, at this stage, you could consider whether you see any differences between them.

Deindustrialisation describes the shift of employment away from primary and secondary industry towards the service sector.

Change is an ever-present feature of any market economy. The UK economy has experienced a remarkable transformation during the 20th century. There has been a major shift from employment in primary and secondary industries such as agriculture and manufacturing towards the service sector. This process of deindustrialisation has been caused by a combination of factors, among which changing technology and competitiveness have been of prime importance.

Today less than 2% of the work force is employed in agriculture whereas over 60% are employed in the service industries.

Capital markets consist of organisations or institutions seeking to borrow or lend money to be used by industry. If there is a general upsurge in business activity and the economy is booming there may be heavy demands to borrow. If there are insufficient funds available the rate of interest, or price that borrowers have to pay, will rise. The market will ration out the available funds.

The market for land reflects the demand and supply of land. Land in city centres is scarce and commands a high price so ice cream factories will set up on the outskirts of towns, perhaps on an industrial estate, where land will be much cheaper. High land prices will also affect the prices of houses which are built on the land.

Two key differences between land and the other factors of production are that first, land is immobile and cannot be moved around in response to a shortage and secondly, the total amount of land is fixed in supply. This means that the prices of land will be particularly sensitive to changes in demand and that investing in property can be a very risky business.

REVIEW

This chapter has introduced the idea that markets exist for products, services and factors. An understanding of markets is essential if we are to go on to develop an understanding of how market economies work. Markets will have certain features in common in that the forces of supply and demand will be influential but each market will have its own special characteristics. The interdependence of markets describes the way in which markets are linked together and a change in one market will affect others. The analysis of markets is the subject of this section of the book.

REVIEW TASK

Investigating markets – a coursework task

A profile of a market

1   Select a market ripe for investigation. You could start with a fairly broad based market such as cars but then see if you can identify different market segments such as small family or luxury cars.

2   Assemble information which sheds light on the kind of market under investigation. This should cover:

- the total size of the market;
- whether the market is growing or contracting;
- information about the buyers and sellers;
- the factors affecting the decisions of buyers;
- the market share of each supplier;
- any special characteristics of the market;
- any recent changes or shocks to the market.

You could present this information as a market profile in report form or as a wall display. If you are working as part of a group, you could present your findings to the rest of the group and then begin to make comparisons between markets. You may be surprised to find that markets such as petrol, chocolate or banks can have many things in common.

How do you affect markets?

Who buys your jeans?

This year approximately 45 million pairs of jeans will be sold in the UK worth £1.5 billion. Levi Strauss is the market leader with 23% of sales and most of these will be sold to 15–24 year olds. So it quickly becomes clear that the market demand is made up of thousands or millions of individuals making decisions about whether to buy or not to buy jeans. To understand how this market works, we need to find out how individuals make decisions to buy goods or services. What is going on in their minds?

TASK 5.1

When was the last time you bought a pair of jeans? How did you do it? What factors did you take into account before making your decision? What were the jeans like? How many pairs of jeans do you already own?
Before reading on, try answering questions like these. If you are working with other students you could compile results for your group and discuss your different responses. Do any general principles emerge?

Preview

In this chapter we shall investigate the following key areas:

- the law of diminishing marginal utility;
- the principle of equi-marginal utility;
- applications of utility theory;
- indifference curve analysis.

Markets are made up of people

To understand how markets work we need to understand what motivates people since it is people who make the decisions which govern how markets function. It is obviously the case that people act differently to each other. We each feel that we are individuals. However, observation of how people behave reveals certain things that they have in common. If we are ever to be able to predict how people will act, we have to make assumptions about what drives people to action.

First, we assume that people act rationally. That is, they use common sense and logic when making decisions. It is probably correct to say that we all act irrationally or on impulse sometimes but for most of the time we do act sensibly making sensible choices.

Secondly, people aim to maximise the total satisfaction or utility they get from their decisions. This means that, given a choice, we will always prefer more rather than less satisfaction.

People have a range of wants which, if satisfied, would generate satisfaction or utility. However, we cannot satisfy all of those wants. We face constraints which limit our ability to maximise our satisfaction despite our best efforts. Our incomes are limited, and this prevents us from buying all the things we would like. Often we lack all the essential information we might need in order to make a rational decision.

This, occasionally, leads us to make incorrect decisions, and making well thought out decisions also requires time which we do not always have. Hence, we end up making the best decisions we can given these constraints.

Given a choice, we all might prefer to drive a Jaguar, Mercedes or Ferrari. Unfortunately, a limited income prevents us from buying them. We therefore have to make do with a lesser machine but we may never know whether we have made the right choice of alternative. There may just be too much information to consider and we often have to buy a car without a full consumer test of all of the possibilities. All we can do is to do our best to make the right decision at the time.

What happens when people make spending decisions?

Most people, when asked why they bought a particular pair of jeans, might reply 'it was because I liked them'. As economists we can read a little more into this answer. Every time a person spends money it tells us about the value they place upon the utility gained from buying the product. If a consumer parts with their money, it tells us that they must have felt that the product was worth at least as much as the price paid. If they hadn't thought this, then why should they have bought the product? In some cases the consumers feel that they have gained good value, that the product was a bargain and that the product was worth more than had been paid for it. On other occasions, we are less certain. Making the decision about whether to buy or not to buy is more difficult. We may just decide to buy, but if we feel that the product is not worth the asking price we don't buy, or we try to get a reduction.

Consumer Surplus is the amount by which total utility exceeds total expenditure on an item.

Every time we buy something we seem to be comparing its value to us (the utility) with the price.

If your last pair of jeans cost you £30, you must have felt that you were getting at least £30 worth of utility from them. If you felt that the jeans were particularly fine and that you would not be seen out without them on, then you could have estimated that they were worth more than £30 to you, perhaps £70 or £80. If you paid £30 for something giving you £80 worth of satisfaction , you are gaining a consumer's surplus of £50 and this could be seen as the amount by which the value of the total utility gained is greater than the total expenditure on the product.

Utility is the satisfaction gained from the consumption of a good or service.

Consumer's surplus is the amount by which the total utility received from the consumption of a good exceeds the expenditure on that good. It is shown on a diagram by the gap between the marginal utility curve and the total expenditure (see Task 5.3).

*The **law of diminishing marginal utility** states that as more of a good is consumed, the satisfaction gained from each additional unit will decrease.*

In practice we make these kinds of consumer decisions every day with very little conscious thought and without bothering to calculate the size of any consumer's surplus. But it is still there. Businesses are certainly aware of its existence. If they detect that consumers are prepared to pay high prices for a product, they can increase profits by raising prices. When shops hold sales they are trying to persuade people to buy products which, at the old prices, would not have produced any consumer's surplus for the buyers.

At this point, an understanding of the law of diminishing marginal utility might deepen our knowledge of what is going on.

The law of diminishing marginal utility

When shopping for jeans, most people buy a single pair. We do this because we do not have unlimited amounts of money to spend on jeans. Even if we did have excessive amounts to spend, we might prefer to buy a wider variety of clothes rather than 10 or 11 pairs of jeans. Try Task 5.2 to work out what is happening as the consumption of any product increases.

TASK 5.2

The Rolo experiment

Try this experiment on your own or with a class of other students.

Step 1 Buy a fun-sized pack of your favourite sweets. Mars, Twix, Creme Eggs are fine but Rolos are best.

Step 2 Find a quiet spot and proceed to eat six bars, one after another. After finishing each bar or packet of Rolos you must stop to record how much satisfaction or utility you gained from its consumption. This, in itself, is quite a problem. You need to decide how you are going to measure utility. It will help if you come up with a system which allows scores to be added to each other. One way, for example, might be to award marks out of 10, a system similar to that used to judge gymnastics or ice skating. Think very carefully before you award marks and make sure that you record your score.

Step 3 When you have completed the exercise you should reflect on what happened to your scores as you ate more packets. If you continued to eat more and more sweets, what would you expect to happen to the value of the utility you gain from each extra packet you eat? How many sweets would you need to eat before you gained no utility from your eating? When would you start to feel ill from eating sweets or, in other words, when would you start to experience negative utility from eating sweets?

TASK 5.2

Step 4 Draw a graph of your utility scores. Plot utility on the vertical axis and the number of packets of Rolos eaten on the horizontal axis. Join up the points with a curved line. What kind of curve emerges? If you are working in a group you could calculate some average values for the group which might provide you with a smoother curve.

(If you couldn't afford the Rolos, you will still be able to imagine what might have happened to your utility.)

The issue you now have to consider is whether what you have found happens when Rolos are consumed will also happen when other goods are consumed. If it will be the same for all goods and services, you are on the brink of discovering an economic hypothesis or law. You could try writing down what you think the law might say. Economic laws will apply to other situations but you will have to identify the assumptions we made when undertaking the experiment.

Once you have formed your hypothesis you can begin to test it and even modify it if necessary.

Economists have addressed problems similar to the 'Rolo experiment' and developed a theory about how people behave and this is known as the law of diminishing marginal utility.

This states that as more of any good is consumed, the satisfaction or utility gained from each extra unit will decrease.

Hopefully, this was pretty similar to your own thoughts in answering Task 5.2.

As with any law in Economics, the law of diminishing marginal utility is dependent on certain assumptions:

● All of the products consumed were exactly the same in every respect – they were homogeneous. Each packet of Rolos was exactly the same as every other packet of Rolos.

● The products were consumed in one time period. You were not allowed to spread your eating of Rolos over six days.
● There was only one product to purchase, in our experiment – Rolos.

Life is not quite like this. We space out our consumption over time. We may own four pairs of jeans but it is unlikely that we bought them all at the same time either because we do not have sufficient income or because we know that we could get more satisfaction by buying one pair of jeans and some other clothes. Jeans come in different colours. It is unlikely that a person buys four pairs of the same colour because they would get greater satisfaction from a wider variety. Test this out with a 'jeans' survey' of your class mates or friends.

Actually measuring utility is more difficult. There is no accepted method of measuring utility. The best we can do is to get consumers to estimate the value of the satisfaction received when a product is bought. This can be seen in the price a consumer would be prepared to pay for a product. In a traffic jam on a hot summer's day, a driver might be prepared to pay £1 for a cold drink and this is a measure of the level of satisfaction the driver might expect to receive from the drink. Having had one drink, the driver would not be prepared to pay the same price for another. The more drinks consumed, the less the driver would be prepared to pay for an additional drink. In theory, we can draw up a schedule showing the value of the driver's marginal utility or satisfaction gained from each extra drink. This is shown in Box 5.1 and Task 5.3.

BOX 5.1

The principle of marginal utility

Drinks consumed	Marginal utility (£)	Total utility (£)
1	1	1
2	0.75	–
3	0.50	–
4	0.25	–
5	0.10	–
6	0.05	–
7	0	–

TASK 5.3

The marginal utility column in Box 5.1 measures the value of the satisfaction gained as the driver consumes drinks.

1 Complete the total utility column.
2 Using the data given, draw the driver's marginal utility curve using the graph below.

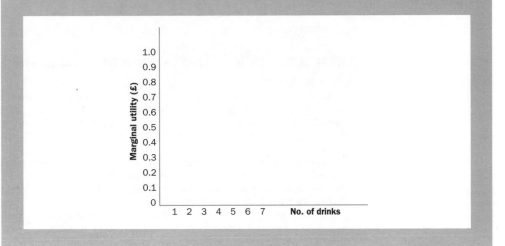

3 Assume that drinks are being sold at 50p each. Draw a horizontal line across from 50p.
4 How many drinks would you expect the rational driver to buy?
5 How many drinks would the consumer have to drink to gain the maximum amount of utility?
6 What would happen if the driver bought more than 7 drinks?
7 When consuming 3 drinks, how much is spent? What is the total utility obtained from 3 drinks? What is the difference between these two figures? Shade this area in on your graph.
8 How many drinks would the driver buy if the price fell to 10p? In this case, what would be the value of the consumer's surplus?
9 What would happen to the consumer's surplus if price rose to 80p?

If the drivers act rationally, they will continue to buy drinks as long as the value of the satisfaction is greater than the price of the drinks. In Box 5.1 this point is reached at a price of 50p when three drinks would be bought. Here the driver is spending £1.50 to buy three drinks which give £2.25 worth of utility. The gap between the total utility and the total expenditure is the consumer's surplus and, in this case, is worth 75p, the shaded area on the graph.

Most of the time people do not go around calculating the size of their consumer's surplus but they generally know if they have bought a bargain or not. Every time we get a sense of good value we are also sensing the presence of a consumer's surplus.

BOX 5.2

IT'S *good* TO TALK

Marathon talk-in leaves Mercury red in the face

Alex Bellos

A handful of chatterboxes helped to turn a telephone company's high-profile Christmas campaign into a fiasco when they embraced a rival's slogan, It's Good To Talk, a little too wholeheartedly.

Thousands of shoppers bought Mercury One-2-One mobile phones in the last two months on the promise of unlimited free calls on Christmas Day to anywhere in the world.

But many of those who took up this offer appear to have been unable to get through to anywhere on Sunday – partly because of a small number of phone-hogs.

At least 20 people spent more than 12 hours on the phone on Christmas Day and another 20 had made more than 2,000 calls between them, conceded a Mercury One-2-One spokesman last night. "Some people will not have got through because of the congestion on the lines," he said.

He was unable to comment on the location of the marathon callers, but he admitted that a "significant number" of other customers were "unhappy".

Andrew MacKinlay, Labour MP for Thurrock, said he would be writing to the Trade Secretary,

BOX 5.2

Michael Heseltine, because customers had been "thwarted in their efforts due to excessive demand and inadequate Mercury planning and facilities".

A Mercury One-2-One spokesman said the company had not expected such huge demand, but thousands of people were able to use the service. "Sixty per cent of our customer base used the network and a large number of these would have been new users. But we recognise that some people were frustrated in their attempts and that makes us disappointed, because we want to keep those customers.

"We are dealing with the complaints case by case, and we will recompense with credit calls those who – from their records – were unable to use their phone. We experienced 10 times the average number of calls usually made on a Sunday."

The free offer was made only to people who bought telephones after November 8.

*Source: **Guardian** (27 December 1994).*

TASK 5.4

How does a knowledge of marginal utility theory help you to explain what happened when Mercury dropped its charges?

The principle of equi-marginal utility

So far we have assumed that there is only one product to be bought. In practice, there are hundreds or thousands of goods available and the consumer faces the difficult problem of how to spend or allocate their fixed income so as to maximise satisfaction.

The consumer unconsciously compares the satisfaction obtained from each good with its price and then makes a comparison between different products. The consumer is looking to see where the best use of income can be made.

If consumers achieve the objective of maximising satisfaction from spending income then they will not be able to increase total satisfaction by transferring any expenditure from one item to another. At this point the economist can add a degree of precision because this combination will occur where the marginal utility (MU) of each good divided by the price of each good is equal.

In effect the consumer is attempting to compare the utility obtained from the last penny spent on each item.

To find this, the MU must be divided by the price.

In order to simplify this, we assume that the consumer is choosing between buying two goods: cola and crisps. Satisfaction will be maximised if income is divided between the two products in such a way that:

$$\frac{\text{MU of cola}}{\text{Price (P) of cola}} = \frac{\text{MU of crisps}}{\text{Price (P) of crisps}}$$

If it is the case that these fractions are not equal then consumers will be able to increase total utility by readjusting their pattern of expenditure. Box 5.3 shows an example of the principle.

BOX 5.3	**The principle of equi-marginal utility**			
	Cans of cola	MU of cola (p)	Packets of crisps	MU of crisps (p)
	1	120	1	70
	2	90	2	60
	3	60	3	50
	4	40	4	45

The price of cola is 60p a can and crisps are 30p a packet. The consumer has £1.20 to spend on food.

TASK 5.5

1 Using the principle of equi-marginal utility, what combination of cola and crisps will the consumer buy?
2 Calculate the consumer's total utility from this combination of cola and crisps.
3 Why might the consumer not buy 2 cans of cola?
4 Use the principle of equi-marginal utility to show how consumers would change their pattern of consumption if they decided to allocate £2.40 to spending on food.

In practice people have many more than two products from which to choose but the same principle applies. Satisfaction will be maximised when

$$\frac{\text{MU good A}}{\text{P good A}} = \frac{\text{MU good B}}{\text{P good B}} = \frac{\text{MU good C}}{\text{P good C}}$$

The main weakness of the principle of equi-marginal utility is that it still requires us to be able to measure the value of utility. The principle attempts to analyse what is going on in people's minds rather than precisely measuring the precise magnitude of the values involved. Other techniques are available (notably, the use of indifference curves: see appendix on p.77) which rely on a person's ability to compare the utility obtained from the consumption of goods rather than actually measuring it. However, these techniques are still dependent on the basic law that as more of any product is consumed the marginal utility falls.

Individuals and the market

The individual's marginal utility curve shows the amount of utility the consumer obtains from each extra unit of the product consumed. We measured utility in terms of the amount the consumer might be prepared to pay for each item. So, the MU curve shows the individual's demand for the product over a range of prices or the individual's demand curve. If price falls, the consumer will be prepared to buy more; if price rises, the consumer will buy less. In Box 5.3, if the price of cola was £1, one can would be bought but if the price fell to 75p two cans would be bought.

In 1994 over £440 million was spent on Coca-Cola alone which means that a whole lot of individuals were making the decision to buy Coke. Each of those individuals had their own demand curve for Coke and when these individual curves were added together, a market demand curve was formed. Because the individual demand curves were downward sloping, we would expect the market demand curve to be downward sloping. Box 5.4 shows an individual's and a market demand curve for Coca-Cola. By convention, we always measure the price on the vertical axis and the quantity demanded on the horizontal axis. The slope of the market demand curve can be explained by the law of diminishing marginal utility.

BOX 5.4

The process of revenue allocation

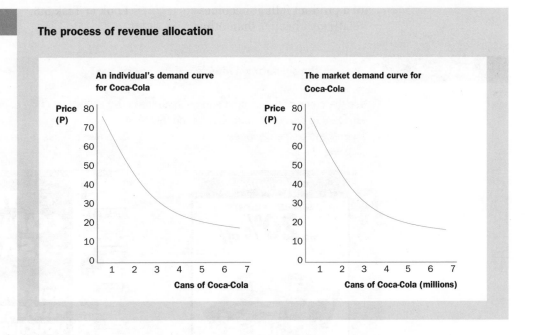

An individual's demand curve for Coca-Cola

The market demand curve for Coca-Cola

Income and substitution effects

Market demand curves for most products slope downwards from the top left. Apart from the law of diminishing marginal utility, this can be explained by two important factors: the income and substitution effects.

● **The income effect** – as the price of a product falls the real income of the consumer increases. This means that the consumer can now buy more items with the same income and is, therefore, better off. The consumer may choose to spend some of the extra real income on buying more of the same good and so demand increases as price falls.

● **The substitution effect** – as the price of a product falls it becomes relatively cheaper than other products whose prices have not changed. The consumer may now choose to substitute the cheaper, more attractive product for the more expensive products and so demand rises.

Whenever the price of a product changes there are likely to be both income and substitution effects. In many cases these effects will work together so that as the price of an item falls people will buy more because of the income effect and more because of the substitution effect. However, in some circumstances the effects may work against each other with the net effect on demand depending on the relative strength of each of the forces. Look at Task 5.6.

TASK 5.6   **Income and substitution effects**

Use the ideas of the income and substitution effects to explain how demand might be expected to change in response to the following price changes:

1 *Holidays to the Canaries going cheap*

2 *Lowest prices in the universe*

*Source: **Guardian** (27 December 1994).*

*Source: **Guardian** (27 December 1994).*

Modern applications of marginal utility theory

1 Utility and broader decision-making

Much of the work done by economists is based on the assumption that people act rationally. This assumption has attracted much discussion and has led to research into alternative theories such as Game theory, the theory of second best and Chaos theory which also seek to explain the behaviour of individuals and firms. Nevertheless, it still seems fair to make the assumption of rationality about the vast bulk of human activity.

The American economist Gary Becker earned a Nobel Prize for Economics in 1992 for the work he has done in this field. He extended the idea that people seek to maximise utility into all areas of human decision-making. He argued that decisions such as whether to get married, whether to have children, whether to stay in education or whether to commit a crime could all be investigated through an appreciation of utility theory.

People are constantly comparing the benefits of an activity with the costs or, in other words, the marginal utility with the price. Becker therefore argues that issues such as the high birth rates in some countries can be explained by reference to the costs associated with bringing up children. In most developed countries these costs are high because children spend a long time in education and do not start earning money until fairly late in life. As they delay having children, women obtain higher paid jobs, and as this happens the cost of having children increases further. Partners take into account the opportunity cost of lost pay plus the effect of a career break on potential future earnings. In poorer countries children will often be contributing to the family income at a very early age, their costs of upkeep are low, infant mortality rates are high and there is no state pension or care for the elderly. So a decision to have a large family can be seen to be perfectly rational. Look at Box 5.5.

Read the following article about the predicted rises in the size of the world's population.

BOX 5.5

The POPULATION *problem*

Global population 'could double by the year 2050'

John Gittings

Significant changes in human life during the next century are predicted in a United Nations report which warns that the world population could double by the year 2050.

The UN Population Fund (UNFPA) annual survey says the most optimistic estimate is that the current total of 5.7 billion will rise rapidly to 7.1 billion in the next 20 years. The rate of growth should then slow down to give a total of 7.8 billion by the middle of the 21st century.

But it warns that, without much greater efforts at education and family planning, these predictions could be wildly wrong. The high prediction for the year 2050 is 11.9 billion.

Next century's world will be increasingly urbanised. By the year 2015, nearly 56 per cent of the population will live in urban areas, against less than 45 per cent at present.

In real terms this means that the world's urban population will grow by half – from 2.6 billion to 3.9 billion – in 20 years.

The increase will be particularly sharp in many developing countries as people leave the countryside and migrate to the towns.

The report acknowledges that significant gains have been made in the past 30 years in education, health care and population policies but says that huge numbers of people are still poorly provided for.

Contraceptive use has quadrupled since 1965–70, yet 350 million couples still lack proper access to modern family planning.

Two-thirds of the world's 960 million illiterate people are women, and 90 million girls fail to attend primary school.

UNFPA calls for continued efforts to place women on equal terms with men. Too often, it says, women are considered "less valuable" and are not consulted about development projects.

The fund praises community programmes to educate men about their family obligations. These include a bi-weekly television soap opera in Zimbabwe called *"You Reap What You Sow"* about male participation in family planning.

Issued on World Population Day, the report seeks to put the best perspective on last year's Cairo population conference, which called for spending on population to be tripled in the next 20 years. Critics complain that many governments have failed to back up their pledges with new cash.

Halfdan Mahler, secretary-general of the International Planned Parenthood Federation, says the challenge at the UN conference on women in Beijing in September will be "to convince governments that, without their leadership and their money, the plight of women will never dramatically improve."

On Monday the Pope issued a defence of women's rights in society and apologised for the past role of the Roman Catholic Church in their oppression.

He also called for compassion towards women who had suffered what he called the "atrocity" of rape in war or peace and had decided to have an abortion.

But he insisted that "in these cases the choice to have an abortion is always a grave sin".

The State of World Population, 1995, available from UN Population Fund, 220 East 42nd Street, New York, NY10017, USA.

Source: **Guardian** *(12 July 1995).*

TASK 5.7

1 What explanations are offered to account for the growth in population?
2 How might the ideas of Gary Becker on maximising utility help to explain the problem?
3 List five solutions available to solve the world's population problem. Which of those solutions you have suggested seem to be the most practical and realistic?

Crime is another area of human activity which could be explained using utility theory. It could be argued that the lives of many young people are extremely bleak today with little prospect of a job, suitable training, a reasonable income or good housing conditions. Is it then a surprise if many with so little to lose turn to crime for a possible form of excitement and way out? Box 5.6 gives more information about crime and the young.

BOX 5.6

THATCHER'S CHILDREN
turn to crime

Barry Hugill

A 'forgotten army' of teenagers, living in acute poverty, is resorting to violence and lawlessness, according to three new surveys. The findings, which include soaring crime figures, widespread unemployment and falling wages for under-18s in work, present a bleak picture to the half a million teenagers who left school on Friday.

Research by Oliver James, a clinical psychologist, shows an unprecedented increase in violent crime by and against young people. He reports a 41 per cent increase since 1987 – when all other types of crime have been decreasing.

His finding comes days after the publication of a five-year study of a thousand 11– to 16-year-olds in Cleveland which shows that many teenagers regard the world as such a threatening place they routinely carry weapons for self-defence.

And an investigation by the Children's Society reveals that more than 150,000 17-year-old school-leavers last year have never worked and have no known means of support. The Society estimates that a similar number of this year's leavers will find themselves in a similar position.

Dr James, whose research will by published this week, has found that since 1987 juvenile crime figures have risen at a rate of 12,000 crimes a year, three times faster than the average of 4,000 for 1979–86 and four times the average yearly rise of 3,000 since 1950.

He links the escalation of violence to government social and economic policies since 1979. In particular, he cites the increasing number of boys raised in low-income families. 'Thatcher's children (boys who reached seven in 1987) are dramatically more violent than their predecessors because more of them were raised in violence-inducing, low-income homes,' he claims.

Since the Eighties, the gap between rich and poor has widened: 'The disadvantaged are the losers. When they leave school they drift into unemployment or badly paid unskilled jobs. The winner-loser culture has caused a change in the way the poorest section of British society act – it may have made them more likely to respond with physical violence.'

The Children's Society claims thousands of school-leavers are opting for further education colleges rather than joining 'slave labour' training schemes. More than 90 per cent of those who find jobs are paid below the Council of Europe's decency threshold (about £200 per week).

Under-18s are the only group in Britain whose average weekly wage has fallen since 1992. Wages before tax for young men fell by nearly 1 per cent to £112.80 and for women there was a drop of 5.9 per cent to £103.30.

The Youth Training allowance has been frozen at £29.50 a week for 16-year-olds since 1989 and £35 for 17-year-olds since 1986. In 1988, all welfare payments to 16– and 17-year-olds were axed.

Source: **Observer** (23 July 1995).

TASK 5.8

'Thatcher's children?'

1 What does the article suggest has caused the rise in teenage crime?
2 How could it be argued that crime could be considered to be a rational choice?

2 Utility and modern marketing methods

Major companies have traditionally used the mass media of newspapers or television to advertise their products. This makes sense if a company is selling a consumer product aimed at a wide cross-section of the population. It is often said that 50% of advertising expenditure is effective; the problem is identifying which is the effective 50%. Advertisers attempt to target their advertisements more precisely through narrow casting. They select particular magazines or programmes to carry advertisements which are read or watched by an audience with an appropriate buying profile. However, the process is still rather hit or miss.

Changes which have happened in your local supermarket give a clue to the next moves by advertisers. Stores now issue customers with their own personal store card. Stores are then able to record every purchase made by an individual shopper. Shops will know the kinds of goods which give you utility so they can then direct advertising and special offers relating to specific products straight at the potential buyers. The response to a particular promotional campaign can be measured very precisely and so future campaigns can be made even more effective. Task 5.9 gives examples of the Tesco, Safeway and Sainsbury store cards.

TASK 5.9

Store cards wars

1 What advantages do supermarkets' loyalty cards have for customers and the stores?
2 What is the link between the introduction of these cards and utility?

The new way to save at Sainsbury's

How you save money

Once you've earned Points, you can save money on future purchases in store. Just tell the cashier how much money you want to save and your bill will be adjusted accordingly. *But don't use your Points too soon. It's much better to save them up, because then you'll be entitled to Bonus Points which mean even bigger savings!*

Spend	Points Saved	New Bonus Points	Total Points	Total Value
1 x £10	5	–	5	**5p**
40 x £10	200	100	300	**£3**
80 x £10	500	300	800	**£8**
120 x £10	1,000	600	1,600	**£16**
160 x £10	1,800	1,200	3,000	**£30**
200 x £10	3,200	1,800	5,000	**£50**

TESCO'S CLUB CARD *comes up trumps*

By Hamish Champ

Wallets are bulging with more and more plastic – credit cards, debit cards, charge cards and now, increasingly, loyalty cards. Tesco's revelation last week that it had recruited five million card-holders in the space of two months, helping to boost its underlying sales growth to twice the industry average, has renewed interest in the loyalty card as a marketing device.

Tesco is quietly building up a useful database on its card-holding customers. Every card-holder's bill is scanned to check which areas of the store have been visited – wines and spirits, meat counter, and so on – and a picture is built up of the shopper's preferences. Tesco then writes to these customers giving details of store promotions which reflect their own shopping routines.

For some, the loyalty card is becoming an essential accessory on every shopping trip. Once consumers start to acquire discount points, little will persuade them to switch to another retailer, even if a tin of beans or a bottle of wine is advertised as cheaper elsewhere.

This is the key to a scheme of the Tesco type. For the competition, it restricts the value of using price reductions in order to attract custom away from card-operating retailers.

But the problem comes when everyone offers loyalty cards. Then the marketers have to come up with a fresh gimmick.

*Source: **Independent on Sunday** (16 April 1995).*

SAFEWAY *ABC* ADDED BONUS CARD

Sign up for the Safeway Added Bonus Card Scheme and earn an added bonus when you shop.

Just present the card at the checkout and you will receive one point for every pound you spend. Then, for every 100 points you earn, you'll save £1 off your shopping.

You can either use them on your next shopping trip or save them up for later. It's automatic, so there are no vouchers to remember. It's free to join, so why not pay us a visit soon.

SAFEWAY lightening the load.

Source: Portsmouth, 'The News' (30 March 1995).

Some consumer goods producers are adopting a similar strategy. Heinz are seeking to make contact with their buyers so that brand loyalty can be improved as a way of fighting off competitors. Companies are likely to find out much more about their consumers in this way and this may lead to more sophisticated pricing techniques. Habitual buyers could be charged a higher price than those consumers likely to defect to other brands if price rises. Companies will then be moving towards their main objective of profit maximisation.

3 Utility and taxation

Much of the recent debate concerning taxation has been about shifting the burden of taxation from taxes on income (e.g. income tax and company taxation) to taxes on expenditure (e.g. VAT, tobacco and petrol duty). From 1979 Conservative governments set out to do this by reducing the top rates of income tax: down from 83% to 40%, whilst increasing the rate for VAT: up from 8% to 17.5%. This policy has been supported from two angles. First, it decreases the government's interference in the labour market and second, it improves incentives in the economy. This should result in people being prepared to work harder, take jobs rather than remaining unemployed and set up their own businesses. However, one consequence of the shift is that the tax system has become less fair; taxes on goods hit the poor harder than they do the rich.

'Fairness' is a difficult concept in economics. There is no single view of how to define fairness but a knowledge of utility theory may help us make a judgement.

There are basically three kinds of tax:
- Progressive taxes which take a higher percentage of the incomes of the higher income earners such as income tax.
- Proportional taxes which take the same percentage of everybody's income.
- Regressive taxes which take a higher percentage of income from the lower income earner than the high income earner. The poll tax was a good example of this but VAT and tobacco and alcohol taxes are also regressive.

But which is the fairest?

One view of 'fairness' is that we should not look at the amount of tax paid but at the sacrifice forced upon the tax payer. If we are all making a similar sacrifice then we have a fair tax. To achieve this, the rich would have pay a higher percentage of their income in tax. Most would accept this although the degree of progressiveness in the tax system is still a matter of debate. Support for this view can be found in marginal utility theory. If it is the case that as we consume more of a product the utility from each extra unit consumed declines then the same idea can be applied to the units of income earned. The first £5000 we earn will give us more satisfaction than the next £5000 and this will give more satisfaction than the next £5000, and so on. This is shown in Box 5.7.

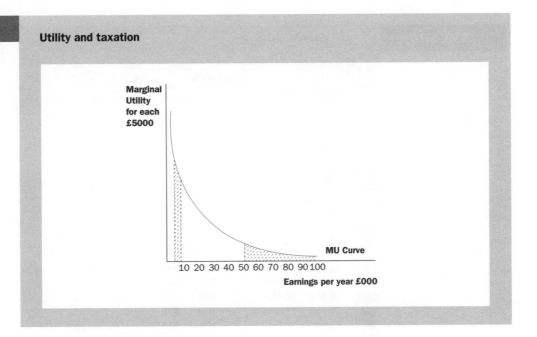

BOX 5.7

Utility and taxation

Box 5.7 shows that if £1000 is collected in tax from a person earning £5000 the sacrifice in terms of lost utility is shown by the shaded area. For a person on £100 000 a year to make a similar sacrifice, they would have to pay approximately £50 000 in tax. This points towards a progressive tax being the fairer type of tax.

We do need to remember that 'fairness' is not the only factor determining the choice of a tax. Not all the tax revenue needed by modern governments can be raised by "taxing the rich until the pips squeaked" (as was said by a former Chancellor of the Exchequer). There has to be a spread of taxes so that we all make some contribution to the costs of government and the tax burden is shared.

4 Utility and pricing

Firms recognise that many people are prepared to pay high prices for a product. If the firm can find ways of charging consumers different prices for the same product it can take over the consumer's surplus and convert it into profit. Rail companies know this, and so push up the prices charged to passengers wanting to travel in the rush hour and lower prices to people travelling at off-peak times. Consumers are being charged different prices for the same product, rail travel, and this is known as price discrimination. Look at Task 5.10.

TASK 5.10

Price discrimination

1 How does the following holiday brochure extract illustrate that the holiday company is using price discrimination?

2 What are the advantages of price discrimination to the tour operator?

Accom. Name	CRETA PARADISE	
Accom. code	9318	
Board Basis	HB	
Party Size	2	
No. of nights	7	14
1 Apr – 14 Apr	379	489
15 Apr – 23 Apr	339	449
24 Apr – 30 Apr	345	459
1 May – 12 May	325	485
13 May – 19 May	375	525
20 May – 26 May	379	529
27 May – 30 May	409	555
31 May – 17 Jun	385	535
18 Jun – 24 Jun	389	579
25 Jun – 1 Jul	435	679
2 Jul – 8 Jul	489	735
9 Jul – 15 Jul	495	739
16 Jul – 21 Jul	499	745
22 Jul – 15 Aug	505	749

DEPARTURES ON OR BETWEEN

Accom. Name	CRETA PARADISE	
Accom. code	9318	
Board Basis	HB	
Party Size	2	
No. of nights	7	14
16 Aug – 23 Aug	515	739
24 Aug – 2 Sep	515	729
3 Sep – 12 Sep	499	739
13 Sep – 22 Sep	485	705
23 Sep – 4 Oct	455	609
5 Oct – 18 Oct	379	495
19 Oct – 31 Oct	359	–

Supplements per person per night	TW MB £4 TW MB+SV £8 BUNG £14 SGL £16 SGL MB £20
For 3-weeks Add	£239 (£269)
Child Reductions	25%
3rd Person Reductions	10%

Attempts by firms to boost demand for their product often are dependent on cut price offers. Firms understand the law of diminishing marginal utility, the income and substitution effects. As a result of cutting prices some consumers will buy more in order to equate marginal utility to the price. Others will buy more due to the increase in real income or may buy more as a substitute for other goods. Task 5.11 contains two examples of companies using price to influence the demand for their products. If you look around you will see many other examples yourself.

TASK 5.11

'Price cuts and utility'
Explain what each of these advertisements has to do with an understanding of utility.

"Once again we've reduced our prices. Here's the lowdown"
Every call over 35 miles has been brought into a single price band

We have abolished the higher 'b' price band for calls of 35 miles and more. This change will bring savings of up to 25% on the price of many national long distance calls.

Previously, only calls made over a few of the network's routes were charged at the lower (b1) price band. These routes were the busiest in the BT national network, and we were able to reduce the price of calls to reflect cost savings resulting from heavy usage.

Now, with the widespread use of advanced technology in BT's phone network we can offer the same low prices for all long distance calls.

So now a 3 minute direct-dialled long distance call to anywhere in the UK will only cost 30p on weekdays (8am – 6pm, Monday to Friday), 20p in the evenings (6pm – 8am Monday to Thursday, 6pm – midnight on Friday and midnight – 8am on Monday), and still only 10p at weekends (midnight Friday – midnight Sunday). Or, as a quick reminder, '30-20-10, weekdays-evenings-weekends'.

Exclusions to this are calls which are not distance related, e.g. to mobile phones or information and entertainment services.

TASK 5.11

DOVER-CALAIS • PORTSMOUTH-LE HAVRE • PORTSMOUTH-CHERBOURG • CAIRNRYAN-LARNE
BOOK EARLY.
SAVE 20%.
This year, we'll help pack your most important item. Your wallet. Book and pay for your crossing on any P&O European Ferries route* before 31 March 1995 for travel between 16 April and 31 December, and we'll give you a full 20% off the brochure price.
The offer also applies to Club Class and cabin accommodation.
For bookings and further details of terms and conditions, pop into your travel agent or just phone 0990 980 980. See you on board.
P&O
European Ferries
BRITAIN'S No.1 FERRY COMPANY.

REVIEW

This chapter has looked at the way in which individuals make consumer decisions. We assume that individuals will always aim to maximise satisfaction and so will constantly be comparing the marginal utility obtained from the consumption of a good with its price. In choosing between a range of goods and services, a consumer will, unconsciously, be employing the principle of equi-marginal utility. The concept of utility is a powerful one and can be used to explain most of human activity. A major problem is the difficulty of measuring utility and this, at least in part, is solved by the use of indifference curves.

REVIEW TASK

Investigating utility – a coursework task

The aim here is to study a context within which the idea of utility is important. To do this you will need to investigate the effects of a price change and then examine the way in which the demand for the good or service will be affected.

Research could be done in your own school or college canteen. You could establish what the existing level of sales of a particular product is, and then monitor the effects of a price change on expenditure patterns.

You could research the percentage of students choosing to eat lunch in the canteen compared to the percentage of students bringing a packed lunch or eating lunch off site. This should reveal information about people's perceived utility from different forms of eating and what your canteen might have to do to boost sales.

You could also investigate the effects of a change in the price of a widely used product such as newspapers. You could establish current patterns of newspaper buying and then monitor the impact of a price change of a particular newspaper. This could affect existing consumers of that newspaper, but could also affect readers of other newspapers. If you then find that a cut in price leads to no change in buying habits, you need to explain why demand has not responded in the expected way.

Appendix: Indifference curves and the income constraint

Indifference curves

- If you were offered a choice between a ham sandwich and a cheese sandwich, which would you choose?
- Would you prefer to watch *Neighbours* or the 'News' on television?
- Would you prefer to spend time studying Economics or Chemistry?

These questions do not ask you to measure the amount of satisfaction you get from ham sandwiches, *Neighbours* or Economics, but they ask you to compare the satisfaction you might obtain from each activity. Most of us can do this quite easily.

Spending decisions can be viewed in this way. We are each trying to maximise satisfaction from our spending decisions by making utility comparisons. We are faced with a wide selection of goods from which to choose and we are looking for the combinations which are likely to give us maximum

*An **indifference curve** shows different combinations of goods which give the consumer equal satisfaction. If a number of indifference curves are shown on the same diagram, each represents a different level of satisfaction and the diagram is called an indifference map.*

satisfaction. What we find is that there are different combinations which will give us equal amounts of satisfaction. In other words there are different combinations to which we will be indifferent.

Box 5.8 simplifies a family's expenditure into food and non-food items. Indifference curve I_1 represents

one level of satisfaction and shows that 60 food items and 10 non-food items will give the same level of satisfaction as 20 food items and 40 non-food items. The consumer is indifferent about which of these two combinations is consumed and all points on the indifference curve represent other combinations which give the same level of satisfaction.

BOX 5.8

Indifference curves

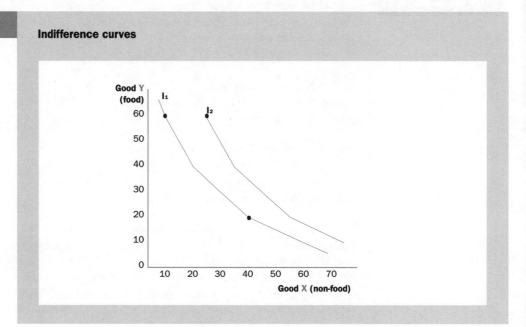

Indifference curve I_2 represents a combination of food and non-food products which give a higher level of satisfaction. 60 units of food and 25 units of non-food items will logically give more satisfaction than 60 food and 10 non-food items. Once a number of indifference curves are drawn

representing a consumer's different levels of utility we have the consumer's indifference map. Each consumer will have an infinite number of indifference curves which could be drawn but, of these, only two are shown in Box 5.8.

Key points about indifference curves are:

- They are always convex to the origin of the graph because of the effect of the law of diminishing marginal utility. If consumers give up the first units of any product they will need more of the other product to compensate for the lost utility.

- Each higher indifference curve represents a higher level of satisfaction.

- Indifference curves can never cross. Since all points on an indifference curve indicate one level of satisfaction, they could not touch another indifference curve which must be representing a different level of satisfaction.

The income constraint

*A **budget line** shows all the combinations of goods and services which can be bought at given prices with a given income.*

Consumers have a fixed income which limits the spending decisions they are able to make. In Box 5.9 it is assumed that the average price of food items is £1 and the average price of non-food items is 80p. If a family has an income of £50 to spend then the line AB represents all the combinations of food and non-food items which can be bought. This is known as the family's budget line.

Wanting to maximise utility, the family

is looking to reach the highest possible indifference curve. This will be I$_3$ which just touches AB. Point C indicates the combination of products that the family can buy and will yield the highest level of utility. This indicates that if the family buys 30 units of food and 25 units of non-food, utility will be at a maximum.

BOX 5.9

The budget line

Good Y (food)

Food = £1
Non-food = 80p

Good X (non-food)

Box 5.9 becomes useful because we can begin to consider what effect changes to the situation will have. For instance, if the income the family could spend increased to £60 the budget line would shift upwards to DE and allow the family to purchase a different quantity of goods on a higher indifference curve.

The effects of changing relative prices can also be shown. For example, if, from the original position, the average price of non-food products rose to £1 then the budget line would pivot from AB to AF so that, again, the family would change its consumption pattern and move on to a lower indifference curve. The changes in the budget line and prices are summarised in Box 5.10.

BOX 5.10

Changes in the budget line

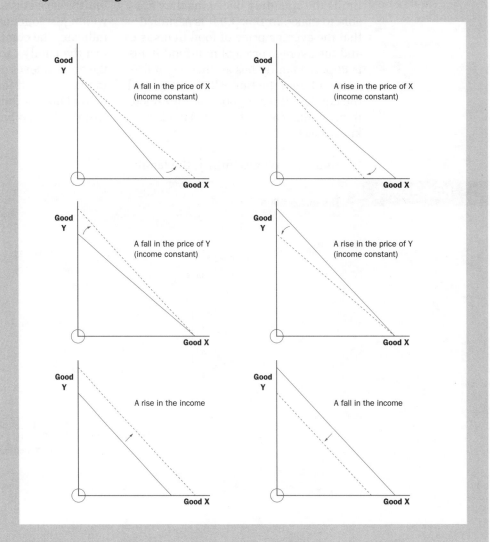

The strength of using indifference curves is that they do not rely on the need to measure utility and that they can be used to analyse a variety of situations when demand, income or price are changing with a greater degree of precision. Indifference curves embody the principles of the law of diminishing marginal utility and provide an alternative approach.

Multiple choice

1 **The aim of a rational consumer, in allocating income, is to achieve**

A   a position where the marginal utilities of all purchases are equal

B   a position where the marginal utilities of all purchases are zero

C   a position where the marginal utilities of all purchases are less than their prices

D   the maximum amount of total utility

(ULEAC, January 94)

2 A consumer allocates expenditure between three goods, **X, Y** and **Z.**
The table shows the prices of the goods and the consumer's marginal utilities.

good	X	Y	Z
price (£)	20	15	5
marginal utility (units)	40	20	10

How should the consumer's expenditure be reallocated in order to maximise utility? Expenditure on:

	X	Y	Z
A	more	less	less
B	more	less	more
C	less	more	more
D	less	less	more

(IB, May 1995, Subsid. level)

QUESTIONS

3 The diagram shows a student's demand for rail travel. The student is given a railcard free of charge which enables her to travel at one half of the standard fare OF.

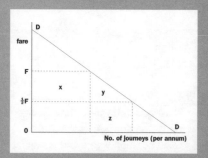

Which area measures the net gain in benefit that the student derives each year from using her railcard?

A x
B x + y
C y
D y + z

(IB, May 1995, Subsid. level)

How are prices decided?

FOCUS

Seen any good films lately?

Plenty of people seem to have done. In fact the cinema is undergoing a revival. Cinema audiences reached their peak after the Second World War when each person, on average, went to the cinema 22 times a year. By 1984 the average annual attendance was down to about once a year. At this time it looked as if cinema was on its way out but audiences began to pick up. From a low point of 54 million annual visits, there has been a steady rise to 120 million in 1994. 1995 has not been quite so good. For the first time in 10 years audiences are down.

Why the change? The reasons are uncertain but there are a number of possible explanations. Competition has broken out amongst cinemas with the building of the relatively new multi-screen complexes. These provide the filmgoer with more choice and a higher quality experience together with buckets of pop-corn. The competition has kept prices down as city centre cinemas have attempted to hang on to their audience. At the same time the cost of going to a pub and other alternatives has risen, making a trip to the cinema seem a relatively cheap evening's entertainment.

People have more income to spend these days, especially the young who make up the bulk of the cinema audience. But also older people, brought up on the weekly visit to the pictures, are now returning. More leisure time has also helped. Interest in the cinema has certainly grown. The expansion of cable and satellite channels and video might have been expected to hit cinema audiences hard but they seem to have generated a greater enthusiasm. Film companies seek to maximise exposure for new films through huge promotions. They also look for lucrative sales of various spin-offs such as stickers, film-branded products and videos. The media has latched on to the appeal of film stars to sell newspapers and magazines and the number of film-based television programmes has multiplied.

Film makers have tried to identify trends in viewing taste and then cash in by producing more of the same: hence the number of film sequels such as *Star Trek Generations, Batman Forever, Beverly Hills Cop 3* or *Police Academy 47*. Big money is at stake when a film is made and if a film company sees the prospect of making increased profit, they go for it.

The industry is dominated by Hollywood and European film makers have called for a subsidy to boost the number of films coming out of European studios.

1995 has not been quite so good. For the first time in 10 years audiences are down. One explanation for this may be the introduction of the National Lottery. People buying scratch cards have a similar profile to cinema goers. The Lottery is mopping up £3 billion a year, much of it in cash. 60% of cinema's business is done in cash.

1 Explain why cinema audiences might have fallen between 1946 and 1984.
2 What factors have led to the revival in cinema audiences since 1984 and the fall in 1995?
3 How have film makers and cinema owners attempted to increase the audience?

Preview

In this chapter we shall investigate the following key areas:

- demand and supply;
- the conditions of demand and supply;
- elasticity of demand and supply;
- dynamic markets.

In answering the questions in Task 6.1, you have probably listed a whole range of points mentioned in the Focus, but as economists we try to provide ourselves with a framework for analysing not just the market for films, but any market. We look for the factors influencing the *demand* and the *supply* of the product. In free markets the interaction between these determines the price of the product. There are close links between demand and supply but, in the first instance, it may help our understanding to think of them separately.

Factors affecting the demand for a product

1 Price

Both demand and supply are affected by the price of the product. Generally, we expect more of a good to be demanded at lower prices than higher prices. As prices fall people will substitute less expensive goods for more expensive goods and so demand will rise. This is known as the substitution effect. Also, as prices fall a person's income will go further: it will buy more goods, real income has increased and demand may rise. This is known as the income effect. Remember Chapter 5.

So, for any product, we expect there to be an inverse relationship between price and demand (as price rises, the quantity demanded falls and vice versa). This can be shown on a graph, as in Box 6.1.

BOX 6.1

A demand curve

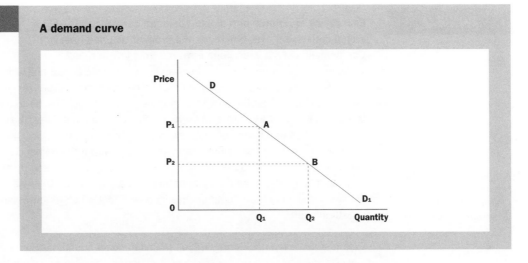

*An **extension of demand** is an increase in demand caused by a fall in price.*

In Box 6.1 D_1 represents a demand curve (we still call them curves even if they are drawn as a straight line). It is drawn on the assumption that only price has changed and everything else has remained the same. This is an important assumption to note. In reality many factors are changing at the same time but if we are to analyse the factors causing change in a market, we first need to try to isolate each of the factors. This assumption, sometimes known as ceteris paribus or 'other things being equal', enables us to do this.

*A **contraction of demand** is a fall in demand caused by a rise in price.*

Effective demand is the desire for a good or service at a given price and over a given time period.

In Box 6.1 if we pick a price, we can read off the level of demand. At price $0P_1$, $0Q_1$ is demanded. At a price of $0P_2$, $0Q_2$ is demanded. As price falls there is an increase in the quantity demanded, there is a movement from point A on the demand curve to point B on the demand curve: this is known as an extension of demand.

If cinemas cut their prices, more people will go to the cinema. If supermarkets cut the prices of selected goods, they will sell more of them.

If price rises from $0P_2$ to $0P_1$, there will be a reduction in the quantity demanded from $0Q_2$ to $0Q_1$. This is shown by a movement along the demand curve from point B to point A. This is known as a contraction of demand.

If fish rises in price, less fish will be sold.

If the price of a product changes there will always be a movement along the demand curve, either an extension or a contraction of demand. For virtually all products we expect the demand curve to slope from top left to bottom right, indicating that more will be demanded as price falls. Look at Box 6.2.

BOX 6.2	**Exceptions to a downward sloping demand curve:**

Would consumers ever buy more of a product as price rises?
Can demand curves ever slope upwards from left to right?

In some poor countries the people often live on a basic diet of rice which is very cheap plus a few more expensive vegetables or some much more expensive meat. In such societies, if the price of rice rises then the people may well decide to buy more in order to substitute it for the more expensive vegetables and meat. There has been an increase in demand in response to an increase in price. Sir Robert Giffen first noticed this phenomenon. In the nineteenth century he saw that the demand for potatoes increased in response to the rises in the price of potatoes caused by the great potato famines in Ireland. Hence products of this kind are known as Giffen goods. With such products there is a negative income effect which far outweighs any substitution effect.

*A **Giffen good** is a product where as price rises, demand rises due to the negative income effect.*

Examples of Giffen goods are difficult to find in richer countries. Some text books do suggest that after-shave or perfume come into the same category but this is not the case. With these products a rise in price is often interpreted by the consumer as an increase in quality and so they may decide to buy more, thinking that they are buying a superior product. There may be psychological factors at work. The economist Veblen carried out research into this and concluded that the price of a product conveyed more than just value information for the consumer; it also represented status and exclusivity. These products which appear to experience rising demand with rising price are known as Veblen goods.

*A **Veblen good** is a product where as price rises, demand rises due to the consumers' changed perception of the product.*

Factors other than price can cause the demand for a product to change. These are sometimes known as the conditions of demand. However, if there are changes in the conditions of demand there will not be a movement along the demand curve but a shift in the position of the demand curve. This shows what happens when other things are not equal, i.e. the effect on demand if anything other than price changes.

2 Taste

The demand for a product will be affected by consumers' taste. Over time fashions change and tastes change. This is particularly important in the clothing industry, for example, where new fashions emerge each season. As one type of clothing comes into fashion, the demand curve shifts to the right indicating that more of the good is being demanded at every price. In Box 6.3, the demand curve has shifted from D_1 to D_2, showing an increase in demand. This means that at the price of $0P_1$, $0Q_2$ will now be demanded instead of $0Q_1$. If tastes had changed causing the level of demand to fall, the demand curve might have shifted to level D_3, which would mean that $0Q_3$ is now demanded instead of $0Q_1$.

BOX 6.3

Shifts in the demand curve

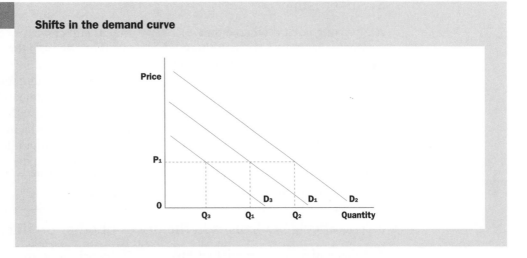

Changing taste has become a feature of many different industries. Fashion has become important in the car industry, home decorating, food and agriculture, leisure activities and holidays.

It would be comforting to think that consumers are acting entirely out of their own free will, and that every change in taste is picked up by an eager manufacturer ready to respond to the next popular whim. This is surely what consumer sovereignty is?

In fact, producers have a vested interest in promoting dissatisfaction from the consumer in today's products, since this opens up new markets for the producer to exploit. A successful marketing campaign persuades the consumer that

they cannot do without a new product which they didn't even know they wanted a few weeks previously. A few years ago people seemed to be perfectly happy choosing from corn flakes, Frosties, Shredded Wheat, Weetabix and porridge for their breakfast. Today the choice is vast. Was the consumer going along to supermarkets, asking to see the manager and demanding new breakfast cereals with a hint of honey, a touch of nuts and made into a circle? Doubtful. It was manufacturers, through their market research, who saw the opportunity for greater profit if they broke down the market into different segments producing cereals specifically designed to appeal to children and adult consumers.

3 Advertising

Advertising is vital when a new product is launched since without basic information about the product the consumer will not buy. In addition, successful advertising campaigns do persuade people to buy and this has the effect of shifting the demand curve for the product to the right (the same as shifting from D_1 to D_2 in Box 6.3). Negative stories in the press about a product have the opposite effect, and can cause a decrease in demand. Reports that a newly introduced washing powder called Persil Power had damaged clothes led to a fall in demand and eventually to the company withdrawing the product and replacing it with Persil Original, a milder alternative. This would cause the demand curve to shift to the left from D_1 to D_3 in Box 6.3.

4 The effects of changes in the prices of other products

The demand for one product will be affected by changes in the prices of others. If one supermarket runs a special offer on fresh salmon then it is likely that it will sell more salmon. But other supermarkets will be affected as their sales of salmon will be hit: demand will fall even though there has been no change in the price of their product. Relative prices have changed. In this case, the two products are close substitutes for each other and a fall in the price of one causes the demand for the other to fall. This would cause the demand curve to shift to the left – in Box 6.3, from D_1 to D_3.

If the price of a substitute product rose then we would expect the demand curve of the original product to shift to the right. If the price of Coca-Cola increases, sales of Pepsi-Cola will rise.

If two products are complements or in joint demand, a rise in the price of one will also affect the demand for the other. A significant rise in the price of foreign holidays will decrease the demand for them, but it will also decrease the demand for sun-tan cream. In this case the demand curve for sun-tan cream will have shifted to the left: demand will be lower at all prices.

5 Expectations of price changes

The behaviour of buyers is affected by what they expect to happen to prices in the future. If buyers expect prices to rise then they may try to buy before prices have risen. This often causes a surge of buying before the Chancellor announces the Budget changes in November. In the expectation of rises in taxes on cigarettes and spirits, people stock up to take advantage of pre-Budget prices. Also during times of inflation, when prices generally are rising, consumers tend to increase their spending in the knowledge that prices will never be as cheap again. The demand curve for these products shifts to the right. If people expect prices to fall, they may put off their buying decisions and wait for prices to change. The holiday industry engages in an annual game where the tour operators try to persuade holiday makers to book early to avoid disappointment whereas the holiday maker often puts off booking in the hope that there may be last-minute bargains.

6 Population change

A rising population generally brings with it rising levels of demand. This often means that the numbers of young people in the population is growing, and this can have a major influence on patterns of demand. Growth in the birth rate means that Mothercare does well and there is a growing demand for health care and education. Companies catering for the taste of young people expand. A population may grow by a fall in the death rate. It will be an ageing population. The demand for hearing aids, rest homes and bowling clubs will increase.

6 The season and the weather

For many products, demand will change according to the time of year or the climate. Umbrella manufacturers will undoubtedly increase sales during the winter or downpours during the rest of the year. Ice cream sales peak during the summer and hot weather. Accurate weather forecasts are becoming more important to supermarket chains, as they try to predict the likely daily demand for barbecue foods or lettuces. Greetings card manufacturers are victims of the seasonal nature of their business. At Christmas over 1.3 billion cards are sold whereas the next most popular time of year for card sales is Mothers' Day when just less than 40 million are sold. This variation in demand causes major shifts in the demand curve and creates serious problems for the production planning departments.

Factors affecting the supply of a product

1 Price

Effective supply is the quantity of a good or service offered for sale at a given price and over a given time period.

Firms supply goods to a market because they want to make profits. They may well have other aims but, unless the firms are sufficiently profitable, they will eventually go out of business. The entrepreneurs running businesses seek out opportunities to make profits and will try to sell into more profitable markets rather than less profitable markets. This means that if prices are low, few firms will be able to sell and still make a profit: therefore supply will be low at low prices. At high prices more profit can be made and so firms will be wanting to sell more into the market: the quantity supplied will increase. This can be shown on a supply curve in Box 6.4.

BOX 6.4

A supply curve

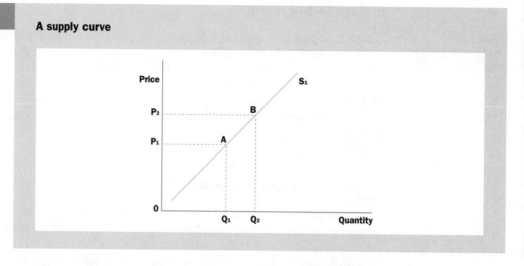

*An **extension in** supply is an increase in the quantity supplied caused by a rise in price.*

*A **contraction of** supply is a reduction in supply caused by a fall in the price.*

The supply curve S_1 in Box 6.4 allows us to read off the quantity of goods supplied at different prices. At price $0P_1$ the quantity $0Q_1$ would be supplied in the market but as the price rises to $0P_2$ there is a rise in supply to $0Q_2$. An increase in supply caused by a rise in price is shown by a movement along the supply curve from point A to point B. This is known as an extension of supply.

If price fell back to $0P_1$ the change in supply could be shown by the movement back down the supply curve from B to A. This is known as a contraction of supply.

Factors other than price will affect the supply of any good or service. These factors are known as the conditions of supply. If any of these change it will cause a shift in the position of the supply curve and not a movement along the supply curve.

2 The costs of production

If any of the costs of production rise then firms may choose to pass on those cost increases to the customers in the form of price rises. In Box 6.5, S_1 is the original supply curve.

BOX 6.5

Shifts in the supply curve

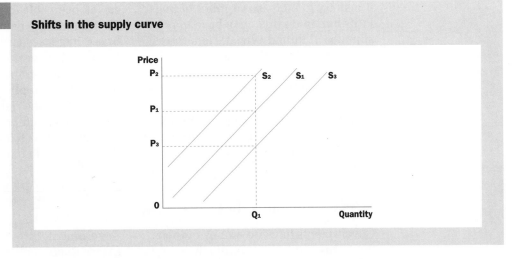

At price $0P_1$ in Box 6.5 producers are willing to supply a quantity of $0Q_1$. If now raw material or wage costs rise, the firm will wish to pass these onto the customer and so will now only be willing to sell $0Q_1$ at a price of $0P_2$. The change in supply costs will have affected the price at which firms will be willing to supply at all prices and so the supply curve will have shifted upwards to the left to S_2.

If costs had fallen due to the introduction of new technology or greater efficiency, firms might be willing to pass on the benefits to customers by lowering prices. In this case the supply curve would shift its position to S_3, and firms would be prepared to supply $0Q_1$ at a price of $0P_3$.

Costs in agriculture are greatly affected by the climate. During good years the yield from crops increases and the costs per tonne fall. This means that farmers are willing to sell at much reduced prices and the supply curve shifts to the right. Bad harvests result in a major fall in supply. Costs per tonne increase and farmers are then only willing to sell at higher prices: the supply curve has shifted to the left.

Other producers may face disruptions to supply. Firms may encounter industrial action which can reduce supply to zero. Raw material producers or manufacturing companies may find that supplies will be affected by wars or trade sanctions. Each of these will cause the supply curve to shift upwards to the left.

3 The prices of other products

The supply of any product will be affected by its price because sellers are interested in making profits. Firms may well find that the conditions of demand change and this has an impact on the prices they can charge. If firms find that the prices of some products are rising

then it is likely that they will want to increase the supply of those products, which could mean that the supply of others will decrease. Such goods are in competitive supply. If a cereal manufacturer notes that consumers have become desperate for Sugar Puffs, it may try to increase supplies of Sugar Puffs but, to do this, may have to reduce supplies of Puffed Wheat. Here the supply of Puffed Wheat has shifted to the left in response to the rising demand and price of Sugar Puffs.

Products may also be in joint supply so that if there is an increase in the supply of one, there must be an increase in the supply of the other. Farmers have not,

as yet, been able to produce a legless chicken. As the demand for chicken breast increases farmers supply more. But with the increase in the supply of breast comes an increase in the supply of legs. The supply curve of chicken legs shifts to the right as the supply curve of chicken breasts has shifted to the right. If Box 6.5 was representing this, the supply curve would have shifted from S_1 to S_3.

4 Taxes and subsidies

Governments have no money of their own. Any money a government spends must be raised from taxes and an important source of revenue has been taxes on goods known as indirect taxes. Most products carry some form of taxation through VAT but some products are selected for special attention, such as cigarettes, alcohol and petrol. In the first instance the

Government, through the Customs and Excise Board, collects this tax from firms. It is then up to the firms to decide how to pay this tax. They could choose to pay the tax out of their own profits but they are much more likely to pass the tax on to the consumer by adding it on to the price of the product. The effect of this is shown in Box 6.6.

BOX 6.6

The effects of taxes and subsidies

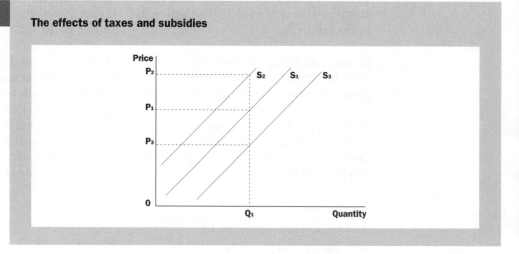

Before the introduction of a tax, firms were willing to supply a quantity of $0Q_1$ at a price of $0P_1$ (see Box 6.6). If the price was £1 and then the Government decided to introduce a 20p tax on the product, the firms raise price by the 20p to £1.20 or $0P_2$. The new tax would have raised the price of the product at all prices so here the supply curve has shifted upwards to the left from S_1 to S_2. The amount of tax levied is represented by the vertical distance between S_1 and S_2.

The type of tax shown in Box 6.6 is a specific tax set at a fixed amount for every unit sold. VAT is slightly different in that it is a percentage-based tax. The percentage of tax stays the same but that percentage represents a larger amount of tax on more expensive items. VAT of 17.5% on a product costing £1 equals 17.5p, on a product costing £1000 it is £175.

Subsidies act in the reverse way. If the Government wishes to encourage the consumption or supply of a particular product, they could offer a subsidy to the manufacturer. This could then be passed on to the consumer in the form of lower prices. In Box 6.6 a subsidy would shift the supply curve down to the right. Goods which were previously supplied at $0P_1$ might now be supplied at $0P_3$. Suppliers would be willing to sell the same quantity, but at a reduced price.

It can be argued that the financial incentives given by the Government to some companies such as Nissan and Toyota are in effect subsidies which enable those companies to compete unfairly. The European Commission monitors this and seeks to control the level of subsidies given by governments to ensure fair competition within the EU.

5 Time

The length of the time period has an important influence upon the ability of supply to react to a change in price. In the short run it is only existing firms in the industry which can respond to a change in price by raising supply, but in the long run new firms may decide to enter the industry. This means that in the short run an increase in supply will be shown by a movement along the supply curve but in the long run the whole curve can shift its position. If the price of steel rises existing steel operators will no doubt try to increase output by selling off stocks and increasing efficiency. It is only in the long run that new firms can enter the steel industry or existing firms can increase capacity by building new steel works.

Demand, supply and price

If we now bring the demand and supply curves together we can represent the market on a graph.

Box 6.7 attempts to show how the market for mushrooms might develop.

BOX 6.7

The market for mushrooms

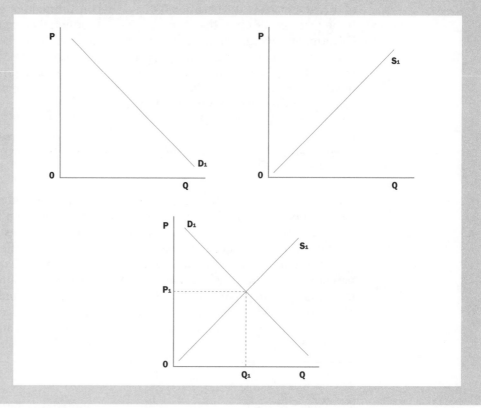

*Equilibrium price is the
price at which supply
equals demand. This is the
same as the market
clearing price.*

D_1 is the demand curve for mushrooms, S_1 is the supply curve for mushrooms. When demand and supply are brought together in Box 6.7 the interaction between demand and supply determines the price. $0P_1$ is known as the equilibrium price or market clearing price since price should tend to move towards that level and when price is there, all the goods supplied to the market will be bought.

On the graph in Box 6.7, if price is above $0P_1$ the supply will be greater than demand. There will be a lot of mushrooms on the shelves but few buyers. In these circumstances the price of mushrooms is likely to fall and move towards $0P_1$. If price is below $0P_1$ then demand will be greater than supply. There will be few mushrooms around but a lot of people trying to buy them. In these circumstances sellers will be able to raise prices and price will move towards $0P_1$.

The equilibrium price is not a fixed price. It will constantly be changing as the conditions of demand and supply change. Changes in the conditions are known as shocks to the market. They have the effect of shifting price away from its current level. The effect of changing market conditions is shown in Box 6.8.

BOX 6.8	The effects of changing market conditions on price

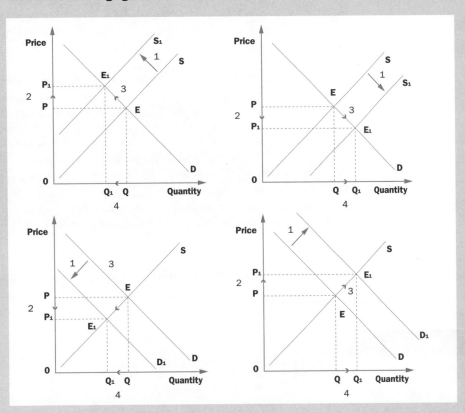

KEY
1   Shift (caused by changed conditions)
2   Change in price (caused by shift)
3   Contraction or extension (caused by price change)
4   Change in quantity
E   First Equilibrium
E1 Equilibrium following change

*Source: Harrison, Smith and Davies, **Introductory Economics** (Macmillan, 1992).*

It is important to remember that the equilibrium price is not necessarily the same as the market price. Firms do not have the complete picture about what is happening in the market. They may be searching for the equilibrium price without knowing precisely what the equilibrium level is. Markets are dynamic – they change over time and we would expect price to change in response to changing conditions. Look at Task 6.2

TASK 6.2

Super Hot Mints

1 Reflect on your answers to Task 6.1. Now try to use the ideas of demand and supply to explain what has happened to the market for films in recent years.
2 Using appropriate diagrams, explain how the market for Super Hot Mints might be affected by the following shocks to the market:

(First decide whether the shock would affect the demand or supply, then decide in which direction the demand or supply curve would be shifted as a result of the shock. You can then predict the overall effect the change will have on price. State what you think will happen to the price and the quantity bought and sold in the market.)

A The sugar price rockets (sugar is a vital ingredient in making Super Hot Mints).
B Super Hot Mints runs a successful advertising campaign promoting mints.
C Super Cool Mints, a close rival of Super Hot Mints, cuts its price.
D A health report slams mints for causing tooth decay.
E The Government, in response to the health report, introduces a special tax on mints.
F Super Hot management cuts the wages of employees by 10%.

Elasticity of demand and supply

Look at Box 6.9.

BOX 6.9

The INVESTIGATOR

Shocks to the market

PRESCRIPTION CHARGES UP AGAIN
On 22 February 1995, the Health Minister Mr Gerald Malone announced a 10.5% increase in prescription charges from £4.75 to £5.25. This increase was three times the rate of inflation. Mr Malone defended the increase by saying that 81% of prescriptions were dispensed freely to people who qualified, the average cost of a prescription was £8.80 and that the £300 million raised could be put towards other priorities in health service spending.

PRICE WARS BREAK OUT IN THE NEWSPAPER INDUSTRY
A 50% cut in the price of *The Times* to 20p caused sales to increase by 48%. This had the effect of reducing sales of the *Independent* by 16% and forcing it to cut its own price. The *Telegraph* also followed suit and cut its price to 30p.

RISING UNEMPLOYMENT HITS THE HOUSING MARKET
House prices have failed to increase as the UK has come out of recession. One of the main reasons for this is that the number of full time jobs has continued to decline and unemployment in this group has risen further.

BOX 6.9

MADNESS IN THE HOLIDAY PRICE WAR

Lunn Poly with its 731 shops was the first to cut prices offering 11% off everything. Going Places with 551 shops then offered 12% off 5 million holidays and Thomas Cook followed up with 15%. Lunn Poly and Going Places then had to cut their prices by 15% to keep in line.

TASK 6.3

The picture on page 97 shows many discounted prices. Consider what has caused prices to change and explain what the effects of these changes might be.

Price elasticity of demand

We have already noticed that a change in price will bring with it a change in demand and a change in supply but, as yet, we have not considered the importance of the size of those changes. This is of key importance. Firms are constantly reviewing prices and are making judgements about whether to increase or decrease them. How are they to decide?

Price elasticity of demand is the responsiveness of demand to a small change in price.

Much depends on the way demand responds to the change in price, and this is known as the price elasticity of demand (Ep).

In some cases a change in price produces very little response from the consumer, whereas in others the change in demand is considerable. The concept of price elasticity adds precision to these ideas. The response in demand can be measured using the following formula:

Price elasticity of demand =
$$\frac{\% \text{ change in quantity demanded}}{\% \text{ change in price}}$$

For example, if a firm raises price by 10% from £1 to £1.10 and as a result demand falls from 1000 to 800 then the price elasticity of demand equals

$$\frac{20\%}{10\%} = 2$$

The number is significant. If it is greater than 1 then it is said to be elastic, if it is less than 1 it is inelastic and if it equals 1 it is unit elasticity.

There is an inverse relationship between price and demand, so if one goes up, the other goes down. This means that when calculating the coefficient of elasticity, either the percentage change in demand or the percentage change in price will be negative. If a negative is divided by or into a positive figure, the answer must always be negative so, technically, the coefficient for elasticity must also be a negative figure. Perhaps because we always know that this must be the case, we often fail to include the negative sign.

Price elasticity can be represented graphically. The two extremes of elasticity are shown when demand is either perfectly elastic, meaning that even a small rise in price will cause demand to drop to zero, or perfectly inelastic, where a change in price causes no response in demand – the same level of demand is present in the market whatever the price. This does not mean that any particular product faces either a perfectly elastic or inelastic demand curve but they are limiting extremes. Some products may encounter a perfectly inelastic demand curve but it will only be over a small price range. If the price of cigarettes went up by 1p, demand might not be affected at all but if price went up by 50p there would certainly be some reduction in demand.

Naturally, for most products, demand is neither perfectly elastic nor perfectly inelastic. It is somewhere in between the two extremes. But what exactly happens to price elasticity as price falls? Try the experiment in Box 6.10.

BOX 6.10

Elasticity and the straight line demand curve

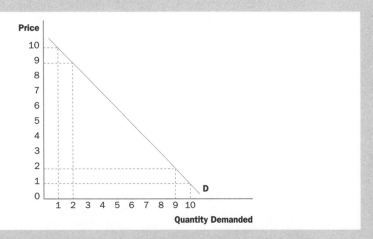

Now, look at your demand curve and try to work out what will happen to elasticity as price falls. (A typical, and quite reasonable suggestion is that the elasticity will stay the same along the demand curve.)

Now, test out this hypothesis. Select a change at a high price and a change at a low price. Make sure the change in price is the same e.g. £10–£9 and £2–£1.

Now, calculate the price elasticity of demand as price falls. You should find that elasticity of demand is high at high prices and low at low prices. In other words the elasticity is not constant but decreases along the demand curve. To test whether this always happens, try drawing your own demand curve and do your own elasticity calculations.

At the middle point of your demand curve, the elasticity will equal 1.

You might consider why, on reflection, this does seem logical. If you are not convinced, a section on the determinants of price elasticity is coming up to help convince you.

Whenever we see estimates of price elasticity, we must always recognise that a major assumption has been made: that it is only the price of the product which has changed and everything else has remained the same. This creates difficulties because when the price of a product changes it takes time for demand to adjust. Over time many other factors can be changing such as incomes, the prices of other products and taste. This makes it more difficult to measure precisely the effects of a price change on the demand for a product and means that any figure representing elasticity will, inevitably, be subject to error.

For example, when *The Times* cut its price and its circulation increased it was easy to attribute the whole of the rise in circulation to the price cut. In fact, at the same time, *The Times* was improving its quality and introducing extra supplements, other newspapers were cutting their prices and changing their look. *The Times* was gaining a lot of additional advertising through its tactics. So, how much of the increase in circulation was directly caused by the cut in price is difficult to tell. Look at Box 6.11.

BOX 6.11

Demand curves and elasticity

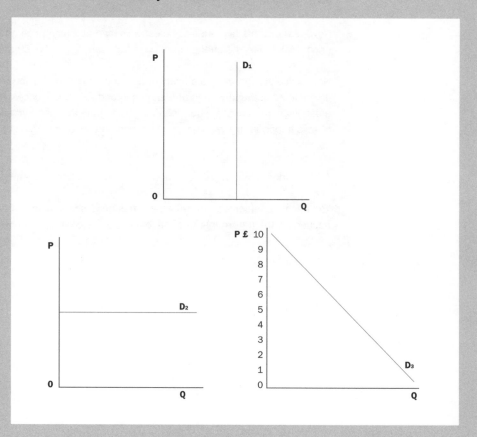

TASK 6.4

1 In Box 6.11, which is the perfectly elastic and inelastic curve – D_1, D_2 or D_3?

2 For demand curve D_3, what would you expect to happen to price elasticity as price falls? Will price elasticity remain the same at all prices, or will it change? Test out your hypothesis by calculating the price elasticity over the price range £1–£2 and £5–£6. Now you should be able to say what happens to price elasticity as you move along a straight line demand curve. Was your original hypothesis correct?

3 Price elasticity can also be measured by looking at how the total revenue a firm gets from selling a product changes in response to a price change.

   A Work out what happens to total revenue in the following table:

Price (£)	Demand (sales)	Total Revenue (£)	Elasticity when price falls	Elasticity when price rises
10	100			
9	120			
8	140			
7	160			
6	180			
5	200			

   B Calculate the price elasticity as price falls from £10 to £9 and £9 to £8, etc.

   C Calculate the price elasticity now when price rises from £5 to £6 and £6 to £7, etc.

   D Why are your answers to C) and D) different?

   E Now look at the total revenue column and the figures for price elasticity you have calculated. How are the figures for elasticity linked to the total revenue figures? If price falls and total revenue increases, what does this tell you about the price elasticity? If price falls and the total revenue remains the same, what does this tell you about price elasticity?

   F You are a manager considering raising the price of a product you are selling with the aim of increasing sales revenue. Under what circumstances will you be confident that your strategy will be successful?

4 Why might you expect the price elasticity of demand to be

   A Greater for a particular brand of new car than it is for new cars generally?

   B Greater for fish than for cigarettes?

   C Greater for video recorders than for salt?

   D Greater over a long period of time rather than a short period of time?

5 A Why might a company want to make the demand for its product become more price inelastic?

   B What could a company do to make the demand for its product become more price inelastic?

6 In only one case will a demand curve have unit elasticity throughout its length and this is known as a **rectangular hyperbola**. This is shown in Box 6.12.

   How would the firm be affected by changing price either upwards or downwards?

BOX 6.12

A rectangular hyperbola

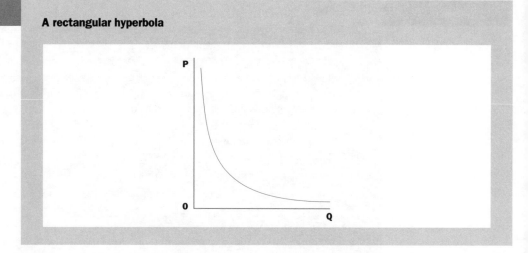

What factors determine the price elasticity of demand?

1 The availability of substitutes

If a product has close substitutes it is relatively easy for the consumer to switch demand away from one product and divert it to another. If the price of one brand of chocolate bar goes up consumers may well switch to buying a rival brand. The substitution effect is strong in this case and the demand for the particular bar will be highly elastic. However, if the prices of all chocolate bars go up then there are few substitutes for chocolate and so demand will be less elastic.

2 The proportion of income spent on the product

Very cheap items such as matches or salt are likely to have an inelastic demand. If their prices rise there will be little impact on the spending power of the individual and so no need to change spending patterns. For larger items of expenditure, the consumer will be more inclined to weigh up the purchase more carefully. Often consumers can put off a purchase and do not have to buy, e.g. replacing a hi-fi system can be quite expensive. If a shop cuts its prices it can have a great influence on buyers and sales may take off. Here the income effect is a powerful influence on demand.

3 The number of uses of a product

If the demand for a single use product, such as lawn mowers, falls there is no other use which might lessen the impact of the change in demand. However, a multi-use product may be protected. The demand for flour may be relatively inelastic because it is used to make a wide range of other products.

4 The addictive nature of a product

The demand for cigarettes is likely to be inelastic. As price rises the evidence seems to suggest that smokers will continue to smoke with little change in their habit. However, even with this product it is probably the case that if price rose to £5 or £10 for 20 cigarettes there would be a greater impact upon demand and demand would become more elastic. Goods which people regard as necessities are likely to have an inelastic demand although it is difficult to define exactly what a 'necessity' is.

5 The time period

For some products it is difficult for consumers to change their pattern of consumption in a short time. There may be a need for time for people to search out alternatives. In this case demand might be relatively inelastic in the short term but more elastic in the long term. This is of particular importance to importers of goods. If the prices of foreign goods rise it may take some time before they can find other suppliers to provide goods at a cheaper price.

Income elasticity of demand

Income elasticity of demand is the responsiveness of demand to a change in income.

A change in income levels will also affect demand. The income elasticity of demand (Ey) can be measured using the following formula:

Income elasticity of demand =
$$\frac{\% \text{ change in quantity demanded}}{\% \text{ change in income}}$$

For example, if there is a 5% increase in incomes and this leads to a 10% increase in demand then
the income elasticity of demand = $10\% \div 5\% = 2$

For most products we would expect demand to rise as incomes rise and these are known as normal or superior goods. But there are some goods which may experience falling demand as income rises. Sliced bread and sometimes supermarkets' own brands might be in this category, and these are known as inferior goods. Look at Task 6.5.

TASK 6.5

Income elasticity

1 Calculate the income elasticity of demand for a product where a 2% fall in income creates a 5% increase in demand.
2 How does a knowledge of income elasticity of demand help to explain the growth of cheap discount supermarkets such as Aldi during the recession of the early 1990s?
3 The latest Government forecast states that the economy will grow by 3% next year. How might a company respond to this information if it already knows that its products have an income elasticity of demand of 2?

Cross-elasticity of demand

Cross-elasticity of demand is the responsiveness of the demand for one good to a change in the price of another.

Cross-elasticity (Ec) can be calculated using the following formula:

Cross elasticity of demand =
$$\frac{\% \text{ change in the quantity demanded of product A}}{\% \text{ change in the price of product B}}$$

So, for example, a bus operator might realise that when a rail company had raised prices by 10%, the demand for the bus service rose by 5%. In this case the cross elasticity of demand
$$= 5\% \div 10\% = 0.5$$

Look at Task 6.6.

TASK 6.6

Cross-elasticity

1 How would you expect the cross-elasticity of demand to be different between two products which are close substitutes compared to two products which are not linked to each other? Think about the way in which the demand for lamb might change in response to a change in the price of pork.
2 Why might a business be interested in finding out what the cross-elasticity of demand for its products might be in relation to competing products? Think about the price of renting videos and the price of going to the cinema.

Elasticity of supply

We already know that supply will change in response to price changes. But if prices rise, by how much will supply rise, and how quickly?

If there is an increase in the demand for a particular make of new car, why will it be relatively easy for the producer to increase the supply whereas, if there is an increase in the demand for fresh flowers, it will be far more difficult for producers to respond?

Elasticity of supply is the responsiveness of supply to a change in price.

Elasticity of supply (Es) can be calculated using the formula:

$$Es = \frac{\% \text{ change in the quantity supplied}}{\% \text{ change in price}}$$

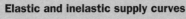

For example, if the price of a product rises by 10% and supply is able to increase by 5%, then

the Es = 5% ÷ 10% = 0.5

In this case supply could not match the change in price.

As with demand, there are the extremes of elasticity. Supply can be perfectly elastic or perfectly inelastic and such curves may be shown on a diagram as in Box 6.13.

BOX 6.13

Elastic and inelastic supply curves

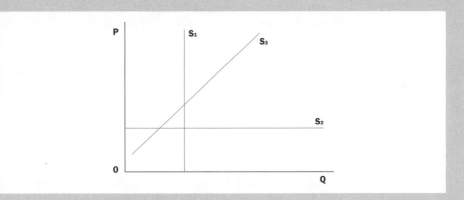

TASK 6.7

1 In Box 6.13, which curve represents a perfectly elastic and inelastic curve?
2 Work out what happens to the elasticity on supply curve S₃ as price rises (it will help to draw this out on a piece of graph paper).
3 Draw any other straight line supply curve starting at the origin of the graph and calculate its elasticity as price changes.
4 Can you now make any broad statement which would apply to all supply curves starting at the origin of a graph?

What factors affect the elasticity of supply?

1 Time

*The **short run** is that period of time in which at least one factor is fixed in supply. The actual period of time will vary from one firm to another. For a window cleaner the short run may be half an hour (the time it takes to buy an extra bucket) but for a steel company the short run could last for seven years or more – the time it takes to build a blast furnace.*

Time is of obvious importance. It is always going to be difficult for supply to increase over the next day but it should be able to increase considerably over the next year. In the short run, firms can increase supply by running down levels of stocks held, taking on more variable factors such as unskilled labour, working longer hours, working more efficiently or making better use of machinery. However, it may be difficult to bring about significant changes to supply.

In the long run, existing firms will be able to expand, build new factories and train up additional skilled labour. New firms can enter the industry, imported goods can be bought from overseas suppliers and so there is little to restrict the growth of supply.

2 The nature of the product

*The **long run** is that period of time in which the quantities of all factors can be varied.*

Firms producing manufactured goods or providing services find it easier to adjust supply but farmers find great difficulty. Once a crop has been planted, that's it. The farmer cannot suddenly plant more halfway through the season because prices have edged up. Often agricultural produce is perishable and difficult to store so it all has to be put on the market at one time; there is very little that can be done to affect supply apart from destroying a surplus crop. The difficulties farmers face have been the main inspiration behind the development of the Common Agricultural Policy (CAP) and this will be discussed in Chapter 11.

3 Ease of entry to the industry

If it is possible firms may find it beneficial to restrict supply because this will keep prices and profits high. They may therefore try to prevent new firms from entering an industry by establishing some barriers to entry.

These can take the form of take-overs and mergers, heavy spending on advertising or new technology or adopting a pricing strategy deliberately designed to keep new firms out.

4 The production process

The nature of the production process is also important. Increasing the supply of a catering service may be relatively easy since it is fairly simple to recruit the kind of staff needed. A jewellery manufacturer will find it far more difficult to recruit the kind of staff needed, and so supply will inevitably be inelastic. What is important here is the ability of factors to move between different jobs or the mobility of factors. If mobility is easy, supply is likely to be elastic; if factors are immobile, supply will be inelastic.

REVIEW

This chapter has investigated the mechanics of markets. Markets are made up of buyers and sellers and it is the interaction of demand and supply which determines price. The demand and supply curves for most goods and services have much in common but each market will be affected by different conditions. Shocks to a market will bring changes in price. How a market responds to changes in price will be dependent on the concept of elasticity. Markets are constantly affected by change and so the ideas of elasticity are extremely useful to economists across a range of contexts.

REVIEW TASK

Using your economic understanding, explain and analyse the following articles about markets. In each case you should be able to identify:
A   what kind of shock has affected the market
B   what the effect of the shock has been.
In each case use a diagram to illustrate what is happening in the market and, in your explanation, try to use the economic terms and ideas you have encountered in this chapter.

The market for oil

The price of oil rose steadily in 1994 from $12.75 early in the year to $19 by the end. Commentators expect the rise to continue. These expectations have been assisted by a cold snap in the USA and a heat wave in Japan where the increased use of air conditioning has led to a 4.6% increase in demand since 1993. Added to this, Japan, the USA and the UK have been emerging from recession. Continental Europe is following the UK out of recession and the Asian–Pacific economies are continuing to show fast growth. The supply of oil is stable at the moment at around 25 million barrels a day and there may be pressure on the petroleum exporting (OPEC) nations to allow output to rise.

The market for diamonds

Russia produces about a quarter of the world's diamonds but it has an agreement to sell virtually all of its production to De Beers, the South African mining giant. Through controlling the supply, De Beers can effectively control the price at which rough cut diamonds are sold throughout the world. Now Russia is in greater need of foreign currency and is planning to sell more of its own production on the open market. The shake-up in the market could be enormous.

REVIEW TASK

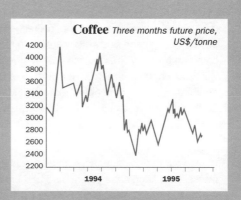

Coffee *Three months future price, US$/tonne*

The market for coffee

Commodities dealers are braced for heavy trading later this week, following a meeting of Central America's top coffee producing nations in Bogota, Colombia tomorrow.

The meeting, initiated by the Colombians, is widely expected to ratify a decision to suspend export registrations to drive up world coffee prices, which have fallen by more than 40 per cent during the last year. Brazil, the world's biggest producer, is not expected to attend.

Central American producers have been feeling the pinch, but analysts point out that much of the price fall is a correction from last year's rises, when the key three-month future price hit $4,100 a tonne in the wake of frosts in Brazil.

Meanwhile, coffee prices tumbled to their lowest point for more than a year at the London Commodities Exchange yesterday. The key three-month futures price closed down $30 a tonne, to $2,358 – **Ian King.**

*Source: **Guardian** (5 July 1995).*

Multiple choice

1 **The quantity demanded of an inferior good always falls**
  I   as income increases
  II as price falls
  III as supply increases

  A I only
  B I and II
  C II and III
  D I, II and III

(IB, May 1995, Higher)

2 **A normal good can be distinguished from an inferior good because a normal good has**
  A positive price elasticity of demand
  B negative price elasticity of demand
  C positive income elasticity of demand
  D negative income elasticity of demand

(AEB, Summer 1994)

3 The diagram below shows the relationship between the quantity demanded of Product **X** and the price of Product **Y**.

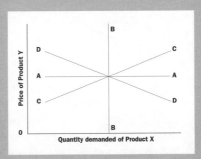

Which of the lines (A, B, C or D) represents a positive cross-elasticity of demand greater than zero but less than infinity?

(AEB, Summer 1994)

4 In the diagram below, **D** represents the demand for the currency of country **X** and **S** represents the supply of the currency of country **X** (on the foreign exchange market).

Everything else remaining the same, a shift from S to S₁ would arise if

A   other countries became became less willing to invest in country **X**
B   exchange controls were imposed in country **X**
C   country **X** devalued its currency
D   country **X** increased its sales of currency on the foreign exchange market.

(AEB, Summer 1994)

5 **The demand curve for petrol shifts to the right. This could have been brought about by an increase in**

A   public transport fares
B   new car prices
C   the price of crude oil
D   the rate of VAT on petrol
E   the standard rate of income tax

(ULEAC, January 1995)

6 **Given that the demand for water is inelastic with respect to price, a change from flat-rate charges to the metering of supplies (i.e. a charge for each gallon used) is likely to**

A   encourage water companies to build more reservoirs
B   be more likely to cause water shortages
C   discourage consumers from conserving water
D   reduce the amount of water demanded by consumers
E   increase consumers' surplus

(ULEAC, January 1995)

7 When the manager of a cinema halved the price of admission she was surprised to find that, despite reducing prices by such a large amount, her weekly takings actually rose. This was because

A the demand curve was inelastic
B average revenue was greater than average cost
C the demand curve was elastic
D average revenue was increasing
E marginal cost was declining

(ULEAC, January 1995)

8 Product X is estimated to have a price elasticity of demand of -1.5, an income elasticity of -0.5, and a cross-elasticity in relation to product Y of -2.0. It can be inferred from this information that

1 the demand for **X** is price inelastic
2 **X** is an inferior good
3 **X** is complementary to **Y**
A 1 only
B 1 and 2
C 2 and 3
D 1,2 and 3

(ULEAC, January 1995)

9 When demand is price elastic and price is falling,

1 total revenue will be rising
2 marginal revenue will be positive
3 sales will be increasing
A 1 only
B 1 and 2
C 2 and 3
D 1,2 and 3

(ULEAC, January 1995)

10 If the income elasticity of demand for bread is -0.2 and that for wine is +2.3, then a 10% increase in real incomes will lead to a

A 2% decrease in demand for bread and a 2.3% increase in demand for wine
B 0.2% increase in demand for bread and a 2.3% increase in demand for wine
C 0.2% decrease in demand for bread and a 2.3% increase in demand for wine
D 2% increase in demand for bread and a 23% increase in demand for wine
E 2% decrease in demand for bread and a 23% increase in demand for wine

(ULEAC, January 1995)

QUESTIONS

11 In the diagram below DD is the market demand curve for gin, SS is the market supply curve, and StSt is the market supply curve after a specific indirect tax has been imposed on gin.

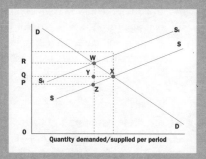

The equilibrium price will

A rise to OT
B rise to OR
C remain on OQ
D fall to OP

(ULEAC, January 1995)

12 Question 12 refers to the following diagram.

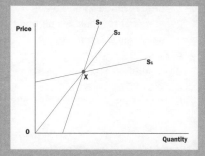

In the above diagram S_1, S_2 and S_3 are supply curves. At point X

A **S_1** has the largest elasticity of supply
B **S_2** has the largest elasticity of supply
C **S_3** has the largest elasticity of supply
D all three have equal elasticity of supply

(IB, May 1995, Higher)

13 The cross-elasticity of demand of Good **X** with respect to Good **Y** is +0.5. The cross-elasticity of demand of Good **Y** with respect to Good **Z** is +2.5. This suggests that

A   **X** and **Y** are closer complements than **Y** and **Z**

B   **Y** and **Z** are closer complements than **X** and **Y**

C   **X** and **Y** are closer substitutes than **Y** and **Z**

D   **Y** and **Z** are closer substitutes than **X** and **Y**

(IB, May 1995, Higher)

Data response

Study the diagram and text below

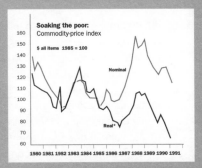

The collapse of commodity prices is good news for industrial economies, as it helps the fight against inflation. But cheap commodities add to the woes of those developing countries struggling to introduce economic reforms and to service their debts. Low commodity prices constrain their investment and growth: the OECD calculates that real GDP per head grew by an average of only 0.2% a year between 1965 and 1987 in poor countries which depend on non-fuel commodities for at least 60% of their exports, compared with average growth of 2.7% in all developing countries. If commodity prices regained their average real level of the 1970s and 1980s, then the export revenues of poor countries which are non-fuel commodity exporters would be a third higher.

For food-exporting poor countries the best hope for a recovery in prices lies with the rich. If rich countries cut back farm protection and subsidies significantly, world grain and meat prices, for example, would bounce back. The prices of many other commodities, particularly metals, have been depressed by overcapacity created by heavy investment in the early 1980s when prices were high. And, while prices may pick up over the next couple of years, there are reasons for expecting the long-term slide in prices to continue.

QUESTIONS

(a) The shift within developed countries from heavy industry to computer and
service businesses means that a given increase in GDP produces a smaller
increase in the demand for basic metals. Meanwhile, demand in developing
countries will remain constrained by low incomes.

(b) Technological advances have both increased supply (e.g. higher crop yields)
and cut demand thanks to cheaper substitutes. Artificial sweeteners replace
sugar; plastics replace metal; fibre optics replace copper wire, and so on.

Thanks to these two trends, the world today uses about a quarter less copper per
unit of GDP than 20 years ago, 40% less iron ore, and 50% less tin. And that
demand is lost forever.

*Source: Adapted from 'Raw Deal for Commodity Producers', **The Economist** (London) (13 April 1991).*

a What is meant by the word 'commodity', as used in this extract?
Give an example.

b Explain how a collapse in commodity prices might help 'the fight against
inflation' in industrial countries (paragraph 1).

c Define 'income elasticity of demand' and explain how it contributes to the
problems described in point (a).

d Using demand and supply analysis, suggest reasons for
(i) the volatile nature of commodity prices in the short run
(ii) the downward trend in commodity prices in the long run.

e Paragraph 2 suggests that rich countries should act in order to help economic
recovery in the poor countries. What incentives are there for them to act?

f What actions could developing countries take in order to overcome the problems
outlined in the passage?

(IB)

All for profit?

A statement from Unilever

Unilever is a major British and Dutch owned multi-national company making a wide variety of products which range from Persil to PG Tips, Calvin Kline to Walls, Birds Eye, Flora and Oxo. In 1994 it employed 304 000 people world-wide and sold goods worth nearly £30 billion. The company's most recent statement makes the following comments about its performance over the last year:

"Turnover and operating profit increased by 8%."

"£584m was spent on buying other companies."

"A major restructuring programme and expenditure on new technology has led to considerable savings in costs."

"Future profitable growth will hinge on technological innovation."

"Our policy is continuously to improve environmental performance in all our activities."

"Our business in Central and Eastern Europe continued to grow strongly and we gained market share."

"Following a major reassessment of corporate strategy, we have increased focus on those product categories and regions which we believe offer the greatest potential for profitable growth."

"Good progress has been made towards the goal of enabling every employee to use his or her talents to the full."

"The Chief Executive earned over £800 000 but at the same time owned 23 000 shares and had options to buy a further 151 000 shares."

FOCUS

What do these statements tell us about the business objectives of Unilever? What is the business aiming to do?

Preview

In this chapter we shall investigate the following key areas:

- Business objectives;
- Short- and long-run costs;
- Mergers and take-overs;
- Small businesses;
- Location.

Business objectives

Businesses may have a variety of objectives depending on the type of firm. Charitable organisations, such as Oxfam, are set up to meet an identified need, often work on a shoestring and aim to cover their costs. They often rely on volunteers and are financed by donations from the public. With publicly owned corporations, such as the Post Office, the objectives are set by the government of the day. These corporations are owned by the state, i.e. all of us, and the government could decide that their primary role should be to provide a satisfactory service for the public and not aim for maximisation of profit. During the period of the Conservative Government since 1979, the dominant thinking was that it was not the government's business to be providing services. This was better done by the private sector so most of the public corporations were sold off. Privately owned firms generally see profits as the main driving force but there may be a range of alternative objectives. The following could be listed as the main objectives a company might have.

Making or maximising profits

Businesses clearly aim to make profits. Firms need an incentive to produce any goods or services and, in most cases, that incentive is the profit they can make. Headlines such as "BP seeking profits of $3 billion", "Stagecoach profits gallop ahead" and "BT makes £100 a second in profit" indicate the importance and interest there is in profit performance. Profits provide the owners of businesses with a reward for the risks they have taken. They provide one way of judging the success of the management of a firm and the policies it has followed. The performance of companies can be compared and profits are a major source of capital for any business. A successful profit figure keeps shareholders happy and wanting to hold on to shares or buy more. This keeps the share price up and makes a firm less vulnerable to a take-over bid.

Knowing that profits are at the heart of business and that firms devote most of their time to creating more profit, economists often make the assumption that firms set out to maximise profits. Businesses do have other objectives, but it is fair to say that making profit is the major concern of businesses. Given a choice, all firms would prefer more profit to less profit and without profit there would be no firms in a free market economy.

Increasing sales

Businesses may see rising turnover (the revenue from sales) as the key to success. There will be a close link between growing sales and growing profitability but firms may be prepared to accept a lower profit level today by charging lower prices in order to make higher profits tomorrow when they are better established in the market. When a firm introduces a new product to the market, such as a new type of tooth paste, it knows that unless it is able to get customers to try the product, there will be no future for it. Firms are therefore prepared to accept a low price to launch a product with the hope that this will cause an instant rush for the product. When the market is growing then prices can rise and the firm can begin to focus more on profit.

Increasing market share

An increase in a firm's share of the market will be a clear indicator that the company is beating the rivals and becoming more successful. As a firm grabs a bigger share of a market it stands a better chance of being able to dominate the market and increase profits further. If market share remains static it could mean that other firms are gaining and that control of the market will be lost. Reducing risk is of major concern to firms and less risk comes with a larger market share.

Achieving growth

Many firms regard growth in the size of the business as a key objective. Growth may occur within particular markets in which case it has the advantages of rising sales. However, internal growth may be slow because time is needed to build the success of products and so firms often look to speed up the process by merging with other companies.

Merging or taking over rival companies has the added bonus that it may well reduce the competition at a stroke. Chief executives and top managers of modern companies also appear to enjoy the increased power, prestige and status associated with running a large company.

Embracing modern technology

Successful businesses are often those which are able to cope with the process of change. The economy, markets, products, competitors and, particularly, technology are constantly subject to change. Firms may have little control over some of these but they can get a grip on new technology. New technology allows a firm to lower costs and to develop new products which can grow into market leaders. Firms in the computing, telecommunications and electronics industries are at the sharp end of this at the moment but technology ripples through the industrial sector and presents one of the few ways in which manufacturers can hope to compete with the businesses of the Far East. Again, Chief Executives derive considerable prestige from operating the most modern and efficient plants. Look at Box 7.1.

BOX 7.1

Windows TO HIGHER PROFITS

Lucrative window on the world

Microsoft's new program will change the face of the computer industry,

says Jack Schofield

Windows 95 could be the biggest launch of all time. The sales revenues that are riding on it dwarf those of the most popular films, books and records, and its unstoppable success is helping to drive the American stock market towards record highs.

Three weeks before its launch on August 24, Windows 95 is already the cover story on dozens of magazines, and broadsheet newspapers are planning to devote multi-page supplements to it – not something they did for ET or Jurassic Park.

Yet, it's not even a very original computer program, just the long-awaited upgrade to Microsoft's hugely-successful Windows 3. It should have appeared 18 months ago, and it's already scheduled for replacement.

But technical considerations have become almost irrelevant. Windows 95 will change the face of the computer industry – worth around $360 billion (£225 billion) a year – and is expected to confirm Microsoft's dominance in desktop software, where it has 80 per cent of the market, and project it into the online services business. Microsoft's boss, Bill Gates, is worth about $13 billion but Windows 95 could make him seriously rich.

Microsoft has already shipped 80 million copies of Windows. If only 10 million users upgrade at $100 each; that's $1 billion worth of business to start with. We can assume about 50 million personal computers will be sold in the next year, most of those loaded with Windows 95 too.

Licensing deals are secret and subject to discounts, but such "pre-loads" could be worth another $2 billion a year.

And Windows 95 is only the start. Microsoft will also be selling a Plus Pack that adds useful features, including the software needed to connect to the Internet; then there's a new version of Microsoft Office, which includes popular programs to take more cash from upgraders.

To an extent, revenues from Windows 95 and Office 95 will simply replace those from current versions of the software in Microsoft's $6 billion annual turnover.

Attorney General for Antitrust, could still try to block Microsoft, but the commercial and political fall-out would be fearful. A lot of American politicians don't think the government should be interfering with the way bright, young American multi-billionaires do business.

Of course, Microsoft has always expanded by moving into new areas. It started in 1975 with three employees and a version of the Basic computer language it wanted to turn into an industry standard. It expanded into operating systems in 1981. Gradually it took the lead in the applications software business, while previous market leaders crumbled and were taken over. Microsoft is now working hard to gain a big share of the home market with "edutainment" and productivity packages: on-line services are just next.

Lots of firms try to do the same. However, outside Japan, very few have Microsoft's long-term vision and determination. And while Microsoft has its enemies, many firms see it not as a shark but as a pond. IBM has lost out after spending a decade fighting Windows, in spite of investing vast sums in rivals.

Source: Guardian (31 August 1995).

TASK 7.2

1. What is the driving force behind Microsoft ?
2. How does Microsoft seek to manage change?

Creating a rising share price

Stakeholders are the groups of people with a direct interest in the success of a company such as employees, customers, creditors, suppliers and shareholders. Of these, the shareholders have a particular importance. If they are not kept happy, there is a risk that they will sell shares, causing the price to fall. If this happens other competitors may see an opportunity to buy up a rival cheaply and launch a take-over bid. Shareholders' loyalty can be bought, to some extent, with a rising share price and regular dividends and so Boards of Directors will be working to this end. In addition, today the payments to Chief Executives of major companies are often linked to the share price. Their pay may be related to the share price since this can be taken as a judgement of the share market about the success of the company. Giving the option to buy shares at a later date is frequently seen as a way of providing an incentive for directors to perform their duties well. Share option schemes may also be used by firms to generate loyalty from workers and give modest financial bonuses. At the top end there has been some abuse of this and the Greenbury committee, set up by the Government, recommended some tax changes to prevent the worst excesses.
Look at Box 7.2 and Box 7.3.

BOX 7.2

Stakeholders

Firms serve a number of different communities. It could be said that each of these communities has an interest or stake in the performance of the firm and so can be regarded as stakeholders in that firm. In 1996 the Labour leader, Tony Blair, recognised their importance by promoting the idea of a 'stakeholder economy'.

Shareholders are the owners of the firm and expect a return on the money they have placed in the shares of the firm. They are therefore mainly interested in the short-term profitability of the firm because they look for high dividends and a rising share price. If a firm performs poorly, it is likely that the shareholders will not campaign for a change of strategy by the management but will simply sell their shares and move their money on to a different firm.

Creditors are organisations which have lent the firm money. These could be banks who have given the firm loan or overdraft facilities but might also be suppliers who are seeking payment in the near future. Creditors will be expecting firms to be prudent in the management of their finances. They will be expecting prompt payment of interest charges and will be prepared to intervene if this does not happen. It is often the creditors who force firms into liquidation when interest payments are not met.

Debtors of a firm are those people who owe the firm money perhaps because they have bought goods from them. These are also stakeholders. Their main concerns will be for the quality of the goods provided and for the continuity of supply.

BOX 7.2

Employees have a major stake in the success of any company. They will have expectations about the continuity of employment, regular wage payments, fair treatment, concern for health and safety, training, that their views are listened to and job satisfaction.

The management of a firm will have their own expectations. They will be seeking the increased opportunities for promotion and responsibility which come from a growing firm and often want to be part of a successful team. Some of their pay may well be related to the performance of the firm and so they will be keen to see rising profits and a rising share price, particularly if they have been given the option to buy shares at a favourable rate.

The local community has a stake in the firms in its area. The prosperity of a region is very much tied up with the success of its local firms. Growth of a firm will create other jobs in the area but may also bring more traffic congestion and more pollution. Firms recognise the need to create good relations with the local community and to be thought of as a 'good neighbour'. They contribute to local good causes and often encourage their employees to get involved with local community projects or schools.

Central government and the state could also be considered to be stakeholders. Firms pay taxes to the Government. If they shed workers a cost will be imposed on the state through additional benefit payments and the state may have to deal with problems such as pollution created by firms. Governments also see the prosperity of the nation tied up in the success of its businesses and will attempt to provide an economic framework within which firms can flourish.

TASK 7.3

Think about your own school or college and one local business.
Who are the stakeholders in those organisations and what role do the stakeholders play?

BOX 7.3

Electricity market gets a SHOCK

£2.5BN BID FUELS ELECTRICITY BILLS ROW

Fury at Hanson power swoop

£4.3bn killing for top Eastern men

Lisa Buckingham

Top executives of Eastern Group stand to make a £4.3 million killing on their collective share options following the take-over bid from Hanson.

That is on top of the sizeable share option profits which a number of directors realised in the last financial year. It means that, on top of their salaries, the board will have scooped the equivalent of nearly £1 million a year since privatisation.

John Devaney, the chief executive, is the largest options beneficiary with a potential profit of £1.24 million. Mr Devaney, whose salary increased from £341,000 to £377,000 in the year to March, will net another £10,000 from his fully-owned shareholding.

Eastern's chairman stands to make almost as spectacular a gain. He should garner £1.03 million on top of a £472,317 gain from cashing in options last year.

In addition, Mr Smith's 8,477 owned shares will be worth £84,350, bringing his possible gains from the company – which paid him £141,000 last year – to £1.58 million.

*Source: **Guardian** (1 May 1995).*

TASK 7.4

1. To what extent do you feel that the directors of Eastern Electricity have earned their rewards?
2. What are the economic effects of these payments?

Being regarded as a good member of the community

With increasing concern for the environment, firms like to be seen as caring and environmentally friendly. Firms achieve this by supporting local activities, sponsoring worthwhile events, donating to charity or adopting practices which show a high level of concern for the environment. Firms may cynically exploit their environmental credentials as part of their marketing strategy – 'its good to be green' – but many show a genuine desire to operate responsibly. Indeed, some companies such as The Body Shop or the Co-operative bank, give the environmental objective a very high profile. Look at Box 7.4.

BOX 7.4

The Body Shop trading charter

The way we trade creates profits with principles.

We aim to achieve commercial success by meeting our customers' needs through the provision of high quality, good value products with exceptional service and relevant information which enables customers to make informed and responsible choices. Our trading relationships of every kind – with customers, franchisees and suppliers – will be commercially viable, mutually beneficial and based on trust and respect. Our trading principles reflect our core values.

We aim to ensure that human and civil rights, as set out in the Universal Declaration of Human Rights, are respected throughout our business activities. We will establish a framework based on this declaration to include criteria for workers' rights embracing a safe, healthy working environment, fair wages, no discrimination on the basis of race, creed, sex or sexual orientation, or physical coercion of any kind.

We will support long term, sustainable relationships with communities in need. We will pay special attention to those minority groups, women and disadvantaged peoples who are socially and economically marginalised.

We will use environmentally sustainable resources wherever technically and economically viable. Our purchasing will be based on a system of screening and investigation of the ecological credentials of our finished products, ingredients, packaging and suppliers.

We will promote animal protection throughout our business activities. We are against animal testing in the cosmetics and toiletries industry. We will not test ingredients or products on animals, nor will we commission others to do so on our behalf. We will use our purchasing power to stop suppliers animal testing.

We will institute appropriate monitoring, auditing and disclosure mechanisms to ensure our accountability and demonstrate our compliance with these principles.

TASK 7.5   Is Body Shop's Trading Charter in conflict with the objectives of maximising profit?

Survival

Whilst most firms aim to make profits, a more basic instinct is to survive. If profits turn to losses firms may need to undertake drastic action to save themselves from bankruptcy. Large firms engage in restructuring or downsizing in order to reduce labour costs; small firms generally have to be nice to bank managers, renegotiate loans and try to persuade them not to pull the plug on the business. The need to survive can persuade firms to change direction and move away from what was their previous core business if the prospects in that industry look grim. Look at Box 7.5.

BOX 7.5

TARMAC *pulls out of housing*

Tarmac, a major building firm, is concerned that if it stays in the house-building industry, its future profits and possibly its future survival may be at risk

TARMAC melts out of house building

OUTLOOK/Market gloom is only part of the reason says *Roger Cowe*

As if the housing market has not taken enough of a battering over the past few years, and with the threat of an interest rate rise hanging over it, Tarmac has now dealt a further blow with its announcement on Wednesday that it wants to stop building houses.

The construction conglomerate will either sell its house-building division or float it on the stock market, just as Hanson did with Beazer last year.

The move is full of irony, though not necessarily full of significance for the industry or for housebuyers.

First, the group, which has always been best known for the black stuff which gives it its name, and for other construction interests, struggled hard in the 1980s to get the message over that it was in fact the country's largest house builder.

It succeeded in winning that recognition just as the housing market collapsed at the end of the decade. And now it has shrunk so much that this year it will probably only rank as number four in the housebuilding league table, behind George Wimpey, Beazer and a resurgent Barratt.

Second, at a time when thousands of people find they cannot afford their house, Tarmac has concluded much the same. Building houses, like buying one, eats up cash. And Tarmac thinks it can find better things to do with the money.

But that says more about Tarmac than it does about the industry. It is true that building new houses is not the licence to print money it was in the late 1980s. A clampdown on Housing Corporation finances has killed the tentative recovery in public sector housing by which housing associations had begun to substitute for the collapse in local authority building.

In the private sector, the volume of new houses is only about three-quarters what it was at the peak – 222,000 in 1988. Worse, the lack of inflation in house prices, plus low consumer confidence, makes it impossible to get near the sort of prices that were achieved then. Buyers

BOX 7.5

know prices will not go up if they postpone a decision, and might well come down if the builder is keen to sell. Builders are usually keen to sell because they don't want cash tied up in completed houses, and Tarmac is renowned in the industry for dropping its prices to get houses off its books.

But the new house market is not in as bad a state as might be imagined. The number of new houses bought with building society mortgages – only about an eighth of the total mortgage market – was back to the 1990 level last year, and has stayed at that level so far in 1995. In fact the total of private housing starts is now well past that level, back to the scale of the mid-1980s, as the chart shows.

The problem for Tarmac is primarily that its other businesses also demand capital, and it believes it can make more money in aggregates, breeze blocks and ready-mixed cement. That view is affected by a gloomy analysis of profit margins in housebuilding, based on rising land costs and static selling prices.

*Source: **Guardian** (4 August 1995).*

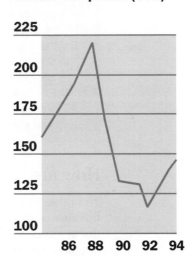

HOUSING STARTS
Private companies (000)

TASK 7.6   What has Tarmac pulling out of the housing market to do with the company's survival?

Satisficing

Most of the above objectives can be described as being maximising objectives – maximising profits, maximising sales, maximising growth or maximising the use of technology in a business. People in charge of a business may decide to achieve a satisfactory performance across a range of indicators and not to maximise any one of them. This approach is more likely to keep all of the firm's stakeholders happy and is known as 'satisficing'.

Firms can see all of the objectives being linked to each other and contributing to the profits of the firm. There is an obvious connection between increasing sales and growth with profit but others can also improve profit performance. New technology is not introduced for fun. It is a way of improving competitiveness and so increasing profit. Even concern for the environment is not totally altruistic. 'Greenness' is a quality that can differentiate one producer from another and, in effect, it becomes part of the marketing budget aimed at shifting more product and making more profit. Look at Task 7.7.

TASK 7.7

Present your own company profile

1   Check out the performance of a major company.

Look at the company report of a major company (you can write for these yourself or consult the copies held in your school/college/local library). Find out the following:

A   the turnover of the company for the last two years;

B   the profits for the last two years;

C   the objectives of the firm (for this you will need to read the Chairperson's statement which is normally included at the start of the report);

D   What can you say about the success of the firm? Is it doing better or worse than the previous year? Can you explain this change in fortune?

E   Are there any business objectives which are not mentioned in the company report? Why do they not get a mention?

How are costs linked to profit maximisation?

To understand the behaviour of businesses, economists generally make the assumption that firms aim to maximise profits. If firms stick to this objective it will be possible to say something about the prices they are likely to charge, the levels of output they are likely to produce and the amount of profit they are likely to make. We will then be able to make comparisons and to assess which types of firms and which forms of competition are best.

Profits are calculated by looking at the difference between the money earned from the sale of goods or services (revenue) and the cost of producing those goods and services (costs). So to understand profit, we first must take a closer look at costs.

Look at Box 7.6.

BOX 7.6

The costs of running a car

TASK 7.8

1   List the costs of running a car

2   Divide the costs between those which will stay the same no matter how many miles you drive (fixed costs) and those which will increase as you drive more miles each year (variable costs)

3   When calculating the cost of driving between two towns, car owners often will just work out the cost of the petrol. Is this a correct valuation of the cost of the journey?

BOX 7.6

Saloon Car

FOR Good secondary safety; comfortable; good to drive; 1.6-engine models reliable

AGAINST 1.4 engine noisy; non-PAS steering heavy; diesels troublesome

CAR FACTS

Length	(m) 4.22-4.37	Model	1.4	1.6	dsl	1.6auto
Width	(m) 1.94	Mpg	36	32	44	33
Boot	(litres) hatch 315/705;	Insurance	8	11	9	11
	Saloon 385; Est.405/805	Monthly cost (£)	120	150	–	150
Tank	(litres) 55	Depreciation	mid	mid	mid	mid
Service	(mls) 12,000; d6,000	Top Speed (mph)	104	115	95	112
Diy	easy	0-60mph (sec)	13.0	10.1	17.6	12.3
Getting		Safety	5.5	7.5	6	6
spares	easy					

Source: Consumer Association,
WHICH? *guide to new and used cars (1995).*

Fixed costs are those costs which do not change in the short run.

Variable costs are those costs which will change as the level of output changes in the short run.

In answering Task 7.8 you will already have considered the main types of costs which firms face. To produce any goods or services, a firm has to employ factors of production which have to be paid for their work. Some costs have to be paid regardless of how much is being produced, and these are known as fixed costs (businesses also refer to these as overhead costs or indirect costs).

These costs will be the same if the firm produces one item or 1000 items, and one example of a fixed cost might be the rent a firm has to pay for the use of its premises.

Some costs will rise as the firm produces more of goods or services, and these are known as variable costs (businesses also refer to these as direct costs or prime costs).

E.g. as hairdressers deal with more customers they are likely to need to spend more on shampoo. So shampoo costs are a variable cost.

Time is important here. Firms use a combination of fixed and variable factors to produce output. The fixed factors cannot be changed over a period of time and we refer to this length of time as the short run or short period. It is of no specific length of time but will vary from one firm to another – as mentioned in Chapter 6 for a window cleaner the short run could be half an hour: the time it takes to go to a shop to buy another bucket; but for a steel producer the short run could be 5–7 years: the length of time it might take to build another blast furnace.

Therefore, in the short run the firm can only increase its output by adding variable factors to its fixed factors. In the long run a firm can change all the quantities of all of the factors it employs and so it can change the whole scale of its operation.

It can move into or out of new industries and can choose to produce at its lowest long run costs. Some costs are neither totally fixed nor totally variable: they are a combination of the two. These are known as semi-variable costs. One obvious example would be a company's gas bill. Part of the charge is a fixed charge and remains the same regardless of how much gas is used. The customer is then charged a set amount for each therm of gas used: a variable cost. Look at Box 7.7.

*The **short run** is that period of time when at least one of the factors of production is fixed in supply.*

*The **long run** is a period of time over which it is possible to increase the quantities of all factors of production.*

BOX 7.7

Hospital television

Hiring televisions to hospital patients formed the basis of the Hospital Entertainment business started up by David Watts and Ian Bradley in the early 1990s. They found a gap in the market because, at the time, the big TV renting companies seemed only interested in long-term contracts not at all suited to the short-stay hospital patient. Their company, Hospital Entertainment, was born. Initially David and Ian needed to borrow to get started. They now operate from Kingston in Surrey making contracts with individual hospitals and then supplying them with the 14-inch televisions with radio, remote control and headphones. The business has grown rapidly and it now employs around 100 people.

TASK 7.9

1 Which factors of production does the business need to employ?
2 In the short run, which of those factors are likely to be fixed in supply, and which variable?
3 List the fixed, variable and semi-variable costs that Hospital Entertainment is likely to face.
4 What difficulties might Ian and David encounter if 15 new hospitals telephoned to ask for the television service to be put in place in the next month?
5 Explain how you think Hospital Entertainment might fix its daily hire charge for a television.

What happens to output in the short run?

We have seen that all companies need to know their costs in order to calculate profit. How would we expect costs to behave? Will they rise, fall or stay the same as output rises? This will be important information for firms trying to set their production levels to maximise profit.

First we need to consider the conditions firms encounter in the short run. Let us imagine that the room in which you are reading this book is a factory, a factory you have set up to make wooden tables. You have some machinery to use already in place, you have a supply of wood and the other raw materials you might need. All that you lack is a supply of labour to make the tables for you. A quick phone call to the local Job Centre solves this problem as they give you the names of 20 equally well qualified and skilled carpenters who are ready to start work immediately. But you are still unsure about how many people to employ. You decide to conduct an experiment. You decide to employ one worker on the first day, two on the second day, three on the third day and so on to see what happens to the production of tables.

The daily output figures are given in Box 7.8.

| BOX 7.8 | **The output of wooden tables** | | |

No. of Workers	Total daily output of tables (Total output)	Extra output added by additional worker (Marginal product)	Average output per worker (Average product)
1	2	2	2
2	5	3	2.5
3	9	4	3
4	12	3	3
5	14	2	2.8
6	15	1	2.5
7	15	0	2.14

TASK 7.10

1. a Look at the total product figures. Explain why we might expect two workers to produce more than double the output of a single worker (think back to the work done on the effects of division of labour and specialisation).

   b Remembering that the quantity of the fixed factors stays the same, explain why it seems reasonable that the growth in the output of tables slows down as more workers are employed.

   c What happens to production as your company employs the seventh worker?

2. Explain how the average product and marginal product figures are calculated.

The figures show the actual output of tables and so can be called the total, average or marginal physical product. A graph showing this data is given below.

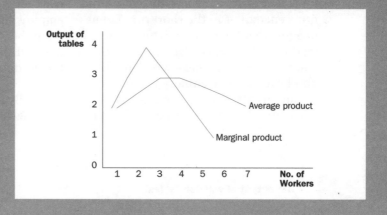

As the marginal physical product figures show the difference between, say, the output of tables when one or two workers are employed, the figures on the graph are marked half way between the points one and two on the horizontal axis.

What do you notice about the relationship between the average and marginal physical product curves? Marginal product increases at first, but then declines. This means that as variable factors are added to the fixed factors total output rises but the output obtained from each extra unit of labour will eventually diminish. The firm gets a smaller and smaller increase in output as it employs extra people.

Of greater importance is the fact that this will not just happen with your imagined firm but will apply to all firms, big and small, operating in the short run. The law of diminishing returns or the law of variable factor proportions describes this process. In the short run, as more variable factors are applied to fixed factors, then the returns (or extra output) obtained from each extra unit of the variable factor may increase at first but must eventually diminish.

Logic confirms to us that the law must apply to all firms. If it did not apply, then a company could continue to increase output by employing more variable factors which would mean that from your own bedroom or classroom you could produce all the tables the world requires by adding more variable factors. This may be an awesome prospect but obviously not feasible. However, we need to be aware of the assumptions we are making when stating the law of diminishing returns:

- The variable factors are all of exactly the same quality – they are homogeneous.
- The variable factors can be varied by one unit at a time.
- The marginal product can be measured.
- There is only one variable factor.

In practice, it is difficult to find situations in which these assumptions are found. We know that, for example, workers vary in quality. It is often difficult or even impossible to change the quantity of the variable factor by a single unit at a time (think about a car manufacturer where a team of workers is required to complete a set process. With the required number of workers, production goes ahead smoothly but with one less worker, any production may be impossible). The value of the output of an extra worker can be extremely difficult to measure (what would be the value of an extra police officer or nurse?) and there may well be more than one variable factor at any one time. Despite this, the law does govern the way firms behave in the short run: firms are constantly battling to achieve higher output by using their resources more efficiently in the knowledge that they cannot do this just by hiring a few more workers.

What happens to costs in the short run?

So far we have seen what to expect from output in the short run but we need to give some monetary values to the factors to be able to calculate what happens to costs. If we assume that the firm has fixed costs of £100 per day and that each worker costs £40 per day to employ we can work out the costs of the tables.

These are shown in Box 7.9.

BOX 7.9		Short-run costs £									
	Workers	TP	AP	MP	FC	VC	TC	MC	AC	AFC	AVC
	0	0	–	2	100	0	100	20	–	0	–
	1	2	2	3	100	40	140	13.3	70	50	20
	2	5	2.5	4	100	80	180	10	36	20	16
	3	9	3	3	100	120	220	13.3	24.4	11.1	13.3
	4	12	3	2	100	160	280	20	21.6	8.3	13.3
	5	14	2.8	1	100	200	300	40	21.4	7.1	14.3
	6	15	2.5	0	100	240	340	–	22.7	6.6	16.1
	7	15	2.1	–	100	280	380	–	25.3	6.6	18.7

Notes:
TP: Total Product
AP: Average Product
MP: Marginal Product
FC: Fixed Cost
VC: Vatiable Cost
TC: Total Cost
MC: Marginal Cost
AC: Average Cost
AFC: Average Fixed Cost
AVC: Average Vatiable Cost

TASK 7.11

1 What is the link between FC, VC and TC?
2 How are the AFC and the AVC calculated?
3 What is the link between AFC, AVC and AC?
4 If it was now necessary to pay the carpenters £50 a day, what effect would this have on the FC, VC, TC, MC, AC, AFC and the AVC?

We can now transfer some of this information to a graph (see below)

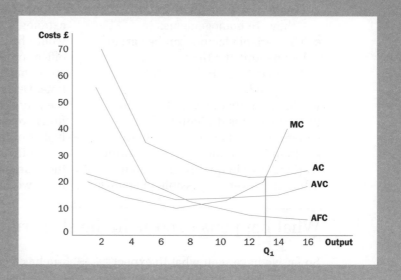

TASK 7.12

1 Reading from the graph, measure the amount of AC, MC, AFC, and AVC when output is at 10 tables.
2 What can you say about the point at which the marginal cost curve cuts the average cost curve? In fact the marginal and average cost curves should always cross in the way shown in Task 7.11. As long as the cost of producing an extra product is below the average cost, the average cost must be pulled down. If the marginal cost is above the average cost, the average cost curve must be rising. When MC = AC, then the AC curve is at its lowest point i.e. this is the firm's lowest cost output or most efficient level of output. On the graph in Task 7.11 this is shown at output level OQ₁ and this is the firm's optimum output.
3 As more tables are produced, what happens to the average fixed costs? If total fixed costs remain constant, explain why this happens.
4 What must the gap between the average cost curve and the average variable cost curve be equal to?

Optimum output is a firm's most efficient or lowest cost level of output. It is always the output when the average cost curve is at its lowest point.

The main general point to emerge here is that because all firms are subject to the law of diminishing returns, all firms will face U-shaped cost curves in the short run.

What happens to costs in the long run?

In the long run, the constraint of a fixed factor no longer exists. Firms can now decide what is the best size or scale of operation. They can build new factories, train more skilled labour, buy more sophisticated equipment or move into new markets, all of which would have held back expansion in the short run.

Firms grow for a variety of reasons. They may see size as an effective way of competing with other companies or reducing risk, but it is also a way of reducing costs. If firms rely on internal growth, that is, financing growth through using their own profits, the process can be slow. Some firms adopt that cautious but prudent approach. Marks & Spencer was in existence for over 100 years before it made its first acquisition, of Brooks Brothers in the USA. Hanson plc only started 30 years ago but through a series of adventurous take-overs has become a major player in the tobacco, coal, plastics and brick-making industries. It has also moved into the electricity industry and has become one of the UK's largest firms.

Whatever the method of growth, firms find themselves moving from one short run situation to another and then to another. Marks & Spencer's or Tesco's or Sainsbury's sales are limited by the amount of shop floor space they have available. So, in the short run, they face a fixed sales area. If these companies wish to grow, they may want to open new stores but this will take time. But as new stores open, each company would expect its average or unit costs to fall. A new store would be supplied from the same warehousing space, with the same lorries and very little extra cost. The store group would now be operating on a larger scale, with lower unit costs but with, once again, a larger but still fixed selling space. This effect is shown in Box 7.10.

BOX 7.10	An envelope curve

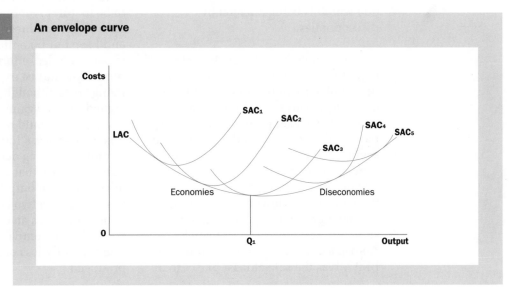

In Box 7.10, SAC_1 represents the short-run average costs of a group with a fixed number of stores. As the group expands, it is able to increase its output or sales and moves onto SAC_2. Because the firm is able to save on its costs, SAC_2 shows that the firm can produce more but at lower cost. The firm's optimum output has increased. Here the firm is achieving economies of scale.

As firms expand they will expect to see costs continuing to fall, but this process will not continue forever. Costs will continue to fall for some time but, eventually, costs may start to rise. Firms can become too large. They become more difficult to manage efficiently, communication slows down, they respond more slowly to changes in the market and this causes costs to rise. The firm is experiencing diseconomies of scale.

In Box 7.10, SAC_3 represents the level of costs when the firm is operating at its long-run optimum output. SAC_4 and SAC_5 show the costs of a larger firm but one which is being affected by diseconomies.

As firms grow they obviously never expect to encounter diseconomies but the problems can be seen after the event. Firms do see difficulties and several have been prepared to sell off parts of the company if the anticipated savings fail to materialise. When British Aerospace bought Rover, there was much talk of a new 'synergy' resulting from the new group. However, when cash became tight, the magical synergy suddenly disappeared and British Aerospace was prepared to sell out to BMW. Was the sale at least partly to do

with a recognition of the existence of diseconomies of scale? Even Hanson has decided to demerge some of its business.

In Box 7.10 we can show the long-run trend in costs by drawing an envelope curve which just touches the short-run cost curves. $0Q_1$ represents the firm's long-run optimum or lowest cost output. As the firm expands up to that level of output the firm is achieving economies of scale which reduce costs. As the firm expands beyond $0Q_1$ the firm encounters diseconomies of scale and costs rise.

However, in some cases a growing scale of production does seem to bring with it constantly decreasing costs. What diseconomies there may be are outweighed by further economies and the long-run average cost curve continues to decline. These conditions are likely to be found in the provision of some national services such as electricity generation, gas distribution or the railways. Such industries appear to be 'natural monopolies' because costs for a single producer will be very low and keep out potential competitors. In these examples, efforts to break up the industry could be expected to lead to rising costs although it can still be argued that the gains from greater competition could off-set this trend. Box 7.11 shows a long-run cost curve of a company facing decreasing long-run costs. It shows that if a large company operating at an output level of $0Q_1$ is split up into two companies, each of which produces an output of $0Q_2$, the costs of each company will rise. Consequently less efficient output is produced.

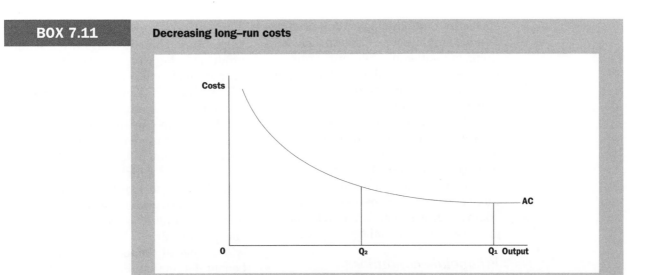

BOX 7.11 **Decreasing long–run costs**

What are economies and diseconomies of scale?

Internal

Economies of scale are the savings in costs which result from the growth in the size of the firm in the long run. There are two types of economy: internal and external economies. Internal economies result from the firm's own decisions to grow and are achieved within the firm. They can be divided into several broad categories:

Economies of scale are savings in costs which result from the growth in the size of the business. They are often divided into two kinds: (a) internal economies, which are achieved through the firm's own decisions and (b) external economies, which are achieved through a growth in the size of the industry. Economies of scale can only be gained by firms in the long-run.

Technical economies

Cost savings result from the use of expensive machinery and equipment and these are known as technical economies. Generally the latest technology is more efficient but new technology can be extremely expensive to introduce. It may be only larger firms which can invest in the latest technology and so the large firms will benefit by seeing costs fall.

Machines do not all work at the same speed. A large firm can employ the right combination of machines to ensure maximum efficiency. For example, a small brewery will not produce enough beer to justify operating its own canning plant. A large brewery with a wider range of products will be able to justify investment in such equipment and achieve the associated cost savings. Getting the most efficient combination of machines is known as the principle of multiples.

Some large pieces of equipment can only operate efficiently if produced on a large scale, e.g. steel-producing electric arc furnaces are unlikely to be operated by a small business working out of a lock-up garage. They cannot be produced in a mini version and so cannot be used by smaller firms. All firms can benefit from the cost savings associated with specialisation and the division of labour. Firms specialise in producing certain products and the employees of firms specialise in doing particular jobs but large firms employing mass production techniques can benefit to a greater extent.

Large firms can afford to pay the high wage levels necessary to employ the best managers. They may also be able to employ specialist advisers to assist managers in their decision-making and may be able to economise on the number of managers needed when a company grows in size. These factors give rise to managerial economies.

Financial economies

Financial economies arise out of the fact that large firms are able to raise money more cheaply than small firms. First, if they are plcs, they will be able to raise finance through the Stock Exchange. Secondly, they will often be able to borrow money more cheaply from banks than small firms because of the smaller amount of risk. Thirdly, large firms stand a better chance of raising money internally and so avoiding high rates of interest. Large firms often act as a holding company for a range of businesses. The businesses pay money into the holding company which then channels it to different parts of the company in need of a cash injection.

Marketing economies

Large firms achieve savings when selling products in large orders. They take proportionately less administration and fewer sales staff. There are economies to be made when buying supplies in bulk and large firms can afford the more expensive but more effective forms of advertising such as television. Such advertising has a high initial cost but it is likely to reach a far wider audience in a more effective way and so, in terms of its cost per unit of sales, it is relatively cheap. Large firms often produce a wider range of products and so can benefit if a reputation built up with one product helps to sell others. Marks & Spencer's reputation for quality in underwear has allowed them to move successfully into other areas where quality is important such as pre-prepared meals. These marketing economies all lead to lower costs.

With their wider product and market spread, large firms are able to reduce the risks they face. If one product has a poor year, others may be doing well; if one market is in recession, others may be experiencing a boom. Small firms are more likely to go under because their success is totally dependent on the fortunes of one or two products. Thus, risk spreading economies enable the larger firm to have better chances of survival.

External

External economies are the savings in costs which result from a growth in the size of the industry rather than a growth in the size of individual firms. They result from decisions outside the firm's direct control.

Economies of concentration

If firms in the same industry set up in the same area there will be economies of concentration to be made. Japanese motor manufacturers like to collect supplying companies around them. This reduces transport costs but also enables communication between companies to be improved. Japanese firms favour Just-in-Time production systems which require suppliers to provide goods exactly when they are needed. This reduces the costs associated with holding large quantities of stocks and leads to greater efficiency.

An area may develop a pool of labour with the skills needed by the local industry which will reduce training costs. Local colleges and universities may well run courses with the needs of the industry specifically in mind and the firms in the industry might set up or finance common research projects. The area could develop a good reputation for high quality products and this, in effect, would provide firms with free advertising. Growing industrial areas will also attract the interest of Government and there may be moves to improve the local infrastructure to the benefit of all local companies.

Splitting up the production process can save costs. Rather than trying to produce all the components needed for a particular product, a firm can benefit by buying in some components from specialist manufacturers. The specialists will be selling to a wider range of customers and so will be able to achieve many of the internal economies which would not be available to a smaller producer.

This is illustrated in Box 7.12.

| BOX 7.12 | The economies of dis-integration |

Economies of information

As an industry grows there is generally an associated growth in the number of trade or specialist journals catering for the needs of the industry. Information about the industry becomes more widely available from which all firms in the industry can benefit. There may even be television programmes made about the industry which will provide free publicity. This reduces the costs of generating information for the firm and creates economies of information.

Diseconomies of scale

Diseconomies are the rises in costs which may result from a company growing too large. Economies and diseconomies can be shown on an envelope curve.

Again, these may be divided between internal and external diseconomies.

Internal

Internal diseconomies result from a firm becoming too large.

If a firm expands into too many unrelated industries there may well be a dilution of management expertise and a lack of the necessary management skills to hold the larger group on track for higher profits. When trading conditions toughen up, the management of large companies have often chosen to concentrate on the core business and sell off peripheral activities. This is a recognition that internal inefficiency, or X-inefficiency, creeps into larger firms. Inevitably, as a company grows in size, it becomes more difficult for central management to keep in touch with all of the firm's activities. A growth in the number of tiers of management or levels of hierarchy makes decision-making slower and so companies respond more slowly to market changes; another example of X-inefficiency. IBM, the major American-owned computing giant, did not respond sufficiently quickly to the popularity of personal computers. It stuck with its dominance in main frame computers and this allowed much smaller companies to gain competitive edge and forced IBM completely to rethink its strategy.

Firms employing thousands of workers are likely to find industrial relations much more of a problem. It's more difficult to retain the loyalty and motivation levels experienced by smaller firms. Trade unions will be more active in large firms and tensions may arise. Any interruption to production will mean that output is lost and unit costs will rise as fixed costs will be spread over a smaller output. Japanese-owned firms have tried to reduce this problem by making single union agreements with trade unions and no-strike deals. The EU has attempted to address the problem through requirements in the Social Chapter of the Maastricht Treaty for larger firms to set up Works Councils.

When large firms make mistakes they can be very costly. For example, the development of a new car can cost up to £500 million. If the manufacturer gets the market wrong, the company can be left with a hefty debt. Such are the financial implications of these kinds of mistakes that companies simply cannot afford to make them. If consumers fail to see the great benefits of a new product they must be persuaded to change their minds through massive advertising campaigns. Even so, sometimes there is no alternative, in the face of consumer resistance, but to withdraw products. It is at this point that heads roll. It is estimated that when Unilever had to change the formula for its new washing powder Persil Power, the mistake had cost the company approximately £257 million, which included research and marketing costs.

External

External diseconomies may occur when firms in the same industry choose to concentrate in the same part of the country. Whilst this can lead to a fall in some costs it may also lead to costs rising. There may be competition for labour and land which drives up costs. Firms trying to recruit labour will have to offer higher wages and other local firms may have to raise their own wage rates to their existing work force in order to prevent them being attracted to competitors.

As an area grows it will experience many of the external costs associated with growth. There will be higher levels of pollution locally, traffic congestion may become a problem, house prices may rise and local schools and hospitals become more crowded. All of this may be accepted by the local community whilst the industry is expanding and jobs are being created, but difficulties will be experienced if the industry moves into decline. Then local unemployment will rise and this will affect other local businesses. People may begin to move away, causing further decline and new firms may be reluctant to move to an area heavily dependent on one industry. These describe the kinds of problems faced by many of the former coal-mining and steel-producing areas of the country. Box 7.13 illustrates some of the problems of size found amongst building societies.

BOX 7.13

JUST BIGGER, *Not Better*

Roger Cowe on the wisdom of society weddings

The fashion for building society mergers has reached its peak with Abbey National's admission yesterday that it has been eyeing National & Provincial. This comes hard on the heels of plans to put together the Halifax and the Leeds as well as Lloyds Bank's take-over of Cheltenham & Gloucester.

Fashions change and it may be that in 10 years' time the urge to merge appears as misguided as so many other financial industry fashions over recent decades.

Building societies have been immune from many of the worst fads – such as Third World debt, highly-leveraged buyouts and huge property loans – because they have been very tightly controlled. But they are not entirely immune, having been heavily implicated in the scandal of endowment mortgages and as keen as anybody else to get into pensions and investments.

As with all fashions, there are seductively powerful, if familiar, arguments in favour of merger. Essentially they are about economies of scale, especially in light of the indisputable fact that there are too many financial services outlets littering Britain's streets, which severely limits growth possibilities.

One big organisation needs only one chief executive and company secretary, thus halving those overheads incurred by two separate bodies. Bigger business can also buy more cheaply, whether the item being purchased is stationery or television advertising. And larger budgets create more marketing clout, allowing a merged business to build a bigger database and use it more lavishly.

These arguments have justified mergers in all sectors for years, from the creation of the "big four" clearing banks to the takeovers in the television industry and, recently, consolidation in the privatised bus sector.

There are two problems. First, there are small organisations in all sectors which operate with lower unit costs than the big brothers supposed to enjoy those economies of scale.

And second, there are always diseconomies of scale. The bigger the organisation the more difficult it is to prevent the growth of bureaucracies, which add nothing, and to avoid expensive mistakes in information technology, distribution and elsewhere which arise because managers become too remote from the operational "sharp end". Furthermore, the experience of the banks over the past 25 years has been that being bigger makes it possible to lose larger amounts on the latest folly.

On the other hand, those in the medium-sized bracket in any industry often face a squeeze: too big to benefit from smallness and the attachment to a particular customer group, locality or region, but too small to benefit from scale. They get the bureaucracies without the benefits.

Thoughts like these persuaded the Cheltenham & Gloucester board that the only move which made sense would be to join a different organisation – Lloyds Bank – which would provide benefits other than economies of scale through its different services and different customer base.

The same thought may have struck N&P, which might look to banks in Scotland or further afield rather than falling into the clutches of Abbey National.

*Source: **Guardian** (24 May 1995).*

BOX 7.13

Top mortgage lenders

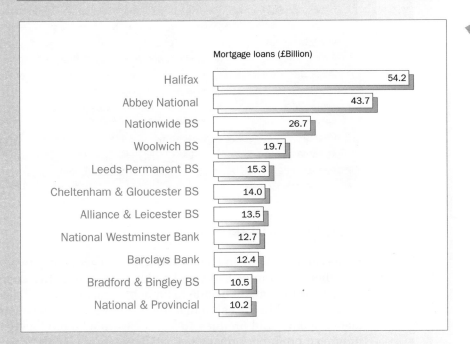

Mortgage loans (£Billion)

Lender	£Billion
Halifax	54.2
Abbey National	43.7
Nationwide BS	26.7
Woolwich BS	19.7
Leeds Permanent BS	15.3
Cheltenham & Gloucester BS	14.0
Alliance & Leicester BS	13.5
National Westminster Bank	12.7
Barclays Bank	12.4
Bradford & Bingley BS	10.5
National & Provincial	10.2

*Source: **Council of Mortgage Lenders** (1990).*

TASK 7.13

1 How does the building societies article explain the growth in the number of mergers between building societies?

2 Why is it that small organisations can operate with lower unit costs than their big brothers?

3 What particular disadvantage does Roger Cowe see facing large financial organisations?

TASK 7.14

Coursework investigation: mergers

Analyse the arguments around a merger that you have seen in the newspapers or on television. Set yourself the task of deciding whether you believe that the resulting merged company will be operating in the public's interest. You will need to consider the criteria you might apply in order to judge the outcome of a merger. Large take-over bids can be referred to the Monopolies and Mergers Commission so you may first have to check the sections of this book on competition policy. Also, today many mergers are influenced by the needs of the Single European Market. The very large mergers can be investigated by the European Commission. Try to analyse the economic logic of the merger. Firms may be merging to achieve economies but, often, it is competitive pressure which pushes firms together. Look at the mergers from the point of view of the customers, the competitors, the employees, the government and the efficient allocation of resources.

Mergers and take-overs

Firms can be bought and sold. If firms see others performing badly and making low profits they might decide to launch a take-over bid in the belief that their management could produce an improved profit performance.

But take-overs take different forms. There are different types of mergers. Firms at different stages in the production of a particular product may join together and this is known as vertical integration, e.g. if an oil company buys out a chain of garages this moves the group towards the consumer (forward vertical integration); if a coffee manufacturer buys up some coffee plantations this moves the group towards the raw materials (backwards vertical integration).

Horizontal integration occurs where firms at the same stage of production making the same kind of product join

together e.g. two retail chains merge or two computer manufacturers merge. Sometimes firms in the same industry merge but those firms may not be producing the same kind of product, e.g. a car manufacturer merges with a truck manufacturer or a sausage maker merges with a drinks manufacturer. These are examples of lateral integration.

During the 1980s there were many examples of firms in different industries and with, apparently, different interests merging to form groups based in a range of industries, e.g. an aircraft manufacturer merges with a car manufacturer and the group then merges with a property company. The major advantage that such groups possessed was that they could wield tremendous financial power and could spread risk. Such groups are termed conglomerates. Look at Box 7.14.

BOX 7.14

BRAINCHILD *of the backroom boy*

Roger Cowe

The bid for Eastern may be seen in some quarters as Lord Hanson's swan-song, but it is in reality the first major move of his anointed successor, Derek Bonham.

This quiet accountant, who has wielded the financial levers in the background for more than 20 years, has gently emerged as the man who might be able to save Hanson from the fate it has handed out to so many groups over the years. If so, this takeover is the first evidence that the group has a future beyond the piracy of the 1980s which made Hanson such a feared predator.

In seven years from 1979, the nerve and judgement of Lord White and the steely grip of Lord Hanson saw the group rocket to the top of the business tree. But Imperial Group – the most bitter UK battle, in 1986 – was the last successful contested takeover bid the group made. There has been a series of friendly acquisitions, many such as ConsGold and Quantum Chemicals being very large, but the buccaneering days are long gone.

Hanson's share price has never reached the heights it achieved in 1985. A huge rights issue

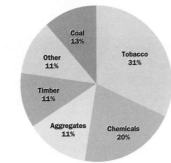

Hanson before electricity

Tobacco 31%
Coal 13%
Other 11%
Timber 11%
Aggregates 11%
Chemicals 20%

and two enormous acquisitions helped see to that, but the market's disillusionment with its former darling was increased by worries about how the group had produced its previously brilliant record. In any case, conglomerates went out of fashion with the 1980s, as investors questioned the rationale of paying people like Lords Hanson and White so handsomely for what were effectively the investment decisions fund managers are paid to make.

Lords Hanson and White made one last stab at the old takeover game with their assault on ICI in 1991, but they were forced to retire hurt. Since then, unable to trade on its shares, the group has been forced to capitalise on its role as a cheap source of finance. Thus Beazer was put out of its misery, and Quantum Chemicals was bought because Hanson could save millions by refinancing its massive debts.

Mr Bonham has sold off a string of smaller companies acquired over the years, culminating in the demerger last year of 34 US businesses.

The result is a different kind of Hanson. It remains an opportunistic conglomerate, but one consisting of a small number of large interests rather than many smaller operations, focused much more clearly than before on primarily energy or resource-related industry.

But Hanson after Eastern Electricity will also be a group with heavy debts and high interest costs. Eastern will bring steady cash flow to help whittle away those debts, but continued shareholder indifference could provoke a more dramatic response if the low share price is not to entice some latter-day Hanson to offer to break up the disjointed empire.

The first step to such a radical transformation could be a major sale or the flotation of a business such as the coal mining company, Peabody. That could wipe out debts at a stroke, though it might not erase the doubts about the logic of the rest remaining together.

*Source: **Guardian** (1 August 1995).*

TASK 7.15   What are the advantages and disadvantages of a group such as Hanson?

Some of today's firms have resulted from mergers spanning across national borders so that a multi-national or trans-national firm results, e.g. an electrical appliance manufacturer in the UK merges with a similar company based in Italy. These kinds of firms have increased particularly with the development of the Single European Market, where firms have seen mergers as a quick way of penetrating overseas markets.

Box 7.15 gives examples of mergers which have taken place in recent years.

BOX 7.15

Merger mania

A   In 1992, British Airways bought Dan Air and then went on to buy 25% of US Air and Quantas.

B   Dixons, the electrical retailers, bought Currys.

C   In 1983 Bass, the large brewery group, bought Augustus Barnett, a growing off-licence chain of stores.

D   In 1995 Lloyds Bank bought out the Cheltenham & Gloucester Building Society.

E   The merger between Cadburys and Schweppes happened in 1969 and since then the company has formed an agreement with Coca-Cola to distribute their products in the UK.

F   Kingfisher, the company which owns Woolworths also owns the Comet chain of stores.

G   Local breweries own chains of pubs.

H   In 1988 Nestlé, the Swiss based company, bought Rowntree and in 1995 BMW bought Rover.

I   Trafalgar House owns Cunard, the cruising company, the Ritz hotel and John Brown Engineering company amongst others.

TASK 7.16

1   Look at the list of mergers above and classify them into the appropriate group.

2   Look at an example in each of the groups and try to identify what might be the advantages of such a merger (the work covered on economies of scale should help but also think about the effects of the merger on competition in the industry).

How important are small firms in the economy?

The information about the advantages of large firms could suggest that there is no place for smaller firms in the economy, but this could not be further from the truth. Of the 2.7 million firms in the UK, 2.3 million employ less than six people. We need to ask the questions: why are there so many small firms and how important are they?

Defining the small business

The Bolton Committee which reported in 1971 investigated small businesses and defined them in terms of their number of employees but they could also be defined by their turnover, market share or type of ownership. Box 7.16 presents some data about firms in the UK for 1991.

BOX 7.16

Business data

Number and % of firms by employment size and total employment, 1991

Employment Size band	No. of firms (000)	% of firms	Total employment (000)	% share of employment
1 – 10	2496	92.6	5730	28.2
11 – 99	182	6.7	4529	22.2
100 – 499	16	0.6	3413	16.7
500+	3	0.1	6683	32.8

Number and % of firms by turnover

Turnover size band (£000)	No. of firms (000)	% share of firms	employment (000)	% share of total employment
1 – 100	2211	77.6	4032	19.9
100 – 1000	215	19	4001	19.6
1000 – 5000	72	2.6	3093	15.2
5000+	22	0.8	9230	45.3

Source: adapted from G. Bannock, **Small Business** data.

TASK 7.17

What does this data tell you about the importance of small firms in the economy in the areas of employment and contribution to the turnover of business?

Small firms are of great importance to the economy. Whether measured in terms of employment or turnover, the vast majority of firms are small. Over 98% of firms employ less than 100 people, and these are responsible for 50% of all employment. Less than 1% of firms have a turnover of more than £5 million, but these contribute nearly half of all sales.

It is in the field of job creation that small firms are even more significant. Graham Bannock (see Box 7.16) suggests that, since 1987, firms employing less than five people have increased their employment by over 30% whereas firms employing over 10,000 people have increased employment by less than 5%. Large companies will not be the source of huge job creation in the future. They are locked into competitive battles with foreign companies which tend to demand restructuring or downsizing which has the result of stripping out tiers of management and reducing employment opportunities. In the future the small business sector is likely to be the major source of new jobs.

Why do small firms survive?

Small businesses are the seed corn for the future. All businesses start small. The successful ones expand to become the large firms of the future. The growth in unemployment in the 1980s meant that many older workers found that self-employment was the only realistic option to being on the dole. They could plough redundancy payments into a new business venture or organise management buyouts of their existing business.

Reductions in the higher rates of income tax may have provided the incentive for some people to start businesses. The Government has also attempted to reduce the red tape associated with running a company and given subsidies to encourage the unemployed to start their own firms.

The Government has been concerned that in the UK a smaller percentage of people are employed in small firms than in many of our European partners. In the EU about 13% of people are self-employed in the non-agricultural work force whereas in the UK the figure is nearer to 10%. This could mean that in the UK there will be less job creation potential and less flexibility to change. The Conservative government was also concerned that to establish a vibrant, free market economy it is essential for new firms to be setting up.

Changes in technology, particularly the personal computer, have meant that small firms have been able to compete more effectively with larger companies. Technology has reduced the optimum size of a business. This has even been recognised in larger firms which often now choose to organise themselves into small business teams. They find that this improves communication, increases the responsibility of the work force, provides a tighter control of costs and improves quality. It is an organisational response to the possible threat from diseconomies of scale. So large companies, in effect, become a group of small units with only certain functions such as finance and research which are retained centrally.

In the recession of the early 1990s when trading was tough, many large firms adopted the strategy of concentrating on their core business. This involved them selling off fringe activities, some of which went to existing employees who became the owners of separate companies which were now suppliers to the parent company. IBM, the American computer giant, adopted this strategy. It sold off a computer manufacturing plant in Hampshire to the managers and this business now trades under the name of Xyratex. The result was the emergence of a new breed of small companies spawned by the larger companies.

It is often small firms which are the most innovative. They often introduce new products or ideas because the owners have set the business up with the specific intention of filling a particular gap in the market. Once the idea has proved itself, the firm often gets bought up by a larger firm with the resources to develop the product.

Where markets are small, small firms will flourish. Often such markets require specialist skills, and consequently there are no benefits from economies of scale. A glance through the Yellow Pages will tell you that there are a large number of firms in the area of personal services such as builders, electricians and plumbers, and the professions such as accountants, solicitors and architects and in any 'designer' activity such as fashion, music and art. Creativity cannot be mass produced and there is still a place for small businesses.

How does the location of a firm affect its costs?

The choice of location for a firm can have a considerable effect on the firm's chances of success. It can help to reduce costs, making the company more competitive and increase the demand for the products produced or supplied.

Firms will take into account a range of factors, including the access to markets or suppliers, the costs of land, labour and transport and any financial assistance which might be available from the Government or the EU which would help to cut costs. Firms may also look at whether an area is already favoured by other firms in the industry. This could bring with it additional advantages but could be a reason for going elsewhere.

The impact of modern technology and energy sources has meant that firms are now much freer to select their most favoured sites rather than being restricted to particular parts of the country. Firms will look at the whole range of facilities an area has to offer. Given a choice most people will choose to live in pleasant rather than unpleasant areas as long as there are good communications.

The development of the Single European Market has been of growing importance, with companies considering where best to base themselves. This has attracted a large number of foreign, particularly Japanese, companies to set up in the UK but has also persuaded some UK firms to move headquarters to Brussels or Paris. Box 7.17 is a good example.

TASK 7.18

Read the two articles. The first is about a supermarket chain's decision to set up a new store and the impact this has on the local area. The second is about the decision of a Japanese company to locate in the North of England

BOX 7.17

Location decisions

TO LET: *One Market Town*

Traders fear superstores are killing places such as Ludlow, Reports **Cal McCrystal**

The medieval town of Ludlow is slowly dying, victim of a decline in similar market towns across the country. Many shops have already closed, due partly to recession but also to an out-of-town shopping centre which has drawn trade away from the centres of both Ludlow and Leominster, 12 miles to the south. More than 30 Ludlow businesses are up for sale. But worse is to follow: plans to build a Tesco within Ludlow will, local traders say, "kill the town". Two years ago, the Secretary of State for the Environment, John Gummer, turned down a developer's application for a shopping centre on a by-pass outside Ludlow on the grounds that a similar by-pass shopping centre had deadened the heart of Leominster. Yet the idea of an "in-town" supermarket is no less controversial. Ludlow's objectors to the Tesco believe it would "change the existing polarity" of the town (by driving shoppers from the upper part of town to the lower).

"Most of the chamber of commerce are against the supermarket," said Brian McKibben. "We believe it could kill the town. Visitors like to come here to gawk at the blue Civic Trust plaques and interest themselves in our niche retailing which is part of the town's vitality."

Ludlow's fledgling Green Party agrees. Last week, having carried out a survey of local food shops, it predicted devastation if Tesco came to town. It said that "in the most likely scenario, a 44 per cent reduction [in turnover],... 82 per cent of businesses would be closed".

When Stanley Jones moved to Ludlow from Birmingham 17 years ago, "it was as nice a place as any in the UK. Look at the centre now. You will see six or seven charity shops in premises that went bust. I have not heard anyone come up with a solution, even though the Government seems to be worrying about it at last. But I feel we are doomed."

*Source: **Independent on Sunday** (19 February 1995).*

POKER GAME pays out Samsung jobs

The Government has awarded Samsung, of South Korea, one of the largest packages of government aid ever given to a foreign investor to set up a European bridgehead in Teeside.

This brings to 10 the number of South Korean companies that have come to the UK, representing virtually half of all the south-east Asian country's manufacturing investment in the European Union.

At £58 million in grants and soft loans, the aid package has only been bettered by the £75 million awarded to the car company Ford nearly 20 years ago for expanding to Halewood car plant on Merseyside and setting up its Bridgend engine plant in South Wales.

Samsung's first phase plans a factory by August next year, making up to a million computer monitors a year and 1.3 million microwaves. A second phase will see facilities to make 250,000 fax machines, 250,000 computers and three million TV cathode ray tubes by 1999. The Samsung package had to be large enough to lure the £450 million investment, with its associated 3,000 jobs, to Britain.

The Department of Trade and Industry gives most of its grants under the umbrella "regional selective assistance" scheme. Regional aid is supposed to be tailored to the creation or preservation of jobs in pre-determined areas, but contains provisions that allow ministers to consider other factors, such as whether the projects will displace existing jobs.

But ministers can also consider the scale of subsidy offered by other countries, the impact on existing companies, the beneficial affect of new technology after the investment, and the long-term viability of the scheme.

The Trade minister, Tim Eggar, said yesterday: "All the other governments in Europe and throughout the world are in the business of offering grants to attract companies making inward investment and we should rightly be in the position to do exactly the same.

The grants are undoubtedly a critical element in attracting large overseas investments."

Professor Garel Rhys, of Cardiff Business School, said the result is "like a game of poker", with the DTI trying to secure the investment while paying as small a subsidy as possible.

Ford recently disclosed it has opened negotiations with the DTI over plans to build its new small Jaguar car in Britain. It hopes to exert pressure on officials to concede more taxpayers' cash.

THE INCOMERS

NEC: £530 million on semiconductor plant at Livingston, Scotland, adding 430 people to existing workforce of 900, September 1994

Motorola: £250 million on semiconductor plant in East Kilbride, creating 250 jobs, September 1994

Digital Equipment: £90 million expansion at Ayre and South Queensferry, 800 jobs, early 1994

Honda: £350 million at Swindon, 1,300 jobs, 1992. Planned to invest further £330 million by late 1990s

Bosch: £100 million on car parts plant in south Wales, 1,220 jobs, 1991

Toyota: £700 million on car and engine plants in Derbyshire and north Wales, 3,000 jobs, 1989

Fujitsu: £400 million at semiconductor plant in County Durham, 600 jobs, 1989. Further £300 million, announced this year, to employ 1,200

Nissan: £900 million at Sunderland car plant, 4,250 jobs, since 1986

The DTI argues that regional selective assistance has proved an effective means of job creation. It spent £89.2 million in 1993–94, up from £71 million the previous year. £101 million is planned next year, rising to £108 million in 1996.

This spend is small compared with the recent past, and reflects the efforts of the Conservatives to rein in industrial sponsorship. The aid was awarded in those days as regional

BOX 7.17

development grants, schemes now scrapped because they were inflexible and awarded to companies for capital investment, not job creation.

Today's DTI has tried to side-step budget problems by working more closely with local agencies to attract overseas investment. Professor Rhys predicts that British state handouts will never be able to compete head-on with the spend available in Ireland, the Iberian Peninsula and southern Italy where European rules allow high levels of subsidy.

Instead the DTI is trying to sweeten its packages by offering soft loans, training, improvements in the local infrastructure, and access to cheap land. Samsung is to get up to £20 million in local aid packages on top of central government funds for infrastructure and training schemes.

But the CBI points out that the Government's regional aid policy still offers less than is available elsewhere in Europe.

TV ONLY PART OF PICTURE

Empire spans ships and chips, **Nicholas Bannister** reports

For most people, Samsung is just a name on televisions or videotape recorders at the local Dixons. But consumer electronics is only the tip of an empire which employs 187,000 people and is the world's largest maker of memory chips, a key component in electronics and computers.

The flagship business is Samsung Electronics, which takes in semiconductors, consumer electronics, tele-communications, watches and computers. But it also has interest in aerospace, shipbuilding, construction, engineering and petrochemicals, insurance, hotels, department stores, hospitals, newspapers and museums.

It was founded in 1938 as a small export firm called the "Samsung Store". Today Samsung Electronics alone accounts for about 8 per cent of South Korea's exports, far outstripping the equivalent figure for Britain's top exporter, British Aerospace.

The electronics business is forecasting sales of £8.8 billion by 1996 and £16.5 billion by 2001. It is the leading microwave oven manufacturer and makes about a quarter of the world's VTRs.

The Samsung group battles with Hyundai to be the country's largest company. Both groups have been in the forefront of South Korea's drive into international markets.

Lee Kun-hee, chairman of the company founded by his father, has sought to prepare Samsung for a more competitive market as South Korea gradually dismantles trade barriers ahead of OECD membership in 1996. A company video tells workers: "If we fail to open our door to foreigners, both Korea and Samsung will perish."

Samsung has been investing heavily overseas. Earlier this year it announced that it was setting up semiconductor and domestic appliance plants in Suzhou, one of China's biggest industrial cities. It is also keen to exploit cheap labour in North Korea, but has cooled its ambitions because of concern about the regime there.

Samsung aims to be one of the world's top five electronics groups in the 21st century. It is concentrating R&D on video products, optics, information systems, semiconductors, computer system integration and software, and environmental and energy systems.

*Source: **Guardian** (18 October 1994).*

BOX 7.17

In each case, identify what you consider to be the main factors influencing the location decision and what the impact of the decision will have on the local area.

Coursework Investigation

1   Concentrate on a local industrial estate and attempt to analyse the factors which have persuaded firms to move onto the estate. You should be able to find out the background to the development of the estate from the local authority's Planning Department. In some parts of the country you may be able to focus on the development of an Enterprise Zone – areas set up during the 1980s to attract firms to certain areas often to provide jobs to replace the loss of a major employer such as a steel works.
You could show your understanding of location issues by devising a brochure to attract new firms to the area.

2   Select a company new to your area and analyse the factors which influenced its location. News of new firms setting up will be carried in your local newspaper so this would be a good place to start. Often a decision of a company to move to an area has external costs and these can be of major importance. Supermarket chains establishing out-of-town shops are particularly good examples of this. You could conduct a survey of the feelings of local residents and shopkeepers so that you are able to identify both private and external costs and benefits of the development.

REVIEW

In this chapter we have seen that businesses may have a range of objectives but central among them will be a desire to make profit. Profit will result from a difference between costs and revenue. This chapter focused on costs. All firms face similar forces acting upon costs in the short and long run. In the short run it is the law of diminishing returns which determines the U-shape of the cost curves. In the long-run it is the economies and diseconomies of scale which determine the U-shape of the average cost curve. Despite the existence of economies of scale, small firms continue to survive and play an important part in the economy.

Improving transport systems and the development of the Single European Market are having an effect on location decisions. The choice of an appropriate location can still generate some cost advantages.

Multiple choice

 Question 1 refers to the following diagram

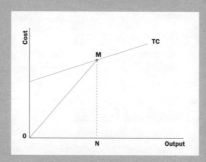

As the output of a good is increased, total cost (TC) increases as shown in the above diagram.
At output N, the gradient of the line 0M measures

A   Marginal cost
B   Average variable cost
C   Total variable cost
D   Average total cost

(IB, May 1995, Higher)

2 **A policy of encouraging industry to move to areas of high unemployment has the advantage of**

1   Reducing the problems associated with the geographical immobility of labour
2   Making better use of the available social capital
3   Securing the full advantage of the localisation of industry
Answer this question with reference to the following:
A   1,2 and 3 are correct
B   1 and 2 only are correct
C   2 and 3 only are correct
D   1 only is correct

(AEB, Summer 1994)

QUESTIONS

3 In the diagram below, **TC** is the total function of the firm.

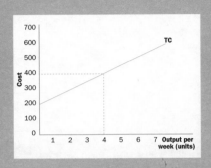

At an output of 4 units, average variable cost is

A £400
B £200
C £100
D £75
E £50

(ULEAC, January 1995)

4 A firm has fixed costs of £90,000. Its marginal costs are contained at £2 per unit of output. If the market price of this product is £5 a unit and the firm is a price taker, then to reach its profit target of £30,000 the firm would need to sell

A 10,000 units
B 18,000 units
C 30,000 units
D 40,000 units
E 60,000 units

(ULEAC, January 1995)

How do firms compete?

FOCUS

Fizzy (or carbonated) drinks:
Manufacturers' shares of the market

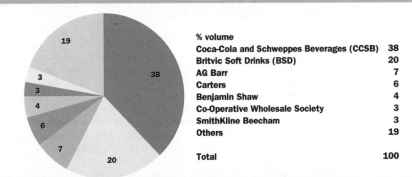

	% volume
Coca-Cola and Schweppes Beverages (CCSB)	38
Britvic Soft Drinks (BSD)	20
AG Barr	7
Carters	6
Benjamin Shaw	4
Co-Operative Wholesale Society	3
SmithKline Beecham	3
Others	19
Total	**100**

Carbonated drinks form part of the soft drinks industry which also includes concentrates such as fruit cordials and squashes. Carbonated drinks made up 57% of the total market.

Public houses
The article below describes some of the changes affecting pubs.

From THE BOOZER TO THE BRAND PALACE?

Most developed-country beer markets are dominated by two or three brewers and a handful of brands, quaffed mainly at home. But in Britain, uniquely, around three-quarters of beer is drunk in pubs — many of them owned by brewers. How long can that last?

In 1989, in the name of breaking up a cosy cartel, the British government ordered brewers to reduce their estates of tied pubs, and to allow their tenants to stock "guest" beers. This helped a movement already under way to turn what critics (e.g., women) claimed were seedy boozers with sidelines in curling sandwiches into modern service businesses.

Typical of the new breed is JD Wetherspoon, a specialist operator, which runs upmarket city-centre pubs with large clear windows, no-

smoking areas and food all day. But even the big brewers are ploughing money into their remaining pubs and increasing the number that they manage directly. A quarter of the takings in Whitbread's pubs now comes from food. This year Whitbread will spend £85m ($135m) building another 50 large "Brewers Fayre" family pubs: apart from an ugly name, each has a children's playground and nappy-changing facilities.

To succeed, pubs need to be clearly segmented, targeting such groups as young families or retired people, argues Whitbread's boss, Peter Jarvis. The catch, say critics, is that pub-beer prices have continued to outpace inflation. Brewers give discounts of up to a third to large outside purchasers, but sell beer to their tenants at full list price. Some brewers claim to compensate their tenants by charging them only a nominal rent.

Next week the director of the Office of Fair Trading may order changes to pub leases, after complaints by tenants of Inn-trepreneur Estates, a joint venture between Courage and Grand Metropolitan, a food and spirits firm. The European Commission, which will look at the issue in 1997, may be more radical, but any attempt to abolish the tie would face widespread opposition – particularly from small regional brewers.

Though the top four brewers will have 85% of the market after Scottish & Newcastle succeeded in buying Courage, concentration still lags most of the rest of Europe. Britons' lingering preference for drinking a range of dark ales in pubs means that the economies of scale required for megabrand marketing are hard to achieve. "If you read today's trends, you have to project the demise of the British pub," says Mr Jarvis: "But it will take a very long time." And since the number of young, blue-collar men – still the pubs' core customers – should rise again after 2000, it may never happen at all. Thank God.

Source: **The Economist** (13 May 1995).

Gas

British Gas was state-owned up to 1986. The government then sold off shares in the firm, moving it into the private sector of the economy. At the time of privatisation its main businesses were the extraction of gas from the North Sea, the distribution of the gas to households and businesses through pipelines, the sale of gas appliances through the gas show rooms and the servicing of the system. Up to 1986 all gas had to be supplied by British Gas but now other companies such as BP can supply their own gas to customers using the British Gas distribution network. These companies only supply around 20% of the total supply. In the absence of direct competition, the gas watchdog OFGAS was set up to monitor the performance of British Gas. It has the power to control prices and to impose performance targets. In 1994 British Gas made profits of £1.245 billion or about £40 a second.

| **TASK 8.1** | Using the information given in Focus 2.8, compare the market structure of the three industries. In what ways are the industries the same and in what ways are they different? |

Preview

In this chapter we shall investigate the following key areas:

- an introduction to different forms of competition;
- perfect competition;
- normal and supernormal profits;
- the shut down point;
- economic efficiency;
- contestable markets.

How does the structure of a market affect prices and supply?

The structure of any market describes the way in which a particular good or service is supplied to the market. It may be judged according to a range of criteria:

- the number of firms in the industry and whether any of those firms possess a dominant position in the market;
- the share of the market held by each company or by the largest four or five companies;
- the ease with which new firms can enter the market;
- the extent of price competition in the industry and the flexibility of price in the market;
- the use of forms of competition other than price competition, such as advertising;
- the level of profits made by firms in the industry;
- the nature of the product supplied by each firm;
- the level of knowledge of the market held by the participants.

The data in Focus 2.8 gives some of the information needed to compare the structure of three industries – fizzy drinks, public houses and gas.

Monopoly is a single supplier of a good or service; in practice a firm can possess monopoly power without being a single supplier (see Chapter 3.13).

Imperfect competition describes all types of competition between the extremes of perfect competition and monopoly.

Oligopoly is a market structure where the industry is dominated by a small number of large firms producing similar products or services.

Monopolistic competition is a market in which there are a large number of sellers of differentiated products.

It is clear that different levels of competition exist in different industries. The challenge for the economist is to understand the forces at work under different circumstances and to predict the behaviour of firms when faced with similar conditions. If we can do this it will become possible to advise on whether more or less competition is preferred, and then to devise policies that might change the market structure if required.

The first task is to see if Economics can provide us with models which may help us to understand the different forms of competition we encounter in practice.

There is a spectrum of competition. At one end of the spectrum is the single supplier of a good or service. The water companies supplying water to a particular area of the country seem to be in this monopoly situation.

At the other extreme is an industry where production is spread between a large number of firms all producing or supplying similar products. Firms compete by changing their prices and this is known as perfect competition.

Between the two extremes there is a whole range of competition which could be labelled imperfect competition.

Within this, some industries will be dominated by a small number of large firms supplying very similar products and this is referred to as oligopoly.

An industry consisting of a large number of firms but with each trying to convince the consumer that their product is, in some way different and, better than the competitors' is termed monopolistic competition.

BOX 8.1

The spectrum of competition

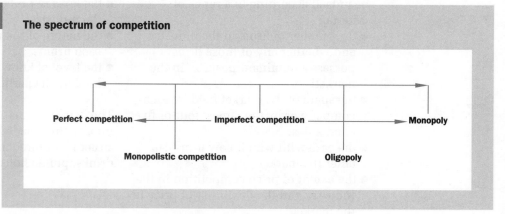

In each market the price and output chosen by firms will be influenced by the degree of competition faced.

Perfect competition

Perfect competition is a market structure in which there are many buyers and sellers of a homogeneous product; there are no barriers to entry or exit from the market and no individual buyer or seller can influence price.

The foreign exchange market is often quoted as an example of 'perfect competition'. In this market there are thousands of dealers around the world seeking to make a profit from buying and selling different currencies. The pounds sterling bought from any one dealer are exactly the same as the pounds sterling bought from any other dealer. Banks which are involved in most of the trade can easily appoint more dealers. Dealers are constantly trying to outthink the market. If they think that the value of a currency is about to fall, they will try to sell before the price has fallen. They may even sell currency they don't have in the expectation that they will then be able to buy back the currency at a lower price and make a profit on the deal. If they expect prices to rise, they will want to be buying the currency so that they can resell at the higher price and make a profit. The price of one currency is measured in terms of how much of another currency it will buy. So when the news reports that the value of the pound sterling has fallen from $1.6 to $1.58 it is giving important information to the foreign exchange dealers. Dealers' expectations about price movements are affected by a wide range of factors both economic and political.

The article in Box 8.2 reports some changes in the market.

BOX 8.2

Assault on the pound

Since leaving the Exchange Rate Mechanism (ERM) in September 1992, the pound sterling has floated relatively freely on the foreign exchange markets. Over 90% of the trade in currencies comes from speculators making a profit from their business. The graph shows the value of the pound since 1992.

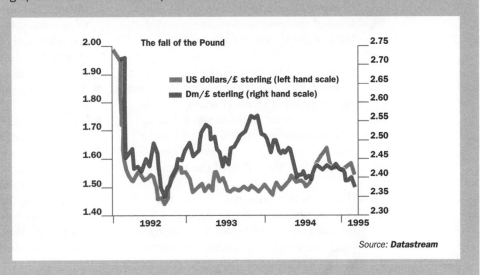

Source: **Datastream**

The value of the pound is influenced by the forces of supply and demand.

If people overseas want to buy British goods or services they need to demand pounds because British companies want to be paid in pounds so that they, in turn, can pay their workers and suppliers. In addition, the demand for pounds will come from dealers seeking profits in the market. If dealers believe that the value of the pound will increase, they will want to buy pounds now in the expectation that the price will rise and they can sell pounds at a profit.

Equally, if British people want to buy foreign-made goods or services, they will have to buy foreign currency to make the purchase. In order to buy another currency, the British will have to supply pounds. But dealers will also be selling pounds if they believe that the value of the currency will fall.

If they sell before the fall, they will be able to buy back the currency at a cheaper price and make a profit. This kind of speculation makes up about 90% of the demand for pounds.

Dealers will be analysing every scrap of news which could have an influence on the price of pounds. They sit with screens in front of them reporting the latest headlines and then will buy or sell on the strength of information which could affect the value of the pound.

If UK interest rates drift below the returns offered in other countries it may be that banks will take their money and put it on deposit in countries where interest rates are higher. This flight of 'hot' money out of the UK could reduce the value of the pound. Political uncertainty or weakness could induce the same effect, as could a rising inflation rate. On the other hand, the pound could be strengthened if other currencies come under pressure and dealers buy pounds in preference to those currencies.

In applying the criteria set out at the start of this chapter to the foreign exchange market, it becomes clear that the market displays most of the characteristics of a perfect market:

- There are a large number of firms active in the market.
- Each firm holds a very small share of the total volume of currencies traded on the market.
- Banks are able to set up more dealers fairly quickly if they so wish.
- Competition is concentrated on the price at which a deal is made. The only reason to buy from one dealer rather than another is the price at which the deal can be made. Dealers are constantly in search of low prices at which to buy and high prices at which to sell.
- Advertising makes no impact on the market.
- If dealers make excessive profits, this should attract new people and organisations into the market. Dealers can make high profits but can also make losses. The activity can be seen as gambling and certainly high risks are at stake but, essentially, dealers are pitting their judgement against that of the market.

- The currencies sold by any dealer are exactly the same in every respect as those sold by any other dealer.
- The dealers depend on having access to any information which could impact upon the foreign exchange market. Dealers face banks of screens which can report the latest news from around the world. They can even tune into other dealing rooms to pick up the trading mood elsewhere.

However, one distinguishing feature of the foreign exchange market is the fact that the buyers of currencies are also the sellers of currencies. In most markets the buyers and sellers are different people.

It is extremely difficult for an individual dealer to affect price on his or her own although there are the occasional exceptions. In September 1992 George Soros, a Hungarian-born speculator made £1 billion profit by selling pounds sterling in the expectation that the pound's value would fall. His massive selling of the pound undoubtedly contributed to the government's

decision to leave the Exchange Rate Mechanism (ERM), and, as a result, he became known as 'the man who broke the Pound'. More generally, it is the actions of the dealers as a whole which force the value up or down.

Each dealer has to accept what the market price is – they are price takers. If the pound sterling is trading for $1.5 a trader will not be able to sell pounds at $1.6. Why should a trader buy pounds sterling at $1.6 when they can buy them cheaper from other dealers?

Each dealer or set of dealers employed by a bank will incur costs. Chapter 7 showed that firms, no matter how small or large, will face standard U-shaped cost curves in the short run. The market is dynamic and constantly subject to change. The dealers will get a feel for the equilibrium price but will still need to determine how much of any currency they should buy or sell. Here we must remind ourselves of the assumption that businesses will be aiming to maximise profits.

Normal and supernormal profits

Imagine that you have decided to open a shop selling clothes. You work away for a year and produce your accounts. These show that your business has made £1 profit for the year. Would this be enough for your business? Would it be an acceptable level of profit? Probably not. In running a business you may well have your own capital at risk, you could lose everything and so it might be fair to assume that £1 profit would not be enough. The next year you would, no doubt, be determined to raise substantially your level of profits.

At the end of the next year your profits show a massive increase; they are now £2. Would this be acceptable? Probably not. If you continued to run your business for these levels of profit it is likely that you would decide to close the business down since you are not receiving an adequate return on your business. So, as economists, we would say that a business must make a certain level of profit if it is to continue in business in the long run. If a business fails to make that level of profit, it will close down, exactly in the same way as if it had not been able to pay its interest charges on a bank loan or its suppliers. In this sense, the level of profit the firm must make to ensure that it continues in production is a cost that the firm must meet. This is known as the normal profit of the firm.

Normal profit is the reward a firm must make if it is to remain in its existing line of production in the long run.

Supernormal profits is the rewards in excess of the normal profits received by a firm.

The actual size of these profits will vary from one firm to another. For a shop the normal profit might be £10,000 whilst for a large multi-national business it might be £100 million. The amount will be dependent on the nature of the company and the industry it operates in, the levels of risk it faces and the returns which could be achieved in alternative activities. Normal profit is regarded as a cost and is included in the total costs of the firm. Hence, when a firm is just able to cover its costs

(total revenue = total cost)

and is at its break-even point, we know that the firm is making a normal level of profit.

Any profits a firm makes over and above a normal profit represents its supernormal profit (sometimes known as abnormal or economic profit).

It is the prospect of making supernormal profits which draws new companies into an industry.

The position experienced by the industry and the individual firms can be shown in Box 8.3.

BOX 8.3

The firm and industry in perfect competition in the short run

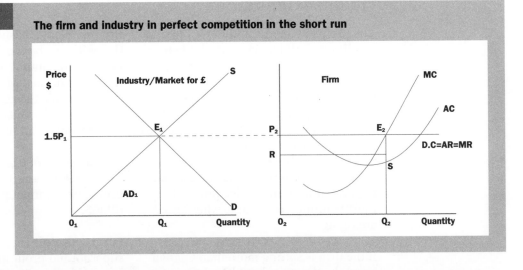

TASK 8.2

On the graph in Box 8.3 try to work out what level of output will secure maximum profits for the firm.

For the industry, as has been previously stated, the price will be determined by the forces of supply and demand. In this case the pound sterling's equilibrium price is $1.5 or OP_1 (see Box 8.3), although this will change as the supply and demand factors change. The individual dealers have to accept the market price for the pound and will trade it at around about the $1.5 level. Unfortunately for the dealers they are in constant search for the equilibrium price. Nobody arrives at work each morning to post the equilibrium price on a notice board. People may have suspicions about the price of the pound for the day but they will not know for sure. It may change by the minute.

Let us assume that this is a particularly quiet trading day and that the price of the pound sticks at around the $1.5 level. The dealers need to decide how many pounds they are prepared to sell during the day. What will be the profit maximising level of sales?

Here the firm needs to consult its costs and these we shall assume are shown as curves AC and MC. The line drawn across from P_1 represents the firm's demand curve since the firm can sell as many pounds sterling as it wishes at that price. If the firm tries to sell at above that price no buyers will choose to buy from it and so sales will decrease to zero. If the firm sells at below the equilibrium price it will be swamped by all the other dealers ready to accept an easy profit. There is no incentive for the firm to sell below OP_1 since it can sell as many pounds as it wishes at OP_1.

The firm's demand curve is also its average revenue curve showing the average amount it will get from selling pounds. If it is selling all of its pounds at $1.5 then the average amount of revenue received from each sale must be $1.5. In addition, if the firm sells an extra pound sterling then it will obtain $1.5 for it so, in this case, the average revenue is equal to the marginal revenue.

Profit maximisation

The profits of any firm under all market conditions will be maximised when marginal cost (MC) = marginal revenue (MR).

Consider the reason for this. As the firm produces up to point Q_2 MR > MC. This means that each extra product or pound sold generates more in revenue than it costs to make the sale and so adds to the total level of profit. Assuming that the firm aims to maximise profit, it must continue to produce when profits are rising.

If the firm is selling more than Q_2 then it will be the case that MC > MR, i.e. it cost more to sell the last pound sterling than it generated in extra revenue. If this happens, the total level of profit must decrease and the firm must reduce sales to achieve profit maximisation. The output at which the firm is maximising profit is known as the equilibrium output.

If firms set profit maximisation as their prime goal, then firms will always be trying to fix output at the equilibrium level.

The point at which MC = AC is the firm's optimum output, where it is producing most efficiently at minimum average cost.

Equilibrium output is the level of output at which profits are maximised. It is always found at the point at which MC = MR.

Optimum output is the level of output at which costs are minimised. It can always be found on a diagram at the lowest point on the average cost curve.

But there is no reason to believe that this will also be the firm's profit maximising output. Remembering that the firm's normal profit is included in the firm's AC, the abnormal profit will be indicated by the difference between total revenue and total cost.

At sales level of 0_2Q_2, the TR = $0_2P_2E_2Q_2$, the TC = 0_2RSQ_2 so the firm's supernormal profit = the area RP_2E_2S.

In this example the firm is able to make supernormal profit in the short run but, as long as there is free entry into the industry, the situation will not last. As new firms begin to sell pounds the supply curve for the industry will shift to the right, causing the price of the pound to fall. As price falls the abnormal profits of the individual companies will be competed away. Firms will only stop entering the market when they see no prospect of making any abnormal profits, i.e. when the firms in the industry are making normal profits. The long-run position is shown in Box 8.4.

BOX 8.4

The firm and industry in perfect competition in the long run

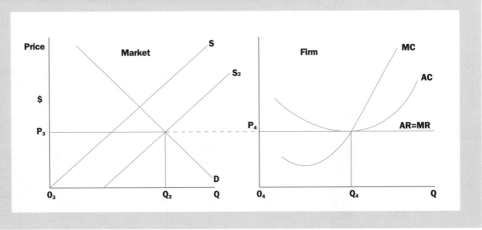

Here the supply curve for the industry in Box 8.4 has shifted from S_1 to S_2, causing the price of pounds to fall to P_3. This means that individual firms now have to lower their price to that prevailing in the market. As price falls the profits of each firm fall until firms are just making normal profits. At this point new firms will not be attracted to the industry. In the long run the firm sells $0Q_4$ quantity of pounds at a price of $0P_4$. The firm must be maximising profits because MC = MR and these must be normal profits because

$$AC = AR.$$

Shut-down point

What would happen if price fell below $0P_3$? The firm would no longer be able to cover its costs. Whilst a company could put up with this situation for some time, it would not be able to keep going in the long term without covering costs and at least making normal profits. Firms would begin to leave the industry and the supply curve would shift to the left. As this happens, the equilibrium price would rise and the firms left in the industry would return to making normal profit.

The process of adjustment is shown in Box 8.5.

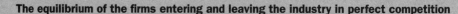

BOX 8.5   **The equilibrium of the firms entering and leaving the industry in perfect competition**

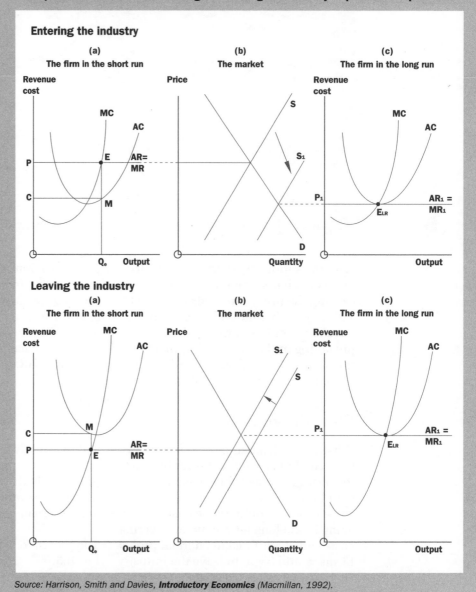

Source: Harrison, Smith and Davies, **Introductory Economics** *(Macmillan, 1992).*

In the short run, whether a firm remains open or closes is dependent on its ability to cover its variable costs. If a firm stays in production, it has to pay both fixed and variable costs. If it shuts down it will have to meet just its fixed costs. Therefore, if the firm's revenue can more than cover its variable costs, its losses will be less than if it stopped production completely. As soon as the firm is not able to generate sufficient revenue to cover its variable costs it must shut down because it would then be making a bigger loss by continuing production than it would if its production ceased. The situation is illustrated in Box 8.6.

BOX 8.6

Shut-down point

How can a firm decide whether to stop production or to remain in production?

There could be four situations comparing costs with revenue which firms could face:

Situation 1 – a firm's weekly total revenue = £1000

the firm's weekly total costs = £800

Result – the firm should keep going in the long run: it is making supernormal profit.

Situation 2 – a firm's weekly total revenue = £1000

the firm's weekly total cost = £1000

Result – the firm should keep going in the long run: it is making a normal profit.

Situation 3 – a firm's total revenue = £900

the firm's weekly total cost = £1000

the firm's fixed cost = £200

the firm's variable cost = £800

Result – the firm should keep going in the short run since its revenue is greater than its variable costs. It is not covering its total costs by £100 so, if this continued, it would have to close down in the long run, it would not be making normal profit.

Situation 4 –a firm's weekly total revenue = £700

the firm's weekly total costs = £1000

the firm's fixed cost = £200

the firm's variable cost = £800

Result – the firm will shut down in the short run. If it keeps producing its losses will be £300 whereas if it shut down its losses would only be £200.

TASK 8.3

1. Consider the relevance of the above ideas to A) a supermarket's decision about whether to open on a Sunday, B) a bus operator's decision about whether to run a late night bus service and C) an airline's decision whether to run a flight for which only half the seats have been sold.

2. Identify two business situations where you feel the distinction between fixed costs and variable costs is of importance.

3. A firm producing shampoo also produces its own plastic shampoo bottles. At present the bottle production section of the plant contributes £1 million towards covering the firm's fixed costs. What factors might make the firm consider closing down its bottle production and buying in bottles from another company?

4. In April 1995 Thorn EMI closed all 285 Rumbelows and 36 Fona electrical retail stores with the loss of 2900 jobs. Sir Colin Southgate, chairman of Thorn EMI said the closures were due to tough market conditions and a move away from the high street to out-of-town superstores. The parent company has wide interests in the music and television rental industry and recorded profits of £343.7 million for the nine months leading up to December 1994. Why should a profit-making group finally take the decision to close such a large chain of stores as Rumbelows?

Perfect markets: a summary

A market can be described as a perfect market if it conforms to the conditions or assumptions of perfect competition.

These conditions are:
- a large number of firms in the industry, none of which is sufficiently large to influence the market;
- a homogeneous product (all products produced by all the firms in the industry are exactly the same in every respect);
- perfect knowledge in the market (firms are instantly aware of innovations made by other companies and are aware of their profit levels; consumers are rational, seek to maximise utility and know the prices of all goods on sale in the market);
- free entry of new firms into the industry and free exit if they wish to leave the industry;
- the firms are price takers (they have to accept the ruling market price and have no control over price).

Such conditions are rarely, if ever, found. The foreign exchange market certainly displays many of these characteristics, as does the market for company shares. If you or your parents decide to buy the shares of a company, you will probably do this through a bank or share shop. These will buy through market makers who deal in shares all day, every day. The market makers employ analysts to study different markets and they make special studies of the performance of companies. In this respect, the dealers do develop pretty close to perfect knowledge. Each ordinary share is exactly the same as all other ordinary shares of that company so that buying from one dealer is entirely dependent on price. There are a large number of firms and each of them is a price taker. Freedom of entry could be a problem.

Commodity markets such as the markets for copper or tin and some agricultural markets such as those for coffee and tea also broadly possess the desired characteristics. These products may not all be the same but can be graded to establish products of specific qualities. Products within certain grades will then trade for the same prices regardless of the country of origin. Look at Task 8.4.

TASK 8.4

The hunt for perfect competition

The market for fresh eggs
Consider the market for fresh eggs. Visit a couple of supermarkets to check on the prices of eggs and the way in which they are sold. To what extent does this market display the characteristics of perfect competition?

Perfect competition and economic efficiency

Economic efficiency consists of allocative and productive efficiency.

Allocative efficiency is a state in which resources are distributed in such a way that nobody in the economy can be made better off without making somebody else worse off. (The idea of using resources to maximise the well being enjoyed by citizens was developed by Vilfredo Pareto in 1890s. He saw that overall welfare might be increased if the gainers from a change in society were able to compensate the losers, creating a net improvement. The difficulty here is measuring the impact changes have on society. If an economy reaches the position when nobody's welfare can be improved in this way, then it is said that the economy is operating at Pareto optimality.)

Productive efficiency (also described as technical efficiency) is a situation where all goods and services are produced at minimum cost. This means that the minimum quantity of resources are used in production, leaving surplus resources to be used to produce alternative types of output.

Static efficiency is the state of efficiency achieved by an economy at a particular point in time. As technology changes, what is efficient at one time may well be inefficient at another.

Dynamic efficiency is the level of efficiency achieved within an economy which will change as economic conditions change.

The scarcity of resources is the basis of the study of Economics (remember Chapter 1). The problem of scarcity will be best tackled if we can be sure that resources are used to meet the demonstrated needs of consumers and not wasted. Also it is important that any goods and services produced are provided using the minimum quantity of resources so that any spare resources can be used to produce other goods and services to satisfy other wants. These two points represent the different dimensions of economic efficiency. The first is known as allocative efficiency and the second is productive or technical efficiency.

In theory, perfect competition should achieve both allocative and productive efficiency. Any change in the demands of the consumer will be reflected in a shift in the demand curve for a product. This will, in turn, cause the price to change which will provide the signal for producers to supply either more or less to the market. The industry will be in equilibrium if there is no tendency for firms to enter or leave the industry.

This will only occur when firms in the industry are making normal profits and Box 8.4 shows that this does occur in the long run under perfect competition. In the industry price settles where supply equals demand. The demand curve is constructed from the individual marginal utility curves of the consumers and the supply curve is derived from the marginal cost curves of the individual firms in the market.

Therefore, when supply equals demand, the benefit from the last units consumed is just equal to the cost of producing the last units of output. The price is equal to the marginal cost of the industry and the total amount of welfare could not be increased by producing one more or one less unit of output.

Also, by referring to Box 8.4, it is clear that firms produce at the level of output where average costs are at a minimum. This means that they are producing at the most efficient level of output and so productive efficiency will be achieved.

Contestable markets

In the 1980s the American economist W. J. Baumol developed the argument that the benefits of perfect competition might be achieved without all of the conditions being met. In theory, perfect markets lead to low prices, high quality products and choice for the consumer: all highly desirable characteristics. Baumol suggested that these qualities could be achieved within a market as long as there was the potential for new firms to enter the industry. The number of firms in the industry was not crucial.

To achieve true contestability, a market needs to have low entry costs so that it is easy for firms to move into and out of the industry.

The air travel industry is often quoted as an example of a contestable market. Airlines can choose to open up new routes by diverting aircraft from other destinations. If these routes appear unprofitable they can pull out. The airlines do not have to spend huge sums of money to get into the industry, there are no large sunk costs or irrecoverable costs to concern the companies.

This is important since if a company has to spend large sums of money developing capital to be used in the industry, it is less able to take the entry decision. The main problem with the airline industry is that, in order to fly a route, the companies need to command the appropriate slots at airports. Today airports often operate at near to full capacity and there are just not the flying slots for new entrants to take. This is one of the main reasons for airline mergers. Access to flying slots opens up new through routes which could appeal to potential travellers. This does limit the level of competition in the industry.

Implications of Baumol's theory

Baumol's theory implies that, given ease of entry to and exit from an industry, monopoly or oligopoly firms will behave as if they actually existed in perfect competition; that is they will
● equate MC with MR to maximise profits;
● only earn normal profits in the long run because if supernormal profits were made, new firms would be attracted into the industry increasing supply and driving down price; and if losses are made, some firms will be forced to leave the industry causing supply to fall and price to rise back to a level consistent with the making of normal profits;

● operate with productive efficiency on the lowest point of the average cost curve where AC = MC. If this were not the case, new firms could enter the industry producing at the most efficient output level, pricing their goods more competitively and forcing existing firms out;
● The theory seems to offer 'the best of both worlds.' As long as there is a threat of competition, consumers will be protected from the worst abuses of monopoly power whilst, at the same time, firms will be able to reap the benefits of large scale production and will operate in accordance with the criteria for economic efficiency.

The advantage of contestable markets to governments is that they require little intervention. As long as new firms have access to the market, it is the competition which will control firms' actions, and this makes it unnecessary for any further legislation. If perfect markets may be unattainable in practice, at least contestable markets may be a more realistic ideal. It can then be argued that policies such as privatisation will still be of great benefit to the consumer if contestability is a feature of the newly established market. Contestable market theory could be considered to be a more useful theory because it takes into account the impact that potential competition might have on firms. Traditional monopoly theory tends to ignore this and just looks at the number of firms currently in the industry. Contestable market theory may, therefore, offer a better guide to firms' pricing and output behaviour.

Criticisms of contestable market theory

The extent to which the theory of contestable markets may be applied in practice is limited. In reality, sunk costs may be extremely high, even at a time when the mobility of capital appears to be relatively easy. For example, the Ford Motor Company would find that there were considerable costs if it was to move production from one country to another and it is these costs which act as the barrier to entry. Once established in a country, the high sunk costs would make Ford very reluctant to pull out.

The level of technical knowledge required to enter an industry may be high, and this knowledge is unlikely to be freely available to any company considering entering the industry. Firms protect themselves by taking out patents on products and certainly do not make the results of their research and development widely available.

The theory ignores the possible aggressive actions of existing firms to potential entrants. In a market where cost barriers to entry and exit are low, existing firms may behave like monopolists by charging high prices and making supernormal profits. However, they may also make it very clear to any potential entrants that they are prepared 'to fight them to the death' should they decide to set up in competition. They could do this by predatory pricing, cutting prices drastically as soon as a new firm appears on the scene. One illustration of these kinds of practices is shown in Box 8.7.

BOX 8.7

Dirty work on the buses

Bus Firms BRANDED AS PREDATORS

Rebecca Smithers
Political Correspondent

Two of Britain's biggest bus operators, Stagecoach and Go-Ahead, were yesterday strongly rebuked in a report by the Government's Monopolies and Mergers Commission which concluded that some of their activities in the North-east were "against the public interest".

Both will be asked to give undertakings to the Office of Fair Trading to prevent further predatory behaviour.

Sir Bryan Carsberg, director general of fair trading, asked the MMC to carry out the investigation into bus services in the North-east, after complaints from local operators about alleged anti-competitive behaviour by the two operators.

The 240-page report looked at five cases where smaller local operators had accused their larger rivals of predatory pricing and "overbussing" in an attempt to force them out of business. Three of these cases concerned Busways, owned by Stagecoach, in Darlington, South Shields and Sunderland, and two concerned Go-Ahead in North Durham. In the area, over 90 per cent of bus services are supplied by subsidiaries of four large groups.

The report looked at events which prompted the long-running bus war in Darlington, which triggered the inquiry and about which Sir Bryan had expressed particular concern. Stagecoach's subsidiary Busways moved into the town as the 90-year-old municipal bus company, Darlington Transport (DTC), collapsed.

"It was the combination of Busway's action in recruiting so many of DTC's drivers so quickly, registering services on all its routes and running free services which caused DTC's final collapse."

The MMC said these actions were "predatory, deplorable and against the public interest".

Also under scrutiny were allegations of anti-competitive behaviour by Stagecoach in South Shields, where a family-run bus company, Hylton Castle Motors, found itself in competition with Busways. It rejected an attempt by Stagecoach to buy the company and subsequently reported its suitor to the OFT for predatory pricing.

Busways denied threatening or targeting Hylton and said that its fare reductions had been an experiment in market pricing in an attempt to stop a fall in passenger numbers.

But the MMC concluded that "Busways did threaten Hylton and that its price cuts, which had the effect of reducing Busways' revenue, were predatory and against the public interest". A similar complaint against Busways' action in Sunderland was not found to be predatory.

Stagecoach rejected the Commission's view that it had acted in a predatory manner in South Shields.

A North Durham small operator, Classic Coaches, complained that in its attempts to establish new services it had encountered "anti-competitive tactics" by the larger operator, Go-Ahead. These were ruled "predatory and against the public interest".

Jonathan Evans, Competition and Consumer Affairs Minister, said he accepted the MMC's findings and had asked the director general of fair trading to seek undertakings from Stagecoach and from Go-Ahead to prevent predatory behaviour against competitors.

Alan Milburn, Labour MP for Darlington, said: "This is not the first time that Stagecoach has been condemned for its anti-competitive tactics. While it is welcome that the MMC has confirmed that Stagecoach acted in a predatory fashion, history will repeat itself unless central government takes action to properly regulate the bus industry."

Source: Guardian (4 August 1995).

TASK 8.5

1. What is meant by 'predatory pricing?'
2. Why would bus companies use predatory pricing?

Supporters of free markets see contestable market theory as very attractive. The benefits of competition appear to be secured without the need for major government intervention and without the need to create the large numbers of firms we would expect to see under perfect competition. This standpoint may be challenged on the grounds that even if perfect contestability exists, which is by no means certain, government intervention in the free market may be justified for a whole raft of other reasons developed in Chapter 12.

REVIEW

In this chapter we have seen that the degree of competition a firm faces will affect the output it produces and the prices it can charge. Perfect competition is a theoretical form of competition and is useful as a standard by which to judge the level of competition existing in any market. Advocates of free markets argue that any movement towards perfect competition will bring benefits for the consumer in terms of lower prices and more choice. Critics would argue that perfect competition is a theoretical state, never achieved in practice and, even if it were, would not produce the claimed benefits. These criticisms of perfect markets will be developed in Chapter 12. An important way of judging the success of a particular market structure is to consider to what extent it contributes to achieving economic efficiency.

Contestable markets provide an alternative view about how markets work. A government's role becomes one of ensuring that there is free access to any market. If this is achieved, firms will behave as if there is competition and the consumer will receive the benefits of competition without the need for further intervention. Look at the Review Task.

REVIEW TASK

Judging contestability

The INVESTIGATOR

In October 1994, Woolworths launched its 'Genuine American Cola' to be followed in November of that year by Virgin Cola. Virgin does not produce its own cola but buys it in from the Canadian Cott Corporation which already supplies own-brand products to other supermarket chains mainly in the USA.

The ingredients of cola are widely known. They are mostly water and sugar with added caramel, phosphoric acid, cocoa leaves and caffeine. Coca-Cola also adds its famous 7X formula which consists of a secret mix of natural oils.

Pepsi claims that its tests prove that its product does taste better than the competitors but taste may not be the most important factor. The soft drinks industry spends heavily on marketing and promotion and this may well be a more powerful persuader of consumers than taste or price.

To what extent, do you believe, is the cola market a contestable market?

Multiple choice

1 **The abnormal profit earned in the short run by a firm under perfect competition is a form of**

A   consumer surplus

B   transfer earnings

C   economic rent

D   opportunity cost

(AEB, Winter 1994)

2

In the perfect competition model, the total revenue curve of the firm is drawn as a straight line sloping upwards from the origin. This indicates that

1   the demand curve of the firm is perfectly elastic

2   the firm is a price-taker

3   the marginal revenue of the firm is equal to its average revenue

A   1 only

B   1 and 2

C   2 and 3

D   1,2 and 3

(ULEAC, January 1995)

3 **Question 3 refers to the following diagram**

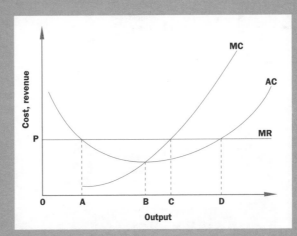

The above diagram shows the cost curves of a firm operating in a perfectly competitive industry. **OP** is the market price. At what level of output will the firm maximise its profits?

A

B

C

D

(IB, May 1995, Higher)

Data response

The data below includes an adaption of an article published in *The Financial Times* on 6 March 1991. Study the data carefully, then answer each of the questions which follow.

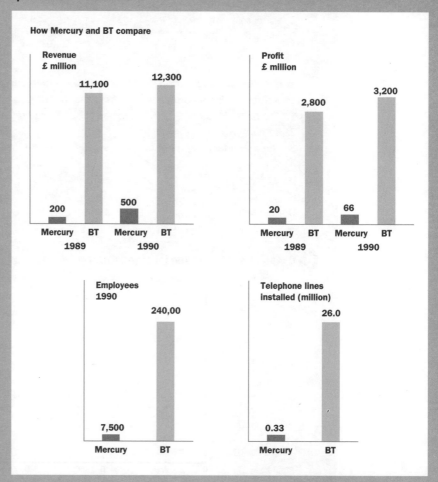

How Mercury and BT compare

From 1984 until 1991 only two companies, British Telecom (now known as BT) and Mercury Communications, were allowed to supply telephone services in the UK. In March 1991 the Government announced plans to allow more firms to enter the telecommunications market. It was concerned about BT's 95% share of the domestic telephone market.

The basic problem of increasing competition is the cost of installing cables, amounting to several hundred pounds per house. BT already has cables to most

QUESTIONS

British homes. Users have to buy a special phone to use the Mercury system. The principle of 'equal access' is seen as vital to create competition. BT would be forced to allow other companies to use its lines (as Mercury currently does). Each company would have a short code which the caller would dial before the main phone number. The caller would therefore be able to choose between different suppliers without needing to buy a new phone.

In Hull, where equal access already exists, Mercury has a much higher market share than in the rest of the country. It is argued that equal access would create genuine competition in the domestic telephone market.

Another way of encouraging new entrants (apart from BT and Mercury) would be to allow them to use their telephone lines to transmit cable television programmes. BT and Mercury will not be allowed to supply cable television until at least 2001.

*Source: Adapted from **Financial Times** (6 March 1991).*

(a) Using the data, compare BT and Mercury's
   (i) size
   (ii) success
(b) Explain the possible difficulties of increasing competition in the supply of domestic telephone services.
(c) Why should `equal access' create advantages for consumers?
(d) Why might potential new entrants into the telecommunications market benefit from being allowed to supply cable television programmes?

(ULEAC, 1993)

What is a labour market?

Recent labour market trends

Part-time, temporary and self-employed workers as a percentage of all employees/ workforce; Great Britain, 1971 – 1994

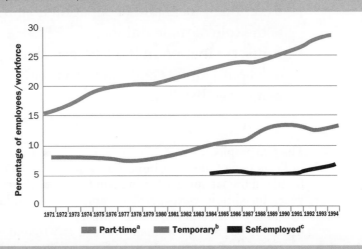

a Part-time employees as a percentage of all employees, June, seasonally adjusted.
b Temporary employees (self-defined) as a percentage of all employees, spring.
c Self-employed as a percentage of the workforce in employment, June, seasonally adjusted.

*Source: Adapted from **Labour Force Survey** and ED Statistics.*

*Source: Adapted from **Labour Force Survey.***

Part-time employment

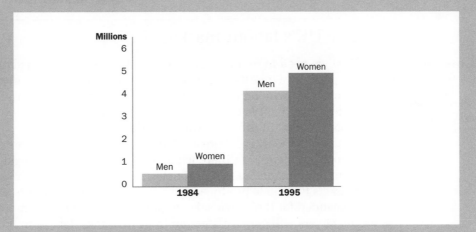

Preview

In this chapter we shall investigate the following key areas:

● national, local and occupational labour markets;
● the role of trade unions;
● discrimination in the labour market;
● labour markets and the individual;
● income distribution.

The two graphs shown in Focus 2.9 indicate two of the most important trends in the labour market in recent years: the shift towards part-time and temporary work and the greater impact this trend has had on women workers.

● Are these trends good or bad?
● Who gains and who loses from these trends?
● How do the trends affect individuals, families, firms and the economy?
● Have all age groups been affected in the same way?
● Have all ethnic groups been affected in the same way?

● Have all parts of the country been affected in the same way?
● Have all countries been experiencing similar trends?

To understand fully what is going on here, we need to recognise that there is not just one labour market, there are several in which people may participate. There is:

● the labour market of the UK;
● a labour market in each region or local area of the UK;
● a labour market for each occupation or skill;
● an individual's labour market.

The UK's labour market

Derived demand is when the demand for one item is dependent upon the demand for another. This applies to the demand for all factors of production.

First we need to remind ourselves what we mean by a 'market' – it is a mechanism which brings buyers and sellers together. We can think of the labour market in the same way we think of any other market. There are buyers of labour but there is a difference here from product markets. In product markets the goods produced are demanded for their own sake, because the buyers will gain satisfaction from their consumption. With labour, employers buy it not for its own sake but because there is a demand for the goods or services produced by the

labour. This is known as a derived demand – the demand for labour is influenced by the demand for the finished goods or services.

There are sellers of labour. These are people who need money to live and only have their skills, talents and time to sell to others. As wage levels rise, it is likely that more people will offer their labour to the market. If we bring the supply and demand together, we have a labour market and we can show this in Box 9.1.

BOX 9.1

The labour market

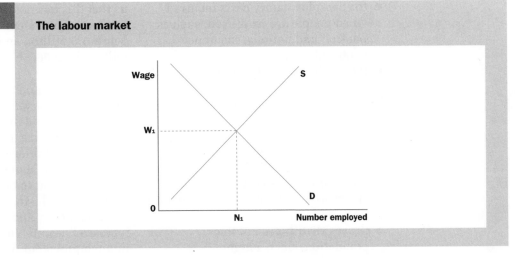

Considering the labour market as a single market may, on occasions, be useful. Box 9.1 shows that the wage paid in the market is recorded on the vertical axis. The number of people employed is shown on the horizontal axis. The graph indicates that the demand curve for labour will be downward sloping, meaning that as wages fall so more people will be employed. This could be for two reasons. First, as wages fall so labour will be used instead of machinery – a substitution effect; and secondly, as wages fall so the costs of the employer fall and prices fall. This generates an increase in demand for the goods or services produced by the labour and so employers want to take on more workers.

The supply curve is upward sloping, indicating that as wages rise so more people will be willing to offer their services to employers. At very low wage levels few people would be prepared to offer their services to others but, as wages rise, so more will be willing to give up their leisure time to work. Where supply equals demand will determine the equilibrium wage rate at

$0W_1$, where $0N_1$ people will be employed.

This analysis can be helpful in allowing us to predict changes likely to affect the whole of the labour market. For example, if there was a general fall in the demand for labour, perhaps because it was being substituted by new technology, there would be a downward shift in the demand curve and we might expect wage levels to fall. Also, if there was an increase in the numbers of people wishing to work, we might expect the supply curve of labour to shift to the right and, again, wage levels might fall.

The demand for labour would be affected by:

- the price or wage of labour;
- the demand for and prices of the goods or services produced by labour; this will be determined by the strength of demand in home and overseas markets;
- the price of other factors of production, such as capital, which could be substituted for labour;

- the complementary costs incurred when people are employed, such as pension and national insurance contributions;
- the productivity of labour.

The supply of labour would be affected by:

- the price or wage of labour;
- the size and age distribution of the population, because the work force comes from certain age groups within the population;
- the sex distribution of the population, since a higher proportion of men than women work in paid employment;
- the number of hours people are prepared to work;
- the quality of the work force, since a better educated and trained work force would be able to offer higher quality work;
- legislation which affects the numbers in the work force, such as the school leaving or retiring ages;
- participation rates: the percentage of males and females active in the work force;
- the activities of trade unions, which could influence the supply of labour to the market.

As with other markets, a change in the price of labour leads to a movement along either the demand or the supply curve whereas a change in one of the other factors causes the supply or demand curve to shift. In theory, if the free labour market is allowed to flourish, the wage level should always move towards the equilibrium and the market should clear. If the market clears then this must mean that there will be a minimal level of unemployment. But the UK's recent economic history tells

us that this has not been the case. Since 1980 unemployment has never been below 1.5 million and rose to over 3.25 million in 1986.

If the labour market had been operating freely, another expectation would be that wages would fluctuate according to market conditions, rising when there were labour shortages and falling in times of labour abundance. Again, this does not appear to be the story which emerges from history. In each of the last 15 years money and real wages have increased despite the exceptional rises in unemployment. Wages certainly rose during times of economic growth but then seemed to stick there and did not fall back during recessions.

The lack of flexibility in the labour market has been of major concern to the Government since 1979. Undoubtedly it has been the case that flexibility has improved and this has been caused by a variety of factors:
- changing product markets with increased competition from the rest of Europe and the emerging economies has forced firms to keep a tighter control on costs, particularly labour costs;
- changing technology has meant that many traditional unskilled jobs have disappeared and heightened the need for a more flexible work force;
- the process of deindustrialisation has meant that jobs in the traditionally male-dominated primary and manufacturing sectors have declined whilst jobs in the service sector have increased. This has opened up opportunities for female labour and brought with it the need for people to work more flexible hours;
- Government policy has attempted to free up the labour market.

Employment protection has been weakened and wages councils, which decided the wage rates for many occupations, have been abolished. Trade union legislation has been radically reformed, making strike ballots and the election of officials compulsory and introducing controls on picketing, the closed shop and use of members' funds. The unemployed have been encouraged more actively back into jobs or training programmes under threat of the withdrawal of benefit. Pay deals have been encouraged at a local rather than a national level and this has been assisted by the privatisation programme. The replacement of unemployment benefit by job-seekers' allowance attempts to ensure that job-seekers do not have unrealistic employment or wage expectations and are therefore prepared to take on the jobs which are available. The Government also refused to accept the employment implications of the EU's Social Chapter which would require the Government to introduce a minimum wage as well as other social legislation.

For their period in office from 1979, the Conservative Government's view has been that jobs will be created by successful private sector companies. It is not the role of the government artificially to create jobs and, as long as wage levels fall, more jobs will be generated. There is much debate about this line of thinking, particularly focusing on the role of a government in the economy.

The flexible labour market

The flexible labour market describes a labour market which is able to respond quickly to shocks to the market. Its characteristics are that workers are prepared to work different hours, acquire a range of skills and be mobile. Firms are able to hire and fire quickly if there are changes in the market which have to be met.

The Conservative Government could claim that its policy of attempting to introduce greater flexibility or freedom into the labour market has been a success.

There has been a tremendous growth in the number of people working part-time or on temporary contracts and it is now easier for employers to hire and fire workers. There is more flexibility in the work force in terms of the skills people possess and their willingness to become multi-skilled.

There is a greater acceptance of lower wage settlements and local negotiation and the number of self-employed people has increased substantially from 7.5% of the work force in 1979 to 13% in 1994.

Unemployment now appears to respond far more quickly to changes in the state of the economy. For example, traditionally unemployment has been seen as a lagging indicator of recessions; it has tended to follow changes in the economy with a 6–12 month lag. As the economy emerged from the recession of the early 1990s unemployment began to fall far more quickly than had been expected and one explanation of this is the increased levels of flexibility in the labour market.

Trade union membership has fallen substantially since 1979 from over 13 million to around 7 million today and the power of trade unions has undoubtedly been weakened. Industrial relations have calmed and trade unions are less influential in the determination of wages.

The job creation record in the UK is good especially when compared with other EU members, although the bulk of new jobs created are part-time or temporary.

The fundamental question to address is whether the labour market should be able to function like product markets. Here there are important differences of view to consider.

Karl Marx in his influential book *Das Capital* highlighted the power struggle inherent in the labour market. In a capitalist system, Marx's view was that the owners of capital would exploit the workers in order to cream off the surplus amount of value produced for

themselves. He felt this exploitation to be part of capitalism, and consequently called for the "Workers of the world, unite!" against the system.

Free markets assume that there is a balance of power between buyers and sellers and, if anything, a shift in favour of the consumer through the notion of consumer sovereignty. In the labour market the employers are the consumers of labour and there is a lack of balance of power in the relationship between employer and employee. Although the best companies succeed in developing a partnership between management and the rest of the workers, it is still the case that divisions do exist. Look at Box 9.2.

BOX 9.2	**Marxism and the gas industry: May 1995**

Shareholders at the Annual General Meeting of British Gas agreed the 75% pay increase for its Chief Executive: Cedric Brown. This brings his salary up to £475 000. At the same time as this pay increase was announced there were plans to cut the wages of the staff working in the gas shops and to increase their working hours.

Other assumptions

Product markets also assume that all units of the product sold are homogeneous. This is not the case with people. There are many different levels of skills, qualifications, motivation, experience and effort. This makes it difficult to think in terms of a single labour market and we should think rather of a range of separated labour markets.

One other assumption is that the main driving force of supply in the product

market is price and profit. With people, the wage paid is important but there is a wide variety of other factors which can motivate people to work. These might include the style of leadership adopted, the degree of job satisfaction obtained, the working conditions provided and the personal ambitions of the worker. Work is a central part of most people's lives. It still defines what kind of person you are and so cannot be fully explained by simple market forces.

Working in a flexible labour market: the impact on women workers

Flexibility would seem to be a desirable asset if the labour market is to function efficiently and unemployment is to fall, but in whose interests does the market operate? The employer gets a cheaper, more pliable work force who can be called upon when required but the employee gets lower wages, greater insecurity, temporary jobs and fewer promotion prospects.

The flexible labour market has had a particular impact upon women workers. In 1993, 50% of women were part of the 'flexible' work force (either in part-time, temporary or self-employed work) whereas only 27% of men were in this category. But within these groups, 75% of the self-employed are men, 85% of part-time workers are women (4.4 million women compared to 0.4 million men) and 56% of people in temporary work are women.

A survey for the Employment Department each year attempts to discover why people are accepting part-time work. In 1994, of all females working part-time, 87% said that they did not want a full-time job, 10.1% said they could not find a full-time job. This looks like a remarkable endorsement of part-time work by women but may have as much to do with women's conditioning and expectations. Undoubtedly some women will prefer the part-time option particularly when they are the prime carer for either small children or elderly relatives but, given adequate child care arrangements, more sympathetic males and a less discriminating work place, it would be the case that more females would seek full-time jobs.

When comparing the average hours worked by people in the UK with the rest of the EU, the figure is roughly comparable. In 1992 the EU average was 37.2 hours per week and in the UK it was just on the average at 37.1, but this masks a considerable difference between men and women. In the UK, unlike in many EU countries, there are no limits on the length of a working week so men tend to work long hours: an average of 43.3, the highest in the EU. Women worked on average 30.2 hours per week, the lowest in the EU apart from the Netherlands and well below the EU average of 33.1.

Data concerning wage levels of men and women are shown in Box 9.3.

BOX 9.3

Gross weekly earnings of male and female workers, 1994

	Average weekly wage (£)		Average weekly wage (£)
All males	358.1	All females	259.2
Manual males	277	Manual females	180.6
Non-manual males	425	Non-manual females	276.1

Source: **Employment Department,** figures extracted from Social Trends (1995).

TASK 9.1

The data in Box 9.3 illustrate the gap between male and female earnings.

1 List as many reasons as you can which could explain the 'wage gap'.
2 What would you predict would happen to the gap between male and female earnings over the next 20 years? Explain the reasons for your prediction.

Part of the story could be related to discrimination, and this will be considered later in the chapter.

Women have become a more important part of the work force over the years.

Box 9.4 shows the composition of the work force since 1984.

BOX 9.4

Distribution of the work force, 1984–94

Employment

Distribution of the workforce
At mid-June each year

	1984	1985	1986	1987	1988	1989	1990	1991	1992	1993	1994
									Thousands, seasonally adjusted		
United Kingdom											
Workforce1	**27 296**	**27 702**	**27 828**	**28 107**	**28 422**	**28 712**	**28 770**	**28 554**	**28 393**	**28 156**	**27 875**
Males	16 378	16 508	16 443	16 462	16 506	16 531	16 473	16 334	16 178	15 957	15 696
Females	10 918	11 194	11 385	11 645	11 916	12 181	12 297	12 220	12 215	12 199	12 179
Unemployed²	**2 897**	**3 019**	**3 120**	**2 836**	**2 294**	**1 786**	**1 615**	**2 300**	**2 732**	**2 915**	**2 643**
Males	2 040	2 100	2 153	1 978	1 599	1 276	1 191	1 743	2 094	2 240	2 024
Females	857	919	967	857	694	510	424	557	638	675	620
Workforce in employment³	**24 399**	**24 683**	**24 708**	**25 272**	**26 128**	**26 926**	**27 155**	**26 254**	**25 661**	**25 241**	**25 232**
Males	14 338	14 408	14 290	14 484	14 907	15 255	15 282	14 591	14 084	13 717	13 673
Females	10 061	10 275	10 418	10 787	11 222	11 671	11 873	11 663	11 577	11 524	11 559
HM Forces⁴	**326**	**326**	**322**	**319**	**316**	**308**	**303**	**297**	**290**	**271**	**250**
Males	310	309	305	302	300	291	286	278	270	252	232
Females	16	16	16	16	16	16	18	19	20	19	18
Self-employed persons (with or without employees)⁵	**2 669**	**2 767**	**2 782**	**3 056**	**3 204**	**3 486**	**3 537**	**3 383**	**3 196**	**3 166**	**3 266**
Males	2 038	2 090	2 109	2 300	2 424	2 673	2 696	2 582	2 423	2 372	2 453
Females	631	677	673	756	780	813	840	801	773	794	814
Employees in employment⁶	**21 229**	**21 414**	**21 379**	**21 586**	**22 266**	**22 670**	**22 893**	**22 220**	**21 851**	**21 493**	**21 397**
Males	11 895	11 908	11 748	11 705	11 978	11 999	12 040	11 514	11 186	10 899	10 786
Females	9 334	9 506	9 631	9 881	10 288	10 671	10 852	10 706	10 664	10 594	10 611
of whom											
Total, production and construction industries	7 080	6 992	6 777	6 688	6 746	6 753	6 657	6 149	5 836	5 580	5 432
Total, all manufacturing industries	5 424	5 377	5 242	5 171	5 215	5 208	5 121	4 720	4 521	4 369	4 330
Work Related Government Training Programmes⁷	**175**	**176**	**226**	**311**	**343**	**462**	**423**	**353**	**325**	**311**	**319**
Males	95	100	127	177	205	291	260	217	205	195	202
Females	80	76	99	134	138	171	163	136	125	117	117

Source: **Annual Abstract of Statistics** (1995).

1 Describe the main trends in the distribution of the work force over the period shown.
2 What does the data tell you about the role of women in the work force?
3 What factors explain the main changes you have noted? (Review the other material covered so far in this chapter to give yourself some ideas.)

The effect of a minimum wage

A main reason for the Conservative Government rejecting the idea of a minimum wage being imposed was because it would disrupt the labour market and cause unemployment to rise. The logic is simple. If the labour market is in equilibrium, then the quantity of labour supplied will equal the quantity of labour demanded.

Anything which pushes wages above the equilibrium level will cause a contraction in the demand for labour and, at the same time, an extension of supply. A gap opens up between the quantity of labour demanded and supplied which will represent the unemployed. This is shown in Box 9.5.

BOX 9.5

The effect of the introduction of a minimum wage

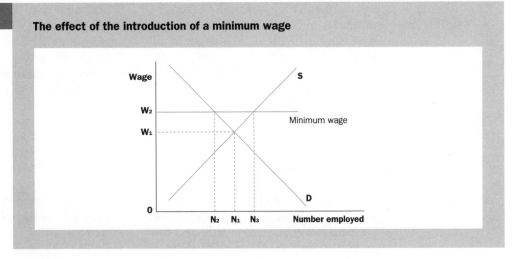

On the graph in Box 9.5 the equilibrium wage equals $0W_1$ and the number of workers employed equals $0N_1$. If the minimum wage is introduced at level $0W_2$ then the supply of labour equals $0N_3$ but the demand for labour at that wage level equals $0N_2$. N_2N_3 represents unemployment, hence the belief that the introduction of a national minimum wage will cause unemployment.

However, the minimum wage would only affect those at the bottom end of the pay scale. There have been suggestions that the wage might initially be around £4 per hour. Looking at average pay rates, the main groups to be most affected by a wage of this level are female manual workers under the age of 20 and male manual workers under 18, although there will also be particular individuals of all ages in all kinds of low grade jobs receiving very low pay. We need to consider the assumptions underpinning the minimum wage analysis.

It is assumed that all people currently being paid less than the new minimum wage will be sacked because they are not now worth the wage that they have to be paid. This may not be the case. The workers may have been exploited, i.e. paid less than their worth, and the employers may be prepared to increase the wage and continue to employ the same people. Workers may be kept on but at lower hours. But, more important, is the notion of an 'efficiency wage'. If wages are forced to rise then employers cannot be so wasteful with their workers. They may now see their workers as a more valuable asset and may train the workers or provide them with more equipment to increase their productivity. Low wages may lead to higher labour turnover (more people leave because of the low wages) and this gives rise to costs of recruitment and training workers. A minimum wage could bring a more loyal work force and a more productive work force.

It is assumed that if people on the lowest pay scales receive an increase then others further up the pay chain will want a pay rise to restore the differentials between pay levels. This will greatly depend on the level at which the minimum wage is introduced. If it is geared to help the lowest paid it should not have much effect on the overall pay structure within a company.

It is assumed that if wage rates in the UK rise then fewer overseas companies will choose to invest in the UK, meaning fewer jobs created. This assumption is by no means certain. Firms making decisions to invest in a country consider a wide range of factors of which wages may be only one. The importance is unclear. The presence of cheap labour may mean that low skill, low productive work is attracted to the UK and other research-based work will go elsewhere.

It is always assumed that if people at the top end of the pay scale are paid more this will act as an incentive for them to work harder. Presumably the same argument can be applied to people at the bottom of the pay scale. A higher wage may encourage them to work harder and, consequently, increase their value to the employer.

It is assumed that if the UK allows its wage rates to rise then the costs of UK firms will rise, causing our inflation rate to rise and our international competitiveness to be lost. This will open the door for more imports to flood the UK market and again threaten jobs.

But however low wage costs fall, they will never reach the levels now found in some of the developing countries or Eastern Europe. The UK has always had to accept that its wages will be higher than many countries. Competitiveness is not just dependent on wage costs but also on technology, innovation, creativity and exchange rates. High productivity will be the key to success.

It is assumed that if the UK's wage rates rose compared to our EU partners, competitiveness would be lost. This should not be the case since all of the other members of the EU will be applying minimum wage rates to their firms and, indeed, most of them have had minimum wage rates for many years.

It is assumed that some businesses will not be able to afford to pay higher wages and so will go bust, causing a larger number of people to lose their jobs. Some firms may be affected by this but the impact depends on their reaction and the numbers involved. Every year some businesses cease trading so any rise in this number could be marginal.

The message here is that the impact of the imposition of a minimum wage is not clear cut. Employers oppose any change which could have the effect of increasing costs. Groups representing the low paid cannot wait for its introduction. Countries which already have the minimum wage in place have not suffered exceptionally high unemployment relative to ours but they do seem to be accepting that there may be a case for freeing up the labour market to some extent. Some research by David Blanchflower and Andrew Oswald at the MIT studied the relationship between wages and employment for 3.5 million people in 12 countries. The results showed no link between higher wages and lower employment and nowhere did lowering wages lead to higher employment in the long run. Look at Box 9.6.

The minimum wage debate

Employers resist wage floor as public begins to feel good again

CBI PLAYS DOWN STUDY BACKING *minimum wage*

Richard Thomas

At a conference today, the confederation will publish a report containing evidence that a minimum of £4.10 an hour would result in substantial job losses and £4.5 billion additional payroll costs.

But the internally prepared paper also shows that a modest floor of £3 an hour would not result in redundancies or significant additional expense for companies.

Despite this finding, CBI members have voted overwhelmingly against the idea of a minimum wage at any level – and the study concludes with a strong denunciation of the policy.

CBI insiders said employers were opposed in principle to government regulation of pay and were afraid that once the mechanism was in place a Labour government would quickly ratchet up the level.

Some employers are also said to be concerned that a minimum wage would make it harder for them to boost productivity through performance related pay. Today's paper states that:

● A minimum wage could fuel price pressures. "The squeezing of pay differentials is likely to bring pressure for higher wages across the board, with inflationary consequences."

● A national minimum wage would not help the poor, because low-income families generally have nobody in work.

● Top-ups to wages, via the Family Credit system, are the best way to help households with a low-paid worker: "The CBI believes that Family Credit is the most appropriate mechanism for tackling poverty among those with low pay," the report argues. The paper also backs moves to extend the benefit to single people.

*Source: Adapted from **Guardian** (18th July 1995)*

Briefing **RUTH KELLY**

THE TIME MAY HAVE COME TO BRING IN A *minimum wage*

Despite rising unemployment and the increasing visibility of the nation's poor and homeless, Mrs Thatcher believed to the end of her days as Prime Minister that the 1980s witnessed an economic miracle and that "everyone in the nation... benefited from the increased prosperity – everyone". But there is increasing evidence that the reverse is true.

Not only have the unemployed swelled their ranks, but of those in work nearly half now earn less than the Council of Europe's "decency threshold". And the gap between rich and poor is widening. So how can we protect the low paid against poverty? Should there be a minimum wage?

BOX 9.6

Britain was certainly turned on its head in the eighties. Figures released from the Inland Revenue on the day before Mrs Thatcher's resignation show that the richest quarter of the population increased their share of the nation's wealth from 72 per cent in 1979 to 75 per cent in 1988. Earnings data tell the same story: the Low Pay Unit estimates that 28.3 per cent of full-time workers earned less than the Council of Europe's decency threshold (68 per cent of the average wage of full-time workers) in 1979. By 1990, the proportion had risen to 37 per cent. And it may well be that the position of some low-paid has deteriorated not only in relative terms but in absolute terms as well.

But the political debate surrounding the introduction of a minimum wage has focused primarily on its economic implications. The driving force behind the Government's economic policy has been the belief that the unemployed price themselves out of jobs. Thus David Forrest entitled his critique of minimum wages "Low Pay or No Pay" and in the same spirit the Government introduced numerous measures designed to reduce wages and make the market work "more freely".

But it is not clear that the unemployed do price themselves out of jobs. In fact, the Policy Studies Institute have recently released a study which examines the characteristics of those entering and leaving unemployment. The picture revealed is substantially different from that assumed in the Government's analysis. It shows that the people entering unemployment had generally worked in "low paid, low skilled and manifestly insecure" jobs. And even though they tended to come from low paid jobs, they often went on to take a pay cut in their subsequent jobs.

"They are", it says, "permanently denied access to the rising incomes, living standards, intrinsic rewards from work and job security enjoyed by the bulk of the working population."

But how can the position of the low paid be improved? In a recent House of Commons debate, the Prime Minister, John Major, reaffirmed the Government's belief that 750,000 jobs would be lost if the Labour Party went ahead with its proposal to introduce a minimum wage. If true, this would amount to a devastating criticism of minimum wage policy.

But in the original Treasury paper from which the information was taken, the officials admit that the results "depend critically on a system of adjustments [about company profitability and investment] which is entirely arbitrary and has no empirical basis".

In fact, using slightly different assumptions, but with the same Treasury model, researchers from the University of Warwick estimated that less than a tenth of that amount would be affected.

A potentially more damaging argument is that the introduction of minimum wages would be self-defeating. If there were an increase in salaries at the lower end of the wage scale, then, it has been claimed, other workers would seek to restore their former position and bargain for higher wages to restore the differential. Not only would the relative position of the low paid remain unchanged, but we would be left with higher inflation. Thus some commitment to narrowing differentials is a pre-requisite of minimum wage policy.

However, the case for a minimum wage is reinforced by Chris Pond and Steve Winyard who argue in a pamphlet for the Low Pay Unit that Britain cannot afford to remain a low pay economy. Not only do the low paid suffer the effects of poverty, but the community pays dearly in economic terms for the inefficiency and lower productivity that results.

The argument hinges on the attitudes of firms to low-paid workers. Pond and Winyard maintain that employers fail to plan ahead and invest in training and capital equipment if there is a constant threat from other firms seeking to gain short-term advantage by the use of cheap labour. With little incentive to invest in capital equipment or training, or to maintain a stable workforce, the efficiency of the whole economy suffers.

Set at half average earnings, the Low Pay Unit would expect the introduction of a national minimum wage to have no significant adverse effect on employment or prices.

We know, so far at least, that many of the nation's workers are suffering the consequences of an economic policy based on low pay. Perhaps the time for a minimum wage has arrived.

*Source: **Guardian** (7 January 1991).*

TASK 9.3

Put the case for and against a minimum wage from the perspective of:
A   the chief executive of a major manufacturing company, and
B   a trade union leader working for the same manufacturing company.

Regional labour markets

The wage rate emerging from a national labour market has a limited value if you happen to be living in Sunderland, Swansea or Stirling. The characteristics of the local or regional labour market may be very different from the national market. The area will probably specialise in a different range of industries with different labour demands. The structure of the local population will be different and local labour markets can be influenced greatly by the decision of a major manufacturer to set up in the area. Box 9.7 shows a broad picture of the wage rates around Great Britain.

BOX 9.7

Average gross weekly earnings,[1] by area, Great Britain, April 1994

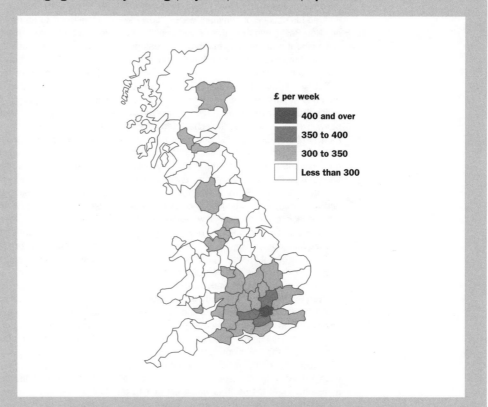

£ per week

■ 400 and over
■ 350 to 400
■ 300 to 350
□ Less than 300

1 *Full-time employees on adult rates whose pay was not affected for the survey period by absence.*

*Source: **Employment Department.***

We need to be careful interpreting this data. It looks as if there is a greater scarcity of labour in the South-East but differences are more likely to be caused by the nature of the industries represented in each area. In the financial services sector in Central London, wages are high and this would boost the average figures for the area. In rural Cornwall or Wales, firms may pay lower wage rates because they happen to be less productive. However, wage rates will reflect the location decisions of firms and the pull of the European market could well mean that more companies will choose to move to the South-East.

The free market should mean that, as wage differentials grow wider between the regions, more firms should move out of the London area and relocate to the West country, Wales or Scotland. Some firms have made this move but the market takes a long time to adjust and may need a helping hand from government or EU regional policy. Look at Box 9.8.

The north-east and Siemens

BOX 9.8

German firm BRINGS **1,800** JOBS TO NORTH

Where the cash comes from

Company and country of origin	Date of decision	Amount of Investment £m	Location of Investment	Number of Jobs
Siemens, Germany	Aug 96	900.0	Newcastle	1800
Samsung, Korea	Oct 94	450.0	Wynyard	3000
NEC, Japan	Sept 94	530.0	Livingston	430
Honda, Japan	June 94	330.0	Swindon	1000
Toyota, Japan	Mar 95	200.0	Burnaston	1000
Valence Tech., US	Sept 93	147.2	Newtownabbey	660
Sony, Japan	May 91	147.0	Bridgend	1400
Motorola, US	Sept 94	250.0	E Kilbride	250
SCA, Sweden	Mar 94	250.0	Aylesford	100

BOX 9.8

Chris Barrie and *Martyn Halsall*

Up to 1,800 jobs are to be created in one of the North-east's worst unemployment black spots following the announcement that Siemens, the German electronics group, is to invest £1.1 billion in a semiconductor plant on north Tyneside.

The investment, one of the largest by an overseas company in Britain, was quickly seized upon by Michael Heseltine, the Deputy Prime Minister, as proof of an upturn in the economy and the forerunner of a revival in Conservative Party fortunes.

Speaking at a London press conference called by Siemens and vigorously promoted by Mr Heseltine himself, he said the investment proved that the British economy now held out the prospect of "solid jobs, solid investment and a brighter future".

Mr Heseltine said Britain was "seeing a breakthrough in economic performance that all governments would welcome as a major achievement". There would be higher living standards over the next two years and these would be "associated with rising political fortunes".

The investment, Mr Heseltine made clear, had been secured after his intervention with assistance from the Prime Minister.

The factory, part of a global expansion plan, will be built at Wallsend, which fought off fierce competition from Austria and Portugal. The Government has pledged aid worth £30 million and a £15 million package of training and infrastructure assistance is in the pipeline.

Jurgen Gehrels, chief executive of Siemens in Britain, said the company had been offered larger grants overseas during its three month search. But Britain had the right combination of a skilled and flexible workforce and a "pro-business" environment.

He denied that Britain's opt-out from the European Union's social chapter had been a factor but admitted that low labour costs were attractive: "We can operate our factory for three shifts a day, seven days a week, without restriction. People will work long shifts here."

Mr Gehrels rejected allegations that the jobs were part of the sweat shop economy. The factory would employ highly skilled engineers, he promised. If low wages were the only reason for the investment's location, Siemens would have chosen a Czech plant where labour costs were 10 per cent of those in Britain.

The factory will make sophisticated integrated circuits for telecommunications equipment, smart cards and multimedia applications and will improve the country's balance of payments by £900 million a year.

Construction of the first, £680 million, phase begins in November, with production due to start 16 months later, creating 1,000 jobs. A second phase will start shortly afterwards, costing £450 million and creating 800 jobs.

Brian Flood, leader of North Tyneside Council, welcomed Siemen's plans as "the most significant development on Tyneside for a generation".

The region has seen 1,500 job losses in the past 18 months following the closure of the Swan Hunter shipyard and cuts in the offshore oil platform yards. Stephen Byers, the MP for Wallsend, said the investment would bring new hope.

Tony Parker, project worker at the Wallsend People's Centre, said new jobs were welcome but former Swan Hunter workers were asking why government support had not been available to the last major shipyard on the east coast of England.

Siemens, one of the largest electronics companies in the world with 370,000 employees, also announced yesterday that it was expanding semiconductor plants in Germany, Austria and the Far East, and was planning to invest in China.

Demand for semiconductors is growing furiously as even mundane products, such as fridges, turn to electronics for control systems. With 100 plants to be completed across the world in the next two years alone, some reports suggest that semiconductor manufacturers will invest over £20 billion this year.

By opting for Britain for its new factory, the company follows in the footsteps of other electronics giants such as Samsung, NEC and Digital.

According to Brian Arthur, director of components and manufacturing at the Federation of the Electronics Industry, Britain is the prime location for electronics investors because it offers a skilled workforce not working under the social chapter, good communications by air and English-speaking engineers.

English is the international language of the electronics industry, and air travel is vital for transporting these high technology parts across the world for final assembly and installation in products.

*Source: **Guardian** (5 August 1995).*

TASK 9.4

The article describes the decision of Siemens to set up in the North East.
1 What were the main factors which influenced Siemens' decision to locate in the North East?
2 How important were the wage levels in the North East to the decision?
3 Comment on the effect of Britain's opt-out of the EU's Social Charter.

TASK 9.5

Coursework investigation: your local labour market

Why is the labour market in your region different to the national labour market?

To answer this question you will need to identify the characteristics of both the local and national labour markets. The national picture can be found from *The Annual Abstract of Statistics, Social Trends* or the *Employment Gazette*. There may be special local studies contained in reports from local Training and Enterprise Councils (TECs) or even local universities. Once you have gained the data you will need to attempt to analyse the reasons for the differences between the two areas.

Much will depend on the pattern of employment in your area. Find out the distribution of jobs between primary, secondary and tertiary industry, the level and duration of unemployment.

The labour market for a particular occupation

Most of us are not sufficiently talented to be able to do all jobs and so we are not able to apply for all jobs. The supply of workers for some jobs will be much greater than for others and so it seems fair to think of the labour market as being made up of a network of separate labour markets for different types of jobs. Since there are separate markets we should expect different prices or wages to develop in each market. Box 9.9 lists some of these markets.

BOX 9.9

Wage differentials

Below are listed 10 jobs:

1 Receptionist
2 Doctor
3 Nurse
4 Waiter/waitress
5 Secondary school teacher
6 Mechanical engineer
7 Bricklayer
8 Cleaner
9 Solicitor
10 Carpenter

TASK 9.6

Place the jobs in the order in which you think they are paid, i.e. the job you think is highest paid first and so on.

The actual order of pay will be found at the end of this chapter in Box 9.19. How did you get on?

People in different jobs are paid different wages. Economists explain this by analysing the markets for different types of occupations. Box 9.10 contains some job advertisements.

BOX 9.10

Job advertisements

> **WALTER'S ENGINEERING**
> require
> Young Person to train as
> # MACHINE OPERATOR
> *Starting £6,500 p.a.*
> **Telephone
> 01351 556023**

> # STUDENTS, HOUSEWIVES, ANYBODY!
> If you are 18 plus and have a good telephone voice then we will pay you an excellent salary plus bonuses to use it for just 18 hours per week.
> *Our friendly office works
> Mon – Fri 6 pm – 9pm and 3 hours Saturday.*
> **If you want to earn £150 plus from a part time job phone on 01351 556024 5 pm – 9 pm NOW.**

TASK 9.7

Using the information contained in the advertisements, explain why the jobs offer different wages. Identify the supply and demand factors involved.

Each of the jobs in Box 9.10 seems to be directed towards different types of people and it would be highly unlikely that the same person would apply for all the jobs. In each of these markets there will be a demand for labour and a supply of labour. Firms want to buy labour because of the value of that labour to the company. This value is measured in terms of the output produced by the labour or its productivity. As was explained in Chapter 7, as more units of labour are employed so eventually the output gained from each extra unit of labour will decrease. This process was explained by the law of diminishing returns.

In deciding how many people to employ, firms will attempt to compare the value of each extra worker (its marginal revenue product (MRP)) with the wage that has to be paid. As long as the MRP is greater than the wage then it seems sensible to continue employing workers. Employment will continue up to the point at which the marginal revenue product is equal to the wage. This is shown in Box 9.11.

BOX 9.11

Marginal revenue product and the wage

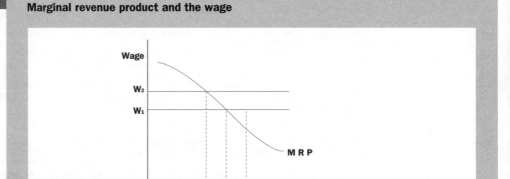

In Box 9.11 $0Q_1$ workers will be employed at a wage of $0W_1$. It would not be worth employing more than $0Q_1$ workers since then the cost of employing the last worker (the marginal cost) would be greater than the benefit obtained from their employment (the marginal revenue product). If the wage paid increased to $0W_2$ then it would be rational for the firm to reduce its workers to $0Q_3$ and unemployment would rise, as was predicted under the minimum wage argument.

However, it is important to remember the assumptions implicit in the argument. First, it is assumed that marginal revenue product can be measured precisely. Second, the units of labour can be varied by single units to allow this measurement to take place. Third, all units of labour are assumed to be of equal ability. Fourth, the marginal revenue product curve is assumed to be static and fifth, it is assumed that as many workers as are required can be employed at the going wage rate. Sixth, it is assumed that employers pay all workers up to the value of the marginal revenue product.

In practice, few of these assumptions may be found. MRP is difficult to measure, especially in the service sector. Therefore wages are often determined by the process of collective bargaining; negotiation between management and the work force. It is often difficult or impossible to measure the contribution of an individual worker since he or she forms part of a team of people. The productivity of labour is not fixed. It can be improved considerably by appropriate training and motivational strategies as well as the application of machinery and new technology. The MRP curve is not static. Firms will pass on wage increases to the consumer in the form of price increases. Since the value of the MRP is calculated from the volume of output multiplied by the price, if the price rises then the value of the MRP must also increase, i.e. the work force are now more valuable and worth paying more.

In the job advertisements, the demand for labour will be affected by the value of that labour to the employer. Value can be measured directly, as in the case of sales staff where a large part of the wage is directly linked to the level of sales achieved through commission. Value may also be measured in terms of the responsibility a job carries, and this might be related to the number of people a person is responsible for, the size of the budget controlled or the importance of decisions made to the success of the business.

The supply of labour for a particular job will be affected by the age or experience a job requires, the qualifications or skills needed, the attractiveness of a job, its location and working conditions, the type of personality required and the relative wage offered. Trade unions can have some impact here by limiting the numbers of potential employees. They can do this by insisting on minimum lengths of time in training, or by operating a closed shop whereby union membership is a condition of employment (the ability of unions to operate closed shops has been much reduced by recent legislation).

Jobs with high value but with few realistic applicants are likely to command high salaries while low value jobs with many applicants will command low wages. Look at Box 9.12.

BOX 9.12

Average weekly wage and the level of educational attainment, 1994

	Men (GB average £338) (£)	Women (GB average £247) (£)
Above A' levels	464	350
A' levels or equivalent	317	225
GCSE or equivalent	309	210
Other qualification	271	198
No qualification	249	181

TASK 9.8

1 What does Box 9.12 tell us about the link between a person's education and the wage they are likely to receive when in employment? What might explain this?
2 Look back at the list of jobs in Box 9.9. Using the actual pay levels given, explain why the wage differentials exist. See also Box 9.19.
3 Select a high paid and a low paid job and use a supply and demand diagram to help explain the wage differences between the two jobs.

Trade unions and the labour market

A trade union is an organisation of working people which has the objective of increasing the standard of living of its members. By representing groups of employees, trade unions aim to redress the power balance in the work place. Membership of trade unions has fallen in recent years and now stands at approximately 9 million. This decline has been caused by a number of factors:

- the changing structure of UK industry with the shift away from primary and secondary industry along with the growth of self-employment;
- the creation of more female jobs in the service sector (women are less likely to be trade union members);
- the increased number of unemployed in recent years has hit membership;
- the growth in the number of part-time jobs has reduced membership;

- the power of the trade unions has been weakened by a series of laws which have restricted what trade unions can legally do;
- trade unions have been slow to up-date their image and services provided;
- trade unions have been shut out of the government's decision-making process since 1979.

Despite their decline, it can still be argued that the trade unions play an important role. Although only about a third of workers are members of trade unions, a much higher percentage are covered by employment contracts and wages deals which have been negotiated by trade unions. Wages may be the major concern of the unions but they do try to promote many other important issues such as health and safety, equal opportunities, training, good working conditions and good race relations.

Economically, trade unions may be seen to have positive and negative effects. Their impact on the labour market may

well be to push up wages or to prevent them falling in line with market forces. In doing this, the unions may be raising living standards of members but may also be creating unemployment. In Box 9.13 the impact of trade union activity is shown.

BOX 9.13

The effect of trade unions on wages and employment

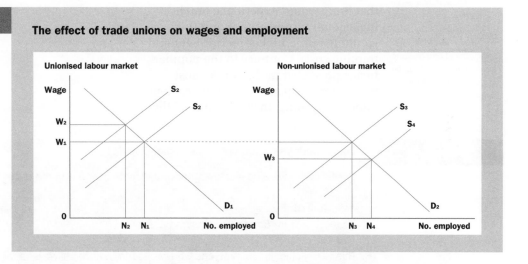

The labour market can be divided between that sector covered by trade unions and the non-unionised sector. In the unionised sector, unions attempt to restrict the supply of labour and this will push up wages in that sector from $0W_1$ to $0W_2$ in Box 9.13. The effect on employment is that fewer people will be employed in that sector. Unemployment rises by N_1N_2. But these people do not give up on work. They attempt to gain jobs in the non-unionised sector of the economy so, in that sector, the supply curve shifts from S_3 to S_4. The effect of

this is to reduce wages in the non-unionised sector and there is a misallocation of labour between the two groups of industries. If trade unions prevent wage levels reaching their equilibrium point, they can be charged with causing unemployment.

However, there is a strong argument in their support. The exit-voice theory emphasises the importance trade unions can have in saving costs.

Exit–voice theory provides an explanation of the role of trade unions in the work place. If workers have a grievance, they have two choices: 1 leave the company or exit the firm and 2 discuss the grievance or give voice to the problem. If, whenever there was a grievance, workers left companies there would be high recruitment and training costs. Therefore it can be argued that trade unions help to reduce firms' costs.

The theory states that if workers encounter problems at work they face two choices: they can leave the company (exit) or they can raise the issue with management (voice). The trade unions provide a mechanism through which problems can be aired and solved. The alternative might be that firms would experience much higher staff turnover rates and this would result in higher recruitment and training costs. Contrary to the popular image presented in the press, most union time is spent in solving problems rather than going on strike. In this, they are assisting management although it can be argued that if the quality of management were better there would not be the need for trade unions. Look at Task 9.9.

TASK 9.9

Coursework investigation: an industrial dispute

The following extracts give a flavour of a dispute over pay in the rail industry.

Aslef Rail Strike
A message from British Rail Chairman

This is to apologise to everyone who wanted to use the railways today but who cannot do so because....

Move to halt rail strike

After meeting members of ASLEF's negotiating team yesterday, Paul Watkinson, BR's personnel director, made it clear BR could not improve on its 3 per cent offer throughout the industry. But if drivers were prepared to come up with other ideas, BR would look at them.

Last night this statement led to an invitation from Lew Adams, ASLEF general secretary, to BR negotiators to meet at the union's Hampstead, north London, headquarters to examine ideas.

TASK 9.9

First rail strike on as talks fail

Keith Harper – Transport Editor

The first of a series of one-day rail strikes will start at midnight tonight after talks between ASLEF, the train drivers' union, and British Rail to avert the stoppage ended in failure.

BR immediately condemned the drivers for imposing "untold misery" on the travelling public. A further five stoppages are planned, running through August and into September.

BR yesterday refused to increase its 3 per cent offer, which has been accepted by all BR passenger staff except the drivers. BR's attempt to sugar the pill with bonus payments of up to £200 at the end of the next financial year were rejected by ASLEF during two days of informal talks at the union's headquarters in north London.

*Source: **Guardian** (11 July 1995).*

Strikes off as BR cuts hours

Two-year deal to lift pay by 5pc

*Source: **Guardian** (14 July 1995).*

Follow an industrial relations dispute covered in the press. Identify the economic issues associated with the dispute and the arguments used by management and workers. Explain why the dispute arose and why it might be difficult to resolve. You will need to consider the background to the current dispute and you could present your findings as a newspaper report or a script for an investigative documentary. If you identify a local dispute try to talk to the parties involved.

Ethnic groups and the labour market

In Britain today 5.8% of the population of working age are members of ethnic minority groups. This represents nearly 2 million people. So how has the labour market worked for them?

A first response to this question must be: not very well. If there was an absence of discrimination we would expect the unemployment rates of the different groups within society to be approximately equal. What we find is that ethnic groups suffer from double the unemployment rates of their white counterparts. In 1993, 12% of all white men were unemployed compared to 24% of men in ethnic minority groups and 7% of white women were unemployed compared to 17% of women from ethnic groups.

As economists we would look for explanations for this. Some can be found. Not all ethnic groups have encountered problems to the same extent. Indians have done relatively well because nearly two thirds of them are in managerial, technical and professional occupations, all areas of work which have suffered less from unemployment. It may be that the older generation are less well qualified and so tend to be found in lower paid, less secure jobs. The black population are less likely to start their own businesses in their communities and so this reduces a potential source of employment. But after this, explanations become more difficult. The young generation are equally as well qualified as white groups and the current differentials in unemployment rates should not persist; but they do.

Despite long standing anti-race discrimination legislation, discrimination still seems to be present in the labour market. If there is prejudice in the market we would expect the demand for black workers to fall, causing their wage levels to fall. Eventually firms' profits would suffer if they did not employ the cheaper labour so that eventually the demand for black workers would rise. In this case the market solution is not acceptable and action is needed to persuade all employers that workers should only be judged on ability. Look at Box 9.14.

BOX 9.14

Data on ethnic groups in the labour market

Income by ethnicity and age, 1990
Probability of low income, %

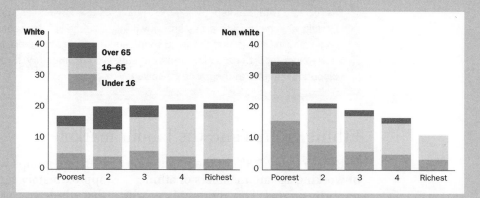

In 1990 only 18 per cent of the "white" population was in the poorest fifth of the population, against more than a third of the "non-white". "We are particularly concerned at what is happening to the non-white population," the inquiry states, and there are "alarming" disparities between ethnic groups. In 1988–90 only 21 per cent of all those aged 16–24 had no qualifications, but the figure rose to 48 per cent for Pakistanis and 54 per cent for Bangladeshis. Over the same period, 8 per cent of white men were unemployed, but 14 per cent of all ethnic minorities and 22 per cent for Pakistanis. Among women the gaps were even greater: 66 per cent of white women were in work, 48 per cent of all ethnic minority women, but only 16 per cent of Pakistani women.

*Source: **Employment Gazette** (May 1994).*

An individual's labour

Individuals face a choice about how they use their time. They can use it to work for somebody for themselves or they can choose to have their time as leisure. The more time they work, the less time they have to use as leisure. People look for a balance between the two, as shown in Box 9.15.

The choice between work and leisure

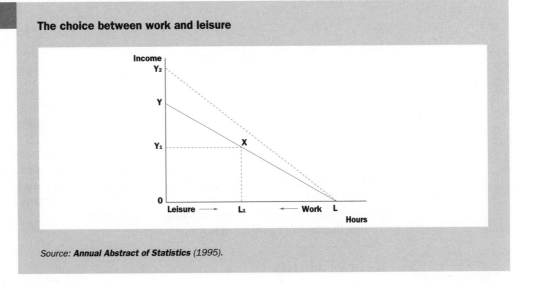

*Source: **Annual Abstract of Statistics** (1995).*

Box 9.15 shows all the options facing an individual. The person could choose all leisure, in which case they would be at point L and would have no income, or they could choose to work all hours of the day, maximise income but have no leisure and be at point Y. The line YL represents all the combinations of work and leisure that could be chosen. A person is more likely to choose a combination of the two and might choose point X where they receive $0Y_1$ income and have $0L_1$ hours of leisure.

This analysis is useful in helping us to predict how people will respond to a wage increase. The government is certainly interested in encouraging us to work harder and so may consider tax cuts if it likely to have the desired effect. This strategy is at the heart of the free market/supply siders' approach to the economy. Lower taxes mean more work which means more income which means people pay more tax which can then be used to improve public services – it is a virtuous circle.

Assuming that the person in Box 9.15 is already paying tax, a cut in tax would shift YL to Y_2L. How will the individual respond? He or she could decide to work longer but, equally, they could decide to take more time off work and spend longer on the golf course. There is evidence that individuals could follow both strategies. As wage rates reach much higher levels it seems reasonable that people will not want to continue to work longer and longer hours. The effect is the backward sloping supply curve shown in Box 9.16.

The backward sloping supply curve is a supply curve which shows a negative relationship between the wage and the supply of labour. It occurs when wages rise to higher levels and the worker wishes to substitute leisure time for work time.

BOX 9.16

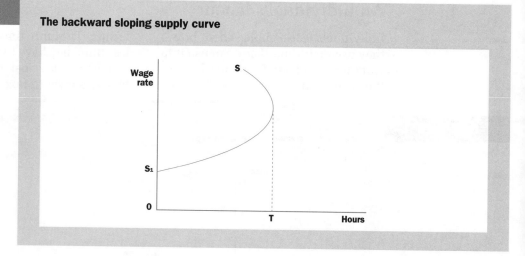

The backward sloping supply curve

In Box 9.6 the individual will not work for less than $0S_1$ wage. As wage rises then the individual is prepared to increase the number of hours worked up to a maximum number of hours of $0T$.

If wage continues to rise the individual prefers to have more free time and the supply curve turns back towards point S.

Rent of ability

Some people possess unique talents. The supply of their services must, therefore, be perfectly inelastic. If their talents are in demand then they will be able to command high fees. Top sports stars, entertainers, singers, bands, film stars or business high flyers all try to make the most of their abilities and are often able to earn way above what they could expect to earn in their next best form of employment. These surplus earnings are known as economic rent or the rent of ability.

Box 9.17 gives some background to one earner of rent of ability.

BOX 9.17

The rent of ability?

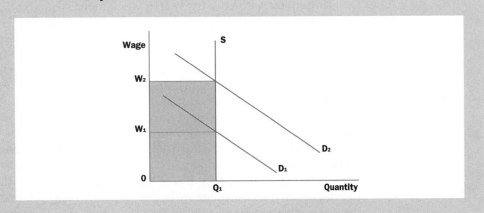

£1m RADIO DEAL FOR DJ CHRIS

(That's 50p for each listener)

EXCLUSIVE

Richard Wallace

Radio 1 golden boy Chris Evans has been offered a £1 million deal to stay with the ailing pop station.

That's 50p for each of the two million new listeners the star DJ has put on since taking over the breakfast show from Steve Wright in April.

Radio 1 chief Matthew Bannister has begged him to stay when his eight-month £400,000 contract runs out at the end of the year.

Evans, 28, and his company Ginger Productions, are mulling over the offer.

He turned down more than £5 million in contracts from all four mainstream TV stations to come to the rescue of Radio 1. But he is undecided if he will give up his TV career for a further 12 months.

Evans has made a fortune from selling the format of his hit Channel 4 game show *Don't Forget Your Toothbrush*.

His near-the-knuckle three-hour radio show is a ratings hit.

And Evans is said to be "more than happy" to stay if the price is right.

"Chris has had a great time on the show and he's very keen for the relationship with Radio 1 to continue," said a pal.

"No final decision has been made and to say he has already signed on the dotted line is wildly inaccurate."

Source: **Daily Mirror** (16 June 1995).

TASK 9.10

Explain how Box 9.17 helps to explain the income of Chris Evans.

207

Income distribution

One consequence of a relatively free labour market is that gaps open up between the high and low income earners. The Rowntree Report of February 1995 examined what had been happening to the income distribution over time. Its conclusion was that greater inequality had emerged during the life of the Conservative Government. From 1979 to 1992 the poorest 10% ended up worse off in actual and relative terms. In the 1970s, 6% of the population had incomes below half of the average wage whereas in the 1990s more than 20% were in that position.

One view of this trend is that it is a natural consequence of a market economy. As an economy grows, the rich will get richer but they will be engaging in wealth creation activities which will create jobs for other members of society. The trickle down effect eventually benefits all of society and the poor are now better off in absolute terms. Any attempt to discourage the rich from prospering will discourage enterprise and will persuade the rich to look around the world for more sympathetic régimes such as Monaco or the Cayman Islands. The belief is that everybody stands an equal chance of achieving high wages and without differences there will be no incentive for people to strive to improve their lot.

Alternatively, the unequal distribution of income can be seen as a major example of market failure. In a market system those with money dictate the way in which resources are used. If there is a demand for cars to be built costing £500 000, they will be built regardless of whether this seems an efficient use of resources. Eventually civil unrest may be the result as people at the bottom end see no prospect of improvement and it might be considered the mark of a civilised society that it is able to care for those less fortunate members of society. Advocates of the free market would no doubt label these ideas as the politics of envy.

Box 9.18 presents some of the information from the Rowntree inquiry.

BOX 9.18

Income distribution, 1979–91

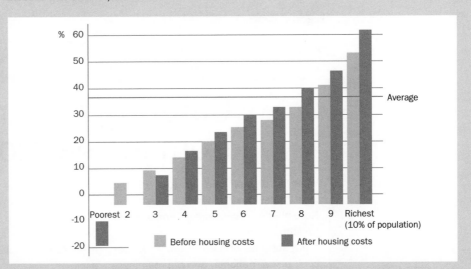

Between 1979 and 1992 the bottom 10 per cent became worse off in real terms. Average incomes rose by 36 per cent, but only the top 30 per cent saw a rise that large or larger. The richest tenth saw their incomes increase by 62 per cent.

*Source: **Independent** (10 February 1995).*

REVIEW

This section has looked at the way in which the labour market operates. Although the market has some similarities with product markets there are some important differences. The demand for labour is a derived demand and, because the market involves the buying and selling of people's time and skills, people's motives and desires get tangled up with the actual transactions. Market imperfections which lead to discrimination or the unequal distribution of income are examples of market failure and give cause for concern and suggest a strong case for some form of government intervention. Income distribution is further considered in Chapters 5.31 and 5.32.

REVIEW TASK Read the extracts below and answer the questions which follow.

Wages at Centre Parcs

EXTRACT A

Catering suffers from indigestion

What a dismal tale is told of the local hotel and catering industry in November's Wiltshire Employment Update.

Pay for jobs offered is low – 35 per cent below national average earnings. And it is increasing at one per cent a year below the rise in the economy as a whole.

Jobs involve shift work, split shifts, week-end and evening work.

These unsocial hours are said to be a major cause of staff recruitment problems.

Less than 20 per cent of jobs offer flexible working hours and only 43 per cent offer a pension scheme.

Not surprisingly some 49 per cent of companies surveyed said they had recruiting difficulties particularly for trained chefs and waiters, followed by cleaners and receptionists.

One of the most frequent reasons given for these problems was the low status of catering in this country compared with the rest of Europe.

This is clearly an industry with its head buried deep in the sand. It could be that because it lacks competition it appears so complacent. It may be in for a jolt.

Competition for staff could be on its way. The go-ahead has already been given for a huge holiday village in the Cotswold Water Park on the county's northern boundary. Soon a decision will be taken on the similar Center Parcs project at Longleat. If approved, this will contain 600 villas and offer up to 750 jobs, similar to the Cotswold figure.

There could be 1500 jobs available, most of them in the hotel and catering market.

The only way to get them filled will be to pay over the odds, and Center Parcs will offer round-the-year employment as opposed to seasonal work.

Source: Adapted from an article by D. Kingman in **The Wiltshire Times***, 29 November 1991.*

REVIEW TASK   *EXTRACT B (from a letter written in response to EXTRACT A).*

Centre Parcs jobs 'will not boost wage rates'

Mr Kingman suggested that any increase in the number of jobs brought about by the development would lead to an improvement of wages and working conditions in the hotel and catering industry in Wiltshire. To recruit and retain workers things would have to improve. On balance he is probably wrong.

Firstly, Center Parcs, if it goes ahead, will need to remain competitive with other similar establishments in the UK.

If it decided that in order to attract enough local workers, wages would need to be raised by £1 an hour, then at least £1 million a year would be added to its wage bill. Couldn't this also lead to some of our existing hotels closing down?

Raising wages in a labour intensive industry is not consistent with remaining competitive.

Secondly, post 1992 a vast reservoir of unskilled labour, anxious to learn English and work here, will be available in Southern Europe. For a company with Center Parcs' pan-European experience recruiting cheap labour from abroad will be no problem.

When I asked Center Parcs' managing director how much he would be paying workers at the Longleat development he replied: "The going rate" which I took to mean £2.75 an hour which is what cleaners and cooks are paid in the local area.

South-West Wiltshire will have a declining number of young people in the 1990s. Perhaps Center Parcs may be relying on further changes to the Social Security system which could force more people who are at present able to claim benefits into taking very low wage jobs or face losing benefits.

*Source: Adapted from a letter in **The Wiltshire Times**, 13 December 1991.*

a Using the data show how the demand for labour in the hotel and catering industry is a derived demand.

b Describe the factors that could affect the supply of labour to the hotel and catering industry.

c (i) Briefly explain how raising wage rates by £1 an hour could add at least £1 million a year to the wages bill of Center Parcs (line nos. 13-17) in EXTRACT B.

   (ii) Examine the possible effects on the local economy of this increase in wages.

d Using the data and economic theory, discuss how future wage levels in the hotel and catering industry in Wiltshire are likely to change.

Multiple choice

1 **If all other things remain equal, an increase in productivity will always lead to a reduction in the**

A   number of workers employed.

B   average cost of production.

C   price of the product.

D   supply of the product

(IB, May 1994)

Questions 2 to 5 should be answered with reference to this key:

A   1,2 and 3 are correct

B   1 and 2 only are correct

C   2 and 3 only are correct

D   1 only is correct

2 **The graph below illustrates the way productivity in a country's farming changed between 1983 – 1993.**

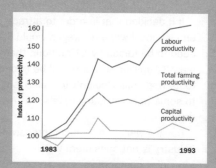

It follows from the graph that, over the period as a whole,

1   demand for labour has increased

2   technical efficiency has improved

3   labour input relative to output has fallen faster than capital input relative to output

(AEB, Summer 1994)

3 **The relationship between the government's total tax revenue and the average tax rate (taking account of all taxes) is shown in the diagram below**

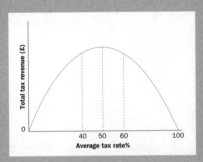

If the current average tax rate is 50% then

1 an increase in the average tax rate may be expected to create disincentives to effort and entrepreneurship

2 a decrease in the average tax rate will be likely to increase tax avoidance and evasion

3 a decrease in the average tax rate must reduce the government's budget deficit or increase its surplus

(AEB, Summer 1994)

4

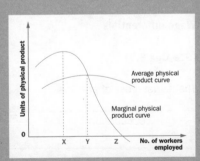

The diagram represents the short-run situation facing a firm with respect to the employment of workers. Which of the following conclusions can be drawn from the situation shown?

1 output per worker is maximised when OX workers are employed.

2 Only after OX workers are employed does the law of diminishing marginal returns begin to operate.

3 Total output would decline if more than OZ workers were employed.

(ULEAC, January 1995)

QUESTIONS

5 **The diagram shows how the total product (TP) of the variable factor will change as additional units of a variable factor are applied to a certain quantity of a fixed factor.**

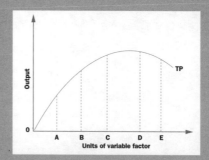

From the diagram it can be deduced that

1 marginal product is zero between D and E
2 marginal product is rising between O and A
3 marginal product is falling between B and C

(IB, May 1995, Higher)

BOX 9.19

Wage differentials

(See Box 9.9)

The actual order of pay was

	Occupation	Wage (1994) (£ per week)
1	Doctor	746
2	Solicitor	569
3	Mechanical engineer	511
4	Secondary school teacher	427
5	Nurse	316
6	Carpenter	261
7	Bricklayer	252
8	Receptionist	182
9	Cleaner	180
10	Waiter/waitress	157

*Source: **Department of Employment.***

2.10 How are markets linked?

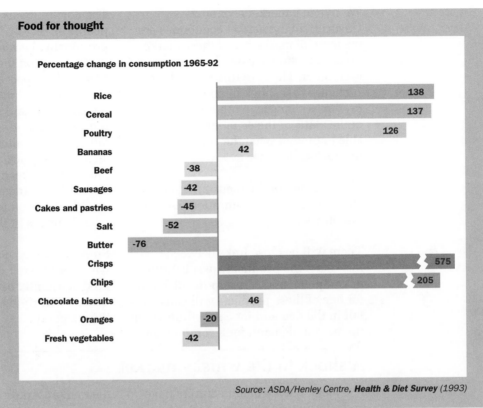

Food for thought

Percentage change in consumption 1965-92

Rice	138
Cereal	137
Poultry	126
Bananas	42
Beef	-38
Sausages	-42
Cakes and pastries	-45
Salt	-52
Butter	-76
Crisps	575
Chips	205
Chocolate biscuits	46
Oranges	-20
Fresh vegetables	-42

*Source: ASDA/Henley Centre, **Health & Diet Survey** (1993)*

TASK 10.1

1 How would you expect the markets for rice, cereals and poultry to have been affected by the increase in demand for these products? (You might think about using supply and demand curves to help your analysis.)

2 How would the markets for beef and sausages have been affected by the changes in demand?

Preview

In this chapter we shall investigate the following key areas:

- how changes in one product's market can affect other products' markets;
- changes in product markets will cause changes in factor markets;
- the ability to predict the effects of a given change on the economy.

We live in a market economy. Unsurprisingly, market economies are made up of markets. But these markets do not function separately from each other. They are linked together. A change or a shock in one market produces changes in other markets. One of the skills of the economist is to be able to predict what the consequences of shocks might be.

The information in Focus 2.10 shows changes in food consumption over the last 30 years.

There will be close links between markets if the products are substitutes or complements. A rise in the demand for one of these products will cause a fall in the demand for a substitute or an increase in demand for a complement.

The data in Focus 2.10 shows that many people are eating less butter today, presumably because they are attempting to cut down on their fat intake. We would expect that the demand for substitutes for butter, such as low fat margarine and spreads, would have increased. These shifts in demand for butter and the alternatives would have affected the prices of both butter and the various spreads which replace butter. The markets are interdependent, i.e. what goes on in one market affects what happens in the other.

Since market economies are dynamic we expect there to be changes of this kind constantly occurring and each change will ripple its effects through the economy.

A shock to the whisky market

For years whisky manufacturers have had an unwritten agreement not to advertise their product on television but, because of unexciting sales figures, they have now decided to take advantage of television advertising. This could produce a major change to the market. An economist might be asked to predict the likely outcome. What would you expect to be the economic effects of the decision?

We can identify different groups which will be affected by the decision.

The whisky distillers

Initially it is likely that the major advertisers will be the companies with the well known brand names. We will assume that there is a net increase in advertising and that the money spent on television advertising is not withdrawn from other forms of advertising.

Advertising on television is an expensive business and we would expect the larger companies to have the resources to be the first onto the screen.

If some companies begin to advertise, others will be forced to join in to prevent the loss of market share. The major whisky manufacturers accept an initial increase in their marketing costs but, if successful, can expect there to be an increase in sales – the demand curve will shift to the right. With heavy sales promotion, this will make demand more inelastic and allow manufacturers to push up prices. This is shown in Box 10.1.

BOX 10.1

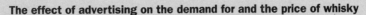

The effect of advertising on the demand for and the price of whisky

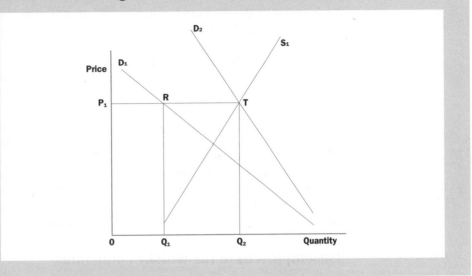

In Box 10.1 the whisky manufacturers have been charging a price of $0P_1$. This price was above the equilibrium price and so stocks equal to Q_1Q_2 built up. You might ask, why didn't the whisky producers just lower price to the equilibrium level? Manufacturers of what they regard as premium products often do not wish to engage in price cutting. First, it could give the wrong signals to the consumer who may equate quality with price and second, it could spark off a price war between manufacturers which could threaten profit levels.

Advertising has shifted the demand curve from D_1 to D_2. This has the effect of equating supply and demand at the price of $0P_1$ and also gives the producers more control over price since they can raise it with less risk that there will be a major cut in demand.

The producers generate additional revenue equal to Q_1RTQ_2.

Not all whisky manufacturers will be successful but jobs will have been generated in the advertising industry and jobs safeguarded at distilleries. A number of companies promoting the product could awaken much more interest in whisky drinking generally and the sales of all manufacturers might start to increase. Rising profitability could have a beneficial impact upon the share price of these companies which could help in future attempts to raise capital or fight off take-over bids.

Whisky manufacture is an interesting production process. The supply available today depends on how much was distilled 8-12 years ago since it has to have time to mature. The reason the companies are engaging in advertising now probably means that they have seen unsold stocks accumulating. Also it is the case that most of the major distilleries are owned by three huge drinks conglomerates – Guinness, Grand Metropolitan and Allied Domecq – which may be keen to see profits rise from the product's sales.

The competitors

An increase in the demand for one product generally means a decrease in the demand for others. In this case it might be the unadvertised brands of whisky which will suffer or supermarket own brands, although there is likely to remain a market for a cheaper substitute product. These supermarket own brands on some occasions act like an inferior product: in recessions when money is tight, sales increase as people substitute the cheaper for the more expensive product. When the economy emerges from recession and incomes start to rise, then consumers move back to buying what they regard as the superior product.

The demand for other less-close substitutes such as gin or brandy may be hit and there could be an effect elsewhere. If the annual sales of whisky increase by £100 million then there is an opportunity cost to consider. That £100 million cannot be spent on alternative products so the sales of these products, whatever they might be, will fall.

The employees of the whisky companies

If the increased emphasis on promotion is carried through into export markets there will be a tremendous potential for growth in sales in the future. Whisky is a unique product to Scotland (although other countries do have their own variations). Many jobs are dependent on the industry. Any upturn in sales will help to preserve jobs and even create jobs. If the profits of the whisky makers increase then there would be a strong argument for a wage increase for the workers to match.

Scotland

The retention of jobs in the whisky industry is vital to the economy of Scotland. Areas where there are distilleries often lack alternative forms of employment so a distillery closure can be devastating to local communities. More jobs in the industry will have multiplier effects on the local area. There could be expenditure on new buildings or equipment and if unemployment falls, people will have more money to spend so that local shopkeepers and other businesses may benefit. It is possible to calculate the size of the local multiplier. More interest in whisky drinking may even lead to more tourism as people decide to visit the places where their favourite tipple is made. This could benefit local providers of bed and breakfast, cafés and people running fishing trips.

External costs

There is always the risk that more advertising of whisky could lead to worse problems of alcoholism, under-age drinking of whisky and drunken driving. These will impose extra costs on society which will be paid for out of taxation and, again, there is an opportunity cost to consider. There is a concern that as more is spent on advertising whisky drinking, there should also be more advertising of the dangers associated with drinking excessive amounts of alcohol.

The analysis could be taken further and once the amounts to be spent on advertising are known, more precise figures could be given to the estimates of the effects of the changes. What is important is to note that the shock affected the whisky market first, then other product markets and then factor markets. If the industry did undergo a major revival then we could expect to see the wages of employees in the industry responding to the increased demand for their services. Although the initial shock was specifically confined to the whisky industry, its effects could reverberate around the Scottish economy. Look at Boxes 10.2 and 10.3.

BOX 10.2

Shocks to markets

In January 1995, a headline in the Grimsby Evening Telegraph read: **1000 JOBS TO GO — KP TO SHUT GRIMSBY FACTORY**. The background to the story was that increased competition between supermarket chains meant that they were trying to drive down the costs of suppliers. United Biscuits, the owners of the KP brand, were responding by trying to cut their own costs through closing a factory. The supermarkets were also finding that people were buying more of their own brand crisps.

TASK 10.2

Explain how you would expect the following to be affected by the story:

A shoppers in supermarkets;
B other producers of branded crisp products;
C the employees at the KP factory;
D wage levels in Grimsby;
E the Grimsby economy?

BOX 10.3	**The big milk shake**

In November 1994, the Government changed the way in which milk is sold. Up until then the Milk Marketing Board, a government agency, had bought all the milk produced by farmers and paid a single price for it. The Government decided to deregulate the market and open it up to competition. In response to this a group of farmers set up a voluntary co-operative known as Milk Marque to buy farmers' milk and to sell this on to the food processing companies and the supermarkets. There follow some extracts of newspaper stories about the change.

Milk GIANT AXES 2,000 JOBS

Northern Foods puts blame on supermarket competition and shake-up of milk distribution system as doorstep delivery share of total sales plunges.

Roger Cowe

Britain's biggest milk company, Northern Foods, announced yesterday that 1,100 jobs would go in its milk bottling operations as doorstep deliveries dwindle, plus a further 1,100 jobs in its food business because shrinking sales in local shops have made van deliveries unviable.

Northern Foods – which owns Northern and Express Dairies – said supermarkets were killing doorstep delivery. The 2,200 job losses are in addition to 1,250 already announced, and are likely to be repeated in other food companies.

Northern Foods has not yet decided where the axe will fall. It is negotiating with other milk companies to try to re-allocate milk rounds, removing competition and leaving each company with profitable operations in its own areas. A final decision is expected by summer.

The closures will cost the company £91 million and were blamed by Northern Foods on the Government's shake-up of the milk distribution system last year, as well as the growing supermarket share of grocery sales.

The chairman of Northern Foods, Christopher Haskins, said: "The new system which replaced the Milk Marketing Board is totally flawed. It is an unregulated private monopoly over a raw material which is rationed because of European Union milk quotas."

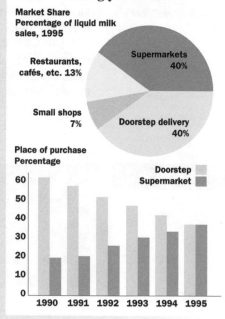

Losing your bottle

Market Share
Percentage of liquid milk
sales, 1995

- Supermarkets 40%
- Restaurants, cafés, etc. 13%
- Small shops 7%
- Doorstep delivery 40%

Place of purchase
Percentage

Doorstep
Supermarket

Source: Guardian (24 March 1995).

BOX 10.3

DAIRIES *mount challenge on milk shake-up*

Roger Cowe

Dairy companies have demanded a judicial review of the Government's shake-up of the milk industry, warning that the abolition of the Milk Marketing Board will result in higher milk prices and the loss of thousands of jobs in the dairy industry.

Predicting an extra 2p on a pint, and much higher increases for milk products such as cheese, the Dairy Trade Federation (DTF) said the Government's scheme, to be introduced on November 1, had resulted in an unregulated monopoly which would devastate the industry.

Milk round up

Approximate prices per half litre, converted into pence

UK:	(supermarket)	25p
	(doorstep)	37p
Belgium:		18p
France:		43p
Greece:		36p
Ireland:		30p
USA:		18p

"By making our milk the most expensive in Europe, it will wipe out the industry's profitability, place jobs and investment at risk and open the door to imports. We could see the prices of some dairy products rising by as much as 18 per cent," said DTF president Jim McMichael-Philips.

The DTF said cheese prices could rise by 15p a pound, while the price of butter in the shops could increase by even more than that.

Nevertheless milk companies Unigate and Northern Foods (which owns Express Dairies) warned that the new regime would knock millions of pounds from their profits. They said the power of the supermarkets, which buy much of their output, and the supermarket price wars, would prevent their passing on the full cost increases.

Northern Foods chairman Chris Haskins claims the new regime has added more than 1p per litre to prices of raw milk for sale as drinking milk, and as much as 3.5p per litre to the price of milk for making cheese. "The whole thing is flawed," he said.

The DTF said Milk Marque had made British milk the most expensive in Europe. It said British farmers will get 24.8p per litre, an increase of 10 per cent over the past year. Farmers in Denmark where milk has traditionally been most expensive, will get 24.25p.

Fresh milk is difficult to import, and with European Union quotas restricting production it is impossible for farmers to produce more to meet demand and keep prices down. But milk products such as cheese and yoghurt are open to much greater international competition, and dairy companies fear they will be undercut by imports from Ireland and the Continent.

*Source: **Guardian** (23 August 1994).*

BOX 10.3

As second and third generation dairy farmers we read your articles on milk (August 23) very carefully and became very angry.

Milk Marque was set up as a voluntary co-operative and it promised the dairy farmers of England and Wales to take their milk wherever they were and however big or small their output was. Approximately two-thirds of dairy farmers agreed to join because the individual companies, which wanted to buy direct from them, could not convince them that they would get the market value for their milk. The large dairy companies are furious that farmers were not going to sell their milk at one of the lowest prices in Europe anymore.

The price at which Milk Marque will sell is obviously the market price because the dairy companies wanted even more at these prices.

But, as quotas are in force, there is not enough milk for the excess manufacturing capacity in this country. The manufacturers will have to put their house in order and not expect the dairy farmer to subsidise their inefficiency. They are complaining bitterly but do not be deceived by their rhetoric. Dairy farmers have not been.

Milk Marque has done nothing wrong and will trade reasonably throughout England and Wales. We wish it well as it is our co-operative and the future of all dairy farmers depend on it.

Mary and Bruce Large
Grange Farm,
North Hykeham,
Lincoln.

Source: Letter, **Guardian** (5 September 1994).

TASK 10.3

Using the information, analyse the economic effects of the change to the way milk is marketed. You could produce a set of arguments in support of the change and a set of arguments against.

Course work investigation: Shocks to markets

BOX 10.4

The cross-Channel transport market

The cross-Channel transport market is one which has seen a major shock in recent years. The building of the Channel Tunnel and the introduction of a fixed rail link between London, Paris and Brussels has brought a new dimension to cross-Channel travel. You could investigate what the economic impact of the Tunnel has been.

First, you will need to research the characteristics of the market. What is the size of the market, who are the buyers and sellers? To what extent can it be described as a perfect market?

Second, what have been the effects on the competition for passengers? How have the ferry companies responded to the threat posed by the Tunnel? How do prices compare? How important is non-price competition? What are the strengths and weaknesses of each form of transport?

Third, what has been the effect of the building of the Tunnel on the local area and how have ferry ports been affected? Who has gained and who has lost?

The building of the tunnel has been a huge engineering project managed by EuroTunnel. All the capital required has had to be raised through the banks and shareholders. The loans are so large that interest charges run at the rate of £2 million a day. There is a possibility that the company could collapse under the weight of debt. If that happened, it is likely that the government might be forced to step in and take over at least some of the debt and the company would then be bought by another firm which feels that it could manage the project profitably. If this did happen, it is interesting to speculate what the outcome might be. That would provide a mega shock to the industry. In September 1995 Eurotunnel announced that it was suspending interest payments to its creditors.

Investigations do not have to be about such major, high profile projects. In every town there are developments which illustrate the way in which markets are linked. Local authorities use planning committees to make decisions concerning new buildings where there is local disagreement about whether a project should go ahead. The reports and votes of these committees generally make big news locally. One example that almost all parts of the country have experienced is the development of large, out-of-town superstores. The following article gives one example from Portsmouth.

Planning application for new store

The INVESTIGATOR

Planning bombshell: planning application for new store turned down

Portsmouth planning committee turned down the application by RailTrack, Hyperion and Safeway to redevelop Fratton rail freight yard. The development was an important one because the decision is tied up with the redevelopment of Portsmouth Football Club's famous ground at Fratton Park.

The Taylor Report required all football clubs in the first two English divisions to move towards all-seater stadiums. Portsmouth FC had already had major plans to relocate the club on a green field site turned down and now was proposing a more modest redevelopment of its existing ground. This plan had gained planning approval but the developers were willing to go ahead on condition that the rail goods yard site would be used for the location of a new supermarket. It is this last proposal which has just been scuppered.

A spokesman for the developers said that there was no evidence that the new supermarket would force other local firms out of business. The regeneration of the yard would bring a strategic link road, the future security of the football club and 1000 jobs in an area of high unemployment.

Opponents argued that the new store would cause an existing Co-op store to lose an estimated £3.5 million of trade or 16.7% of its turnover. Other local shops would also be affected and the existence of the superstore would undermine the future of town centre shopping throughout the area.

Councillor Tony McCarthy said: "It all sounds so tempting but what we want is real jobs in the city centre not jobs diverted from one store to another."

This type of local story gives a good lead into an investigation. It opens up the possibility of speaking to local shopkeepers and residents and evaluating evidence. A report could be produced under the title: 'What would have been the economic effects of the granting of planning permission for the new supermarket at Fratton?'

Major infrastructure projects such as building new motorways have a significant impact on a number of different markets and are worthy of investigation. The building of motorways or by-passes creates jobs in the construction industry but the projects may be opposed because of their impact on the local environment. A main difficulty here is evaluating the amount of damage done. The government may commission a cost/benefit study to be undertaken which will attempt to identify and put a value on the various effects a decision may have. Sometimes the government will hold a public enquiry to ensure that all points are heard and a fair judgment made.

A change in licensing laws

The following article looks at the effects of the change in law which came into effect on 6 August 1995.

Licensing laws

BOX 10.6

Sunday DRINKERS ROLL OUT THE BARREL

Tomorrow, many public houses will be open all day. Lisa Buckingham and John Glover test the commercial waters

Gis Liverani is perplexed. The Italian executive, who recently moved to London, was visiting Windsor Castle with his wife last Sunday. Having taken in the sights, they headed for the pub. They got the food they wanted but were refused the beer. "You just have to accept it, I suppose, but it's absurd," he said.

It has taken more than a century to achieve, but this weekend England and Wales will finally remove that absurdity, putting paid to the old Monty Python gag that the pubs shut every time you are thirsty.

After casting off the weekday noose in 1988, from tomorrow pubs will be allowed to serve drinks all afternoon on Sundays. "We are expecting some increased trade, but don't think it will be dramatic," commented Ansells, the pubs arm of Allied Domecq. "We don't see this as the great fightback by the pub, but it will help to create a more level playing field. It will give more flexibility and should be good for the tourist trade."

That is certainly the experience of T. E. Dingwalls in Camden, north London, which has been opening all day on Sunday since the start of May after a handful of pubs in the area were liberated under the terms of the 1964 Licensing Act, which gives greater flexibility to premises around market areas.

"It's been absolutely crazy," said Paul Lewis, deputy manager of the pub which led the campaign by Camden hostelries for their new found freedom.

"Customers are coming out of other pubs at closing time and then heading for us. It's all tourists and we are making an absolute fortune. You can safely say that in the extra three hours we are doubling our take."

Mr Lewis accepts, however, that his pub, owned by Regent Inns, may be lucky. It has a large beer terrace overlooking Camden Lock – with temperatures topping 90 degrees in the centre of London it is little wonder that parched tourists find their way to his oasis.

Camra, the Campaign for Real Ale whose beer festival is under way, argues that extended Sunday opening will make little difference to overall beer sales, which account for almost £14 billion a year, although average consumption has fallen from 200.4 pints a year in 1989 to 180 pints today.

"I don't think it will alter demand significantly," said a Camra spokesman. "When all-day opening was introduced in 1988, people drank more in the first couple of weeks and there was a kind of euphoria. But that soon died down and consumption has remained static."

A similar experience was true in Scotland, where fears of drunks carousing through Glasgow on a Sunday afternoon have not materialised.

"It's a return to normality," said Ben Petersen, manager of the Continental-style Harry's Cafe and Wine bar on Quayside in

BOX 10.6

Cambridge. "After all, we're open all day the other six days of the week. People just don't understand why they can't get a drink on Sunday afternoons.

"I'm expecting to increase sales by anything between one and two thousand pounds if Saturday is anything to go by, and that's quite an improvement."

At a table by the window, looking out over the River Cam, a group celebrating a wedding sit with a few glasses of wine and some beer. They work in catering and Sunday afternoon is their only chance to go to the pub together. However, they have no plans to guzzle more.

"We might go out on a Sunday if it's nice, rather than staying in with a bottle of wine, but really we'll just drink differently," said one of the revellers.

So are the pubs heading for an experience similar to that of the high street, where Sunday opening has meant almost no rise in overall income but groups like Marks & Spencer have to spread six days of sales over seven days of overheads?

Will the industry find itself backtracking on a potential opportunity, as bookmakers such as Ladbrokes have done with their decision to keep all their betting shops shut on the next two Sunday racing days after only six Sundays' experience?

Or will the industry surprise itself and register a significant increase in business which spreads beyond chocolate-box-style venues on pretty waterfronts and lasts longer than the few brief weeks of summer?

Martin Robinson, marketing director of Scottish & Newcastle, which has experience of longer opening hours north of the border, says he expects a mixed outcome. The company will be opening about two-thirds of its managed estate tomorrow. Large outlets in top tourist destinations such as Covent Garden, London, are expected to increase their take by up to £5,000, but this is untypical. A popular country

pub with a potential tourist catchment might see £1,000 of extra business, but some of the "community" pubs which S&N will also keep open are unlikely to see any increase in trade at all.

"In many of our community pubs, customers are on a fixed budget and are likely to spend the same in three hours as they normally do in two and that makes the economics of staying open less attractive to us," Mr Robinson said.

Up in the Baron of Beef, on Cambridge's Bridge Street, landlord Dave Westwood is expecting a 25 per cent increase in overall takings on Sundays. "I suppose we'll get an extra £100 in drink sales and another £200 from food," he predicted.

Next door in the Mitre Tavern, which a board on the wall proclaims has been a licensed house since 1755, manager Martin Tinkler doesn't expect the new arrangements to make any great difference to him. He already has a restaurant licence.

"The only difference it's going to make to us is that we'll stop doing the table service and serve food at the bar like every other day of the week," he said.

The Brewers and Licensed Retailers Association predicts that although some pubs will benefit, particularly when the weather is sunny, overall consumption is unlikely to reverse its slow downward trend. "It is more a question of customer expectation," said a spokesman.

"People now expect to be able to drink when they want to without having to eat a meal."

Whitbread, whose Brewers' Fayre pub restaurants already open all day Sundays, claims there is a bottleneck at many ordinary pubs on Sunday lunch-times and thinks traditional outlets will benefit, if from nothing else, from an end to the confusion over which pubs are allowed to stay open and for how long. Whitbread Inns also reckons to do about 40 per cent of its business at weekends. Managing

BOX 10.6

director Wess Van Riemsdijk commented: "All day Sunday opening, combined with children's certificates, is bringing pubs into the modern age, allowing them to compete on an equal footing in the leisure market."

Pubs and pub restaurants are already the most popular venue for Sunday lunch — accounting for about 50 per cent of the total market — and the big groups clearly think there is more to play for. But overheads will increase and margins could worsen, particularly as many pubs which plan to remain open on Sunday afternoons will be providing more food (less profitable than drink) and could sell a lower margin mix of beverages.

Pub owners, however, maintain that the increase in costs will not be too steep. Employees already tend to remain on the premises until about 4.30pm, closing up after the lunchtime session, and will return again at about 6.30pm to prepare to re-open. Even at Sunday rates, most part-time bar staff are none too handsomely rewarded, which allows executives such as Mr Robinson to claim that "costs will not increase by as much as you might think".

Although pubs are showing some restraint in their predictions for Sunday opening, there is clearly a hope that it will not only improve their competitive edge against other leisure pastimes such as sport, cinemas and rival restaurants but will allow them a tilt at clawing back some of the business they are losing to drinking at home.

From their vantage point in the Eagle's window seat, near the Cambridge Corn Exchange, six American women shake their heads when asked if they understand the licensing laws.

Sundays may be simpler from now on, but there is still plenty to keep the foreigners guessing.

"I'm kind of surprised at how early your pubs close during the week," said Megan Cooper. At home in Cincinnati she and her friends don't go out to a bar until 10.30pm or 11pm.

Source: Guardian (5 August 1995).

TASK 10.4   Analyse the economic effects of the change in Sunday licensing laws.

This again could open up an opportunity for a local investigation to try to judge the impact of the change of law after it has had time to be accepted by pub owners and customers.

A major shock: the National Lottery

One novel change to the British life style has been the introduction of the National Lottery. When first introduced, the main motive seemed to be a desire to raise more money for good causes; those kinds of worthwhile activities which government funds were just too tight to cover. But its impact has been far greater. Box 10.7 gives some information about the effects of the introduction of the Lottery.

BOX 10.7

THE NATIONAL LOTTERY
A magnet for the nation's loose change

A recent study indicates annual spending on the game will exceed £3bn. Diane Coyle reports

Just as the Great Wall of China is big enough to be seen in satellite photographs, the phenomenon of the National Lottery can be spotted as a bulge in Britain's economic statistics.

According to new official figures, the lottery added about 0.2 per cent to total consumer spending in its first six weeks – equivalent to about £200m in extra spending, and big enough to make a noticeable contribution of 0.1 per cent to economic growth in the final quarter of 1994.

The detailed Henley Centre study reports that on an annualised basis, spending of just over £3bn on the lottery amounts to almost 1 per cent of incomes after essential spending, such as tax and housing costs.

This is equivalent to £2.59 a household every week.

*Source: **Independent on Sunday** (26 March 1995).*

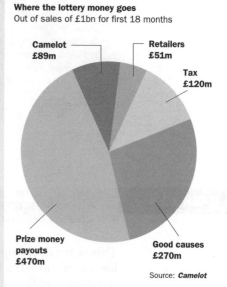

Where the lottery money goes
Out of sales of £1bn for first 18 months

Camelot £89m

Retailers £51m

Tax £120m

Prize money payouts £470m

Good causes £270m

Source: *Camelot*

BOX 10.8

The Lottery: WHAT WE SPEND

- Sales exceed £1 for every UK citizen in the lottery's first 10 weeks.
- It is estimated 58 per cent will play every week and a further 6 per cent at least once a month. The average spend is £2.08 per head.
- Sales from the draw are expected to reach £3.1 billion in year one, with sales of £4 billion by 1997. Scratch cards are expected to raise at least £1 billion a year.
- Two groups with relatively high discretionary incomes, the 25–34 pre-family group and the 45–59 post-family group, will become key to the lottery's success.
- Before the lottery there were 15 million regular gamblers in the UK. Now there are 25 million.
- Eighty-seven per cent of prize-winners have won £10 for matching three numbers, with one-fifth reinvesting their money in more lottery tickets; 12 per cent bought gifts for their family;

20 per cent put winnings into the household budget; 20 per cent saved them.
- The lottery has created up to 12 million new shopping trips each week; sales in shops with terminals are up 20 per cent.
- Foodstores have gained 5,000 customers per week; confectionery, tobacconists, newsagents and convenience stores 2,700.
- Saturday night TV-viewing has risen by 20 per cent because of the BBC1 draw programme.
- Pools firm takings have fallen by 10–15 per cent a week and Saturday bingo attendances are down.
- Charities expect donations to drop by £172 million.

Source: Lottery Fallout (Henley Centre and GAH Partnership, £1,250)

*Source: **Guardian** (22 March 1995).*

So a disproportionate amount of lottery junkies come from lower income households – and if the British experience follows that of established lotteries, the game's appeal will become concentrated on a core of committed regular players.

It is the nightmare scenario espoused in advance by the lottery's critics; the poor being encouraged to waste their money to subsidise the pastimes of the rich. But the concerns of Churchmen and women and those engaged in the voluntary sector have been drowned out by the ringing of cash tills. Retailers with terminals – 15,000 across the country – are enjoying a substantial bonanza; the margin on ticket sales is only 5 per cent but it is achieved with

minimum effort. According to the marketing people, the 5 per cent achieved is "almost pure profit, which goes straight to the bottom line".

Only a handful of stores have pulled out of the lottery, despite concerns by many retailers about the level of disruption being caused by large crowds on Friday and Saturday, when 70 per cent of ticket sales take place.

Before the lottery launch, Saturday was the busiest day of the week for most retailers, accounting for 25 per cent of the week's sales. The lottery has skewed trading even more towards the weekend, with two-thirds of trade concentrated into the last two days of the week.

BOX 10.9

Charities warn OF £57M LOSS AS DONORS TURN TO THE LOTTERY

Andrew Culf
Media Correspondent

Charities are warning they face a net loss of £57 million income this year because of the effects of the National Lottery.

Charitable donations have fallen from 81 per cent of the population to 67 per cent during the first 20 weeks of the lottery, the National Council for Voluntary Organisations says.

An NOP survey discovered that the most popular fund-raising methods, raffle ticket sales and street collections, have dropped from 32 per cent of the population to 17 per cent and from 32 per cent to 23 per cent respectively.

Source: *Guardian* (31 March 1995).

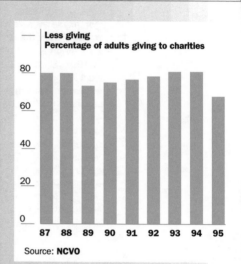

Less giving
Percentage of adults giving to charities

Source: **NCVO**

Lottery IMPACT COSTS POOLS JOBS

Dan Atkinson and Stephen Bates

Britain's second-largest pools company, Vernons, is losing 95 jobs at its Liverpool head office in response to a 15 per cent crash in revenue caused by the National Lottery.

Source: *Guardian* (26 January 1995).

BOX 10.9

Cinema CROWD THINS OUT

In 1994, attendances were up another 10 per cent, having risen 10 per cent the previous year.

Figures for the first quarter of this year tell a different story, however. After climbing 11.9 per cent in January on the same period a year ago, audiences fell 22 per cent in February and 33.3 per cent in March. For the first quarter as a whole, they were down 17.5 per cent. The decline continues, with the most recent figure for April, released last week, down 11.5 per cent.

So far this year, cinema attendance is running at an average of 2.14 million admissions a week, from 2.59 million a week in 1994. One possible scapegoat is the National Lottery. John Wilkinson, of the Cinema Exhibitors Association, says that scratch card punters have a similar profile to cinema customers, although he admits the link is unproven.

*Source: **Independent on Sunday** (28 May 1995).*

TASK 10.5

1 Identify which markets have been affected by the introduction of the Lottery.
2 What have been the economic effects of the Lottery? (Think about other product markets and factor markets.)
3 Do you feel that there is any need for changes to be made in the way the Lottery is run or how its funds are distributed? (Think about this question from different points of view: Camelot's, the Government's, the ticket sellers', the ticket buyers', charities and other businesses affected by the Lottery.) Explain the thinking behind your answer.

Governments and markets

The Government plays a direct role in many important markets. Some of these will be considered in Chapter 11 but we will look at one of its interventions now to illustrate the point that markets are interdependent.

An interest rate is a price paid for the use of money. If banks or building societies want to persuade you to deposit your money with them they need to offer you a return or interest rate. If people want to borrow money from a bank they will be asked to pay a rate of interest, a price to use the money. In the economy there is a whole structure of interest rates and the level at which these are set is determined by the Government's monetary policy. The Chancellor of the Exchequer has a monthly meeting with the Governor of the Bank of England to decide whether there will be any change in rates of interest. If rates are pushed up then this will affect all other rates around the banking system.

Now let's track through what the impact of a rise in interest rates might be.

Interest rates rise.

↓

This raises other interest rates such as the rates paid to savers and the rates demanded of borrowers.

↓

Savings rise and borrowing falls.

↓

The level of consumption or aggregate demand in the economy falls and this affects the markets for a range of consumer products.

↓

With demand rising more slowly, firms find it harder to raise prices so the rate of inflation slows.

↓

At the same time lower levels of demand require firms to cut costs if profits are to increase. Firms shed labour to improve efficiency and unemployment rises. This further decreases the level of aggregate demand and unemployment rises again. The labour market has been affected.

↓

Mortgage interest rates also rise so the cost of borrowing to buy a house increases. This affects the housing market.

↓

This reduces the demand for houses which also hits the demand for house-related products such as carpets, curtains and furniture.

↓

House prices rise more slowly or even fall. This could contribute to people feeling less well off and causes consumption to fall further. The markets for consumer goods are affected further.

Rising interest rates could make it more attractive for money to be placed on deposit in the UK so banks and multi-national firms move money into British banks. This is known as 'hot' money.

A rising demand for the pound sterling causes the price of the pound to rise. The exchange rate appreciates. The foreign exchange market is affected.

A rising pound causes export prices to rise and import prices to fall making it more difficult for firms to sell their goods abroad. Imports now seem more attractive so more will be bought. Britain's balance of payments (a record of all transactions between the UK and the rest of the world) worsens.

More imports mean that firms selling on the home market face more competition. This could lead to a further loss of jobs. Alternatively it could force UK firms to become more efficient. They must do if they are to survive.

As these effects begin to take effect, the Government may decide that interest rates can be allowed to fall a little and this will spark off changes to a wide range of markets. Managing the economy is a complex balancing act.

The point is that a change in one market (the money market) had an important effect on the consumer goods market, the housing market, the labour market, the market for the pound sterling and the markets for imports and exports. All of these markets were interdependent and governments need to appreciate the level of interdependence which exists when making policy changes. This movement in markets is a constant feature of a dynamic market economy. More extensive coverage of the relationship between policy changes and the economy will be considered in Sections 4 and 5.

REVIEW

Changes in the forces of demand and supply affect individual markets and the prices prevailing in those markets. However, to understand how a market economy works we need to remember that markets are not isolated. Changes in one market will affect others and it is by understanding the links between markets that we can begin to predict the changes that might occur in an economy following a given shock.

REVIEW TASK

The Net Book Agreement (NBA) was a voluntary agreement between book sellers and book publishers in the UK and Ireland to sell books at the price recommended and stated on each book by the publisher. It meant that, whether you BOUGHT a book in W.H. Smith or a small local book shop, you would pay the same price. There has been some pressure by some book sellers and the Office of Fair Trading to end the NBA.

Box 10.10 gives an extract from some material printed by The Booksellers Association putting the case for retention of the NBA.

BOX 10.10

Books – worth fighting for
We get education, knowledge and enjoyment from books.
Book buyers today can choose from over 500,000 titles on just about any subject under the sun: from novels to poetry, gardening to nuclear physics.
Over 3,300 bookshops in towns and cities all over Britain offer a huge range of choice and specialist services.
Many are among the best in the world.
Britain is acknowleged as having a world class publishing industry, producing outstanding books at reasonable prices.
Fight for choice
This rich diversity is only made possible because of the NET BOOK AGREEMENT, the mechanism that stimulates competition between publishing firms and also between booksellers, while ensuring that a book will cost the same price wherever you shop.
The NBA is a VOLUNTARY arrangement which allows each publisher to decide the prices at which its books are sold.
Because booksellers know their competitors are not permitted to discount net books, they are encouraged to stock the widest selection of titles, making more books available.
Fight for value
The NBA has worked well to promote value and choice over nearly a century. Now a few short sighted economists and journalists want you to believe that without the NBA, books would be cheaper.

Source: *The Booksellers' Association* (1995).

TASK 10.6

1 What is the case given in support of retaining the NBA?
2 Explain how you would expect the market for books to be affected by the ending of the NBA.
3 How might other markets be affected by the change in the market for books?
4 The first steps in the abolition of the NBA occurred on 1 October 1995 when W.H. Smith and Dillons began to offer big discounts on a range of best sellers. Economists predicted the following:

● W.H. Smith, which sells 25 per cent of all consumer books in the UK, would lose £7 million from profits.
● The effect of the abolition of the NBA would hit W.H. Smith harder because Dillons is owned by Thorn EMI, the electrical giant.
● There will be a bloody price war. Bankruptcies are inevitable — and probably on a large scale.
● The big book publishers will get bigger and the large bookselling chains will get larger.

Explain and analyse the economic thinking behind each of these statements.

QUESTION

Multiple choice

'If the price of Good **X** rises, demand falls; then after demand falls, the price of Good **X** falls. Therefore price returns to its original level.'

This statement is
A true, because it suggests that Good **X** follows the law of demand
B true, because it shows that price eventually settles at equilibrium
C false, because Good **X** might be an inferior good, and so would not follow the law of demand
D false, because it confuses movements along and shifts of a demand curve.

(IB, May 1995, Higher)

2.11 How do markets affect the UK?

The housing market

Housing white paper backs couples but raises fears for most vulnerable

Gummer LAUNCHES PUSH TO EXTEND HOME OWNERSHIP

Source: *Guardian* (26 June 1995).

NUMBER OF EMPTY HOMES HITS *500,000*

Source: *Guardian* (12 April 1995).

GARDEN FLAT
FOR SALE
Winkworth
0181-788 9295

FOCUS

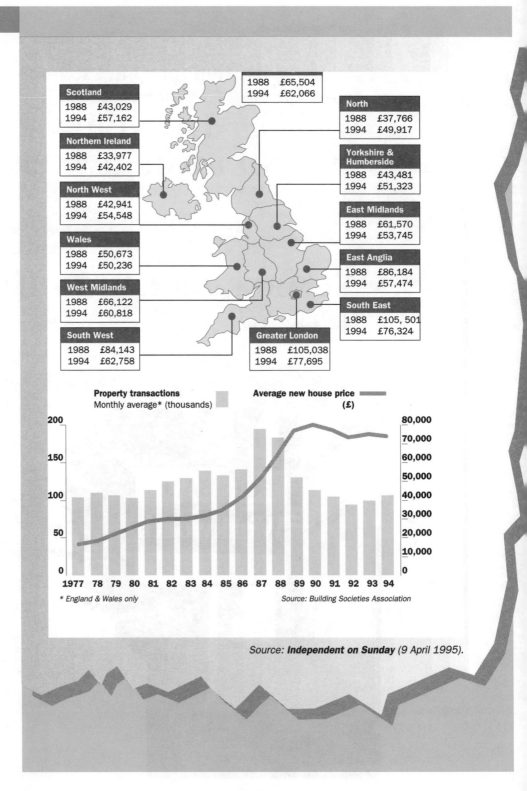

Scotland
| 1988 | £43,029 |
| 1994 | £57,162 |

1988 £65,504
1994 £62,066

North
| 1988 | £37,766 |
| 1994 | £49,917 |

Northern Ireland
| 1988 | £33,977 |
| 1994 | £42,402 |

Yorkshire & Humberside
| 1988 | £43,481 |
| 1994 | £51,323 |

North West
| 1988 | £42,941 |
| 1994 | £54,548 |

East Midlands
| 1988 | £61,570 |
| 1994 | £53,745 |

Wales
| 1988 | £50,673 |
| 1994 | £50,236 |

East Anglia
| 1988 | £86,184 |
| 1994 | £57,474 |

West Midlands
| 1988 | £66,122 |
| 1994 | £60,818 |

South East
| 1988 | £105, 501 |
| 1994 | £76,324 |

South West
| 1988 | £84,143 |
| 1994 | £62,758 |

Greater London
| 1988 | £105,038 |
| 1994 | £77,695 |

Property transactions
Monthly average* (thousands)

Average new house price
(£)

200
150
100
50
0

80,000
70,000
60,000
50,000
40,000
30,000
20,000
10,000
0

1977 78 79 80 81 82 83 84 85 86 87 88 89 90 91 92 93 94

* England & Wales only

Source: Building Societies Association

Source: **Independent on Sunday** (9 April 1995).

FOCUS

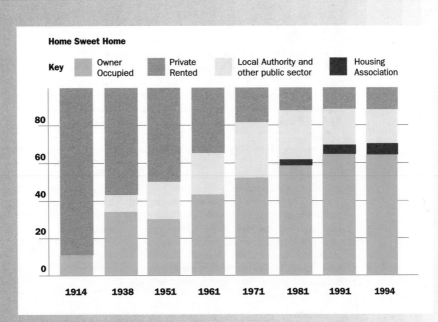

Home Sweet Home

Source: *Guardian* (12 April 1995).

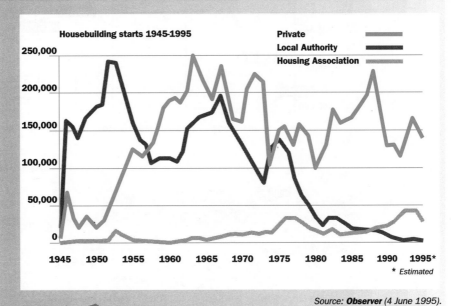

Source: *Observer* (4 June 1995).

Negative Equity: THE ROLLERCOASTER TO HELL

The Tory Government's ideal of creating a home-owning democracy has been shaken to its foundations.

Nearly 1,000 families a week are losing their homes while 250,000 are behind with their mortgages.

Now the Tories have given home-owners another kick in the teeth.

Chancellor Ken Clarke's decision to cut DSS payments to first-time buyers who lose their jobs after October will force homebuyers to take out costly unemployment insurance to qualify for a mortgage. It could add £30 a month to a £60,000 repayment mortgage.

Around one million homeowners will not even qualify for cover, because they're on short-term contracts or are not in perfect health.

Here we chart how Jon and Julia Camden's house in South Norwood, Surrey, rose and then slumped in price.

We also suggest ways of escaping the negative equity trap by improving your home or switching to a more flexible mortgage package.

Mirror Money will keep fighting on your behalf so if you've got problem with negative equity write to: NEGATIVE EQUITY, Mirror Money, 1 Canada Square, Canary Wharf, London E14 5AP.

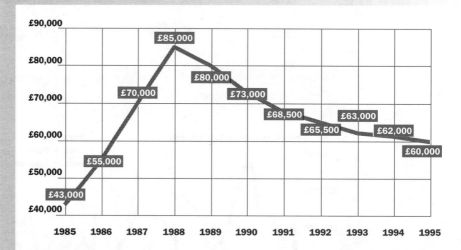

Source: **Daily Mirror** (13 June 1995).

Mortgage MISERY

More than a million home-owners trapped by negative equity are desperate for some relief from the nightmare of falling house prices.

TASK 11.1

1. What are the problems which have been seen in the housing market in recent yrears?
2. What is meant by 'negative equity' and how are families affected by it?
3. Should the government do anything about negative equity? If so, what? Here you need to justify yourself using economic arguments.

Preview

In this chapter we shall investigate the following key areas:

- the housing market;
- the markets for agricultural products;
- the Single European Market;
- the money market.

Markets are a central feature of market economies. Some markets are of particular importance to the UK economy and this chapter will investigate some of these.

The housing market: What causes house prices to change?

We all need somewhere to live. The housing market is therefore important to us as individuals but also important to the economy as a whole. Spending on housing is one of the main items of expenditure of families. A house is the most expensive item a person will ever buy and, for most people, a house is where the bulk of their wealth is kept. A well housed population will be a healthier population and a roof over our heads is one of those basic rights we have all come to expect.

Focus 2.11 raises some of the important questions which arise out of any investigation of the housing market. Why is a government minister promoting home ownership when we have one of the highest ownership ratios in the EU? What is the significance of the different forms of home ownership? Why are fewer people buying houses today than in the 1970s? Why have house prices fallen? Why are more than a million people in negative equity, and what does this mean? If there is a shortage of housing and 800,000 people homeless, why are there 850,000 houses lying empty? Why has house building (particularly local authority house building) slumped in recent years? Why do house prices vary so much between one region and another?

First it is vital to understand what kind of a market the housing market is.

What are the characteristics of the housing market?

- Houses are not homogeneous products. All houses and flats are, to an extent, individual – though some are more individual than others.
- Houses are immobile and cannot be moved around. If there is a shortage of housing in one part of the country, houses cannot be rolled in from somewhere else.
- Houses are bought for the service they provide, i.e. somewhere to live, but they are also bought as a form of saving in that house owners hope that the value of their property will increase over time.
- New houses represent a very small proportion of the total housing stock. There are 24 million houses in the country and, at present, about 180,000 new houses are built each year (just under 1% of all houses are therefore new). Most of the market is a second hand market. People like buying old houses.
- The buyers of houses are also the sellers of houses. When buying a house, most people are selling their own house although there are always a group of first-time house buyers.
- Most purchases of houses are financed by borrowing long term

through mortgages. A mortgage is a special type of loan where the lender, normally a building society or a bank, retains ownership of the property as security for the loan. Most lenders will allow borrowers to take out loans 2–3 times their annual salary.
- The rented housing sector provides an acceptable substitute for the owner occupied sector so these two markets are likely to be highly interdependent. The rented sector has been in decline in recent years.
- There are major transaction costs every time a house changes hands. These include estate agents' and solicitors' fees as well as the actual costs of removal.
- The housing market is politically sensitive and attracts the intervention of governments in a variety of ways. The government, through local authorities, has been a major provider of housing and has encouraged home ownership through giving tax incentives.
- The complexity of the market makes it extremely difficult for buyers or sellers to feel that they have anything approaching perfect knowledge of the market.

What factors affect the demand for and supply of housing?

Since the buyers of houses are also the suppliers of housing, we can list a series of factors which will affect decisions to buy or sell.

Price and price expectations

As with other products, we might expect the demand for houses to increase as prices fall but so much depends on people's expectations about the future movement of prices. If prices fall it will be cheaper to buy a house but if people expect prices to fall further they will put off buying now and wait until prices have fallen further.

As prices rise we might expect more people to want to sell in order to make a profit on their property. However, this may not happen, because people need somewhere to live and so would need to buy somewhere else which would now be more expensive. There is a paper rather than a real profit to be made.

If prices are expected to rise, people will be looking to move into the property market. Any decision to delay will mean that it will be more difficult to buy in the future. If prices are rising faster than the inflation rate there is a great incentive to move savings into housing rather than into some lower yielding form of saving. In a rising market people will be looking to trade up their house and to move into better accommodation. Expectations of house price rises would also increase supply since people wanting to move would have to supply before they could buy. The market would generally be more buoyant with more transactions completed.

Higher prices will stimulate more building of new houses as construction firms do see the prospect of increased profits. But because the number of new houses represents such a small proportion of the total housing stock, the costs of building a house have little to do with the final price.

Box 11.1 represents the housing market. We can present the market using a simple demand and supply diagram where the equilibrium price equals OP_1. Any change in one of the conditions of demand could be shown by a shift in the demand curve to D_2 or D_1, causing price to rise or fall. However, the particular characteristics of the market make this diagram of limited use and only suitable to analyse the general trends affecting house prices.

BOX 11.1

The price of houses

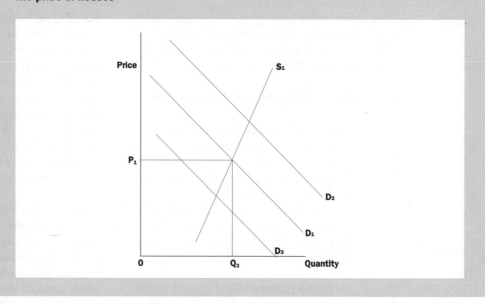

TASK 11.2

Use Box 11.1 to show what you would expect to happen to the prices of houses if
A   there was a massive programme to build 1 million houses a year;
B   there was an expectation that house prices would fall;
C   another half million homes become empty.

The price of substitutes

Houses will have close substitutes in the form of other houses. Unlike in other markets, house buyers often prefer to buy used or second hand houses and so these are a very close substitute for new houses. This contrasts with other markets such as the markets for shoes and socks, where there is very little demand for used products and a second hand sock is not seen as a good substitute for a new sock.

The demand for owned property will be strongly influenced by the market for rented accommodation. If rents are high then people will wish to buy houses whereas if rents are low, they may wish to rent instead. There must be a close link between the rented and the bought markets. Look at Box 11.2

BOX 11.2

The bought and rented markets

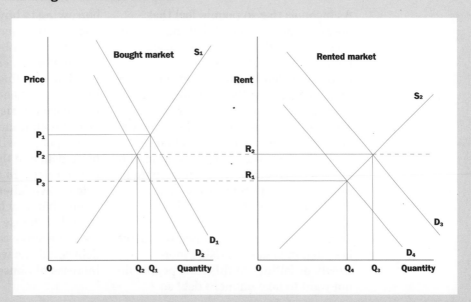

Box 11.2 shows the markets for bought and rented houses. We need to remember that buying, as opposed to renting, brings with it additional transaction costs such as the costs of estate agents and solicitors as well as search time. The diagrams show that the cost of renting a house per month at **OR$_1$** is cheaper than buying a house which would cost **OP$_1$** per month. If this was the situation, we would expect more people to want to rent property. This would shift the demand curve for rented property to the right and cause average rents to rise to **OR$_2$**. At the same time the demand for owner occupied houses would fall from **D$_1$** to **D$_2$**, causing the cost of buying a house to fall to **OP$_2$**. So the cost of renting and buying should move together towards an equilibrium position. In practice, rents will remain above mortgage repayment costs due to the importance of the transactions costs. Many people do not want to be tied down by these costs which will also include the costs of decoration and maintenance which, in rented property, remain the responsibility of the landlord.

Incomes

As incomes rise so people feel that they can spend some of that increase on housing. The demand for houses is highly income elastic. Finance institutions lending mortgages normally relate the amount they are prepared to lend to the income of the borrower. They will lend perhaps 2.5 or 3 times a person's income. This means that a rise in income of £1,000 per year might allow a person to borrow £3000 extra to put into house purchase, giving a considerable boost to demand.

During recessions when unemployment is rising, incomes are rising more slowly or falling. At this time people do not want to take on more debt so borrowing to buy houses decreases. People experiencing difficulties may wish to sell their house to boost their personal finances but they will face the problem that there will be few buyers in the market and selling a house will not be easy. If rising unemployment brings with it more job insecurity then, again, people will not wish to accept more debt and this will feed through to house prices. In the 1990s when house prices have fallen, many people have found that they have borrowed more than their house is now worth – they are in negative equity. This makes their debt problems worse and has led to an increase of house repossessions.

Interest rates

The amount people are prepared to borrow is greatly dependent upon the monthly payments required. Any increase in interest rates increases the monthly payments from a mortgage and will discourage people from borrowing so much money. This will exert downward pressure on house prices. However, if interest rates fall, borrowing becomes more attractive and demand for houses may increase.

Availability

If banks and building societies make more money available to finance house purchases the demand for houses will be boosted. De-regulation of the housing finance market in the 1980s led to an explosion of mortgage lending. Competition between banks and building societies meant that they were falling over themselves to lend and this, consequently, fuelled a major rise in house prices. In the past banks have seen mortgages as a fairly safe form of lending since it carries the security of the house.

Tax relief

The government has encouraged house purchase through giving buyers tax relief on the interest on the debt. This means that if you have a £30,000 loan at 10% interest you will be expected to pay £3,000 interest each year. The government has chosen to encourage home ownership by subsidising house buyers by giving tax relief. On an interest payment of £3,000 borrowers can claim back 15% in the form of a tax rebate. This represents a government subsidy of £450. This kind of financial inducement is not available for any other kind of loan and does encourage house buying. Any reduction in the level of tax allowance given will make it more expensive to borrow and hit the housing market.

Selecting one kind of borrowing to qualify for special tax treatment does distort the market and is a move away from free markets. Hence, advocates of free markets argue for the removal of this subsidy, but this would undoubtedly hit the housing market. If the housing market is in decline many other sectors of the UK economy are affected and, certainly, the political prospects of the government are damaged.

Population

People tend to buy houses at a particular time in their lives: between their 20s and 40s. If there are more people in those age groups then the demand for houses is likely to be higher. More single-parent families and old people will increase the demand for certain kinds of housing.

Box 11.3 gives some information about what has been happening in the housing market in recent years.

BOX 11.3

Changes in the housing market

House prices set to drop again

Every time one housing expert makes a prediction that house prices are about to rise and sellers hold on to wait for the recovery, down they go again. Since 1990 more than 300,000 houses have been repossessed and over 1 million people live in 'negative equity'.

There seems to have been a government plot against home owners in recent years.

The 1980s saw the government's enthusiasm for a property owning democracy bearing fruit. Council house sales had been a roaring success. De-regulation of the financial markets meant that the banks were now given the freedom to pump money into the mortgage sector and home loans jumped from about £26 billion per year to over £40 billion. Tax cuts kept the fire burning and the house price boom looked as though it would continue forever.

But the decision of the Government to enter the ERM at a high rate for the pound required interest rates to be pushed up to record levels just as the Government was reducing the tax subsidy to home owners in order to produce a freer market. Rising unemployment in the recession of the early 1990s started to affect the middle classes as firms restructured. Changing working patterns produced a far less secure work force and the demand for houses collapsed.

Living with falling house prices is a painful experience for many households who long for the days of leaping house prices to return.

TASK 11.3

1 Describe the trend in house prices in recent years.
2 What factors account for the trend you have identified?
3 Explain why
   A similar houses command different prices in different parts of the country and
   B different regions have experienced different rates of house price inflation.
4 What effects might falling house prices have on the rest of the UK economy?
5 If the government wished to stimulate the prices of houses, what policy options might it be able to use?

The housing market is a very important market for the UK economy. The building industry is still a labour-intensive industry and so when the industry expands, jobs are created and this helps the whole economy to expand. People have most of their wealth tied up in housing and so when house prices are rising they feel wealthier which is likely to release more spending. However, rising house prices can lead to inflation which governments attempt to keep in check. The main method of controlling inflation has been interest rates, and any change here directly has an impact upon the housing market.

Agricultural markets

The markets for food products should, theoretically, approach the model of perfect competition. There are large numbers of buyers and sellers, the product is homogeneous, competition should be by price, firms are price takers and it is quite possible for farmers to enter or leave markets by planting more or less crops on their land.

Reality is different. In fact, agriculture is one of the most heavily controlled industries largely through the existence of the Common Agricultural Policy (CAP) of the EU. Agriculture tends to be an unstable industry. The demand for food is relatively inelastic – we eat more or less the same amount of food as prices move up or down. The supply of food is also highly inelastic – once a crop is harvested supply cannot change even if prices change. Agricultural yields are determined to a great extent by weather conditions and so the supply curve may shift from year to year. The market for a food product is shown in Box 11.4.

BOX 11.4

The market for an agricultural product

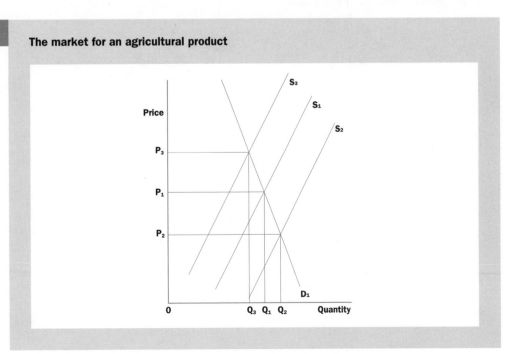

In Box 11.4 the effect of the supply curve shifting to S_2 in a year of good harvests and S_3 in a year of bad harvests is that price fluctuates wildly, causing farmers' incomes to fluctuate wildly. In bad years when growing conditions are poor, many farmers could decide to leave the land; in good years when crop yields may be high, prices may be so low that farmers could still decide to leave the the land. Consumers may be faced with shortages and high prices one year and abundance and low prices the next.

Farmers have always been a very influential group within the European Community (EC). There probably would have been no European Community without the support of the farmers. After the deprivation of the Second World War, member states believed that it was in all our interests to stabilise prices, guarantee farmers a reasonable income and to safeguard food supplies. To do this, some intervention system was required.

The Cobweb theory

Further instability comes from the way in which farmers adjust their use of land to changing product prices. Farmers will make decisions about the allocation of their land to different crops based on previous year's prices and price expectations. Once planted, a crop cannot be changed mid-season. There will be a supply regardless of the price at the time when the crop is harvested. The market for a food product is shown in Box 11.5.

The Cobweb

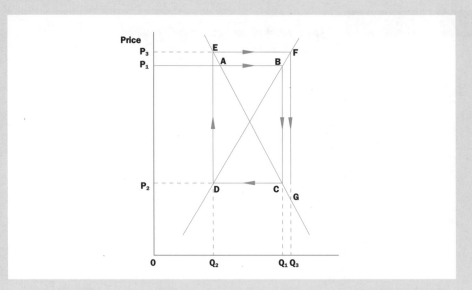

Farmers expected the price of the product to be $0P_1$ (see Box 11.4) and had decided to supply $0Q_1$. The price they were expecting was not an equilibrium price and demand was only P_1A at that price. To sell $0Q_1$ the farmers would have to lower price to $0P_2$ because the demand curve indicates that this is the price needed to stimulate this level of demand. This price will then affect the farmers' decisions for the next year. At a price of $0P_2$ the farmers would plan to produce $0Q_2$ but, if the demand curve retains its position from the previous year, there is now excess demand over supply and price will be forced up through competition from buyers to $0P_3$. It is this price which will affect planting decisions for the next year when supply will rise to P_3F. The process of instability continues tracing the cobweb ABCDEFG and so on. The price fails to settle at an equilibrium level and further instability is caused.

The role of the Common Agricultural Policy – does the CAP fit?

The central idea of the CAP was to set target prices which would guarantee even the less efficient farmers of the EC a reasonable income. The prices for different crops would be set so that farmers could make informed decisions about planting. If the market price failed to reach the target price all of the countries of the EC, acting through the CAP, would buy up any surpluses and store them. If the intervention prices were above world prices for the products, a levy or tax was placed upon non-EC goods to raise their prices at least to the level of EC produce. Look at Box 11.6.

BOX 11.6

The effect of the CAP

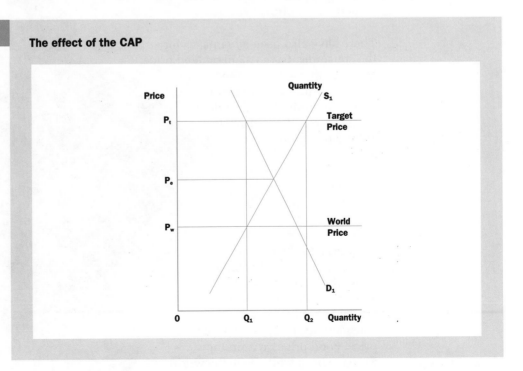

In Box 11.6 D_1 and S_1 represent the demand and supply curves of an agricultural product within the EU. P_e is the equilibrium price in the market but the target price is set at P_t. P_t is a minimum price below which price is not allowed to fall. Consumers will only wish to buy $0Q_1$ at that price and so there will be a surplus of Q_1Q_2 on the market. This will be bought by the EU. $0P_w$ is the world price for the product and so a levy equal to P_wP_t is placed on imports from outside the EU.

The advantages to farmers were that their income was stabilised, price rises were given each year to secure rising incomes, farmers were kept on the land (very important in the rural parts of the EU) and away from the areas of high unemployment in the urban areas. Farmers are a politically important group within many of the EU countries and keeping their support has been essential for political success.

There have also been advantages for the consumer. Given a guaranteed price, farmers have seen that the way to increase profits is to increase output and this they have done magnificently. From 1970 to 1990 cereal production almost doubled, oil seed rape and sugar increased by 50% and milk production by 25%. This has secured food supplies and the EU is at least self-sufficient in staple agricultural products. Variety and choice of food products available has increased considerably. But there has been a price. Food prices within the EU have been well above the world prices which has increased the cost of

living for every family. The food surpluses have cost a lot to finance.

The cost of running this policy always gives concern. In 1993 49.3% of all EU spending, or about $130 billion, was used to support agriculture and this money had to be raised from the levies imposed on imported products and 1% of the revenue raised from VAT. This has pushed up prices elsewhere for consumers.

In addition, whenever the surpluses were sold off on world markets they had to be subsidised to bring them below the world price.

Concern about the rising cost of the CAP has encouraged members to review the policy with the intention of cutting its cost. The demand for

(© UN)

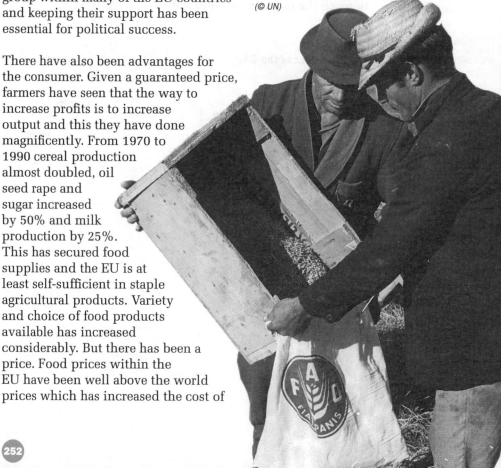

food has been steady over the years whilst production has increased by approximately 2% per year causing food surpluses to grow. Reforms have been put in place. Prices are to be controlled or reduced, e.g. cereal prices will fall by 30% between 1993 and 1996. Cereal producers are being paid to take up to 15% of their land out of production in so-called 'set aside'. The actual effect on the market may be less than anticipated. Farmers will take their least productive pieces of land out of production and then may farm what is left even more intensively so that crop yields will not fall by much.

There has also been some encouragement for farmers to adopt more environmentally friendly methods to curb the growth of yields and there is financial help for farmers leaving the land.

These changes are having an effect and the huge food mountains which built up in the 1970s and 1980s have virtually disappeared. The aim is that by 1999 the CAP will take up 45% of the EU's budget so that money can be released for other purposes such as support for the regions.
Look at Box 11.7.

BOX 11.7

CAP data

Cereal yields 1970—90 (100 kg/hectare)

Country	1970	1990
Germany	33.4	57.9
France	33.8	60.7
Italy	26.9	38.4
Netherlands	37.6	69.3
Belgium	33.6	59.7

Agricultural output as a % of GDP

Country	1973	1990
Germany	2.51	1.11
France	6.13	2.81
Greece	16.96	11.71
Ireland	15.76	7.2
Spain	8.93	3.99
Portugal	7.26	4.07
UK	2.44	1.16

Source: **Eurostat** data.

TASK 11.4

1 Using diagrams, explain how you might expect the reforms to the CAP to affect the markets for agricultural products.
2 Argue the case for the CAP from the point of view of a farmer in rural France and the case against the CAP from the point of view of a British consumer.

The Single European Market (SEM)

The SEM was ratified in Britain by the Single European Act of 1987 and was signed on behalf of the UK by Prime Minister Thatcher. The aim was to produce a single market within the EU from 1 January 1993 and to guarantee the four freedoms:

- the free movement of people;
- the free movement of goods;
- the free movement in services;
- the free movement of capital.

The EC had been established as a customs union in 1957. This meant that internal trade barriers between member countries were scrapped and all the members adopted a common strategy towards trade with countries outside the customs union. A single Common External Tariff (CET) was imposed on goods entering the EC from other countries.

Despite this apparent free trade, there were still many national rules and regulations which effectively prevented trade from taking place. The Act required the member states to pass 280 separate pieces of legislation to draw the countries' trading systems together. Instead of passing a single set of rules, the EU has moved towards the mutual recognition of standards in each of the member states.

Alongside the development of the market, there has been a movement under the Treaty of European Union (or

Maastricht Treaty) of 1992, towards a Social Chapter and a single currency. The Social Chapter gives workers guarantees of various rights including health and safety, working conditions, consultation and minimum wages. The UK negotiated an opt out for this part of the Treaty.

This Treaty set out a deadline for the achievement of a single currency by 1999. The UK participated in the first stage and joined the Exchange Rate Mechanism (ERM). The value of the pound sterling had previously floated freely on the foreign exchange market but in 1990 it was tied into the ERM. This fixed the value of the pound at between DM2.78 and DM3.10 so a maximum and minimum price were placed upon the pound. If the pound showed signs of dropping through the floor, central banks around the EU would step in and buy the pound in order to force the price up. If the pound showed signs of pushing through the ceiling, central banks would sell the pound.

The main objectives were to achieve stability in the values of currencies and to fight inflation. Unfortunately, for the UK, the pound came under enormous pressure, interest rates had to raised heftily but eventually the selling pressure was too great and the pound's membership of the ERM had to be suspended. Look at Box 11.8.

BOX 11.8

The single currency

Experts divided ON WORTH OF EUROPEAN MONETARY UNION

Two reports have ignited the single currency conflict again, as Richard Thomas reports

To be, or not to be, was the question yesterday. Should the UK be part of a European single currency?

Economists, business leaders and politicians entered the fray as two reports published yesterday, the Kingsdown inquiry and a paper from the Institute of Directors, set out different views.

The first argues that Britain's interests will be damaged if we stay out. The second states the opposite.

The most contentious issue is control over monetary policy – the setting of interest rates. Lord Kingsdown, the former Governor of the Bank of England, argues that if the UK stands alone, the markets will see a door left open to devaluation of the pound, which could be seen as a last resort to help British business.

Investors, especially those in the foreign exchange markets, would demand a higher return on their holdings while joining would mean enhanced credibility and a lower cost of borrowing.

"Britain ought to be able to look forward to lower inflation and lower interest rates inside a European monetary union," he concludes.

The Institute of Directors, by contrast, argues that EMU could lead to an inappropriate stance for the UK because of structural differences between the British and continental economies. A pan-European interest rate, for instance, could be too high for Britain which, as a result of its high level of owner-occupation, is sensitive to interest-rate changes.

On the other hand, the trade structure of the UK, not so geared towards Europe as others – less than a third of our trade is with the "core" EU countries of Germany, France, Austria and Benelux – alters the effect of any change in the value of a single currency. A weaker currency stokes inflation by making imports dearer, and a higher proportion of the goods we buy from overseas are not European.

As a result, says the IoD: "A depreciation of a European single currency would amount to a greater relaxation of monetary policy in the UK." The different trade structures also mean that any reduction in transaction costs and unpredictability resulting from holding separate currencies would be less important for Britain.

The second key issue is unemployment. The IoD argues that many EU countries are simply too poor to join EMU successfully and give up the escape route of currency devaluation, without huge transfer payments to offset the social costs. This would mean higher taxes for Britain to protect, for example, the Greek labour market from the single discipline.

Any increase in transfer payments would give more power to the EU over fiscal (tax-and-spend) policy, too, the IoD argues. Monetary union would ultimately mean fiscal union — the third bone of contention — and would lead to political union.

Lord Kingsdown goes some way towards conceding this argument, but says that none of the other rich nations would want to shell out either. "To the extent that sceptics are opposed to EMU, because they fear that Britain's right to tax and spend could be pre-empted, it seems too plausible to suppose that British interests in this respect would coincide closely with those of other, responsible, hard-core countries."

In any case, the inquiry argues, the real answer to high unemployment and a low level of efficiency is to remove regulations, reduce costs on employers and encourage labour market "flexibility".

*Source: **Guardian** (9 June 1995).*

TASK 11.5

1 Produce a supply and demand diagram to explain how the ERM operated with its maximum and minimum price for the pound sterling.
2 The UK Government secured an opt out clause for membership of a single currency so that it could decide whether to join a single currency at a later date. To what extent would the creation of a single currency contribute towards the development of a single market? (Here you could think about the UK itself, which is a single market with a single currency.)
3 What will be the advantages and disadvantages of the single market to UK businesses and consumers?

A single currency would assist the development of a single market. The UK is a single market with a single currency; the USA is a single market with a single currency; the EU is attempting to become a single market but without, as yet, a single currency. However, the objective of achieving a single currency remains in place. The third stage of monetary union requires that the economies of at least six of the member states meet certain 'convergence criteria'. These cover the inflation rate (rates should be no more than 1.5% above the best three performing countries), interest rates (rates should be no more than 2% above the average of the best three performing countries), the government deficit which should be no more than 3% of GDP with total government borrowing less than 60% of GDP and exchange rates which should remain within the prescribed limits set by the European Monetary System (EMS) for two years. There is the possibility that these criteria may never be achieved by some countries, or at least not achieved for several years. This may open up a number of possibilities and hasten the establishment of a 'two-speed Europe'. Box 11.9 shows some of the countries' progress towards achieving the criteria in 1994.

BOX 11.9

The convergence criteria

Who's ready for EMU?
Meeting the Maastricht Treaty convergence criteria for monetary union

	Inflation	Long-term interest	General gov't lending (+) or borrowing (-)	General gov't gross debt %	Exchange rate stability
	Not more than 1.5% above the average of the best three. Ceiling 3.4% on 1994 figures	Not more than 2% above the average of three countries with the lowest inflation. Ceiling 9.13% on 94 figures	Public debt not exceeding 3% of GDP.	Public debt not exceeding 60% of GDP.	Two years within normal ERM margins without undue pressure. Current ERM regime not in place long enough to meet strict criteria.
1994					
Belgium	**2.4**	**7.7**	-5.5	140.1	✔
Denmark	**2.0**	**7.8**	-4.3	78.0	✔
Germany	3.0	**7.0**	**-2.9**	**51.0**	✔
Greece	10.8	20.8	-14.1	121.3	✘
Spain	4.7	10.0	-7.0	63.5	?
France	**1.6**	**7.2**	-5.6	**50.4**	✔
Ireland	**2.4**	**7.9**	**-2.4**	89.0	✔
Italy	3.9	10.6	-9.6	123.7	?
L'bourg	**2.1**	**6.4**	**1.3**	**9.2**	✔
N'lands	**2.7**	**6.9**	-3.8	78.8	✔
Portugal	5.2	10.4	-6.2	70.4	✘
UK	**2.4**	**8.1**	-6.3	**50.4**	?

Key   Pass (Bold text)   Fail (Light text)

Scoring done on basis of ignoring two year time condition.
Britain, Italy and Greece not in ERM.

*Source: **Guardian** (5 April 1995).*

TASK 11.6

Refer to Box 11.9 and also to Box 30.7
Compare the UK's performance in achieving the convergence criteria with other countries. Which countries are doing best, and which worst?

In theory, the creation of a single market should help to develop the advantages associated with free trade and free markets. There should be more competition, with companies competing on a more equal basis. Markets in any one member state will be opened up to firms from any of the other member states. However, trading in other countries may not be so easy. There are still different customs, tastes and practices which will continue to present barriers to trade. One response of businesses wanting to extend their penetration of markets is to engage in cross-union mergers. The BMW/Rover merger is perhaps the best known example of this so far. Another response is for firms to reorganise their operations to treat Europe as a single market possibly shifting the centre of gravity of the company to Brussels. Look at Box 11.10.

BOX 11.10

Is the Single Market a reality?

Much effective work can be done monitoring the impact the Single Market has had on local businesses. After the initial high profile of the development of the Single Market, less is now heard of its impact. Research could be undertaken into a particular firm or a number of firms to establish to what extent they have responded to the challenge of the Single Market. Are there tangible benefits for the consumer? Has it created jobs? Has it secured longer production runs and brought costs down?

The money market

Financial intermediaries are any financial institution which accepts deposits from savers and makes loans to borrowers

Interest rate is the price paid for money

There is a market for money because there are some people wanting to save money and some wanting to borrow. It is difficult in today's society for savers to be directly in touch with borrowers and so there is a need for number of institutions to act as financial intermediaries.

These accept deposits from those wishing to save and then lend to the borrowers. In this market there is a price which borrowers have to pay in order to be able to use somebody else's money, just as there is a price that the financial intermediaries have to pay to persuade people to deposit money with them. This price is the rate of interest.

BOX 11.11

A selection of interest rates

PERSONAL LOANS

	Telephone	APR	Fixed monthly payments £3,000 for 3 years	
Unsecured				
Midland Bank	Local branch	15.40	£116.54	£103.14
N&P BS	0800 808080	15.50	£118.22	£103.29
Yorkshire Bank	0113 231 5324	15.50	£119.34	£103.34
Secured			Max adv %	Max term
First Direct	0800 242424	10.30	80	Up to 40 years
Royal B of Scotland	0800 121121	10.90	70	3 years – retirement
Midland Bank	Local branch	11.40	80	5 to 30 years

TYPICAL OVERDRAFTS

	Telephone	Authorised EAR %	Unauthorised EAR %
Barclays Bank	Local Branch	19.20	29.80
Lloyds Bank	Local Branch	19.40	26.80
Nat West Bank	Local Branch	18.90	33.25

CREDIT CARDS

	Telephone	Card	Min income	Rate pm %	APR %	Annual fee
Standard						
R Fleming (S&P)	0800 282101	Mastercard/Visa	–	1.00	14.60	£12
Royal B of Scotland	0800 161616	Mastercard	–	1.14	14.50	–
TSB	Local branch	Mastercard/Visa	–	1.38	17.90	–

APR – *Annualised percentage rate.*   EAR – *effective annual rate.*

'Best savings rates'

	Telephone Number	Account	Notice or term	Deposit	Rate %	Interest Interval
INSTANT ACCESS						
Yorkshire BS	0800 378836	1st Cl Access	Postal	£1,000	6.05	Year
Skipton BS	01756 700511	3 High Street	Instant	£2,000	6.10	Year
Northern Rock BS	0500 505000	Go Direct	Postal	£20,000	6.70	Year
Leeds & Holbeck	0113 243 8292	Albion Inv Acc	Postal	£50,000	6.80	Year
NOTICE ACCOUNTS						
Bradford & B'ley	0345 248248	Direct Notice	30 day P	£10,000	6.65	Year
Scarborough BS	01723 368155	Scarborough 50	50 day P	£1,000	6.60	Year
Coventry BS	0345 665522	Postal 50	50 day P	£40,000	7.40	Year
Northern Rock BS	0500 505000	Postal 90	90 day P	£5,000	7.30	Year
TERM ACCOUNT S						
Portman BS	01202 292444	Fixed Int Bond	1 year	£500	7.00F	Year
Woolwich BS	0800 400900	Fixed Rate Bond	2 year	£500	7.50F	Year
Woolwich BS	0800 400900	Fixed Rate Bond	3 year	£500	7.75F	Year
Norwich & P'boro	01733 391497	5 Yr Fxd Rte Bond	5 year	£10,000	8.05F	Year
NATIONAL SAVING **Accounts & bonds (gross)**						
INVESTMENT ACCOUNTS			1 month	£20	5.25	Year
				£500	5.75	Year
				£25,000	6.00	Year

*Source: **Independent on Sunday** (6 August 1995).*

1 How do borrowing rates of interest compare with savings rates of interest rates?
2 What factors seem to influence the rate of interest you might have to pay if you were borrowing money?
3 What factors seem to influence the rate of interest you might expect to receive if you were saving money?

*The **structure of interest rates** is the range of interest rates existing within an economy. Rates will tend to be low for savers and higher for borrowers.*

__Base rates__ represent a standard rate of interest which acts as the bench mark for all other interest rates charged by banks

It is clear from Box 11.11 that there is no single interest rate but a range or structure of interest rates.

Financial institutions are in business to make profit and they do this by charging borrowers higher rates than they pay to savers. Interest rates will either rise or fall dependent on the level of banks' base rates which are themselves, determined by the supply and demand forces in the money market and by the policies of the government.

The financial intermediaries

The financial intermediaries consist of the banks and non-banks. The banks include:

● The clearing banks (also known as retail, commercial or joint stock banks) which consist of the high street banks such as Barclays, Lloyds, Midland and National Westminster. They deal directly with customers, accept deposits, lend, provide methods of payment, foreign exchange and give financial advice. They have developed the full range of financial services such as insurance, fund management, pensions, mortgages and a wide variety of savings schemes. They all use the clearing system whereby, each day, cheques paid between banks are set off against each other and the day's adjustments are made to the banks' deposits held at the Bank of England.

● The merchant banks are wholesale banks often with famous names such as Rothchilds. They generally deal with corporate finance and advise companies on all financial matters including raising capital in the UK and abroad, take-overs and mergers, chasing the highest interest rates for surplus funds and trade and foreign currency deals. They also accept (or insure against non-payment) bills of exchange which are short-term loans to firms sometimes used to finance trade transactions.

● The discount houses are a set of nine banks based in the City of London unique to the British banking system. They are specialists at borrowing for very short time periods and then lending for slightly longer time periods, thus making a profit. They borrow surplus cash that the banks may have on a daily basis and so, make sure that money is mobilised. The terms of such loans are that they can be called in when required by the banks and, if necessary, the discount houses can sell bills back to the Bank of England to raise the required amounts of money.

- The Bank of England is the country's central bank and has overall responsibility for the banking system. It was set up in 1694, was nationalised in 1946 and is one of the few public corporations not to have been privatised. It supervises the issue of bank notes and coin through the banking network and acts as the banks' bank. In this capacity, the Bank licenses any organisation wishing to operate as a bank and monitors their performance. It requires the banks to hold nearly 0.5% of their assets in the balances held at the Bank and can issue directives to the banks to govern their lending strategy.

The Bank of England is also the government's bank. It keeps the accounts of various government departments, advises on and implements monetary policy and believes that its prime responsibility is to protect the value of the pound, i.e. to lead the fight against inflation. It manages the government's borrowing through the sale of government or gilt-edged securities and Treasury bills. It also is responsible for the management of the National Debt. The Bank may be called upon by the government to intervene in the foreign exchange market either by buying or selling the pound.

The Bank acts as lender of last resort to the banking system. If the clearing banks need liquid assets they may recall loans given to the discount houses who, in turn, can raise this by selling bills to the Bank of England.

There is often tension between the Bank of England and the Treasury. The monthly meetings between the Governor of the Bank and the Chancellor of the Exchequer often consist of a frank exchange of views and, under the present system, it is for the Chancellor to decide the extent to which the advice of the Governor is heeded. Conflict may arise because the Bank's main concern is to keep the pressure on inflation whereas the Chancellor may be concerned about a broader range of economic and political objectives. Some of this tension is shown in Box 11.12.

BOX 11.12

Tension at the bank

Bank GIVES NEW INFLATION WARNING

Pauline Springett

The dispute between the Chancellor and the Bank of England over interest rates is set to flare up again this week as the Bank issues a renewed warning over inflationary pressures in the economy.

The Bank's inflation report, due out on Wednesday, will argue that, unless there is an increase in interest rates, inflation will breach the Government's target of 1–2.5 per cent in the run-up to the next election. Kenneth Clarke, the Chancellor, has resolutely resisted the Bank's pressure to raise rates, for fear of further slowing down the economy, and has held them at 6.75 per cent since February.

Last week Mr Clarke again crossed swords on the issue with Eddie George, the Governor, when the two men held their monthly meeting, the last before the summer recess. Now their argument has taken on added momentum within industry and commerce.

Sir Brian Pitman, the chief executive of Lloyds Bank, openly sided with Mr George when he said he would like to see the Chancellor more actively curbing inflation. Other leading businessmen back Mr Clarke's steadfast resistance to raising rates.

In an early release from Wednesday's publication, the Bank today adds weight to its stance by reporting that business investment is likely to strengthen, after failing to recover in 1994. "With capacity pressures growing, profitability high and signs that balance sheet adjustment may have been completed, however, investment is likely to strengthen this year," it says.

The Chancellor's view receives strong backing from the Chartered Institute of Marketing, which today points to growing control of inflation. It predicts a 6.3 per cent growth in sales volume over the next year, compared with a 5.4 per cent rise in the past 12 months.

The CIM adds that prices will increase by 2.1 per cent, compared with planned rises of 2.5 per cent, and that the upsurge in inflation triggered by the weak pound and last year's price boom could be over.

"This is especially important since the Governor of the Bank of England has been arguing that the risk of accelerating inflation pointed to the need to raise rates," it says. "The evidence is that the Governor's fears are exaggerated. If evidence emerges that collaborates the results of this survey, the case for cutting interest rates will start to build."

The Chancellor might also look for support from the latest statistics from the Royal Institution of Chartered Surveyors, which reports that there has been a fall in confidence in the market for business property over the past three months. The RICS says this is further evidence of uncertainty.

*Source: **Guardian** (31 July 1995).*

The Evening Standard presented the debate more succinctly

Ken and Eddie AT WAR ON BASE RATES

Source:*Evening Standard* (31st July 1995).

TASK 11.8 Why is there a possible difference of view about monetary policy between the Bank of England and the Chancellor?

An independent central bank?

One possible solution to the kinds of problem indicated in Box 11.12 is to grant the Bank of England independence from the government. This would mean that the Bank could be left with its prime responsibility of squeezing inflation out of the system free of any political interference. We would then have a system similar to that used in Germany, a country which has had spectacular success in keeping inflation rates low. We might also be in better shape to move towards a single European currency where control of the Euro would be passed to the European Monetary Institute (EMI) working through the individual central banks of the member states.

The difficulty here is that the elected government's control over the economy is diminished. There could be occasions when a little more inflation might be acceptable if the trade off was a little less unemployment. Independence to the Bank would take away such

choices. There is also an important assumption behind any decision to hand over responsibility for the control of inflation to the Bank. It is that inflation is entirely a monetary phenomenon and that the only weapon to be used in its fight is interest rates. It denies the effective role that fiscal policy can play in countering inflation and the other anti-inflationary policies which are available to a government.

● **Many** overseas banks **set up branches in the UK, often based in the City of London. They locate here to participate in the international money markets and handle accounts for overseas residents.**

● **The** National Savings Bank **is run by the government and operated through the post office network. It is mainly attractive to small savers who may never have had full blown bank accounts.**

Non-bank financial intermediaries include:

- The building societies, **which were traditionally set up as non-profit making friendly societies with the sole purpose of promoting home ownership. The 1986 Building Societies Act opened up a wider range of markets to them and they** have been able to offer more effective competition to the clearing banks. The first to convert itself into a public limited company was the Abbey National and a series of mergers is creating a group of large scale operators performing virtually the same functions as the banks. Look at Box 11.13.

BOX 11.13   **Change and the building societies**

Mortgage lenders CHANGE
WITH THE TIMES

By Clifford German

There was a time, about 20 years ago, when building societies used to lend money exclusively for people to buy homes, and banks used to lend money for production, consumption, investment – in effect, everything else. The two did not really compete. Banks tended to advance mortgages only to their own staff, and the main competition for building societies came from local councils.

Mortgages were long-term loans, committed for 25 or 30 years, while bank credit was short term. Even the rates of interest were different. Bank base rates followed the lead given by the London money markets and the Bank of England, while the building societies offered a standard rate for deposits from small investors, who provided the overwhelming bulk of their funds.

The societies all charged identical rates for their mortgages as decided by the industry's trade body, the Building Societies' Association.

The BSA controlled the supply of mortgages by raising or lowering its rates to savers, which in turn determined the availability of money. When savings rates were attractive, savings flowed in to the building societies' extensive network of branches, and mortgages were plentiful but rather dear. When savings rates were low, the inflow of savings fell back and

mortgages were relatively cheap but, in effect, rationed. Borrowers could wait for months to get a loan.

But these cosy cartels were shaken up. First, the bigger societies started to offer premium rates of interest for long-term money outside the control of the BSA and to lend it out again to borrowers willing to pay a premium for larger loans. Then the incoming Conservative Government took a hand by allowing banks to enter the mortgage market and pressing the BSA to reduce and then abolish its powers to dictate rates for savings and mortgage.

In return, the building societies were allowed to make personal loans and further advances for a variety of purposes in competition with the banks – and to raise an increasing amount of the money they needed to finance their business in the London money markets, where interest rates were often significantly cheaper. At first, the banks concentrated on the top end of the market, making larger loans at higher rates of interest. But they quickly moved down-market to compete directly with building societies.

By 1985, local councils had been virtually squeezed out of the mortgage market, but the big London and Scottish clearing banks were competing vigorously for market share. Other

BOX 11.13

banks such as Bank of Ireland, Citibank and Banque National de Paris also entered the market enthusiastically.

At the same time, a new group of specialised mortgage companies were being set up, including the National Home Loans Corporation and the Household Mortgage Corporation. They raised their money exclusively in the London money markets and lent through the mortgage brokers, independent financial advisers, estate agents or insurance companies.

The last two saw mortgage packages as a perfect way to sell homes and endowment policies – which suddenly became the popular alternative to plain repayment mortgages in helping borrowers repay their mortgages.

In 1985, building societies accounted for three-quarters of the £150bn market in mortgages outstanding and 80 per cent of the net lending done that year. The banks had about 15 per cent of the balances outstanding and about 20 per cent of the new business. Since then, the balance has fluctuated as the banks have soft-pedalled on mortgage loans when there was plenty of demand in the rest of the economy and returned to them during the recession.

In 1993, the banks took over 50 per cent of the market in new mortgages for the first time, but last year the building societies took advantage of their increasing commercial freedom and commercial skills to regain market share. Many of the non-clearing banks found the business increasingly competitive, and both Bank of America and BNP have sold their mortgage portfolios.

Competition has also forced an increasing number of building societies to seek mergers

LINE-UP OF THE BIG LENDERS

Largest 20 mortgage lenders, 1993	Residential mortgage loans outstanding (£ billion)
1 Halifax	54.2
2 Abbey National	43.7
3 National BS	26.7
4 Woolwich BS	19.7
5 Leeds Permanent BS	15.3
6 Cheltenham & Gloucester BS	14.0
7 Alliance & Leicester BS	13.5
8 National Westminster Bank	12.7
9 Barclays Bank	12.4
10 Bradford & Bingley BS	10.5
11 National & Provincial BS	10.2
12 TSB Bank	8.3
13 Britannia BS	7.6
14 Lloyds Bank	6.8
15 Midland Bank & First Direct	6.5
16 Northern Rock BS	5.8
17 Bristol & West BS	5.7
18 Bank of Scotland	5.4
19 Royal Bank of Scotland	4.6
20 Yorkshire BS	4.2

Source: Council of Mortgage Lenders

and takeovers to minimise their operating costs and stay competitive. The number of building societies has fallen steadily over the last few years from 300 in 1979 to just 80, and the process is far from finished. The remaining smaller societies have been increasingly driven to team up with insurance companies or mortgage brokers to market their loans in combination with insurance policies, pension plans, PEPs and unit trusts.

*Source: **Independent on Sunday** (23 April 1995).*

BOX 11.13

Summarise the main changes which have affected the mortgage lenders in recent years.

- Finance Houses specialise in hire purchase lending but also deal in some special kinds of finance for industry.
- Insurance, assurance and pension funds are amongst the largest raisers of capital on a day to day basis. They have millions of pounds deposited with them each day and look to maximise returns for members. These institutions often place their money in shares and could, potentially, be an important source of influence in the boardrooms of industry.
- Unit and investment trusts collect in the savings of individuals and then are able to achieve higher gains through placing the money on different markets around the world. For the individual it represents a safer form of saving than trying to pick winning shares from the newspapers.

The determination of interest rates

In looking at the information in Box 11.11, we were assessing comparative rates of interest but we were not considering the overall level of interest rates. Why should the banks' base rates be set at 6.75%, 6%, 8% or even 15%? Our knowledge of markets can help us here. If an interest rate is the price of money then we might expect it to be determined by the normal forces of supply and demand. In this case the supply of money comes from those wishing to save whilst the demand for money comes from those wishing to borrow. The interaction between these could determine an equilibrium rate of interest. Look at Box 11.14.

The loanable funds theory of the rate of interest

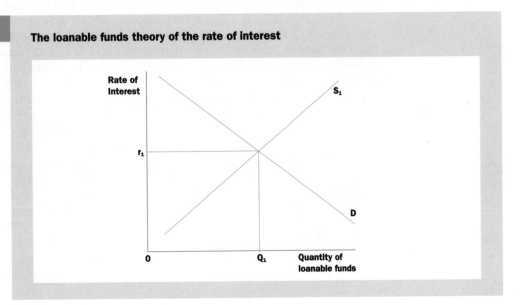

A main weakness of this theory is that savers and borrowers may not respond to changes in interest rates as Box 11.14 suggests. Interest rates may be important in influencing the decisions of firms and individuals to borrow but they may not be the most important factors. This was particularly evident during the 1930s when interest rates were very low but there was still very little demand for money. The reason for this appeared to be that firms would only borrow if there was a reasonable expectation that profits could be made. When the economy is in recession, profit expectations decline.

An alternative theory was developed by the economist John Maynard Keynes. His view was that people faced a choice about how to hold their assets. These could be held in cash (but cash earns no interest) or in a form such as government securities which do earn interest. Keynes suggested that there were three reasons or motives for holding assets in a liquid form:

- People need to hold some cash either in notes and coin or with instant access from a bank in order to buy things, and this is known as the transactions motive. This will not respond to changes in interest rates; it is interest rate inelastic.

- People need to have access to some funds to meet the unexpected and these liquid assets will be held for precautionary purposes. This will also be interest rate inelastic.

- People will prefer to hold cash and liquid assets if they believe that prices are about to fall. In this case they will choose to hold on to cash and then buy the asset once price has fallen. This is the speculative motive for holding cash because people are acting on the basis of expectations about future prices. This form of demand will be interest rate elastic since if interest rates rise, government security or bond prices fall and at this stage people will dash for cash. This is because the interest paid on bonds is fixed but the price of bonds varies according to the forces of supply and demand. If interest rates rise to 10% elsewhere, the demand for a particular bond carrying, say, 5% interest will fall causing the price of the bond to fall until the yield on the bond is equal to 10%, e.g. If a bond has a price of £100 and carries 5% interest it earns £5 per year. If interest rates rise to 10%, the price of the bond will have to fall to £50 because it is only at this price that the yield on the bond is the equivalent to 10%.

The three motives added together give the demand for liquid assets and this is shown in Box 11.15. The liquidity preference curve represents the demand to hold liquid assets but, to determine a price or interest rate, we need to add the supply of those liquid assets or the supply of money. This is shown at 0M in Box 11.15 and interest rates will be determined where the supply and demand curves cross.

BOX 11.15

The liquidity preference curve

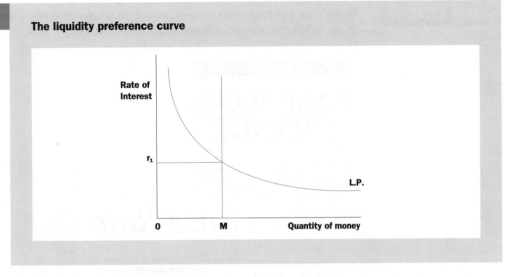

This analysis of interest rates suggests that they may be affected by either a shift in the liquidity preference curve or by a shift in the supply of money.
The Bank of England could control the money supply by issuing directives to control the amount of money the banks can lend but it has chosen, in recent years, to adjust interest rates to influence the market. The Bank can control the level of interest it pays on Treasury bills and a movement up in this market acts as a signal to all the banks that interest rates should also be pushed in the same direction and generally all the banks make an announcement of the change at the same time; as if in a cartel.

As interest rates rise so the demand for money contracts and the supply of money shifts as shown in Box 11.16.

BOX 11.16

The effects of a change in interest rates

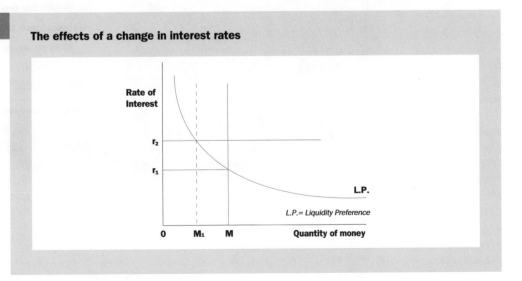

BOX 11.16

Please note that these Notices are a sample illustration of a rate change notice and do not reflect the position of these institutions as at today's date.

The **CO-OPERATIVE BANK**

BASE RATE CHANGE

With effect from close of business on Thursday 2nd February 1995, Co-operative Bank changes from 6. to 6.75% p

THE CO-OPERATIVE
PART OF THE CO-OPERATI
1 Balloon St., Manchester M60 4E

Base Rate

With effect from close of business on
2nd February 1995,
Base Rate is increased from
6.25% p.a. to 6.75% p.a.

All facilities (including regulated consumer credit agreements) with a rate o linked to Yorkshire Bank Bas will be varied accordingly

Yorkshire
Head Office: 20 Merrion Way, L

+ Girobank

Girobank announces that

with effect from

close of business

on 2 February 1995

its Base Rate was

increased from 6.25% to

6.75% per annum.

Girobank plc, 10 Molk Street LONDON EC2V 8JH
Reg. No. 1950000

*Source: **Guardian** (3 February 1995).*

The Government may wish to change interest rates for a range of reasons. It may wish to reduce the rate of inflation, influence the level of investment in the economy, affect the level of unemployment or the value of the pound sterling on the foreign exchange market. The decision to change interest rates is always finely balanced and creates the kind of controversy indicated by Box 11.17.

BOX 11.17   **The interest rate dilemma**

Slowing economy 'could be tipped into recession'

Interest Rates MUST NOT RISE, SAY FIRMS

Richard Thomas

British business delivered a sharp warning to the Government yesterday that higher interest rates could tip an already slowing economy into recession.

Unveiling its latest health-check of small and medium-sized firms, the British Chambers of Commerce said an unhealthy housing market and job insecurity were squeezing new orders and dampening business optimism.

"Economic activity appears to be delicately poised between the sustainable growth that is desired and a lower stagnant level of growth,'"said BCC president Robin Geldard, adding that "any further tightening of monetary policy could tip the economy towards the low growth scenario."

The BCC stopped short of following the lead of Treasury "Wise Man" Patrick Minford, who yesterday advocated a cut in the cost of borrowing, although the organisation's quarterly survey of over 8,000 firms confirmed that interest rates remained high on the list of company worries – topped only by fears of rising raw material prices.

City analysts said the BCC survey reinforced Chancellor Kenneth Clarke's stand against Bank of England pressure for dearer borrowing than the current level of 6.75 per cent. Robert Barrie, of brokers BZW, said Mr Clarke was unlikely to tighten monetary policy further in any case. "The BCC are pushing at an open door," he said.

Mr Barrie pointed to evidence in the BCC survey of a slowdown in the growth of export orders. "These figures show that we're not simply exporting our way out of the slow-down, as many people imagine."

The BCC said the gap between the number of manufacturing firms reporting higher overseas orders and those with emptier order books was 33 per cent between April and June, down from 37 per cent in the first quarter of the year. Exports are "clearly past their peak" the forecast warns. Meanwhile, domestic demand continues to weaken.

Against a background of slower growth in both domestic and export orders and a historically high cost of borrowing, firms have trimmed their plans for investment and recruitment, the BCC said.

The positive gap between the number of companies planning to increase spending on

BOX 11.17

new plant and machinery and those expecting to reduce expenditure fell from 27 per cent in the first three months of the year to just 20 per cent by the second quarter of 1995.

But Mr Geldard remained hopeful that investment intentions would strengthen again once bosses were convinced the economy is not heading into a slump.

The need for new investment was highlighted by the BCC's finding that pressure on firms' output capacity has increased to the highest level for over six years, with 39 per cent of companies reporting no spare capacity in the second quarter, compared to 36 per cent between January and March.

Firms are also reluctant to hire new staff because of fears about future demand, with companies in all sectors revising down sharply their recruitment expectations.

Despite reduced demand for labour some enterprises are having difficulty recruiting.

*Source: **Guardian** (21 July 1995).*

TASK 11.10   Analyse the conflicting views about whether interest rates should be changed.

REVIEW

This chapter has focused on four markets: the housing market, the market for agricultural products, the Single European Market and the money market. It should be the case that you are now beginning to see that a common set of principles can be applied to whatever market is under the spotlight. Free markets are generally seen as beneficial in that they generate a greater degree of competition between firms which should improve productive efficiency by driving down costs. The consumer should benefit through lower prices, higher quality and more choice. However, we have seen that on some occasions markets left to themselves create problems or fail to achieve these desired effects. It is then that governments may choose to intervene in a market to correct this market failure. This is the main topic for Section 3 of the book.

Multiple choice

1 **Other things remaining equal, an increase in the supply of money will tend in the short run to reduce**

A   prices
B   national income
C   aggregrate demand
D   interest rates

(IB, November 1994)

2 **All other things remaining equal, which one of the following is most likely to bring about a rise in interest rates?**

A   A reduction in the money supply
B   A reduction in government borrowing
C   A fall in unemployment
D   An increase in the proportion of income saved

(IB, May 1995, Higher)

3 **Which of the following is not generally regarded as a function of a central bank?**

A   Influencing interest rates
B   Supporting a government's anti-inflation policy
C   Attempting to achieve full employment
D   Supervising commercial banks

(IB, May 1995, Higher)

Questions 4 and 5 should be answered with reference to this key:

A   1 only is correct
B   1 and 2 only are correct
C   2 and 3 only are correct
D   1,2 and 3 are correct

4 **A rise in house prices can be caused by**

1   a decline in house building
2   an increase in lending by building societies
3   a rise in mortgage interest rates

(ULEAC, January 1995)

5 **Which of the following government actions would assist in keeping the price of a good at a level above market equilibrium price?**

1   A tax on producers of the good
2   Intervention purchasing of the good
3   Rationing the consumption of the good

(IB, May 1995, Higher)

Data response

 The data below include an adaptation of an article published in *The Financial Times* on November 23, 1991. Study the data carefully, then answer each of the questions which follow.

HARD TIMES FOR THE KING OF FISH

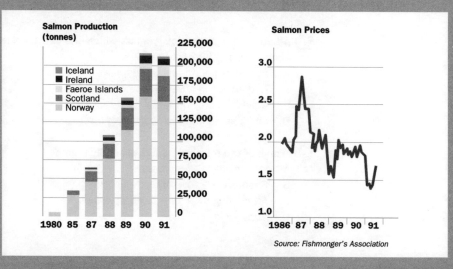

Source: Fishmonger's Association

Norway's salmon, the king of fish, is not having a happy time this winter. After years of investment in the industry that made the country the leading farmed salmon producer in the world, the recent glut has led to prices collapsing.

What was once a luxury product has become one of the cheapest fish in the supermarket, as a result of a surge in Norwegian salmon production dating back to the mid 1980's. In 1985, the Norwegian Government made it easier to get a licence for salmon farming. Low interest rates and high returns on capital compared to other industries helped to fuel the growth.

The industry developed in the hope that consumption would rise (it takes 3 years to produce a fully-grown salmon). Production increased to 115,000 tonnes by 1989.

But in 1989 with Scottish and Irish farms also building up production the market collapsed. At the end of the year FOS (the Norwegian Fish Farmers Sales Organisation), the banks and the salmon exporting companies established an intervention buying system. This system involved FOS guaranteeing to buy a salmon at a minimum price above the free market equilibrium.

QUESTIONS

Two abnormally warm winters have led to increased production and Norway's output in 1991 is likely to be almost as great as in 1990. Some farmers sold illegally outside the system at up to 30 per cent below the official price.

FOS was unable to sell all the fish. From June 1991 onward the organisation was unable to pay the farmers, about 200 of whom have gone bankrupt in the past 23 months.

The Norwegian salmon industry is now considering whether to set up a new organisation or to accept the case, strongly supported by the larger farmers, for abandoning the intervention buying system altogether.

*Source: adapted from **Financial Times** (23 November 1991).*

A) Explain how the Norwegian Government's economic policies led to increased salmon production.
B) Explain, with the aid of a diagram, why the price of salmon fell after 1987.
C) Why did FOS's intervention buying system fail?
D) Explain two possible effects of abandoning the intervention buying system.

(WJEC, 1993)

2 **Study the table and extract below about the Spanish potato industry.**

Anti-inflation policy ruins the potato producer
Cultivation of, and external trade in potatoes

	Area	Production	Imports	Exports
	Thousand hectares	Thousand metric tonnes	Metric tonnes	Metric tonnes
1984	347.5	5980.7	82.257	128.518
1985	330.9	5927.0	49.552	94.056
1986	296.7	5124.5	153.506	72.139
1987	298.4	5603.1	357.458	112.605
1988	285.0	4574.2	446.447	115.314
1989	278.0	5366.0	415.574	111.827
1990	271.3	5330.7	341.794	103.177
1991	264.6	5178.8	412.978	153.042
1992*	266.3	5194.5	217.074(i)	109.296(i)

*Ministry of Agriculture prediction.   *(i) First half of 1992.*

1   In a full potato crisis, when producers do not receive more than eight pesetas a kilo, and threaten to harden their protest actions, an important chain of supermarkets announces a grand sale this week of potatoes at 25 pesetas a kilo, in 10 kilo bags. It costs the consumer more than three times what is paid to the producer, and this breaks the rules of the free market.

2   The agricultural organisations warn that all of the fight against inflation by the socialist administration since 1986 has been centred on the agricultural sector 'and all brought about by a measure as simple as allowing the entry of imports without restriction.' The measures in sectors such as services, which are accused of being the true culprits of inflation, pass the years without being anything more than promises.

3   At the same time this economic attitude has not been accompanied by adequate planning by the Ministry of Agriculture, which has not created producer organisations which could intervene in the functioning of the markets.

4   **Agricultural Income**
The final result was a global drop in agricultural income, more than 200,000 farmers and sellers abandoning the sector each year, and a drop in production.

5   It has caused the ruin of many farmers, who invested heavily at the start of the eighties, and later, while nobody was buying potatoes from them, have had to waste their machinery and irrigation installations.

6   **Subsidy of 15 pesetas a kilo**
The imports, mainly from France and Holland, have arrived in Spain at 10 pesetas a kilo, when the cost of transport was 10 pesetas a kilo and the producers in those countries received more than 15 pesetas a kilo. These calculations indicate that for every kilo sold in Spain the operators have lost 15 pesetas which, presumably, has been paid by their respective governments or the European Community.

7   To the Spanish producers this is clearly dumping, totally illegal, and it would be much better and less costly to send the produce to Somalia.

Source: Adapted from an article in **Cinco Dias (Madrid)** *(24 August 1992).*

QUESTIONS

a   **Explain the meaning of the following terms:**

   i   Subsidy (paragraph 6)
   ii   Dumping (paragraph 7)

b   i   Give a possible reason why potatoes are sold in shops at three times the price received by the producer (paragraph 1).
   ii   Why might it be said that this `breaks the rules of the free market' (paragraph 1)?

c   Paragraph 3 suggests that a producers' organisation could intervene in the functioning of the markets. Using a supply and demand diagram, explain how this might be done.

d   Do the figures for 'area' and 'production' in the table indicate that Spanish farmers have become more or less efficient? Briefly explain your answer.

e   i   Why might a policy of unrestricted free trade be regarded as an 'anti-inflationary policy', as is implied by paragraph 2?
   ii   Give a reason why such a policy might harm the agricultural sector more than the service sector (paragraph 2).
   iii From your reading of the article as a whole, including the figures in the table, is it your opinion that the author makes a convincing case for the idea that it is govenment policy and unrestricted imports that have ruined the potato farmer, or could there be other causes? Justify your answer.

(IB, 1994)

Section 3
Market Failure

3.12 Are markets so wonderful?

'Tide turns on Tories' market philosophy' *Will Hutton*

FOCUS

It was the market philosophy that provided the policy weapons to slay trade unions and nationalisation, and the same philosophy gave us a deregulated banking system and credit boom that passed as an economic miracle. But just as that has dissolved into a painful recession, so the attempt to extend the market principle across almost every facet of our economic and social life is running into the sand.

For there was always a cancer at the heart of this market-based enthusiasm. Markets can fail. More that that, they have extremely weak self-regulating properties and very little tendency to stability. Here are just a few examples:

Markets are biased to the predictable immediate future.
In a free market, economic agents are rewarded for responding to price signals, and prices are reckoned to contain all the relevant information needed to make rational decisions. But there is a problem when the rule is extended for services which have long-term paybacks. Why should today's buyers pay a higher price for benefits that accrue to someone else tomorrow?

The answer is that they do not, which is why companies find it so difficult to persuade shareholders to value research and development as highly as dividends paid today. It is hardly a surprise that teaching hospitals in the NHS's internal market find themselves having the same problem as a Pilkington or Rolls Royce has with the stock market. Why should buyers pay for tomorrow's doctors when the service they want is on offer more cheaply elsewhere? The market builds in a bias against investment, yet little of this was recognised by the health system reformers. The internal market requires regulation and a long term banker. The Government is providing neither.

Markets are unstable because they are poor at dealing with uncertainty.
Prices do not reflect the possibilities of an unknowable future. Economic agents, who know how little they individually know, try to protect themselves against this by playing safe, reducing irrational outcomes alongside a tendency to instability.

So it is that in the foreign exchange market, dealers assume that the trend of the last few hours, days, and weeks will continue. They trade on that basis, so producing systematic over-and under-shooting. This is damaging enough, but ruinous if transferred to an educational market of opted-out schools. Parents crowd their children into schools with a proven track record and shun those that are failing, so reinforcing the success of the first and downward spin of the second. The theory is that the system is self-correcting, as poor schools attempt to turn themselves round; free market economists once used the same argument to justify floating exchange rates, saying that contrary speculation would prevent too much overshooting. It was nonsense then and it is nonsense now. Unless we are to accept a two-tier education system, the abandonment of educational opting-out is inevitable.

There are certain goods which markets cannot provide.
There are some economic phenomena whose characteristics defy opening up to competition. The most obvious examples are water distribution and the electricity and

FOCUS

gas grids. It would be economically irrational to have competing reservoirs, gas pipelines, and electricity cable – and although privatised, the industries have remained natural monopolies whose sole instruments of public accountability are small regulatory offices.

The intellectual pendulum, having swung the way of market forces, is swinging back before the logic of events, but not necessarily to a world with which we are particularly familiar. There will be more effort to correct market failures, certainly, and more regulation and scope for government. But the basic gains of privatisation, competition, and price incentives will be retained, so that government initiative will have to be cleverer and more accountable than that which Westminster and Whitehall has habitually provided.

*Source: Adapted from **Guardian** (1993)*

Preview

In this chapter we shall investigate the following key areas:

- the essence of the market system;
- the process of resource allocation;
- market failures because of:
  - unrealistic assumptions
  - the existence of externalities
  - the provision of goods which benefit society as a whole
  - national economic objectives.

The market system revisited

Classical Economics is the body of economic thought which began with the publication of the Wealth of Nations by Adam Smith in 1776, and other works of the mid-nineteenth century, and whose other major practitioners included David Ricardo, Thomas Malthus, John Stuart Mill, Jean Baptiste-Say and Nassau Senior; its underlying belief was in free competition and minimal government interference.

As we have already seen in Chapter 8, the 'ideal' free market economy is one in which a number of conditions exist: there are a large number of sellers, such that none of them is powerful enough to exert any control over its respective market; there is an even larger number of buyers for whose custom the sellers compete; self-interest abounds in the form of producers trying to maximise their profits, and rational, knowledgeable consumers trying to maximise their satisfaction from the things that they buy; sellers increase their supply when prices rise and lower it when they fall; buyers generally do the opposite, demanding less when prices rise and more when they fall; firms can easily enter or leave markets in response to changes in profitability; and a state of permanent full employment exists.

For Adam Smith, the father of Classical Economics, and his present-day disciples such as Milton Friedman, the pursuit of self-interest by buyers and sellers, guided by the 'invisible hand' of the market, would ensure, albeit unintentionally, the maximum welfare for society as a whole.

BOX 12.1

Adam Smith and Milton Friedman

Adam Smith

As every individual, therefore, endeavours as much as he can both to employ his capital in the support of domestic industry, and so to direct that industry that its produce may be of the greatest value, every individual necessarily labours to render the annual revenue of the society as great as he can. He generally, indeed, neither intends to promote the public interest, nor knows how much he is promoting it ... he intends only his own security... he intends only his own gain, and he is in this, as in many other cases, led on by an invisible hand to promote an end which was no part of his intention. Nor is it always the worse for the society that it was no part of it. By pursuing his own interest, he frequently promotes that of the society more effectually than he really intends to promote it. I have never known much good done by those who affected to trade for the public good.

*Source: Adam Smith, **The Wealth of Nations** (1776).*

Milton Friedman

Adam Smith's flash of genius was his recognition that the prices that emerged from voluntary transactions between buyers and sellers – for short, in a free market – could coordinate the activity of millions of people, each seeking his own interest, in such a way as to make everyone better off. It was a startling idea then, and it remains one today, that economic order can emerge as the unintended consequence of the actions of many people, each seeking his own interest.

*Source: Milton Friedman, **Free to Choose** (1980).*

Thus firms in this scenario may not set out to provide consumers with high quality products at low prices – their main aim is to make the largest profit; but the only way that firms will be able to realise this goal, given the relentless pressure of competition, is to keep prices low and quality high, lest customers are lost to rivals. In a fruit market, for instance, a vendor attempting to sell inferior quality cucumbers at a higher price than others might fool some consumers in the short term, but eventually shoppers would realise, perhaps because of painful stomach upsets, that they had wasted their money and they would switch to buying from other stall-holders. The message would be clear: the only way to make a profit is to operate efficiently, keeping costs low so that prices will be low, ensuring that consumers are provided with the high quality goods and services that they require. However, even then businesses would not be able to rest back on their laurels: competitors, eager to get a slice of the action, will try to improve their products through the constant process of invention and innovation, and surplus profits may prove to be a very temporary phenomenon as consumers switch their allegiances, with the emergence of new firms and products.

The process of resource allocation

As we have seen in Chapter 1, the central problem of economics is one of scarcity of productive resources relative to the unlimited potential demand which could be made upon them. It therefore follows that every society, be it centrally planned or based upon markets, has to have some mechanism by which its resources – that is its land, labour and capital – are allocated amongst all the numerous uses to which they could be put. So, by what process are resources deployed so as to ensure that consumers obtain exactly the right amounts of frying pans, ice-creams, jeans, etc. that they require? Well, under a system of central planning the answer is not too difficult to ascertain – the state planning authority decides upon its priorities and directs resources to those lines of production which are deemed to be most important; but, in the absence of a central planning authority, how do consumers magically obtain those goods that they want in just the right quantities? Here the answer is slightly less obvious – essentially, it is through the interaction of demand and supply. But how, exactly, does this interaction perform the allocative function?

The short answer to the above question is that it is through movements in prices which act as a link between demand and supply. These changes in price indicate and motivate – the so-called signalling function. Changes in price indicate the relative strength of consumer demand and signal to producers changing consumer tastes; they also indicate changes in supply which enables producers to signal to consumers what is available on the market, and on what terms. Rising prices of goods, which in turn increase profitability, motivate producers to respond to increases in demand by increasing supply; producers will decrease supply when demand, prices and thus profits all fall. Likewise, labour will be motivated to supply more factor services as its price, that is the wage rate, rises, and vice versa. This process can be illustrated in Box 12.2.

BOX 12.2

The process of resource allocation

Consumers switch their demand from sandals to wellington boots.

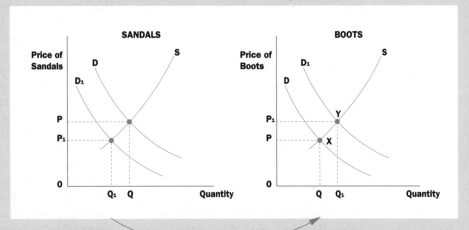

THE SANDALS SECTOR

Demand for sandals falls

Price falls

Revenue and profit fall

Sandals producers cut output

Demand for sandals workers fall

Wages fall (or do not rise)

Fewer workers are needed

THE WELLINGTON BOOTS SECTOR

Demand for boots rises

Price rises

Revenue and profit rise

Boots producers increase output

Demand for boots workers rises

Wages rise

More workers are needed

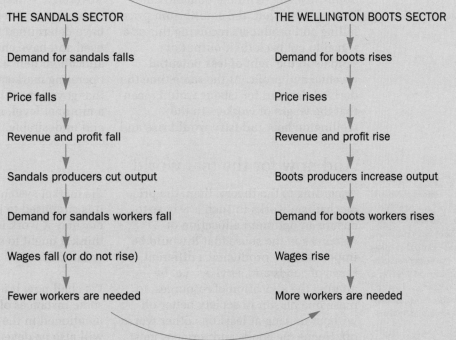

Mobile resources are bid away from sandals production to boots production.

In Box 12.2, consumers, who are assumed to be rational, knowledgeable and sovereign, decide, perhaps because of more inclement weather, to switch part of their demand from sandals to wellington boots. The increased desire for wellington boots means that consumers would be willing to pay more for them at each and every price, and the demand curve would therefore shift out to the right. This would cause the equilibrium price of boots to rise and boot producers, spurred on by the prospect of greater revenues and greater profits, to increase their output of boots, indicated by a movement along the supply curve from point X to Y. The fall in demand for sandals has the exact opposite effect, with the demand curve shifting to the left, the equilibrium price falling and producers receiving this as a signal to cut back their output of sandals in the light of less potential revenue and profit. At the same time the derived demand for labour would mean that the wages of workers in the wellington boot industry would rise and those of workers in the sandals industry would fall.

Through this mechanism, prices act as a link between consumers and scarce resources. Those sectors of the economy in which demand, prices and profits are rising will be able to commandeer resources away from declining sectors of the economy by paying more for labour, land and capital. The resources of the economy, which are assumed to be perfectly mobile, are therefore allocated to those sectors where consumers want them to be employed, in our example, to the wellington boots industry. Here, the consumer is said to have 'called the tune', to be 'king' or 'sovereign' – despite having no direct command over resources, consumers have determined how they should be used and have ensured their optimal allocation: hence the case for freely operating markets and the argument that government intervention, beyond a minimal level, is both unnecessary and undesirable.

And now for the real world

Market Failure is a situation in which the free market leads to a misallocation of resources in the sense that either overproduction or underproduction of a particular good occurs, leading to a less than optimal outcome.

According to the theory, then, the price mechanism works in such a way as to ensure an optimum allocation of resources in the sense that it would be impossible, by producing a different range of goods and services, i.e. by altering the allocation of resources, to make one person in society better off without making at least one other worse off. Hence the goods and services most desired by society would all be produced. However, in the real world, a suboptimal allocation of resources is likely to arise for a variety of reasons: the market system may neither work as it is supposed to in a mechanical sense, nor may it work in a way that we think it ought to so as to ensure equity or fairness.

We shall now briefly examine some instances of 'market failure', mentioned in the Preview, which will also be developed more fully elsewhere in this section. These are general reasons why markets might not work in true textbook fashion.

Unrealistic assumptions

We can identify three assumptions for discussion here: perfect factor mobility, competitive markets and consumer sovereignty.

● Perfect factor mobility

In Box 12.2, we explained how an increase in demand for wellington boots would, via an increase in price, increase the profitability of that industry and induce producers to increase their output. As a result, additional resources would be attracted away from the declining sandals industry from which resources in less demand would be released, higher wages in the boots sector providing the necessary inducement. In fact, the smooth and quick movement of labour and capital in response to price signals from one line of production to another, is a prerequisite for an efficiently operating price system. But how likely is this in practice?

There are two types of mobility: occupational, the movement of factors from one occupation to another, and geographical, the movement of factors from one area to another. Unfortunately, in reality, resources, for a variety of reasons discussed previously, tend to be highly immobile. In our example, if sandals were produced in the Highlands of Scotland and wellington boots in Leyton, East London, it is most unlikely that Scottish workers would be either willing or able to move south in response to price signals; it is more likely that they would remain unemployed in the area in which they were released.

Even when market forces do work so as to reallocate resources from declining to expanding sectors of the economy, they may do so very slowly, causing considerable pain and social distress in the process.

TASK 12.1

The INVESTIGATOR

Killing coal digs a pit for the economy

There would be little debate about the restructuring of the coal industry if we were in a recovery, as unemployed miners would easily be able to find jobs. Although there may be personal upheaval, when the pattern of demand changes in the context of a dynamic, expanding economy, people need to adapt; if this was not the case we would all still be footpads, ostlers, smiths and maids. However, the situation is absolutely different in a situation of recession and mass unemployment when there is no alternative work for miners to do: the miners' output is lost to the economy; the government loses the taxes and national insurance contributions; and the government has to pay social security and redundancy payments.

Even in purely financial terms, it is unlikely that the Treasury will be better off. What a sad and terrible mess!

*Source: Adapted from **news reports**, (October 1992).*

A *Explain why the author says that 'when the pattern of demand changes in the context of a dynamic, expanding economy, people need to adapt'.*
B *How does the existence of recession and mass unemployment affect this argument?*
C *Examine some of the general reasons why miners as a group of workers might be occupationally and geographically immobile.*

● **Competitive markets**

BOX 12.3

Adam Smith on monopolists

Our merchants and master manufacturers complain much of the bad effects of high wages in raising the price, and thereby lessening the sale of their goods at home and abroad. They say nothing concerning the bad effects of their own gains. They complain only of those of other people.

People of the same trade rarely meet together, even for merriment and diversion, but the conversation ends in a conspiracy against the public, or in some contrivance to raise prices.

Source: Adam Smith, The Wealth of Nations.

A most important assumption of the ideal free market economy is that markets within it are competitive, so that a large number of competing firms passively take the price that is set in the market as a whole and either increase or decrease their output in response to shifts in consumer demand.

However, as we shall see in Chapters 13 and 14, markets may be dominated by a single producer of the good or service, in which case a situation of monopoly exists, or by a few producers, in which case an oligopoly exists. In either situation, producers may not be content to take a price set in the market. Having significant control over supply, firms in pursuit of maximum profits may attempt to make the market price higher than it would otherwise have been by restricting output. The outcome for consumers may therefore be that they are paying a higher price for a smaller output. This would represent market failure and a misallocation of society's scarce resources, as the economy would be deprived of some of the output which would be valued more highly than that currently being consumed.

Also, in a situation of monopoly or oligopoly, profits may not perform the function that they are supposed to in the 'ideal' free market situation. Here, the making of profit is deemed to be a sign of efficiency; that is, the goods that are being produced are precisely those that consumers want and of a suitably high quality, and because firms cannot influence price, the profit has been achieved by operating efficiently, with costs being kept below the ruling price. However, given the power of firms in monopoly and oligopoly to restrict output to keep price artificially high, the making of profits may reflect market power and dominance rather than efficiency. In fact, as we shall see in Chapter 13, monopoly may involve both allocative and technical inefficiency.

● **Consumer sovereignty**

Consumer SOVEREIGNTY

Signal failure to understand what consumers are really looking for

We all had a good laugh back in the seventies when Milton Friedman and friends mounted a legal challenge to US price controls on the grounds that a price is a piece of information and therefore protected by freedom of speech. A blink of an eye later, and our own economy was being masterminded by goggle-eyed think-tankers droning on about free markets being "information rich". The Government, they intoned, should never try to second-guess the near-instant transmission of data between consumer and producer which occurs with free pricing. One hates to spoil the party, but 12 years after the death of the Prices Commission, the view at pavement level is rather less rosy. Let's start in a suitably Friedmanite location, the London street market. Every customer knows that the biggest hazard of using these fine institutions is the propensity of the stallholders to hassle even the most casual shopper – "Only a fiver, COME ON SIR!" And five minutes' observation would show that this hustling is 100 per cent counter-productive, causing, as it does, the potential buyer to scuttle off at the speed of light.

Yet somehow the market information is simply not getting through. Nothing will convince the stallholder that the best technique is to shut up and let the browser browse. On to the pub, for a nerve-steadying pint. The beverage's therapeutic effects are, however, counteracted by the filling-rattling volume of the music. Everybody hates it. Survey after survey proves the fact. But brewers and landlords just will not turn it down (or, better still, off).

Around the corner, the bank has responded to deregulation by sacking the manager and installing a young man called Steve as "personal product adviser". He sits behind a plastic desk while customers queue for the one open cash window. Here, too, the infallible market signals have been scrambled.

Nor can one help but remember that our telephone service responded to arrival in the information-rich market place by producing a new generation of universally-loathed pay-phone kiosks.

Final proof, in my own case, that the system is driven by something other than the bleep-bleep of consumers appearing on the producer's sonar came recently, when the local Wine Rack closed for the day because its computerised tills had stopped working.

Price signals will not clean the streets, clear slums or deter the creation of hideous "leisure developments" on farmland. On the other side of the fence, producers are at least as motivated by fashion, technology and the drive for dominance as they are by a desire to respond passively to "market signals".

The "information standard" of the price system is as irrational as the gold standard of the thirties, a doomed attempt to run our economy on remote control. Bleep-bleep and out.

*Source: Dan Atkinson, **Guardian** (10 February 1992).*

Explain what the author means when he says that the system is driven by something other than the bleep-bleep of consumers appearing on the producer's sonar.

Consumer Sovereignty is a state of affairs which exists when the allocation of society's resources is determined by the spending patterns of consumers, rather than by state direction or manipulative producers.

According to the theory of perfect competition, consumers 'rule the roost': they have knowledge of all prevailing prices, such that any producers trying to 'pull a fast one' by selling goods above the market price, or of inferior quality, would soon receive their 'come-uppance', as rational consumers would simply withdraw their custom. So, in this way, consumers, acting so as to maximise their satisfaction and in an entirely free, calculating and informed manner, determine the way in which scarce resources should be used; for example, in Box 12.2, it is assumed that consumers switch their demand from sandals to wellington boots of their own free will, perhaps because the weather has got worse or because they decide that boots are now more fashionable than sandals.

However, the reality might be rather different, with consumers not always behaving in an entirely rational manner, as they may not have perfect knowledge of either prices or quality. Prices of similar goods and services may vary between regions, within regions and from shop to shop, and it may in practice be extremely difficult to keep abreast of such variations. An even more challenging problem for most consumers is to make sensible, well informed choices when it comes to quality. This is particularly the case when we buy technologically sophisticated products such as computers, vacuum-cleaners, dish-washers, CD players and the like. Few

consumers possess the necessary scientific know-how to make really well-informed judgements about these types of goods, although consumers' magazines such as *Which* obviously help in this respect. It may also be a hazardous business trying to make sensible choices even amongst such day-to-day household goods as soap powders: faced with a bewildering array of brands on the supermarket shelves, how exactly do we know which one is going to clean best of all, with the least damage being done in the process?

Another problem for consumer sovereignty is the role of advertising and other forms of non-price competition (examined more fully in Chapter 14), where the aim may frequently be to persuade consumers rather than to inform them, with the result that the pattern of demand and resource allocation in the economy may not so much reflect the autonomous desires of individuals, as the skill of corporate marketing departments in shaping our tastes to accord with their production plans. Thus, in reality, large companies with considerable market power may decide what they want to produce and then set about convincing consumers that this is what they ought to buy, instead of simply reacting to changing price signals as in the theory.

Finally, there is the problem of consumer sovereignty being very unequally held. Look at Box 12.4.

BOX 12.4

BILLIONAIRES

So you thought the party was over for the rich? Don't you believe it. Between 1987 and 1993 the number of billionaire families and individuals more than doubled, from 98 to 233. In 1967 the richest $1/5$ of the world's people were 30 times richer than the poorest $1/5$. By 1991 they were 61 times richer. **Fortune,** the in-house magazine for the seriously rich, complains that the dollar-billionaires' club is getting less exclusive. The world's richest 101 individuals and families now control wealth valued at some $452 billion. This is more than the total yearly income of the entire population of India, Pakistan, Bangladesh, Nigeria and Indonesia put together: 1 billion people in all.

*Source: Adapted from **New Internationalist** (September 1994).*

Advocates of a freely operating price system often liken it to a political democracy where all voters can cast their votes for the candidates of their choice, with everyone who is eligible having an equal say: the price system, according to this line of reasoning, is a consumers' economic democracy: every time we go out and buy a particular good, we are affecting the demand for that good, and hence also its profitability and supply. Hence, the simple act of buying a good is akin to casting a 'vote' in favour of the production of that good, and is the way in which consumers determine how scarce resources should be allocated.

Unlike the political democracy, however, in which each person has equal voting rights, the consumer democracy described above, given the unequal distribution of income that exists in most capitalist economies, is unlikely to be one in which all have an equal say – clearly voting power is directly related to income, so that the rich would have many more votes, and thus a much greater pull on resources, than the poor. Consequently, the resulting pattern of resource allocation may overlook the pressing, often life and death needs of the poor, and reflect instead the more trivial wants of the rich. In the economics of the market place, human wants are those that are supported by effective demand, i.e. demand backed by the ability and willingness to pay the market price. Human needs, however, if unaccompanied by the wherewithal to pay, are simply ignored. This is the overriding reason for the existence of malnutrition and starvation in the world today: it is not that there is an overall shortage of food – there is more than enough in total terms to feed everyone; the problem, quite simply, is that those who need the food lack the money to pay for it.

Hence the 'free' market, given the degree of inequality which typically exists, is likely to be one in which many people are severely disadvantaged in terms of their market power. 'Electoral successes' will be the fast cars, exquisite jewellery and luxury hotels, etc. for those who can pay, with basic health care, education, safe drinking water and nutritious food for the poor almost certainly 'losing their deposits'. Clearly, some consumers are a lot more 'sovereign' than others!

In Section 5 we examine the question of inequality in greater depth.

BOX 12.5

The MYTH of the MARKET

Supporters of capitalism have always insisted that the laws of supply and demand and the price mechanism – the laws of the market – are not only "generally satisfactory" but the best possible "means of determining provision and consumption".

They have based this argument on three key claims.

First, that the market is economically democratic, that it enshrines the sovereignty of the consumer and obliges producers to give people what they want.

Efficiency

Second, that it maximises efficiency. The width of market competition, it is claimed, means that efficient productive firms prosper while inefficient unproductive firms fall by the wayside.

Third, that the market, by restricting the power of the state, is the best economic system for guaranteeing political democracy and freedom.

The notion of consumer sovereignty is false because it assumes the equality of consumers. In fact, the economic power of consumers is exactly equivalent to the amount of money they have. All that the market does is ensure priority for the needs of the rich over the needs of the poor.

It is more profitable, for example, to meet the demand for giant office blocks for multi-national companies than the demand for houses for homeless people, and to manufacture and sell arms to warring governments than to provide food for their impoverished populations.

Consumer sovereignty is a myth because the laws of the market ensure that consumption as a whole is subordinated to production, and production is subordinated to the accumulation of capital.

It is the drive to accumulate capital, imposed on every capitalist by the logic of competition, that comes to dominate the whole of society.

Which brings us to the question of efficiency. Market competition maximises efficiency in one sense only, making a profit. This does involve producing goods that people need but is quite different from maximising either the physical production of goods or the satisfaction of human needs.

On the contrary, the laws of the market frequently dictate the holding back of production so that much of industry works at less than its full capacity. Goods are often destroyed in order to maintain price levels (hence the dumping of wheat in the sea and the EEC food mountains).

Indeed as capitalism develops so the gap between what is actually produced and what potentially could be produced, even with existing levels of technology, grows ever wider.

Moreover, the anarchy of the capitalist

BOX 12.5

market contains within itself (as Marx demonstrated in *Capital* a century ago), a built-in tendency to crisis and recession.

In recession the economic system ceases to be efficient even in capitalist terms. Countless millions are wiped off share values on the stock exchanges, company after company goes bankrupt, machines stand idle and millions of workers are thrown onto the dole.

Finally the idea that there is some special relationship between the free market economy and political freedom and democracy is complete nonsense theoretically and historically.

No control

On the one hand the dominance of the market means that even where an elected parliament exists it has no control over the key factor in the life of any society, namely the economy. On the other hand a free market economy has no difficulty in coexisting with the most vicious dictatorial and authoritarian forms of rule.

In Britain the capitalist market dominated the country for over 200 years before working men even had the right to vote (women had to wait another 40 odd years).

In Spain the fascist Franco presided over a free market for over 40 years. In Chile in the 1970s and 1980s the murderous military dictatorship of General Pinochet was one of the world's most ardent advocates of market forces.

*Source: Adapted from **Socialist Worker** (20 February 1988).*

The existence of externalities

Externalities are those external costs (negative externalities) or external benefits (positive externalities) which are initiated by producers or consumers, but experienced by others, and which are not reflected in free market prices.

Externalities are costs (negative externalities) or benefits (positive externalities) which are not reflected in free market prices. In a free market, consumers and producers make their respective consumption and production decisions on the basis of money prices and their own private costs and benefits. However, these prices may not always reflect the true value of the product to society or the true cost of producing the good. Often the production and consumption of certain goods affect other firms or households who were not the initiators of these costs or benefits, and this is an important source of market failure and misallocation of scarce resources – if costs are imposed on others and not included in the market price of the good, from society's point of there will be overproduction of that good, whilst the consequence of ignoring the generation of external benefits will be underproduction of the good.

In Chapter 18, we will consider the topic of externalities in greater detail, together with possible forms of government intervention.

In small groups, discuss and make a note of the likely external costs and benefits for you of the following:

a) the siting of a major new airport near your house;

b) the removal from your area of all local bus services;

c) the creation of additional parkland in your local authority;

d) the operation of refuse collection in your neighbourhood on a 'pay as it's collected' basis.

The problem of providing goods which benefit society as a whole

Merit goods are goods which are deemed to be socially desirable, and which are likely to be underproduced and underconsumed through the market mechanism.

Demerit goods are goods which are deemed to be socially undesirable, and which are likely to be overproduced and overconsumed through the market mechanism.

Public goods are goods which when consumed by one person can be consumed in equal amounts by the remainder of society, and where it is impossible to exclude others from their consumption.

The market mechanism, as pointed out previously, is a system by which resource allocation is facilitated through changes in demand and supply, which in turn bring about changes in prices and profits. The problem, however, is that the system by itself is unable to make judgements about which goods and services are desirable, and which are undesirable from the standpoint of society as a whole, and it may have difficulty in providing a number of goods which are difficult to price. For private producers, the main criterion for producing a good is that there should be a demand for it, and ultimately a profit to be made. Hence the existence of effective demand for hard drugs, pornography and cigarettes would almost certainly be met, given the prospect of lucrative profits. Such goods are known as demerit goods, and are characterised by the fact that they impose costs on society (negative externalities), in addition to those borne by the individual consumer (see Chapter 19). From the point of view of society as a whole, it is likely that such goods, in the absence of any government intervention, will be overproduced and overconsumed.

Conversely, there are certain goods, such as health care and education, which confer benefits on society in excess of those conferred on individual consumers, which the free market is likely to underproduce and underconsume. Such goods are known as merit goods (see Chapter 19). The degree to which such goods should be provided by the state out of general taxation is a significant area of disagreement between economists on the right and left of the political spectrum, with the former favouring greater market provision, and the latter favouring greater government provision.

Whilst the free market might underprovide certain goods which are considered socially desirable, it is likely that another category of goods, known as public goods, may not be provided at all (see Chapter 19). Examples of such goods are street-lighting and defence, and, in these cases, government provision is usually required as the market would be incapable of distinguishing between those who would and would not be willing to pay the market price – all benefit irrespective of whether they pay or not, and there would thus be little inducement for individuals to pay anything at all. This involves the so-called free-rider problem.

The problem of national, macroeconomic policy objectives

Most countries have been subject to alternate periods of boom and slump in which the level of economic activity has lurched from peaks to troughs in the manner of a fairground roller-coaster. This phenomenon is known as the trade or business cycle.

Interventionist or Keynesian economists would argue that the market left to itself is more likely to worsen economic instability than provide a cure for it. Indeed, Keynesians would argue that markets can 'clear', with the economy being in 'equilibrium', with a state of mass unemployment. Alternatively, the boom period of the cycle, in the absence of government intervention, may be characterised by high inflation. In addition, given the openness of most markets to international trade, the free market may give rise to balance of payments problems.

These matters are considered in more detail in Section 4. In the following chapters, we take some of the issues raised above and examine them in greater detail, as well as investigating the idea of 'government failure'.

REVIEW   In the chapter title, we posed the question, 'Are markets so wonderful'? The foregoing discussion has attempted to demonstrate that there is a great deal of difference between the ideal, perfect market of the economics textbook and that of reality, in which a variety of 'market failures' may lead to a less than optimal outcome.

REVIEW TASK   Explain how the price system allocates resources in a market economy. Under what circumstances might the price system fail to allocate resources in an efficient way?

(IB, May 1995, Subsid. level)

3.13 What is monopoly?

COMPETITION, MONOPOLY *and* WORKERS

Supporters of capitalism, and particularly supporters of the "free market" and privatisation, often concede that capitalism is based on greed and inequality.

But they say capitalism means competition and competition makes for greater efficiency, productivity and better service all round.

They claim the whiff of competition destroys the old dead wood, clears out the tired and inefficient and makes space for the new, dynamic, innovative and thrusting entrepreneur.

Supporters of capitalism are fond of words like "dynamic", "innovative" and "thrusting".

What is more, they say, market forces ensure "the sovereignty of the consumer".

Businesses have to sell their goods and this means they have to produce what people want to buy. This in turn leads to variety and choice.

True, they admit, capitalism does lead to a bit of exploitation, poverty, homelessness and unemployment. These facts are hard to deny when you have to "step over the homeless as you leave the opera".

But these minor misfortunes are a small price to pay compared with the immense benefits conferred by capitalist competition in terms of general prosperity and freedom of choice.

Karl Marx, who had studied Adam Smith and innumerable other pro-capitalist economists, was well aware of these arguments.

He was also well aware of the dynamism of youthful capitalism compared with feudalism and other earlier economic systems.

He paid tribute to it in the Communist Manifesto:

"It has been the first to show what human activity can bring about, it has accomplished wonders far surpassing Egyptian pyramids, Roman aqueducts and gothic cathedrals. The bourgeoisie has created more colossal productive forces than have all proceeding generations together."

But to glorifications of capitalist competition and the market Marx had a simple reply – under capitalism competition turns inevitably into its opposite, monopoly. He describes the process in Capital:

"The battle of competition is fought by cheapening of commodities. The cheapness of commodities depends on the scale of production. Therefore the larger capitals beat the smaller.

"It always ends in the ruin of many small capitalists whose capitals partly pass into the hands of their conquerors, partly vanish. One capitalist always kills many."

War

Thus capitalism may have begun as a system of "free competition" between numerous small entrepreneurs but it has long since become a system dominated by a few giant corporations.

As production has become more inter-nationalised, so the position of these giants has been further strengthened.

It becomes increasingly difficult for merely national or local companies to compete with those operating on a world scale.

Lenin, writing in 1916, also had something to say on this: "Here we no longer have competition between small and large, technically developed and backward enterprises.

"We see here the monopoly throttling those which do not submit to them, to their yoke, to their dictation."

A perfect example of what Marx and Lenin

were talking about is now taking place among Britain's newspapers.

Rupert Murdoch's world media empire, News International, is attempting through price war to crush two of its British rivals, the Independent and Daily Mirror.

Murdoch can do this because the size of his empire lets him sell the Times and Sun at a loss for a period.

If the Independent or the Mirror is driven out of business he can then put prices up again with a larger share of the market.

When new technology was developed in the print industry Murdoch used it to smash the unions and move to Fortress Wapping.

He claimed at the time to be pioneering a new era of free competition and choice and many foolish political commentators of both right and left believed him.

That was how it began.

How it ends is with him "throttling" all those who do not submit to his yoke and reducing, not widening, the choice available to the consumer.

It was the same story with Murdoch's conquest of BSB.

Faced with facts like these some people dream of a return to the past.

They talk about stimulating small businesses, of legislation to limit media ownership, of inquiries and referrals to the Monopolies Commission.

But in the long run this is precisely dreaming. Ultimately no government policy, no legislation, is more powerful than the basic economic laws of capitalist production.

There is no road back from the rule of the giant monopolies, only a road beyond it to democratic social ownership and control.

*Source: **Socialist Worker** (September 1993).*

Preview

In this chapter, we shall investigate the following key areas:

- the nature of monopoly;
- the sources of monopoly power ;
- the neoclassical theory of monopoly;
- monopoly compared to perfect competition;
- and the implications of monopoly for economic efficiency.

The nature of monopoly

Monopoly, as a market form, is at the opposite end of the spectrum to perfect competition (see Chapter 8). In the literal sense, a monopoly exists when one single firm, or a small group of firms acting together, controls the entire market supply of a good or service for which there are no close substitutes. This is a situation of pure monopoly, which like the case of perfect competition, is rarely easy to identify in reality. Moreover, whether an industry can be classed as a 'monopoly' will depend on how narrowly the industry is defined; for example, the London Underground has a monopoly on the supply of underground travel within London, but does not have a monopoly on all forms of public transport within London: people can also travel by bus or overground trains.

A market concentration ratio is the proportion of a total industry accounted for by a certain number of its largest firms.

Thus in practice, less stringent definitions than 'single producer' tend to be used and economists focus instead on the degree of monopoly power which exists rather than absolute monopoly power. In the UK, a firm is legally regarded as being a monopolist if it controls 25 per cent or more of the total market supply of a particular good or service.

A market concentration ratio is used to measure the degree of concentration within a particular industry or group of industries. A commonly used ratio is the five firm concentration ratio, which indicates the proportion of the industry's output produced by the five largest firms. We consider concentration ratios in more detail in Chapter 14.

The multinational, monopoly nature of real world markets

In all the major capitalist countries of the world, 'perfect markets', even approximating to the textbook models, are extremely difficult to find beyond a very limited sector of the economy, typically stock and financial securities exchanges and parts of retailing and agriculture. Increasingly, giant 'multinational' or 'transnational' corporations have come to dominate markets on a world scale. The United Nations defines such corporations as

A multinational or transnational company is a company which possesses and controls means of production or services outside the country in which it was established.

associations which possess and control means of production or services outside the country in which they were established.

Although they operate in different countries, most of such corporations are controlled from a national base from which a global system of integrated production, sales, research, marketing and finance is facilitated.

BOX 13.1

John Kenneth Galbraith on the multinational company

❝ The two parts of the economy – the world of the few hundred technically dynamic, massively capitalised and highly organised corporations on the one hand and of the thousands of small and traditional proprietors on the other – are very different. It is not a difference of degree but a difference which invades every aspect of economic organisation and behaviour, including the motivation to effort itself. It will be convenient ... to have a name for the part of the economy which is characterised by the large corporations... I shall refer to it as the Industrial System. The Industrial System... is the dominant feature of the New Industrial State. ❞

*Source: John Kenneth Galbraith, **The New Industrial State** (1967).*

Thus, in a world in which giant corporations control 70 per cent of the world's trade, carry out the bulk of new research and development (R&D), shape international markets through their advertising and exert a great deal of influence over price, it is difficult to find very much evidence of the perfectly competitive market of the economics textbook. The nineteenth century revolutionary, Karl Marx, was one of the few economists to correctly predict this growth of big business. While mainstream, orthodox economists mainly focused their attentions on markets with large

numbers of buyers and sellers, with none large enough to influence price, Marx centred his attention on the likely growth of huge aggregates of capital having significant control over their markets, and with the ability to eliminate many of their smaller rivals: a process in which the stronger and more profitable 'mop up' the weaker, making for giant monopolies with enormous economic, and even political, power.

The extracts in Box 13.2, taken from the New Internationalist, provide some interesting facts and figures about the multinationals.

BOX 13.2

Facts and figures from the *New Internationalist*

The big players

- The combined sales of the world's largest 350 multinationals total nearly one third of the combined gross national products of all industrialized countries and exceed the individual gross national products of all Third World countries.
- More than 90% of all multinationals are head-quartered in the industrial world. France, Germany, Japan, the UK and the US account for 70% of all foreign investment by multinationals and about half their total number.
- The largest multinationals operate in dozens of countries and employ thousands of employees. PepsiCo, the world's biggest beverage company, has more than 500 plants and 335,000 workers in over 100 countries. Nestlé, the giant Swiss food manufacturer, operates in 126 countries with more that 200,000 employees.

BOX 13.2

Biggest companies in the world ranked by industry (1991)

Industry	Company	Country	Company Sales ($ billion)
Aerospace	Boeing	US	29.3
Apparel	Levi Strauss	US	4.9
Beverages	PepsiCo	US	19.7
Building materials	Saint-Gobain	France	13.3
Chemicals	El du Pont	US	38.0
Computers, office equipment	IBM	US	65.3
Electronics	General Electric	US	60.2
Food	Philip Morris	US	48.1
Forest products	International Paper	US	12.7
Industrial/farm equipment	Asea Brown Boveri	Switzerland	28.8
Mining/crude-oil	Ruhrkohle	Germany	14.9
Motor vehicles/parts	General Motors	US	123.7
Petroleum refining	Royal Dutch/Shell	UK/Netherlands	103.8
Pharmaceuticals	Johnson & Johnson	US	12.4
Publishing/printing	Bertelsmann	Germany	9.1
Rubber/plastic goods	Bridgestone	Japan	13.2
Scientific/photo equipment	Eastman Kodak	US	19.6
Soaps/cosmetics	Procter & Gamble	US	27.4
TobaccoRJR	Nabisco	US	14.9
Toys/sporting goods	Yamaha	Japan	3.6

Merger mania
- The 1980s was a decade of corporate cannibalism as companies sought to buy out or build strategic alliances with competitors.
- Nearly $1.3 trillion was spent on corporate mergers in the 1980s, more than the annual economic output of the UK. About 90% of all mergers were between companies from the industrial world.
- The inter-relationships between corporations can be Byzantine. All major auto manufacturers now have alliances with competitors. Ford owns 25% of Mazda; Chrysler owns 24% of Mitsubishi; GM has joint ventures with Toyota.

Hot money
- Investment brokers, mutual funds, managers and multinational banks now control the fate of nations. National currencies rise and fall according to how closely governments tailor their economic policies to the interests of corporations.
- Every day nearly $1 trillion-worth of currencies is traded on world financial markets without any regulation. Huge flows of speculative capital wash around the world as central banks vie with each other, increasing interest rates to stem the outflow of capital.

BOX 13.2

More players, fewer winners

- There are now 35,000 multinationals with some 150,000 foreign affiliates. The largest 100 manufacturing and service companies accounted for $3.1 trillion of world assets in 1990; about $1.2 trillion of that was outside the multinationals' home countries.
- Multinationals control 70% of world trade; much of that is inter-firm trade, ie between branches owned by the same parent firm.
- Although the total number of multinationals is increasing, a small number of companies continue to dominate most major areas. The top five companies typically account for 35–70% of total sales across a range of industries.

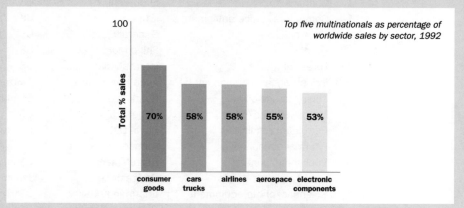

Top five multinationals as percentage of worldwide sales by sector, 1992

Source: ***New Internationalist*** (August 1993).

Sources of monopoly power

One of the features of monopoly is that, unlike perfect competition, supernormal profits may be made in the long run. If there were free entry to the market this could not of course happen, as the arrival of new firms would have the effect of shifting the market supply curve to the right and lowering the market price until the supernormal profits were eliminated. The existence of long-run supernormal profits therefore implies the presence of barriers which prevent the entry of new firms into the industry. Indeed the basis of monopoly power is the ability to prevent entry of new firms, and we now turn to an examination of these various barriers.

TASK 13.1

The INVESTIGATOR

Small brewers droop in face of pub monopoly

Steve Dugmore and Phil Burke represent the new breed of brewer, meeting a mainly local demand for distinctive tastes. But they retain their day jobs as a laboratory assistant and a chemistry teacher at the same school because of the riskiness of their business.

The 1995 Good Beer Guide lists 204 micro-breweries, but about half of those that started in the 1980s have collapsed, so the chances of all 204 being in business in a year's time is somewhat remote, in spite of the fact that sales of real ale have risen by 9 per cent over the past 12 months.

The problem, unsurprisingly, is that the big boys are winning the fight hands down for what is, overall, a shrinking market. The Monopolies and Mergers Commission recommended various reforms at the end of the 1980s, but these have not, in practice, weakened the vice-like grip of the national brewing conglomerates on the beer market, who have expanded by buying up pubs, making sure that their beverages feature prominently on restricted guest beer lists.

Dave Roberts, Chairman of the Small Independent Brewers' Association, bemoans the way that the door is being closed on the micro-breweries. In 1982, he opened his Pilgrim Brewery in Reigate, Surrey.

'Allied Breweries owned most pubs here at that time. I could sell in one pub and a few clubs. When Lord Young said he was going to break the big brewers' monopoly and force them to take guest beers, we thought we were in business at last. But the pubs they sold off were bought up by smaller, but still substantial companies, such as King and Barner and Greene King. And they were under no obligation to take a guest beer.'

Stuart Elliott, a small brewer from Warwickshire notes that:

'More often than not, free houses and clubs tell you they can't take your beer because they have an agreement with one of the big boys. But I went into this with my eyes open and I'm prepared to hassle and chase business.'

The alternative is indicated by the name of his strong ale: Gravedigger.

*Source: Adapted from **The press** (October 1994).*

By what means have the 'big boys' in the brewing industry attempted to restrict competition?

Legal restrictions

A monopoly may be granted by law in the form of a patent. This gives inventors complete control over the production and sale of their goods for a set period of time as other firms are prevented from producing an identical good for the duration of the patent. Similarly, copyrights afford protection in the field of literature and music. Legal protection may also occur where only one firm is granted a licence to operate in a particular activity, e.g. bus routes and broadcasting, or where a public sector service is established as a statutory monopoly. With the large-scale privatisation that has occurred in the UK since 1979, examples of the latter are increasingly difficult to find, but, at the time of writing, it is illegal to compete with the Post Office in the delivery of letters, although not parcels.

Capital costs

For certain industries, e.g. aircraft building and motor manufacturing, initial set-up costs may be very high due to the enormous capital outlay required. In such cases the minimum efficient scale of production might be so great as to form an effective barrier to entry for firms unable to afford the high fixed costs necessary to enter the industry.

In addition, where the industry is likely to benefit from substantial economies of large-scale production, it may sometimes be the case that the market would be most efficiently supplied by a single producer. This situation is sometimes referred to as a natural monopoly, and this will occur if the market is such that it will sustain only one firm benefiting from full economies of scale in the long run.

'Utility' industries such as gas, electricity and water may be regarded as natural monopolies because of the wasteful duplication that would be involved in having competing firms all serving a particular geographical area with rival pipes and cables. Before the Conservative Government of 1979 came to power, these industries were publicly owned and operated as state monopolies. They were privatised during the 1980s and now operate as private monopolies which are subject to public regulation. We consider this regulation more fully in Chapters 16 and 17.

Natural monopoly is a market situation in which average cost falls over large ranges of output so that the market is most efficiently served by a single supplier.

Limited sources of supply

For climatic or geological reasons, certain products are only found in particular parts of the world and this may give rise to control over supply. This would apply to primary commodities such as diamonds from South Africa, coffee from Brazil and nitrates from Chile. In these cases, particular countries would have a monopoly in the supply of certain commodities due to natural factor endowments, and it would not be possible to obtain supplies of the commodity from a large number of other sources.

The supply of a good may also be limited to a certain geographical area if transport difficulties or ownership of private property rights within a certain area exclude other firms from the market.

Agreements between producers to limit competition

A cartel is an agreement between sellers of a good to coordinate the amount they produce in order to affect sales, prices and profits.

It is possible that a number of firms may act together to establish control over the production or sale of their goods or services, perhaps to increase their profits or to eliminate the uncertainties of competition. The most highly formalised type of agreement is the cartel, in which firms jointly agree the level of output for each member of the cartel and the price to be charged for the product.

The best known example of a cartel, in this case an international one, is the Organisation of Petroleum Producing Countries (OPEC). Such agreements are, however, illegal in the UK.

Another possible form of joint action to limit competition is the merger where independent firms combine together under the control of one management. Although the firms may retain their individual names, they in effect become a single company with a unified policy. Their combined economic power may enable them to more effectively prevent the entry of new firms into the market.

Non-price competition as a barrier to entry

Non-price competition is a form of competition in which firms attempt to establish a competitive advantage over their rivals by strategies other than lowering prices.

Non-price competition includes advertising, product differentiation, constant introduction of new brands and attractive after-sales services.

The effects of these various non-price strategies on the ability of new firms to enter markets and on consumer sovereignty, is examined more fully in Chapter 14. However, suffice it to say at this stage that the range of marketing strategies employed by the large established firms have the effect of making it very much more difficult for newcomers to join the marketplace – smaller firms would find that they were

simply unable to afford the minimum levels of advertising and product promotion necessary to induce the large retail chains to stock their product; and even if the retailers could be persuaded, the chances of success for one new product against numerous well-established brands, without the necessary level of promotion, is likely to be very slim. How successful, for example, is a new manufacturer of tooth-paste likely to be in dislodging our existing brand loyalties without spending a fortune on television advertising and free-gift offers?

Tariffs and quotas

*A **tariff** is a tax imposed on imported goods. A **quota** is a quantitative limit placed on specified imported goods.*

A firm may have achieved a dominant position in the domestic market, but may be subject to much competition internationally. A tariff has the effect of raising the price of goods imported into the domestic economy and reducing demand, depending on elasticities; a quota places a physical restriction on the amount that can be imported. They both, therefore, potentially protect domestic industry from international competition and can act as sources of monopoly power. We discuss the question of import controls more fully in Section 5.

BOX 13.3

Newspaper industry told to SEEK MORE OUTLETS

A Monopolies Commission report on the supply of national newspapers has found that restrictions on shops that may sell papers operate against the public interest; and newspaper suppliers have been told to find ways of supplying newspapers to more outlets wishing to sell them.

60 per cent of all applications by retailers to sell papers have previously been refused; wholesalers and publishers have claimed that if all shops wishing to sell papers were permitted to do so, sales would become extremely fragmented and home-delivery and early opening hours would be threatened.

Rupert Murdoch's News International, publisher of the Sunday Times, The Times, Today, the Sun and the News of the World, controls 31 per cent of the newspaper market, while W. H. Smith has in excess of 30 per cent of the wholesale market as well as being a retailer. More than 12 million newspapers are distributed each night through wholesalers to retailers in England and Wales. 10 publishers produce 22 daily and Sunday papers, which are distributed through almost 80 wholesalers, with each publisher having about 180 distribution areas, each with a single wholesaler given exclusive distribution rights.

Whilst the market positions of News International and W. H. Smith may be defined as monopolies, the Commission concluded that neither is against the public interest; nor, they found, is the complex monopoly arrangement involving the display of prices on the cover of papers, the setting of a common retail profit margin plus exclusive distribution arrangements.

Source: Adapted from
***Daily Telegraph** (10 December 1993).*

TASK 13.2

A To what extent is the national newspaper market a monopoly?

B What barriers to entry exist in this market?

C Do you agree with the view of the Monopolies Commission that, although a situation of monopoly does exist in the national newspaper market, this is not against the public interest?

Also use the Focus article at the beginning of this chapter to answer this part of the question.

The Neoclassical theory of monopoly

The monopolist's demand curve

In our analysis of perfect competition in Section 2, we showed how there is a distinction between the demand curve of the individual firm and that of the market as a whole – the existence of many firms each competing against each other means that each one has no influence over price, and has to take the price that is determined in the market through the intersection of the demand and supply curves. The demand curve for each firm is therefore horizontal: an infinite amount is demanded at one price, with nothing at all being demanded at a higher price and with the charging of a lower price being inconsistent with the goal of profit maximisation.

However, under monopoly, there is only one firm in the industry; thus there is no difference between the demand curve for the industry and the demand curve for the firm. As the monopolist is subject to the normal law of demand, the monopolist's demand curve will be downward sloping so that to sell more, price would have to be lowered (Box 13.4). In comparison to other types of market, the monopolist's demand curve is likely to be relatively inelastic as close substitutes may not be available if price is raised. Indeed, the availability or non-availability of close substitutes is one of the key factors determining the monopolist's power in the market.

BOX 13.4

The monopolist's downward sloping demand curve

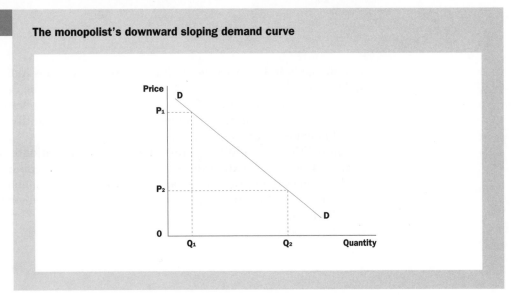

The demand curve shown in Box 13.4 presents the monopolist with a choice. The monopolist can either choose to make the price or the quantity, but cannot do both; for example, if the monopolist chooses to set a price of OP$_1$, the market dictates that only a quantity of OQ$_1$ could be sold; however, if the monopolist chooses to set a quantity of OQ$_2$ to be sold, clearly the demand curve tells us that this could only be achieved at a price of OP$_2$.

Marginal revenue and average revenue under monopoly

The table in Box 13.5 assumes that the monopolist faces a normal demand schedule, and from this the revenue curves are derived. (To make sure that you understand these concepts, cover up the figures for total, average and marginal revenue and try writing them down yourself.)

BOX 13.5

Marginal revenue and average revenue in monopoly

Output/sales	Price	Total revenue	Marginal revenue	Average revenue
1	20	20	20	20
2	18	36	16	18
3	16	48	12	16
4	14	56	8	14

From the table in Box 13.5 two points can be seen:

a   As price has to be lowered to increase sales, marginal revenue is not equal to price as in perfect competition: the additional revenue gained from each extra sale is always less than price or average revenue, and thus the MR curve will always be below the AR curve in monopoly.

b   As price is identical to average revenue, the demand curve is also the curve relating average revenue to the quantity produced.

The information in Box 13.5 can now be shown in diagrammatic form to show the relationship between the average and marginal revenue curves.

BOX 13.6

The monopolist's marginal revenue and average revenue curves

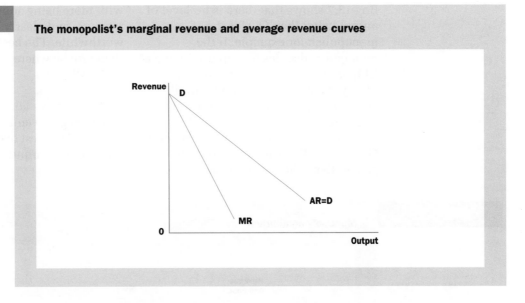

Monopoly equilibrium

Like the firm in perfect competition, the monopolist will maximise profits where
Marginal cost = Marginal revenue
(MC = MR)
This indicates the best or profit-

maximising level of output.
When the average cost and average revenue curves are related to each other, they indicate the level of profit

BOX 13.7

Equating MC with MR in monopoly

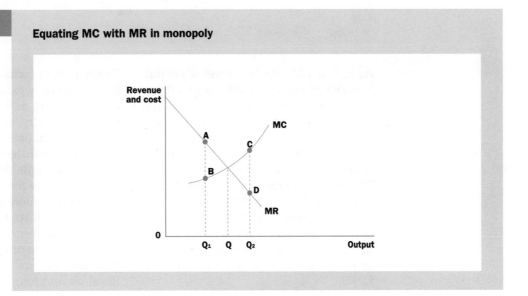

Box 13.7 shows that there is no level of output better than OQ for the monopolist; for example, if the monopolist decides to stop producing at OQ_1, then MR would be greater than MC by the distance AB, and output could be expanded, with more being added to revenue than to cost; if the monopolist decides to produce beyond OQ, say to OQ_2, then MC would be greater than MR by the distance CD,

with more being added to cost than to revenue, and clearly this would not be worthwhile. The best output would therefore be where
MC = MR.

In Box 13.8, we add the average cost and average revenue curves to show the monopolist's best output and level of profit at that output.

BOX 13.8

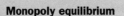
Monopoly equilibrium

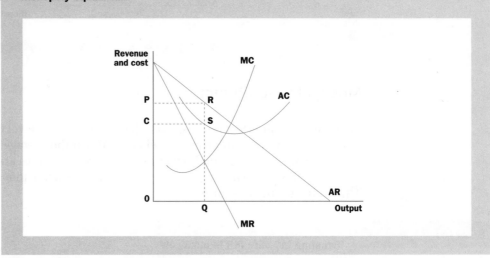

As in Box 13.7, the best level of output is at OQ where MC = MR. To find the price or average revenue, a vertical line is taken from OQ to the demand curve (the monopolist 'charges what the market will bear'), and a horizontal line is drawn across to the revenue/cost axis. The price is therefore OP or QR. The level of profit is indicated by the amount by which AR exceeds AC: AR = QR; AC = QS; so RS is the profit per unit of output, and the total supernormal profit is given by the area CPRS.

Under perfect competition, supernormal profits can only exist in the short run, as in the long run new firms are attracted into the industry, and the abnormal profits are competed away as the market supply curve shifts to the right and the market price falls. However, under monopoly, new firms are unable to enter the market as there are various barriers to entry which are the very source of monopoly power. Thus a single firm may remain the only supplier, and supernormal profits may persist in both the short and long run; in monopoly, there is therefore no distinction between short and long run equilibrium.

Although the existence of such long-run abnormal profits implies a considerable degree of market power, the fact that the monopolist cannot control both the supply of the good and its demand means that complete control does not exist. As we show in Chapter 14, corporations devote an enormous amount of time, money and effort trying to mould our demand to fit in with their long-term corporate plans: a situation which might be described as producer sovereignty; however, provided the demand curve is not completely inelastic, some element of consumer sovereignty will still remain.

You should note that a monopolist will always produce at a point where demand is elastic, and will achieve this by restricting output to keep price in the upper price ranges (in Chapter 6, we demonstrated how the elasticity of demand on a straight line demand curve varies from infinity at the top left section of the curve to nought at its bottom right section). Box 13.8 shows that the MR curve falls continuously as price falls, eventually becoming negative. It can be seen, however, that although the MC curve falls and rises, it is always positive as there will always be some cost involved in producing any economic good. It would therefore follow that where MC = MR and the firm is in profit-maximising equilibrium, MR will be positive, and where this occurs demand is always elastic.

Monopoly compared with perfect competition

In the discussion that follows, we shall draw extensively upon several concepts that were introduced in earlier parts of the book: that is, the perfect competition model, consumer surplus and the various types of economic efficiency, static, dynamic, productive and allocative (see Section 2). If you are unsure about the meaning of any of these concepts, it would be advisable at this stage to refer back to Section 2 of the book before proceeding.

Consumer and producer sovereignty

Because of the conditions of perfect competition – many buyers and sellers, perfect knowledge and freedom of entry – firms would be forced to produce those goods and services which consumers most wanted. Any firm or even group of firms not behaving in this way would be unable to survive for very long as the competitive pressures from those firms who were responding to consumers' wishes would soon drive them into extinction. From this point of view it could be argued that consumers are 'sovereign' in as much as it is they who 'call all the shots'. However, as described previously, monopoly producers may well decide on which types of goods they are going to supply and at what prices, and then set about manipulating and moulding consumers' tastes, via their marketing activities, to match their pre-determined output plans – a situation in which the producer and not the consumer is sovereign.

Under monopoly, price is likely to be higher and output lower as compared with perfect competition.

Box 13.9 can be used to predict the effect of a monopoly taking over a perfectly competitive industry, making the assumption that costs would be unchanged in the process of monopolisation.

BOX 13.9

Perfect competition compared with monopoly

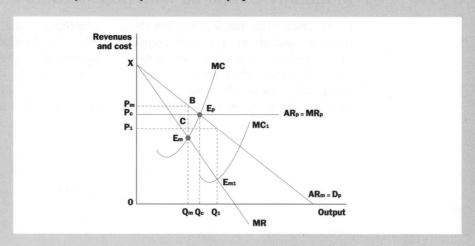

AR$_m$(D$_p$) is the monopolist's demand curve and the market demand curve under perfect competition. MC is the combined marginal cost curve of all the firms in the perfectly competitive industry. As the competitive firm's marginal cost curve is also its supply curve, this combined marginal cost curve must also represent the industry's supply curve. Equilibrium occurs where demand equals supply, and therefore in perfect competition OP$_c$ would be the equilibrium price and OQ$_c$ the equilibrium output of the industry. If the industry is monopolised and costs are unchanged, the monopolist would produce where MC = MR, giving an equilibrium price of OP$_m$, higher than OP$_c$, and an equilibrium quantity of OQ$_m$, lower than OQ$_c$.

It can also be seen from Box 13.9 that consumer surplus falls as a result of monopolisation from P$_c$XE$_p$ to P$_m$XB. Area P$_c$P$_m$BC represents a direct transfer of welfare from consumers to the producer, while area BCE$_p$ is lost to both groups and is known as a deadweight loss.

Deadweight welfare loss is the loss of consumer surplus resulting from the monopolisation of a perfectly competitive industry.

Its existence implies that society's resources are not being used in a way that would achieve maximum allocative efficiency.

However, if monopolisation of a perfectly competitive industry leads to the reaping of economies of scale, as may well be the case when several small producers are replaced by one large producer, then lower prices and a greater output might result – the opposite of what we originally predicted. In this case, it is possible to predict a social gain from monopolisation. In Box 13.9, the gaining of economies of scale is indicated by a downward shift of the marginal cost curve from MC to MC$_1$, and where MC$_1$ intersects with the MR curve a new and greater equilibrium output is obtained at OQ$_1$, with a price of OP$_1$, which is lower than the perfectly competitive price of OP$_c$. However, the monopolist has still not achieved full allocative efficiency as price is above marginal cost; neither has it achieved full productive efficiency as it will not be operating on the bottom point of its new average cost curve.

Economic efficiency in perfect competition and monopoly

● Productive efficiency

As explained in Chapter 8, this refers to a situation in which output is being produced at the the lowest possible cost, i.e. where the firm is producing on the bottom point of its average total cost curve. Since the MC curve always passes through the lowest point of the AC curve, it follows that productive efficiency is achieved where MC = AC.

BOX 13.10

Equilibrium in perfect competition and monopoly

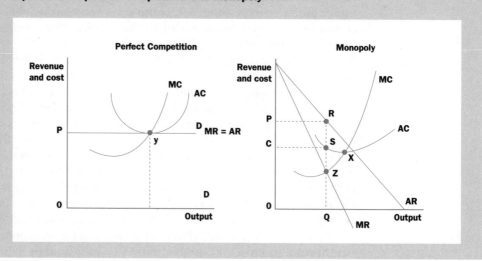

Box 13.10 shows the long-run equilibrium positions of the firm in perfect competition and the monopolist. We can clearly see that for the perfectly competitive firm, productive efficiency automatically arises, as in long run equilibrium, MC = AC at point Y. However, in the case of monopoly, the firm is not operating on the lowest point of its AC curve (point X), but is instead operating on some higher point (point S). We can therefore conclude that in contrast to perfect competition, and assuming an absence of economies of scale, the monopolist will be productively inefficient.

Allocative efficiency

As explained in Chapter 8, this occurs where price equals marginal cost in all parts of the economy.
Again, with reference to the graphs in Box 13.10, it can be seen that, in perfect competition, MR = MC, and MR = price. MC therefore = price (at point Y), and allocative efficiency occurs. However, the monopolist produces where MC = MR, but price does not equal MR. It can be seen that at the equilibrium output of OQ, price is greater than MC by the distance RZ, and the monopolist could thus be said to be allocatively inefficient.

Dynamic efficiency

Both productive and allocative efficiency are examples of static efficiency in that they are concerned with how well resources are being used at a particular point in time. However, it is also important to consider how efficiently resources are being allocated over a period of time, when, for example, there may be technological advances, and this is the concern of dynamic efficiency.

Monopoly has been justified on the grounds that it may lead to dynamic efficiency. This is because the supernormal profits made will not only enable the monopolist to finance expensive research and development programmes, but may also provide the necessary inducement to undertake such programmes in the first place. In contrast to this, firms operating in a perfectly competitive environment may lack the incentive to finance expensive R&D programmes, as open access to the market would mean that their competitors would immediately be able to share in the fruits of any success. The greater certainty of being able to earn supernormal profits in the long run also explains why levels of investment in capital projects may be greater in more monopolistic markets.

We also discuss the dynamic potential of monopoly in Chapter 14 in relation to product innovation.

BOX 13.11

Summary of the disadvantages and advantages of monopoly

Disadvantages
1 Producer as opposed to consumer sovereignty
2 A higher price and a lower output as compared with perfect competition
3 Productive inefficiency
4 Allocative inefficiency

Advantages
1 Large scale production may result in economies of scale, offering the possibility of lower prices
2 Avoids the wasteful duplication of distribution costs in the case of utilities
3 Dynamic efficiency
4 Abnormal profits may be used to consumers' advantage in providing funds for research and development

REVIEW

In this chapter, we have considered the various aspects of the theory of monopoly. We have demonstrated how this market form differs sharply from the textbook model of perfect competition, and the implications of this divergence for price, output and efficiency in particular markets; we have also tried to broaden your perception of monopoly through the use of material contained in Focus 3.13 and Boxes such as 13.2, which set the topic in a social, political, historical and factual context, rather than a purely economic one.

Multiple choice

The following three questions are based on the diagram which shows the cost and revenue curves of a public sector monopoly with spare productive capacity.

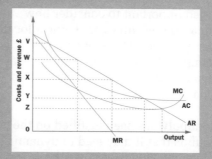

1 If the monopoly wishes to maximise profits it will set price at level

A   OV

B   OW

C   OX

D   OY

E   OZ

(ULEAC, June 1993)

2 If the monopoly wishes to maximise revenue regardless of profit it will set price at level

A   OV

B   OW

C   OX

D   OY

E   OZ

(ULEAC, June 1993)

3 If the monopoly wishes to maximise production subject to not making a loss it will set price at level

A   OV

B   OW

C   OX

D   OY

E   OZ

(ULEAC, June 1993)

4 **A profit-maximising monopolist will certainly**

A   produce less than a competitive industry would have produced

B   charge more than a competitive industry would have charged

C   charge different prices in different markets

D   make more than 'normal' profits

E   equate marginal revenue with marginal cost

(ULEAC, June 1993)

5 Below is a diagram showing costs and revenue of a firm.

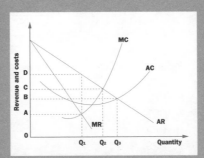

If a public corporation, faced with the costs and revenues shown in the diagram, wishes to break even it will sell at price

A   OA

B   OB

C   OC

D   OD

(AEB, June 1990)

6 **If a monopolist charged a price which maximised profit**

A   the price would equal the cost of the last unit produced

B   total revenue would be at a maximum

C   production would take place at an optimum level of output

D   the revenue received from the last unit provided would equal the cost of producing that unit

E   all economies of scale would be gained by the monopolist.

(ULEAC, June 1993)

7 The diagram below represents the market conditions faced by a monopolist.

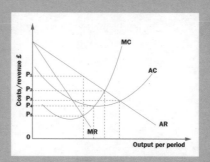

Productive efficiency occurs at a level of output at which the price is

A   OP1

B   OP2

C   OP3

D   OP4

E   OP5

(ULEAC, June 1993)

8 In the diagram, MC(C) represents the combined marginal costs of perfectly competitive firms in the market, and MC(M) represents marginal cost after the firms have amalgamated to form a monopoly and rationalised their production methods.

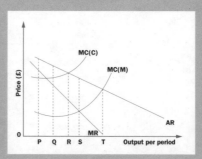

What would be the profit maximising output if the original firms had amalgamated but not changed their production methods?

A   OP

B   OQ

C   OR

D   OS

E   OT

(ULEAC, June 1994)

9 A monopoly is a profit maximiser. It discovers that at its present output level marginal cost is greater than marginal revenue. Which one of the following decisions would increase its profits?

A   Increase price and decrease output

B   Decrease output and leave price unchanged

C   Increase price and leave output unchanged

D   Decrease price and increase output

(IB, November 1994)

The following graph shows the cost and revenue curves of a monopolist.

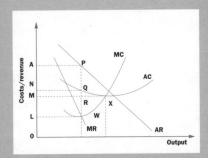

At the profit-maximising output of the firm its abnormal profits are represented by the area

A   NQRM

B   APRM

C   APQN

D   APWL

(AEB, June 1992)

10 If a profit-maximising monopolist is subject to a 50% tax on his abnormal profit he will

A   raise price and reduce output

B   lower price and increase output

C   leave price and output unchanged

D   raise price and leave output unchanged

(AEB, June 1993)

Data response

THE FLYING MONOPOLISTS

Should Boeing and Airbus be forbidden to team up to build a super-jumbo?

In some businesses, the high cost of developing new products raises a barrier to would-be competitors. That day has already arrived in civil aerospace. America's Boeing and the partners of Europe's Airbus Industrie are the only companies capable of building a range of commercial jets. Once arch-rivals, they are now thinking of building an 800-seat super-jumbo together.

The idea poses a dilemma for governments. Without collaboration, and perhaps without public money as well, the super-jumbo may never be built – which would be a pity. But suppose the partnership goes ahead. If it succeeds, and the super-jumbo is much in demand, the partners will have a partial monopoly – one which they may seek to extend. This could hurt airlines and their customers, the travelling public. If the partners fail, and the super-jumbo loses money, any public investment in it will have been wasted. This trade-off between innovation and competition will become increasingly troublesome. Many of the industries governments care most about – high-tech, high-wage industries with a claim to be "strategic" – are suited to international, and anti-competitive, collaboration. The plans for the super-jumbo are a test case. How should governments respond?

Just good friends?

Entirely new commercial airliners are already too costly for any one producer to develop on its own. To bring a super-jumbo to market could cost $15 billion. A partnership, as Boeing and Airbus point out, would spread the risk. The aircraft makers also say that the super-jumbo serves a public interest: it would help to relieve overcrowded airports. That, they say, is why they should be allowed to collaborate, and perhaps be given some public money, too.

The case for a public subsidy is weak. Some argue that financial markets are short-termist and therefore mistakenly discriminate against big projects of this kind. But the record of governments in judging the viability of such undertakings is abysmal – witness Concorde. Financial markets may be imperfect, but in matters of this sort, they are a lot better than governments. Once governments become involved in highly publicised schemes involving the "national interest", politics takes over and wishful thinking overrides economic reality.

A public subsidy for the super-jumbo venture should therefore be ruled out. A harder question is whether to forbid the collaboration altogether. The crucial issue is whether the new super-jumbo would have a monopoly, or whether competition could be left to regulate its price. If the partners tried to exploit any monopoly power by charging too high a price for the new aeroplane, you might think, airlines could use smaller aircraft. The trouble is, these smaller aircraft are also produced by the partners. They would be tempted to set the prices of their existing aircraft to make their super-jumbo viable. In short, collaboration on the super-jumbo would be both the reason and the means to build an aircraft-pricing cartel.

Boeing may be trying to protect the monopoly-of-sorts it already enjoys with the 747. Airbus had considered making its own, slightly smaller, super-jumbo. This would have stolen sales from the 747. The defection of one or two Airbus partners to the Boeing camp could break up the European consortium.

All this suggests that a partnership should be forbidden on competition grounds. In that event, the super-jumbo may never be built – but that may not be such a bad thing. Airbus and Boeing would continue to build bigger jets.

In aerospace, as in other industries, competition remains the most reliable spur to innovation. In this case, and in the many others that are sure to arise, governments should be guided by a simple rule: do not be drawn into supporting partnerships that are chiefly attempts to corner a market.

*Source: adapted from **The Economist** (June 1993).*

a What is meant by a monopolist?
b The passage states that 'the high cost of developing new products raises a barrier to would-be competitors' (lines 1–2).
i Why does the 'high cost of developing new products' (line 1) act as a barrier to entry?
ii Briefly explain one other barrier to entry which could occur in the aircraft manufacturing industry.
c Evaluate the arguments put forward to support the creation of this monopoly.
d The passage suggests that neither companies nor governments are very good at assessing the desirability of investments. Discuss two different ways by which economists would try to determine whether an investment, such as building this new aeroplane, should take place.

(AEB, June 1995)

N.B. Part (d) should be attempted after you have read Chapter 3.18.

Essays

1 Discuss the view that monopoly markets are inevitably inefficient and undesirable.
(WCEJ, June 1994)

2 a What is meant by economic efficiency?
b Can monopolies ever be efficient?
(AEB, June 1992)

3 Analyse and comment upon the pricing and output decisions of the firm and the industry in perfect competition and monopoly.
(Cambridge, June 1992)

3.14 What is oligopoly?

FOCUS

The INVESTIGATOR

Market Shares

The data below indicate the market shares of various large companies in the chocolate market.

The UK chocolate market, % share of sales, 1992	
Cadbury Schweppes	30
Nestlé	28
Mars	26
Jacobs Suchard	2
Ferrero Rocher	2
Others	12

Source: ***Adapted from press reports***, *1992.*

1) To what extent do you think that this market is competitive?
2) What do you think are the most important ways in which the companies in this market compete against each other?

Preview

In this chapter, we examine the market form known as oligopoly. In particular, we shall investigate the following key areas:

- the nature of oligopoly;
- how it can be measured;
- the various forms of non-price competition under oligopoly.

The nature of oligopoly

Oligopoly is a market form in which there are only a few firms in the industry with many buyers; so market supply will be concentrated in the hands of relatively few producers, although an industry might still be said to be oligopolistic where several smaller firms existed alongside the few large firms that dominate; the wholesale petrol market provides a suitable example of the latter. The markets for cigarettes, records, confectionery, motor vehicles, fizzy drinks, high street banks, airline carriers, domestic appliances, soap powders and supermarket chains all provide good examples of oligopoly in the UK and elsewhere.

Where the few firms produce an identical product, this is known as perfect oligopoly, and where, more commonly, the products are differentiated, this is referred to as imperfect oligopoly. The case of duopoly, where there are only two firms in the industry, is a special case of oligopoly.

However, the absolute number of firms in the market is less significant than the way in which they behave and the relationship between the firms that comprise the industry. In the case of the monopolist, for example, independent price and output decisions can be made, with the only consideration being the customer's reaction to the change in price. However, in oligopoly, where there is competition amongst the relatively few, each firm has to also try to assess the reaction of its rivals to a change in price, as each firm will occupy a sufficiently important position within the industry for its particular price and output decisions to have a significant impact on its competitors. Thus if an oligopolist is thinking of raising the price of its product, it has to assess whether its rivals will do likewise or keep price down in order to gain more custom. Oligopoly is therefore characterised by interdependence between the firms that comprise the industry, and by reactive market behaviour.

The extent of oligopoly

Oligopoly has emerged as the most prevalent market form in the industrialised world. This can partly be explained by the existence of economies of scale, especially in manufacturing, encouraging the growth of large-scale production; inevitably, as firms grow in size, the number of firms supplying the market falls, and hence the tendency towards oligopoly power. Moreover, once established, this power may be sustained by various barriers to entry, similar to those that exist under monopoly.

Economists use concentration ratios to indicate the increased importance of

large, usually oligopolistic, firms to the UK economy. Two types of concentration ratio are used.

- An aggregate concentration ratio
  This indicates the proportion of total economic activity in the UK, usually in terms of output, accounted for by the 100 largest firms in the manufacturing sector. Census of production figures indicate that the degree of aggregate concentration rose from a figure of 16 per cent at the turn of the twentieth century to 41 per cent in 1981, before declining to 36 per cent in 1991.

● A market concentration ratio
Market concentration ratios are used to measure the degree of concentration within a particular industry. 2,3,5 or 100 firm concentration ratios may be used:

For example, the 5 Firm Concentration Ratio =

$$\frac{\text{The output of the largest 5 firms}}{\text{The output of all the firms in the industry}}$$

It thus shows the the proportion of an industry's total output which comes from the five largest firms.

The table in Box 14.1 shows the concentration ratios for the five largest firms in a variety of UK industrial sectors in 1990.

BOX 14.1

Concentration ratios for the five largest firms in various UK industrial sectors, 1990

Industry	5-firm concentration ratio (%)
Tobacco industry	99.1
Iron and steel	94.8
Motor vehicles and engineering	87.3
Aerospace equipment	77.1
Agricultural machinery and tractors	75.1
Soap and toilet preparations	56.3
Brewing and malting	45.1
Telecommunications equipment	33.1
Specialized chemicals	27.6
Wooden containers	17.3
Clothing, hats and gloves	16.4
Wooden and upholstered furniture	14.5
Processing of plastics	9.6

Source: **Central Statistical Office** (1992).

However, although concentration ratios provide a first approximation of the degree of concentration in an industry, they cannot always be relied upon to provide a complete picture of the competitiveness of an industry. This is because such ratios do not take account of the extent of competition from abroad (e.g. the UK motor industry faces significant import penetration), nor do they allow for the possibility of regional, sometimes almost total, monopoly power within a country (e.g. the various regional water and electricity boards in the UK).

Non-price competition

BOX 14.2

Changing BRAND POSITIONING

Is the Persil brand undergoing a sex change?

If Persil were a human instead of a soap powder, she would be a nice, friendly mum and **Daily Mail** reader, so numerous qualitative research groups conclude. The brand's feminine qualities were for years promoted by the strapline:
"Washes whiter and it cares."

"Part of the enduring appeal of Persil as a brand over the years was a personality that its target market warmed to," Paul Southgate, chief executive of the design agency, Wickens Tutt Southgate, and author of the recent book, **Total Branding by Design**, says.

And the strategy certainly seemed to work. Throughout the early 80s, Persil maintained a healthy 10 to 20 percentage point lead in market share over the rival Ariel in the UK. But product innovation helped Ariel to catch up – notably in 1986, when it launched Ariel Liquid and closed the gap with Persil to a couple of points.

Southgate argues that with Persil Power, Unilever has adopted a risky strategy by dramatically changing Persil's brand position-

ing. "I'm sure it was an extremely well-thought strategy on the part of Lever Brothers, which is an extremely experienced and astute marketer. But if a brand like that [caring, feminine Persil] launches a product called Persil Power, whose entire proposition is built around a powerful cleaning action, whose design uses more masculine colours and which then attracts controversy over the robustness of its cleaning action, then there is a danger that the brand is inadvertently undergoing a sex change," he says.

Tim Hammond, detergents marketing director at Lever UK, does not agree that there has been a fundamental shift in positioning: "I'd say there was maybe a shift in emphasis, but nothing too dramatic. The Persil brand, in the minds of consumers, stood for excellent cleaning results as well as excellent care. This particular launch focused direction more on the cleaning message. After all, the single biggest consumer requirement is to get clothes clean."

*Source: **The Campaign Report** (November 1994).*

BOX 14.3

DISSATISFACTION *and need*

FRANCIS WHEEN EXAMINES OUR INSATIABLE APPETITE FOR INVENTIONS WE DON'T NEED

Marxism is dead. It has been disproved, debunked, exploded. It has rung down the curtain and gone to join the choir invisible. It is an ex-parrot.

Or so we are told. But every time I see an Innovations mail-order catalogue – and it's hard to avoid them at this time of year, as they fall out of magazines like so many autumn leaves – I realise that Karl Marx was largely right. Capitalism, he pointed out, depends for its survival on constantly extending people's needs. To quote from Ernest Mandel's excellent summary, The **Marxist Theory of Alienation**: 'The system must provoke continual artificial dissatisfaction in human beings because without that dissatisfaction the sales of new gadgets which are more and more divorced from genuine human needs cannot be increased.'

Marx's only mistake was to assume that consumers would eventually become so alienated by this process that they would rebel against it. Instead, they have embraced it as an invaluable source of Christmas gifts, jamming the credit-card hotline with their orders for revolving shoe-racks, pyjamas that glow in the dark, a see-through alarm clock ('highly original'), a clock with no face or hands, an hourglass with 'digital sand' ('uses two button-cell batteries') and a 'gleaming FM/AM/LW radio' which not only looks like a motorbike but also emits 'the emotive throb' of a Harley-Davidson when switched on. (Quite why anyone would want the background noise of a revving engine while listening to **The Archers** or **This Week's Composer** is not explained, though I can see that it might come in useful for drowning out the pious platitudes of **Thought For The Day**.)

Even old Karl might have raised a bushy eyebrow at the ingenuity with which capitalism continues to create 'needs' that don't exist. Look at the treats on offer from Innovations this autumn: 'The world's first microchip-controlled home Drinkscentre' dispenses gin and tonic 'at the touch of a button' and costs £149.99. Thanks a lot. For a fraction of that price, one could buy a bottle of Gordon's and several litres of Schweppes, unscrew the tops, tip them into a glass and get stuck in.

Or how about the Micromix? 'This beautifully simple British invention automatically stirs food while it cooks in the microwave. Perfect for dishes like scrambled egg.' There is, of course, an even more beautifully simple way of making scrambled eggs: put egg mixture in saucepan, heat, stir with wooden spoon – and eat.

*Source: **Observer Life Magazine** (September 1994).*

TASK 14.1

Use boxes 14.2 and 14.3 to evaluate the view of Ernest Mandel that 'the system must provoke continual artificial dissatisfaction in human beings because without that dissatisfaction the sales of new gadgets which are more and more divorced from genuine human needs cannot be increased'.

As we shall see from our forthcoming discussion of oligopoly, an important feature of oligopolistic markets, i.e. ones dominated by a few large firms, is the tendency towards relative price stability Lack of price movement will occur most obviously where firms collude with each other to collectively fix their prices, but it may also occur in a situation of what is known as non-collusive oligopoly, where no such price agreements exist; interdependent firms may well come to the conclusion that, in the longer term, there is no point in 'cutting each other's throats' by engaging in price warfare as this could be disastrous for all the combatants, although there may well be a tendency towards occasional short bursts of price cutting. However, this absence of price competition does not necessarily mean an absence of competition: oligopolistic firms are likely to compete in a variety of non-price forms.

Non-price competition occurs where firms attempt to win a competitive advantage over their rivals by strategies other than reducing prices. Non-price competition inevitably involves product differentiation

Product differentiation is a strategy adopted by firms to create real or perceived differences in the goods they offer, which are essentially the same as those of their rivals.

Here, oligopolistic competitors try to carve out separate markets in which they can command **consumer loyalty** through the creation of actual or imagined differences in the goods or services they offer, which are essentially the same as their rivals. This is in contrast to perfect competition where the good on offer, perhaps an agricultural one, is homogeneous, and product differentiation is difficult – e.g. one carrot is pretty much the same as another.

Product differentiation is extremely widespread amongst the whole variety of consumer goods and services that we buy – washing machines, television sets, home computers, motor cars, washing powders, soft drinks, packaged holidays and financial services, to name but a few. These are all differentiated one from another in a variety of ways, including shape , size, quality and image.

Non-price competition may take a variety of forms, including:

- Advertising;
- Branding;
- Product innovation;
- Packaging;
- The provision of after sales services, e.g. product guarantees;
- Free samples and gift offers.

We shall examine the first three of these – advertising, branding and product innovation – in greater detail, whilst Box 14.4 provides an example of a recent gift offer which did not go quite as planned!

BOX 14.4

BUYING THE DREAM
Sucker punch

Hoover's ill-fated flight of fancy has dealt a fresh blow to the image

To the group of senior executives sitting at Hoover's UK headquarters in South Wales last summer, it seemed like a terrific idea.

There they were, wondering how they could drum up sales in the recession and all too aware that the company was about to enter its traditional lean pre-Christmas period.

In marketing jargon, Hoover products – vacuum cleaners and washing machines – are "distress purchases". People may buy a new one as a treat – when moving house, say – but usually an appliance has to go on the blink before it is replaced.

Christmas is especially difficult: vacuum cleaners and washing machines do not appear on many present lists. And this Christmas, in the midst of recession, would be terrible.

The executives' scheme was simple: promotions with Air Miles and air tickets were all the rage, so why not follow suit? They called in a firm of travel agents and drafted a plan. They narrowed the offer down to two flights to a choice of six European cities, required a customer to spend at least £119 – the price of the cheapest qualifying Hoover vacuum – and reckoned on 50,000 applicants.

Last week, Hoover fired the two senior executives responsible for the scheme: Brian Webb, vice president of marketing UK, and William Foust, head of Hoover UK and European president. Michael Gilbey, director of marketing services, was also made redundant but the company said this was not connected with the offer.

Their attempt to boost sales in a flat vacuum cleaner market had exceeded their wildest expectations – so much so that triumph turned to disaster.

Instead of 50,000 applicants, there were 200,000 (including an additional 100,000 for a second promotion for flights to the US, launched before the first offer turned sour). Shops could not get enough Hoover products to cope with demand. The company was forced to draft in extra manpower to help on the travel side and it put the factory on a seven-day week.

Management has had to find at least an extra £20m to buy the air tickets. One industry expert estimated that for every 4,000 responses, Hoover would have to pay £1.75m (4,000 x two people x the £220 average air fare).

Worst of all, the good name of Hoover has been pilloried in the media as complaints from customers anxious to obtain their free flights have flooded in.

And the Hoovers that were hard to find in the shops are now easily available – in the classifieds in Exchange & Mart and local newspapers.

The fiasco has ceased to be just Hoover's problem. Sales for other vacuum and washing machine manufacturers dipped as customers plumped for Hoovers and brought forward their purchases. But after Hoover, the £10bn promotions industry has been hit hardest.

The public, already deeply suspicious of sales "gimmicks" and far less gullible than marketing personnel suppose, have had their prejudices confirmed by Hoover's deliberate, if failed attempts to stop their customers from flying: sales promotions are a con.

*Source: **Independent on Sunday** (April 1993).*

Advertising

Advertisements are usually classified according to whether they are informative or persuasive.

● **Informative advertising**

As the name implies, this type of advertising is concerned with the dissemination of information about products or services, e.g. as regards availability, price or performance, and such information would be of a factual type. For instance, an advertisement for a car could focus on such things as its fuel consumption, its safety features, the time it takes to reach certain speeds, its price, the names and addresses of main dealers, etc.

BOX 14.5

Sweet taste of success...
Mars barmy

TV POLICE OUT TO BAN FAVOURITE CHOC ADVERTS
By Dominic Mills – Editor of Campaign Magazine

The television watchdogs have bitten again, but this time their victim is not sex, violence or four-letter words, but the humble chocolate bar.

Tough draft guidelines published by the Independent Television Commission would ban some of our best-loved confectionery advertisements from our television screens, because they claim they are bad for our health.

It could mean unemployment for the Milky bar kid and a sticky end for the Flake girl. Creations such as the Harry Enfield character who loads his shopping trolley with Dime bars would never see the light of day.

For the proposed rules include banning all adverts showing people eating two or three confectionery bars, or a whole box of chocolates, at one sitting.

The watchdogs believe children are eating too many sweets and snacks that are unhealthy for them – and the telly ads are to blame.

The unspoken message is "These ads are too persuasive and you have to tone them down."

A 65g MARS A DAY GIVES YOU...
● 295 calories – 2.6g protein, 45.2g carbohydrates (nearly all sugar), and 11.4g fat (53 per cent saturated).
● NO fibre, 17 per cent of the recommended daily amount of calcium, 17 per cent of the RDA of Vitamin B2 (Riboflavin) and 14 per cent of the RDA of iron.
● NINE Mars bars would give an average man all the calories he needs a day.

MARS BAR FACTS
● MARS bar was launched in 1932.
● MARS makes three million bars a day – on average we each eat one bar every 3 – 4 weeks.
● THE Mars slogan "A Mars a day helps you work, rest and play" was dreamt up in 1959. In 1992 it was examined for accuracy by the ITC and given the all clear.
● SOLDIERS use Mars bars in their survival rations. A mountaineer stuck for five days on Mount Elbris, Eastern Europe, survived on a diet of mostly Mars bars.
● A MARS bar is a convenient source of glucose for diabetics at risk of going into a low sugar coma.

*Source: **Daily Mirror** (October 1994).*

TASK 14.2   Do the tougher rules on T.V. advertising introduced by the Independent Television Commission represent an increase or decrease in consumer sovereignty?

● **Persuasive advertising**

Informative advertising is that advertising which confines itself to the dissemination of information.

Persuasive advertising is that advertising whose primary purpose is to persuade rather than to provide factual information.

The main feature of persuasive advertising is that it provides consumers with little, if any, meaningful information about the products being advertised; rather it seeks to persuade consumers to buy one particular brand of a product rather than another through a combination of 'catchy' jingles and appealing images.

If the advertising is successful, the images and jingles register into our consciousness and create strong brand loyalty; e.g. the lines, 'A Mars a day helps you work, rest and play', and 'Coke, the real thing' are extremely widely known, but provide consumers with absolutely no information on the sugar, fat and chemical contents of the products in question.

Often the images are sexual and are intended to lead consumers to believe that their relative attractiveness to the opposite sex will be enhanced by the consumption of the good. Many advertisements for such things as cigarettes, alcohol, cosmetics, sports cars and even ice-cream fall into this category (remember Chapter 4)

TASK 14.3   **Are you informed or persuaded?**

The next time you watch commercial television, make a note and brief summary of the advertisements which appear during your first hour of viewing.

Classify these advertisements into informative and persuasive. Which type of advertising predominates?

The table in Box 14.6 provides a summary of the potential advantages and disadvantages of advertising to consumers, firms and the economy as a whole, although its overall impact on such factors as prices, costs, competition and resource allocation is, as with many aspects of economics, very much a matter of judgement.

BOX 14.6

The advantages and disadvantages of advertising

	ADVANTAGES	DISADVANTAGES

For consumers	1 Acts as a medium of communication between sellers and buyers, provides information on product availability and facilitates wider choice
	2 May lead to lower prices if
	  a larger sales and production levels result in economies of scale and lower unit costs
	  b the advertising is based on price competition
		1 Persuasive advertising may render consumer choice irrational and destroy consumer sovereignty
		2 Through its portrayal of a fantasy, largely affluent world, it creates unnecessary wants by generating feelings of inadequacy and greed
		3 May lead to higher prices because
		  a there may be higher costs, particularly if economies of scale are not achieved
		  b advertising may act as a barrier to the entry of new firms and thus increase monopoly power, particularly where established firms engage in saturation advertising which cannot be matched by smaller firms

For firms	1 If successful, advertising will
	  a shift the demand curve to the right
	  b make the demand curve more inelastic
	2 It may enable firms to maintain their monopoly power through the creation of brand loyalty and barriers to entry
	3 Greater profits may be earned if higher sales and output levels lead to economies of scale and lower costs
		1 Lower profits if costs of production are increased without raising sufficient extra revenue, or without shifting the demand curve making demand more inelastic

For the economy as a whole	1 A greater level of employment if the level of sales and production increase 2 Certain sectors of the economy only survive because of the revenue which advertising earns e.g. commercial radio, newspapers and magazines	1 Advertising may lead to a misallocation of society's scarce resources as the pattern of production may reflect the skill of the advertisers in manipulating consumers' tastes, rather than what consumers actually want/need 2 The generation of negative externalities through tasteless or unsightly advertisements

Branding

BOX 14.7

The top 20 European stature brands

Rank	Brand name
1	Coca-Cola/Coke
2	BMW
3	Adidas
4	Mercedes-Benz
5	Philips
6	Kodak
7	Sony
8	Volkswagen
9	Gillette
10	Pepsi Cola
11	Ford
12	Ferrari
13	Levi's
14	Colgate
15	Volvo
16	Rolls Royce
17	Renault
18	Lego
19	Audi
20	Nestlé

These are the brands that Y&R says European consumers are most familiar with and hold in the highest esteem.

Source: **Y&R's BrandAsset Valuator**, based on field work in ten countries in Europe

Source: **Campaign Report** (November 1994).

The creation of consumer loyalty to particular brands is mainly achieved through advertising, and it is in oligopolistic markets where branding, backed by extensive product promotion, is most prevalent. The markets for soap powders, cereals, cars, confectionery and cosmetics provide a few notable examples.

The main aim of branding is to make particular goods, produced by particular firms, appear as if they have unique features which the products of competing firms do not possess. On occasions these features may be real, e.g. the distinctive quality of a Rolls Royce car. However, often the 'uniqueness' may only exist in consumers' minds, but a difference, real or imagined, in how consumers perceive branded products, may be sufficient to allow goods to be sold at very different prices – well known brands of soft drinks, sports-wear, bars of soap and shaving creams are all sold at higher prices than their 'own brand', or lesser-known, equivalents.

Thus, if successful, branding will reduce the degree of substitutability for the good, make its demand more inelastic, allow for higher prices and profits to be earned and enable the brand to become unassailable.

Multiple branding is the practice whereby firms produce several brands of the same product, e.g. soap-powders, in order to make it more difficult for potential new market entrants to compete.

Moreover, the practice of multiple branding serves as a very effective barrier to entry of new firms. Go to any supermarket and you will see several brands of soap-powders on the shelves, although these are are mainly produced by just two firms, Unilever and Procter and Gamble. The costs of breaking into such a market would be formidable as any new entrant would have to compete against numerous brands of soap-powder, requiring an enormous outlay on advertising; obviously, if Unilever and Procter and Gamble only produced one brand each, the task of contesting the market would be made considerably easier.

Product innovation

Non-price competition in oligopoly may also take the form of product innovation whereby rival firms attempt to gain a larger slice of the market by constantly seeking to improve the quality and/or style of their existing products, or by developing entirely new products. This innovation usually has to be backed by extensive research and development (R&D), and has the effect of causing rapid obsolescence of consumer durable goods, a renewable source of demand and certain decline for those firms unwilling or unable to engage in such innovation. Most car manufacturers, for example, are constantly in the process of changing the design and other features of particular models so as to generate new demand, and the few large firms that dominate the pharmaceuticals industry are locked into a perpetual struggle to develop new and better drugs.

This process fits well with the writings of Joseph Schumpeter (1883–1950) who took a long-run, dynamic view of monopoly to argue that, over time, it would be far more efficient than perfect competition. He argued that the static method, i.e. taking a point in time

approach, of comparing perfect competition with monopoly, overlooked the likelihood of technical advances which may lower costs and prices as output expands. Although Schumpeter's analysis relates specifically to monopoly, it is appropriate to apply it to contemporary oligopolistic markets.

Schumpeter identified two main reasons why monopolies would be more innovative than competitive industries: first, because of the earning of long-term supernormal profits, the monopolist would have greater access to the funds necessary to finance inevitably expensive R&D programmes which are the basis of most innovation; and secondly, the monopolist would have a far greater inducement to undertake R&D in the first place – in highly competitive markets, any technical advantage gained by one firm would only permit the earning of high profits to be made for a relatively short period of time, as new entrants and existing firms copy the innovation and bid any abnormal profits away; the monopolist, however, would be the sole beneficiary of technical advance and would thus be able to reap the benefits of lower costs and higher profits indefinitely.

However, empirical evidence on the subject suggests that whilst smaller firms, i.e. those not possessing substantial monopoly power, tend to undertake little R&D, no clear, positive relationship exists between the amount of R&D spending and company size beyond a certain minimum size of enterprise.

REVIEW

In this chapter, we have introduced the market form known as oligopoly. We have demonstrated how it contrasts very sharply to perfect competition; whereas in perfect competition numerous firms compete amongst each other, producing a homogeneous product, in oligopoly, the relatively few firms which dominate the market tend to devote a good deal of effort to making their products heterogeneous through the various types of non-price competition.

REVIEW TASK

As a group task, in a formal debate, discuss the following motion:

This house believes that goods which have to be advertised ought not to be produced at all.

Select 2 main speakers to support the motion and 2 speakers to oppose it. Other class members should prepare points either for or against the motion so that they can contribute to the proceedings when the discussion is thrown open to the 'floor of the house'.

Multiple choice

In the UK, the five largest firms in the brewing and malting industry produce nearly 40% of the industry's total output. In the vehicle and engine manufacturing industry the five largest firms produce 90% of the industry's output.

It can be concluded from this information that

a   firms are larger in brewing and malting than in motor vehicle and engine manufacturing

b   there are more economies of scale in motor vehicle and engine manufacturing

c   the concentration ratio is higher in motor vehicle and engine manufacturing

d   small firms have more chance of survival in motor vehicle and engine manufacturing than in brewing and malting

(AEB, Specimen Paper)

Essays

1 a   Explain, and illustrate with examples, how advertising and product differentiation can enable a firm to achieve monopoly power.

   b   Discuss whether or not advertising and product differentiation are against the interest of consumers.

(AEB, June 1994)

2 a   Why do firms advertise?

   b   Critically discuss the view that advertising promotes market imperfection and is against the interests of consumers.

(AEB, June 1992)

3 'Advertising is an unnecessary cost of production and distorts the allocation of resources in a market economy.' Discuss.

(AEB, November 1991)

4 a   With reference to examples, show how firms compete other than by price.

   b   Examine the economic consequences of firms competing in this way.

   c   Is there any case for government regulation of non-price competition?

(ULEAC, June 1992)

5 a Why might a firm advertise its product?

  b To what extent does the consumer benefit from advertising?

  c Why is advertising likely to be more significant in some market structures than in others?

  (ULEAC, June 1991)

6 a Why may firms wish to reduce competition by colluding with each other, for example, by forming a cartel?

  b Is such collusion in the public interest and what might be the economic effects of prohibiting collusion?

  (AEB, June 1990)

7 a Why might firms compete through advertising campaigns rather than through price competition?

  b Examine the economic effects of firms competing through advertising campaigns rather than through price competition.

  (ULEAC, January 1994)

8 a Explain the benefits a firm might expect to derive from expenditure on research and development.

  b Discuss the view that the government ought to provide financial incentives to firms to encourage them to increase their spending on research and development.

  (AEB, June 1995)

.15 How do oligopolists behave?

The INVESTIGATOR

4 Star Wars

Prices at the pumps

Company	Four Star	Unleaded	Diesel
BP	57.1p	51.9p	51.4p
SHELL	61.9p	56.9p	55.9p
ESSO	61.9p	56.9p	55.9p
TESCO	53.8p	48.3p	47.9p
SAINSBURY	55.5p	49.5p	48.5p
SAFEWAY	53.9p	48.9p	48.9p

Maximum recommended retail per litre
Other prices based on national averages compiled by companies

*Source: **The Daily Mirror** (October 1994).*

Giant oil company BP yesterday pledged to match the cheap prices at supermarket petrol stations, vowing: "We're taking them on." Supermarkets were quick to counter: "You'll never beat our prices."

The ignition of a petrol price war looks certain to benefit the forecourt customer, with significant savings to be had from shopping around.

Preview

In this chapter, we shall investigate the following key areas:
- the different models of oligopoly;
- the various forms of pricing under oligopoly, including a detailed discussion of price discrimination.

Theories of oligopoly

A central aim of market theory is to make predictions about firms' price and output decisions in different situations, and, under such market forms as perfect competition and monopoly, economists can be fairly certain about likely outcomes. In the case of the former, price is set in the market through the free interaction of demand and supply, and individual firms passively take this price and equate marginal cost with marginal revenue to determine the best output; in the case of the latter, the firm will still equate MC with MR, but can restrict output and raise price in so doing.

However, under oligopoly no such certainty exists – where the number of firms in the industry is small and much interdependence exists between these firms, there will be a whole variety of

Collusive oligopoly is an oligopoly in which some agreement exists between the firms that comprise the market with respect to price, output and other policies.

Non-collusive oligopoly is an oligopoly in which the few firms pursue a particular strategy, without colluding with each other.

ways in which individual oligopolists may respond to rivals' price and output decisions. Consequently, several different models of oligopoly have been developed, underpinned by different analytical approaches and assumptions about the nature of oligopolistic, reactive market behaviour.

Unfortunately, therefore, for students of economics, there is no single, general and all-embracing theory of oligopoly to explain the nature of the business world around us! Particular theories of price and output determination under oligopoly should therefore be seen as illustrative of what might happen under certain sets of assumptions about the reactions of rival oligopolists.

The various models of oligopoly can be classified under two main headings: non-collusive or competitive oligopoly and collusive oligopoly.

We shall consider each in turn:

Non-collusive or competitive oligopoly

In this case, each firm will embark upon a particular strategy without colluding with its rivals, although there will of course still exist a state of interdependence, as possible reactions of rivals will have to be considered.

There are three broad approaches that might be adopted by firms in a situation of competitive oligopoly:

- Observe the behaviour of rival firms, but make no attempt to predict their possible strategies on the basis that they will not develop counter-strategies. This was the essence of the earliest model of oligopoly developed by Cournot as far back as 1838: each firm acts independently on the assumption that its decision will not provoke any response from rivals; this is not generally accepted nowadays as providing a useful framework in which to analyse contemporary oligopoly behaviour.

- Make the assumption that a given strategy will provoke a response from competitor firms, and assess the nature of the response using past experience. This is the basis of the kinked demand curve model, described below, in which it is

assumed that any price cut by one oligopolist will induce all others to do likewise, whilst a similar price increase would not be matched.

- Formulate a strategy and try to anticipate how rivals are most likely to react, and be prepared with suitable counter-measures.

This is the basis of Game Theory, in which competition under oligopoly is seen as being similar to a game of chess, every potential move must be regarded as a strategy and possible reactive moves by opponents and subsequent counter-moves must all be carefully considered. The application of the theory of games to economics was first introduced in 1944 by J. von Neuman and O.Morgenstern. Games theory involves the study of optimal strategies to maximise payoffs, taking into account the risks involved in estimating reactions of opponents, and also the conditions under which there is a unique solution, such that an optimum strategy for two opponents is feasible and not inconsistent. A zero-sum game is one in which one player's gain is another's loss, and a non-zero-sum game is one in which a decision adopted by one player may be to the benefit of all.

In this discussion of non-collusive oligopoly, we shall focus our attention on the second of the three broad approaches identified above.

The kinked demand curve theory

This theory of oligopoly was first developed in 1939 by Paul Sweezy in the USA, and by R. Hall and C. Hitch in the UK, to explain why oligopolistic markets would be characterised by relatively rigid prices, even when costs increase.

As mentioned previously, the kinked demand curve model makes the assumption of an assymetrical reaction to a change in price by one firm: a decrease in price by one firm will cause a similar reduction of price by other firms eager to protect their market share, whilst a price increase by one firm will not be matched and its market share will be eroded. This is shown in Box 15.1.

BOX 15.1

The oligopolist's 'kinked' demand curve

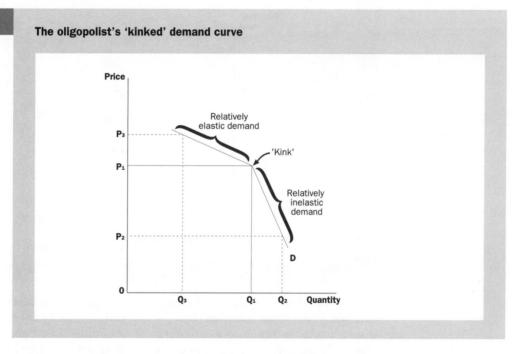

Price is initially set at OP_1, at the kink of the demand curve, and the oligopolist sells an output of OQ_1. If the firm tries to reduce price to OP_2 in order to sell more, other firms would match this reduction so that sales would increase only slightly, or more technically, by a less than proportionate amount, to OQ_2. The demand curve would be inelastic and the reduction in price would not represent a sound strategy as total sales revenue, and probably profit levels, would both fall; clearly the area OP_1 X OQ_1, representing initial revenue, is greater than OP_2 X OQ_2, the producer's revenue after the reduction in price. The alternative ploy of raising price to OP_3 would also be unsound as none of the other oligopolists would follow suit, and a large or more than proportionate fall in demand would follow.

Here, the demand curve would be elastic, and the change in price would again cause total revenue to fall – $OP_3 \times OQ_3$ is smaller than $OP \times OQ$. The logical conclusion from this analysis would therefore be that oligopolists would benefit from keeping prices stable so long as all could enjoy reasonable profits at the established price. The kinked demand curve theory also has other implications. A normal demand curve becomes less elastic as price falls, but the oligopolist's demand curve becomes less elastic suddenly at the kink. Mathematically, this causes the MR curve to suddenly change to a different position, as can be seen in Box 15.2, so that a discontinuity exists along the vertical line YZ above output OQ_1.

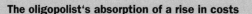

BOX 15.2

The oligopolist's absorption of a rise in costs

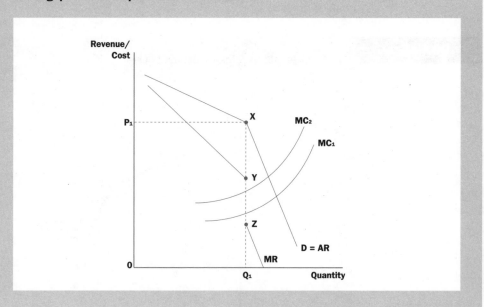

This implies that the MC curve can increase or decrease between this discontinuity, without necessitating a change in the profit maximising output OQ_1 or price OP_1 – the oligopolist will absorb the higher costs. According to normal demand and supply analysis, an increase in costs would cause a fall in output and an increase in price. An example of cost absorption in practice is when the price of crude oil rises and petrol companies wish to increase price, but do not as no company wants to be the first to do so.

Criticisms of the kinked demand curve theory

- The theory assumes that oligopolists perceive a kink at the current market price, i.e. at point X, but it does not explain how or why the original price was chosen. As a theory, it is therefore incomplete as it does not deal with price determination.

- Price stickiness or rigidity in oligopolistic markets might, in practice, be more apparent than real; for example, in the market for new cars, published catalogue prices may remain constant over relatively long periods, but the common practices of offering discounts, and items such as free insurance, cash-back deals and interest-free credit all amount to ways of reducing price. In fact, the theory takes no account of the various forms of non-price competition which characterise most oligopolistic markets.

- There is little empirical evidence from firms operating in oligopolistic markets to substantiate the kinked demand curve hypothesis that a change in price by one firm will always evoke a predictable and uniform response from its rivals. In practice, a very wide range of possible reactions is probable.

- Any perceived stability in prices in oligopolistic markets may not be due to the existence of a kinked demand curve, but may occur for other reasons such as the administrative expense and inconvenience of altering prices too regularly.

Cut-price competition

Although oligopolistic markets tend to be characterised by relative price stability in the longer term, occasionally short bursts of price warfare break out. This typically occurs when the dominant players attempt to defend and/or raise their market shares because the total level of demand in the market is insufficient to enable all to achieve their intended level of sales, and overcapacity results. The price cutting has the effect of reducing the profits of all the combatants in the short run, with consumers gaining the temporary benefit of lower prices.

However, the likely outcome is that the weakest firms, i.e. those with the highest costs, will be driven into bankruptcy, with a new era of relative price stability eventually emerging. If too many casualties are caused, consumers are likely to face greater monopoly power and possibly higher prices. There have been numerous examples of price wars in recent years with the most notable battles occurring on the petrol forecourts and in the retail grocery and travel businesses.

Collusive oligopoly

A central feature of competitive or non-collusive oligopoly is the existence of uncertainty amongst the interdependent firms. Although these firms may utilise informed guesswork and calculation to cope with such uncertainty, they can never be entirely sure as to how their competitors will react to any given marketing strategy. Thus instead of living with uncertainty, firms may adopt a policy of reducing, or even eliminating it by some form of central coordination, cooperation or collusion. Such collusion may occur where firms attempt to **maximise their joint profits**, by reaching agreement on their price, output and other policies, or where firms seek to **prevent the entry of new firms into the industry** so as to protect their longer run profits.

BOX 15.3

The INVESTIGATOR

Marketing monopoly is the name of the game

The greatest present difficulty of the De Beers diamond empire is the renegotiation of its agreement to sell the majority of Russia's diamonds – the deal expires in 1996.

It is obviously in the interests of both parties to reach an agreement on prices and marketing as De Beers produce 50 per cent of the world's gem diamonds and Russia about 25 per cent. Neither De Beers nor the Russians want a return to the diamond price crash of the inter-war years – a crash which induced De Beers to form the worldwide marketing monopoly of its Central Selling Organisation to stabilise prices.

When announcing his departure from De Beers' board, Harry Openheimer optimistically noted:

'The demand in the world for diamonds is stronger and more firmly established than it has ever been and co-operation among all the major producers is beyond doubt in the interests of them all... For just that reason there will, in the long run, be co-operation.'

TASK 15.1

For what reasons is co-operation amongst the world's diamond producers 'in the interests of them all'?

We now consider the forms that such collusion may take.

Forms of collusion

Formal collusion

The most common type of formal collusion is through the cartel; where a small number of rival firms, selling a similar product, come to the conclusion that it is in their joint interests to formally collude rather than compete, they may establish a cartel arrangement in which they agree to set an industry price and output which enables them to achieve a common objective. This is likely to involve the setting of agreed output quotas for each member in order to maintain the agreed price.

A successful cartel arrangement, from the point of view of the participating firms, would be one in which the cartel acts like a single monopolist to maximise profits of individual members. This is illustrated in Box 15.4.

BOX 15.4

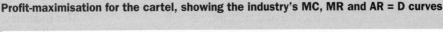
Profit-maximisation for the cartel, showing the industry's MC, MR and AR = D curves

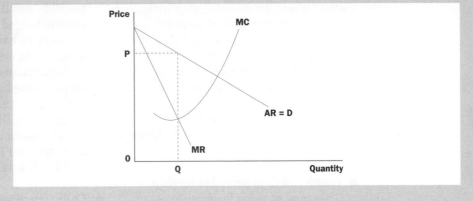

Box 15.4 is the familiar monopoly diagram, with each curve representing the aggregated situation for all the firms in the cartel. In order to maximise profits, MC is equated with MR and a price of OP is set, with an output of OQ, which represents the potential level of sales. The allocation of this market quota between members could be decided by such criteria as geography, productive capacity or pre-cartel market share; or cartel members, having set a price of OP, could engage in non-price competition to each gain as large a slice of OQ as they can.

In practice, cartels may tend to be rather fragile and may not last for very long. This is because individual members may have an incentive to renege on the agreement by secretly undercutting the cartel price. The almost inevitable necessity to limit output to keep price high will tend to leave individual firms with spare productive capacity, and provide the temptation to increase profits by expanding output. Such an expansion would not only generate profit on the additional sales, but would also increase the profits on existing sales, as average fixed costs would fall as output expanded.

As the end result of successful collusion will be to create a situation similar to monopoly, with its consequent drawbacks and loss of economic efficiency, cartels are illegal in many countries, including the UK and the USA. Various cartels do, however, operate internationally, the most famous of which is OPEC. Another example of an international cartel is IATA (The International Air Transport Association) which has sought to set prices for international airline routes. However, the experience of both these cartels has been one of price cutting amongst its members, particularly during periods of declining product demand and competition from non-members.

Informal or tacit collusion

The most usual method of tacit collusion is price leadership, which occurs where one firm sets a price which is subsequently accepted as the market price by the other producers. There need be no formal or written agreement for this to happen; it is sufficient that firms believe this to be the best way of maintaining or increasing their profits. Price leadership may take various forms.

- **Dominant firm price leadership**
  This type of price leadership occurs where a firm, probably by virtue of its size, comes to dominate an industry in terms of its power to influence market supply. The dominant firm sets a price to suit its own needs, and the smaller firms then adjust their planned output in line with the market price that has been set for them. An example of such price leadership is provided by Ford motor company, who have often been the first to raise prices in the car industry.

- **Barometric price leadership**
  A barometric price leader need not necessarily be the dominant firm in the industry; rather it will be a firm, possibly small in size, which is acknowledged by others in the industry as having an informed insight into current market conditions, perhaps because it employs the best team of accountants and market analysts. The firm's reputation will therefore enable it to act as a 'barometer' to others in the industry, and its price movements will be closely followed.

- **Collusive price leadership**
  This involves a form of tacit group collusion in which prices within an an industry change almost simultaneously, and is linked to price parallelism where there are identical prices and price movements in a given market. In practice, collusive price leadership might be difficult to distinguish from dominant firm leadership, especially in circumstances where the price leader is quickly followed.

Tacit collusion may also occur where firms in the industry follow a set of 'rules of thumb' instead of a price leader. Such rules may be designed to prevent destructive competition and thus maintain longer-term profitability, although some short-run profitability may be sacrificed as the rules do not require MC and MR to be equated. One such rule of thumb is cost-plus pricing.

- **Cost-plus pricing**
  This is also known as average cost pricing, mark-up pricing and full-cost pricing, and empirical evidence suggests that it is the most common pricing procedure adopted by firms.

It involves firms setting price by adding a standard percentage profit margin to average costs, so that

Price = AFC + AVC + Profit margin

Cost-plus pricing is consistent with the idea of relatively stable oligopoly prices as, provided costs are stable, prices will also remain stable in the short run, even though demand might be changing. Conversely, if costs rise on average by 5 per cent, then prices in the industry will also be rising by a similar percentage

TASK 15.2

Coursework

Choose one particular market to study, e.g. the market for soap-powders, chocolate-bars, personal computers or any other of your choice.

Investigate:
- the degree and nature of competition in your chosen market;
- and the implications of this for producers and consumers.

Other forms of pricing

Transfer pricing

This occurs when multinational corporations set internal, as opposed to market prices, for transactions between semi-autonomous subsidiaries of the company which are likely to be based in a number of different countries; for example, the setting of prices for the sale of components from one subsidiary to another.

Transfer prices may be artificially set above or below market prices so as to minimise the tax or tariff liability of the the corporation on a global scale; for example, multinationals may

deliberately overstate costs for subsidiaries operating in countries with high profits taxes so as to shift profits to subsidiaries in lower tax countries. This can be achieved by over-invoicing exports to, or under-invoicing imports from, high tax countries. Thus profits can be declared where taxes on company profits are lowest. This is one of the main ways in which world famous multinationals are able to pay a very low effective rate of corporation tax in the UK and elsewhere, despite being immensely profitable concerns.

BOX 15.5

Price discrimination

LEYTON ORIENT F.C.
SEASON TICKET PRICES
1995/6

AREA	BEFORE 31st May	1st June Onwards
MAIN CENTRE		
Adults	£165.00	£200.00
Children/OAP's/Women	£110.00	£130.00
MAIN NORTH WING		
Adults	£145.00	£170.00
Children/OAP's/Women	£80.00	£100.00
WEST STAND		
Adults	£115.00	£140.00
OAP's/Women	£50.00	£75.00
Children under 16	£10.00	£10.00
TERRACE/ENCLOSURE		
Adults	£100.00	£120.00
Children/OAP's/Women	£40.00	£50.00

*COVERS ALL ENDSLEIGH LEAGUE MATCHES.
* LEYTON LINK – DISCOUNTS STILL APPLY.

OFFICIAL SPONSOR
ACCLAIM entertainment, inc.

Source: **Leyton Orient Football Club**

TASK 15.3

In small groups:
a before reading the section on price discrimination, discuss and write down some possible economic justifications for Leyton Orient's structure of season ticket prices for the 1995/6 football season;
b after reading the section on price discrimination, using economic analysis, try to add further points to your analysis.

Price discrimination is carried out primarily to increase the profits of the discriminating firms.

It occurs where different consumers are charged different prices in different markets for the same product or service, or where the same consumer is charged different prices for the same product,where the different prices are not due to differences in supply costs.

Necessary conditions for price discrimination

- There must be some imperfection of the market. If there were perfect competition, price discrimination would be impossible since the individual producer could have no influence on price. At least some degree of monopoly power is therefore necessary so that producers have some ability to make rather than take the market price.

- The discriminating supplier must be able to split the market into separate sections and keep them separate, such that it is difficult to transfer the seller's product from one sector to another; i.e. there must be no 'seepage' between markets in the sense that goods can be bought in the cheaper market and re-sold in the dearer.
  Barriers between markets may be:

  - geographical in that customers are separated by distance; e.g. the international dumping of cheap goods, where goods are sold overseas at prices below those in the home market, and often below the cost of production; e.g. the East European Communist bloc countries used to sell their exports to the West at lower prices than those prevailing

in domestic markets to earn hard foreign currency.

  - temporal in that customers are separated by time; e.g. it is cheaper to travel on the London Underground after 9.30am than before 9.30 am, and the two markets can be kept separate as ticket office staff will not sell the cheaper tickets until after this time;

  - according to customer type so that customers are separated according to some easily identified feature of the customers themselves, e.g. age, sex, income or occupation; examples of this would include cheaper theatre tickets for children, old age pensioners and the unemployed, reduced price rail travel for students and higher Harley Street physician consultation fees for those who are perceived as being able to pay more. The two conditions discussed so far would make price discrimination possible, but, for it to also be profitable, a third condition must also be satisfied.

- Price elasticity of demand in each market must be different; if this were the case, the discriminating supplier would increase price in the market with an inelastic demand curve, and reduce price where demand is elastic in order to increase total revenue and profits. If the elasticity of demand in each market was the same at each and every price, a common price would be charged in both markets as this price would represent the profit-maximising price in each market where MC = MR. You might wish to refer back at this stage to Chapter 6 where we discussed the relationship between price elasticity of demand and total revenue.

BOX 15.6

It isn't always price discrimination when firms charge different prices for different products

Consider the following examples, which are often given as instances of price discrimination.

● The differences in price for first class and standard class rail travel.
● Different rates for the consumers of off-peak and peak-time electricity.

In the first example, passengers are receiving the same product in the sense that they are travelling to the same destination. But are they all receiving exactly the same service? First class seats are larger, more comfortable, and have more leg room than standard class seats. The costs of running a first class carriage are therefore shared among fewer passengers than those of a standard class carriage. In addition, passengers who travel first class often receive additional comforts, such as waiter service.

British Rail could argue that these services cost more and that these costs should be reflected in a higher price. On the other hand there might be an element of price discrimination if the price differences are not entirely justified by cost differences, but it cannot be argued that the difference between first class and standard class ticket prices is completely due to price discrimination.

With respect to the second case, the demand for electricity fluctuates throughout the day and it cannot be stored. Demand is heaviest in the evenings when people come home from work, turn on the lights and television, cook their tea, and heat the water to wash up. The electricity generating companies must keep plant and equipment in reserve able to cope with the heaviest demand on the coldest and darkest day of the year. For much of the time, this is spare capacity which is idle and unused. It can therefore be argued that on-peak consumers impose higher costs on the industry than off-peak consumers, and that on-peak charges should reflect these higher costs.

Thus Powergen and other electricity suppliers do not practice price discrimination by charging different prices for peak and off-peak consumption of electricity. They are merely trying to use their generating capacity more efficiently by matching supply more closely to demand.

● Lower cost travel on British Rail

Imagine you are travelling from Bristol to London on the train. You have bought a ticket using your Young Person's Railcard. The man opposite you is a soldier returning from leave; his ticket has been obtained using a Forces Travel Warrant. The gentleman next to him has bought a 'Super-saver' ticket. The lady next to you has used a coupon cut from a detergent packet, and her young daughter has a cheap travel voucher because she belongs to the 'Rail Riders Club'. On the other side of the aisle the girl's grandmother is travelling with a Senior Citizen's Railcard. These passengers are sharing a substantially similar service; all are imposing similar costs on the provider; and yet six different customers have paid six different prices.

Source: **Introductory Economics**, Harrison, Smith and Davies (Macmillan, 1992)

First degree price discrimination

First degree or perfect price discrimination is where each unit of the good is sold for the maximum price obtainable.

This is sometimes known as perfect price discrimination, as discrimination takes place to the extent that each unit is sold for the maximum price obtainable. It takes place when different consumers are charged different prices for the same product, or when the same consumer is charged different prices for the same good. This is illustrated in Box 15.7.

BOX 15.7

Perfect price discrimination

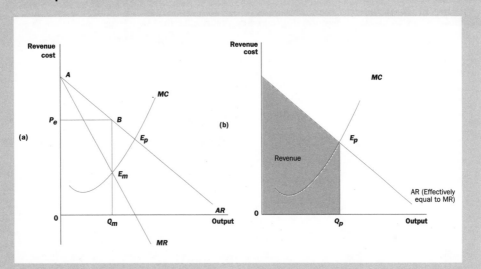

The monopolist charges all customers the same price P_e, and produces at point E_m where MC = MR. If each unit of output can be sold at a different price, then extra units of output can be sold without reducing the price of existing units. This means that the demand curve AR also becomes the marginal revenue curve, and the perfectly discriminating monopolist will increase both output and profits by producing at point E_p. The monopolist can not only gain an extra revenue of ABP_e from selling output Q_m at differentiated prices, but he can also make extra profit of BE_mEP by expanding output and sales from Q_m to Q_p.

*Source: Harrison, Smith and Davies, **Introductory Economics** (Macmillan, 1992).*

Here a different price is charged for each unit sold, and as greater revenue is earned for any given level of output as compared with the charging of a single price, overall profit is increased. However, to charge each consumer the maximum possible amount for a good, and to extract all consumer surplus, very accurate information on consumers' ability and willingness to pay different prices would be needed. In practice such information is unlikely to exist, making perfect price discrimination most unusual.

Second degree price discrimination

Second degree price discrimination is where the consumer is charged different prices for different blocks of consumption.

This occurs where consumers are charged different prices for different blocks of consumption, with a relatively high price for the first block and lower prices for subsequent blocks. Domestic consumption of electricity in the UK provides an example of this. Here, unlike first degree price discrimination, only a part of consumer surplus is extracted, so much less consumer information is required. This is illustrated in Box 15.8.

BOX 15.8

Second degree price discrimination

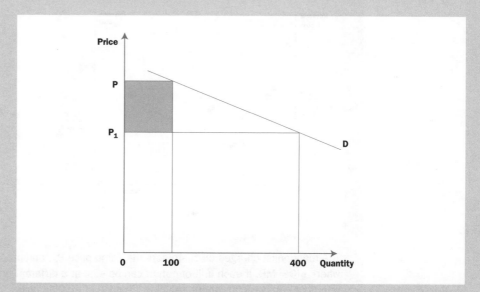

The hatched area shows the revenue gain compared with selling 400 units at the single price of P1.

*Source: Harrison, Smith and Davies, **Introductory Economics** (Macmillan, 1992).*

Box 15.8 shows the demand for a certain good over a given time period by an individual household. The first 100 units are sold at a price of OP and the next 300 units are sold at a price of OP_1.

The revenue obtained by selling a given quantity of output is increased through discrimination and profits are therefore greater.

Third degree price discrimination

Third degree price discrimination is where the same product or service is sold at different prices to different consumers.

This is the most common form of price discrimination, and it occurs where the same product or service is sold at different prices to different consumers. Look at Box 15.9.

BOX 15.9

Third degree price discrimination

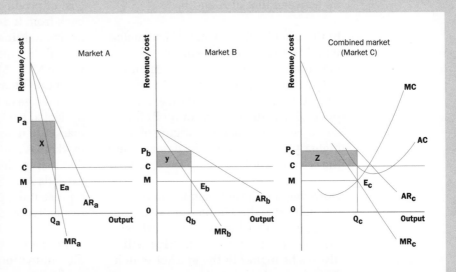

The profit gain from price discrimination is (x + y) - z

*Source: Harrison, Smith and Davies, **Introductory Economics** (Macmillan, 1992).*

In Box 15.9 there are two distinct markets, Market A and Market B. A third market, Market C, which is the combined market, is obtained by the horizontal summation of the individual AR and MR curves from A and B. Market A has an an inelastic demand curve, whilst Market B has a more elastic demand curve. The gradient of the combined market demand curve will lie between that of A and B.

In the combined market, MC is equated with MR to give a single profit-maximising price of OP_c with an output of OQ_c, and a total profit equal to to the shaded area z is earned. With a single price, this is the maximum profit that could be earned as the charging of a higher price would reduce demand and the area of profit, z.

However, total profits can be increased through price discrimination, with the total output OQ_c being sold at different prices in markets A and B. **Price will always be higher in the market with a more inelastic deman**d as consumers will be less responsive to price changes.

As price discrimination only occurs where the differences in price are not associated with any cost differences, the combined market MC curve will also apply to markets A and B, and the output of each sub-market is therefore determined by equating MR in each market with the marginal cost of producing OQ_c units of output. Thus in Box 15.9 it can be seen that the marginal cost of production, OM, is projected back from the combined market as a horizontal line to enable the monopolist to find the equilibrium points E_a and E_b where MC = MR in each of the individual markets, A and B. Similarly the average cost of production, OC, is projected back from the combined market to determine the area of profit in markets A and B. As the level of profit is denoted by the amount by which AR exceeds AC, the areas x and y will represent the total profit for A and B respectively.

From the producer's standpoint, price discrimination will be a success if total profits increase as a result. In the diagram, it can be seen that **Area x + Area y is greater than Area z**, so the producer has succeeded.

BOX 15.10

Ball Bearings

DAVID BATES, UK Marketing Manager for racket sports and team sports, Wilson Sporting Goods Ltd., explains why the cost of premium quality tennis balls in this country is higher than other markets, particularly the USA.

"How can you justify the difference in tennis ball pricing in the UK and the US?" A question that if I had been paid £1 for each time it was asked, I would be a rich man.

When one compares the average price in the US to the UK it is easy to understand why it is such a popular question.

According to Sports Marketing Surveys the average UK three ball can price is £5.16 (£1.72 per ball). The Wilson US Open three ball can, the best selling ball in the US, sells from $2.99 to $3.99 (£0.70 to £0.90 per ball).

At first glance it looks ridiculous. However, when one considers all the factors, including most importantly, product and size of market, it begins to weigh up.

The US tennis consumer mentality is very different from its UK equivalent. Tennis balls are played with for a day and then given to the family dog to play with. Durability is not a key issue with the 'disposable' US market. US product is manufactured to a durability standard that meets this product usage.

Whilst meeting ITF specifications, adhesive, felt and core components are used to the relevant needs.

In the UK, however, the durability and quality requirements are very different. Most regular UK club players expect balls to last until the loss of pressure, when the ball goes 'flat', making it unusable. Higher product expectation, in terms of durability, gives rise to higher production costs, resulting in higher consumer costs.

The US market is approaching half the world market in tennis balls. Volume sales with few product variables enables lower production costs – another benefit to the US in terms of price.

The UK market – approximately 400,000 in top grade durable balls, that are generally used by regular club players – is tiny in comparison to the US.

*Source: Adapted from **Serve and Volley** (November 1994).*

TASK 15.4

1 Explain how the theory of price discrimination may account for the different prices of tennis balls mentioned in the article.

2 What other factors, besides price discrimination, might contribute to the different prices of tennis balls?

Disadvantages and advantages of price discrimination

Disadvantages

- The main disadvantage will be experienced by consumers, particularly those having to pay the higher prices who may object to the discrimination against them; e.g. users of peak time public transport. It could be argued that price discrimination represents a transfer of welfare from consumers to producers and is a way in which producers gain at the expense of consumers through the extraction of consumer surplus. In the extreme case of perfect or first degree price discrimination, no consumer receives any consumer surplus at all.

  In more general terms, the higher profits earned through price discrimination could be viewed as an unjustifiable redistribution of income in favour of profit takers with higher prices reducing consumers' real incomes.

Advantages

- Producers of course benefit from the higher profits as previously shown. It could also be argued that if such profits are re-invested, consumers might derive long-run benefits in terms of increased efficiency and lower costs and prices.

- Those consumers paying the lower price may be able to obtain a good or service that they might not otherwise have been able to afford; e.g. half-price tickets for children at football matches.

- Consumer and producer alike may gain if a loss-making firm is turned into a profitable one. This is illustrated in Box 15.11.

BOX 15.11

Profits and losses (a) without and (b) with discrimination

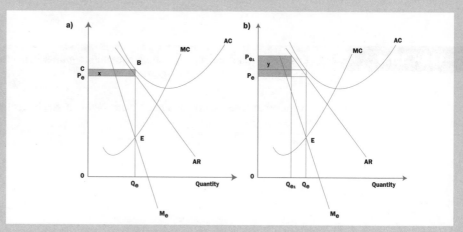

*Source: Harrison, Smith and Davies, **Introductory Economics** (Macmillan, 1992).*

In Box 15.11, the producer's best output, where MC = MR is at OQ_e, but the price of OP_e does not cover the average cost of OC or Q_eB, and a loss, equivalent to the rectangular area, x, is made. However, a loss can be transformed into a profit by charging those consumers who are prepared to pay a higher price of OP_{e1}. The shaded area y shows the additional revenue that accrues to the firm from charging a two-part tariff. As area y exceeds that of x, the loss-making firm is now able to make a profit at the current output level.

In the absence of price discrimination, this good would probably not be supplied in the long run, which would particularly represent a loss to society if it were one which generated positive externalities; e.g. a doctor in a remote area charging wealthier patients more than the less affluent ones.

BOX 15.12

Summary table: the main features of oligopoly

- Few producers, interdependence and reactive market behaviour

- Barriers to entry and a high degree of market concentration

- Non-price competition

- Non-collusive or competitive oligopoly
  - Relatively stable prices in the longer term (the kinked demand curve);
  - Occasional short bursts of price warfare.

- Collusive oligopoly
  - Formal collusion (cartels);
  - Informal collusion (price leadership).

- Other forms of pricing, including price discrimination.

REVIEW

In this chapter, we have investigated the market form known as oligopoly which most corresponds with the major real world markets. Whereas the perfect competition model can be neatly represented in a number of key diagrams, the study of oligopoly cannot be reduced to such simple dimensions. This is because the actual business world is exceedingly complex, and no one, all-embracing, conventional economic theory exists to fully explain it. Instead, different theories of price and output determination are used, depending on what particular set of assumptions are made about the nature of oligopolistic market behaviour.

REVIEW TASK

The following passage is adapted from an article by Antony Thorncroft entitled 'How Companies Fix Prices'.

Pricing in practice is exceptionally far removed from the view of traditional economic theory on how companies fix their prices. According to traditional economic theory, price is determined at the level of output at which marginal revenue equals marginal cost. But a recent survey by Industrial Market Research, into how 220 manufacturing companies fix their prices, suggests otherwise. Many prices are 'cost-plus' prices, arrived at by taking a view on the average costs of producing a particular output and then adding a profit margin. Only a third of companies investigate the acceptability of their prices before fixing them. Few companies make use of price in their advertising; they see price as important rather than as vital in overall marketing strategy. As the report says: 'Price is seen as a handicap that has to be carried in the competition stakes while the race itself is won or lost on the basis of quality, applicational engineering or reputation'. Companies increase prices when costs go up, but rarely reduce them if costs ever fall. Price changes are not seen as a means of expanding market share and seldom are scientific methods used to assess the impact of pricing decisions. Hardly any of the firms investigated tested prices.

a i   Explain the statement: "According to traditional economic theory, price is determined at the level of output at which marginal revenue equals marginal cost."
   ii Suggest reasons why firms may adopt 'cost-plus' pricing.
   iii If prices are usually determined on a cost-plus basis, has the traditional theory of the firm any relevance?

b Why may firms use methods of competition other than price changes in order to expand their market share?

(AEB, November 1987)

Multiple choice

1 **A firm operating in an oligopolistic market believes that it faces the demand curve shown below. The firm is currently charging a price OP for its output OQ.**

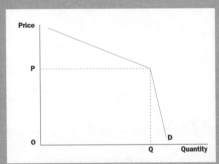

The shape of the demand curve facing the firm could be explained by the fact that if the firm

A raises or lowers its price then its rivals will introduce similar price changes

B raises its price then its rivals will do the same but if it lowers its price they will keep their prices unchanged

C lowers its prices then its rivals will do the same but if it raises its price they will keep their prices unchanged

D raises or lowers its price then in both cases its rivals will keep their prices unchanged

(AEB, June 1992)

2 **The 'kinked demand curve' leads to the conclusion that prices in oligopolistic markets will tend to be rigid because rival firms would**

A not follow price increases but would follow price cuts

B follow price increases but would not follow price cuts

C tend to follow a price leader but no other firms

D collude together to follow a joint profit maximising strategy

(AEB, November 1991)

3 **A monopolist is considering splitting the market into two separate sections and adopting a policy of differential pricing. Which of the following items of information is the most necessary in deciding whether or not this policy will increase profits?**

A The effect on marginal cost of a rise in output

B Whether price elasticities of demand differ between the separate markets

C Whether the price elasticity of demand in the combined markets is greater than unity

D The relationship between marginal cost and marginal revenue in the combined markets

E The income elasticity of demand in both markets

(ULEAC, January 1993)

4 **A price discriminating monopoly is both possible and profitable only when**

A two or more markets with different price elasticities of demand for the product can be separated

B there are several markets for the product and the size of the production unit is well below the optimum

C the absolute elasticities of demand for the product in the different markets are the same

D the monopolist is producing at the level of output where he is obtaining the maximum advantages from economies of scale

E In none of the above situations

(ULEAC, January 1992)

5 **A firm that is practising price discrimination is most likely to be**

A charging different prices for the same product which do not reflect cost differences.

B charging different prices in the same market for the same product, because of cost differences.

C buying in a lower priced market and selling in a higher priced market.

D buying different products from the same supplier at different prices.

(IB, May 1995)

6 **An oligopolist with a 'kinked' demand curve increases output slightly. This is most likely to be in response to an increase in**

A marginal costs

B fixed costs

C price

D demand

(IB, May 1995)

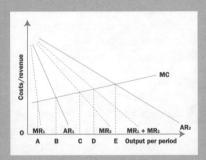

7 **The above diagram shows the marginal cost and the marginal and average revenue of a discriminating monopolist selling in two distinct markets. The profit maximising total output will be**

A OA

B OB

C OC

D OD

E OE

(IB, May 1995)

QUESTIONS

Essays

1 a Describe the various ways in which firms compete to increase their market share.

 b Is such competition always in the interest of the consumers?

(AEB, November 1994)

2 Discuss the various factors which a firm operating in an oligopolistic market is likely to take into account when deciding upon the price to charge for its product.

(AEB, June 1993)

3 a Explain how firms in oligopolistic markets are affected by inter-dependence and uncertainty.

 b What action might firms in oligopolistic markets take to reduce uncertainty?

(AEB, June 1991)

4 a Carefully explain why a firm may charge different prices for the same product.

 b Discuss whether such a pricing policy is in the interest of the firm's customers.

(AEB, November 1992)

5 Economic theory makes certain assumptions about market conditions, in order to study how firms decide on prices and output. Are these assumptions realistic, and do firms always behave in the real world as Economics textbooks predict?

(IB, May 1995)

6

Representative prices of compact discs in selected countries in 1992:	
Irish Republic	£17.13
Denmark	£16.73
France	£15.41
Germany	£13.14
United Kingdom	£12.78
USA	£9.70

 a Outline the theory of price discrimination and explain how price discrimination may account for the different prices of compact discs shown in the table.

 b Briefly discuss any other factors, besides price discrimination, that might contribute to the different prices of compact discs.

(Open University, October 1994)

QUESTIONS

7 In February 1992 the Monopolies and Mergers Commission reported that the price of a Rover Metro car was £2000 lower in Amsterdam than in Birmingham where the car was made. Use the theory of price discrimination to explain how such a pricing policy may increase profits for the Rover group.

(Open University, October 1992)

8 a Using economic analysis, explain why British Rail charges some customers more than others for inter-city journeys such as that between Glasgow and London.

b Examine the likely economic consequences of British Rail's pricing policy for:
i other public transport operators;
ii the travelling public.

(ULEAC, January 1994)

QUESTIONS

Data response

1 **The demand for rail travel on a suburban railway line at different times of day**

a Explain the demand relationship, shown in the diagram below:
i when the same price is charged at all times of day
ii when different prices are charged at different times of day.

b Discuss the advantages and disadvantages of the two pricing systems.

c Discuss what might happen to demand if the price were raised from 20p to 50p per passenger mile at all times.

(AEB, June 1987)

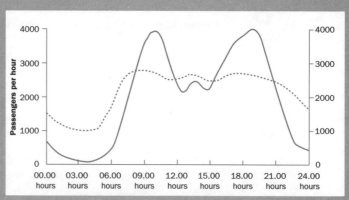

Key:

〜 Demand for rail travel when a price of 25 pence per passenger mile is charged at all times.

•••••• Demand for rail travel when a price of 40 pence per passenger mile is charged during morning and evening peak periods and a price of 15 pence per passenger mile is charged at other times.

2 Study **Table 1** and **Extract A** below and answer all the questions which follow.

Early in 1994, a few months before the opening of the Channel Tunnel to passenger traffic, the prices shown in Table 1 were announced by the main cross-Channel operators for the summer and winter months in 1994/95. The passage in Extract A has been adapted from a newspaper article published at the time.

Table 1

Return Standard Fares: Dover to Folkestone to Calais, Car plus passengers			
	Winter off-peak	*Summer off-peak*	*Summer peak weekend*
Le Shuttle (operated by Eurotunnel)	£220	£280	£310
Stena Sealink car ferry	£126	£220	£320
P&O car ferry	£139	£139 – £221	£289 – £320
Hoverspeed hovercraft ferry	£142	£297	£338

*Source: **Independent** (12 January 1994)*

Extract A

"The market from which Eurotunnel needs to carve itself a share is perhaps 20 million passengers a year. The company has suggested that, by 1996, it might be carrying 8 million car passengers. But this makes a huge assumption: it assumes that ferry prices will not be slashed in order to try to win back some of the 8 million people who have gone underground. But ferry prices are bound to fall – the real cost of crossing the Channel has been falling by 3 or 4 per cent annually for years.

Eurotunnel insisted yesterday that it is not interested in a price war with the ferries. Instead it feels that it can attract sufficient takers by promising a 35-minute crossing time with no weather hold-ups and no sea-sickness. When Eurotunnel opens there is going to be a vast increase in cross-Channel capacity for people, cars and freight. But if there is no price war, there is little reason to think that there will be any large increase in the volume of traffic carried. In other words, the total revenue to be divided up between the rival operators will not be greatly different from today's. And what if there is a price war? The volume of traffic may well increase as more people will be tempted to cross the Channel. But because each crossing is at a lower average price for the operator – be it a ferry operator or Eurotunnel – the total amount of money will not go up as steeply as the traffic volume."

*Source: adapted from **Guardian** (12 January 1994).*

QUESTIONS

a   What market structure amongst cross-Channel travel operators is suggested by the data? Explain your reasons.

b   Explain why the cross-Channel travel operators charge different prices at peak and off-peak travel times as shown in **Table 1**.

c   In the light of the information in the data, discuss whether it is realistic for Eurotunnel to aim for a market of 8 million car passengers by 1996 (**Extract A**).

d   In January 1994, Eurotunnel stated that the company was 'not interested in a price war with the ferries' (**Extract A**).
Taking account of both short run and long run factors, evaluate the case that it would not be in the interest of the cross-Channel travel operators to engage in a price war.

(AEB, Specimen question)

3.16 How does the UK deal with monopoly?

FOCUS

Monopolies and mergers

'Firms which are in a very strong market position may try to get away with high prices or poor service. And they may use unfair tactics to keep others out of the market, or distort the market in their favour. Agreements among firms to fix prices or share markets harm customers by increasing prices and limiting choice.

Source: **Competition Policy – How it works** (DTI HMSO, 1989).

Super merger WILL HIT JOBS

BIFU cautions against plans

BANKING union BIFU warned yesterday that thousands of jobs would go after the Halifax and Leeds Permanent building societies announced plans to merge.

The new merged company with £87 billion assets will then be floated on the stock exchange.

About 2.36 million borrowers and eight million investors are set for a shares bonanza from the flotation set for sometime in 1997.

But banking union BIFU warned that massive cutbacks would flow in the wake of the link.

"Going for size does not necessarily give the customer a better service and often means big job cuts," said negotiating officer Joe Hoedemaker.

The building societies said that the new company – to be known as Halifax – would have a workforce of 27,000 – made up of the current 22,000 staff from the Halifax Building Society and 5,000 from Leeds. Its head office will be in West Yorkshire.

A Halifax spokesman admitted that job losses would be likely from the group's combined workforce, but refused to give a figure.

"But there is no doubt that these will be achieved from natural wastage or, if not, from voluntary redundancy," he claimed.

In a separate statement, the societies said that the conversion to a public company would enable them to take a greater share of the expanding personal finance markets as well as allowing greater flexibility to raise capital to meet lending needs.

However, the Building Societies Members Association "unhesitatingly" condemned the merger.

"This idea is born of greed for profits. People need more choice not less. If the merger plans make progress we shall certainly see that it is referred to the Monopolies and Mergers Commission."

Economic Secretary to the Treasury Anthony Nelson said that he could not rule out a reference of the "Yorkshire high society marriage" to the Office of Fair Trading and hence the Monopolies and Mergers Commission.

The plan is to be put to members in the spring and requires a 75 per cent majority of investors and a 50 per cent majority of borrowers.

Previously, the Halifax was the country's biggest building society. It has more assets than all the banks apart from Barclays and NatWest.

Source: **Morning Star** (26 November 1994).

Preview

In this chapter, we examine the various weapons at a government's disposal to tackle the problem of monopoly/oligopoly power.

In particular, we shall investigate the following key areas:
- competition policy;
- some general approaches to monopoly;
- a brief history and evaluation of UK monopoly policy.

Competition policy

Competition policy is that part of a government's industrial policy which is specifically concerned with the problems arising from monopolies, mergers and restrictive practices.

The underpinning basis of competition policy is the belief that the best interests of the economy, in terms of a wide range of economic indicators, such as efficiency, competitiveness, growth and living standards, are best served by markets which most closely correspond to the model of perfect competition.

Competition policy is an important strand of the UK government's broader industrial policy, and is specifically concerned with the problems arising from monopolies, mergers and restrictive practices

As such, it forms part of the government's microeconomic policy which is designed to facilitate improvements on the supply side of the economy. Supply-side policies are also considered in Section 4.

Some general approaches to monopoly

Different governments, in different countries, at different times have adopted a variety of policies in confronting problems of competition and monopoly. The range of choices available can be categorised into two main levels: first the type of policy and secondly the policy aim

Types of policy

Four broad types of approach may be identified:

- A non-interventionist or laissez-faire approach
  This is the ultimate market approach, which has not generally been adopted, in which the government does not intervene at all, with resource allocation being left completely to market forces. Government policy is therefore one of no policy. A more likely, 'half-way house' policy in reality, known as conditional laissez-faire, would be where significant areas of economic activity are exempted from government regulation on the grounds that they are so unconcentrated as to warrant no attention.

● A per se approach
This type of approach is the direct opposite of the laissez-faire approach, in that strict rules are applied against monopolistic behaviour or structures on the basis that the latter would per se, or in itself, be undesirable, as it prevents the achievement of perfect competition. Likely outcomes of such an approach could involve automatic policy laws to prevent mergers and restrictive trading practices and to disband existing monopolies, with little or no discretion for exceptions to be allowed. This approach has found greater favour in the USA than in the UK and Europe.

● A discretionary or rule of reason approach
UK monopoly policy has convention-ally been of this type. The view has been that each instance of suspected

or alleged monopoly abuse should be judged on a case-by-case basis. Thus there are no firm rules or laws about what is and is not allowed; rather, each particular problem is dealt with in a pragmatic manner, with recomendations being made as to whether or not any policy interventions are deemed necessary.

● A mixed per se and discretionary approach
This is the basis of EU competition law in which prohibitions exist on certain company practices, e.g. collusive price fixing, but a discretionary element exists in that exceptions can be allowed if proof of substantial benefits of such practices can be shown, with the burden of proof being on the firms involved; failure to provide such proof can result in fines, with damages being awarded to affected parties.

The policy aim

As well as deciding upon the broad type of monopoly policy to use, governments also have to decide on whether they are going to attempt to influence the behaviour of businesses or the market structures in which they exist, although in reality policies are likely to involve some combination of the two. UK and EU monopoly policy has traditionally tended towards the 'behavioural' approach on the basis that mere existence of monopoly power, i.e. structure, does not constitute a

problem in itself; it is the mis-use of such power which requires regulation. However, towards the end of the1990s in the UK, there was something of a shift towards a 'structuralist' approach; for example, prior to privatisation in 1990, in order to create a more competitive environment, the Central Electricity Generating Board (CEGB) was restructured into four different companies: National Power, Power Gen, Nuclear Electric and the National Grid Company.

TASK 16.1	**GROUP TASK**
	In small groups, using your knowledge of perfect competition and oligopoly, try to resolve the following paradox: When all firms in a particular industry charge similar prices, this could indicate either the existence of a great deal of competition or very little at all!

Monopoly policy in the UK: a brief history

BOX 16.1

The main instruments of UK monopoly policy

Institution	Founded	Monopoly policy functions	Main Acts/Provisions
DEPARTMENT of TRADE and INDUSTRY (DTI)	1973 (Formerly the Board of Trade)	Secretary of State can refer existing firms and proposed mergers to MMC	**1948**: Monopolies and Restrictive Practices Act – Monopolies Commission created
MONOPOLIES and MERGERS COMMISSION (MMC)	1948 (Monopolies) 1965 (Mergers)	Investigates and reports on monopolies and mergers (if referred)	
RESTRICTIVE PRACTICES COURT (RPC)	1956	Decides whether referred agreements are against the public interest	**1956**: Restrictive Trade Practices Act – Restrictive Practices Court established **1965**: Monopolies and Mergers Act – Provision for monopolies to be referred to the Monopolies Commission
OFFICE of FAIR TRADING (OFT)	1973	Director-General can initiate an investigation into 'anti-competitive' practices, and can refer agreements to RPC	**1973:** Fair Trading Act – Director-General of Fair Trading established **1980:** Competition Act – Provision for the MMC to undertake efficiency audits of the nationalised industries **1989:** Companies Act – Modified and strengthened previous merger legislation
EUROPEAN COMMUNITY (EC) (NOW EU)	1957 Treaty of Rome (Britain joined in 1973)	European Commissioner for competition has powers to prevent various restrictive practices, monopolies and mergers	**Article 85:** Agreements prohibited which affect trade between member states and prevent, restrict or distort competition **Article 86:** Abuse of a dominant position within the EU prohibited **Articles 92-94:** Prohibit government subsidies to industries or individual firms which will distort, or threaten to distort competition **Merger Control Regulation 1989:** 'Tightened' article 86 with specific guidelines on referral of mergers to the Commission
REGULATORY AUTHORITIES	1980s/1990s (on privatisation)	Act as 'Watchdogs' on privatised industries	Establishment of: **1984:** Office of Telecommunications (OFTEL) **1986:** Office of Gas Supply (OFGAS) **1987:** The Civil Aviation Authority (CAA) **1989:** Office of Water Services (OFWAT) National Rivers Authority (environment) (NRA) **1990:** Office of Electricity Regulation (OFFER)

Box 16.1 lists the main institutions which are concerned with the implementation of monopoly policy in the UK.

Attitudes towards monopoly have changed over time according to different economic and political conditions, and it is possible to categorise UK monopoly policy in the twentieth century into four main phases:

● Before the Second World War, both private monopolies (limited companies) and public monopolies (nationalised industries) were encouraged, in the hope that this would help to protect British industry against international competition and reduce the effects of the economic depression of that time; for example, such large, present-day enterprises as the BBC and British Airways can trace the history of their current organisation back to the 1930s, when the government of the day encouraged them to take up a monopolistic position.

● Immediately after 1945 private monopolies were discouraged by the then Labour Government which was committed to a policy of export-led growth and full employment – economic theory predicts that private monopolies will reduce output and increase prices. However, in line with the government's policy of nationalisation, certain public monopolies were encouraged, e.g. railways and coal. During this period a two-pronged approach to private monopolies was developed through the establishment of the Monopolies Commission and the Restrictive Practices Court, whilst public

monopolies were excluded from these bodies' terms of reference.

● During the 1960s and 1970s there was a confused and contradictory approach both to public and private monopolies. By now it was realised that the control of potential monopolies which could be created by mergers and takeovers was just as important as the control of actual monopolies. Consequently, the Monopolies Commission had its powers extended to become the Monopolies and Mergers Commission (MMC). However, in the 1960s, government policy towards mergers was particularly ambiguous. There was a discretionary, case-by-case approach in which some mergers were referred to the MMC, whilst others were not; for instance, the Westminster Bank was allowed to merge with the National Provincial Bank to form the National Westminster Bank, but a proposed merger between Lloyds and Barclays Banks was disallowed after an unfavourable report by the MMC. Meanwhile, an organisation, known as the Industrial Reorganisation Corporation (IRC), was created by the government in order to encourage mergers! The IRC was particularly active in the motor industry, assisting car manufacturers to amalgamate in order to become more internationally competitive.

By 1970, the disbandment of the MMC was widely predicted, but it was given a new lease of life by the UK's entry into the EU (then known as the Common Market) and the need for the UK to adopt European standards of monopoly control.

● During the 1980s and early 1990s, when privatisation and deregulation were central to Conservative government policy, public monopolies were discouraged and largely eliminated, but a contradictory policy towards private monopolies remained. In 1990, the powers of the MMC were extended to cover the nationalised industries, and the MMC also benefited from the growth of 'consumerism', with increased public awareness of monopolistic practices and a general demand for government action to protect the interests of the consumer. However, the MMC was still restricted by the traditional discretionary, case-by-case approach of UK governments towards monopolies. At the same time, mergers between large firms reduced competition and the power of multinational conglomerates grew. There was also a trend towards joint ventures, for instance between British and Japanese car manufacturers, which might reduce competition, and there was a growing awareness that action by single countries to limit monopoly power was no longer sufficient: there had to be action on an international scale, for example, within the EU.

The current position

The Monopolies and Mergers Commission

The MMC investigates cases of dominant firm monopolies, where a firm controls 25 per cent or more of the output of an industry, which are referred not only by the Secretary of State for Trade and Industry/President of the Board of Trade (who is a politician), but also by the Director General of Fair trading (who is a permanent public official).

The MMC might recommend, for instance, that a firm's prices should be reduced, or that costs should be lowered. It is then up to the Secretary of State to either accept or reject the Commission's recommendations. The MMC will not always criticise a monopoly, as it is empowered to support it if the public interest is likely to be served; e.g., if consumers can benefit from economies of scale which would be lost if the monopoly were broken up.

With respect to mergers, the MMC can only investigate those mergers which are referred to it by the Secretary of State/President of the Board of Trade, and only a small percentage of mergers are in fact referred. The government is sometimes accused of failing to have a consistent policy on mergers, and often there is considerable controversy when amalgamations occur, for instance the BMW takeover of Rover in 1994.

The Restrictive Practices Court

A restrictive trade practice is an agreement between two or more firms to undertake restrictions on such factors as output, prices, quality of goods traded or distribution channels.

The court was set up in 1956 to consider restictive trade practices, or agreements between firms; for example, an agreement between two petrol companies to increase their prices at the same time might be viewed as a restrictive trade practice.

Any agreement between firms has to be registered with the Director General of Fair Trading. The agreement is automatically assumed to be against the public interest unless it can satisfy at least one of eight conditions known as 'gateways'; for example, it could be claimed that an agreement is necessary to protect jobs, promote exports, protect the public against injury or to provide specific benefits to consumers. However, the Court has, in practice, found against most agreements which have come before it, and many agreements are voluntarily abandoned before they come to court.

European Union (EU) Legislation

Prior to 1989 there were only two brief rules in existence to deal with anti-competitive behaviour in the EU: Articles 85 and 86 of the Treaty of Rome. Article 85 is concerned with restrictive practices and all types of oligopolistic collusion, whilst Article 86 bans firms from the 'abuse of a dominant position' within the EU market. The articles mainly concern trade between firms in EU member countries, and do not therefore apply to companies operating solely within a member country. The European Commission can refer firms to the European Court of Justice who appear to be contravening the provisions of either of the articles. In addition, Articles 92–94 prohibit government subsidies to industries or individual firms which will distort, or threaten to distort, competition.

Articles 85 and 86 were mainly designed to control restictive practices and unfair competition rather than mergers as such, although by 1983 the Commission had developed the principle that mergers could also be dealt with under Article 86.

However, a large wave of mergers in Europe in the the 1980s convinced the Commissioners that the two Articles were inadequate in themselves to tackle the growing amalgamation phenomenon, and the Merger Control Regulation of 1989 was formulated. Under this regulation, a merger is referred to the Commission if:

- the merging firms have a combined world-wide turnover exceeding 5 billion Ecu (£3.6 billion);

- at least 250 million Ecu of turnover is generated within the EU.

If the above two criteria are satisfied, but each of the firms concerned achieves more than two-thirds of its total EU turnover within one and the same country, then such a merger would be dealt with under that country's merger policy and not under EU legislation.

Some common criticisms of UK monopoly policy

- The process of investigation by the MMC is cumbersome and time-consuming, and only a very small proportion of all mergers are ever examined.

- The whole approach has been too 'gentlemanly', and has lacked 'real teeth' as regards the imposition of sufficiently stiff penalties for offending firms; for example, industrial lobbying and negotiating has often been able to secure favourable deals for the firms involved, even where clear recommendations have been made.

- The definition of what comprises the 'public interest' in the 1973 Fair Trading Act is too vague, and the burden of proof should be changed so that companies involved would have to positively demonstrate the benefits of a merger to the public before it could proceed, rather than merely proving that it would not be against the public interest.

- Regarding restictive practices policy, whilst open collusion has largely been eliminated, tacit collusion on such matters as price fixing is likely to be widespread, is very difficult to prove and even if proved carries a relatively light penalty.

- The MMC does not consist of permanent staff and its members are frequently changed. This has led to a lack of continuity and differences in emphasis and interpretation as between different investigations, depending on the personnel involved.

- The discretionary, case-by-case approach has led to arbitrariness in terms of selecting which mergers should be referred, and the decisions of the Secretary of State/President of the Board of Trade, which may be based on purely political considerations.

- From a free market viewpoint, it has been argued that the MMC attempts to regulate industries and businesses which are better left to the market.

Box 16.2 is a case study on the market for petrol.

BOX 16.2

The market for petrol

The MMC investigated petrol prices in some depth at the end of the 1980s, and published its report in 1990. It arrived at the following conclusion:

"that the wholesale petrol market is competitive. In most areas of the country consumers have available in their neighbourhood a range of petrol prices and standards of service from which to choose. Pump prices are highly visible, being clearly displayed outside outlets, enabling the motorist to be aware of relative prices and make a choice... The price that the wholesalers pay for petrol, since they are based on Rotterdam prices, are similar; equally their wholesaling costs, while they vary, are unlikely to be moving differently. Thus at a time of rising prices they all face similar pressures... A move by one is likely to be followed by changes of very much the same size by the others. This speed of response is helped by the transparency of prices in the market; our study of two periods of price changes during spring 1989 showed that principal wholesalers became aware of competitors' movements in a matter of hours... Neither the absolute levels of retail prices in the United Kingdom nor the way in which these prices have reacted to international price changes suggest that the wholesalers have been securing unjustified margins or that they collude in setting prices."

*Source: **MMC** 1990*

In this chapter, we have examined how UK governments have dealt with the problem of monopoly power: the approach adopted has essentially been discretionary, with each suspected instance of monopoly abuse being judged on a case-by-case basis. Such an approach has by no means met with universal approval, and has in fact been criticised from several standpoints. Look at the following extract.

The Brewers: what a crazy way to make the law

Before 1989 the brewing industry was monopolised by a cartel of 6 big brewers, who also controlled most of England's pubs. The Monopolies and Mergers Commission decided that what was needed was greater competition and consumer choice and cheaper prices. Changes were implemented. So what is the situation now?

Brewers' market share

Scottish Courage 25%

Bass 23%

Rest 17%

Carlsberg-Tetley 17%

Whitbread 13.5%

Imports 4.5%

Well, instead of the big 6 brewers controlling 76% of all beer output, there is now a 'big 5' controlling 82%; and beer prices have risen, sales have fallen, thousands of pubs have closed and hundreds of publicans have gone bankrupt and/or committed suicide.

All this has cost the industry an estimated £500 million, with no serious benefit to the average drinker. The beer industry seems to provide a formidable cautionary tale on what happens when governments start to meddle with the market. As Sir Peter Kemp, a former permanent secretary in the Cabinet Office has noted, Whitehall is now 'littered with policies that do not work'.

So, how did this beer chaos arise? The MMC recommended that the big breweries should only be allowed 2000 pubs each, and that they would have to sell half of all their pubs over this limit – it would mean that thousands of pubs would have to change hands. But the big brewers did not take all this lying down – tenants were served notice to quit, or were forced to accept less favourable contracts and the brewers restructured their operations to circumvent the Order's intention. For instance, Courage sold all its pubs, Grand Met sold all its brewing interests, but they sold them to each other, so that the Beer Orders did not cover them. As Roger Protz of the Campaign for Real Ale explains: Grand Met can have as many pubs as it likes because it's not a brewer. And in Grand Met pubs, in the main, they just sell Courage.

REVIEW TASK

The most fundamental criticism is directed at the Government's overall approach to competition. Monopolies enquiries may be conducted where any industry has a structure which is deemed to operate or may be expected to operate against the public interest; and no evidence is required of consumers' interests actually being harmed.

As Professor Kim Warren of the London Business School points out: Industry structure is presumed to explain and predict public outcomes. This is a dangerous assumption. Real markets are too complex to be understood by simple models.

Source: *Adapted from Daily Telegraph* *(20 November 1993).*

1 What criticisms of the government's competition policy are implied by the article?
2 Do you think that this case study makes the case for a more laissez-faire approach? Give reasons for your answer.

How could the UK deal with monopoly?

The OFT and extended warranties

OFT TO SLAM RETAILERS OVER WARRANTIES

Antony Barnett

If you are planning to buy an electrical appliance this Christmas, chances are that the retailer will try to sell you an extended warranty – a three or five-year insurance policy to cover repairs after the manufacturer's guarantee expires.

Anyone tempted by this should think twice – a cheaper warranty can probably be bought direct from the manufacturer.

The lack of consumer information about extended warranties prompted an Office of Fair Trading investigation into the practice last February. Its report, due to be published shortly, is believed to be critical of High Street retailers such as Dixons – which owns Currys – and Comet for providing inadequate information about the choice of alternatives.

At the time of the investigation Sir Bryan Carsberg, Director-General of Fair Trading, called for 'greater transparency' in the process. He said: 'Consumers are often asked to make snap decisions about taking out extended warranties without the benefit of shopping around.

'It seems likely that many retailers do not inform their customers of the availability of extended warranties from other sources including the manufacturer. It is also unclear how much consumers are aware of limitations and exclusions.'

The consumer lobby is likely to welcome any move by the OFT to increase information available to customers. But the Consumers' Association has questioned the need to take out an extended warranty in the first place.

For instance, its test on machine reliability in 1992 found that a television has a one-in-four chance of going wrong in the first four years, with average repair costs of between £40 and £50. The average price of a four-year warranty in 1992 was £70.

The CA concluded: 'The message is clear: you are likely to save money by not taking out the extended guarantee and running the risk of needing a repair, not the other way round.'

*Source: **Observer** (4 December 1994).*

Preview

In Chapter 16, we considered some of the general approaches that a government could adopt to the control of monopoly/oligopoly. In this chapter, we shall investigate the range of specific strategic approaches that could be deployed, including the following key areas:

- the discretionary approach;
- use of the law;
- taxation of monopoly profits;
- subsidies;
- price controls;
- nationalisation;
- privatisation;
- deregulation.

The discretionary/investigatory approach

This involves the approach previously described in Chapter 16, and at its heart, in the case of the UK, is the role of the Monopolies and Mergers Commission. Since its inception in 1948, the UK's monopoly policy has been variously described as regulatory, discretionary, rule of reason, pragmatic, case-by-case, investigatory or 'watch-dog', and involves the process of investigating monopolies and mergers when abuse of market power is suspected and referring such abuse to the MMC or the Restrictive Practices Court. Each investigation undertaken involves a cost-benefit analysis on a case-by-case basis to determine whether or not the situation referred is in the public interest. As pointed out in Chapter 16, only a very small proportion of companies and amalgamations are ever investigated, but it is argued that the mere existence of a 'watch-dog' should act as a sufficient deterrent against monopoly abuse. There are, however, several criticisms of this view, as we saw in Chapter 16.

Use of the rule of law to enforce the break-up of monopoly

On the presumption that the very existence of monopoly power is against the public interest and something which is likely to adversely affect economic efficiency, the government could enforce the compulsory break-up of a monopolist into smaller units. This is the per se approach to monopoly control, as described in Chapter 16, which has never found favour in the UK.

It does, however, depict the much less flexible, more vigilant approach adopted in the USA since the Sherman Anti-Trust (the American term for monopoly) Act of 1890, in which monopolies were considered illegal from the outset, and were required to be broken up. The Act prohibited 'contracts and conspiracies in restraint of trade', and an early victim of the legislation was the Standard Oil Company which was broken up by the Supreme Court. Three of the major seven world oil companies of today Esso, Mobil and Chevron – began life as subsidiaries of Standard Oil.

The effect of the government enforcing such an automatic policy law would obviously depend on the nature of the monopoly in question and the size of the market in which it exists: for example, the breaking-up of a cartel is likely to yield far greater welfare gains than the breaking-up of a natural monopoly or one with a relatively large minimum efficient scale of production, and, in the case of the USA, the vast size of the domestic market permits corresponding vast company size, without the anti-trust legislation necessarily being infringed.

The taxation of monopoly profits

In order to improve equity, by returning some consumer surplus to taxpayers, the government could levy a tax on super-normal monopoly profits. However, in theory, such a tax is likely to leave the monopolist's price and output unchanged, and therefore not lead to an improvement in allocative efficiency where price equals marginal cost. This can be explained as follows:

Suppose a government decided to levy a lump-sum tax of 50 per cent of monopoly profits. It might appear intuitively that the monopolist's best course of action would be to raise price. However, inspection of the figure in Box 17.1, the familiar monopoly equilibrium diagram, suggests that this would not occur.

BOX 17.1

Monopoly price and quantity

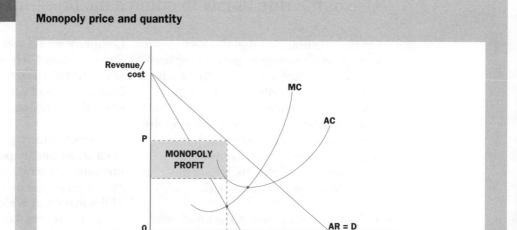

In Box 17.1, the monopolist will maximise profit at output level OQ, where MC = MR. If the firm increases price, it moves from its equilibrium position and profit will fall. The monopolist will therefore leave price and output unchanged as, in this case, it would be better to have 50 per cent of maximum profits than 50 per cent of less than than maximum.

In general, the specific taxation of monopoly profits has not been used in the UK as a tool to control monopolies, although special taxes have on occasions been imposed where 'windfall' gains have been made.

The granting of subsidies

The direct opposite course of action to the imposition of taxes on profits would be the granting of a subsidy to firms per unit of output produced. The aim here would be to reduce the marginal cost of production, to shift the MC curve downwards so as to equate it with price and to create allocative efficiency.

However, aside from the technical difficulties inherent in a policy involving accurate knowledge of the firm's cost and revenue curves, the provision of state subsidies to the

private sector might run counter to EU legislation (Articles 92–94, see Box 16.1), as well as flying in the face of 'free-market philosophy', based on the 'survival of the fittest' and the need to allow businesses and individuals to 'stand on their own feet'.

The following are some of the general arguments for and against state provision of subsidies:

Arguments for

- As noted above, in order to achieve allocative efficiency in a particular industry, it may be essential for the government to grant a subsidy to enable marginal cost to fall so that it can be equated with price.
- Although counter to the EU's policy of free trade within its internal market (see Chapter 30), subsidies, which have the effect of lowering price and raising domestic output, may help the balance of payments by making exports more price competitive and imports less price competitive; i.e., they act as a form of protection.
- Similarly, subsidies may be used to protect infant industries until they are strong enough to face the full force of international trade; it is argued that many industries in the early stages of development,

particularly those in developing countries, might never actually reach 'adulthood' unless in receipt of such assistance. This argument is considered in the context of international trade in Chapter 28.

- Subsidies may be used to increase the output of merit goods which tend to be under-produced in a free market economy (see Chapter 19).
- The same argument as above can also be applied to those goods which confer positive externalities on society (see Chapter 18).
- Subsidies may provide the necessary temporary financial assistance to protect employment in a particular industry, which, in the absence of such assistance, may face serious retrenchment or even closure.

Arguments against

- In free market terms, a subsidy represents an interference with the free interplay of the forces of demand and supply, and would inevitably lead to a misallocation of society's scarce resources, which will be overallocated to those sectors in receipt of subsidies.
- Subsidies may encourage inefficiency – firms in need of financial support cannot, by definition, be operating efficiently, and as such the government would be pursuing a policy of supporting 'lame ducks' which should be allowed to die.
- Payment of subsidies may have to be financed through higher taxation which may cause distortions elsewere in the economy in terms of disincentive effects, higher inflation

in the case of indirect taxes or general inequity, as not all the people who pay the taxes will benefit from the subsidy; e.g., a subsidy to the railways would be financed by all tax payers, but only enjoyed by rail-users.

- Any flow of money from the public to the private sector will involve an opportunity cost in terms of other forms of government expenditure forgone, or in terms of private expenditure forgone if taxes have to be raised.

The use of price controls

Price controls in such forms as minimum and maximum prices, and prices and incomes policies, represent an interference with the free interplay of market forces, and as such have not carried favour in recent years with successive 'laissez-faire' Conservative governments. However, in the case of the privatised utilities, such as British Telecom, gas, water and electricity, it was realised by the government that these 'natural' monopolies, once freed from state ownership and control, would be in a very advantageous position to abuse their very considerable monopoly power and exploit the consumer. Consequently, special regulatory bodies were established at the time of privatisation to act as 'watch-dogs' over the performance of the formerly nationalised utilities (see Box 16.1). The main regulatory bodies are the Office of Telecommunications (OFTEL), the Office of Gas Supply (OFGAS), the Office of Water Services (OFWAT) and the Office of Electricity Regulation (OFFER).

The power of these regulatory bodies lie in the terms of their operating licences, which set out the duties of both the privatised utility and the regulator. In all the utility industries, the regulators are duty-bound to liberalise entry to the market by promoting effective competition. However, the most important feature of the licensing system is the pricing formula set out in each industry's licence which in effect sets maximum prices for the privatised monopolies which are usually linked to the rate of inflation. The price control operates mainly via the 'RPI minus X' formula, where RPI represents the rate of inflation and 'X' is set by the

regulatory body. The prices charged by the privatised utility are effectively 'capped' as average price rises have to be limited to 'X' percentage points below the rate of inflation, as indicated by the Retail Price Index (RPI); for example, with an inflation rate of 3 per cent, a price limit of RPI minus 2 would lead to a price rise of 1 per cent, whilst an 'X' factor of 4 would require the industry to reduce prices by 1 per cent. The exact nature of the formulae applied to the privatised utilities has varied from industry to industry.

BT is regulated by OFTEL

Various strengths and weaknesses
of the regulatory system have been claimed:

Strengths of the regulatory system

- The 'RPI minus X' formula could provide the impetus to increase efficiency and reduce costs as a lowering of costs below the 'X factor' is likely to lead to higher profits.

- The regulatory system dove-tails well with the largely discretionary nature of the older established agencies of monopoly control, such as the OFT and the MMC – it allows for a pragmatic approach to be adopted in which pricing formulae can be adjusted to prevailing circumstances.

Weaknesses of the regulatory system

Regulatory capture is a situation in which the regulator operates in the interests of the monopolist rather than seeking to protect the interests of the consumer and society at large.

- The constant need to lower costs to maintain profitability may manifest itself in the form of a worsening of workers' conditions of service and/or a policy of redundancies. British Gas was recently criticised for pursuing such a policy whilst simultaneously granting a 75 per cent pay rise to its Chairman.
- If the 'X' factor is initially set too low, the utility might be able to make excessive profits, and higher values for 'X' would then be set for subsequent years. This 'removal' of profit could thus lessen the industry's incentive to lower costs.
- The power of the regulators has gradually increased and their record of greater intervention in the utility industries has led to calls for more public accountability of the regulators themselves.
- The regulatory agencies have been accused of becoming too involved in the day-to-day management of the industries they oversee, whilst lacking both the necessary expertise and the exposure to commercial risk necessary for any genuine management role. Their judgements have been too discretionary, and not

based upon common principles about the degree to which markets should be structured to promote competition, and about how the returns to justify investment should be computed.

- The phenomenom of regulatory capture may occur. This is a situation in which the regulator operates in the interests of the monopolist rather than seeking to protect those of the consumer. This may occur over time as the regulator is 'captured' by senior managers and manipulated to accept their values and view of the world which may well be at odds with consumers' and society's interests.

Will Hutton of the *Guardian* newspaper (12 December 1994) argues that "regulation has proved weak, inconsistent and biased towards the interests of the shareholders. The public interest has been improperly served. There has been widespread misallocation of resources. Monopoly profits and executive pay have boomed, the security of employment and levels of training have deteriorated".

Look at Box 17.2.

The Water Companies

BOX 17.2

The INVESTIGATOR

OFWAT canes 3 water companies

OFWAT has accused three of the largest water companies of delivering poor standards of service: Anglian and Thames were rapped over the knuckles for delivering the poorest quality of service in OFWAT's annual review, with Yorkshire being rebuked for supply interruptions.

Anglian managed to acquire 43,000 complaints last year, an 8-fold increase, but denied any links between its poor performance and the decision to axe 900 jobs. Thames Water's response to bill queries and written complaints was described as 'very poor' by OFWAT, and along with Yorkshire Water and Anglian, they were also rebuked for causing customers to have their supplies cut off.

The INVESTIGATOR

Liquid gold

Imagine turning on the tap and millions of pounds pouring out. An impossible dream? Not if you're the boss of a water company.

Shadow Chancellor, Gordon Brown revealed that since water was privatised, 28 of these bosses have shared in a £20 million bonanza.

But for water customers charges have rocketed and many water workers have lost their jobs.

There seems to be a strong argument for turning off the tap.

Taking private monopolies into public ownership: nationalisation

Nationalisation is the act of transferring privately owned enterprise into the hands of the state.

One solution to the abuse of private monopoly power arising from the goal of profit maximisation is for the government to 'socialise' the enterprise by taking it into state ownership, i.e. by nationalising it. Nationalisation is therefore the act of transferring privately owned assets into the hands of

the state, and a nationalised industry is a public corporation, i.e. one which is owned and controlled by the government.

Box 17.3 indicates the history of nationalisation in the UK.

BOX 17.3	**The major nationalisations in the UK 1926–77**	
	Business	**Date first nationalised**
	Electricity	1926
	Airways (British Overseas Airways Corporation)	1940
	Bank of England	1946
	Road Haulage, Coal	1947
	Railways	1948
	Gas, Iron and Steel	1949
	Airports	1966
	Aero Engines (Rolls Royce),	1971
	Oil (British National Oil Corporation)	
	Car Manufacturing (British Leyland)	1976
	Aerospace, Shipbuilding	1977

Privatisation/Denationalisation is the act of transferring state owned enterprise to the private sector.

Most nationalisation in the UK took place during the Labour government of the period 1945–51, e.g. coal, railways, gas and steel, and the nationalised industries continued to play a very important part in the economy up until the early 1980s, when the newly elected (in 1979) Conservative government, ideologically committed as they were to the laissez-faire philosophy, started to pursue their programme of denationalisation/privatisation.

At this time, the nationalised industries accounted for approximately 10 per cent of the nation's GNP, employed 1.5 million people and accounted for 15 per cent of total fixed investment. However, by 1995, the only nationalised industries remaining in the UK were the Post Office, which the government had previously planned to privatise, but were forced to temporarily abandon in the light of fierce opposition, and the railways, which were partly privatised.

Arguments for nationalisation

A variety of arguments were used to support the transfer of industries from private to public ownership:

Political arguments

The political case for nationalisation is that it is a key element in achieving a more just, socialist society, which is incompatible with the private ownership of the means of production. The old Clause IV of the Labour Party made an unequivocal commitment to public ownership (see Box 17.4).

Although the current leadership of the Labour Party have 'remodelled' this clause in trying to formulate 'New Labour', the founders of the Labour party saw nationalisation as an effective means of achieving the transition from capitalism to socialism. In practical terms, Labour's nationalisation programme developed into a programme of trying to take control of the key industries in the economy, sometimes referred to as the commanding heights.

BOX 17.4

The pre-1995 Clause IV of the Labour Party

"To secure for the workers by hand or by brain the full fruits of their industry and the most equitable distribution thereof that may be possible upon the basis of the common ownership of the means of production, distribution and exchange, and the best obtainable system of popular administration and control of each industry or service."

Labour Party Constitution Clause IV (4)Labour

From a political point of view, it was also believed that nationalisation would bring about a fairer society, in that resources could be more equitably distributed: capitalist society is one based upon antagonistic class divisions – there are the capitalists and their agents who own and contol the means of production, and those who do not, i.e. workers; capitalist profit is derived from the expropriation of surplus value created by the efforts of the working class, and nationalisation was seen as a way of seizing back these profits, and using them for the benefit of all, in the form of higher real incomes for the employees of the nationalised industries and lower prices for consumers.

It was also believed that nationalisation would bring about improved industrial relations as the class conflict (i.e. between capitalists and workers) of privately owned industry would give way to greater cooperation between managers and workers who would share a common interest. However, the form of nationalisation adopted in the UK actually did very little to facilitate worker participation in the running of their industries, let alone anything to bring about worker control!

Management of the economy and post-war reconstruction

Linked to the idea of capturing the commanding heights of the economy was the belief that an extension of public ownership would provide the most direct and effective means of influencing the performance of the whole economy. Nationalisation was seen as a movement towards socialist planning of the economy, and on the basis that 'you don't own what you don't control, and you don't control what you don't own', and in the general context of an unstable market economy, it was viewed by its supporters as the only way of ensuring the achievement of a high level of employment, stable prices and a faster rate of economic growth.

Moreover, after the Second World War, some of the UK's key industries, e.g. coal and railways, had become extremely run-down under private ownership, and it was felt that the only way that they could be saved and regenerated would be through a state take-over, and a subsequent large-scale injection of capital investment, which would be most unlikely to be forthcoming from the private sector. Paradoxically, this same type of argument has been used in reverse to justify privatisation!

Natural monopolies

Until recently, it was believed that the utility industries such as telecommunications, water, gas and electricity were 'natural monopolies' in the sense that the total market size, combined with the existence of substantial economies of scale, meant that there was only room for one firm in the industry:

competition in these sectors would lead to wasteful duplication, a reduced level of efficiency and a massive waste of society's scarce resources; and private monopoly control would provide enormous potential for consumer exploitation. State monopoly control was therefore seen almost universally as the most common-sense solution.

Externalities and public interest

An important argument for nationalisation is that publicly owned industries can operate in the interests of society at large by taking into account the external costs and benefits associated with their production decisions. This is in sharp contrast to the privately owned corporation whose primary obligation will be to its shareholders, whose long-term goal is likely to be profit-maximisation and whose basis of operation would necessarily have to accord to strict commercial criteria – i.e. that private revenues exceed private costs.

Thus, a nationalised industry, unlike its private counterpart, could provide socially important, but unprofitable, services, which may generate substantial positive externalities; for example, a railway line serving a remote outlying rural community is unlikely to be commercially viable but would almost certainly confer considerable social benefits on the community in question in terms of keeping the community alive. Similarly, the publicly owned industry is likely to take greater account of the generation of negative externalities, e.g. in the case of atmospheric pollution or workers' safety standards.

Strategic arguments

Some industries are of strategic importance to the economy, and this might provide an important reason for taking them into public ownership; e.g. coal was an extremely important indigenous source of power, Rolls Royce engines were considered to be of great importance to the interests of Western defence in 1973 and the atomic energy industry was, in the past, deemed to be too potentially hazardous to be in private hands.

The privatisation of state monopolies

Successive Conservative governments since 1979, in line with their belief in supply-side, new classical, laissez-faire economics, have been unswervingly committed to a programme of privatisation in their desire to fundamentally and irreversibly alter the balance of the mixed economy in favour of the private sector. Box 17.5 indicates the various strands of the government's privatisation programme, although the discussion under this heading refers specifically to denationalisation; i.e. the transfer of ownership of businesses from the state to the private sector. Boxes 17.6 and 17.7 show the major privatisations which have occurred since 1979, and the extent of the financial proceeds raised.

BOX 17.5

The various strands of privatisation

Type of policy	Examples
Privatisation: the transfer of ownership of public sector assets to the private sector.	● the conversion of nationalised industries into public limited companies through sales of shares, (denationalisation) e.g. British Telecom in 1983 and British Coal in 1994 ● the sale of government shareholdings in otherwise private companies, e.g. the sale of BP shares ● the sale of various government owned assets e.g. council houses
Deregulation or liberalisation: the removal of government regulations on the activities of businesses in order to promote greater competition	● the encouragement of import competition for those goods which are traded internationally ● the ending of legal monopolies for solicitors in the conveyancing of house property and for opticians in the sale of spectacles ● the 'Big Bang' of 1986 – the deregulation of the London Stock Exchange ● bus services and broadcasting
Contracting-out, competitive tendering or franchising: the process by which private firms are invited to submit tenders, to undertake services previously carried out within the public sector	● the franchising of railway lines ● local authorities contracting-out road cleaning, refuse collection and the maintenance of parks ● schools and colleges contracting-out cleaning and catering services
Marketisation or Commercialisation: The increased market provision of services previously undertaken in the non-market sector of the economy and/or the introduction of market criteria, e.g. efficiency and competition, in the provision of certain state funded services	● greater private provision of health care and education and less public provision ● the introduction of the 'internal market' into the NHS ● the incorporation of local authority colleges

BOX 17.6

Major UK privatisations since 1979

Business	Date
British Aerospace	1981/2, 1984/5
Cable and Wireless	1981/2, 1984/5
Britoil	1982/3, 1983/4, 1985/6
Enterprise Oil	1984/5
British Telecom	1984/5, 1985/6, 1986/7, 1993
British Gas	1986/7
British Petroleum	1979/80, 1981/2, 1983/4, 1987/8
British Airports Authority	1987/8
Rolls Royce Aero Engines	1987/8
British Steel	1988/9, 1989/90
Water	1989/90, 1990/1
Electricity	1990/1, 1991/2, 1994/5
British Coal	1994
British Rail	1994 onwards

BOX 17.7

Privatisation proceeds since 1979 (£ billion)

Year	Proceeds	
1979/80	0.4	
1980/81	0.2	
1981/82	0.5	
1982/83	0.5	
1983/84	1.1	
1984/85	2.1	
1985/86	2.7	
1986/87	4.5	
1987/88	5.1	
1988/89	7.1	
1989/90	4.2	
1990/91	5.3	
1991/92	5.3	
1992/93	8.1	
1993/94	5.4	
1994/95	5.5	⎫
1995/96	1.0	⎬ Projected figures
1996/97	1.0	⎭

Arguments for privatisation

In the same way as socialists would regard public ownership, of at least the commanding heights of the economy, as inherently more efficient and equitable than any corresponding private ownership, people on the political right, and even the political centre, would tend to believe the exact opposite; i.e. that industry will always function more efficiently under private ownership. Some of the specific arguments advanced in favour of privatisation are as follows.

● Increased competition and efficiency
  Probably the most important argument advanced in favour of privatisation is that the break-up of the 'sleepy' state monopolies would expose these industries to the forces of the free market, and consequently expose them to greater competition and impel them to become more efficient. Thus, driven by the profit motive, operating under competitive market conditions and faced with the constant threat of takeover, instead of being 'feather-bedded' by the government, the privatised concern would be forced to:

– keep its costs and prices to a minimum, and produce high quality goods and services so as to compete effectively in the goods market, with consumers reaping the benefit in terms of greater choice and lower prices;

– increase efficiency, and thus profits, to satisfy the wishes of its shareholders to whom it is ultimately accountable;

– further ensure efficient utilisation of resources as it will be competing in the capital market for funds, which are only likely to be forthcoming if investors perceive its performance favourably.

● Less government interference
A major problem faced by nationalised industries was that successive governments, in order to achieve their macroeconomic objectives, would constantly interfere in these industries' employment, investment and pricing policies in the form of overmanning, delayed decisions on new investment projects/external financing limits and price controls. Privatisation would eliminate this type of intervention, allow managers to manage and improve performance overall.

PSBR is the amount by which, in a particular year, the expenditure of the whole public sector exceeds its income.

● Increased government revenues and a reduction in the PSBR
The public sector borrowing requirement (PSBR) is the annual overdraft of the whole public sector, including central government, local government and the public corporations; i.e. the amount by which, in a particular year, the expenditure of the public sector exceeds its income. It can be seen from Box 17.7 on the proceeds of privatisation, that considerable sums of money have been raised by the government through the transfer of assets to the private sector, and this has obviously reduced the amount the government has needed to

borrow. This has been viewed favourably by successive Conservative governments, not only because they have regarded the size of the PSBR as being of significance in itself, but also because it is believed to influence such key factors as the money supply and inflation and the level of interest rates and investment. A reduction in the size of the PSBR might also permit a reduction in income tax rates, which has been a central plank of government policy.

● Wider shareholding and the promotion of popular capitalism
As part of the 'culture of enterprise' and 'peoples' capitalism', which were promoted particularly vigorously by Conservative governments during the 1980s, individuals were not only permitted to become part of the 'property-owning class' through the acquisition of council houses, but were also encouraged to become shareholders through the purchase of shares in the newly privatised public limited companies. As these companies were all extremely well known, it was argued that many individuals who had not previously been shareholders would acquire shares for the first time, which would considerably widen share ownership away from the large financial institutions, and give members of the public a real stake in the major industries of the UK, as well as the free market economy in general.

Arguments against privatisation

The case against privatisation can be made in two main ways:

First, by restating the case for nationalisation:

- **Political arguments**
  For those who believe that socialism represents a superior form of society to capitalism, the movement towards the complete privatisation of the means of production would be one that was in the totally wrong direction, and one which would inevitably lead to greater class conflict, greater exploitation of workers and a more unequal and unfair society in general.

- **Management of the economy**
  The same point can be made in relation to socialist planning – a privatised, laissez-faire economy is one which is likely to be particularly prone to the vagaries of the market and the violent swings of the trade cycle: a point which the peoples of the new market economies of Eastern Europe would all too readily appreciate!

- **Natural monopolies**
  The case aqainst private ownership of the utility industries rests upon the enormous potential for monopoly abuse in terms of high prices and poor quality service for consumers, worsened conditions and redundancies for employees, with high dividends for shareholders and high salaries for senior managers.

The weak control of the utilities through the regulatory bodies has not helped to overcome the above criticism.

Look at Box 17.8

Power Firms' PROFITS FUEL POPULAR ANGER

A WOMAN who'd been a Tory voter all her life said it all as she confronted the television cameras outside the polling station at Dudley: "A few people getting very rich, most of us struggling on." Even John Maples, Tory vice-chairman, wrote in his recent report that, for most Tory voters, privatisation meant directors and shareholders getting rich "off the backs" of everyone else. Every week, it seems, a new batch of privateers recklessly fills its pockets, oblivious of the rage and hatred which is building up in the country. Last week, a series of regional electricity companies revelled in vast increases in profits and dividends for the first half of the financial year.

Northern Electricity led the field with dividends up 30 per cent. Share prices rocketed at the prospect of a take-over by Trafalgar House – a company which has never looked back since its subsidiary, Cementation, employed Mark Thatcher in the early 1980s. Scanning the reports, I couldn't find any reference to the amount of electricity distributed. There must, surely, have been fantastic increases in distributed electricity to justify such enormous hand-outs. A jolly press officer helped me out. In the first half of 1991–92, the first year of privatisation, Northern Electricity distributed 6,730 gigawatts of electricity; in 1992, 6,735; in 1993, 6,831; in 1994, 6,793.

*Source: **Guardian** (19 December 1994).*

● Externalities and the public interest
Advocates of the government's privatisation programme would argue that the above need not be a problem, provided there is adequate regulation. However, this argument might be challenged by reference to the unimpressive record of the regulatory authorities to date, and the goal of long-run private profit-maximisation which is ultimately likely to subordinate all else, including externalities and the public interest.

A second way of arguing against privatisation is to challenge the particular arguments for privatisation and to criticise the policy implementation:

● Privatisation has mainly taken the form of converting public monopolies into private monopolies, e.g. gas and water, which largely nullifies the 'increased competition and efficiency' argument. However, aware of this criticism, the government has gone to great and complex lengths to ensure competition in the more recent privatisations such as electrity and the railways.

● Whilst the benefits to consumers and employees have not always been transparent, the merchant banks handling the floatation of shares have unambiguously benifited in terms of the large fees received. Box 17.9 shows the issuing institutions' income from four major privatisations, which can be seen to be substantial!

BOX 17.9

The costs of four UK privatisations

	British Telecom (£m)	British Gas (£m)	British Airways (£m)	Rolls Royce (£m)
Underwriting/placing commissions	74	60	8	13
Selling commissions	13	9	3	4
Clearing bank costs	20	45	8	11
Marketing (includes advertising)	14	40	6	4
Advisers' fees	6	5	4	2
Overseas offer	30	23	5	-
Total	157	182	34	34

*Source: **Institute of Economic Affairs** (1992).*

- Profitable, nationally owned assets have been sold at 'knock-down' prices. It is alleged that in its haste to transfer publicly owned companies to the private sector, the government seriously undervalued the corporations it was offering for sale, and therefore underpriced the privatisation programme in general, denying the nation as a whole of immense funds.

- Linked to the above point, the tendency to underprice the share issues of the newly privatised public limited companies led to the general expectation that their share prices would rise immediately (this was in fact the situation in all but one case, that of British Petroleum in 1987, in which shareholders incurred an immediate loss). Consequently, many of the new members of the shareholding class 'cashed in their chips' very soon after acquiring them, with the shares falling into the hands of the large financial institutions. This had the effect of concentrating share ownership, with institutional investors increasing their proportion of shareholdings at the expense of the individual investor. This situation led critics to claim that the government was running the economy like a casino.

- The government has used the sale of capital assets, e.g. factories, offices, plant and equipment, to fund current public expenditure, e.g. payment of public sector employees' wages – a practice akin to selling your house to pay for the shopping! It is what the late Conservative Prime Minister, Harold MacMillan, labelled a policy of 'selling off the family silver'. Moreover, being profitable assets, the Exchequer, and thus the country as a whole, would lose any future returns which such assets might generate, possibly necessitating higher taxes and a higher PSBR to finance any given level of public expenditure. Thus the beneficiaries of profitable enterprise would be the private shareholders instead of the nation at large, representing a redistribution of income in the form of dividend payments, from tax-payers to shareholders.

- Many thus feel that the government has perpetrated a fraud of vast proportions upon the citizens of the UK. Whilst claiming that 'popular capitalism' has returned industries to the public, the opposite has been the case. When an industry is nationalised, it is jointly owned by everyone in the country. Privatisation therefore represents a process of selling shares in assets to people who already own those assets, a confidence-trick which if carried out by any individual, would carry a stiff custodial sentence! At the same time, those individuals who are either unable or unwilling to purchase the shares are in effect compelled to relinquish their assets.

- The large-scale sale of shares to the public has had a distortive, 'crowding-out' effect on financial markets. Money used to buy shares was diverted from financial institutions such as building societies, possibly depriving other potential borrowers of funds.

TASK 17.1

Coursework

Undertake a study of an industry which has been privatised. Using a range of criteria, e.g. productivity, profits, employment, prices, investment, the public interest, etc. assess the performance of the industry now in relation to its performance when it was in the public sector.

Deregulation

Deregulation refers to the removal of government regulations on the activities of the business sector. Although privatisation and deregulation may occur at the same time and have the same type of aims, i.e. the promotion of competition and a reduction in the level of state influence, they are not exactly the same thing. Privatisation involves a change in the ownership of assets, whilst deregulation implies that markets have been opened up to greater competition. Two examples of simultaneous privatisation/deregulation are the de-regulation of bus services also involving the privatisation of the National Bus Company, and the privatisation of British Telecom occurring at the same time as the telecommunications market was deregulated by allowing Mercury Communications to have access to BT's landlines.

Deregulation may therefore be seen as complementary to privatisation as a weapon for dealing with the problem of monopoly power – although privatisation is supposed, by its advocates, to create a more competitive environment, it may not be able to do so on its own as it may merely involve the transformation of a state monopoly into a private one – e.g. BT – with the likelihood of monopoly abuse still remaining.

The establishment of the various regulatory bodies was clearly designed to deal with the latter problem.

However, supporters of laissez-faire economic policy, and, in particular, advocates of the theory of contestable markets (see Chapter 8), might take the view that regulatory policies are unnecessary and undesirable, representing as they do a new form of government interference, a type of reregulation. All that is necessary, they would argue, is that the government should identify which markets are potentially contestable, and then implement suitable deregulatory policies so as to ensure freedom of entry and exit, and in consequence a highly competitive environment.

An oft-quoted good example of deregulation is that of bus services in the UK. Regulation here had been based on a system of 'closed licensing' which limited the number of operators in a given area of service, and was intended to prevent wasteful duplication of services and to help in the enforcement of safety regulations. Competition was, however, restricted as a consequence, because new businesses wanting to enter the market often found it difficult to obtain licences. In addition, the government had introduced a system of controlled fares which were designed to protect bus passengers against possible exploitation. However, these were often set at levels which eroded operators' profits and, despite increased government subsidies for operators, contributed to a decline in the number of services.

Bus deregulation took the following form:

- In 1980, long distance coach travel was deregulated so that the existing nationalised monopoly supplier, The National Bus Company, had to compete with new entrants to the market. The NBC was privatised in 1986, involving a transfer to private ownership and a breaking up of the company into independent competing subsidiaries.
- 'Open licences' were introduced allowing new operators to set up services.
- Controlled fares were abolished.
- General network subsidies were abolished, but government subsidies for socially necessary services continued.

As is the case with privatisation and nationalisation, the 'beauty', or otherwise, of deregulation is very much in the 'eyes of the beholder', with those on the political right being its most enthusiastic advocates.

Advantages of deregulation

The advantages of deregulation are based on the general arguments for a freely operating price system and the virtues of economic liberalism, i.e. laissez-faire and individualism:

- the promotion of competition and enterprise;
- greater efficiency;
- lower prices and wider choice for consumers;
- 'getting the state off the backs' of businesses by the removal of 'red-tape' and bureaucracy.

Disadvantages of deregulation

These are based on the general disadvantages of a freely operating price system, which is the subject area covered by this section of the book:

- deregulation might increase market failure in the form of
  - generation of negative externalities;
  - underprovision of merit goods/services;
- deregulation would increase exploitation by those with economic power of those without power; e.g. monopoly exploitation and greater exploitation of workers in the form of lower wages and worsened conditions of service;
- regulation is necessary to ensure equity or fairness in matters such as income distribution.

Look at Box 17.10.

BOX 17.10

The INVESTIGATOR

Taxi de-regulation Swedish style – Who's the taxi for?

Yesterday taxis in Malmö blockaded the city centre 'French style', twenty of them driving around at a snail's pace to protest against poor supervision, oversupply, sharp practices and other effects of the recent deregulation. Nowadays anybody in Malmö can hail a taxi directly on the street. After years of opposition from cab firms and the authorities, what has been taken for granted in New York or London has now become possible here.

Since deregulation in July 1990 the number of taxis in Malmö has almost trebled. Prices have fallen and cab drivers fight for customers. Slow telephone responses, queues and taxi shortages have vanished with the introduction of the market freedom to establish a taxi business.

Is it any surprise that taxi firms in Malmö and

other parts of Sweden are starting to protest? The monopoly which used to guarantee them a non-stop stream of subservient customers at the taxi rank is no more. The sharp practices we now see are nothing new, and hardly due to the fact that the taxi service has been transformed from guild system to effective transport service. Nobody who has frozen in a taxi queue or listened on the phone to a laconic, 'please wait' will understand this talk of over-supply, or see anything odd about taxis chasing customers.

For years the Malmö taxi establishment imagined customers existed for them – rather than the other way round. What happened yesterday in the city centre shows some people still think that.

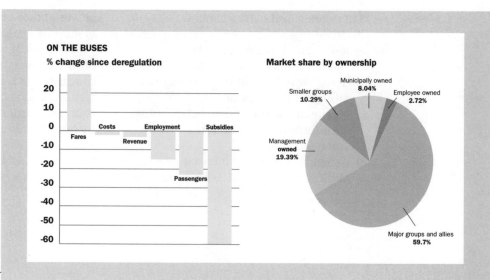

ON THE BUSES
% change since deregulation

Market share by ownership

BOX 17.10

Bus Deregulation SHEFFIELD STYLE

Competition brings chaos on the buses

Six years after deregulation, bus wars are still in full flow in Sheffield.

The 93 bus was waiting at the stop near the bus station. The blue double-decker was in the livery of Sheffield Omnibus. It was, however, in no hurry to move off until another 93, a single decker in the livery of South Yorkshire Transport (SYT), the area's main operator, arrived to chase off its rival.

This 'wing mirror timetabling' is common in Sheffield with competitors trying to claim a dwindling number of passengers. In 1985, the last year of the cheap fares policy which kept tickets to an average 8p, there were 350 million passengers; that has fallen to under 200 million last year.

The average fare is now 48p but bus mileage has remained the same which means there is terrific competition on the profitable routes and the city centre is jammed with competing buses.

Deregulation of the bus industry, like rail privatisation, was intended to increase competition and stimulate new services. The industry, dominated by publicly-owned companies and hidebound by tight regulations, was an obvious target but both managers and unions say that the results have been damaging.

They point to the chaos on the streets, the confusion for the passenger and the lack of investment. Mr. Mayer said: 'You used to be able to buy a time-table for 50p showing all routes and it would be valid for a year. Now services are changed every week.' When the

new £240m supertram is completed next year, SYT will not be allowed to coordinate its services with it because the Office of Fair Trading would argue that this is an anti-competitive activity.

The Government's argument against the cheap fares policy was that the ratepayers of the now defunct South Yorkshire County Council were forced to subsidise the service. Indeed, they paid £80m in 1985, equivalent to about £110m at today's prices. The local passenger transport executive still provides £40m to subsidise socially necessary routes.

However, Mike Smith, the PTE's press officer, points out that this is not a net benefit: 'You have to count this against the awful increase in congestion in the city as more people have taken to their cars and, of course, the extra they are paying in fares.' Both management and unions agree deregulation swept away some restrictive practices. There is, however, a human cost. 'Many drivers are getting in money terms about the same as they did five years ago. And they have to drive for five-and-a-half hours without a break,' Martin Mayer said.

The extra efficiency means South Yorkshire now runs the same number of miles with 750 instead of 1,100 buses and breaks even rather than making a loss.

Mike Pestereff, SYT's director, said: 'I would like to see something similar to France where all the public transport in a town is integrated and then offered by tender to the private sector.'

TASK 17.2

1 Why might taxi deregulation in Sweden be more successful than bus deregulation in Sheffield?

2 What advantages and disadvantages would a French-style franchise scheme have over British free-for-all bus privatisation?

3 Discuss the arguments for and against a return to public ownership of bus transport. Use the data in Box 17.10 to help with your answer.

REVIEW

In this chapter, we have examined the variety of specific approaches that a government might adopt to tackle the problem of monopoly/oligopoly power. However, the discerning reader will have noticed that we have not provided a clear-cut, unambiguous answer to the question that we posed in the title of the chapter ('How could the UK deal with monopoly?'). This is because there is no one definite answer! As is the case in many areas of economics, economists are by no means united in their policy prescriptions, as these are to a large extent influenced by their own political perspectives and value judgements about desirable courses of action.

REVIEW TASK

Nationalised industries' productivity
Annual percentage change

Year	Nationalised industries	Manufacturing industries	Whole economy
1979-80	1.7	0.9	1.2
1980-81	-0.4	-5.3	-3.7
1981-82	0.9	6.9	3.6
1982-83	2.0	6.3	4.8
1983-84	1.3	8.4	4.1
1984-85	6.3	4.5	1.7
1985-86	6.7	2.0	2.2
1986-87	9.6	5.4	4.6
1987-88	8.9	5.9	3.5
1988-89	8.2	5.8	1.4
1989-90	3.7	2.7	0.4
1990-91	1.8	-0.1	-0.1

a Explain what is meant by the term 'productivity'.

b i What conclusions, if any, may be drawn from the productivity figures of the nationalised industries over the period in question?

ii What other information would be useful in assessing the nationalised industries' performance?

iii What problems might arise from trying to use profit as a benchmark of the nationalised industries' performance?

c To what extent does the data support the view that nationalised industries should not be privatised?

Multiple choice

1 **A policy of banning all monopolies and mergers may be preferred to one which considers each on its merits because**

A   a competitive industry must produce a higher output and charge a lower price than a monopolist

B   a monopolist will be inefficient because he does not have any competitors

C   the costs of investigating monopolies and mergers may outweigh the benefits

D   barriers to entry will always lead to excessive profits for the monopolist

(AEB, November 1990)

2

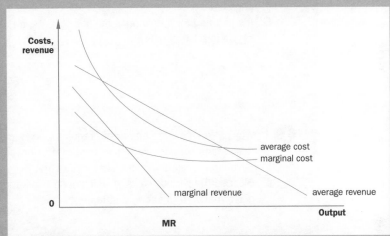

The diagram shows the cost and revenue curves of a nationalised industry.

What is the major implication of a government requirement that this industry should set its price equal to marginal cost?

A   It would make a loss

B   The socially optimal output would be where marginal cost equals marginal revenue

C   It would produce a greater output than consumers are prepared to consume

D   The industry would be producing above the technically efficient output.

(WJEC, June 1994)

3 **To achieve an allocatively efficient use of water resources, the government should try to ensure through regulatory mechanisms that each regional water company charges its consumer a**

A   price equal to the lowest average cost per unit of supplying water

B   price which will maximise the water company's profits

C   price which will ensure the water company just breaks even

D   price equal to the cost of the marginal unit supplied

E   zero price, but makes a flat rate charge to each consumer to cover the total supply cost

(ULEAC, January 1995)

4 In a particular country gas is produced by a monopoly, but its price must be approved by a regulator. The gas company has asked the regulator if prices can be raised so as to increase revenues to offset falling profits. In reply, the regulator has suggested that profits can be restored by lowering rather than raising prices.

Which one of the following is consistent with the above information?
The gas company believes that
A   the demand for gas is price elastic and income inelastic
B   there will be no increase in demand if prices are lowered
C   the demand for gas is price inelastic but the regulator believes it is price elastic
D   the demand for gas is price inelastic but the regulator believes that the supply of gas is price elastic

(AEB, June 1995)

Essays

1 a   Why did the government create regulatory agencies such as OFTEL (for the telecommunications industry) and OFGAS (for the gas industry), when it privatised previously nationalised industries?
 b   Discuss the various ways in which such regulatory agencies can influence the performance of these industries.

(AEB, November 1993)

2 In the last decade the government has privatised gas and electricity, it has reduced its stake in the oil industry and has attempted to increase competition in the market for energy. Do you consider that these changes have been beneficial or detrimental for the British economy?

(AEB, 'S' Level, June 1994)

3 a   How might privatisation policies be used to increase competition and reduce monopoly?
 b   Discuss whether the United Kindom privatisation programme is likely to achieve this result.

(AEB, June 1991)

4 a   Explain with the aid of a diagram or diagrams, the effect on price and output of a government subsidy to a particular sector of an economy.
 b   Discuss the arguments for and against cutting government subsidies to British Rail.

(AEB, A/S Level, June 1993)

5 a Outline the causes of monopoly power.

b Discuss the view that a government's competition policy should primarily be concerned with the removal of barriers to entry and the creation of conditions which allow new firms to enter and contest the market.

(AEB, Specimen paper, 1993)

6 a Explain the benefits which supporters of the government's privatisation programme expect to result from the privatisation of industries such as gas, water and telecommunications.

b To what extent, if any, has the creation of regulatory agencies such as OFGAS, OFWAT and OFTEL minimised the disadvantages of privatisation?

(AEB, June 1995)

7 *'In the United Kingdom, privatisation has often been accompanied by the creation of a regulatory organisation to oversee the newly privatised industry.'*

Using examples to illustrate your answer, discuss the costs and benefits of such a policy.

(AEB, S Level, June 1993)

8 *'Privatisation has created private monopolies.'*
'Privatised monopolies never benefit consumers.'

Critically evaluate these statements.

(ULEAC, June 1994)

9 a What arguments are put forward for the privatisation of state-owned companies?

b To what extent do you feel that experience in the UK has justified the decision to move such firms into the private sector?

(ULEAC, January 1994)

Data response

 Read the extracts carefully and then answer the questions which follow.

PRIVATISATION – THE BRITISH GAS EXPERIENCE
The British Government announced its intention to privatise British Gas in mid-1985 and the necessary legislation completed its passage through parliament in mid-1986. Debate on the right balance between State owned and privately owned enterprises go back into the mists of time. The arguments for public ownership fall into two main groups. First, there has been the argument that the state should control "the commanding heights of the economy". Secondly, there has been the argument that natural monopolies need to be under public control to safeguard the public interest ...

It is worth looking at the objectives of the Government's privatisation programme. These were, I think, fourfold.

First, they believed that efficiency would be improved. Secondly, they were keen to see a substantial increase in the number of small shareholders. Thirdly, they wished to introduce as much competition as possible. Fourthly, they wished to raise as much cash as possible for the treasury ...

British Gas is now operating within the regulatory environment established under the 1986 Gas Act. The main responsibility for administering the regulatory system has been placed upon a Director General of Gas Supply and his office known as OFGAS.

British Gas is also subject to general competition law and is subject to investigation by the Monopolies and Mergers Commission.

Source:Extracted from an After-lunch talk by SIR DENIS ROOKE Chairman, British Gas PLC in October 1988.

In April 1991, British Gas accepted proposals from the Director General of Gas Supply for a tougher tariff formula. In October the Office of Fair Trading concluded that further measures were needed to bring about a fully competitive gas market.

Despite a 3.6% tariff increase in April 1991, domestic gas prices are some 13% lower, in real terms, than when British Gas was privatised in 1986.

In response to a sudden demand for gas for use in power stations, British Gas increased prices for large, long-term interruptible supplies (i.e. those which British Gas can switch off at times when the demand for gas is very high).

Source: Extracted from The Annual Review and Summary Financial Statement
for the year ended 31 December 1991.

QUESTIONS

(a)   **What is meant by:**
      (i) "to privatise British Gas";
      (ii) "natural monopolies"?

(b) **Explain the factors that are likely to influence the prices British Gas PLC charges its various customers.**

(c) **Discuss the proposition that the privatisation of British Gas is likely to have resulted in improved efficiency.**

(AEB, Wessex Project, June 1994)

3.18 Why bother with what's outside the market?

Friedrich Engels and the environment

Although the uneasy relationship between the level of production and the environment has come into particular prominence in recent years due to our growing awareness of such issues as polluted rivers, seas and beaches, global warming and ozone depletion, the problem is not an entirely new one: Friedrich Engels, for example, writing in 1844, drew attention to the great contrasts of the age in terms of the growth of total output, trade and capital accumulation on the one hand, and the miserable conditions of life of the new working class on the other:

'One day I walked with one of these middle-class gentlemen into Manchester. I spoke to him about the disgraceful unhealthy slums and drew his attention to the disgusting condition of that part of town in which the factory workers lived. I declared that I have never seen so badly built a town in my life. He listened patiently and at the corner of the street at which we parted company, he remarked: 'And yet there is a great deal of money made here. Good morning, Sir!'

Source: Quoted in W. J. Barber, **A History of Economic Thought** *(1988)*

Preview

In this chapter, we shall investigate the following key areas:

- what externalities are;
- how externalities cause markets to fail;
- an assessment of what governments can do about externalities, involving an examination of the various forms of intervention:
  - direct government provision of goods and services;
  - extension of property rights;
  - use of taxes and subsidies;
  - tradeable pollution rights;
  - regulation or direct controls.
- the technique of cost-benefit analysis:
  - what it is;
  - the procedures involved;
  - problems likely to arise;
  - an overall assessment.

What are externalities?

In Chapter 12, we defined externalities as being costs (negative externalities) or benefits (positive externalities), which are not reflected in free market prices. Externalities are sometimes referred to as 'by-products','spillover effects', 'neighbourhood effects' 'third-party effects or 'side-effects', as the generator of the externality, either producers or consumers, or both, impose costs or benefits on others who are not responsible for initiating the effect. The key feature of an externality is that it is initiated and experienced, not through the operation of the price system, but outside the market.

Proponents of laissez-faire would argue that externalities particularly arise because of the absence of markets – as no markets exist for such things as clean air and seas, beautiful views or tranquillity, economic agents are not obliged to take them into account when formulating their production and consumption decisions, which are based on private costs and benefits, i.e. those which are internal to themselves. Another way of putting this is to say that individuals have no private property rights over such resources as the air, sea and rivers, and thus ignore them in making their production and consumption decisions.

Private property rights represent the legal entitlement to property and the right to use or sell the property, as well as the rights which other have, or do not have, over the property.

Property rights refer to those laws and rules which establish rights relating to:
● ownership of property;
● access to property;
● protection of property ownership;
● the transfer of property.

Thus a firm may feel free to dump effluent into a river as the spoiling of the environment and the killing of fish is not a cost which it would directly have to bear. Those on the political left would be more likely to argue that such an externality would arise because of the market system which is based upon the private ownership of resources, with individuals acting in their own self-interest and therefore not having to consider what is in the public interest: from such a perspective, the problem is due to an absence of communal property rights and of a system of planned production.

The above example of an externality is one which is commonly cited, but it is important to establish at this stage that there are various types of externalities and that they can be classified in different ways: they can arise from acts of consumption or production, and can thus be production, consumption or mixed externalities, and, as previously mentioned they can be experienced as external costs (negative externalities) or as external benefits (positive externalities). Look at Box 18.1.

BOX 18.1

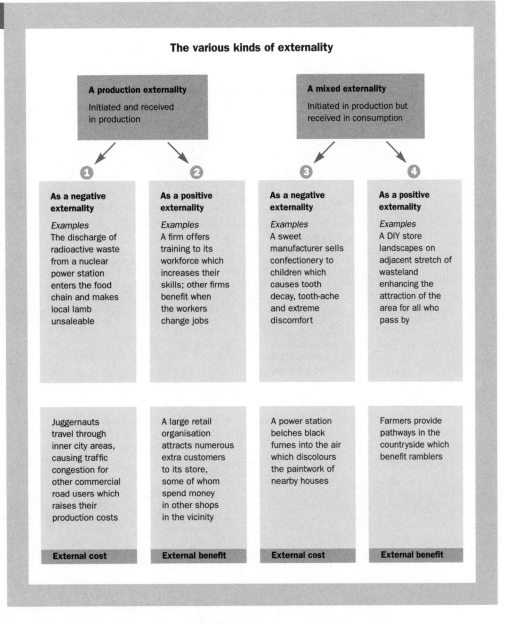

The various kinds of externality

A production externality

Initiated and received in production

A mixed externality

Initiated in production but received in consumption

①

As a negative externality

Examples
The discharge of radioactive waste from a nuclear power station enters the food chain and makes local lamb unsaleable

Juggernauts travel through inner city areas, causing traffic congestion for other commercial road users which raises their production costs

External cost

②

As a positive externality

Examples
A firm offers training to its workforce which increases their skills; other firms benefit when the workers change jobs

A large retail organisation attracts numerous extra customers to its store, some of whom spend money in other shops in the vicinity

External benefit

③

As a negative externality

Examples
A sweet manufacturer sells confectionery to children which causes tooth decay, tooth-ache and extreme discomfort

A power station belches black fumes into the air which discolours the paintwork of nearby houses

External cost

④

As a positive externality

Examples
A DIY store landscapes on adjacent stretch of wasteland enhancing the attraction of the area for all who pass by

Farmers provide pathways in the countryside which benefit ramblers

External benefit

BOX 18.1

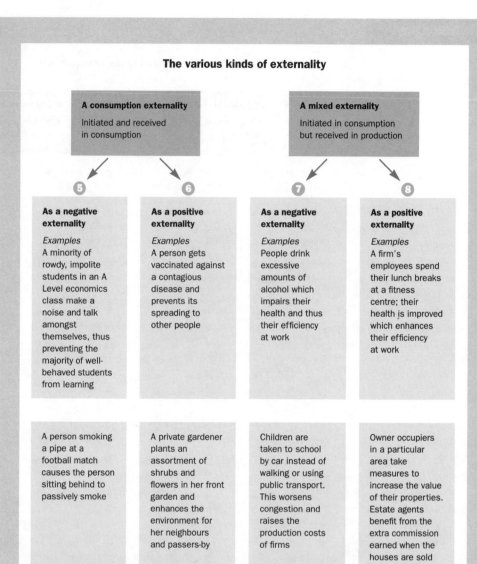

The various kinds of externality

A consumption externality		A mixed externality	
Initiated and received in consumption		Initiated in consumption but received in production	

⑤	⑥	⑦	⑧
As a negative externality	**As a positive externality**	**As a negative externality**	**As a positive externality**
Examples A minority of rowdy, impolite students in an A Level economics class make a noise and talk amongst themselves, thus preventing the majority of well-behaved students from learning	*Examples* A person gets vaccinated against a contagious disease and prevents its spreading to other people	*Examples* People drink excessive amounts of alcohol which impairs their health and thus their efficiency at work	*Examples* A firm's employees spend their lunch breaks at a fitness centre; their health is improved which enhances their efficiency at work
A person smoking a pipe at a football match causes the person sitting behind to passively smoke	A private gardener plants an assortment of shrubs and flowers in her front garden and enhances the environment for her neighbours and passers-by	Children are taken to school by car instead of walking or using public transport. This worsens congestion and raises the production costs of firms	Owner occupiers in a particular area take measures to increase the value of their properties. Estate agents benefit from the extra commission earned when the houses are sold
External cost	**External benefit**	**External cost**	**External benefit**

Box 18.1 summarises the different types of externality and provides some examples. It can be seen from Box 18.1 that there are in fact four different varieties of externality:

- a production externality: initiated in production and received in production;
- a mixed externality: initiated in production, but received in consumption;
- a consumption externality: initiated in consumption and received in consumption;
- a mixed externality: initiated in consumption, but received in production.

Each of these are sub-divided into two, according to whether they are experienced as an external cost or as an external benefit, giving a total of eight varieties.

TASK 18.1

Try adding a further example of your own to each of the eight types of externality given above.

In practice, the most important externalities are those which affect the environment, and it is these which have received widespread adverse publicity in recent years, and which have prompted the rise of 'green' pressure groups and political parties. Indeed, so great has been the impact of environmental pollution, that in addition to the externalities identified in Box 18.1, we can also, in a global context, identify externalities which are transmitted from one country to another, and which may be mutually damaging; the Chernobyl nuclear disaster in 1986 in Russia, for example, not only contaminated the local area, but also polluted other parts of Europe, including the UK; emissions of acid rain from West European nations not only harm the environment in the initiating countries, but also wreak havoc on the forests, lakes and rivers of the Scandinavian countries.

How do externalities affect allocative efficiency?

In Chapter 8, we explained how, given the existence of perfect competition, allocative efficiency would automatically occur where price equals marginal cost in all markets, assuming that neither negative nor positive externalities are present.

Social cost is the private, internal costs plus the value of negative externalities.

So, how do externalities affect our condition for efficiency? We will consider the oft-quoted case of a firm which discharges its waste products into a river. Such a firm would be treating the environment as a free resource, and would be imposing a cost on society as a whole, rather than just on the consumers of the good. The price charged to consumers would not therefore, in this instance, reflect the true cost of the product; if the firm were compelled to install equipment which could treat its effluent and render it harmless to the environment, its production costs and prices would rise and consumers would, as a consequence, reduce their demand for the product in question. Resources would then be reallocated to other lines of production.

In this case there is a divergence between private and social cost;

- The private cost is the internal money cost of production incurred by the firm; i.e. costs such as wages, raw materials, heating and lighting which must be paid to carry out production, and which would appear in the firm's accounts.
- The social cost, on the other hand, is the real cost to society as a whole; it is the private, internal costs plus the value of the negative externalities (external costs).

Similarly, if the firm's production decisions were to generate positive externalities, such as the beneficial effects arising from the provision of employment, then there would be a divergence between private and social benefit:

Social benefit is the private, internal benefits plus the value of positive externalities.

- The private benefit is the money value of the benefits accruing internally to the firm from production activity; e.g. in the form of sales revenues.
- The social benefit, on the other hand, is the private benefit plus the value of positive externalities (external benefits).

TASK 18.2

Explain the difference between:
a social cost and negative externality
b social benefit and positive externality

Now, the significance of this analysis is that allocative inefficiency will occur if private cost or benefit diverges from social cost or benefit. Where externalities exist the condition for allocative efficiency is that

Price = Social Marginal Cost = Social Marginal Benefit;

i.e. the price must equal the true marginal cost of production to society as a whole, rather than just the private marginal cost.

We will now illustrate the above in relation to the firm discharging waste into the river. Consider Box 18.2.

BOX 18.2

Negative externalities causing market failure: overproduction at the free market price

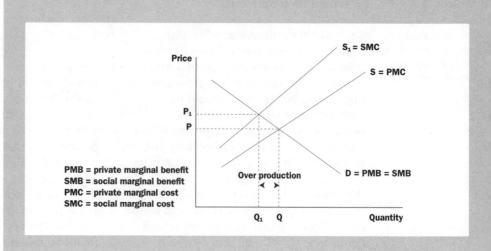

PMB = private marginal benefit
SMB = social marginal benefit
PMC = private marginal cost
SMC = social marginal cost

The firm's demand curve indicates the value that consumers place on each additional unit of the good, and it is thus the private marginal benefit curve. If no positive externalities are present, it would also be the same as the social marginal benefit curve.

The marginal private cost curve indicates the cost of producing an additional unit of output.

If no negative externalities were present, output would settle at OQ, and allocative efficiency would be achieved. However, the dumping of waste into a river imposes an external cost on society as a whole, for which the firm would not have to pay. Clearly, if the firm had to pay the full social cost of its production activities, the additional cost would shift the supply curve, or private marginal cost curve, to the left. Thus S_1 represents the social marginal cost curve, the vertical distance between the two supply curves indicating the value of the negative externality, or the marginal external cost. The intersection of S_1 and D would indicate a reduced level of output at OQ_1. However, if the firm did not pay for the external cost caused, MSC would be greater than price, and overproduction, overconsumption and a misallocation of society's scarce resources would occur.

Conversely, if the production of a good conferred net positive externalities on society, then there would be underproduction and under-consumption at the free market price and again a misallocation of resources. This is illustrated in Box 18.3.

BOX 18.3

Positive externalities causing market failure: underproduction at the free market price

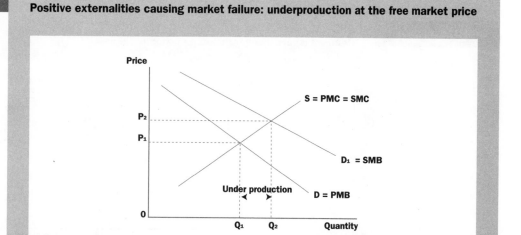

In Box 18.3, S is the private marginal cost curve, and as it is assumed that there are no negative externalities, it is also the the social marginal cost curve. If positive production externalities are generated, for which producers receive no payment, e.g. the beneficial 'knock-on' effects of higher employment, the social marginal benefit would exceed the private marginal benefit. The curve D (private marginal benefit) would shift to D_1 (social marginal benefit), the vertical distance between the two curves representing the value of the positive externality, or marginal external benefit at each level of output. The socially optimum level of production would be at OQ_2 where MSB = MSC. However, if the firm were to ignore the external benefit, which it is likely to do on account of receiving no payment for it, an output of OQ_1 is likely to arise which is less than socially desirable.

Hence externalities cause market failure:

- when a negative production externality is initiated, the firm will not be made to pay for the cost imposed on others, and will therefore have no market incentive to produce less; from society's standpoint it will therefore overproduce;
- when a positive externality arises, the firm will lack any incentive to increase its output to the socially desirable level, as it does not receive any payment for the generation of the external benefit; underproduction therefore occurs.

Look at Box 18.4. It shows how the foregoing analysis can be applied to the problems of traffic congestion.

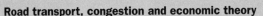

BOX 18.4

Road transport, congestion and economic theory

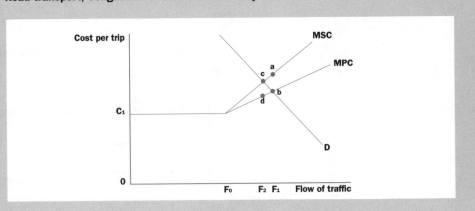

BOX 18.4

The economic theory of traffic congestion

Economic theory can be used to analyse the issues involved in traffic congestion as shown here. The figure indicates the relationship between the cost of travel and the flow of traffic along a particular route. The essence of this theory is based on the fact that, when making a journey by car, a motorist only considers the marginal private cost (MPC). This is the cost directly attributable to him/herself, such as time, fuel and the maintenance of the vehicle, rather than the full cost of the journey, which may include costs imposed upon society such as pollution, noise and time lost due to congestion. When added to the private costs, these are termed the marginal social costs (MSC), the difference between the two representing the externality imposed by the motorist.

In outlining the theory, it is assumed that, when making a journey, congestion is the only externality. As stated, the graph represents the demand for travel along a particular stretch of road over a particular period of time. Up to a flow of traffic F0, there is no congestion, thus there is no divergence between MPC and MSC, although, in reality, such a situation only applies to extremely low volumes of traffic.

As the flow of traffic increases above F0, congestion is apparent and there is a divergence between MPC and MSC. Note that the MSC is equal to the MPC, plus the social cost of congestion.

If demand for travel on this particular route is of the normal shape (represented by D in the graph) and is a measure of the marginal benefit, then the flow of traffic will be determined by the intersection of the demand curve and the MPC curve at F1 and the private cost to the motorist will be C1. At a flow of F1, the social cost, not taken into account by the motorist, is ab (the difference between the MPC and MSC). This means that resources are not being allocated efficiently and that individuals are making more journeys than they would if they were aware of the full (social) costs.

Given the demand curve D, a way to rectify this allocative inefficiency is to make an additional charge for each journey, such that the marginal benefit to the motorist (represented by the demand curve) is equal to the marginal social cost of making that journey, thus alleviating the welfare loss represented by area abc in Box 18.4. Such a charge (a road price) would be equal to an amount cd, and amounts to charging the motorist for the costs he or she imposes on others.

If such a charge were made, the flow of traffic on the route would fall to F2, meaning that marginal journeys would be priced off the road or would be redistributed to other less congested time periods. It is important to note that congestion has not been eliminated completely, and is still present at the optimal flow of F2.

The charge upon motorists for the use of road space can take a number of forms. If they are to meet closely the requirements of the theory, the charge cd needs to be accurately defined. In practice, this is difficult as the flow of traffic on the road is constantly changing, as are the external costs imposed on society. Thus, in the morning rush hour, a charge of CD may be insufficient, meaning that the allocative inefficiencies

BOX 18.4

remain, while in the off-peak period such a charge may be too high, forcing motorists off the road and towards other modes of transport unnecessarily. Because of the difficulties in establishing an optimal charge, simpler methods of reducing congestion have usually been adopted.

*Source: **Economic Review** November 1993*

TASK 18.3

Use Box 18.4 to explain in your own words how traffic congestion leads to allocative inefficiency.
What measures could the government take to remedy such inefficiency?

What can governments do about the problem of externalities?

The outstanding characteristic of a market economy is that production does not occur as a result of some grand, master plan; rather, it is the result of the pulls and pushes of supply and demand; of the numerous uncoordinated decisions of individuals and firms. As individuals are assumed to seek to maximise their own satisfaction, and firms their own profits, decisions made are likely to be strictly on the basis of private costs and benefits and, as previously explained, herein lies the problem: unless the full social costs and benefits of production and consumption decisions are taken into account, so that MSC is equated to MSB, social inefficiency and a misallocation of society's scarce resources will result.

So, what measures can a government take to rectify such inefficiency, and

how successful is it likely to be? As is the case with most important questions in economics, a range of answers are possible, depending largely on the political perspective of the respondent. At one end of the spectrum, governments could 'leave well alone', essentially not interfering with markets but trying to gently persuade firms and individuals to modify their behaviour. At the other extreme, the market could be completely replaced by direct government provision, and in between various policy options are possible. We now turn to an examination of some of these options.

In practice it is the problem of production externalities, particularly environmental ones, which most occupy the attention of governments, and our discussion will mainly, but not exclusively, focus on these.

Direct provision of goods and services by the government

In Chapter 17, we explained how the existence of externalities provides an important argument for the common ownership, or nationalisation of a number of key industries.

The argument is that privately owned firms, in order to survive in a competitive world, necessarily have to put their own interests before those of society at large, for to do otherwise might be inconsistent with the goal of long-run profit-maximisation, or even survival. This harsh reality of the market is likely to manifest itself in the generation of negative externalities such as pollution, as the control of these externalities would involve higher costs and an adverse impact on profits; conversely, production activity which conferred net positive externalities on society might not be undertaken in sufficient quantities if the criterion of private profitability could not be met.

Nationalised industries, on the other hand, on account of being commonly owned, could be operated according to broad social criteria, rather than the narrow commercial criterion of private profitability, and this allows for the possibility of externalities to be fully incorporated into production decisions. Thus, for example, questions of workers' safety standards and atmospheric pollution could be accorded priority status, rather than being ignored on the grounds that to do otherwise would adversely affect profits and competitiveness; and activities such as the keeping open of 'uneconomic' pits and the provision of postal and transport services to remote outlying areas could all be maintained on the grounds that they provide substantial positive externalities to society at large, although not necessarily being profitable in the sense that the private revenues from such activities exceed the private costs.

Similarly, an important argument for merit goods such as education and health being directly provided by the government rather than through the market, is that they not only confer private benefits on individuals, but also significant positive externalities on society as a whole which individuals would tend to ignore when making their consumption decisions. As a result, left to the market, underprovision is likely to occur; for example, individuals would be prepared to buy education through the market if they had to, as substantial private benefits, such as higher life-time earnings, are likely to result; however, a case for a higher level of government provision can be made on the grounds that not all the benefits accrue solely to the individual – society gains from a more efficient and adaptable labour force and perhaps a more tolerant and more aware population. The issue of merit goods is considered more fully in Chapter 19.

The above arguments for direct government provision would of course be strongly contested by free market economists who would argue the case for privatisation, the desirability of using markets to provide merit goods and the extremely poor record of pollution control of the formerly centrally planned economies of Eastern Europe.

The extension of property rights

Property rights concern the legal entitlement to property and the right to use or sell the property, as well as the rights that other people have, or do not have, over the property. It is argued that negative externalities in particular arise because of the existence of incomplete property rights over natural resources such as air, land, rivers and seas; i.e. as property rights are not fully allocated to these areas, as nobody really owns them, individuals and firms are free to impose external costs from their production and consumption activities without having to pay any compensation. The dumping of toxic wastes into the sea and the riding of a noisy motor-bike provide two examples.

Thus, by extending property rights, individuals would be able to stop others imposing costs on them, or to claim compensation if they did so. A person purchasing a house, for example, could also acquire a set of 'amenity' rights which would entitle the owner to peace and quiet in the vicinity of the property, as well as a supply of water and air of a reasonable quality. Any infringement of such rights, e.g. by neighbours playing heavy metal music unduly loudly, or juggernauts emitting excessive exhaust fumes into the air, would give the owner of the amenity rights entitlement to compensation. In this case the externality would be internalised as the initiators of the external costs would be forced to pay for them, and adjust their production/consumption decisions to more socially efficient levels.
However, there may be a number of problems with this solution in practice:

- for compensation to be paid, it must be possible to establish the nature and extent of external costs being imposed; in the case of most types of pollution, for example, this tends to be an extremely difficult thing to do, and so appropriate compensation levels become almost impossible to establish;

- where there are many firms or individuals imposing negative externalities, it would be exceedingly difficult to claim compensation from them all; for instance, if many juggernauts, low-flying helicopters and joy-riding teenagers passed a property, making great noise in the process, it would be somewhat impractical for the property owner to try to claim compensation from them all;

- even if those generating the external costs are few in numbers, the time and cost involved of pursuing the offenders through the courts may be prohibitive for all but the very rich; what chance would an ordinary person have, for instance, in claiming compensation from a large, multinational burger chain, which had permitted the neighbourhood to become unduly littered with burger wrappings?

- the extension of property rights has equity implications; extending private property rights is likely to favour those who already possess property at the expense of those who do not: so, Gypsies and travellers may be prevented from setting up camp, peace campaigners and other protesters could be prevented from holding their demonstrations and ramblers' rights of way in the country-side might be infringed; thus those on the political left tend to favour an extension of communal property rights and a society based more on public ownership and a set of cooperative values which, they would argue, are less likely to cause the problem of negative externalities in the first place.

Taxes and subsidies

The use of taxes and subsidies to tackle the problem of externalities is a market-based method of control as it works through the price system, i.e. through the impact of changes in prices.

If negative externalities exist, and there is allocative inefficiency at the free market price because SMC is greater than price and overproduction is occurring, then the appropriate solution would be to tax the good; if, on the other hand, the market is underproducing because positive externalities are not being taken into account, it would be appropriate for the government to grant a subsidy. We shall consider each in turn.

Taxes

There are two types of tax which may be applied to address the problem of negative externalities: a tax set equal to each firm's marginal external costs and an environmental or 'green' tax.

The policy of taxing firms according to the marginal external costs that they impose on society can be illustrated using Box 18.2. In this example we assumed that a firm was dumping waste products into a river. The government would have to assess the cost to society of such an action, and impose a tax on the offending firm equal to the value of the marginal external cost (or negative externality); in this case the tax would internalise the externality by making the polluter pay. The levying of such a tax would shift the supply curve from S to S_1, which would increase the market price to OP_1, and cause the level of output to fall to OQ_1, where $P = SMC$ and allocative efficiency is achieved.

An environmental tax could be imposed either on a product responsible for creating pollution, or on the inputs to an industry which have caused environmental damage, e.g. carbon producing fuels, which are believed to play the major role in the process of global warming. The aim of a carbon tax on each unit of carbon in fossil fuels would be to: raise the price of those sources of power with high carbon contents, thus encouraging a switching to power sources causing lower CO_2 emissions; encourage greater conservation of energy in general; and stimulate the search for more environmentally-friendly technologies.

Subsidies

Whilst a tax may be imposed on generators of negative externalities, a subsidy may be granted to generators of positive externalities to ensure a higher level of consumption and production than would otherwise arise through the completely free interaction of market forces. This is illustrated in Box 18.3. In this case the government would have to assess the value of the marginal external benefit (i.e. the positive externality) to society and give a subsidy equivalent to this amount. If the good in question were loft insulation, which confers benefits on society in terms of energy conservation, households prepared to lag their lofts could be given a grant, and this would shift the demand curve D(PMB) to the right to D_1(SMB). Allocative efficiency is achieved as SMB = SMC at OQ_1. A similar result could be achieved by subsidising the output of loft insulation which would cause the supply curve to shift to the right until the socially optimum level of production is reached.

Issues arising from the tax/subsidy approach

- Advocates of this approach would argue that it permits the forces of demand and supply to operate. At the same time generators of negative externalities are induced to 'clean-up their act' because the less pollution they create, the less their tax liability; and conversely, grants and subsidies encourage greater output and consumption of those goods involving net social benefits.
- In practice various difficulties are likely to arise:
- For the tax/subsidy solution to work in the way indicated in Boxes 18.2 and 18.3, the exact value of the marginal external cost and the marginal external benefit must be established so that taxes and subsidies, respectively, of exactly the right size can be applied; in reality it is not only extremely difficult to identify external costs and benefits, but it is also an extremely arbitrary matter trying to ascribe a monetary value to them; e.g. how should the emission of black fumes into the air from an industrial chimney be assessed?
- From an environmental point of view a tax on pollution does not solve the problem, as pollution is still allowed to continue; the tax merely provides a market-led inducement to firms to find cleaner ways of producing so as to reduce their costs; moreover, the unwilling third parties who receive pollution as a negative externality are not in any way compensated.
- Taxation of pollution would require regular monitoring of pollution emissions, and as offending firms are likely to be generating different quantities and types of pollution, such monitoring is likely to be administratively complex and very costly.
- Distortions and inefficiencies might arise in terms of the cost of collecting a pollution tax, the inevitable temptation by the less scrupulous to evade paying it altogether and the possibility of an inflationary impact on the price level.

The articles contained in Box 18.5
reveal some of the different perspectives
on the implementation of 'green taxes'.

GREEN *taxes*

Rely on carrot not on stick

IF, as the RAC predicts, the royal commission on environmental pollution recommends an 18p rise in petrol prices as a form of "green tax" later this month, it will have a marginal effect on air pollution.

Very few people will give up their private vehicles in favour of public transport, because our public transport system is too expensive, unreliable and ineffective.

This is not the fault of the workers in the rail and bus industries. It is because of the government's hostility to publicly provided transport, which is run as a service instead of a profit-making enterprise.

It smashed the successful experiments introduced by the Greater London Council and many metropolitan authorities when regular, reliable and well co-ordinated services were introduced and fares were cut and then pegged.

These services were popular and led people to voluntarily choose public over private transport, but because they were at variance with Tory philosophy, they were wrecked.

The carrot of good public services is more likely to win the environmental struggle than the stick of higher petrol prices.

*Source: **Morning Star** (15 October 1994).*

Letter to *The Observer*

Your leader last week supports the Royal Commission on Environmental Pollution's report calling for large petrol price rises to force motorists to drive less often. You advise Ministers to 'intervene with stiffer fuel taxes over and above the 5 per cent already pledged by the Chancellor'.

You appear to believe a majority, or even a significant minority, have another way of getting to work. Where I live, in a distant rural part of the country, it is almost essential to use your own motor vehicle to get to work, should you be fortunate enough to have a job.

Once again, a tax solution to a problem would cause immediate hardship to the less well-off, little difference to the rich, and would be expected to have its desired effect on those in the middle income range.

It would seem reasonable to suggest the proper targeting of those who can choose their method of transport, rather than a swinging price increase in petrol; the only result in this area would be an increase in the cost of living.
J. H. Nicholls, Haverfordwest, Dyfed.

*Source: Letter in **Observer** (23 October 1994).*

BOX 18.5

The INVESTIGATOR

Eco-tax could cut the dole queue?

A report by Dr. Terry Barker of Cambridge University has concluded that half a million jobs could be created over 10 years by taxing pollution rather than employment – a considerable boost to employment would be provided by scrapping employers' National Insurance contributions and raising the money instead from duties on road fuels or a new carbon tax. Most of this boost, the report estimated, would be in the services and construction sectors.

Dr. Barker said the road fuel option would improve the balance of payments and result in greater growth without inflation, whereas the carbon tax would cause some deterioration in industrial competitiveness and add a little inflation.

TASK 18.4 Using the articles provided, as well as any other relevant information, discuss the arguments for and against the introduction of new 'green taxes'.

Tradeable pollution rights

Tradeable pollution rights are emission allowances or permits which can be traded between organisations whose operations generate pollution.

Like the use of taxes and subsidies, tradeable pollution rights (otherwise known as tradeable emission allowances or permits), represent another market-based solution to the problem of negative externalities, in particular pollution. They were first introduced in the USA in 1990 under the Clean Air Act in which the Environmental Protection Agency set a target rate of reduction for power stations' emissions of sulphur dioxide. Initially, power stations were issued with emission permits in proportion to their current pollution levels and were allowed to discharge pollution into the air up to a specified limit. Thereafter, those power stations for whom the cost of reducing pollution was low, could sell their spare pollution permits to generators for whom the cost of pollution abatement, through the installation of appropriate equipment, would be very high. Thus, a market in tradeable pollution rights is created, stimulating pollution reduction through the possibility of making money out of selling surplus permits.

The main argument in favour of such a scheme is that it operates through the market via the price system: firms are given a profit incentive, i.e. through the right to sell spare permits, to find cheap ways of reducing their pollution levels; and such a system should be administratively cheap and simple to implement, as the regulatory agency need have no information regarding firms' costs – it simply has to issue the permits and arrange for their sale; in addition, consumers may benefit if the extra profits made by low pollution power stations, arising from the sale of their spare permits to other companies, are passed on in the form of lower prices.

The main argument against the use of tradeable emission permits is that they do not actually stop firms from polluting the environment; they only provide an incentive to do so – where a degree of monopoly power and relatively inelastic demand exist, the extra cost of purchasing additional permits so as to further pollute the atmosphere could easily be offset by the possibility of charging consumers higher prices; moreover, the system of allocating permits in accordance to existing emission levels could be seen as a reward for the greatest polluters!

Regulation or direct controls

BOX 18.6

The INVESTIGATOR

Gummer's plans for environment agency undercut

In the name of saving public money and freeing industry from government regulation, the Conservative Manifesto commitment to create a tough new environment agency has effectively been abandoned.

The bill proposed by Mr Gummer, the Environment Secretary, has been mauled by the Treasury so that no action can be taken in exercising its powers if substantial public expenditure is involved. The agency will be compelled to take into account the benefits of industrial development, whilst its duty to conserve and protect the environment will be discretionary. Ministers will have far-reaching powers to order the agency to take or not take action on a wide range of issues and will also be able to interpret as they see fit controversial European environment directives on water pollution and other issues.

Mr Chris Smith, Labour's environment spokesman, denouncing the bill's weaknesses, said:

'This is like saying that the watchdog can only bark with the permission of the burglar. It is definitely a watchdog without teeth. The bill creates an agency with fewer powers than the sum of its parts.'

TASK 18.5

To what extent do you agree with the view that the government's new environment agency is like a 'watchdog without teeth'?

In practice, the use of direct controls represents the most common approach to pollution abatement. Such controls can be applied both to individuals and firms and can take a number of forms; for example, restrictions can be imposed on smoke emissions from private homes and firms; restrictions may be placed on all forms of building in designated green-belt areas; minimum environmental standards may be stipulated for air and water quality; laws may be passed to prevent drinking and driving and the sale of alcohol and tobacco to people under a certain age.

Apart from restriction, direct controls can also be used more severely: activities generating negative externalities could be banned completely; for instance, the dumping of waste into rivers or the sea; or an activity which conferred net positive externalities on society could be made compulsory; for example, all children under the age of 16 in the UK must by law receive some form of education, whether it be in a state school, a private school or at home.

The main advantage of regulation is that it is the most direct way of tackling the problem of externalities; for example, market-based solutions such as taxes and tradeable emission permits provide incentives to firms to reduce their pollution levels but do not compel them to do so; as such problems as global warming and the depletion of the ozone layer are thought by many to threaten the very survival of our planet, it is argued that we cannot afford to trust our futures with policies which allow for

the possibility of non-compliance. Provided legal restrictions are backed by inspections which are sufficiently regular and rigorous, they should be effective.

Against this, it is argued that, in reality, the policing of regulations can present great difficulties as the less environmentally conscious firms may attempt to circumvent the controls, e.g. through the generation of pollution during the night. Thus an extremely large number of inspectors might have to be employed to ensure compliance.

It is also claimed that regulation can be a rather blunt, indiscriminate instrument of control; for example, the setting of maximum emission limits does not take into account the fact that the cost of reducing pollution would vary considerably as between different firms, some facing high costs, others facing low costs. Thus a uniform limit applied to all firms would be an inefficient way of reducing pollution, implying as it would a high resource cost. Also it may be the case that once emission targets have been achieved, there would be no further incentive to continue to reduce pollution, as would be the case with a pollution tax.

Regulation may also give rise to the problem of regulatory capture (remember Chapter 17) – those being regulated may be successful in manipulating the regulatory body to act in accordance with the private interests of the firms concerned, rather than in the interests of society as a whole.

BOX 18.7

Britain TO BLOCK NORTH SEA BAN ON TOXICS

Polly Ghazi, Environment Correspondent

BRITAIN will block moves this week to ban the dumping of toxic chemicals into the North Sea, leaked documents reveal.

Most of the eight states at the North Sea Conference in Denmark on Thursday are sympathetic to a Dutch proposal to phase out all hazardous discharges 'within a generation'. The Dutch say there is mounting evidence of the devastating effects of factory and farm chemicals on the sea's wildlife.

But the meeting's confidential draft declaration, leaked to Greenpeace, reveals strong opposition from Britain and France which threatens to split the conference.

Britain, supported only by France, is proposing a watered-down commitment towards a 'continuing reduction' of pollution levels with no timescale attached. But the Norwegian host government has warned privately that if no compromise is reached Holland and the Nordic countries will go it alone with tougher measures, leaving Britain once more accused of being the 'dirty man of Europe'.

Official figures released last week confirmed that Britain remains one of the sea's biggest polluters. The Government has failed to meet its commitments for several pesticides, leaving the UK in the lower half of the eight-nation league table.

Environment Secretary, John Gummer, who will lead Britain's delegation, will also face severe criticism over the decision to allow Shell to dump the contaminated Brent Spar oil rig at sea.

The draft declaration also underlines the lack of consensus on how to tackle the developing crisis over declining fish stocks. Mackerel is now officially classified as commercially extinct, and cod and haddock are expected to meet a similar fate within a decade.

Yet a German proposal that action should be taken to cut back fisheries suspected of damaging the marine ecosystem will be blocked by a majority of governments including Britain.

*Source: **Observer** (4 June 1995).*

TASK 18.6

Suggest economic reasons for the stance adopted by the UK government on the North Sea, which has led Britain to be accused of being the 'dirty man of Europe'.

Cost-benefit analysis (CBA)

What is cost-benefit analysis?

Cost–benefit analysis (CBA) is a technique of investment appraisal, mainly used in the public sector, which evaluates the full social costs and social benefits of a project.

CBA is a technique for evaluating all the costs and benefits, i.e. the social costs and social benefits to society as a whole, arising from a particular economic action or project. It has mainly been used to appraise the net return on major public sector investment projects such as the construction of motorways (e.g. the M1), railways (e.g. the Channel Tunnel Rail link between London and Paris), extensions to the London Underground network (e.g. the Victoria Line) and airports (e.g. the siting of the Third London Airport). However, CBA could also in principle be applied to whole categories of government expenditure such as education and health, changes in taxation (e.g. on cigarettes), as well as private sector projects such as the Channel Tunnel. By identifying all the costs and benefits of a particular project, not merely the private costs and benefits, CBA tries to establish whether the benefits to society as a whole outweigh the costs, or vice-versa, and thus whether or not the project should be undertaken; CBA is therefore an important tool in the evaluation of various types of project, providing guidance on economic decision making.

What procedures must be adopted to conduct a CBA?

There are several stages involved in a cost–benefit analysis:
- all the costs and benefits to be taken into account are identified; i.e. the private costs and benefits and positive and negative externalities;
- the costs and benefits are assessed and a monetary value is given to each;
- a value is given to future costs and benefits, as not all of these will occur at the same time;
- the overall costs are compared to the overall benefits; if the costs exceed the benefits it could be concluded that the project should not proceed, and vice-versa if the benefits exceed the costs.

However, in practice, a number of problems are likely to arise at each stage of the process.

What problems are likely to arise?

● The need for subjectivity in deciding what should be included

The essence of CBA is that it takes into account social costs and benefits which may be ignored in an evaluation of a private sector project; for instance, in evaluating the building of a motorway, costs such as construction and maintenance, pollution, noise, degradation of the environment and compulsory purchase of houses in the path of the motorway are all considered, along with benefits such as savings in journey times, fewer accidents (as new roads tend to be safer than old ones) and less traffic congestion on adjoining roads.

However, this may not be the end of the story, as a number of other more indirect costs and benefits of the project might also need to be considered; e.g.the building of the M25 has, in effect, widened the boundaries of the Greater London area, and has brought increased traffic and economic activity to several places on the route of the motorway, and has thus spawned a subsidiary set of social costs and benefits. So should all of these be included in any CBA of the M25? At what point should the appraisal stop? A full CBA should take account of all direct and indirect costs and benefits, but in practice this would be an impossibility; but the question of which costs and benefits to include is a key issue, and such a question is therefore liable to involve value judgements on behalf of the policy makers.

Shadow pricing is the use of estimated prices in a cost–benefit analysis to assess the opportunity cost of a project.

● It is difficult to place a monetary value on externalities

Whilst reasonably accurate estimates of the private costs and benefits of a particular project may be possible – e.g. in the case of the Channel Tunnel, the building and maintenance costs and likely sales revenues – the task of ascribing a monetary value to externalities is a very much more difficult task: not only are externalities often extremely intangible in nature, but they will also arise over some period of time in the future as a result of an action undertaken in the present. How, for example, can monetary values be placed on such intangibles as increased noise, the destruction of an area of great ecological worth, the spoiling of a beautiful view, or the saving of journey time?

One method is to use a technique known as shadow pricing, which involves the use of estimated prices to assess the opportunity cost of a project. For example, a major social benefit in the building of rail links, tunnels, motorways and underground lines is the saving of journey time. Thus an hour saved travelling to a business meeting would represent an extra hour available for work and could thus be valued at an hour's wages. However, the evaluation of time saving for the person travelling to and from work in his/her own time, or to the person having a day out at the seaside, is obviously more difficult to calculate. In practice, the opportunity cost will rarely be equivalent to the average wage, so placing a value on this variable will necessarily be extremely arbitrary.

Similarly, if a new railway or motorway is responsible for saving human life by reducing the number of fatal road accidents, how should this be assessed? Some would argue that the attempt to put a money value on people is both morally reprehensible and likely to be nonsensical in practice. However, CBA attempts such a task by considering the levels of compensation which are awarded in accidents in which one party is to blame or by assessing the present value of the expected future earnings of the deceased.

Clearly, whichever method is used to evaluate the broader social costs and benefits is going to involve value judgements on behalf of the policy makers as there are usually no objective criteria; for instance, the building of the M11 link road in East London (see Box 18.8) has involved enormous environmental disruption as well as provoking fierce opposition from local people and those with a 'green' perspective on life, but has proceeded nonetheless!

Discounting is the method by which the present value of a future payment or return is calculated, using a given rate of interest.

● Costs and benefits must be valued across time

A major problem for CBA is that the costs of a project are necessarily incurred before the good or service becomes available for consumption, whereas the benefits are likely to be experienced over a considerable period of time; e.g., unless there is some terrible natural or other disaster, the Channel Tunnel could reasonably be expected to outlive most or all of the readers of this book! Thus, the further we project into the future, the more

perilous any attempts at forecasting benefits and costs become – trying to forecast such variables as interest rates, inflation rates and levels of demand and supply in most cases is unsuccessful from one year to the next, let alone 20 or 30 years hence!

Even if the value of future benefits can be estimated, they cannot simply be compared with costs incurred in the present to determine the viability or otherwise of a particular project, for to do so would not be comparing like with like: the value of future benefits must be discounted to their present value; for example, £100 of benefits in 10 year's time is likely to be worth much less than £100 of benefits today, as some return on the £100 could be earned if it were saved or invested; likewise it would be less desirable to have to pay £100 today than to wait 10 years to do so. Thus assuming a compound rate of interest, (discount or return) of 10 per cent each year, £100 saved today would be worth £110 in one year's time, £121 in two year's time, £133 in three year's time, etc. The discounting procedure is the compound interest in reverse; thus £110 of benefits in one year's time, £121 worth in two year's time and £133 worth in three year's time all have a present value of £100.

The problem, however, for CBA is establishing an appropriate rate of discount when a project is expected to have a relatively long life, as the results of any CBA will depend crucially on the rate of interest chosen to discount future costs and benefits.

How can we assess the worth of CBA overall?

CBA has its proponents and opponents:

- Supporters of CBA argue that for all its problems, it remains the best way to appraise investment decisions because all the costs and benefits, not just the internal, private costs and benefits, are identified to form a broad base upon which decisions can be made; private sector project appraisal, on the other hand, only concerns itself with private monetary costs and benefits and therefore fails to take into account what is good or bad for society as a whole. CBA is thus seen as a useful aid to decision taking, indicating as it does whether a particular project is likely to make a socially worthwhile use of scarce resources.

Against this CBA is criticised from a number of different perspectives:

- CBA gives a spurious impression of accuracy, when in fact costs and benefits can be so widely and loosely defined that it is possible to obtain any result required; clearly, the problems of what to include, what monetary value to put on externalities and choosing a suitable rate of discount are so fraught with value judgements and arbitrary decision making that at best CBA is pseudo-scientific, and, at worst, a manipulative device for achieving the results which the investigator desires.

- Those on the political right, including the present Conservative Government, view CBA as a waste of public funds, believing as they do that both private and public sector projects should be judged purely on the basis of commercial criteria, i.e. that private revenues should exceed private costs so that profitability is achieved.

- CBA does not always take account of the distribution of the costs and benefits of the project in question in terms of which groups of people lose and which groups gain; for instance, the building of a new road often involves people having to compulsorily and unwillingly sell their homes as houses have to be knocked down (losers), whilst the building contractors derive considerable revenues from such projects (gainers).

BOX 18.8   **Case study: the M11 Link Road in East London**

Background

Plans to build a road from Redbridge to Hackney go back to the turn of the century, although the current plan was established in the early 1950s. There have been three public inquiries (1962, 1983 and 1989) and after various revisions were made, draft orders were published in 1981, with the final go ahead being given in 1991. Work on the road finally started in 1993. As noted by the Department of Transport, 'this scheme must be about the most talked about, appraised, revised and delayed scheme in the history of road building'.

The road when completed will be 3.5 miles long, and will stretch from the M11 at Redbridge through Wanstead, Leytonstone and Leyton to the A102 at Hackney. The cost will be in the region of £250 million to £300 million.

Protest

A passionate anti-motorway campaign began in 1993, centred around a local beauty spot called George Green, through which the motorway was planned to go. Campaigners occupied a 250-year-old sweet chestnut tree on the Green by building a tree house in its boughs to prevent the contractors from felling it. The tree made legal history when it was acknowledged under the law as a legal dwelling. When the tree was finally felled, a new 'front' was opened in the self-declared 'independent free area of Wanstonia', named after the east London suburb of Wanstead which is bisected by the link road. The 'Wanstonians' appealed to the United Nations for recognition, and constructed elaborate defences to protect their 'homeland'. When this was finally conquered by numerous police and security guards, the protesters moved on to Leytonstone for their last stand, which was finally overcome in December 1994.

Costs

The costs of the road according to the 'No M11 Link Road Campaign':
- The east London communities of Wanstead, Leytonstone, Leyton and Hackney would be carved in half by a 4- and 6-lane express route.
- 350 homes would be lost and 1000 made homeless.
- More noise and air pollution from the additional traffic generated, with accompanying problems such as increased incidence of asthma.
- House devaluation and blight.
- Developments associated with road building.
- 4 years of heavy construction work.
- Subsidence problems for properties near the road.
- Acres of irreplaceable open space and green-belt land, parkland and marshland would be lost for ever without adequate exchange land given in return.

All for a total journey saving time of approximately 7 minutes!

*Source: 'The Roadbreaker', the No M11 **Link Road Campaign Newsletter** (1994).*

BOX 18.8

Benefits

The benefits of the road according to the Department of Transport:

- The road will act as a local relief road which will take heavy trunk road traffic off the local highway network, and will put it largely below ground away from direct interaction with local communities.
- Local travellers as well as longer distance road users will benefit from reduced congestion and delay on other local roads.
- Once the Link Road removes strategic traffic from local roads, the local authorities will have the opportunity to consider pedestrianisation of residential and shopping streets, the provision of childrens' play parks and landscaped areas and the introduction of a variety of traffic calming measures.
- About 10 acres of Epping Forest Land is being taken for the scheme, but 20 acres will be added to the Forest in exchange.
- Stationary vehicles produce more fumes than free-flowing traffic. Opening the link road will relieve existing traffic congestion and so traffic will be able to flow more freely both on it and on local roads. Therefore pollution levels should fall.

*Source: **Link Road Information Office Notes** (1994).*

REVIEW

In the chapter title, we posed the question, 'Why bother with what's outside the market?' We hope that the foregoing discussion has now made the answer fairly plain – the existence of externalities causes markets to fail and a misallocation of scarce resources. How governments should respond to this failure is a matter of debate, and yet another area where values necessarily intrude. Finally, externalities must be carefully considered if an overall assessment is to made of the worth of a particular project to society as a whole.

3.18

ROAD BUILDING *only makes traffic worse*

John Vidal

TRANSPORT professionals yesterday welcomed the Government's acceptance that new roads stimulate traffic, but warned that the problem was not new roads so much as car dependency.

When a new road was built or significantly improved, said Colin Buchan, a consultant, economic savings resulted for a year or two but the benefits declined very quickly.

"The demand for transport in Britain is more or less infinite. Build new roads and you can do longer journeys, you can travel more frequently, and you can substitute journeys previously done by cycling or by train.

"But the economic and social disbenefits start to increase quickly as new traffic is generated."

These "disbenefits" include severe congestion in and out of towns, air and ground pollution, the stimulation in some areas of intense development, and corresponding decline of other parts of the economy, including other forms of transport such as railways.

"You can have a lot of road traffic growth and nothing much happens, but the next 5 per cent increase can lead to gridlock." This, said Mr Buchan, was now happening all over the country. "It's only a matter of time before many small towns experience the sort of congestion that London has long suffered."

Figures from the Department of Transport show that car ownership increased almost 33 per cent between 1983–1993, and passenger miles travelled increased by 40 per cent. The department estimates traffic will double within 30 years.

A recent report commissioned by the British Road Federation showed that even if Britain increased by 50 per cent its spending on trunk roads for the next 15 years, on current trends traffic congestion would worsen rather than improve.

"We must accept that supply of road space is not going to expand in line with demand, and that demand will have to be moderated to meet supply," says Phil Goodwin, head of Oxford University's transport studies unit.

How much traffic is generated by individual road schemes is difficult to quantify. The M25, the largest new road since the war, was billed in the 1970s as taking through traffic away from London and massively improving accessibility, said John Adams of University College, London. But it has become "a ring of intense development" and is now one of Britain's most congested roads.

Research shows that people now use the M25 to travel much further to work and shop, and that in 10 years it has attracted to nearby towns applications for almost as much office space as in the whole of Birmingham.

"But it has also dampened the economy of inner London which is left with inferior access", says Professor Adams.

"We are in the foothills of an inexorable

REVIEW TASK 1

rethinking of trunk road policy", said Professor Goodwin. "It is one thing to ask people to accept some personal sacrifice or environmental loss if it will make things better overall, but on current trends things are clearly not going to get better. Any sacrifice merely slows down the pace at which things get worse."

Source: **Guardian** (20 December 1994).

Data response

In relation to road building, evaluate the extent to which supply creates its own demand.

REVIEW TASK 2

SMOKING *will* KILL 1 MILLION YOUNG PEOPLE

A report by scientists at the Cancer Research Fund and the World Health Organisation has concluded that prolonged smoking will kill around one million British teenagers and children in middle age if present patterns continue, with a further one million dying in old age of tobacco-related diseases. Current trends suggest that 4.5 million young Britons will become regular smokers.

Professor Richard Peto of the ICRF noted:

'In most countries the worst is yet to come. If current smoking patterns persist, then by the time the young smokers of today reach middle or old age there will be about 10 million deaths a year from tobacco – one every three seconds.

The developing countries are sitting on a time-bomb.

Commenting on the government's failure to reduce smoking among children to below 6 per cent, Professor Peto pointed to the Government's refusal to ban tobacco advertising; and its successful lobbying to stop other European governments doing so independently:

'So young people continue to see misleading portrayals of smoking as romantic and sporting. It tells them that lighting up is acceptable. It is no surprise therefore that 90 per cent of smokers start when young.'

Source: Adapted from **Guardian** (20 September 1994).

Data response

1 Identify the possible externalities associated with smoking.
2 Draw a diagram to show the effect of increasing taxation on tobacco.
3 How might such a tax affect economic efficiency and resource allocation?
4 Undertake a cost–benefit analysis of taxing smoking more heavily.

Multiple choice

1 **Production activity as part of an environmental closed cycle implies**

A government activity to internalise the social costs of pollution

B an economic model of resource allocation without a public sector

C an economic model of resource allocation which ignores foreign trade

D the recycling of material as an input into the productive process

(AEB, November 1994)

2 **Which of these would not be included in the social costs of the petroleum industry?**

A The cost of treating illnesses caused by car exhaust fumes

B Surplus profits of oil suppliers during a fuel shortage

C The cost of raising capital for investment in the North Sea

D Traffic hazards caused by transporting inflammable materials in petrol tankers

(AEB, November 1994)

3 **An external benefit is most likely to arise when**

A firms are able to reduce their costs of production by utilising the results of research and development from overseas

B a reduction in corporation tax increases the amount of money firms have available for investment

C the Government subsidises suburban commuter rail services in order to reduce urban congestion

D a firm is able to dispose of waste products into rivers free of charge

(AEB, June 1994)

4 **Markets will fail to allocate resources efficiently when**

A market prices exclude externalities

B there is a high degree of factor mobility

C entrepreneurs aim to maximise profits

D governments control monopolies

(AEB, May 1994)

5 **If waste from a chemical factory kills fish in a river, this is best classified as**

A an opportunity cost

B a private liability

C a negative externality

D a public liability

(AEB, November 1993)

6 **The production of a good results in a negative externality. It is likely that there will be an improvement in economic welfare if the government**

A   gives the producer a subsidy which reflects the marginal benefit derived from the consumption of the good

B   gives the producer a subsidy which reflects the marginal cost of the externality

C   eliminates any restrictions on output to allow market forces to work

D   imposes a tax on the producer which reflects the marginal cost of the externality

(AEB, June 1994)

7 **Cost benefit analysis is used to**

A   equate social costs and social benefits

B   make producers pay for the external costs of a project

C   measure the net social benefit of a project

D   ensure that society pays for the net social benefits it receives

E   minimise social costs

(ULEAC, January 1993

8   A drug which cures an infectious disease is supplied in a free market. The production of the drug pollutes the atmosphere and imposes additional cleaning costs on neighbouring firms. The diagram below shows the costs and benefits of production.

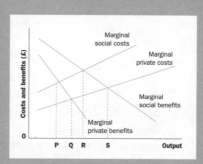

The optimal output of the drug for society would be

A   OP

B   OQ

C   OR

D   OS

(AEB, June 1993)

Essays

1 a What are the costs and benefits of training to
i   the individual?
ii the firm which provides the training?

b Discuss the arguments for and against the provision of grants by the government to encourage an increase in the amount of training which is undertaken by firms in the United Kingdom

(AEB, November 1994)

2 Pollution is an example of a 'negative externality'. Explain what an externality is and comment upon the means available for controlling negative externalities.

(Cambridge, June 1992)

3 The existence of an externality implies market failure and means that the good should necessarily be provided by the government! Discuss.

(Cambridge, November 1992)

4 a Define and give examples of
i   external costs
    and
ii external benefits
b Explain and comment on the policies which a government may adopt to
i   reduce external costs
    and
ii increase external benefits

(Cambridge, November 1991)

5 a Distinguish between private costs and social costs using examples to illustrate your answer.
b Discuss the importance of this distinction for a government considering whether or not to help finance the construction of a new railway line.

(AEB, November 1993)

6 a Distinguish between private and social costs and benefits.

b Explain how an increase in the number of cars on the roads in the UK might lead to a misallocation of resources.

c Indicate what policies the Government might use to remedy this misallocation.

(AEB, A/S Level, June 1991)

QUESTIONS

7 a Explain what is meant by
   i   private cost and
   ii   social cost
   in the production of a good or service.
  b **Discuss the extent to which it is possible and desirable to make private and social costs coincide.**

(Cambridge, November 1993)

8 a **With the aid of examples, explain the terms private benefit and social benefit**

  b **Explain what you understand by 'cost–benefit analysis' and illustrate and discuss its use as a means of resource allocation**

(Cambridge, June 1993)

9 a **Explain the functions that prices perform in a market economy.**

  b **Assess the case for and against using the price mechanism to relieve the problem of traffic congestion.**

(AEB, Specimen paper)

10 a **Explain why it is possible to regard pollution as an economic problem.**

  b **What economic policies might the Government use to reduce the level of pollution?**

  c **Discuss whether it is possible or desirable to completely eliminate pollution.**

(WJEC, June 1994)

11 a **Explain what is meant by an externality.**

  b **Examine the impact of introducing any two of the following:**
   i   pollution taxes;
   ii   legal maximum controls on pollution emissions;
   iii   tradeable pollution licence permits.

(ULEAC, June 1994)

a Briefly explain the following terms:
  i   externalities;
  ii   cost benefit analysis.

b The government is proposing to build a motorway linking a city with a major port; this motorway would cross an area of outstanding natural beauty. Discuss the problems involved in undertaking a cost benefit analysis of such a project.

(ULEAC, June 1992)

13 **a** Define what is meant by the term 'externality'.

b Examine alternative policies to resolve the externality problem in the case of lead pollution from cars.

(ULEAC, January 1991)

14 Examine the economic consequences of the Government imposing regulations on the emission from UK coal-fired power stations of pollutants causing 'acid rain'.

(ULEAC, January 1990)

Data response

 Study the passage below and answer the questions which follow.
The following passage describes a scheme recently introduced in the USA which aims to reduce the pollution caused by coal-burning power stations. The scheme is based on setting, and then each year gradually reducing, maximum limits or ceilings for pollution. Under the scheme, a power station which 'over-complies', i.e. one which cuts pollution by more than is required, is allowed to sell its spare pollution allowances. The allowance or 'permit to pollute' can be bought by an 'under-complying' power station, i.e. one which has cut pollution by less than is required. (**Note:** one allowance equals one tonne of sulphur dioxide.)

A Market in 'Permits to Pollute'
Last month, three US utility companies bravely waded into a national experiment to use market principles for environmental ends and to tackle a problem of 'market failure'. In the first public deal to trade 'permits to pollute', the Wisconsin Power & Light Company sold 10,000 allowances to the Tennessee Valley Authority and between 15,000 and 25,000 allowances to the Duquesne Light Company in Pittsburgh.

The allowances are part of the Clean Air Act of 1990, which requires America's mostly coal-burning utilities to halve their emissions of sulphur dioxide, the key ingredients in acid rain, by the year 2000. The national cap on sulphur dioxide emissions will be achieved in the most economically efficient way by trading the rights to pollute among utilities. Under the Act, those companies which exceed compliance with the emissions standard – by installing new cleaner technology or switching to lower sulphur fuels – can sell their spare allowances, issued by the Environmental Protection Agency (EPA), to those who have not fully complied.

The electricity market is a 'regulatory-driven market'. As yet however, the public utility commissions that regulate the American private power companies have not spelled out who – the consumers of electricity or the companies' shareholders – are to benefit (or lose) from the effects on electricity prices and company costs of the trading of pollution allowances.

At present, surveys show that utility companies are tending towards over-compliance with the new standards – mostly by installing new technology to remove sulphur dioxide from flue gas, and some through fuel switching. The inclination to over-comply means that there will be extra allowances for sale. The price of allowances or 'permits to pollute' should therefore by kept pretty low.

In Phase 1, which runs from 1995 to the year 2000, 110 of the dirtiest plants have been targeted to reduce their emissions. Because most of these power stations are likely to install new technology to reduce emissions in preference to buying extra pollution allowances, the price of pollution permits will probably continue to remain low throughout Phase 1. But after the year 2000, in Phase 2, a permanent annual cap of 8.9m tonnes of sulphur dioxide will be applied to all the electricity generators. Assuming that demand for electricity increases, many power stations will find they are unable to meet demand while keeping within the pollution ceiling – solely by installing clean technology. To meet demand for power, they will have to purchase extra pollution allowances. In Phase 2 allowance prices are expected to rise to about $600 per tonne. This compares with $250–$300 per tonne in the first deal. The EPA's penalty for emitting excess sulphur dioxide is $2,000 per tonne.

*Source: Adapted from Barbara Durr, 'A market made out of muck', **Financial Times** (10 June 1992).*

a Explain briefly why economists regard the formation of acid rain as a 'market failure'.
b Explain
i the statement that the electricity market is a ''regulatory-driven market''
ii how consumers might benefit from the trading of pollution allowances
c With the aid of supply and demand analysis, explain why, according to the passage, the price of pollution permits or allowances is likely to rise from $250–$300 per allowance in Phase 1 to about $600 in Phase 2.
d The passage states that: "The national cap on sulphur dioxide emissions will be achieved in the most economically efficient way by trading the rights to pollute...''.
i Briefly describe one other method, besides the creation of a market in pollution permits, by which sulphur dioxide pollution might be limited.
ii Discuss the advantages and disadvantages of the various methods of controlling sulphur dioxide pollution.

(AEB, June 1994)

QUESTIONS

2 'Economics is concerned with the allocation of resources in the face of all opportunities, costs and risks. The market is a mechanism for transmitting dispersed information unknown to any one central planner or computer and providing individuals with incentives to act upon it.

There has been a long tradition of market-based thinking on the economics of the environment. The standard example of an externality is that of the smoking chimney which inflicts costs for which the polluter does not have to pay. The main reason for externalities is not excessive, but inadequate, use of markets and prices. The chimney owner is unrestrained because there is no price to pay for the harm inflicted by his smoke.

The original economic approach was to put a tax on the owner of the chimney and other polluters. The tax can be high enough to impose whatever standard of purification the legislature desires. There is also a case to be made for some combination of taxes for external costs – and subsidies for favourable spillovers. There are other related ideas, such as marketable "pollution permits". The more modern approach is to say that adverse externalities arise because property rights have been inadequately defined. It is because no-one owns large stretches of the sea that there is an incentive to over-fish. The principle "polluter pays" is an attempt to use the property rights approach. This is not always possible, especially where many people are involved and transaction costs are heavy. The most obvious example crying out for action is for a "congestion tax" imposed on vehicles coming into busy urban areas.'

Source: Adapted from: S. Brittan, 'The green power of market forces', **Financial Times** *(4 May 1989).*

a Explain the meaning of the phrase, 'The main reason for these externalities is not excessive, but inadequate, use of markets and prices'.

b Examine and illustrate with a diagram the impact of putting 'a tax on the owner of the chimney and other polluters'.

c What policy could a government employ to deal with a situation where it feels that the desirable level of pollution should be zero?

d Analyse the economic effects on firms and households of a 'congestion tax imposed on vehicles coming into busy urban areas'.

e Why does over-fishing occur when property rights are inadequately defined?

(ULEAC, June 1993)

.19 Are all goods marketable?

The Health Care Debate

Article 1 – Health care through the market

The NHS is in crisis. Yet those who call for more resources without reform lack credibility. In 1947 the NHS boldly attempted to sever the connection between access to health care and the ability to pay. This system has failed because of the removal of health care from the market place. If a commodity is offered free at the point of consumption there will be excess demand; some rationing device must be found. The NHS uses several; some patients are not treated, some join waiting lists or go private, and more urgent cases are treated according to informal and often arbitrary priority schemes. Not only does this cause inefficiency in the allocation of resources but it also is a cause of constant political embarrassment; the government is blamed for waiting lists and particular failures of treatment as recently we have seen with children in intensive care and the constant claims by doctors of the inadequacy of resources.

On the supply side there is monopoly power and the politicisation of management, whose main object must be seen as forcing the government and taxpayer to provide extra resources. Monitoring of costs by ministers has been handicapped by a lack of power over management, who have a vested interest in denying proper information for control and can engineer a headline scandal of closed wards to frighten off too enthusiastic a search for economies.

In fact the NHS has failed because there is no competition to spur producers into better efforts. Existing vested interests – doctors, nurses, administrators and ancillaries and their unions – continue to share both power and resources. Secondly the consumer has no say in the allocation of resources. GPs have a monopoly of access to NHS resources, leading to a poor quality NHS service, a remoteness of the NHS from patients' demands and excessive waiting times.

Economic efficiency and political considerations both point to a greater role for the market, with government intervention reserved to ensure effective protection of the weak, the poor and the unfortunate.

*Source: Adapted from Patrick Minford, **Economic Affairs** (October – November 1988)*

Article 2 – Health care for free?

Ask almost anyone why we can't have a completely free health service with no charges at all and the answer comes back, "We can't afford it."

Somehow we could afford it from 1948 to 1951, as we were recovering from the most expensive war in history and when national income was much less than half what it is now. But now we can't afford it.

Casting my eye idly over the written questions sections of Hansard, the record of parliament, the other day, I came across this little nugget.

An Ulster Unionist MP asked how much it would cost in extra income tax to get rid of every single charge on health prescriptions including prepaid ones.

Steel yourself for the reply. A fifth of a penny. Yes, a fifth of a penny.

Most people would would hardly notice it. For this really very trivial sum all health charges, which have been raised no less than 17 times since 1979 (when Thatcher said she had "no plans" for increasing them), could be completely dismantled.

Crypto-Tories

The case for the health charges, the Tories have always argued, is that there isn't any reason why "the state" should subsidise the health prescriptions of people who can afford them.

Surely, if well off people pay charges, this saves money for the health service and makes it easier to "subsidise" the health charges for the poor?

This argument used to be confined to Tories. Lately it has been taken up by large sections of the new Labour Party.

It forms the core of the Social Justice Commission which recently delivered a huge report to the Labour Party in effect recommending an end to "universal benefits" such as child benefit – or a completely free health service.

Why do Tories and crypto-Tories in the Social Justice Commission seem to argue for charges for the well off and the rich?

The answer is that they detest the idea of a completely free health service much more than they resent paying charges for prescriptions.

If everyone pools their resources to contribute to a health system available to everyone, what is to stop that idea brimming over into every other aspect of society?

A thriving and free health service threatens the very foundations of the greed and profit society which the Tories have always supported.

A private health service in the United States costs about 13 per cent of the national income, and is far more unfair and inefficient than the British National Health Service, which costs less than 7 per cent of the national income.

Flying in the face of these facts, the Tories have eaten away at the NHS, privatising services, slitting the slender threads which tied its management to elected councils and boards.

*Source: Paul Foot, **Socialist Worker** (17 December 1994).*

TASK 19.1

The 2 articles provide different perspectives on the question of health care and the market.

a Briefly summarise the views of the two authors.
b With which view do you most sympathise? Explain the reasons for your decision.

Preview

In this chapter we shall investigate the following key areas:
- what public goods, merit goods and demerit goods are;
- why the market fails in these cases;
- how the government might respond to this failure;
- the effectiveness of the various responses.

What are public goods?

*A **pure public good** is one which possesses the features of non-excludability and non-rivalry (non-diminishability).*

Pure public goods are ones that when consumed by one person can be consumed in equal amounts by the remainder of society, and where the possibility of excluding others from consumption is impossible.

Examples of public goods are:

- national defence;
- the police service;
- street lighting;
- lighthouses;
- flood-control dams;
- pavements;
- public drainage.

It is likely that the market, left to itself, will seriously under produce such goods, or possibly not produce them at all. This is because the market will only provide goods for which a profit can be made, and pure public goods possess two important properties that together make their production on the basis of private profitability extremely difficult.

These features are:

- non-rivalry (or non-diminishability);
- non-excludability.

First, consider the characteristic of non-rivalry: this means that one person's use of the public good does not deprive any other person of such use or does not diminish the amount available to others; for example, if one person enjoys the benefits of being protected by the police force, a flood control dam or the national defence system, it does not prevent everyone else doing the same; similarly, if one person benefits from walking along a street at night-time which is paved, free of pot-holes, and well-lit, the benefits and the availability to others would not be diminished.

Secondly, consider the characteristic of non-excludability: this means that when the public good is provided to one person, it is not possible to prevent others from enjoying its consumption –

sometimes summarised as: provision at all means provision for all; thus, if a police force, a flood-control dam or a national defence system is successful in offering protection to citizens of a country, once it has been provided, it is impossible to exclude anyone within the country from consuming and benefiting from such goods; similarly, for a paved and well-lit public street – nobody can be prevented from enjoying its benefits.

The concept of a 'public good' can perhaps best be understood by comparing it with its opposite, a private good

*A **private good** is one which possesses the features of excludability and rivalry (diminishability).*

A private good possesses two features, excludability and rivalry, and when consumed by one person, it is not available to others; thus, a person buying a new washing machine can exercise private property rights over it and exclude others from enjoying its cleaning abilities, whilst, at the same time, diminishing the the total stock of washing machines available for sale to others.

Thus, in the case of public goods, the market fails because the private sector would be unwilling to supply them – their non-excludability makes them non-marketable, because non-payers cannot be prevented from enjoying the benefits of consumption, and therefore prices cannot be attributed to particular consumers. This involves the free-rider problem which arises when it is impossible to provide a good or service to some without it automatically and

Free riders are those who enjoy the benefits of a public good without having to pay ,because it is impossible to exclude them.

freely being available to others who do not contribute to its cost. For example, imagine a situation in which you shared an island with five other inhabitants; if you paid privately for an army to defend the island against violent invaders, your five co-inhabitants could 'free-ride' off you by enjoying the benefits of the defence, without having to pay anything towards it; there would probably come a point when you would withdraw your payments and, like the others, leave it to someone else to foot the bill; eventually, the army would not be provided at all.

Hence, in a free market, a whole range of pure public goods may not be provided, and the only answer is for the state to provide them, financed out of general taxation. (Exceptions to state provision are lighthouses on the UK coast which are provided by Trinity House, a registered charity, and public drainage which is supplied by the water companies which are public limited companies.) Moreover, the non-rivalry aspect of public goods means that the cost of supplying one more user, i.e. the marginal cost, is zero; for example, once paving stones have been laid, it makes no difference how many people walk along them, as there is no additional cost involved. As the condition for the achievement of allocative efficiency is that price should be set equal to marginal cost, it would therefore follow that to achieve an optimum level of output and consumption of public goods the state should provide them at zero prices.

Non-pure public goods (quasi-public goods)

*A **non-pure** or **quasi-public good** is a public good for which the two properties of non-excludability and non-rivalry are not completely present; it therefore has a mixed private and public good content.*

In practice, various ways may be devised for excluding free-riders from the consumption of public goods, as the characteristics of non-excludability and non-rivalry may not be completely present. In such cases, the goods would be referred to as non-pure or quasi-public goods; for example, in the case of a motorway, various methods could be used, such as electronic tagging or toll-gates, to make users pay (an impossibility with a pure public good), so excludability would be possible; and, if the motorway were to become sufficiently congested, non-rivalry would not be present; i.e. as the road reaches its full vehicle capacity, as often happens in the rush-hour periods on urban motorways, each extra road user does reduce the availability of the motorway to other motorists and raises the marginal supply cost above zero. (The marginal cost would of course be zero, or near to zero, on an entirely uncongested motorway.)

Thus a non-pure public good is an example of a mixed good, which is one which has both a public and a private good content. A motorway provides an example of a public good with a private good component, and conversely it is possible to identify private goods, with a public good component; e.g. driving a car is an act of private consumption, but when public transport is not available, perhaps because transport workers are on strike, car owners may offer lifts to stranded travellers creating some 'publicness'. Hence, in practice, many public and private goods contain some mix of both.

TASK 19.2

a Identify some other goods which are non-pure public goods, and explain in each case why some excludability and diminishability are possible.

b Why are health and education **not** pure public goods?

The INVESTIGATOR

Debt-laden Tories revive plans to sell motorways

Plans to privatise Britain's motorways have been drawn up in order to raise billions of pounds from their sell-off and to save the Government about £550 million a year in maintenance costs.

Previously, a plan to franchise existing motorways, with private companies paying for their upkeep, was abandoned following vigorous lobbying by motoring organisations. They argued that the scheme would inevitably force traffic on to smaller roads, causing congestion, pollution and more accidents.

Three factors have now encouraged the Government to change their minds:
● A desire to reduce the PSBR.
● The success of the Dartford River crossing, a combined toll-bridge and tunnel on the

M25, which is expected to break-even in 2001, 7 years earlier than predicted.
● The belief that the UK is on the verge of becoming a world leader in developing the technology for high-speed toll roads, which could identify hundreds of vehicles per minute without making them slow down.

Critics of motorway privatisation warn that it would drive up the cost of motoring, making it almost as dear as rail travel and possibly lead to serious environmental problems if motorway tolls divert vehicles to minor roads.

An AA spokesman noted:

"We are a pretty congested island. We might as well use these main arteries. If we put something in their way, it's going to cause enormous problems."

Discuss the case for and against the privatisation of motorways.

What are demerit goods?

Demerit goods are goods which are deemed to be socially undesirable, and which are likely to be overproduced and overconsumed through the market mechanism.

Examples of demerit goods are cigarettes, alcohol and all other addictive drugs such as heroine and cocaine.

The problem arises from the fact that so long as an effective demand is present,

such goods are, in all probability, going to be extremely profitable to produce, and this is all that a price system takes into account – the market neither possesses a 'heart' to enable it to help those in need, nor is it inherently able to make value judgements about which commodities are good or bad for society as a whole: it is prices and profits which act as the 'guiding light' to resource allocation.

However, the consumption of demerit goods imposes considerable negative externalities on society as a whole, such that the private costs incurred by the individual consumer are less than the social costs experienced by society in general; for example, cigarette smokers not only damage their own health, but also impose a cost on society in terms of those who involuntarily passively smoke, and the additional cost to the National Health Service in dealing with smoking-related diseases. Thus, the price that consumers pay for a packet of cigarettes is not related to the social costs to which they give rise; i.e. the marginal social cost will exceed the market price and overproduction and overconsumption will occur, causing a misallocation of society's scarce resources. This is illustrated in Box 19.2.

BOX 19.2

Over-consumption of a demerit good

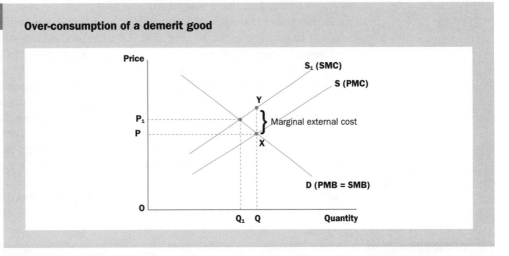

Box 19.2 illustrates how the market fails in the case of demerit goods. At a market price of OP, OQ quantity of the demerit good is consumed, where demand (private marginal benefit) equals supply (private marginal cost). However, at OQ the social marginal cost exceeds the price by the vertical distance XY, the value of the marginal external cost. Social optimality would require a smaller level of consumption at OQ_1, where

Price = social marginal cost = social marginal benefit.

Government measures to correct market failure arising from demerit goods

- The government may attempt to reduce the consumption of demerit goods such as cigarettes, alcohol and addictive drugs through persuasion. This is most likely to be achieved through negative advertising campaigns, which emphasise the dangers of drink-driving, drug abuse, etc. The aim here is the opposite of normal commercial advertising, namely to shift the demand curve for demerit goods to the left.

- A contraction of demand (movement along the demand curve for a demerit good) could be achieved by the imposition of a tax on the demerit good. This would have the effect of shifting the supply curve to the left, raising the price and reducing the amount consumed. If the government could accurately assess the value of the marginal external cost caused by the consumption of the demerit good (e.g. in Box 19.2, it is the vertical distance XY), a tax equivalent to this could be imposed, and a socially optimum outcome could be achieved. However, in practice, ascribing an accurate monetary value to negative externalities is extremely difficult to do, and the demand for such goods as cigarettes and alcohol is often highly inelastic, so that any increase in price resulting from additional taxation causes a less than proportionate decrease in demand.

● The government may use various forms of regulation. In its most extreme form, regulation could be used to impose a complete ban on a demerit good, such that its consumption is made illegal; for example, the Prohition Laws in the USA in the 1930s criminalised the sale and consumption of alcohol, as does the law at the moment in Saudi Arabia; also in the UK today anyone found guilty of selling or consuming heroin can be imprisoned. However, the effect of such regulation is rarely to completely eliminate the market for the demerit good; rather, it is usually driven underground in the form of an unofficial or hidden market.

Less severe regulatory controls might take the form of spatial restrictions; e.g. people may be disbarred from smoking in their place of work, on public transport and in cinemas and restaurants; there may be time restrictions in that it may be illegal to sell alcohol during certain periods of the day, or there may be age restrictions in terms of a minimum age being stipulated at which young people are permitted to buy cigarettes and alcohol.

TASK 19.4   In small groups, discuss and write down the possible economic arguments for and against the legalisation of cannabis.

What are merit goods?

Merit goods are the opposite of demerit goods – they are goods which are deemed to to be socially desirable, and which are likely to be underproduced and underconsumed through the market mechanism. Examples of merit goods include education, health care, welfare services, housing, fire protection, refuse collection and public parks.

In contrast to pure public goods, merit goods could be, and indeed are, provided through the market, but not necessarily in sufficient quantities to maximise social welfare. Thus goods such as education and health care are provided by the state, but there is also a parallel, thriving private sector provision. Indeed, there is considerable disagreement between economists on the right and left of the political spectrum over the extent to which such goods should be provided by the state or the private sector. We consider these arguments later in this section.

Before we proceed with our discussion of merit goods, and in particular the question of why merit goods tend to be underprovided by the market, it would be useful at this stage to consider Box 19.3 which summarises the main differences between public goods, private goods and merit goods.

BOX 19.3

Public goods, merit goods and private goods

Main features	Type of good		
	Public goods	Merit goods	Private goods
Diminishability (rivalry)	Non-diminishable (non-rivalry)	Diminishable (rivalry)	Diminishable (rivalry)
Excludability	Non-excludable	Excludable (but their full benefits are not felt by those who are included)	Excludable
Benefits	Communal (mainly positive externalities)	Individual and communal (strong positive externalities)	Individual (mainly internalities)
Provider	Usually the government	Government and/ or private enterprise	Usually private enterprise
Financed by	Usually taxation	Taxes and/or prices	Usually through the price system
Examples	National defence; law and order; street lights; light houses.	Health; Education; Housing.	Corn Flakes; Clothes; TV sets; etc., etc..

Source: Charles Smith, **Economic Development, Growth and Welfare** (Macmillan, 1992).

Why might merit goods be underprovided by the market?

Merit goods will tend to be underprovided by the market because:

- they generate positive externalities;
- there is an unequal distribution of income;
- consumers may lack perfect information;
- consumers may be uncertain as to their future needs;
- and monopoly power may arise.

We shall examine each of these factors in turn:

Merit goods generate substantial positive externalities

Merit goods confer benefits on society in excess of the benefits conferred on individual consumers; in other words, there is a divergence between private and social costs and benefits, as the social benefits accruing to society as a whole from the consumption of such goods tend to be greater than the private benefits to the individual. This divergence means that the private market cannot be relied upon to ensure an efficient allocation of society's scarce resources. The problem is that individual consumers and producers make their decisions on the basis of their own internal costs and benefits, but, from the standpoint of the welfare of society at large, externalities must be considered. This point can be illustrated in relation to health care and education.

Health care generates a number of positive externalities; for example, if all people receive adequate levels of healthcare, the nation's workforce is likely to be fitter and healthier, fewer working days would be lost through sickness, and this would have beneficial effects on the level of output and economic growth; vaccinations and preventive health care which prevent the spread of contagious diseases such as small-pox and whooping cough, clearly not only benefit the individuals receiving the treatment, but also the rest of society at large. Indeed, a major reason for the relatively weak economic performance of many of the poorer countries of the world is the widespread incidence of ill-health and disease amongst their populations.

Similarly, in the case of education, there are a number of positive externalities from which society at large may benefit, which may not directly accrue to the individual pupil/student. Individuals clearly derive private benefits from higher levels of education as, for example, earning capacity is to a considerable extent a function of educational attainment. However, society at large receives the benefits of a more highly skilled, adaptable and thus more efficient workforce, which is one of the key ingredients of economic success – the West German post-war 'economic miracle' has, in part, been attributed to its highly educated and trained workforce. Society also benefits in less tangible ways as it could be argued that educated people are less prone to crime and racial intolerance, although this argument is obviously not foolproof!

The important point then is that if people had to pay privately through the market for such merit goods as health and education, they would consider only their private benefits and their private costs, and would thus consume too little from the point of view of the best interests of society as a whole. This problem of under-consumption is illustrated in Box 19.4.

BOX 19.4

Under-consumption of a merit good

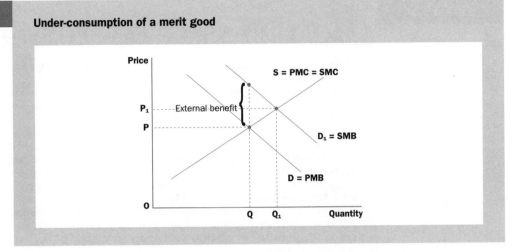

In Box 19.4, OQ is the free market level of consumption as, at this point, individuals equate their private marginal benefit with their private marginal cost. The existence of positive externalities means that the social marginal benefit curve lies above the private marginal benefit curve as the social benefits of consumption exceed the private benefits. Allocative efficiency would require a level of consumption of OQ_1 at which $SMB = SMC$.

There is an unequal distribution of income

Perhaps a more basic reason for the market tending to under-provide merit goods is that, given the highly unequal distribution of income, and the widespread poverty such as exists in the UK today, many people would be unable to afford adequate education, health care and housing in the absence of state provision or subsidy. A market system only takes effective demand into account; that is, demand backed by the ability to pay the asking price. It does not respond to human demand as indicated by peoples' needs, so quite simply the poor may have to go without. Thus, on the grounds of equity, it may be decided that such merit goods as health and education should be provided free on the basis of need rather than according to ability to pay. Underpinning this approach would be the view that all have a fundamental human right to the various merit goods, which should not be determined by the market criteria of prices and profits.

HOMELESS TOTAL TOPS *420,000*

BRITAIN is going through both an economic and a housing crisis. The home ownership boom of the 1980s, which was financed by a rapid growth in consumer credit, has helped to deepen the recession and made the outcome in Britain worse than in most of the European Community.

Homelessness and mortgage repossessions were at record levels this Christmas.

The number of people without a permanent home has reached scandalous proportions.

Official homelessness has tripled since 1978. In 1992 about 150,000 families – over 420,000 adults and children – suffered from homelessness.

Mortgage repossessions are running at 200 a day. Thousands more are sleeping rough or living in squalid, insecure homes.

A quarter of Britain's housing stock is unfit or in serious disrepair.

Many councils, especially in London, are forced to use various types of temporary accommodation.

The most depressing, cramped and often dangerous are hostels and bed and breakfast hotels. Over 20,000 families were expected to spend this Christmas in such accommodation.

The word "temporary" implies that these families are soon found a decent home. But many homeless families have to live in a bed and breakfast hotel for over a year and some for longer.

*Source: **Camden News Journal** (14 January 1993).*

TASK 19.5

Why might housing be described as a 'merit good'?
Discuss the arguments for and against the state reducing its role in the direct provision of housing.

Consumers may lack perfect information

At one level, market provision of health care and education may not provide a socially optimum outcome because consumers may not be aware of all the benefits of such goods, and may behave in a foolish manner – they may choose to spend their money on demerit goods such as cigarettes, alcohol and pornography, rather than making adequate provision for their own and their children's medical and educational needs. In this case, government provision may be justified on the paternalistic grounds of protecting us against our own folly.

At another level, consumers of such goods as health care and education may have every intention of behaving wisely, but because of the particular characteristics of these goods, may not be able to do so. A basic assumption of economic theory is that consumers are aware of their own best interests better than anybody else, and provided they possess full information, will act in such a way as to maximise their satisfaction. Thus, consumers of fresh fruit will not usually experience too much difficulty in establishing the best prices available in the market, and most would be able to make fairly accurate assessments of quality merely by sight and feel; and, if an incorrect decision is made (for instance by purchasing sour satsumas which were perceived to be sweet), the consequences of such a mistaken decision are unlikely to be too catastrophic, as the amounts spent are likely to be relatively small, and the sour satsumas could simply be thrown away.

However, health care and education are considered to be different from other goods, and the sovereignty of the consumer is likely to be considerably less than in the case of fresh fruit, for instance.

A major problem of providing health care through the market is that there is likely, in the overwhelming majority of cases, to be an imbalance between the information possessed by the suppliers, i.e. the doctors, and the consumers, i.e. the patients: medical treatment is usually technically complex, and consumers will rarely possess sufficient information to make rational choices between the alternatives available – most would have to rely on the suppliers of medical care for their information; and it is somewhat doubtful as to whether a profit-maximising supplier could always be relied upon to provide completely impartial information. Also, as many

medical problems only occur once, any information acquired may be of no future use; and finally, in contrast to buying a sour instead of a sweet satsuma, any mistaken choices in the case of health care are likely to involve a far greater cost and to be considerably more difficult to reverse; for example, the consumption of poor quality facial plastic surgery.

Similarly, in the case of education, consumers, usually parents, intending to act wisely, may not be able to do so, and the consequences of mistaken decisions may be extremely great. Education is a multi-faceted, complex process about which there is considerable disagreement, even amongst the 'experts', and obtaining the necessary information on such variables as teachers' qualifications, examination performance, intake according to social class, the incidence of bullying and racial harassment, may be extremely time-consuming and difficult to acquire; moreover, in the case of higher education, it is usually far more difficult for those who have not experienced it to appreciate its benefits and make wise decisions, as compared with those who have. As it is generally accepted that education is a prime determinant of life chances, future earning potential and quality of life, mistaken decisions because of imperfect information can have particularly severe consequences.

Consumers may be uncertain as to their future needs

Not only is a lack of information likely to cause market failure, but so too can uncertainty of information – particularly in the case of health care. A situation in which consumers are uncertain about future market information can lead to allocative inefficiency, with too little health care

being consumed if state provision is not available. Few people are able to predict with any degree of certainty the level and type of health treatment that they will require at some point in the future, as the incidence of serious accidents or ill-health are essentially unknown variables, even for the smartest of medical practitioners. As paying through the market for an operation, hospitalisation or long-term disability would almost certainly involve exceedingly large sums of money, it would be very difficult for individuals to plan their savings and consumption so as to ensure that all future medical requirements could be met; the market in this situation is unlikely to provide the optimal quantity of health care, because at the particular point in time when consumers actually need it, they may lack the wherewithal to pay the market price. Direct government provision of health care, free at the point of contact, overcomes this problem.

A possible market-based solution to this problem would be that of private medical insurance; in the same way that it is obligatory for all motorists to take out some form of car insurance, everybody could be required to purchase a minimum level of health insurance to guard against unforeseen contingencies. However, such a scheme is likely to present a number of problems:

● As all motorists are aware, the quality of insurance cover depends on the premiums paid, and the type of policy purchased; a driver who has the benefit of the more expensive 'fully comprehensive' cover will be guarded against most eventualities; however, a person with the cheaper 'third-party, fire and theft' type of policy will find that they are entitled to no compensation whatsoever for a whole variety of occurrences, for example, damaging a car by driving it into a lamp-post; similarly, and more seriously in the case of health

care, those who have paid the smallest premiums would be entitled to the least insurance cover, which may be insufficient to cover serious ill-health, should it arise; and clearly those who are likely to have the lowest cover would be the poorest, most vulnerable groups in society, who are probably the ones who need health care the most, but who would be least able to afford it.

● Not only are the most needy likely to have the least insurance cover but, as is the case with motor insurance, there are likely to be those who have no medical insurance at all.

● Like other private sector business organisations, insurance companies are motivated by the goal of long-term profit-maximisation, and would thus be reluctant to insure such 'unprofitable' categories of people as the long-term sick, the permanently disabled and the very old; for all these people the market solution is likely to be no solution.

● In contrast to the problems of under-provision for the most needy, a system of health provision, based solely on private medical insurance, is likely to lead to over-provision for those, almost certainly the better off, with the most comprehensive and expensive cover: in such cases, neither doctors nor patients may have any incentive to economise on treatment – fully covered patients may wish to visit their doctor as often as possible to obtain value for money, and doctors may be induced to diagnose the most expensive of treatments to maximise their earnings.

Monopoly power may arise

Spatial monopoly is monopoly power obtained by a business organisation through locating at a distance from its competitors.

In Chapter 13, we demonstrated how under monopoly, price will tend to be higher and output lower compared to the case of perfect competition; and as price will be set at a level above marginal cost, and the firm is unlikely to operate on the lowest point of its average cost curve, neither allocative nor productive efficiency will occur. Thus, where monopoly occurs, the market could not be relied upon to produce an efficient allocation of resources.

If education were provided solely through the market, it is likely that spatial monopolies would arise, as various geographical areas would not be adequately populated to support more than one school, college or university; i.e. monopolistic educational providers would be protected from competition by virtue of distance and such provision may lead to sub-optimality in the market.

Similarly, in the case of health care, market provision would be likely to generate substantial monopoly power, and therefore market failure: as the consumers of medical services lack perfect or even adequate information about the products they consume, scouring the market place for the best deals is not possible, and, in this situation, the suppliers, i.e. the doctors and hospitals, would be able to act like monopolists and raise their prices with relative impunity. Not only might consumers face monopoly pricing, but they might also, on account of their relative ignorance, end up purchasing more health care than they actually need: the 'sound of cash-tills' might induce the less scrupulous practitioners to be over-zealous as regards the amount and type of treatment they recommend. For example, in the USA where a direct charge for childbirth delivery is usually made, many more caesarean deliveries on average are carried out as compared to the UK, where most childbirth is provided free through the NHS.

What role should the government play in the provision of merit goods?

One solution would be for the government to play no role whatsoever and to allow the provision of merit goods to be decided completely through the free interaction of market forces. However, for all the reasons previously mentioned, this would lead to extreme under-provision of these goods and a misallocation of resources from the standpoint of society as a whole. Thus, in practice, governments play a substantial role in the provision of merit goods such as health and education, even where they are ideologically committed to the market system. However, the exact form that such government involvement should take is a subject of much dispute, and we shall consider each of the following in turn:

- direct government provision;
- regulation;
- subsidies;
- a combination of government provision and market forces.

Direct government provision

In the UK, the overwhelming majority of health care and education is still paid for out of general taxation and provided free at the point of contact by the government – for most people, when they visit their doctor, go to hospital, school or college, no direct charge is levied upon them; the private sector still only accounts for a relatively small proportion of all health and education provision. Apart from generating substantial positive externalities and overcoming the problems arising from unequal income distribution, lack of current and future information and potential private monopoly power, direct government provision may also give rise to large economies of scale, and may thus be productively efficient. For example, when a service such as health care is provided to the population as a whole, greater scale economies are likely to arise in terms of capital and labour costs than could be expected to accrue to the private health care sector, whose scale of operations is necessarily much smaller than that of the NHS.

However, the idea of universal provision for all on the basis of need, with prices and profits playing no role, is one which sits very uneasily with the philosophy of market economics, and has thus in recent years come under fierce attack from right-wing, market-oriented economists. They have argued that government provision of health and education has led to an undesirable situation of state monopoly power in these areas and that to increase consumer choice, lower costs and raise the level of efficiency, greater competition is required. This has led the present Conservative Government to implement changes which involve a combination of government and market allocation mechanisms, which have aimed to increase incentives for providers of health care and education to become more efficient, and for consumers to 'shop around' more for the 'best deals'. These changes are considered later in this chapter.

Regulation

The government may also use a range of regulatory devices both to increase the consumption of merit goods and to ensure their quality. In the case of education in the UK, it is compulsory that all children between the ages of 5 and 16 receive some form of schooling, be it in the private or public sector, and quality is controlled in such ways as school teachers being required to have stipulated qualifications before they are allowed to teach; state (but not private), schools being required to follow the national curriculum and a through a system of inspections. In the case of

health care, vaccinations against various contagious diseases could be made compulsory, and medical practitioners such as doctors, dentists, opticians and nurses are required to obtain certain qualifications before they can practice. Bodies such as the British Medical Association (BMA) and the Royal College of Nursing (RCN) engage in various forms of self-regulation of their members. The government could also use regulation to enforce the consumption of a good provided by the private sector which is deemed to be a merit good by virtue of the positive externalities that it generates: the compulsory consumption of seat-belts by motorists provides one such example.

In the case of housing, the use of rent controls on private sector rented accommodation is a means by which the market can be regulated so as to protect tenants from having to pay high rents. Rent controls were introduced by the Labour government of the 1970s, but have since been abolished, in line with the present government's belief in deregulated markets.

Rent controls represent a form of price fixing (see Chapters 2.10 and 2.11). More specifically, they represent an attempt to fix a maximum price below the equilibrium; i.e. a maximum rent that a private landlord may charge for rented accommodation; and, to be effective, rent controls may also have to be accompanied by further regulation preventing the landlord from ousting the tenant once the rent has been fixed. Box 19.6 illustrates the fixing of such a maximum, and the possible longer term problems.

BOX 19.6

The use of rent controls

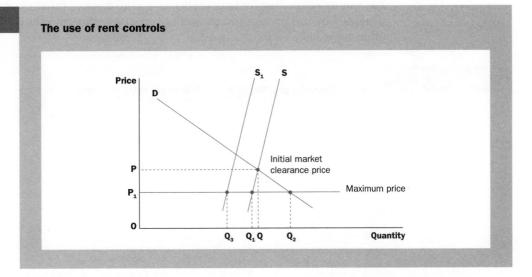

Box 19.6 shows that, with a relatively inelastic supply of rented accommodation, the free market rent would be established at a price of OP, with the quantity demanded and supplied equal at OQ. However, if the government impose a ceiling of OP_1 on the price that landlords can charge, an initial shortage of Q_1Q_2 develops as the short-term profitability of renting-out accommodation declines. In the longer term, if landlords' rate of return falls

below what they could receive from alternative investments, such as government bonds, then existing landlords could be expected to leave the housing market with little new rented accommodation coming onto it. As a consequence, the supply of rented accommodation would shift from S to S_1, and the shortage would increase to Q_3Q_2. Thus, unless the government could shift the supply curve to the right, for example by building more publicly owned council houses, the long-term shortage would worsen, with the existing rent-controlled stock descending into an ever greater state of disrepair, as a result of landlords seeking to reduce their costs by postponing or cancelling repair and maintenance work.

Under the 1988 Housing Act, all new lettings may now be let at market rents, with the social security system providing some protection for tenants in the form of housing benefit income.

Subsidies

Subsidies may be used to increase the output of merit goods, provided both by the private and public sectors, to the socially optimum level.

For example, the theatre is usually provided by the private sector, and is often regarded as a merit good on account of the educative and civilising benefits that it confers on society. The government might take the view that without state assistance to the arts, there would be an unacceptably small number of theatres able to survive. Box 19.7 illustrates how the subsidy would operate.

BOX 19.7

The effect of subsidising a merit good (theatre tickets)

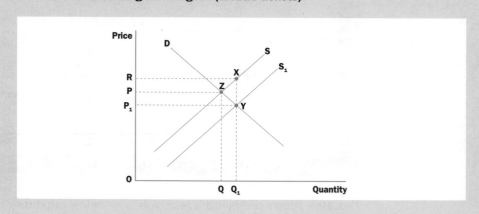

In Box 19.7, the free market price of theatre tickets is established by the intersection of the curves D and S at OP, with the equilibrium quantity at OQ. A government subsidy, equivalent to the vertical distance XY, would have the effect of shifting the supply curve to the right, causing the market price to fall to OP$_1$ and the quantity of theatre tickets demanded and supplied to increase to OQ$_1$. Consumers' expenditure on the theatre increases from OPZQ to OP$_1$YQ$_1$ and the area P$_1$RXY represents the total amount that the government spends on the subsidy.

TASK 19.6

The effect of subsidising theatre tickets on price and quantity will, to a large extent, depend upon the elasticity of demand for theatre tickets. Draw two diagrams, such as the one in Box 19.7, one with a relatively inelastic demand curve, and one with a relatively elastic demand curve. Explain the different effects on price and quantity.

In the case of health care in the UK, the majority of it is provided free to the user out of general taxation, although charges are levied for prescriptions and optical and dental treatment. In these cases the prices charged have been made cheaper than they would otherwise be, with patients only paying part of the cost of treatment and the government making up the difference through the payment of subsidies to suppliers. In the case of housing, owner occupiers receive a subsidy through the receipt of tax relief on mortgage interest repayments, which is not available to those people who rent their accommodation. State education in the UK, like most health care, is provided without direct charges being made, although education vouchers represent an alternative form of market-based, subsidised provision which has been proposed. Box 19.8 focuses on the issue of such a voucher scheme.

BOX 19.8

The INVESTIGATOR

Education vouchers

PAY AS YOU LEARN

Under a new Tory plan, parents would pay £500 to send their children to state schools, who would set their own fees. A typical state secondary school would charge £3000 a year per child with the parents receiving a £2500 voucher.

Families on low incomes would receive a higher value voucher worth the average school fee for the locality. They could either save cash by sending their children to cheaper schools, or they could pay more and send them to more expensive schools, which would probably have the best exam results.

Architect of the scheme, Lord Skidelsky, said the scheme would make parents more education conscious, and that

'the voucher would be set below the cost of the school to enable parents to contribute. You would get an increase in the national education budget without relying on the tax system'.

The teachers' union, NASUWT said:

'It's going to be an extremely expensive enterprise of no use to anyone without a car, or living in an area with poor public transport.'

*Source: **Press Reports** (March 1995).*

BOX 19.8

The INVESTIGATOR

Forth warns of vouchers mismatch

Mr Eric Forth, Minister of State for Education highlighted the drawbacks of a voucher system for the under-fives. In response to pressure from the right-wing Centre for Policy Studies for a free-market solution to the expansion of pre-school services, he warned:

'For every parent with a voucher, there needs to be a school place somewhere, and if there is too much of a mismatch, then the virtues of a voucher scheme will not be forthcoming.'

The INVESTIGATOR

Parental choice not likely to be enhanced

The Early Childhood Education Forum has warned the government, in a draft discussion paper, that a voucher system for 4-year-olds would be unlikely to enhance either parental choice or levels of service, and could undermine Government spending policies.

The discussion paper notes:

'One of the aims of voucher schemes is to stimulate a market for services. The acknowledged problem of voucher schemes is that of 'dead weight', which occurs where those who can now afford to (and choose to) pay 100 per cent of the cost of private provision, subsequently use their entitlement to a voucher to part-pay for the same service. It is likely that this will lead either to increased public expenditure to fund no net increase in provision; to the same level of funding with a net decrease in the volume of provision; or to

the transfer of public subsidy from the poor to the rich (much existing state nursery education is targeted at the needy), which is the most likely outcome.'

The paper also points out that vouchers on their own do not tackle the problem of start-up or capital costs and putting an infrastructure into place; and that there would be an increase in bureaucracy to administer them.

The Primary Education Study Group warn that:

'a voucher system could lead to divisiveness, with schools and nurseries working in competition rather than in co-operation; that planning would become difficult for schools and playgroups as the numbers of children would be unpredictable; and that low-value vouchers could cause the closure of high quality maintained nursery classes and schools, which would be replaced with something cheaper'.

BOX 19.8

Nurseries: ONLY A FEW BENEFIT

THE TORIES announced their plans for nursery provision in a fanfare of publicity last week.

Education secretary Gillian Shephard said £1,100 vouchers will be distributed to the parents of all four year olds in 1997, following a pilot scheme.

John Major promised to provide nursery places "for all four year olds whose parents wish it" before the next election.

But the Tories' voucher scheme will do nothing of the sort.

It will not create a single extra place. All it will do is hand out a £1,100 cash payment to those parents who can already afford a private nursery.

The introduction of vouchers for the first time marks the beginning of privatisation of education. From their earliest years children will be forced into a two tier system.

Children from richer families will be able to attend nurseries and get a head start, while poorer children lose out.

State nurseries will not fill the gap. Local authority nurseries are already massively over subscribed.

Around 100,000 more nursery places are needed for Britain's four year olds. The Tories are leaving an expansion to the market.

Local authorities reacted with fury to the plans as they threaten the existing places provided.

To pay for the vouchers the government plans to cut council grants by £545 million. The Tories are only providing an extra £185 million.

The voucher scheme is a tax on the poor.

It would "begin to destroy pre-school education in this country", says Graham Lane, education chair of the Association of Metropolitan Authorities.

Britain has the worst nursery provision in Europe. Fewer than 3 per cent of three and four year olds have full time state nursery schooling.

Only 25 per cent of three and four year olds get any nursery schooling here, compared with 95 per cent in France.

If childcare was fully subsidised about 70,000 women, mainly lone parents, would have the chance to take a job.

A further 130,000 could work longer hours if they wanted.

*Source: **Socialist Worker** (15 July 1995).*

TASK 19.7   Discuss the arguments for and against an education voucher system.

A combination of government provision and market forces

Successive Conservative governments since 1979 have implemented a number of fundamental changes to the way in which merit goods are provided, all of which have involved greater use of market forces. We shall discuss these changes under two main headings: contracting-out (compulsory competitive tendering or franchising) and marketisation (or commercialisation).

Contracting-out

Before 1988, merit goods such as refuse collection, road sweeping and school cleaning, were financed out of local taxation and mainly provided directly by local authorities. Since this time, local authorities have been required by law to put these services out to competitive tender.

Contracting-out is the process by which private firms are invited to submit tenders to undertake services previously provided within the public sector.

Thus local authorities are no longer free to simply provide the range of services that they have traditionally been responsible for. They are obliged to allow private firms to submit tenders for the right to provide such services in competition with each other, and usually against the local authority's direct labour force. The local authority is obliged to award the contract to the organisation submitting the most competitively priced bid, subject to various quality constraints. The services are therefore still provided free to users by the local authority, but may be undertaken by private sector firms.

The case for merit goods such as refuse collection and road sweeping being provided in this way, is basically the same as that for greater use of the price system in general; that is, the promotion of competition, enterprise, the profit motive and incentives leading to greater efficiency and thus cost savings for local authorities, allowing for the possibility of a lower level of local taxation.

The case against the contracting-out of local authority services is based upon the general arguments against the increased use of market provision; that is, the possibility of private monopoly abuse in terms of the quality of the service provided if the bid price is too low, and perhaps in terms of price itself in the longer term; the generation of negative externalities if quality declines, e.g. roads not being swept properly; the diminution of workers' wages and conditions of service, and/or redundancies in order to achieve competitiveness; and the possibility of higher costs if the benefits of local authority economies of scale are lost.

Marketisation

In the context of merit goods such as health care and education, marketisation may take the form of:

● encouraging increased provision of such services by the private sector alongside the state sector;

● and/or the introduction of market criteria when these merit goods are provided through the public sector of the economy, e.g. through the use of internal markets.

We shall examine each in turn.

Private provision alongside government provision

The encouragement of greater private provision of health care and education alongside direct government provision has been achieved by the government offering various inducements to positively encourage people to 'go private'; for instance, tax relief for various schemes to meet the cost of private school fees and for old age pensioners to purchase private health insurance. People have also been 'negatively' encouraged to purchase private healthcare and education through a more indirect, 'back-door' type of policy, which has operated through stealth: tight controls on government expenditure on health and education, in line with the present Conservative government's policy of 'reining-back' the size of the public sector, have inevitably led to a deterioration, not only in the services provided (e.g. growing hospital waiting lists and larger class sizes), but also in the physical condition of the capital stock (e.g. crumbling, often Victorian, school buildings); this has 'forced' many people, mainly those with adequate financial resources, to opt out of the state system and into the private health and education sectors. In addition, within the NHS internal market, fundholders have the right to purchase medical treatment for patients from the private sector.

Free-market economists would view this development in very favourable terms: They would argue that:

- Greater private provision of health and education allows for the

possibility of reducing public provision and for lowering taxes and the level of government expenditure, which are desirable goals in themselves for the free market lobby.

- The use of prices for health and education, as opposed to universal 'free' provision to users, indicates how strongly consumers actually want these services, and if applied more generally, would more selectively transfer the burden of provision from taxpayers in general to those who use and benefit from the services.

- Increased market provision allows for greater consumer choice, with people enjoying the freedom to decide how they wish to spend their money, and a reduced pressure on the state provided services – if all the private consumers of health care and education suddenly opted for government provided services, hospital waiting lists and class sizes would both dramatically increase.

Against these arguments for greater marketisation of health and education, a number of objections may be raised:

- Private sector health care and education are only able to exist and prosper because of massive subsidisation from the public sector: not only is demand for private sector health and education artificially boosted through the granting of tax relief, but both these industries also receive considerable state aid in the form of 'ready-made' doctors, nurses and teachers who have mainly been trained in the public sector at the expense of taxpayers in general; if the private health and education

An internal market (quasi-market) is a system of resource allocation, used particularly in the case of health care and education, which attempts to combine the best elements of market and government provision – the government remains a subsidiser of services but finances independent suppliers to provide the service concerned, rather than providing it directly.

Note that the term 'internal market' is also used in connection with the 1992 Single European Market Act, and refers to the creation of a market within the European Union in which there is completely free movement of goods, services and factors of production.

sectors had to meet the full cost of training their own staff, their fees would be significantly higher, and their relative attractiveness less.

● Following on from the previous point, larger private health and education sectors would imply a real resource cost for the public sector – expensively trained doctors, nurses and teachers employed in the private sector would not be available for all their time to the public sector; for example, it has been claimed that the widespread practice amongst hospital consultants of dividing their time between the NHS and their own private patients, is an important factor in NHS patients having to 'queue' for their treatment.

● The greater choice provided by the private sector is only available to those who have enough money to pay for this choice: for those lacking effective demand no such choice exists; and because education is a prime determinant of life chances in terms of the access that it provides to jobs, the opportunity for some to buy

better (i.e. more highly resourced) education may be viewed simply as a means of perpetuating inequalities.

● Private consumers of health and education may not themselves be receiving a very good deal for reasons pointed out previously – when purchasing such merit goods, consumers may lack perfect or even adequate information and in the case of health care, may face suppliers with significant monopoly power.

Internal or quasi-markets

In the late 1980s, internal markets were introduced by the Conservative Government for education and health care. Their introduction was in response to the pro-market belief that direct state provision and subsidisation had created unresponsive monopoly suppliers of health and education, whose efficiency would be greatly enhanced by allowing consumers to have more choice, and by compelling providers of such services to compete amongst themselves.

BOX 19.9   **Internal or quasi-markets**

Source: *Hands off our NHS Campaign* (1991).

In the case of education, the internal market was first implemented through the Education Reform Act of 1988. Under the Act, schools continued to receive state funding, but the amount of money each school received would depend on the number of pupils enrolled, with parents, in theory at least, having the chance to send their children to the schools of their choice. A similar system was introduced for colleges of further education in 1993, when the colleges were removed from local authority control and given corporate status. The underlying rationale of the changes was that providers of education would be forced to respond to the wishes of their 'customers' as their funding would directly be determined by the numbers 'signed-up', and the competition between rival providers would generate greater efficiency – efficient, high quality providers of education would prosper and expand, whilst the not so efficient would 'go to the wall'.

Similarly, an internal market within the NHS was introduced in 1989 through the government White Paper, *Working for Patients*. Within the NHS internal market, which is not a private market in the normal sense, 'fund-holding' general practitioners are provided with money by the government to run their own practices and to buy extra services for their patients, either from public sector providers, mainly NHS hospitals, or from private sector providers. GPs' budgets are determined by the number of patients registered with them, and by a 'needs assessment' of each practice which determines funding according to such criteria as numbers of elderly patients. Each hospital then has to compete for customers from the fund-holding GPs and from the District

Health Authorities, the other category of budget holder and purchaser of health care services.

Thus, hospitals are compelled to compete against each other on price, quality and 'speed of delivery' in order to attract customers (patients) and the accompanying funding, with the most successful, cost-effective providers being able to expand and prosper, whilst the 'market-losers' would be forced to contract.

In addition, hospitals have been encouraged to become 'opted out', self-governing trusts, accountable to central government rather than district authorities.

Supporters of the NHS internal market argue that it leads to an increase in efficiency all round: hospitals would have every inducement to reduce costs so as to provide medical services at the most competitive prices to attract customers, whilst at the same time raising the quality of patient care and reducing waiting lists; fund-holding GPs and District Health Authorities would shop around for the best deals in order to make their limited funds go as far as possible.

However, the internal markets for health and education have by no means been universally acclaimed, and have in fact come in for bitter criticism from several quarters. The criticisms have included the following:

● Were the reforms really necessary in the first place? The NHS, for example, judged against the criterion of administration costs as a proportion of total costs, was one of the cheapest and most efficiently run health services in the world prior to the reforms. It has been suggested that this was precisely the reason why the old non-market system had to be replaced – for a Conservative Government, ideologically committed as it is to the market system, a national health service, operated purely on the basis of need, without the use of prices and profits, simply could not be seen to be working well!

● Whilst a key justification for the reforms was that competition would lead to costs being minimised, the drawing-up of contracts and the general management of budgets has led to an explosion in administration costs, with chief executives of colleges and hospital trusts not being at all averse to awarding themselves and their inner-circle of senior managers substantial pay increases and other perks (see Boxes 19.10 and 19.11).

BOX 19.10

The INVESTIGATOR

Spending up £1 billion on NHS bureaucrats

According to data released by the Department of Health, spending on NHS bureaucrats has soared by more than £1 billion since the internal market started in 1991. The figures reveal that whilst nursing salary costs rose by 25 per cent over the period 1989/90 to 1993/94, managerial salary costs in England increased by 284 per cent, with administrative and clerical costs going up by 49 per cent.

Mr Alan Milburn, Labour MP for Darlington, and a campaigner against NHS bureaucracy said:

'The red tape bill in the NHS is spiralling out of control. Precious resources are being diverted from the sharp end of patient care, where they are most needed.'

A Department of Health spokesman said that about two-thirds of the increase between 1991 and 1992, and almost half the increase between 1992 and 1993 was a result of reclassifying many senior nursing, professional and administrative staff as managers.

Source: Adapted from **Press Reports** *(February 1995).*

BOX 19.11

Perks, pay and privatisation

THE TORIES have brought the east European model of privatisation to Britain's further education colleges.

They have simply handed them over to the management and their mates to do as they please.

In college after college principals and top managers award themselves vast pay rises and perks like company cars while staff and students lack basic resources.

For instance in one college twenty of the management team spent two weeks in Los Angeles at the college's expense last year. The college has an executive box at the local football ground.

Luxury suites have appeared for top managers and the institution is crawling with private consultants.

The chair of the governors is also chair of the local opted out hospital. Other governors include bosses from local businesses and a raft of small business owners.

There are no student representatives, no community representatives, no parents, no councillors. There is a single staff representative who is, anyway, a manager.

Britain's further education colleges have multimillion pound budgets but the way they have been privatised means they don't even face the meagre levels of accountability that are legally demanded of business.

Companies, for example, are legally required to declare the salaries of their directors. There is no such requirement on college principals.

Once college chiefs, like other staff members, were paid on a nationally agreed salary scale. Now top managers agree their own pay rises.

The principal of another college last month announced 40 lecturers were to be made redundant while admitting he had just received a five per cent rise.

And managers have little or no knowledge of education.

Language

"You put an educational argument to these people and they look at you like you are speaking a different language," complains one lecturer.

Instead it is the language of US business schools that dominates.

Students have become "clients", "customers" or even "tariff units". There is an obsession with "quality assurance".

*Source: Adapted from **Socialist Worker** (22 October 1994).*

● The reforms do not address the root problem of health and education provision which is one of underfunding – in the NHS the money is supposed to 'follow the patient', but if there is not enough money following patients, then hospital departments inevitably have to close. The criticism is that the overall budgets for health and education have been too small, and in the case of health, the UK spent less as a proportion of GDP in 1994 than it did in the mid-1970s and less than any other OECD country, with the exception of Greece and Turkey; thus, whilst the reforms were supposed to have brought about greater choice, consumers have not had the choice to have more resources devoted to health and education – this has been denied them by a government pursuing its goal of tax cuts and balanced budgets, with providers of health and education having to 'scrap amongst themselves' for an adequate 'slice of the cake'.

● Given the vital importance of education and health care both to the success of the national economy and to people as individuals, a policy of closing wards, hospitals and schools because of a supposed lack of demand, represents a form of 'economic vandalism'; given that the resources exist, they should be used for the benefit of all, and provided as part of a planned adequately resourced health and education system, rather than being left to the vagaries of the market. Look at Box 19.12.

BOX 19.12

War between the colleges

It is almost two years since the incorporation of further education took place – time enough to judge its success or failure.

It is becoming increasingly clear that colleges are having extreme difficulty in meeting the growth targets. Indeed the FEFC has had to extend the timescale.

Behind the polite tones of the joint FEFC/OFSTED Report on 16 – 19 guidance lies the reality that exists in post-school education; a vicious war between schools and colleges for the bodies of 16 year olds. This is the result of league tables and competition and is killing any quality education service for young people.

Education and training is not a commodity to be hawked around the market place. It needs careful and rational planning; collaboration and co-operation between institutions and stakeholders, not warfare.

*Source: The **Lecturer** (the newspaper of the National Association of Teachers in Further and Higher Education, NATFHE) (March 1995).*

- As NHS fund-holders are encouraged to buy health care services from the private sector, tax payers' money will be used to promote the expansion and subsidisation of private providers of health care whose raison d'être is to make a profit, and where access is determined solely by ability to pay (see Box 19.13).

The INVESTIGATOR

NHS private care up 80 per cent

Official figures show that spending of NHS money in the private sector has risen 80 per cent in two years – to almost £400 million.

This large increase will prompt new accusations that the NHS is being privatised by stealth. Ministers, however, will argue that the total amount spent outside the NHS represents a very small proportion of its total budget.

Mr Alan Milburn, Labour MP for Darlington noted:

'The Conservative's market changes in the NHS have given the green light to private medicine. The taxpayer is footing the bill for a massive state subsidy to the private health care industry.'

A Department of Health spokesman said:

'Health care contracts are placed with the independent sector by the NHS only where they offer value for money, best quality and best use of resources. NHS patients treated in the independent sector remain NHS patients, and are not subject to any extra charges'.

- The internal NHS market will lead to a two-tier health service, as hospitals will give preferential (i.e. earlier) treatment to the patients of fund-holding practices in order to honour their contracts with them, 'keep them sweet' and ensure a future supply of business. In addition, to ensure profitability, hospitals will have every inducement to specialise in the financially rewarding types of treatment, such as hip replacements, whilst neglecting the less profitable areas such as care of the elderly and mentally ill.

- Efficiency gains within the hospitals and colleges have largely been achieved at the expense of the workforces, which have become more casualised and more 'flexible' through the imposition of new contracts. These have diminished workers' rights and worsened their conditions of service.

- Hospital trusts and colleges of further education are now run as QUANGOS (Quasi-Autonomous Non-Governmental Organisations – see Chapter 20) which has led to a loss of local democratic accountability – their members are appointed rather than elected, not infrequently on the basis of their allegiance to the Conservative Party, their meetings may take place in secret and they are not accountable to their workers or the local communities that they serve.

A QUANGO is a quasi-(semi-) autonomous (independent) non-governmental organisation; e.g. a college of further education which is controlled by its own board of governors, but which receives part of its funding from the government.

In this chapter, we have attempted to assess how useful markets are in the provision of public goods, demerit goods and merit goods. Clearly there are differences between the three.

In the case of pure public goods, we have demonstrated how markets are unlikely to work at all, and that government provision will usually be required. Such alternatives as full privatisation or franchising might, however, be possible in the case of quasi-public goods such as motorways.

Demerit goods can, and indeed are, provided through markets, but here the question is one of assessing the appropriate form of government intervention to limit their consumption to socially acceptable levels. Extreme free-marketeers might, however, argue that all government interference with the forces of supply and demand is undesirable, irrespective of the nature of the good in question.

Merit goods, such as education and health care, give rise to the greatest controversy. Increasingly, in recent years, economists of the political right have challenged the post-war consensus that markets should only have a limited role to play in these areas, and a Conservative Government, fully in agreement with the latter, have implemented far reaching reforms, such as the internal markets for health and education, as confirmation of their convictions. It is clear that markets can play a substantial part in the provision of all merit goods, but the desirability in these cases of such an allocative mechanism is very much open to question.

1 Formal class debate.

Debate the following motion:
This house believes that education, health care and housing are best provided through the market.

Data Response

2 Elbow grease won't make up for national health service (NHS) funds shortage

The Government says spending on the NHS has increased by almost half in real terms since it came to power in 1979, and health remains high on the political agenda. Such claims can be deceptive. The reason is that costs in the NHS go up faster than they do in the rest of the economy, so that higher prices in the NHS erode much of the real increase in funding before any more services are bought.

The increase in costs in the Hospital and Community Health Service (HCHS) has been calculated by the Government and it is necessary to allow for this if we are to judge whether the volume of services has increased or decreased. The measure of cost inflation takes into account changes in pay and in the cost of supplies of drugs and medical equipment to the NHS. The Department of Health estimates that there was only 7.9 per cent more money available to spend on improving the NHS. Nothing near one half.

REVIEW TASK

DATA RESPONSE

If we take into consideration the increase in need over the period, the picture changes dramatically. The Government itself produces an index of need for the HCHS based purely on demographic changes in the population – it shows a further 11.2 per cent increase in need between 1978–89 and 1990–1.

So what does all this add up to? It seems that the increased demands on the NHS would require an increase in purchasing power of more than 20 per cent since 1979 just to maintain the same level of service. Instead we have seen purchasing power rise by only 8 per cent – a cumulative shortfall of more than £4 billion.

At first sight it appears that demand has out-paced the supply of services and that the NHS is suffering from a severe dose of underfunding. On top of this, we have a nation where average incomes have gone up by 28 per cent since the Conservatives came to power, and who demand better health care for their money. The Government, however, claims that efficiency improvements have been sufficient to compensate for any relative price effect or change in population structure.

Even if true, efficiency improvements alone would be hard pressed to make up the funding gap. They are hotly contested by many academics and by people who work in the NHS who don't see much improvement – just fewer beds.

*Source: Adapted from an article by Ruth Kelly, **Guardian** (2 April 1991).*

a   Use the article and your knowledge of economics to explain why:
   i   the demand for health care has risen over the period 1978 – 91;
   ii   the 'NHS is suffering from a severe dose of underfunding, in spite of real increases in government expenditure on it'.
b   How might 'efficiency' be measured in the NHS?
c   Discuss the possible constraints on the ability of a government to meet the increasing demands of the NHS.

(AEB, A/S, June 1993)

Multiple choice

1 **A certain good is described as a 'demerit' good. It follows that this good**

A   is taxed by the government

B   is a good which people will not pay for

C   does not give any satisfaction to its users

D   has costs which are not fully paid by its users

(IB, May 1994)

2 **Those goods which are likely to be provided by the market mechanism but have such important social benefits that they are often supplied by the government are known as**

A   inferior goods

B   public goods

C   merit goods

D   Giffen goods

(AEB, November 1993)

3 **A good can be termed a public good when**

A   supply to one person does not prevent consumption by another

B   the benefits each user derives is measured by the price paid

C   consumption and production involve no external costs

D   consumption by one person results in the reduction of supply to others.

(AEB, November 1992)

4 **A difference between a merit good and a public good is that**

A   the former is provided by the central government and the latter by public corporations

B   the former has a cost attached to it whilst the latter is provided without cost to anybody

C   the former is in limited supply whilst the supply of the latter is infinite

D   one person's consumption of the former reduces the amount available for others whilst an individual's consumption of the latter leaves the amount available for others unaffected.

(AEB, June 1991)

5 **Market failure occurs when**

   A   companies become bankrupt

   B   companies cannot find a market for their goods

   C   demand falls so that companies need to cut back production

   D   the price mechanism fails to allocate resources efficiently

   E   prices rise so that consumers become worse off

(ULEAC, June 1994)

6 **The principle of non-diminishability applied to public goods means that**

   A   the production of public goods involves increasing marginal costs

   B   public goods must be financed by progressive taxation

   C   the opportunity cost of providing public goods is a positive and constant value

   D   no extra resources will be consumed when marginal consumption takes place

(AEB, June 1995)

7 **A government replaces cash grants paid to students in full-time higher education with a scheme of loans to be repaid by the students from their future incomes earned within the country.**

In the absence of offsetting changes, which of the following is likely to result?

   A   a decrease in the opportunity cost of higher education to the student

   B   a decrease in the private rate of return on investment in higher education

   C   reduced emigration on the part of graduates

   D   a switch in demand by students away from job-related courses

(WJEC, June 1994)

Essays

1 **a** Explain, with the aid of examples, the main characteristics of
  i   public goods;
  ii merit goods.

  b To what extent is it desirable that the government should provide
  i   public goods;
  ii merit goods?

(AEB, June 1994)

2 **a** Explain how the price mechanism assists in the allocation of resources

  b Discuss the case for and against doctors (GPs) charging patients for their services.

(AEB, June 1993)

3 "Prices are the most effective means of allocating resources." In the light of this statement discuss the case for and against the introduction of meters in place of the current system of water rates (flat rate charges) as a method of pricing water.

(AEB, June 1992)

4 **a** With the use of examples, explain the difference between a public good and a merit good.

  b How can a government ensure that the optimal quantity of a merit good is provided and consumed?

(AEB, June 1992)

5 **a** Distinguish carefully between private and public goods.

  b How can public goods be efficiently provided?

(AEB, November 1991)

6 Assess the arguments for and against subsidising public transport.

(AEB, November 1991)

7 In the United Kingdom, refuse collection has traditionally been financed and provided directly by local authorities. More recently, local authorities have been forced to put their refuse collection out to competitive tendering.

   a In what way does the process of competitive tendering involve a greater use of the price mechanism?

   b Discuss the possible advantages and disadvantages of making greater use of the price system for the provision of refuse collection.

(AEB, A/S Level, June 1994)

8 **a** Using examples compare and contrast public goods with merit goods.

   b Discuss how public goods and merit goods could be provided and paid for.

(Cambridge, June 1992)

9 **a** Define what is meant by (i) a merit good and (ii) externalities.

   b Discuss the relevance of these concepts to the subject of health care.

(ULEAC, June 1991)

10 **a** Distinguish between a 'public good', a 'merit good' and a 'private good'.

   b Using defence and education as examples, examine the economic arguments used to justify the provision of public goods and merit goods.

(ULEAC, January 1993)

11 **a** In a market economy prices
    i   give signals to participants in the economy;
    ii act as a rationing device;
    iii provide incentives.
   Explain each of these functions.

   b Evaluate the economic arguments for and against introducing a system where schools charge their own fees and the government gives parents a voucher for each child which is used to contribute towards school fees.

(AEB, June 1995)

.20 Market failure or government failure, or both?

The Use of Knowledge in Society

Hayek

We must look at the price system as a mechanism for communicating information if we want to understand its real function – a function which, of course, it fulfils less perfectly as prices grow more rigid. The most significant fact about this system is the economy of knowledge with which it operates, or how little the individual participants need to know in order to be able to take the right action. In abbreviated form, by a kind of symbol, only the most essential information is passed on and passed on only to those concerned. It is more than a metaphor to describe the price system as a kind of machinery for registering change, or a system of telecommunications which enables individual producers to watch merely the movement of a few pointers, as an engineer might watch the hands of a few dials, in order to adjust their activities to changes of which they may never know more than is reflected in the price movement.

Of course, these adjustments are probably never "perfect" in the sense in which the economist conceives of them in his equilibrium analysis.

The marvel is that in a case like that of a scarcity of one raw material, without an order being issued, without more than perhaps a handful of people knowing the cause, tens of thousands of people whose identity could not be ascertained by months of investigation, are made to use the material or its products more sparingly; that is, they move in the right direction. This is enough of a marvel even if, in a constantly changing world, not all will hit it off so perfectly that their profit rates will always be maintained at the same even or "normal" level.

I have deliberately used the word "marvel" to shock the reader out of the complacency with which we often take the working of this mechanism for granted. I am convinced that if it were the result of deliberate human design, and if the people guided by the price changes understood that their decisions have significance far beyond their immediate aim, this mechanism would have been acclaimed as one of the greatest triumphs of the human mind. Its misfortune is the double one that it is not the product of human design and that the people guided by it usually do not know why they are made to do what they do. But those who clamor for "conscious direction" – and who cannot believe that anything which has evolved without design (and even without our understanding it) should solve problems which we should not be able to solve consciously – should remember this: The problem is precisely how to extend the span of our utilization of resources beyond the span of the control of any one mind; and, therefore, how to dispense with the need of conscious control and how to provide inducements which will make the individuals do the desirable things without anyone having to tell them what to do.

Fundamentally, in a system in which the knowledge of the relevant facts is dispersed among many people, prices can act to co-ordinate the separate actions of different people.

*Source: Adapted from Friedrich Hayek, '**The Use of Knowledge in Society**' (American Economic Review, 35 (September 1945); reprinted in F. Hayek, Knowledge and Society (Routledge, 1976).*

Sugden

Living things are marvellously intricate and elegant solutions to design problems; problems that are far beyond the grasp of human engineers. This used to be taken as evidence of a divine Designer. But we now know that living things are not the product of any designer; they are the unintended consequences of a blind process of evolution. The deepest insight of economics is that we depend for our survival on a network of exchange that in this respect is like a living thing or an eco-system: it is highly ordered, but no one has ordered it … The idea of spontaneous order is fundamental to economics.

Source: Robert Sugden (1992).

TASK 20.1

What views of markets and government intervention in markets are suggested by these two economists?
Do you agree or disagree with the views expressed? Justify your answer.

Preview

In this chapter, we shall investigate the following key areas:
- the background to the idea of government failure;
- possible reasons for government failure;
- and an assessment of these reasons.

From where does the idea of government failure originate?

In the previous chapters in this section, we have considered the various reasons for market failure, including the existence of monopoly/oligopoly power, externalities, public goods, merit goods and demerit goods, and an unequal distribution of income. In addition, in Section 4, we shall address the problem of macroeconomic market failure, which involves the study of Keynesian economics and the idea that markets left to themselves, i.e. without government intervention, are likely to be extremely unstable, with mass unemployment being one possible outcome. Thus, for many economists, mainly of a Keynesian or interventionist persuasion, freely operating markets are likely to contain a variety of inherent problems which prevent them from working efficiently in the absence of state involvement. Such economists tend to view market imperfection as the norm, with market disorder being internally generated; the implicit assumption of this analysis being that government intervention is necessary to correct market failure.

Government failure is a situation in which government intervention in markets leads to worse economic outcomes than if no such intervention had taken place; the attempt to correct market failure results in a new set of government-induced problems.

Economic liberalism is that set of ideas which advocates the greatest possible use of markets and the forces of competition to allocate scarce resources.

However, for an alternative group of free-market, neo-liberal economists, the problems of the UK and other economies have been viewed in terms of too much, rather than too little government involvement in the economy: not market failure, but government failure.

Government failure, in this sense, may be viewed as a situation in which government intervention leads to worse economic outcomes than if no such intervention had taken place, such that the attempt to correct market failure merely results in the emergence of a new set of problems.

For this group of economists market disorders are externally generated, and their vision of the economy is essentially one of efficient, freely operating markets which are only obstructed by outside or external factors, such as 'meddling' Keynesian governments or 'ungentlemanly' trade unions.

After 1945, the consensus throughout the western world, under the influence of the 'Keynesian Revolution', was very much that governments had a large and dominant role to play in the management of market economies, and there were few voices raised against this view during this period. However, for a small number of thinkers, most notably the Austrian economists, Ludwig von Mises and Friedrich von Hayek, and later the American economist, Milton Friedman, the West was seen as disastrously careering down the road to socialism, and they set about reviving the ideas of economic liberalism – essentially a belief in laissez-faire and freely operating markets, unhampered by state intervention. For these thinkers, the 'middle way' offered by Keynesian demand management was a form of 'creeping disease' which could only ultimately lead to economic ruin: the primary responsibilities of government were to preserve individual liberties and the system of private property ownership, which was perceived as being both a moral good and a necessity for progress and prosperity. The Conservative Government, led by Margaret Thatcher, which was elected to office in 1979, was very much committed to these right-wing, pro-market ideas, and from the outset they set about implementing them.

Reasons for government failure

Free market, laissez-faire economists might view government failure from a number of standpoints:
- imperfect information;
- welfarism;
- the growth of state bureaucracy and the erosion of individual liberties;
- conflict of objectives;
- regulatory capture;
- distortions of individual markets.

We shall consider each of these in turn, and in addition, we shall also briefly discuss the Marxist perspective on government failure.

Imperfect information

A particularly influential case against government intervention in economic matters was made by Friedrich von Hayek in a famous article, published in 1945, called 'The use of knowledge in society' (see Focus 3.20, which contains extracts from this article). Hayek was concerned with the familiar economic problem of how scarce resources could best be allocated amongst alternate uses; i.e. through the price system or through central planning. For Hayek, the best method would be that which was most effectively able to use knowledge about people's preferences and about the resources and opportunities available to satisfy them.

This knowledge or information would, according to Hayek, be widely dispersed amongst many different people – each consumer is aware of what it is that he or she wants and their relative personal valuation of various goods and services; similarly, employers and workers possess unique knowledge about their own particular occupations. As no government could possibly have all this infinite knowledge at its disposal, planning would necessarily be based upon highly imperfect information, and government's attempts to perform the resource allocating function would inevitably be doomed to failure.

By contrast, Hayek believed that the price system would continuously coordinate this vast array of dispersed information, and our ever-changing valuations, so that society as a whole could make efficient use of its resources – a free market system would facilitate the satisfaction of existing and new human wants better than any other system known to man; a view that we shall now examine in a little more detail.

In Chapter 2, we discussed central planning as an alternative resource allocating system. The fact that this system suffered total collapse in the Soviet Union and Eastern Europe during the late 1980s and early 1990s is cited by market-orientated economists as the ultimate example of government failure. However, it could be argued that this view is something of an oversimplification: first, the government failures of Communism have now been replaced by a variety of market failures, including high levels of inflation, unemployment and widespread poverty, as well as the emergence of a 'Mafia economy' in which criminalised, unofficial markets, racketeering, extortion and speculation are rife; secondly, it is inaccurate to say that Soviet style central planning was a failure in all respects – there were aspects of the system that were highly successful; this point has been well illustrated by the American economist, John Kenneth Galbraith (see Box 20.1).

BOX 20.1

Central planning

The Soviet economic system and that of the Eastern European acolytes were, indeed, both strong and weak. The basic error in analysing them was in generalisation. Their strength, especially in the Soviet Union, was in basic or heavy industry: steel, petroleum, electricity, transport, chemicals and, needless to say, armaments. In the more than forty years since World War II, the Soviet Union had established itself as an industrial and military power second only to the United States. There were now two superpowers in the world, and the Soviet Union was assuredly one of them. That was no slight achievement.

For heavy industry and armaments, the Soviet command and control system worked with obvious efficiency. The orders went out from Moscow; supplies and components were allocated; finished products appeared and were used. Industrial planning served well, and from this emerged the economic development within the Soviet Union that was visible to the rest of the world. From this also came, quite plausibly, some of the apprehension on the part of those outside. Widely overlooked were those areas of inadequacy and failure that remained and how they affected public attitudes within the country.

The principal failures were in meeting the needs of the Soviet consumer and in agriculture. The successful consumer economy produces or requires a disconcerting number of goods and services. The goods are not only numerous but varied as to nature, style and design and unstable as to demand. The required services are varied as to training and preparation and unstable as to use. The Communist central planning system that worked adequately for steel, chemicals, tanks and nuclear weaponry did not work for consumer goods; it was too rigid and unyielding, incapable of accommodating to variety and change. Thus the inadequacy of the resulting products and services – clothing, house furnishings, restaurants, repair work, entertainment, much else.

Source: Adapted from John Kenneth Galbraith, **The World Economy Since the Wars. A Personal View** *(Sinclair Stevenson, 1994).*

The eulogising of the unfettered free market has led the disciples of Hayek, as well as such organisations as the World Bank and the International Monetary Fund (IMF), to claim that the only route to economic success is via the unregulated price mechanism.

However, as Paul Ormerod (Box 20.2) and the *New Internationalist* (Box 20.3) point out, most of the successful 'market' economies have been those that have experienced substantial levels of state intervention.

BOX 20.2

State intervention in the 'free market'

The advice to follow pure free-market policies seems to be contrary to the lessons of virtually the whole of economic history since the Industrial Revolution. With the possible exception of the first wave of industrialisation in Britain, every country which has moved into the strong sustained growth which distinguishes industrial, or post-industrial, societies from every other society in human history, has done so in outright violation of pure, free-market principles.

Markets, competition and entrepreneurship are all very important, but by themselves they are not enough. Infant industries – even when they have become industrial giants – have sheltered behind tariff barriers; government subsidiaries have been widespread; there has been active state intervention in the economy; and, perhaps most important of all, successful companies have exercised power and control over their markets. Even Far Eastern economies such as South Korea and Singapore, which are held up as models of free-market principles, do not in practice conform to the ideal. The governments of these countries possess a degree of internal power which is far greater than is the norm in Western societies, and they are not afraid to use it.

The World Bank brought out a report in the autumn of 1993 which attempted to challenge the idea that the success of the Far Eastern economies in general was due to extensive co-operation between the public and private sectors, and in particular the idea that government intervention in the economy had been successful. But even this report, which met a barrage of criticism from Far Eastern experts, was obliged to recognise that a key reason for the economic success of the countries was a high level of investment in education by the state, that policies to promote exports, which often involved protection of the domestic market, had worked, and that government intervention in financial markets to support industry had usually been successful.

*Source: Paul Ormerod, **The Death of Economics** (Faber, 1994).*

BOX 20.3

Simply... the alchemy of a miracle'

Spectacular rates of economic growth are spreading from the four tigers of Asia (Singapore, Taiwan, South Korea and Hong Kong) to their Asian neighbours, particularly Thailand and Malaysia. The chemistry of this economic success is a hotly debated topic. Some, like the IMF and World Bank, put it down to the magic of the market. Others point to a heavy government hand behind the emphasis on growth through exports. *NI* looks at the East Asian economic sorcery and finds the reasons for success are not easily separated from the costs of high-speed industrialisation.

RIGGING THE TRADE GAME

'Export at all costs!' is the first commandment of Asia's new miracle economies. Exports like Hyundai cars and Taiwanese electronics are subsidized from the public purse and often sold at low profit margins in order to gain 'market share' and the allegiance of foreign consumers. Undervalued currencies are another way in which Taiwan and the other 'tiger' economies have made sure their exports were cheap and

BOX 20.3

imports too expensive for local consumers. Domestic economies are heavily protected. In South Korea, for instance, almost no-one drives a car that is not made in Korea. And the code for foreign investors is one of the strictest in the world.

COMMAND ECONOMY

Despite eulogies to the market by its partisans, the Asian economic 'miracle' is the product of a highly interventionist state. The use of subsidies to underwrite otherwise uneconomic exports, the control of finance and foreign exchange, centralized economic planning and a large public sector (particularly in Taiwan) are typical of the 'tiger' economies. In its heyday the powerful Economic Planning Board in Seoul could make or break the large 'Chaebol' enterprises that dominate the Korean economy. Rather than reflections of pure market logic, 'tiger' economics has achieved success by 'getting the prices wrong' – through the manipulation of credit and the supply of foreign exchange to achieve export growth.

LAND REFORM

Both Taiwan and South Korea underwent far-reaching land reforms in the 1950s. In South Korea it was to counter the appeal of the Communists; in Taiwan to break the power of the indigenous landed élite so that the mainland nationalist Chinese could take over. Land reform in both places boosted support for the government among small farmers. And, given the precarious economics of small-plot agriculture, a growing pool of cheap labour left the countryside for the cities and export-processing zones. The landlord class that stood as a block to industrial development in Latin America was eliminated early in East Asia.

PLANNED CITIES

Both Singapore and Hong Kong have had several key advantages. As city-states they have been able to control the migration of poor rural dwellers that has overwhelmed almost all other Third World cities. They have taken in workers in boom times and expelled them when they were no longer needed. Their location has also made these two bustling ports into centres of financial and communication services for their surrounding regions.

AUTOCRATIC GOVERNMENT

Three of the Four Tiger societies have not bothered much with the niceties of human rights – being particularly harsh on political opposition and workers organizing independent unions for better wages and working conditions. Singapore's jails are home to some of the world's longest-serving political prisoners. The Korean military massacred hundreds of protesters in the ancient city of Kwangju as recently as 1980. Only in Hong Kong has there been relative political tolerance, although no right to democratic government.

COLD WAR AID

In the early period of their industrial take-off both Taiwan and South Korea, the cornerstones of US anti-Communist strategy in Asia, were recipients of lavish economic and military aid. In the 1950s this aid was equivalent to 95 per cent of Taiwan's trade surplus. Between 1945 and 1978 South Korea got almost six billion dollars in US

BOX 20.3

economic aid, almost as much as all of Africa. This aid helped build up the infrastructure of modern export economies.

HARD WORK

Workers in the East Asian miracle economies work some of the longest hours in the world. Many in South Korea still work 10 or 12 hours a day with one of the highest rates of industrial accidents in the world. In Hong Kong just one week's annual leave for industrial workers is common. With the exception of Hong Kong, organizing independent unions is difficult. In Taiwan and South Korea, company unions have been the norm until very recently. In Singapore the very tight police surveillance on a small island makes democratic unionism an impossibility.

SPOILING NATURE

The environmental costs of boom times have been borne by the ecosystems and citizens of Taiwan and South Korea. The Nakdong and Han rivers in Korea are both badly polluted with industrial waste. Chemical agriculture has poisoned land and water, particularly in densely populated Taiwan where cancer rates have doubled over the last 30 years. It is already the leading cause of death. Both Korea and Taiwan are committed to massive expansion of an already heavy reliance on nuclear power. Urban air quality is so bad in Taipei that motorcyclists commonly wear surgical masks.

Source: **New Internationalist** (January 1995).

The problem of welfarism

Free-market economists would also cite attempts by the state at providing welfare systems as another example of government failure (see Chapters 19, 31 and 32). Apart from causing disincentive/distortive effects, such economists also believe that direct government provision of health and education has a number of adverse consequences – not only is such provision seen as being unresponsive to market forces, and therefore inefficient, but also as something which is likely to create large, unresponsive monopoly suppliers with a tendency to spawn a variety of powerful pressure groups, which would transform the welfare state into a tangle of selfish interests.

The following article by John Molyneux (Box 20.4) considers some of these arguments:

BOX 20.4

Dependent on welfare?

Welfare is bad for you, according to right wingers here and in the United States. Politicians like Republican House of Representatives leader Newt Gingrich argue that welfare leads to a "culture of dependency" where people rely on the state rather than provide for themselves.

In Britain Tories like Michael Portillo and Peter Lilley put a similar argument.
Now, increasingly, Tony Blair's "New Labour" echoes the same theme – talking of people needing "a hand up, not a handout".

The argument runs like this – "welfare dependency" means young men becoming unwilling to work, young women have babies outside marriage, and their kids turn to drugs and crime.

People lose their dignity and self respect, we are told. Morale and morality collapse, society spirals into chaos and it is all the fault of a "nanny state" and its handouts.

Of course, being unemployed, signing on and scraping to get by on the dole is demoralising.

It is far better to have a job and a decent wage.
Similarly, single mothers would undoubtedly benefit from being able to afford childcare and to pursue careers instead of struggling to survive on income support.
But this is not what the right wingers who attack welfare, or the Labour figures who echo their arguments, mean.

They think the unemployed, single mothers and everyone else in need should have benefits reduced or removed. They reckon it would do the poor good to be thrust even deeper into poverty.

If it were not so serious it would be laughable.

Why not suggest that people suffering from malnutrition be cured of bad eating habits by a dose of starvation?

Unfortunately, these callous monsters have power. Therefore we need to have arguments against the propaganda that accompanies these attacks.
An obvious point is that the very people who attack what they call "welfare dependency" are responsible for the unemployment and cuts which leave people on the dole or benefits.

On a plate

These politicians attack single mothers on benefit, but then shut down nurseries, so forcing many to give up jobs and college courses. Another obvious point is that the right are very selective in their opposition to handouts. They never argue that the inheritance of wealth should be abolished because it is bad for the children of the rich to receive such large sums on a plate. Nor do they argue that getting all that money from the civil list is damaging for the royal family.

Somehow it is only "the lower orders" who are led astray by the smallest giro.

The crux of the matter, however, is the idea that the unemployed, single mothers and other claimants voluntarily place themselves in this position, enticed by the prospects of state benefit.

BOX 20.4

This is pure prejudice. It is almost as stupid as claiming people injure themselves to get free NHS treatment.

What is more, it is completely contradicted by the facts. In the early 1930s, unemployment benefit was very low. But it did not stop there being mass unemployment. In the late 1940s and 1950s benefit was higher in relation to average wages. But unemployment was almost non-existent.

The shift from near full employment to the mass unemployment of the last 15 years occurred in three big surges.

The first came in 1970–1, the second in 1975–6, and the third in 1979–82 immediately following the election of Thatcher.

None of these rises had anything to do with more generous benefits. On the contrary, the gap between benefits and average wages rose during this period.

Each surge in unemployment was caused by economic recession. Quite simply, mass unemployment is forced, not voluntary – and the right wing line against the welfare state is a vicious lie.

Cutting welfare penalises the victims of the system for being victims. It can only drive the poor further into despair and make it harder for them and their children to rejoin the mainstream workforce.

To a large extent this has already happened in America, where benefits are even lower than in Britain and where poverty on the scale of the Third World now exists in most inner cities.

The cuts being pushed through by Newt Gingrich will only make a terrible situation worse.

It is for us to ensure, through mass resistance, that their British co-thinkers do not get the chance to do the same thing here.

*Source: John Molyneux, **Socialist Worker** (11 February 1995).*

TASK 20.2

Critically assess the view that welfare leads to a 'culture of dependency' and induces people to rely on the state rather than themselves.

BOX 20.5

The growth of state bureaucracy and the erosion of individual liberties

Friedman

"The existence of a free market does not of course eliminate the need for government. On the contrary, government is essential both as a forum for determining the rules of the game and as an umpire to interpret and enforce the rules decided on.

What the market does is to reduce greatly the range of issues that must be decided through political means, and thereby to minimize the extent to which government need participate directly in the game. The characteristic feature of action through political channels is that it tends to require or enforce substantial conformity. The great advantage of the market, on the other hand, is that it permits wide diversity. It is, in political terms, a system of proportional representation. Each man can vote, as it were, for the colour of tie he wants and get it: he does not have to see what colour the majority wants and then, if he is in the minority, submit."

*Source: Milton Friedman, **Capitalism and Freedom** (Chicago University Press, 1962).*

Thatcher

"Freedom is indivisible. Once the state controls the means of production, distribution and exchange, all of us would become dependent on it." (1986).

Gray

"Hayek's insight is that against a background of stable laws, human individuals, left to their own devices, will produce an order spontaneously which is more complex and more stable than any which could be designed by the human mind. It's also an order...which embodies their purposes and their goals. The moral defence of the market is that it protects freedom and voluntary exchange: whereas the moral hazard of economic planning is that it subordinates the purposes of some to those of the rulers."
John Gray (Oxford University, 1989).

TASK 20.3

1 All three quotes equate 'freedom' with a market system. Explain the reasons that the authors would be likely to give for this.
2 In what ways might a market system not lead to greater 'freedom' for all?

As well as viewing central planning as the example *par excellence* of government-induced economic failure, Hayek and his followers have seen state intervention in the economy as leading down the road to political ruin – government attempts to correct market failure, it is argued, would inevitably lead to an erosion of peoples' individual freedoms and to a totalitarian state: only free-market capitalism can ensure the existence of political liberties.

The experience of the former Communist-bloc countries of Eastern Europe is frequently cited as proof of this argument. However, whilst it is without doubt the case that the latter, 'Stalinist' system did involve an enormous loss of human rights, the converse argument that the free market automatically guarantees human rights simply cannot be sustained: some of the most grotesque abuses of human freedom have occurred in market economies; the cases of Hitler's Germany, Franco's Spain, Pinochet's Chile and Suharto's Indonesia are but a few examples; history has not to date established any clear-cut, causal relationship between type of economic system and political liberties – human freedoms have been widely denied under both market and centrally planned systems.

Moreover, when the followers of Hayek and Friedman talk of 'freedom', the question has to be asked, 'freedom for whom?'; and the answer is, inevitably, 'freedom for those who can pay'. As we explained in Chapter 12, the price system is frequently described as a 'consumers' democracy', in which the demand for goods and services acts as a 'voting' system, determining the way in which society's scarce resources should be used. However, with an unequal distribution of income, as exists in most capitalist economies, the rich will tend to have very much more 'freedom' than the poor: a freedom to buy the goods and services of their choice; furthermore, the important freedoms from such factors as poverty, insecurity, malnutrition and unemployment are rarely considered in the market notion of freedom.

Since 1979, successive Conservative Governments in the UK have been greatly influenced by the ideas of Hayek and Friedman, and have in theory been very much in favour of 'rolling back' the powers of the state in order to reduce bureaucracy and promote individual 'freedoms'. However, whilst the privatisation programme has certainly diminished the degree of state ownership of industry, the growth of QUANGOS (quasi autonomous non-governmental), of which there is now one for every 10,000 people in the UK, has, ironically, substantially increased the extent of bureaucracy in the economy and decreased local democracy. Box 20.6 considers this matter in some detail.

BOX 20.6

The QUANGO *quagmire*

Tony Wright

A few weeks ago I turned up at the monthly meeting of my local NHS trust. I had gone along with the League of Friends at our hospital to ask about the closure of some wards. We were told, ever so politely, that we were not allowed to ask questions and that we were lucky to be allowed there at all. That is one face of the quango state transforming government in Britain.

Another face is the one recently described by the House of Commons public accounts committee, which in an unprecedented report drawing on a series of appalling cases of mismanagement and corruption, declares that standards in the conduct of public business are at their lowest ebb in all the 140 years since the Northcote-Trevelyan reforms had cleaned up the Civil Service and buried the old patronage state. Now a new patronage state is being created, as much in need of democratic attention as its 18th century predecessor.

Its terrain is quangoland. It is extraordinary that the first Thatcher government crusaded against the quangos of the corporate state. Indeed, the assertion is still being made that quangos have had their wings clipped since 1979. A casual reader of *Public Bodies*, the annual compendium of the appointed state, or a careless listener to William Waldegrave, might be inclined to take the assertion at face value.

Yet the official picture is a distortion. It neglects all the grant-maintained schools, NHS trusts and, crucially, all those bodies that have been given a semi-private character (notably the training and enterprise councils) and those that (like housing associations and further-education corporations) have replaced elected local governments in the provision of key services. Once all those structures of appointed government are counted in the picture begins to look sharply different. Some of us have been trying, especially through a vast enterprise of parliamentary questions, to map this unelected state. The results are published today.*

They reveal that nearly a third of all public expenditure – some £46.6 billion in 1993 – is now being channelled through the appointed and contracted-out state. There are some 5,521 quangos (three times the official figures) and over 70,000 quangocrats put there by ministerial appointment (compared to 25,000 elected councillors). Our study shows, in devastating detail, the democratic deficit that lies at its heart. For each body we asked a range of questions in order to compile an accountability index (for example: Does the body meet in public? Are its papers available to the public? Is there a register of members and a register of interests? Is it subject to effective audit?) The answers disclosed inadequate scrutiny and minimal accountability. It is not surprising that this is a world that generates a growing saga of financial irregularity, waste of public resources, and cronyism.

It is a world that demands to be constitutionalised. The fact that it is not tells us much about the political order in Britain. The almost daily appointment scandals (today it is the appointment of two former Tory MPs to the Government's deregulation panel, before that it was the appointment of a Tory businessman to run the Schools Funding Agency, and before that...) are just the expression of a system in which ministerial patronage can be liberally deployed without any scrutiny beyond that of public opprobrium. This was the same system that was in place in the pre-1979 world when quangoland was the preserve of the Great and the Good, the domain of superannuated civil servants, university professors and members of the TUC, but the territory has been expanded and mobilised to carry forward the ideological ambitions of politicians who have confused the public interest with their own interests. There is a nice sentence in one internal government review of the public-appointments system which points to the abundant opportunities for ministers to use public bodies to press forward their political purposes.

BOX 20.6

The temptation for the Labour Party is to follow the same example, and replace the quangocrats with politically acceptable alternatives. In some areas, Labour should have no hesitation in succumbing to that temptation (especially in the health service). But the real task is to constitutionalise the appointive state (and the state itself). The partisan expansion of the quango state has been possible only because there exist such inadequate checks on what governments can get away with. Any serious assault on quangoland therefore becomes a much larger assault on the political system that is its precondition.

The whole process of ministerial appointment to public bodies needs to be overhauled, with a role for a Public Appointments Commission and a ratification process for key appointments by parliamentary select committees. Some appointed bodies will be replaced by elected bodies, others at least by an elective element. Public registers of membership, and of interests, can be introduced. The arrangements for scrutiny, openness and audit can be made subject to the test of public accountability. Administrative law can be used (as in the US and Australia) to underpin the procedures of these bodies in the public interest.

Hopefully, a Labour government will establish a Constitutional and Administrative Commission to provide the standing machinery for constitutional and administrative reforms, for the absence of such a mechanism – again unlike elsewhere – is both a characteristic expression of the unregulated system we have and a crucial absence in terms of a reform agenda.

Finally, it must be remembered that the quangoid growth since 1979 is part of a whole consumerist approach to public services and to government itself. Accountability has been redefined away from politics and towards the market. It is the end of politics with a vengeance. It is a world in which nobody is responsible for anything any more, with individual consumers left to claim their "rights" in an irresponsible public market place of quangos, contractors, providers and purchasers.

The challenge for Labour, though, is not to return to a *status quo ante* in the provision of public services but to build a complementary system of both political and consumer accountability. The choice is not citizen or consumer but citizen and consumer. Thus the Citizens' Charter should not simply be dismissed as a cosmetic irrelevance but trumped by grounding it in enforceable rights for citizen-consumers. In constitutionalising the quango state, Labour can embark on the democratic renewal of the British *ancien régime* itself.

* Ego Trip: *Extra-governmental Organisations in the UK And Their Accountability*, edited by Stuart Weir and Wendy Hall, published by Democratic Audit and Charter 88 Trust, £9.95. Exmouth House, 3-11 Pine Street, London EC1R OJH

Tony Wright is Labour MP for Cannock and Burntwood.

Source: **Guardian** (24 May 1994).

Conflict of objectives

Public choice theory is the body of theory which assumes that politicians and state officials behave so as to maximise their own self-interest, rather than seeking what is best for society as a whole.

The likelihood of a conflict of policy objectives is another strand to the argument that state interference in markets will inevitably lead to government failure. This view can be considered at a macro and micro level. At a macro level, it is argued that interventionist policies will: inevitably fail because the quality of statistical information available to governments is simply not suitable for making the right decisions; and lead to clashes or conflicts between the major goals of economic policy, i.e. between full employment, stable prices, satisfactory economic growth and the balance of payments.

At a more micro level, proponents of the government failure school of thought argue that, whilst politicians might popularly be viewed as altruistic and always seeking to achieve the best for the citizens, the reality might be considerably different – politicians and government departments might be primarily motivated by their own political and personal objectives. This is known as public choice theory.

In the words of Gordon Tullock (Hobart Paperback 9, Institute of Economic Affairs), 'the vote motive in politics is the profit motive in industry'. Thus, instead of serving the public good, politicians may prioritise: the winning of elections, for instance by cutting taxes at strategic points in time to curry favour with the electorate; personal aggrandisement, sexual conquests and 'empire building'; or even personal financial gain, for example by advocating the privatisation of a particular industry, and then taking up a lucrative position on the board of directors of the company. Box 20.7 considers some of these points:

BOX 20.7

Government as it is

William C. Mitchell

1 Since collective choice in the unpriced political process divorces costs from benefits, it is likely to be less efficient than individual choice in the market process where the price mechanism forces the chooser to absorb most, if not all, benefits and costs. Since no-one in politics knows the price of anything, the political allocation of scarce resources is rarely efficient.

2 Most political scientists are at best only dimly aware of the differences in the interconnections between demand and price in state and private consumption and use of resources. This ignorance produces political proposals for the allocation of resources based on 'need' or 'priorities' that are arbitrary, politicised substitutes for pricing.

3 Politicians who plan to pay for 'needs' with other people's money create 'priorities' that are little more than wish-lists that the political process cannot turn into informed, responsible investment decisions.

4 Conventional political science sees politicians and bureaucrats as official altruists; public choice sees them as self-interested utility-maximisers. It does not follow that

BOX 20.7

political people do not serve the public weal, but that it usually takes second place to the personal urge to political survival and power.

5 Political suppliers differ in four main fundamentals from market suppliers. They possess no property rights in their office; do not derive profit from successful activity; must trade with other political suppliers without a currency; and are elected for fixed terms. Such attenuated political markets tend towards politically rational but publicly irrational decisions and choices.

6 The politician characteristically asks not how much consumers value government services sufficiently to pay for them, but how many voters value them enough to vote for him. He considers not the total benefits he can create and their costs, but their distribution among voters.

7 The bureaucrat influences or controls both the supply of and the demand for his service. This unique power will hardly go long unused, because his virtual monopoly of information induces him to over-state the benefit and under-state the costs of the government services that require his participation and buttress his authority.

8 Interest groups press for privileges for themselves, not to end the privileges of others, even if ending privileges creates equal benefits. Politicians find more votes in granting privileges than in cancelling them, even if cancellation does more good.

9 Political science studies the character and temperament of politicians. Public choice analysts do not put alteration in human nature on the political agenda. Nor do they conclude that changing political decision-makers will make much fundamental difference to the efficiency of government.

10 The pathology of politics is far-reaching. The preferences of citizens are never faithfully represented. They are dishonoured because voters are ('rationally') ignorant in policies on production, which they cannot influence or understand, but are well-informed on distributist policies that bring personal gain. Politics is mostly remote from everyday life; political promises evaporate; market products are familiar and can be tested. Politicians, more than businessmen, can exaggerate, obfuscate and suppress relevant information.

11 Politicians act irresponsibly because their products cannot be costed by comparison, and monitoring costs are higher in the political than in the market process. Protest by rejection or escape by exit (emigration) is less feasible or prohibitively more costly than in the competitive market.

12 Voters' preferences can be misrepresented by bureaucratic obstruction and misinterpretation because bureaucrats can influence politicians by timing, withholding or 'processing' information.

Source: **Summary of Hobart Paper**, 109 (IEA,).

Regulatory capture

In Chapters 3.16 and 3.17, we explained how regulatory bodies such as OFTEL and OFGAS have been established to oversee the activities of the privatised utilities. One of the main criticisms of this system of control is that the phenomenon of regulatory capture may occur. We previously defined this as a situation in which the regulator operates in the interests of the monopolist, rather than seeking to protect those of the consumer – over time the regulator may be 'captured' by senior managers and manipulated to accept their values and view of the

world, which may be at odds with consumers' and society's interests. Free-market economists would view this as yet another example of government failure, and would argue that, provided there is sufficient potential for competition within an industry, the government should confine itself to ensuring market contestability through the use of deregulatory policies designed to remove barriers to entry and exit, rather than interfering with the pricing and output policies of firms. Look at Box 20.8.

BOX 20.8

The INVESTIGATOR

Oftel challenged to ditch telecom controls regime

Sir Iain Vallance, chairman of British Telecom, citing the degree of competition which now existed within the industry, has challenged OFTEL, the industry regulator, to abandon its main regulatory controls.

Pointing to the excellent job that telecom regulators had done in fostering competition and innovation, providing Britain with a world-beating telecom industry, Sir Iain said: 'What is now needed is a clear and simple vision of where regulation is set to take us.'

He argued that the regulators should make a commitment towards deregulation of all retail activity from 1997, at which time the current price regime forcing BT to cut its prices expires.

'There should be no price caps and no

constraints on pricing structures beyond normal competition law,' he said.

Sir Iain argued for time limits to be put on measures to aid new competitors to enter the UK market, where more operators, are more active, at more levels in the market than in any other nation.

'The UK has succeeded in attracting substantial investment from British and foreign entrepreneurs... market entry does not seem to be a problem.' Indeed some markets, for example, the City of London where BT, Mercury, MFS, Videotron, Sprint and others are investing in fibre infra structure, might even be showing signs of congestion and overcrowding.

TASK 20.4

Critically evaluate Sir Iain Vallance's view that, in relation to British Telecom, there should be no price caps, and no constraints on pricing structure beyond normal competition law.

Distortions of individual markets

State intervention in particular markets may take a variety of forms, most of which, according to laissez faire economists, are likely to result in government failure; ie a worsening of the situation.

For instance, the government may decide to grant a subsidy to a particular industry. We discussed the general arguments for and against subsidies in Chapter 17. Free market economists would, of course, mainly emphasise the ill-effects of subsidies in terms of, for example, interfering with the free interplay of market forces and thus misallocating resources, allowing 'lame ducks' to survive and the need for higher taxation.

Similarly, governments may intervene in particular markets through price fixing: either a maximum price set below the equilibrium, or a minimum price established above the equilibrium. As we have seen, the general problem of maximum prices is that they tend to create market shortages, and conversely, the general problem of minimum prices is that they tend to create market surpluses (see Section 2).

The Marxist or radical perspective

BOX 20.9	**Two simple truths**

Two simple truths

There are two simple truths about the world we live in: exploitation and class. The rich are rich not because of their ability, or because they allow so much to 'trickle down', or for any other reason save that they have robbed other people's labour.

There would be no wealth at all if no one worked. Labour is essential to everything that is produced. The rich have got rich because they have swiped a proportion of the value of the workers' labour, and because they use that surplus for one purpose only: to increase their own wealth, power and privilege.

This exploitation of labour, by a class of people who have grown rich because of it, is as central a characteristic of society today as it ever was. The 'market' is the economic mechanism by which this system works. It claims to be able to identify what is wanted or needed, and then to produce it. It claims an 'economic discipline' which only produces where a profit can be made. If something makes a profit, it is selling and therefore it is needed. If it doesn't make a profit, it isn't needed or wanted and therefore shouldn't be made.

You may of course need something very badly, but not have the money to buy it – in which case you don't count in the market. Millions of starving people are in this predicament.

BOX 20.9

The market is driven not by reason or need, but by irrationality and greed. In each new burst of investment workers are taken on, and there is a short boom. When the investment is over, workers are laid off and more goods come on the market at prices they can't afford. So there is a slump.

Marx described the market system as a mixture of despotism and anarchy. The anarchy can be seen all over the world today. Vast investment programmes during booms are suddenly scrapped in slump, and whole communities are wrecked in the process. Since the central drive of the market is to enrich the rich at others' expense, its madness and megalomania rivals that of any gang of rulers in all history.

Source: Adapted from Paul Foot, 'The Case for Socialism' Socialist Worker (1990).

Those viewing the world from a Marxist perspective would reject both the 'market failure' approach of Keynesian interventionist economists and the 'government failure' approach of the free-market, neo-liberal economists (also known as monetarists or supply-siders).

Interventionist and free-market economists both accept capitalism as the best economic system known to man, but with fundamental differences as to how to get the best results from it. Interventionists see the problems of capitalism in terms of various internal market imperfections, e.g. the existence of externalities, monopolies and volatile business cycles, which can best be remedied by appropriate forms of state involvement in markets. Laissez-faire economists, on the other hand, view government intervention as the major cause of capitalism's problems, and believe that unrestrained self-interest and freely operating markets offer the only way of promoting the public good. For Marxists, however, capitalism itself is the problem – it is seen as a system which is based upon unequal power relations, the exploitation of one class by another and therefore upon intrinsic inequality; as a system which is inherently unstable and whose entire history has been characterised by periodic economic crises; as a system whose central drive for profit and capital accumulation will inevitably threaten the environment and the prospect of peace between nations; and as a system which, in spite of its vast productive powers, will never adequately feed and house the majority of the world's peoples.

From this perspective, therefore, the only long-run solution to the great problems of poverty, inequality, unemployment, economic instability and environmental destruction would be to replace capitalism by socialism – at best Keynesian interventionist policies would only alleviate temporarily the worst excesses of the market system and humanise it a little, whilst the laissez-faire solution of non-government intervention and allowing market forces completely free rein would be likely to lead to more economic instability, greater disparities between rich and poor and ever greater misery for the mass of the world's people.

In this chapter, we have investigated the various strands of the idea that whenever the state attempts to improve the operation of the free market it makes things worse. We have discussed the different possible theoretical perspectives on this topic, and in so doing have attempted to convey to the reader the rich diversity of thought which forms the fabric of economics as an academic discipline and which, for us, makes it such a lively and exciting subject to study. We would like to think that our readers are beginning to feel the same way!

SOCIALLY REGULATED CAPITALISM does best

DEBATE   Len Doyal and Ian Gough

Which sort of economic system best contributes to human welfare? We believe a mixed one provides the best framework – and that this is borne out when we survey different nations' successes or failures. Today, socially regulated corporatist capitalism is the most successful model.

There can hardly be a more important question in political economy, but orthodox economists have little to say about it. They usually equate welfare with subjective wants, not objective needs.

But the hard-pressed adjust their wants downwards to cope with life; the affluent have new wants created for them. Want satisfaction cannot provide a metric to compare the welfare of different societies.

Our book contests the dominant relativist currents in philosophy and social science. We develop a notion of human need that is objective and cross-cultural. Basic needs for us are those that enable participation in one's social life – physical health and autonomy – mental health, cognitive skills and social opportunities.

They can be satisfied by a variety of goods, services, activities and relationships – "need satisfiers". Yet we can isolate common characteristics of satisfiers – "intermediate needs" which contribute to health and autonomy.

These include adequate food, health care, basic education and physical security. In this way a set of cross-cultural social indicators can be constructed.

In our book we develop a set of procedural and material pre-conditions that would enable a society to prioritise and distribute the most appropriate need satisfiers. We can then see how well different economic systems meet these pre-conditions.

Two extreme forms of economy will fare badly. Free-market capitalism has no system for identifying common human needs (as opposed to wants) and provides no way of granting people the need satisfiers they require. It encounters market failures and cannot foster community-based forms of provision.

State socialism ends up with very different pros and cons, but a similar bottom line. A "dictatorship over needs'' prioritises meeting needs, but distorts their definition to suit the interests of party or bureaucrats. Social rights are not accompanied by political rights, and information and motivation failures distort delivery of the most basic satisfiers.

Neither of these systems embodies our notion of human need – mixed systems offer a better prospect. Here the market, the state and "negotiated co-ordination" can each make an appropriate contribution. Mixed systems can operate with private or public ownership of the means of production, but only capitalist forms are considered here.

Statist capitalism has the potential to correct for the tunnel vision and failures of the market, but it runs the risk of authoritarianism, clientelism and bureaucracy.

Corporatist capitalism, on the other hand, permits the dominant market mechanism to be regulated by government action and collectively-negotiated agreements, and so has the potential to overcome market and state failures but unorganised groups are in danger of being excluded from the corporatist decision-makers.

Nonetheless, our view is that the weight of argument favours corporatist capitalism on both procedural and material grounds, and within this category it favours social over liberal corporatism. Neo-liberal capitalism – a combination of "free market and strong state" – is bereft of the countervailing power of both public authority and networks of public co-operation, and is the least suitable framework, while statist capitalism is indeterminate.

What can research on real-world differences in need-satisfaction contribute to this debate? We know that country levels of welfare vary on average with national income per head, but there are exceptions to this rule.

Can we discern the causes of national variations in human well-being? Ian Gough recently fed in need indicators and economic,

social and political variables for all 128 rich and poor countries with a population of over one million around 1990.

Only mixed capitalist economies were found to be associated with higher need satisfaction levels: neither free market capitalism nor state socialism showed up positive. But many other factors are significant, including national and political independence, the tax capacity and spending priorities of the state, the level of democracy and human rights, and relative gender equality.

These are encouraging findings. They suggest that economic development contributes most to welfare when guided by an effective public authority that guarantees civil, political and social rights to all and is thus open to pressure by effective political mobilisation.

Of course, things are grim in many parts of the real world today but it should not be an excuse for despair. Other countries have achieved unprecedented gains in need satisfaction. Our results are clear; it is those socially regulated forms of capitalism which do best.

This is a summary of part of the Deutscher lecture to be delivered at the LSE tonight by Len Doyal and Ian Gough following the award of the Deutscher prize for their book *A Theory of Human Need* (Macmillan, 1991).
*Source: **Guardian** (21 December 1994).*

1 Explain the authors' distinction between 'subjective wants' and 'objective needs'.
2 Why do the authors believe that the 'two extreme forms of economy will fare badly', and that mixed capitalist economies will perform best?
3 Do you agree with the authors' conclusion? Give reasons for your answer.

Section 4
National Issues

4.21 Does spending lead to prosperity?

4.21

Spending and prosperity

There has been a clear set-back to hopes that the UK economy would move out of recession. Recovery remains heavily dependent on the consumer, whose confidence has been affected by debt overhang, high unemployment and the falling house prices. Indices of consumer confidence have been pointing to a consumer-led recovery for some months but surveys now suggest it is slipping again.'

*Source: Based on **Barclays Economic Review,** (August 1992).*

High street spending rose 1.1% in the first quarter and should now be underpinned by an upturn in the housing market. We now envisage economic expansion of around 3% per annum for the next three years. However we do not see rising inflation because there is unlikely to be pressure on capacity and tightness in labour markets for several years.

*Source: Based on **Barclays Economic Review,** (Spring 1994).*

The Chancellor of the Exchequer says the latest economic figures are quite the best combination of circumstances pointing to sustainable expansion of output with low inflation which he can remember for a long time. But some commentators are saying the government should take action to stimulate spending now if recovery is to continue.

*Source: **National newspaper reports** (July 1994).*

Latest retail figures show the recovery in consumer spending is hesitant and fragile – this poses a threat to our prosperity

*Source: **Retail traders' spokesman,** (July 1995).*

Preview

In this chapter we shall investigate the following key areas:
- setting up a macroeconomic model;
- the Keynesian model;
- the classical model;
- the significance of the Phillips curve relationship;
- the concept of a non-accelerating inflation rate of unemployment (NAIRU);
- the significance of passive, adaptive and rational expectations;
- the 'new' classical model.

Debt overhang is a heavy, and often unexpected, level of debt.

Inflation is a persistent rise in the general level of prices.

A recession is a period when output in the economy turns down and unemployment rises.

As economists, what are we to make of the Focus 4.21 material, which suggests that the level of High Street spending can affect our prosperity? The idea is that more High Street spending would encourage firms to produce more output, leading to more jobs and higher incomes. This assumes that there is sufficient 'slack' in the economy, in terms of labour supplies and machine capacity, to deliver more jobs and output. However in the early 1990s the UK economy was certainly very slack, for it had been undergoing a recession.

As late as 1994 the economy was still estimated to be producing about 6% less than it could have at full capacity. So, provided there was sufficient slack in the economy, greater High Street spending could lead to an expansion of output which would leave people in broad terms 6% 'better off'.

Some economists believe however that – no matter how much slack in the economy there might be – any such gain in prosperity would inevitably be purely temporary. After a year or so it would evaporate in the form of higher prices, which might even damage the economy. So could higher spending help to increase prosperity – or would it lead to inflation? We shall be seeing that one group of economists, known as Keynesians, think that higher spending can deliver lasting prosperity. Another group, known as Classical economists, strongly disagree – any gains will be short-lived. That is what this chapter is about.

Microeconomics and macroeconomics

Microeconomics is the area of economics which deals with the behaviour of individual economic agents.

Macroeconomics is the area of economics which deals with aggregates of behaviour and the workings of the economy as a whole.

Aggregate demand is the level of planned total spending in the economy.

Aggregate supply is the total output of goods and services which businesses are willing to supply.

You will see that the extracts in the Focus look at the state of economic activity not in a particular industry but in the economy as a whole. This gives us an opportunity to remind ourselves of the distinction between microeconomics and macroeconomics.

'Micro' means 'small', and microeconomics is concerned with analysing the behaviour of economic agents 'close-up' in individual areas of the economy – for instance, how a particular firm sets about maximising profit, or why the price of coffee fluctuates so much. It is microeconomics which you have been mainly studying so far in this book. 'Macro', on the other hand, means 'large', and macroeconomics deals with the workings of the economy as a whole.

There is an important reason for dividing economics in this way: assumptions which we can make in microeconomics may not work in macroeconomics. In microeconomics we can often assume that there are self-regulating forces – for instance the inter-reaction of supply and demand – which bring about conditions of stable equilibrium. Thus a fall in the wages of say bricklayers would, other things remaining equal, lead to an extension in their demand and higher employment. However in macroeconomics this style of analysis could break down, since 'other things' may not remain equal. Hence a fall in the wages of employees in all industries might not lead to more jobs. This could be because cuts in wages in one job by reducing demand elsewhere, lead to falls, not gains, in overall output and employment. In microeconomics there will generally be a price which 'clears' the market. In macroeconomics, where we are dealing with inter-reactions and 'feedback' effects between aggregate demand and aggregate supply, this will not necessarily be the case.

Setting up a macroeconomic model

BOX 21.1

The circular flow of income

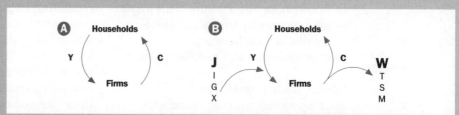

A illustrates a very simple model of the economy. We begin by classifying people as belonging to one of two groups: the 'business sector' (firms) and the 'personal sector' (households). These sectors interact with each other in two ways: there is (1) an employer/employee relationship, and (2) a producer/consumer relationship.
This means that

1 Households go out to work for firms. In other words, they provide factor services (labour, capital, land and enterprise). In return, they receive factor incomes (wages, interest, rent and profit). This gives us a flow of income (Y) from firms to households.
2 Households buy the output of firms, in the form of goods and services. In return there is a flow of consumption expenditure (C) from households to firms.

A 'circular flow' economy such as that in **A** would be one where all income is spent, and all spending becomes income. It would be in a state of 'equilibrium' because there would be no reason for national income either to increase or decrease. There would be no saving or investment, because there is no financial sector to receive or channel flows of money for these purposes. Without a government sector there would be no government spending or taxes. And this is a 'closed economy', i.e. one without international trade, so that there is no expenditure on imports, nor any income from exports.

B shows the effect on the model of introducing these three further sectors. We now have three injections (flows of income onto the circular flow): investment (I), government expenditure (G), and export earnings (X). We also have three withdrawals or leakages (income which is not passed on in the circular flow): saving (S), taxes (T), and import expenditure (M).

We can now see that this economy is no longer necessarily in equilibrium, because the flow of national income (Y) can increase or decrease, depending on the relative size of total planned injections (J), and total planned withdrawals (W). We can predict whether national income is likely to increase or decrease over a forthcoming time period.
    If W>J, then Y will fall;
    if W<J, then Y will increase.
If W=J, then Y will not change (the economy is in equilibrium).

Later in this chapter we will study the 'multiplier principle', which attempts to predict exactly how changes in W and J will affect Y.

*A **model** is a working scheme or hypothesis of how a system operates.*

Consumption is expenditure on consumer goods and services, mainly by households.

The Keynesian model is the macroeconomic model in which it is held that the levels of national output and employment are determined by both aggregate supply and aggregate demand.

Investment is expenditure on capital goods, mainly by businesses.

If we are to make sense of the immensely complex behaviour of the 'macroeconomy' we need a working scheme of how it operates: a model.

A model is made up of three elements:
● a system based on a set of simplifying assumptions;
● a hypothesis about the way the system works;
● a set of resulting predictions which can be used to test how well the model 'fits' the real world.

Models are judged on how successful they are in explaining the real world. Sooner or later evidence is likely to arise which contradicts the predictions of a model. It is then time to 'go back to the drawing board' and modify the model or construct a new one. The two models we shall be looking at in this chapter – Keynesian and classical – both use the concepts of aggregate demand and aggregate supply. The first of these terms refers to the level of planned total spending in the economy, the second to the total output of goods and services which businesses are willing to supply.

An increase in high street spending in the Keynesian model

In the Keynesian model an important role is played by aggregate demand, which consists of four components. First there is household consumption ('High Street spending'), the main component of aggregate demand. Secondly, there is investment expenditure on producer goods, such as factory buildings and machines. Thirdly there is government expenditure on goods and services. Fourthly there is the balance of exports over imports. In Keynes' model the level of national output – the amount of prosperity – is determined by the combined forces of aggregate supply and aggregate demand, as Box 21.3 demonstrates. Previously, economists had assumed that aggregate supply conditions alone would determine this. Some UK 'economic accounts' are shown in Box 21.11 on p 521.

BOX 21.2

The level of national output

National income can be defined as

The total value of factor incomes in one country in one year.

However, economists recognise that national income is created by the output of goods and services, and by expenditure on those goods and services. One person's expenditure is another person's income, and yet another person's output. Thus, if you purchase a new bicycle, this represents expenditure to you, but income to the seller; it also represents a quantity of output from the bicycle industry. Statisticians who calculate national income figures therefore use three methods:

● the expenditure method, which calculates the total amount of spending on goods and services;
● the output method, which estimates the total value of goods and services produced;
● the income method, which measures the total amount of incomes earned.

BOX 21.2

Economists and statisticians have developed the collection of national income accounts into a fine art; indeed, the comprehensiveness and reliability of a government's national income statistics could perhaps be regarded as one test of the 'economic development' of the country in question.

The published figures have two broad uses. First, they can be used to help to chart the economic progress of a country over time; second they can be used to help to compare the progress of different countries. In short, they can be used for both single-country comparisons and international comparisons.

A study of the National Income Blue Book of the UK Government, for example, reveals a wealth of economic data. There is information on spending patterns, earnings, investment, the balance of payments, and much more. Comparing such data with publications from, say, the Indian government would reveal many insights into the different nature of the two economies. In order to assist in such comparisons, economists have attempted over a number of years to standardise the methods of calculation and terminology used in the accounts. In theory, all three methods of calculation should give an identical total; in practice, a number of adjustments have to be made to bring them into equality.

National income is known in technical terms as net national product at factor cost.

- Within this phrase, the word 'product' draws attention to the fact that income is not a purely 'monetary' phenomenon; in other words, creating money does not necessarily create income. What does create income is the output of something real; the production of goods and services.
- The term 'factor cost' indicates that the value of the output is related to the cost of the factors of production used in production. This is not necessarily the same as thing as national product at 'market prices' since market prices can be increased above the level of their true factor cost by indirect taxes, or reduced by subsidies.
- The word 'net' indicates that depreciation or capital consumption has been taken into account. This is necessary because in the production of anything, there is some 'wear and tear' on producer goods, and some national expenditure therefore has to be devoted to the replacement of worn-out plant, machinery, and other items.
- Thus, net national product is invariably a lower figure than gross national product at factor cost, which includes expenditure on all types of investment goods, whether or not this investment is in additional capacity, or merely replaces old items.
- The word 'national' indicates that the figure includes net property income from abroad. This is income earned by assets situated in other countries, owned by domestic residents, less income earned by assets located in the domestic economy and paid to foreigners abroad. These flows of interest and profits arise from international investment. If, for example, a UK resident owns shares in a German chemical company, then the German plant contributes to German national income through providing output, income and employment in Germany; but it also contributes to the UK national income when dividends are paid to the British shareholder.
- Subtracting net property income from GNP gives gross domestic product (GDP) at factor cost; this is a measure of the total value of goods and services produced in a year within the geographical boundaries of a country.

What happens in the Keynesian model when an increase in 'High Street spending' takes place? In the Keynesian model when there is productive slack in the economy, aggregate supply is assumed to be infinitely 'elastic'. Hence when aggregate demand increases this leads to a proportionate improvement in national output with no change in the general price level. However at a very high level of economic activity with many firms operating close to the limit of their capacity, conditions of aggregate supply would become less elastic. A continuing expansion of aggregate demand would thus lead to rising prices and a smaller gain in output ('prosperity'). If aggregate demand were to expand to a level corresponding to full employment of capacity, aggregate supply would become totally inelastic. The effect would be purely one of rising prices, with no gain at all in prosperity. You can follow this Keynesian analysis in graphical terms in Box 21.3.

BOX 21.3

Aggregate demand and supply in the Keynesian model

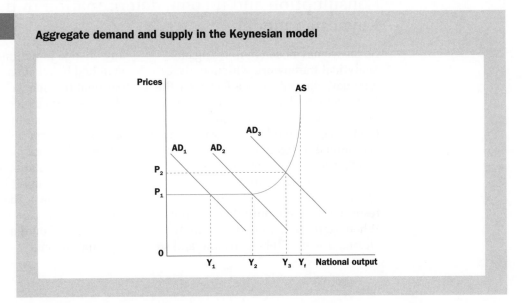

*The **real balance effect** is the change in the buying power of money held by households and businesses as the general price level rises or falls.*

In Box 21.3 the aggregate demand curve is seen to be downward sloping. The main reason for this is the real balance effect: as the general price level falls the buying power of money held by households and businesses increases, so aggregate spending on goods and services is likely to be higher.

The shape of the aggregate supply curve depends on the assumptions we make. As we saw, in the Keynesian model it is only partly upward sloping. At low levels of economic activity, when there is a lot of productive 'slack' in the economy, aggregate supply is assumed to be horizontal and infinitely 'elastic'. However as the level of economic activity rises, and firms operate closer to the limit of capacity, aggregate supply becomes increasingly inelastic. Assume now that aggregate demand in Box 21.3 increases from AD_1 to a new level AD_2. This leads to a proportionate improvement in national output from OY_1 to OY_2, and no change in the general price level. However when aggregate demand increases further, from AD_2 to AD_3, it encounters less elastic conditions of aggregate supply. The rise in national output is therefore less than for the first increase in demand (AD_1 to AD_2), and there is a rise in the price level, from OP_1 to OP_2. If the expansion of supply were to reach the point OY_f, corresponding to full employment of capacity, aggregate supply would become totally inelastic. The entire effect of increased aggregate demand would be in higher prices. Now in 1992–4 the UK economy was as we have seen operating with considerable 'slack'. So in the Keynesian model, higher consumer spending could lead to a significant increase in national output with little or no rise in prices – a period of increased prosperity.

Consumption and income determination in the Keynesian model

So far we have been employing an analytical framework which analyses how national output is affected by the interreaction of aggregate supply and demand. Now we have seen that in the Keynesian model, aggregate supply is assumed horizontal and infinitely elastic over a large span of national output, up to the point where approaching full employment of resources leads to output constraints. When aggregate supply is infinitely elastic, prices will be constant, and so any change in national output will be matched by an equal change in nominal national income. (This is not so in the classical models we examine below where, due to an upward-sloping aggregate supply schedule, there is a different level of prices for each and every level of national output.) In the Keynesian model it is therefore possible to analyse how a change in aggregate demand – for instance higher consumer spending – would affect the level of national income.

BOX 21.4

The consumption function

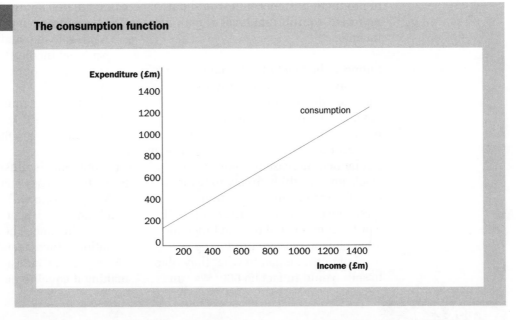

Consider Box 21.4. National income is measured on the horizontal axis, and aggregate demand, represented in this example by consumption, on the vertical axis. It is assumed that the consumption schedule is upward sloping: the more income households have, the more they will tend to spend on consumption (you can read about this in Chapter 22). We also assume for the present that the economy has two sectors only – households and businesses – and that business investment, which is also a component of aggregate demand, is zero.

In our graph the relationship between planned consumption expenditure and income is expressed by an equation or consumption function:

$$C = 150 + 0.75Y$$

where C is planned consumption expenditure, and Y is the level of national income, all variables being measured in £million. The proportion of any change in income which is consumed (0.75 in this example) is known as the marginal propensity to consume.

The equilibrium level of national income in the Keynesian model

By 'equilibrium' we mean a condition of balance where there is no net tendency towards change. Suppose in our current example that the level of national income (paid out by businesses to factors of production) happened to be 400. Households would, according to

our consumption function, then undertake 450 of consumption expenditure. Businesses would now experience an unplanned reduction of 50 in their levels of stock, and would be likely to respond by raising output. This would generate more income for factors of production. Hence 400 would not represent equilibrium level of national income.

Suppose the level of national income was, say, 700. You will be able to calculate that businesses would be paying out more income than they were receiving in the form of consumption expenditure. They would experience an unplanned increase in their levels of stock, and would be likely to respond by reducing output – so national income would fall. It turns out that the equilibrium level of national income, where businesses are producing a level of output equal to what they plan to sell, would in fact be 600. We can calculate this figure using algebra.

We have just seen that at equilibrium:
Aggregate demand (AD) = National income (Y)
However in our current model
AD = C
Therefore for equilibrium, C = Y
Hence 150 + 0.75Y = Y
Therefore Y = 600

This outcome is illustrated in Box 21.5. Since the two axes have the same scale, a 45-degree line will show equal combinations of aggregate demand and national income. The equilibrium level of national income, 600, is where this 45-degree line cuts aggregate demand – making it equal to national income.

BOX 21.5

Equilibrium level of national income

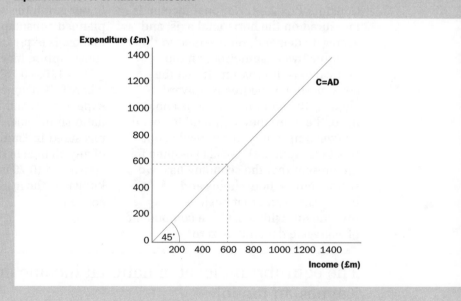

The consumption multiplier

Suppose households were to increase their consumption expenditure from 100 to, say, 200. Aggregate demand will now be higher by 100. How will this affect the level of national income? This increase in expenditure will initially cause an unplanned reduction in business stocks.

Businesses will respond by increasing their output, and factor incomes will rise. Box 21.6 shows us that the final outcome will be a new equilibrium level of national income of 1000: a 100 initial increase in aggregate demand has resulted in a 400 increase in national income.

This comes about by what is known as a multiplier process. In our example factor incomes will rise initially by 100. However some of this will be spent on goods and services, generating a further

increase in income; part of this will in turn be respent, and so on. In terms of our data, the multiplier stream of extra income generated will be:

100 + 75 + 56.62 + 42.19 + ... + = 400

The multiplier factor or coefficient is seen to be equal to 4. The higher the proportion of income consumed, the greater will be the multiplier effect. It turns out that the multiplier coefficient is equal to 1/1-MPC. Hence an MPC of 0.5 would deliver a multiplier of 2, whereas an MPC of 0.9 would result in a multiplier of 10.

In Chapter 23 we shall be looking at an 'investment' multiplier. In Chapter 24 we examine how the multiplier might be exploited, in terms of 'demand management', to stabilise the level of economic output in an economy.

BOX 21.6

A shift in aggregate demand

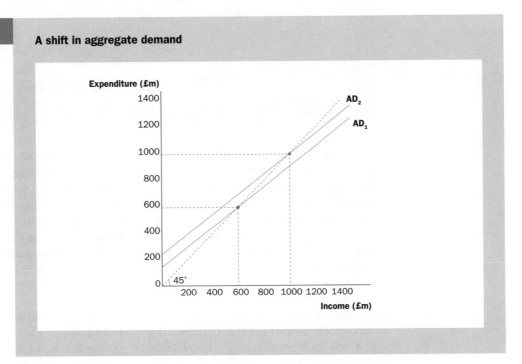

An increase in High Street spending in the classical model

Like the Keynesian model, the classical model also employs aggregate supply and aggregate demand – but with two important differences. First, the aggregate supply schedule corresponding to SAS in Box 21.7 is assumed to be upward sloping at all points. So any increase in aggregate demand will lead to a combination of rising prices and rising output.

Secondly, this aggregate supply schedule is considered to be a short-term one only. In the long run, after a period of one to two years, it gets replaced by a completely inelastic vertical aggregate supply schedule corresponding to what is known as the natural rate of output (we shall be looking at the reasons for these two assumptions below).

BOX 21.7

Aggregate demand and supply in the classical model

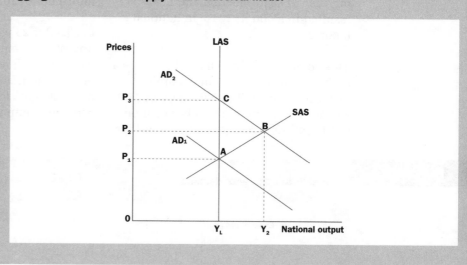

As Box 21.7 shows, the effect of an increase in aggregate demand is different from that in the Keynesian model. In the short run, prices rise more, so the gain in prosperity is less. In the long run, the entire demand effect is eaten up by rising prices and national output reverts back to 'normal'. Initially aggregate demand is given by AD_1 and national output is OY_L (point A). An increase in aggregate demand to AD_2 encounters output resistance, resulting in a less than proportionate increase in output, to OY_2, and a rise in the general price level, to OP_2 (point B). In the long run, however, wages and other unit costs 'catch up' with the higher prices, so profit is squeezed back to its initial level. The output level therefore reverts to OY_L, which is the 'natural' level of national output, and the general price level stabilises at OP_3 (point C). So the long-run gain in prosperity is zero. Going back to the extracts in Focus 4.21 classical economists would argue that it is a mistake to see the economy, and prosperity, as being 'driven' by spending, other than in the short run.

In the long run what spending determines is the general price level. National output, and prosperity, are determined by conditions of aggregate supply and the natural rate of output.

How do the classical economists reach these conclusions? We shall be studying this very important question in the next section, using the concept of the 'Phillips curve'.

Using the 'Phillips curve' to test the Keynesian model

The 'Phillips curve' is the statistical relationship between wage or price inflation, and the level of unemployment.

In 1958 A. W. Phillips examined the relationship between UK inflation and unemployment over a period of years. The data turned out to show an inverse relationship these two variables. In Box 21.8 price inflation is measured on the vertical axis and the unemployment rate on the horizontal axis, and a 'scatter' of points is obtained, each representing the data for a particular year. The line of best fit for the scatter is known as a 'Phillips curve'.

BOX 21.8

The Phillips curve scattergraph, 1955–65

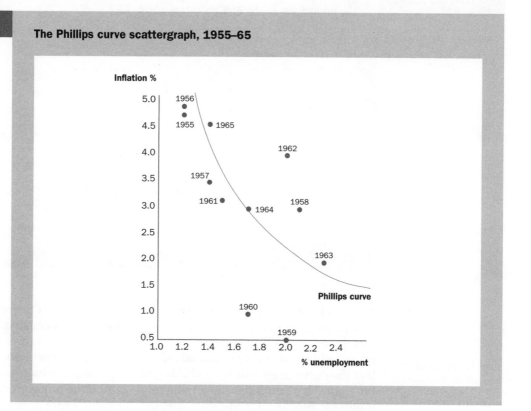

The Phillips curve relationship illustrated in Box 21.8, for example, was consistent with the predictions of the Keynesian model. At very low levels of unemployment (very high aggregate demand) we would expect inflation to tend to be higher. At high levels of unemployment (low aggregate demand) inflation ought to be low or even zero. Box 21.8 shows this to be the case.

The 'breakdown' of the Phillips curve

Stagflation is a situation in which there is simultaneously a high level of inflation and unemployment.

Unfortunately for Keynesians, after the mid-1960s the Phillips curve relationship unexpectedly seemed to break down. The UK and many other countries now found themselves experiencing growing unemployment and higher inflation: what became known as 'stagflation' as in Box 21.9.

BOX 21.9

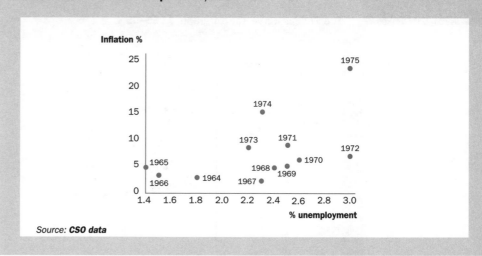

The breakdown of the Phillips curve, 1964–75

Source: **CSO data**

*The **classical model** is the macroeconomic model in which it is held that the level of national output and employment is mainly determined by aggregate supply.*

What had been happening? One way of interpreting the new data was to argue that the original Phillips curve relationship was still operational but that the curve itself had been shifting to the right. This could have been due to economic shocks – for instance, higher oil prices and trade union militancy – imparting an 'upward thrust' to costs and prices in the economy. However as stagflation persisted, a non-Keynesian explanation of the breakdown of Phillips curve, associated with Milton Friedman (whom we met in Chapter 13) and other supporters of the classical model, came to be offered. This we shall now examine.

*The **non-accelerating inflation rate of unemployment** (NAIRU) or **natural rate of unemployment** is the level of unemployment which is consistent with zero inflation.*

Friedman argued that the plum pudding Phillips curve data could best be explained in terms of a vertical long-run Phillips curve. In Box 21.10 the position of this curve corresponds to what Friedman called the non-accelerating inflation rate of unemployment (NAIRU) – also known as the natural rate of unemployment.

At point A unemployment is initially at this natural rate and the rate of inflation is stable at zero. Assume there takes now takes place an increase in aggregate demand due, say, to an acceleration of

High Street spending. What happens? In the short run the increased demand for goods and services leads to a fall in the output stocks of firms. It also has the effect of bidding up the prices of goods and services, leading to a rise in firms' profits. These two effects encourage firms to expand output. To increase output, firms need to hire more workers. They therefore bid up wage rates but, in order to protect their profits, do so by less than the increase in prices. Unemployment falls to U_1, inflation rises to 4% and the economy moves to point B on curve PC.

BOX 21.10

The vertical long-run Phillips curve

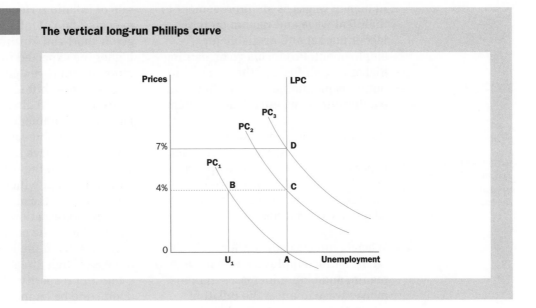

The role of price expectations

What happens in the long run, according to Friedman, depends what kind of price expectations economic agents, including employees, hold. It may be that they hold passive expectations. In the context of the Phillips curve this means they believe (wrongly) that, following any increase in demand, inflation will remain at zero. They suffer from a money illusion that prices are stable when in fact they are not.

*The **money illusion** is the passive expectation that the general price level is stable when in fact it is not.*

Employees therefore interpret their rise in money wages as an improvement in their real wage and remain on the labour market and available for employment. Producers go on earning higher real profits and the increase in output is maintained, with a long-run equilibrium being established at point B.

But suppose, as Friedman asserts to be the case, economic agents learn from experience – for example, employees expect inflation this year to reflect the rate last year. Friedman calls this adaptive expectations.

*The **adaptive expectations** hypothesis is the view that expectations are formed on the basis of past economic behaviour.*

When contracts come up for renegotiation employees will now require and obtain increases in their money wage to offset the inflation which they anticipate. Real profits and real wages will fall to their original level, and output and employment will revert to what they were before the increase in aggregate demand took place. In Figure 21.8 equilibrium is now re-established at the natural rate of unemployment at the point C, on a new Phillips curve PC$_2$ corresponding to the new expected inflation rate.

A further increase in consumer spending would lead to the process being repeated, with the economy moving to say point D on curve PC$_3$ corresponding to a still higher expected rate of inflation. Hence for each expected rate of inflation there will be a given short-run Phillips curve. The higher the expected inflation rate, the more the short-run curves become augmented – shifted outwards. Stable equilibrium will always be at the same natural rate of unemployment and output, at a point somewhere on a long-run Phillips curve LPC. This corresponds to the natural level of national output which we examined earlier. Hence the assumption of adaptive expectations leads us back to, and explains, the classical model of the economy. As in the Keynesian model, increases High Street spending leads to a gain in prosperity. However this is doomed to be temporary. In the long run, due to adaptive expectations, the economy 'goes back to square one'!

TASK 21.1

Convert the data below into a Phillips curve. Does the relationship indicate passive or adaptive expectations? Justify your answer in the context of the economic background for the period.

Year	inflation	Unemployment
(%)	(%)	
1987	4.2	2.82
1988	6.8	2.04
1989	7.7	1.64
1990	9.3	1.84
1991	4.5	2.29
1992	2.6	2.77
1993	1.9	2.90
1994	2.0	2.65
1995	2.4	2.42

Source: **Barclays Economic Review** (Winter 1995).

A third macroeconomic model: the 'new' classical model

Rational expectations is the view that expectations are formed on the basis of the most probable outcome of all currently available information.

In the 1970s a concept known as rational expectations swept through economics.

Adaptive expectations, which we examined above, reflect past data. Rational expectations are founded on the current state of the economy and incorporate all information directly and indirectly available to economic agents, including published indicators and forecasts, newspaper articles, government statements and so on. According to rational expectations:

The 'new' classical model is the macroeconomic model based on rational expectations which holds that levels of national output and employment are at all times determined by aggregate supply.

- Individual economic agents exploit their access to all available information to learn from experience and do not make systematic errors in

forming expectations: any errors will be random reflecting unpredictable events such as economic shocks.
- Economic agents as a whole forecast correctly the outcome of current economic events! How can this be when inevitably they are operating on the basis of information which is bound to be imperfect? It is because individual errors are random and tend to cancel out: on average economic agents will forecast accurately.

Rational expectations led to the development of a 'new' classical model which makes new and controversial predictions about the effects of changes in aggregate demand.

With adaptive expectations, economic agents take time to react to changes in aggregate demand. This was why an increase in aggregate demand could raise short-term national output and employment above their natural level. In the new classical model, with rational expectations, there is no lag in reaction. Following an increase in consumer spending (or any other component of aggregate demand), economic agents predict instantly that output and employment would become re-established at the natural level. Unemployed people are not 'fooled' into entering employment in the incorrect belief of securing higher real wages. Employers, realising that improvements in real profits will not be sustained, do not undertake higher output. Hence in the 'new' classical model there is no improvement in output and employment, following an expansion of aggregate demand, even in the short run! Higher aggregate demand encounters completely inelastic aggregate supply and the immediate outcome is a rise in the general price level – which will have been instantly predicted! The gain in prosperity from greater High Street spending is zero.

TASK 21.2

Study the extract below.

Britain's economic recovery is facing its greatest threat from the possibility of returning wage inflation, the Confederation of British Industry warned yesterday. Business leaders are expressing grave fears that economic recovery is now being threatened by rising inflation due to increasing wage costs. Labour market data shows unit costs rising at an annual 2%, compared with falls of 2% and 3% in Germany and the USA. As employers, they say they must hold the line on labour costs and will only have themselves to blame if things go wrong.

Source: Based on **The Times** (10 June 1994).

1 Does the extract indicate adaptive or rational expectations?
2 What implications might there be in this scenario for the recovery of the economy from recession?

TASK 21.3

In one of his more complex expectations models, Friedman assumes that workers' anticipations reflect the difference between the anticipated inflation rate and the current rate. Thus if the anticipated rate was 6 per cent but the current rate was 12 per cent, workers might revise their anticipated rate to, say, 9 per cent.

On this assumption, use the Phillips curve relationship to predict the outcome of a series of increases in aggregate demand.

Demand management in the three models

Taking measures to stimulate aggregate demand so as to boost prosperity constitutes part of what is known as demand management. We examine fully this important idea in Chapter 27. However it is worth noting here that its outcome depends on which model we select to make sense of the way the economy works. In a long-lasting recession like that of the early 1990s:

- Keynesians say: Taking measures such as tax cuts to stimulate consumer spending (or other components of aggregate demand) can increase long-term prosperity. When the UK economy is operating well below its production capacity, with around 3 million unemployed, aggregate supply will be highly elastic and the risk of inflation from increased demand will be slight. If later the economy does 'overheat', measures can then be taken to reduce demand. In this way the UK economy could be controlled at a high level of prosperity.

- The Classical School disagrees: because of adaptive expectations, measures to increase demand will merely deliver a short-term improvement in output and employment. In the longer run both will revert to their natural rate, at the cost of higher inflation. Any improvement in prosperity will be temporary and costly.

- The New Classical School says: When expectations are rational, economic agents will realise instantly that any improvement in real wages or profits associated with increased aggregate demand would be illusory. They will not be 'fooled' into participating in increased economic activity, and output and employment will remain at the natural level. The effect of demand expansion will be purely inflationary. There will be no improvement in prosperity – not even in the short run.

REVIEW

You may want to ask, 'Surely by now economists must have sorted out which of the three models best fits the real world?' The answer, fortunately or unfortunately, is 'no'. The real world is immensely complex and no model can mimic it or offer more than an approximation to its behaviour. Nor is economics a discipline which lends itself to controlled experiments (such as botanists or chemists can undertake), in which a single variable like a change in aggregate demand could be isolated and studied. This makes it hard to sort out cause and effect and increases the difficulty of eliminating 'wrong' models.

In essence, the outcome of the contest between the three macro models we have been studying largely boils down to what kind of expectations economic agents hold. If these are mainly passive, the predictions of the Keynesian model will apply and, in the 'slack' conditions of the early 1990s, increased High Street spending could deliver long-term prosperity. Adaptive expectations, however, take us to the classical model, which predicts temporary prosperity only, followed shortly by inflation. If the new classical school is right, and rational expectations hold, increased High Street spending does no good at all!

UK governments, and their advisers, up to 1976 employed macroeconomic policies consistent with an assumption of mainly passive expectations on the part of economic agents. Since then macroeconomic policies have largely reflected an assumption of adaptive expectations. At the time of writing some influential elements in John Major's Government – but not he himself or his Chancellor Kenneth Clarke – seem rather hooked on the view that the UK economy is driven by rational expectations.

Remember, however, that you, the reader, are also an economic agent. You spend and may have a part-time job. You know people who are mortgage holders, run businesses, belong to trade unions. What type of economic expectations do they have? Do you think they are representative of economic agents in general? Which of the three models we have looked at would best predict their economic behaviour? The present writer's hunch is that as more and more people get 'clued up' on the economic world around them, expectations will become increasingly adaptive – and might even become rational. When you have completed this book, you could set up a research programme and try to find out more about economic expectations ! For the present, however, the link between increased High Street spending and possible gains in prosperity spending must remain an open question.

REVIEW TASK

In his 'tough' budget of November 1993 the Chancellor of the Exchequer, Mr. Clarke, introduced substantial tax increases, amounting to £8 billion in 1994/5 and £7 billion in 1995/6 in order to cut the PSBR and reduce inflationary pressure. Some commentators strongly criticised this budget, arguing that since the recovery from recession had been almost entirely dependent on consumer spending, it would be threatened if the tax squeeze brought spending to a standstill.

Assuming he was influenced by the classical macromodel, explain, using a graphical analysis, why Mr. Clarke believed his budget
A   Would reduce inflation
B   Would not lead to higher unemployment.

Appendix: National income statistics

BOX 21.11

UK 'economic accounts', 1948–93
Gross national and domestic product[1]: average estimates

£ million

| | At current prices | | | | | | At 1991 prices | | |
| | At market prices | | | less Factor cost adjust- ment[2] | At factor cost | | | Gross domestic product at market prices | less Factor cost adjust- ment[5] | Gross domestic product at factor cost |
	Gross domestic product "Money GDP"	Net property income from abroad	Gross national product		Gross domestic product[3]	Gross national product[4]			
1948	11 835	235	12 070	1 437	10 398	10 633	187 747	23 186	164 317
1953	16 906	229	17 135	1 992	14 914	15 143	214 523	25 760	188 416
1958	22 853	293	23 146	2 629	20 224	20 517	239 571	30 028	209 274
1963	30 586	398	30 984	3 443	27 143	27 541	285 744	36 217	249 257
1968	43 808	359	44 167	5 860	37 948	38 307	335 078	40 814	294 325
1973	74 257	1 327	75 584	8 555	65 702	67 029	396 407	50 222	345 816
1978	168 526	806	169 332	18 981	149 545	150 351	421 073	55 223	365 920
1983	304 456	2 830	307 286	43 231	261 225	440 888	56 631	384 351	405,011
1988	471 430	4 424	475 854	70 002	401 428	405 852	537 215	71 469	465 746
1989	515 957	3 388	519 345	74 198	441 759	445 147	548 940	72 712	476 228
1990	551 118	981	552 099	72 232	478 886	479 867	551 118	72 232	478 886
1991	575 321	-217	575 104	79 421	495 900	495 683	540 308	71 395	468 913
1992	597 121	4 293	601 414	81 094	516 027	520 320	537 553	70 989	466 564
1993	630 023	3 062	633 085	83 903	546 120	549 182	548 599	72 670	475 889

1 Estimates are given to the nearest £ million and in the case of indices to one decimal place but cannot be regarded as accurate to this degree. Estimates at current market prices are affected by the abolition of domestic rates and the introduction of the community charge.

2 Equals taxes on expenditure less subsidies.

3 The factor cost estimate of GDP is obtained from the market price estimate by subtracting the factor cost adjustment.

4 Gross national product equals gross domestic product plus net property income from abroad.

5 Represents Taxes on expenditure less subsidies both valued at 1990 prices.

*Source: **Central Statistical Office.***

BOX 21.11

Gross domestic product: by category of expenditure[1]

£ million, current prices

		Domestic expenditure on goods and services at market prices						
		General government final consumption						
	Consumers' expenditure[2]	Central government	Local authorities	Total	Gross domestic fixed capital formation	Value of physical increase in stocks and work in progress	Total	Exports of goods and services
1946	7280	1861	487	2348	929	-102	10455	1430
1951	10238	1838	684	2522	1919	575	15254	3648
1956	13882	2511	1020	3531	3193	259	20865	4598
1961	18008	3077	1493	4570	4750	279	27607	5380
1966	24373	4270	2401	6671	7063	288	38395	7167
1971	35763	6474	4078	10552	10894	114	57323	12918
1976	76225	16830	10868	27698	24504	901	129328	35090
1981	154274	35017	21495	56512	41304	-2768	249322	67432
1986	241554	50331	30580	80911	65032	682	388179	97885
1988	299449	57522	36119	93641	91530	4333	488953	107273
1989	327363	63294	38502	101796	105443	2677	537279	121486
1990	347527	70108	42826	112934	107577	-1800	566238	133165
1991	364972	76985	47120	124105	97747	-4927	581897	134234
1992	382240	82148	49738	131886	93942	-1932	606136	140477
1993	405639	88226	49998	138224	94715	-197	638381	157999

1   Estimates are given to the nearest £ million, but cannot be regarded as accurate to this degree.

2   This series is affected by the abolition of domestic rates and the introduction of the Community Charge.

Source: **Central Statistical Office.**

BOX 21.11

Gross domestic product: by category of expenditure[1]

£ million, current prices

	Total final expenditure	less imports of goods and services	Statistical discrepancy (expend-iture)[2]	Gross domestic product at market prices[3]	less Taxes on expend-iture	Subsidies	Gross domestic product at factor cost[3]
1946	11885	1825	–	–	1572	386	–
1951	18902	4331	41	14612	2264	470	12818
1956	25463	4554	-143	20766	2811	364	18319
1961	32987	5511	-44	27432	3615	593	24410
1966	45562	7260	68	38370	5380	559	33549
1971	70241	12161	-332	57748	8653	939	50034
1976	164418	36636	-2535	125247	16284	3572	112535
1981	316754	60388	-1439	254927	42465	6369	218831
1986	486064	101221	–	384843	62872	6301	328272
1988	596226	124796	–	471430	76039	6037	401428
1989	658765	142808	–	515957	79980	5782	441759
1990	699403	148285	–	551118	78298	6066	478886
1991	716131	140810	–	575321	85416	5995	495900
1992	746613	149492	–	597121	87506	6412	516027
1993	796380	166266	-91	630023	91361	7458	546120

1 Estimates are given to the nearest £ million, but cannot be regarded as accurate to this degree.

2 This series is affected by the abolition of domestic rates and the introduction of the Community Charge.

3 Gross Domestic Product is estimated in seasonally adjusted form only. No equivalent unadjusted estimates exist.

Source: **Central Statistical Office.**

BOX 21.11

Gross domestic product: by category of income[1]

		Factor incomes							
	Income from employment[2]	Gross Gross trading profits of companies[3,4,5]	Gross trading surplus of public corporations[3,5]	Gross trading surplus of general govern-ment enterprises[3]	Other income[6]	Total domestic income[7]	less Stock appreciation	Statistical discrepancy (income)[8]	Gross domestic product at factor cost[8]
1946	5758	1476	20	90	1639	8983	109	–	–
1951	8501	2483	259	122	2191	13556	750	12	12818
1956	12267	2928	342	130	2798	18465	208	62	18319
1961	16396	3605	639	121	3727	24488	171	93	24410
1966	22842	4483	1042	124	5196	33687	305	167	33549
1971	33489	7016	1523	201	8379	50608	1055	481	50034
1976	78005	14620	4505	152	20014	117296	6681	1920	112535
1981	149737	27341	7974	236	38697	223985	5974	820	218831
1986	212380	47339	8213	155	62020	330107	1835	–	328272
1989	283454	66464	6528	199	92175	448820	7061	–	441759
1990	312358	64748	3801	12	104098	485017	6131	–	478886
1991	329609	58819	1809	-36	107709	497910	2010	–	495900
1992	342215	60140	2415	207	112882	517859	1832	–	516027
1993	352896	73397	3415	294	118160	548162	2359	317	546120

1 Estimates are given to the nearest £ million, but cannot be regarded as accurate to this degree.

2 Wages and salaries, forces' pay and employers' contributions.

3 Before providing for depreciation and stock appreciation.

4 Including financial institutions.

5 Figures reflect privatisations.

6 Income from rent and from self-employment, and the imputed charge for the consumption of non-trading capital.

7 The sum of the factor incomes before deducting stock appreciation.

8 Gross Domestic Product is estimates in seasonally adjusted form only. No equivalent unadjusted estimates exist.

Source: **Central Statistical Office.**

Multiple choice

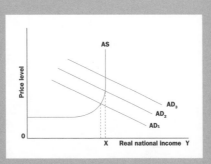

1 **The diagram illustrates an aggregate supply (AS) schedule and three aggregate demand schedules for an economy. Which of the following statements is (are) correct?**

1 The full employment level of real national income is OX.

2 An increase in aggregate demand from AD₁ to AD₂ would be associated with rises in output, employment and prices.

3 An increase in aggregate demand from AD₂ to AD₃ could have been caused by a fall in the marginal propensity to consume.

(IB, 1995)

2 **If an aggregate supply curve is perfectly elastic, this implies that**

A firms experience constant returns to scale

B as real income rises, consumption expenditure is constant

C the economy is in equilibrium

D consumers are indifferent as to whom they purchase output from.

(IB, 1995)

3 **If unemployment is at the 'natural' rate, which of the following combinations of inflation and unemployment would have to exist in the long run?**

	Inflation	Unemployment
A	Zero	Constant
B	Constant	Constant
C	Variable	Constant
D	Constant	Zero

(IB, 1995)

QUESTIONS

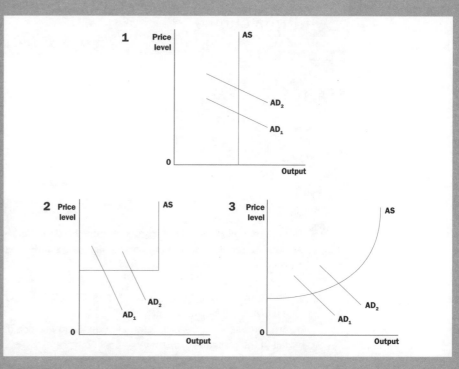

4 Question 4 refers to these diagrams.

Which of the above aggregate supply curves could be said to illustrate a Keynesian view of the effects of an increase in aggregate demand?

A 1 only

B 1 and 2

C 2 and 3

D 1,2 and 3.

(IB, 1995)

5 **According to Keynesian analysis, there might be unemployment at the equilibrium level of income because of**

A nominal wages being too high

B prices being too high

C aggregate demand being too low

D savings being too low.

(IB, 1995)

6 **The Phillips curve is a relationship between**

A the level of unemployment and the rate of growth of output

B the money supply and the level of interest rates

C the rate of inflation and the level of unemployment

D the rate of inflation and the money supply.

(WJEC, 1994)

.22 Falling house prices: good news or bad?

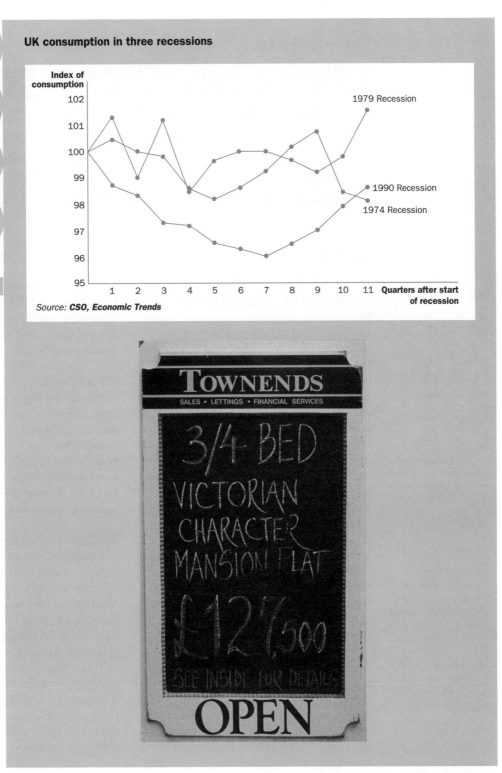

UK consumption in three recessions

1979 Recession

1990 Recession

1974 Recession

Source: **CSO, Economic Trends**

Preview

In this chapter we shall investigate the following key areas:

- theories of consumption behaviour;
- the effect of inflation on consumption;
- the relationship between wealth and consumption;
- the effect on UK consumption of falling house prices and negative equity;
- proposals for stabilising housing markets.

Do fluctuations in consumer expenditure matter?

Consumption is expenditure on consumer goods and services, mainly by households.

We saw in Chapter 21 that fluctuations in consumer spending matter do matter. Keynesians see consumer spending as having an important and lasting influence on the level of real output in the economy, with too low a level contributing to recession and unemployment. Classical monetarists see the primary link as being with price levels: thus increased consumer expenditure in the long run merely generates inflation, though in the short run it may temporarily improve output and employment. The graph in Focus 4.22, which compares the behaviour of consumption in the UK in three recent recessions, indicates that something unusual seemed to happen to consumer expenditure in the late 1980s: it may have 'destabilised'. One of the factors which influences consumer expenditure is the amount of household disposable income.

Disposable income is household income minus taxes paid to government, plus transfer payments received from government.

Recession is a period of falling national output and employment.

During the recession phase of the business cycle we would expect falling income levels to be associated with lower consumer expenditure. However you can see from the graph that during the recession of 1989 – 92 consumer spending fell faster and for longer than is usual.

On the other hand, in the boom of the late 1980s, the rise in consumer spending was unusually high, and greater than most economists and policy makers predicted.

What then does the level of consumer expenditure depend upon – and why may its behaviour have changed? Keynes believed consumer expenditure – consumption – to be a 'stable' economic variable in the sense that its level would relate closely to its main determinant, current household income.

In other words, consumption would be a dependable proportion of household income. Later analysis and research, notably by Duesenberry, Friedman and Modigliani (we examine their models below), suggests however that the level of household consumption could be influenced by other factors too. Changes in these factors might then destabilise consumption, in the sense of 'throwing' it to new and unexpected levels in relation to income. In the remainder of this chapter we will seek to test this proposition.

Keynes' 'absolute-income' consumption hypothesis

In Keynes' model the behaviour of consumption, or consumption function, consists of two elements:

- Induced consumption varies directly with the level of current household disposable income (gross income minus taxes paid to government, plus transfer payments received). Keynes believed also that as income rose, households would be able to afford to save at a higher rate, so that overall consumption, though rising, would be found to decline as a proportion of income.

- A basic or autonomous level of consumption which does not vary with disposable income and which is determined by other factors.

However, empirical data does not really support Keynes' idea of a straightforward relationship between consumption and the level of income: as Box 22.1 shows, consumption ratios can vary quite a lot. More recent theories have therefore focused much more on the nature of autonomous consumption. Some of these theories relate this to non-income factors but we begin by studying, in the next section, two theories which investigate less direct links between consumption and income.

Autonomous consumption is consumption expenditure which does not vary with disposable income and which is determined independently of income level.

BOX 22.1

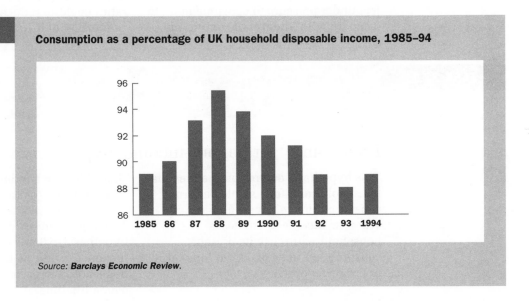

Consumption as a percentage of UK household disposable income, 1985–94

Source: *Barclays Economic Review*.

Duesenberry's 'relative-income' consumption hypothesis

Keynes' view that high income households would consume a lower proportion of income than low income households was supported by early national income data. However data over a period of time when real income per head had risen substantially, also showed that the proportion of income consumed by households as a whole had remained broadly constant. Duesenberry's relative-income hypothesis attempts to resolve this apparent contradiction. It too assumes that when an individual household's income rises, other things being equal its proportion of income consumed will tend to fall. However Duesenberry argues that when everybody's income increases individual households will feel under pressure to consume more to 'keep up with' the rest of community.

So the proportion of income consumed by households as a whole will tend to remain constant.

On Duesenberry's relative-income hypothesis, what would happen to consumption levels when, as in the UK in the 1980s, the distribution of income between households becomes more uneven? The overall proportion of income consumed should rise, because more households will be attempting to 'keep up with the Joneses'. Keynes' hypothesis predicts that the overall proportion of income consumed would fall. This is due to the fact that a redistribution of income from poorer households (who tend to have a high consumption ratio), to richer households (with a lower consumption ratio) ought to reduce the overall proportion of income consumed.

TASK 22.1   Using published national income and other data for the period of the 1980s, test the relative predictions of the absolute- and relative-income consumption hypotheses.

Friedman's 'permanent-income' hypothesis

This hypothesis centres on the idea that households aim for a stable pattern of consumption over a period of time. When its income fluctuates, a household will relate its present consumption to its expected long-term or permanent income.

Permanent income is expected household income over a long period of time.

Short-term changes in transitory (temporary) income will have little effect on permanent income and the proportion of income consumed. On Friedman's hypothesis, factors which reduce expected permanent income,

should lead to a reduced level of consumption – as in fact occurred.

The Modigliani–Aldo life-cycle hypothesis extends the permanent-income hypothesis to take account of a household's expected income stream over a life-time. A typical household will attempt to 'smooth out' its consumption over time, saving in its middle years when income is at a peak, and dissaving in early and late years when income is relatively low.

BOX 22.2

Household income and savings in Japan

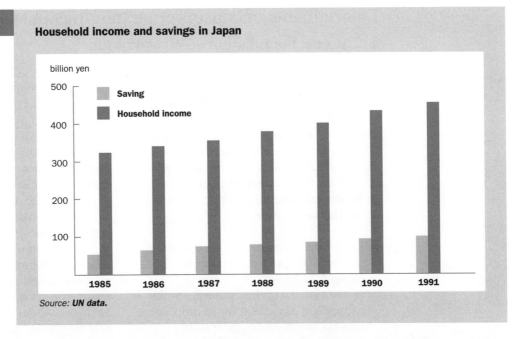

Source: **UN data.**

TASK 22.2

1 In 1993, in order to reduce its borrowing requirement the UK government introduced substantial tax increases. Many people believed, however, that these increases would be reversed by the time of the next general election.

Using the consumption models we have examined, what predictions would you make about the response of household levels of consumption to the 1993 tax increases?

2 Lump sum payments, which are added on to employees' basic salaries are a distinctive feature of Japanese pay arrangements. These awards are very uncertain, and can amount to a third or more of basic salary when a business is doing well – or can be very little in a 'bad' year.

Using the consumption models we have examined, what predictions would you make about household levels of saving and consumption in Japan, compared with a country like the UK which has 'normal' salary arrangements?

Check your prediction with the data in Figure 22.2.

Determinants of consumption: non-income factors

1 The effect of inflation on consumption

Another factor which economists believe influences the level of household consumption is inflation.

The later 1980s saw a sharp increase in UK inflation, after which in the mid-1990s inflation fell to historically very low levels. There are a number of ways in which inflation might affect the level of (real) consumption:

- First, by causing uncertainty about the real value of future household income, inflation may increase precautionary saving and reduce the proportion of current household income spent on consumption.
- Secondly, in times of inflation consumers may experience a partial money illusion, in the sense that they systematically underestimate the rate at which prices are rising. They are therefore repeatedly taken by surprise at 'excessive' increase in the price of specific goods and services, purchases of which they cut back. The effect of (unanticipated) inflation could thus be to reduce consumption. On this view downward pressure on consumption could especially occur in the late stages of a business cycle when prices often 'take off'.

- Thirdly, inflation may have a wage-effect which affects consumption. Money wage rates are generally set once a year, at which point real wages will be at a maximum, falling to a minimum at the end of the period. If inflation is anticipated, households will 'smooth out' consumption expenditure over the year, by saving more early in the period and less later on. If wage contracts are spread over the year, and inflation is constant, then at any given time the extra savings of some households will cancel out the reduced savings of others. So there will be no net overall effect on the ratio of consumption to income. But suppose inflation, and money wage increases, are accelerating. Increased savings by households who have recently received higher wage award will then exceed those of other households still tied to lower wage awards, and so the consumption rati will fall: accelerating inflation could reduce consumption levels.

- Fourthly, inflation affects household wealth. Generally, higher wealth wil encourage consumption (see below). Now other things being equal, inflation will reduce the real value o household wealth held in money-denominated forms, such as bank deposits and national savings. However inflation may be associated with increases in the real value of household wealth in the form of property and company shares. The net overall wealth effect of inflation on consumption expenditure is therefore difficult to determine.

Box 22.3 shows the course of inflation in the UK since 1970. Is the downturn since 1990 a temporary 'blip' or are we seeing the start of a long period of price stability? At the time of writing some commentators are forecasting some increase in inflation from 1996, when the current rapid expansion of aggregate demand (notably of investment and export volume) increasingly encounters bottlenecks in the aggregate supply of skilled labour and capital capacity. However there are a number of reasons why inflation seems unlikely to return to the high levels of 1979 and 1990 (see Chapter 26). So, whereas several of the factors we are examining in this chapter come out as destabilising factors, a low and stable level of inflation in the later 1990s could have a stabilising influence on consumption.

BOX 22.3

Inflation in the UK, 1970–94

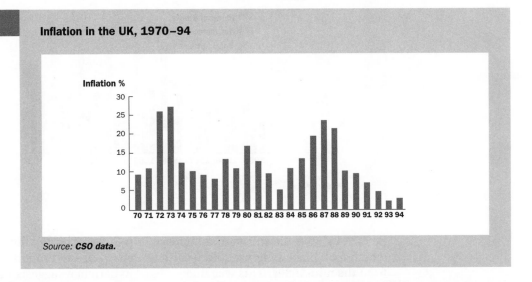

Source: **CSO data.**

TASK 22.3

How would a sharp fall in inflation, such as occurred in 1993 – 4, be likely to affect household expenditure?

2 Wealth and consumption

Net wealth is the value of assets minus liabilities.

In this section we look at the effect of the level of household wealth on consumption. Wealth may be in the form of physical assets (for example a house and contents) or financial assets (such as a bank balance, shares or bonds). A household's net wealth consists of its total assets minus all liabilities, that is, debts.

BOX 22.4

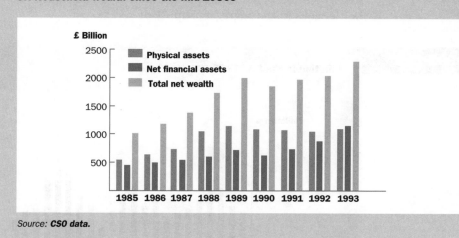

UK Household wealth since the mid-1980s

Source: **CSO data.**

Box 22.4 shows the substantial increase which took place in household wealth from the mid-1980s. This was due partly to high levels of employment and earnings, which afforded many households an opportunity to build up increased holdings of financial and other assets. Secondly, substantial business profits led to rising share prices and a corresponding increase in the value of households' share portfolios, pension funds and assurance policies. Thirdly, there took place a sharp rise in property values. Experience suggests that the greater a household's wealth, the more it will tend to spend on consumption at a given level of income. More wealth increases personal security, thus reducing the need to save for future contingencies, and allowing higher consumption out of current income – for example by selling shares or by borrowing against owned property.

Mortgages and household wealth

Although many households own considerable financial wealth nowadays, this is overshadowed by wealth owned in the form of house property. In the UK about 70 per cent of households now own their dwelling, generally on the basis of purchase through a house loan or mortgage, from a bank or building society.

The operation of a mortgage affects a household's consumable income and its wealth. The monthly mortgage outgoings take away income from consumption. Conversely, assuming no change in the value of the property being bought, the household's wealth increases as it cumulatively repays mortgage debt, until the mortgage loan is finally 'redeemed' – that is, paid off.

*A **mortgage** is a house loan, generally from a bank or building society.*

House purchase as a speculation

Before the 1980s house loans were restricted to a small multiple of the borrower's income and a large deposit was required. In the early 1980s, however, financial markets were 'de-regulated' to make them more responsive to demand. This led to prospective borrowers being offered loans on very much easier terms. Soon, zero-deposit 100 per cent mortgages were common, with loans exceeding the house price commonly being made in the expectation that rapidly rising house prices would soon 'catch up' with the loan. Eventually this led to an explosion of house prices as more and more households trying to 'move up the housing ladder' took out ever-larger mortgages.

Some people began to borrow very large sums to buy houses, not just for living in but also for later resale at a much higher price, with the aim of securing a capital gain after the repayment of their mortgage debt.

Capital gain is the excess of the selling price of an asset over its purchase price.

Many householders exploited the rising net asset value (**equity**) of their homes by taking out a second loan (which building societies and other mortgage-lenders were happy to advance), to support increased consumption on a winter holiday, extra car and so on. This was known as **equity withdrawal**. The rush to buy property was encouraged by a number of factors peculiar to the UK housing market:

- The rented sector – rented private and council housing – was relatively small, hence many people were obliged to look to early home ownership.

- Mortgage loans could be taken out for long periods in anticipation of rising career income.

- Mortgage loans of up to 100 per cent of the house purchase price were common.

- There was no tax on house-wealth or other assets.

- There was no tax on capital gains associated with 'main' house sales.

- Mortgage interest payments were eligible for tax relief.

- Equity withdrawal was relatively easy.

In 1988 UK house prices began to fall and the decline was to continue for several years. It led to a significant 'squeeze' on household consumption through the development of negative equity, as explained in Box 22.5.

Negative equity in the housing market

One of the most distinctive features of the current down turn in the housing market is that prices have fallen in both real and nominal terms. In some regions, most notably the South East, nominal house prices have been falling for nearly four years. This situation has left many households with a home worth less than the value of their mortgage, a phenomenon that has been termed 'negative equity'.

Negative equity is most prevalent among first-time buyers who bought in the South on high loan to value ratios in the late 1980s and have since seen the value of their properties fall substantially.

From information on the size of cash deposits, the number of transactions and regional movements in house prices, it is possible to estimate the number of homeowners who currently face negative equity. Of perhaps more significance than the number of affected households is the value of negative equity. This is the shortfall which must be financed if affected households are to move home.

The phenomenon of negative equity has taken nearly four years to reach its current proportions. To unwind fully, these effects will require either a heightened rate of saving by affected households, or the reversal of the falls in house prices seen since the end of 1988. In either event, the presence of negative equity seems likely to remain an important feature of the finances of many households for some time to come.

For families in the South, the problems raised by negative equity seem unlikely to be short-lived. It would require house price inflation of 10% per annum from early next year to lift all of the affected households out of the equity trap by the end of 1995.

BOX 22.6

Regional profile of negative equity, 1994 (first quarter)

Number of households with negative equity		Negative equity (£ billion)	Average negative equity (£)
Greater London	220	1.7	8000
Rest of South East	510	3.8	7500
South West	180	1.0	5700
East Anglia	80	0.6	6700
East Midlands	100	0.3	2600
West Midlands	90	0.1	1400
Other regions	120	0.1	900
Total	1290	7.6	5900

Source: Bank of England **Bank Briefing** (August 1992) and **Quarterly Bulletin** (May 1994).

3 Negative equity and consumption

Negative equity is a situation in which a property is worth less than the outstanding mortgage debt on it.

As the extracts in Boxes 22.5 and 22.6 show, negative equity had serious effects. One of these was to reduce the geographical mobility of labour. Secondly, the decline in net household wealth, including that resulting from negative equity, was likely to lead to a decline in consumption. Thirdly, a household with negative equity contemplating moving house would be likely to need to save more – consume less – in order to meet a joint commitment both to repay or renew the outstanding mortgage loan and to cover the loss incurred by selling property at a reduced price. Overall, therefore, the development of negative equity was likely to have a marked downward effect on consumption.

TASK 22.4

Explain the decline in house prices in the early 1990s. What predictions would you make for the future trend of house prices in the late 1990s?

'Income gearing' and household consumption in the early 1990s

Income gearing measures the ratio of a household's interest payments to its income.

The higher the income gearing, the less the amount of household income available for maintaining consumption. At the end of the 1980s there took place a sharp rise in mortgage interest rates. The downward pressure of negative equity on consumption and aggregate demand was thus reinforced by the effect of an increase in income gearing for many households. Later, interest rate reductions led to lower levels of household income gearing but in 1994 rising interest rates pointed to possible increases in income gearing and a further squeeze on consumption. Look at Box 22.7.

BOX 22.7

The squeeze on household consumption

There is some evidence that the increase in negative equity has altered the behaviour of households and affected the economy as a whole. Lump-sum repayments to mortgage lenders, other than on loan redemptions, have risen by 140% since 1989, to reach £2.5 billion in 1993 – nearly 5% of personal sector saving. This increase cannot readily be explained by changes in Mortgage rates; rates fell sharply between 1989 and 1993, reducing the incentive to repay debt. A more likely cause was concern about the level of debt, particularly among households with negative equity. But repayment of £2.5 billion is not large compared with the benefit that consumers have enjoyed from lower interest payments; in gross terms, these have increased annual personal income net of interest payments by £18 billion a year between 1990 and 1993.

The severe income-gearing problems faced by some indebted households provide another example of the range of experience within the personal sector; it is illustrated by the large increase in the proportion of mortgages going into arrears and leading to repossessions. But falling asset values do not by themselves explain these increases, unless households are simply unwilling to continue paying interest and capital on secured debt that exceeds the value of the underlying asset. The increase in arrears is more likely to have resulted from lower-than-expected personal income growth or larger-than-expected increases in interest rates. Falling nominal house prices exacerbated the difficulties, however, because negative equity prevented households from trading down and so reducing their mortgage payments to more sustainable levels. Home-owning consumers with no outstanding mortgage debt seem to have reacted to lower interest rates, and lower investment income, by reducing their spending: between 1991 and 1992 real consumption by such homeowners fell by about 11%, whereas spending by households with a mortgage rose by 5%.

*Source: **Bank of England Bulletin** (May 1994).*

1 How does the extract explain the effect of negative equity and increased income gearing on consumption ? What third factor is mentioned as a likely source of downward pressure on consumption?

2 What factors could lead to increasing positive housing equity? What would be the likely microeconomic and macroeconomic effects of increased housing equity?

Could consumption behaviour be stabilised?

Stabilising economic activity through demand management is helped if consumption expenditure is stable and its behaviour over the economic cycle can be predicted and controlled (Chapter 24). What we have seen in this chapter suggests, however, that consumption has become more vulnerable to non-income shocks, notably falling house prices, and less predictable. Are there any ways in which consumer behaviour could to some degree be 'stabilised' and made more manageable? With regard to fluctuations in house prices, the following measures have been suggested:

Capital gains tax is a tax on capital gains on the sale of assets.

- Restrict mortgage loans to a much smaller proportion of the house purchase price, to a level similar to most other countries. House buyers would need to save much more for deposit, and would be less vulnerable to negative equity and high income gearing.

- Introduce capital gains tax on profits made from house sales.

- Abolish all tax relief on mortgage interest payments.

- Introduce measures to reduce the ease with which positive house equity can be withdrawn.

- Re-introduce 'mortgage-loan limits' (see Box 22.8).

BOX 22.8

Mortgage regulation?

Mortgage regulations ... might in principle take two forms: deposit requirements on all mortgages (which would be equivalent to introducing a uniform limit on loan-to-value ratios) and measures specifically targeted at equity extraction.

The case for limits on mortgage lending in order to control equity extraction applies only to those households with equity to extract, and does not include first-time buyers. A simple maximum loan-to-value ratio for buyers who were also sellers would still allow equity extraction. So, any limits that were intended to limit equity extraction would have to take into account sale proceeds from previous ownership.

One of the practical problems in reintroducing restrictions on mortgage lending, would be the extension of the population of lenders. Specialised mortgage lenders, not always based in the UK, have entered the market.

Financial deregulation is the removal or relaxation of controls or rules from financial markets.

Greater competition together with **financial deregulation** has increased the incentive to find ways round controls.

Abolition of exchange controls has made it difficult to control borrowing from overseas lenders. Foreign currency mortgages are freely available. It is difficult to imagine that informal controls or guidance would provide an effective cap on mortgages financed from overseas. A more formal requirement involving sanctions for non-compliance would be needed for such a control to be effective.

Controls are undesirable, not only because they are difficult to enforce, but also because they interfere with loan allocation among borrowers. Their attraction is as a form of emergency brake if credit were thought to be expanding too rapidly – as such they are a policy of last resort.

*Source: **Bank of England Bulletin** (May 1991).*

1 How might mortgage limits be used to stabilise the housing market?
2 Why does the extract recommend that mortgage limits be employed only as 'a policy of last resort'?

REVIEW

It is time to draw together the threads in this chapter. We began by asking what the level of consumer expenditure depends upon and why its behaviour might be changing. We saw that the level of disposable income is clearly a key determinant of consumer expenditure. However, since the 1980s a number of factors may have made consumption behaviour less stable and predictable in terms of income:

- A continually rising increasing number of home-owner households, so that fluctuations in house prices had an ever stronger influence on consumption

- The seemingly inexorable fall in house prices and continuance of negative household equity

- An increasing importance of financial assets – particularly share-ownership – as a source of household wealth, fluctuations in the value of which would have a significant effect on consumption.

- Changes in labour markets leading to greater job insecurity, combined with an increasing number of people dependent on uncertain income from small businesses.

Could consumption behaviour be stabilised again? In terms of the house price effect, we looked at the possible introduction of restricted mortgage loans, capital gains tax on house-sale profits, abolition of tax relief on mortgage interest, and reduced house equity extraction. There seemed a good chance that some at least of these might become part of policy in the later 1990s.

REVIEW TASK

The effect on consumption of 'unfulfilled' permanent income expectations

The pattern of changes in income over time across the distribution of household income suggests that unfulfilled income expectations may have had an important bearing on household behaviour. Households in the top half of the income distribution enjoyed substantial real rises in their income between 1980 and 1988; since then, they have suffered significant real declines. The potential for unfulfilled income expectations is clear, if expected permanent income is affected by actual income. Furthermore, changing permanent income expectations affect the behaviour of younger consumers more than older. So any effect as a result of unfulfilled income expectations probably reinforced that from negative equity (a situation in which a property is worth less than the outstanding mortgage debt on it), which has been concentrated among the young: two thirds of those suffering from negative equity are first-time house-buyers.

REVIEW TASK

The distribution of income and spending patterns across different income groups can have important effects on aggregate behaviour. Because high-income households account for a disproportionate amount of consumption – it has been estimated that the top 4% of income-earners account for almost 15% of all consumer spending – the expectations and behaviour of high-income groups may be particularly influential.

Regional differences also suggest some role for income expectations in the explanation of the movements in consumption, but the evidence is not conclusive. Regional saving ratios show that the consumption boom of the mid- to late 1980s was associated with a sharp fall in the saving ratio of households in the South East. Consumers in northern regions also spent more of their income, but the falls in their saving ratios were generally smaller. Between its peak in 1986 and its trough in 1990, unemployment fell faster in the South East than in the rest of the economy which, other things being equal, would cause the expected income of those in the region to increase relative to other regions; this could in part explain their spending behaviour. Since 1990, however, despite a larger rise in unemployment in the South East than in other regions, the recovery in consumption has been led by a decline in the saving ratio in the South East. This suggests that factors other than income expectations have been more important in determining consumers' behaviour.

Source: **Bank of England Quarterly Bulletin** (May 1994).

1 How does regional data suggest a relationship between income expectations and changes in household consumption?

2 What 'other factors' might have been more important in determining consumers' behaviour?

Data response

1 Study the data below and answer all the questions which follow.

Total for this question: 20 marks

Table 1 UK housing tenure pattern since 1971

	Owner-occupation (%)	Public sector (%)	Private rented incl. housing associations (%)	Housing associations %)
1971	51	31	19	n/a
1981	56	31	13	2
1991	68	22	10	3

Source: *Independent on Sunday* (26 July 1992).

Table 2 Interest rates (nominal)

Clearing Banks' Base Rate (%)					
1987	1988	1989	1990	1991	1992
8.5	13.0	15.0	14.0	10.5	10.0

Source: *British Economy Survey.*

Chart 1 Halifax House Price Index (1983–91)

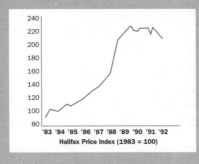

Halifax Price Index (1983 = 100)

Source: Adapted from the *Halifax Building Society.*

QUESTIONS

Chart 2 Unemployed as a percentage of working population

*Source: Adapted from **Datastream***

a i Briefly describe the changes in housing tenure patterns between 1971–1991, as shown in Table 1.

ii Explain two possible causes of the changes you have described in A(i).

b i Using demand and supply diagrams, explain why the changes in rates of interest (Table 2) and unemployment (Chart 2) may have affected the changes in house prices since 1989 shown in Chart 1.

ii With the help of the data, discuss the possible economic consequences that may have arisen from a policy of encouraging home ownership.

(AEB, 1995)

2 **Figure 1 Saving as a percentage of GDP in the UK, 1970 – 89**

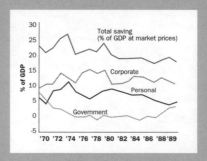

In Figure 1, saving as a percentage of GDP is shown both in total and for each of three sectors of the UK economy.

The government sector comprises central government and local authorities.

The personal sector comprises households, unincorporated businesses, life assurance and pension funds, and private non-profit making bodies such as universities.

The corporate sector comprises industrial and commercial companies, financial companies and institutions and public corporations.

Figure 2 Personal sector saving ratio in the UK, 1970–90

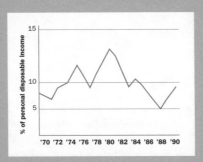

Source: C. Pass and J. Sparkes, **Savings and Investment** (Collins).

a Why are the personal saving ratios different in the two diagrams? Explain your answer.
b With reference to Figure 1, examine factors likely to explain trends in savings by:
   i   the corporate sector;
   ii   the government sector;
   iii the personal sector.
c In the decade after 1980 the personal saving ratio fell to an unprecedentedly low level. Discuss the impact you would expect this changing behaviour to have on the level of aggregate demand.
d In the period after 1988 the UK economy moved into recession and the personal saving ratio started to rise again. In what way does a rise in the personal saving ratio have an impact on an economy moving into recession and on the prospects of recovery from recession?

(ULEAC, 1995)

3 The table gives data relating to personal income, expenditure and saving in Great Britain.

	Total personal disposable income	Consumers' expenditure	Saving ratio (%)
1982	192.3	170.7	11.3
1983	206.9	187.0	9.7
1984	224.9	200.3	11.0
1985	244.8	218.9	10.6
1986	265.8	243.0	8.6
1987	287.1	267.5	6.9
1988	319.9	302.1	5.6
1989	354.1	330.5	6.7
1990	382.1	350.4	8.3
1991	407.2	367.7	9.8
1992	437.3	386.2	11.6

Source: *Economic Profile of Great Britain* (Lloyds Bank, 1993).

a   What is meant by the term 'total personal disposable income'?

b   Calculate the average propensity to consume in 1983.

c   Calculate the marginal propensity to consume between 1991 and 1992. Comment on your result.

d   i   What do you understand by the term 'saving ratio'?

    ii   Analyse the factors which may have influenced the trends in saving during the periods 1984–88 and 1988–92.

(ULEAC, 1995)

Why is investment important?

Fears on investment: CBI survey adds to investment 'short-termism' debate

The Confederation of British Industry's investment appraisal survey which came out today showed that many businesses are setting high hurdles – minimum rates of return – for investment projects and accuses them of 'short-termist' investment strategies. By demanding high rates of return on investment, businesses could be fuelling inflationary expectations and stifling viable investment projects. Many City analysts and businessmen however argue that companies are right to be cautious about inflation in light of past events. Many firms believe that price inflation for goods and services in the shops is only dormant for the time being, and they say that cost inflation on wage rates and materials is already a serious threat to profitability and therefore investment prospects. They are feeling the pinch on profits, caught between suppliers pushing for higher prices and the near-refusal of their own customers to take on board price increases.

The Bank of England and the Treasury disagree, arguing strongly that businesses need to adjust to the new low-inflation and low-risk environment by reducing their minimum rates of return. The Treasury said: ministers have made clear their determination to deliver the government's inflation target, and if companies assume higher inflation they will miss out on construction and investment opportunities.

Eddie George, Governor of the Bank of England, warns that these stiff hurdles will never allow investment to boom again, and that means that continued economic expansion which is needed to eat into unemployment figures, will run into inflation pressures and not be sustainable.

*Source: Adapted from **press coverage** (July–August 1994).*

Preview

In this chapter we shall investigate the following key areas:
- types of investment;
- methods of investment appraisal;
- investment and the product life cycle;
- the effect of changes in investment on aggregate demand and aggregate supply;
- factors affecting levels of investment;
- factors affecting the quality of investment;
- the changing effect of investment on the UK economy.

What are we to make of the extract in Focus 4.23? It amounts to a strong criticism of the investment policies of Britain's businesses in the mid-1990s. What did Eddie George mean, when he asserted that firms were missing out on investment opportunities? Why should low investment threaten that economic expansion would run into inflation and not be sustainable? In this chapter we shall be using economic theory to try to answer these and other questions. We begin by looking at what investment is.

BOX 23.1

UK investments, 1993

Investment (£m) in:	Private sector	Public sector
Vehicles, ships and aircraft	7 533	1 078
Plant and machinery	29 337	3 558
Buildings and land	41 319	13 786
Total investment:	78 189	18 422

Source: CSO, **Economic Trends** *.*

'Real' investment and 'paper' investment

Goods which satisfy wants directly are classified as consumer goods. Goods which satisfy wants indirectly – for example an oil tanker or a machine – are classified as producer goods. Expenditure on producer goods is known as investment or capital formation. Sometimes this is referred to as real investment to distinguish it from 'paper' investment – for instance, when someone 'invests' in the purchase of shares. For an economist, buying shares is an instance of saving and in this chapter we focus on the role of real investment.

Who invests?

In a country like Britain a certain amount of investment, for instance on schools and postal services, is undertaken in the public sector by the government. As Box 23.2 shows, most investment is however undertaken by firms in the private sector and in this chapter we shall be focusing on this 'business investment'.

BOX 23.2

Reasons for investment, % of UK manufacturing firms, 1994:1 and 1979–94

	Expand capacity	Increase efficiency	Replace capacity	Other
1994:1	25	75	52	11
1979–94	23	72	50	7

Source: **CBI** survey data.

Three elements of investment

Firms are required by law or other provisions, to undertaken mandatory capital expenditure in areas such as the environment, health and safety and so on. Firms also however invest, in the following ways, as part of their operations to produce and sell at a profit.

To replace existing capital

The stock of capital employed by firms ages and gets 'used up' – depreciates – over time. At any given time there will be some investment which is geared to replacing existing capital.

To expand capacity

Product innovation is the introduction of new products, often associated with the application of new technology.

If the amount of new or gross investment taking place happened to equal the amount of capital depreciation, the size of the stock of capital employed would remain constant. Any excess of gross investment over depreciation will represent net investment in expanded capacity. In a recession, when sales of output are low, firms may experience excess capacity – they will possess more equipment and other productive resources than are required for current levels of output. In a boom firms often at some stage find they have insufficient equipment to satisfy current output needs, and feel the need to invest in expanded capacity. An important driving force behind the expansion of capacity is product innovation, the introduction of new products and groups of products, often based on new technologies.

Increasing efficiency

Process innovation is the introduction of new production processes, often associated with the application of new technology and 'lean' production.

To be successful in competitive markets firms have to aim for increasing productivity, in their use of inputs. This may well be driven by process innovation.

The greater the pressure and scope for increased efficiency, the more investment firms are likely to to need to undertake if they are to survive and expand. Box 23.2 shows that for UK manufacturing firms, the desire to increase efficiency is a leading reason for investment.

BOX 23.3   Capital widening and capital deepening

Investment may have the effect of capital widening, where extra capital is applied to an increased quantity of labour, with the amount of capital per employee remaining broadly unchanged. Unless it is related to economies of scale this does not necessarily lead to any increase in productivity. Investment may also lead to capital deepening, where the amount of capital per employee is increased, often leading to large improvements in productivity.

How do firms 'appraise' their investment projects?

In investigating if UK investment levels were unnecessarily low in the early 1990s we need to look at how firms evaluate or 'appraise'

investment projects, in terms of profitability and viability. Box 23.4 outlines three leading methods of investment appraisal.

BOX 23.4   Three methods of appraising investment

Recent surveys suggest that companies employ a variety of methods for appraising investment. About 90 per cent were found to use quantitative ways to evaluate investment, based on three main methods. The most popular was the ''pay–back'' method, which assesses a project in terms of how soon a business can recoup investment – only 14 per cent of these used a pay-back period of five years or more. However most businesses used more sophisticated calculations based on "rates of return'' and "cashflow'', often in combination. Among these about two-fifths said their hurdle rate was above 20 per cent.

● **Payback method** This refers to the length of the period before the initial outlay on an investment is recovered out of the stream of profit generated by the project. Other things being equal, an investment project which pays for itself quickly will be preferred to one which takes longer.

BOX 23.4

● **Internal rate of return** This method measures the anticipated stream of profit expected to be earned over the expected lifetime of a project, expressed as an overall annual percentage-rate. An investment project is viable when its internal rate of return exceeds the rate of interest, which measures the 'cost' of financing the investment.

● **Net present value** This method measures over the expected lifetime of a project, the anticipated stream of net cash flows, expressed in terms of their 'discounted' present value. The greater an investment project's net present value, the more viable it will be, compared with other projects.

Investment and the product life cycle

Most products have a finite life cycle which passes through four recognisable stages:

Introduction stage

The first stage of a new product is the launch. Despite usually heavy advertising aimed at promoting market awareness, sales in the launch stage of a product often increase only slowly, particularly if the product is very innovative. Many products fail at this stage, and even eventually successful products may make substantial losses, due to technical problems, inadequate cost control and lack of demand.

Growth stage

Once the product is successfully launched, demand accelerates and, notwithstanding likely competition from newer rival products with lower development costs, losses turn into healthy profits.

Maturity stage

At this stage the product is showing signs of ageing. In a market now saturated with similar competing products, sales slow to a 'plateau'. Very heavy advertising may be undertaken to defend market share and this, combined with falling prices, contributes to declining profitability.

Decline stage

Tastes and fashions having now moved on a long way since the introduction stage; changing demand and innovation lead to entire new families of products. The market size of 'elderly' products contracts, and a combination of falling price and demand lead to increasing losses, and eventually a final stage of decline.

The life cycles of different products do not usually 'synchronise' and so any investment effects are likely to be on a microeconomic scale only. However in the case of a major product – or a group of related products with broadly parallel life cycles – investment required at key stages of the life cycle may be on such a scale as to have a macroeconomic effect on the economy. One example would be the 'white goods revolution' of the 1960s which probably helped to prolong western Europe's postwar boom. Another may be the wide range of investments being triggered in the 1990s by direct and indirect applications of personal computers.

TASK 23.1

Take an example of a well-known product with which you are familiar.
At what stage(s) of its life cycle would investment levels be likely to be particularly
(A) high? (B) low?

The instability of investment

Evidence suggests that investment levels are often likely to fluctuate considerably. Why is this?

Investment involves an assessment of likely profitability over a period of perhaps many years. Hence investment is strongly associated with perceived risk. The greater the risk, the higher the rate of profitability which must be expected if a given investment is to be considered worthwhile. However changes in economic conditions can completely alter perceptions of risk and hence planned levels of investment. In the next section we shall see that this is very important because investment has an influence both on aggregate demand and on aggregate supply.

BOX 23.5

UK net investment as a percentage of GDP, 1979–93

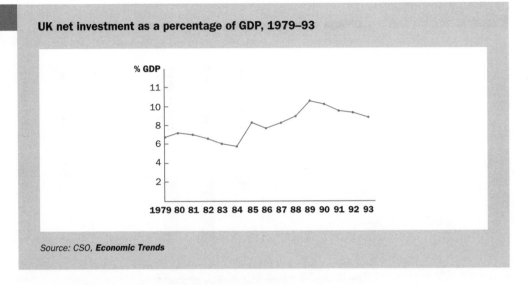

Source: CSO, *Economic Trends*

Investment and aggregate demand

Investment, like consumption, is a component of aggregate demand: year by year gross expenditure on factories, machinery, equipment and so on, amounts to around one-fifth of total UK national expenditure. Just as in the case of consumption, which we examined in Chapter 21, fluctuations in investment have a significant effect on economic activity. As Box 23.6 shows, there was a sharp decline in investment during both the the 1990–2 and 1979–81 recessions, and this had the effect of accentuating the decline in aggregate demand in these periods. However, investment did not rise by nearly as much in the recovery of 1992–4, as it had in 1981–3, which served to delay the recovery of aggregate demand in 1992–4.

BOX 23.6

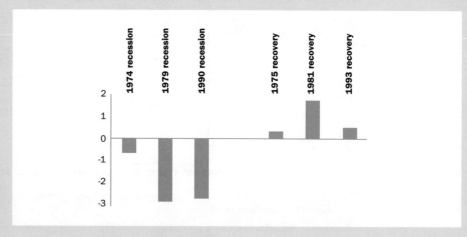

Change in investment as a percentage of UK GDP, 1974–93

Source: Bank of England Inflation review (May 1994)

An increase in investment expenditure will add to aggregate demand. This in turn will tend to lead to an extension of short-run aggregate supply. If conditions of aggregate supply are very elastic, as Keynesians believe to be the case in periods of low economic activity (Chapter 21), there will be little, if any, increase in the general price level. However at higher levels of economic activity, an increase in aggregate demand resulting from higher investment will encounter increasingly inelastic aggregate supply, leading to smaller extensions of output but bigger increases in the price level.

Economists who use the classical model don't agree with the predictions of the Keynesian model. They assert that there is always some inelasticity of short-run aggregate supply. Hence any increase in aggregate demand, due for instance to higher investment, inevitably leads to a short-run increase in the general price level.

In the long-run, investment also affects conditions of aggregate supply and we examine the significance of this a little later on.

The investment multiplier

*The **multiplier effect** is the process which relates changes in the equilibrium level of national income to changes in aggregate demand.*

A change in the level of investment expenditure not only affects economic activity directly, it will also have an indirect income 'multiplier effect'. Investment in a project such as the Channel Tunnel raises income directly through the pay of workers and the receipts of suppliers and contractors.

It also however generates additional income as the initial round of income created becomes re-spent on goods and services, generating a further round of income, and so on. We can employ the framework we used in Chapter 21 to analyse this effect. Assume that there is infinitely elastic aggregate supply, and hence constant prices, so that any change in national output is matched by an equal change in nominal national income.

Consider now Box 23.7, where (as in the corresponding graph in Chapter 21) income is measured on the horizontal axis, and aggregate demand is measured on the vertical axis. We assume that the economy has two sectors – households and businesses. As before the consumption schedule is upward-sloping, and given by the equation
$$C = 150 + 0.75Y.$$

Breakthrough of the UK South landward rail tunnel boring machine at Hollywell Coombe.

© Eurotunnel

Investment in infrastructur

© Eurotunnel

BOX 23.7

Aggregate demand in a two-sector economy

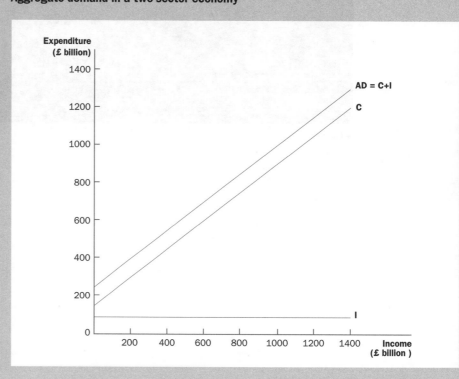

This time business investment, which is also a component of aggregate demand, is no longer zero, for we assume that businesses plan to undertake 100 of investment, shown in the graph as a horizontal line. Note that investment – unlike consumption – is assumed to be constant at all levels of national income. (We shall see below that the level of investment is however related to the growth of national income, as well as other factors.) Our investment equation is thus simply:

$$I = 100$$

We can now combine our consumption and investment equations:

$$C = 150 + 0.75Y$$
$$I = 100$$

Aggregate demand (AD) = C + I
= 150 + 0.75Y + 100
= 250 + 0.75Y

For equilibrium, C = Y
Hence 250 + 0.75Y = Y
Therefore Y = 1000

This outcome is illustrated in Box 23.8. Since the two axes have the same scale, the 45-degree line will show equal combinations of aggregate demand and national income. The equilibrium level of national income, 1000, is where this 45-degree line cuts aggregate demand, making it equal to national income.

BOX 23.8

Equilibrium level of national income

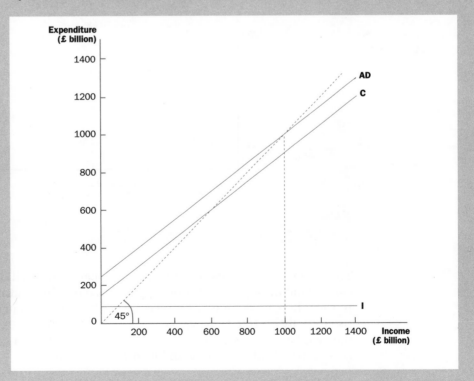

Suppose businesses now increase their investment expenditure from 100 to, say, 200. Aggregate demand will now be higher by 100. The effect of this on national income is precisely the same as when, in Chapter 21, consumption expenditure rose by 100. As before, the increase in expenditure will initially cause an unplanned reduction in business stocks. Businesses will respond by increasing their output, and factor incomes will rise. Box 23.9 shows us that the final outcome will be a new equilibrium level of national income of 1400: a 100 initial increase in aggregate demand has resulted in a 400 increase in national income.

BOX 23.9

A shift in aggregate demand: the multiplier process

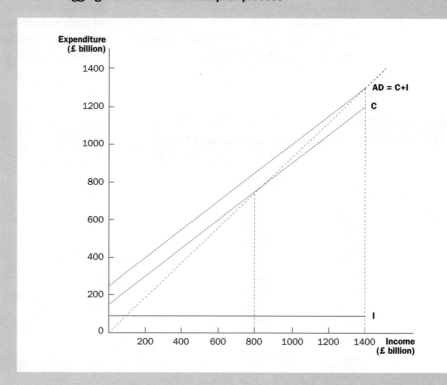

This increase in national income has come about through a multiplier process. In our example factor incomes rise initially by 100. However some of this will be spent on goods and services, generating a further increase in income; part of this will in turn be re-spent, and so on. The multiplier stream of extra income generated will be:
100 + 75 + 56.62 + 42.19 +.... + = 400
The multiplier coefficient is seen to be equal to 4.

Investment and aggregate supply

Unlike consumption, investment also affects conditions of aggregate supply. As we saw earlier in this chapter, a desire to increase efficiency is a prime reason for investment, and increases in the capital stock via investment are undoubtedly associated with improvements in output and productivity. In the long term, in both the Keynesian and the classical models, higher investment has the effect of increasing aggregate supply. In graphical terms, we show this by shifting the short-term aggregate supply schedule to the right. The outcome, for any given level of aggregate demand, is then an increase in the equilibrium level of national output. Additionally, in the classical model the effect of additional investment is to shift to the right the vertical long-term aggregate supply curve, which corresponds to the 'natural rate' of national output and employment (Chapter 21).

Hence an economy with an unnecessarily low level of investment – such as the extracts in Box 23.1 and 23.2 above assert was the case in the UK in the early 1990s – might risk losing out on desirable gains in aggregate supply and competitiveness. Remember then that investment (unlike consumption) has an important effect on both aggregate demand and aggregate supply.

The difference between the predicted effects of an increase in the level of investment in the two models, Keynesian and classical, is one of emphasis. Both point to possible short-term inflationary pressures. Both point to likely long-term improvements in costs and supply, with possible downward effects on inflation, when investments come on stream. On either analysis, an unnecessarily low level of investment, such as that alleged for the UK in the early 1990s, is associated with a loss of prospective long-term gains in aggregate supply and competitiveness, compared with economies experiencing higher investment levels. Hence Eddie George's warning (Focus 4.23) that by rejecting viable investment projects in the early 1990s, Britain's firms were reducing the long-term potential for supply and cost improvements, and so helping to maintain pressures for inflation which they feared in the first place!

TASK 23.2

In the new classical model, short-term aggregate supply is assumed, due to rational expectations, to be vertical and totally inelastic (Chapter 21). Construct a graph to analyse the short- and long-term macroeconomic effects of an increase in investment for the new-classical model, and explain the thinking behind how you drew the graph.

Factors affecting levels of investment

Economists have developed a number of theories to explain the behaviour of business investment, and we now need to examine these and see how they might relate to investment behaviour in the 1990s. The main influences on the level of business investment are considered to be:

- the level of inflation;
- rates of interest, which measure the 'cost' of investing in projects;
- the anticipated profitability of investing in a project;
- the trend of anticipated product demand;
- capital stock adjustment needs;
- business debt levels and the availability of investment finance.

Investment and inflation

The extract in Focus 4.23 criticised British businesses for requiring excessively high rates of profit and cash flow on investment. It argues that since the outlook for inflation in the UK was now better, conditions for investment were more favourable and firms should therefore be going ahead and investing in more projects – to the benefit of themselves and the supply side of the UK economy. How, then, does inflation affect investment decisions? When it is anticipated, high inflation can have favourable effects on investment. It can reduce the burden of debt repayment and may make it easier – at least for a time – for firms to widen profit margins following an investment. However one of the characteristics of high inflation is that it is also likely to be more variable. For instance, in the UK between 1965 and 1990 the level of inflation, at an average value of 9%, was two-and-a-half times higher than in the previous twenty years, but varied four times as much. High and variable inflation is likely to have a damaging effect on investment prospects.

In the first place, high and variable inflation increases the difficulty of assessing economic conditions in future years, leading to greater uncertainty and risk. To offset this, firms will require higher returns and will be likely to reject otherwise viable investment opportunities. Secondly, savers and lenders may require a 'risk premium' in the form of higher interest rates, which will tend to reduce investment. On balance, economists believe that high, and variable, inflation has an adverse effect on investment. Many firms in the mid-1990s doubted that low inflation would really last – so they were sticking to the high investment hurdles they had used in the past.

BOX 23.10

Falling UK inflation

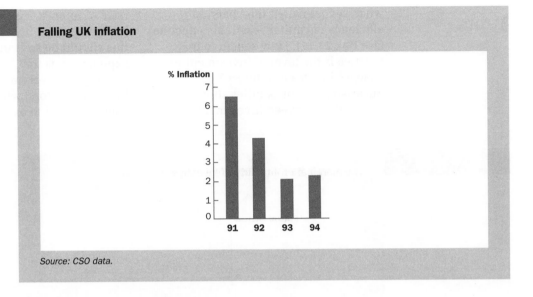

Source: CSO data.

The rate of interest: the 'cost' of investing

In general terms, firms invest to make a profit. An investment which doesn't achieve this will not pay for itself and will turn out unviable. The decision whether to go ahead with an investment project will depend on the relationship between the anticipated rate of return and the expected rate of interest over the life of the project, which measures the cost of financing the investment. If the estimated rate of profit on a project were 15 per cent, then having to pay 20 per cent interest for investment funds would lead to a loss – the project wouldn't be worthwhile. At an anticipated rate of interest of 10 per cent, however, the same project would become viable. The same would apply for investment financed out of a firm's own funds. Here the rate of interest then measures the opportunity cost of employing these funds in alternative

uses. Movements in interest rates can also influence investment by providing an indicator of likely future economic conditions. As we explain in Chapter 26, rising interest rates may be a signal of government action to restrain the growth of demand – which could have a downward impact on firms' sales and returns.

At any given time there will be available a range of potential investment projects over the economy, some expected to yield high rates of profit return, some lower rates, others possibly an outright loss. Other things being equal, the lower the anticipated rate of interest, the greater will be the number of viable projects and hence the higher the level of total investment undertaken. At the same time, the profitability of marginal investment –

what Keynes called the 'marginal efficiency of capital' – will also decline (see Box 23.11). How sensitive in practice is the level of investment to changes in rates of interest ? Surprisingly, most studies show little connection between investment and rates of interest – investment appears to be very interest-inelastic! Quite why this should be so is unclear. One explanation is that investment is actually relatively interest-elastic, but that other factors, which we shall now consider, tend to override this effect.

BOX 23.11

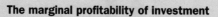

The marginal profitability of investment

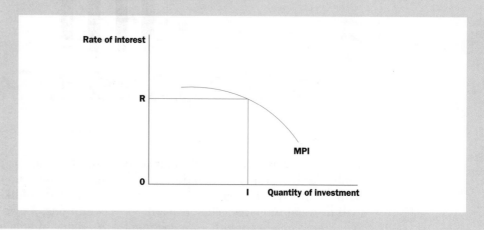

Investment and profitability

Other things being equal, higher profitability will improve the prospects for investment. In the first place, about two-thirds of business investment in the UK is financed out of retained profits, and so the higher their level, the more funds become available for financing investment. Secondly, increased current profits may be taken to indicate a higher return on new, future, capital projects. This could encourage firms to place their funds into investment rather than employing them elsewhere.

Box 23.12 makes clear the improvement in the profit levels of British business in recent decades. We can see that in the 1990s' recession/recovery the average rate of return on invested capital was almost twice as high as in the corresponding stage in the last cycle. There were a number of factors behind this improvement, but one was undoubtedly a strong improvement in labour productivity, relative to wage levels, over the period. (Productivity increased by 36% between 1990 and 1993, compared with a rise of only 9.4% in 1979–82.) It is clear that profit conditions were relatively favourable for investment in the early 1990s, as was the movement in inflation, which we examined above.

BOX 23.12

Profitability in three recessions/recoveries

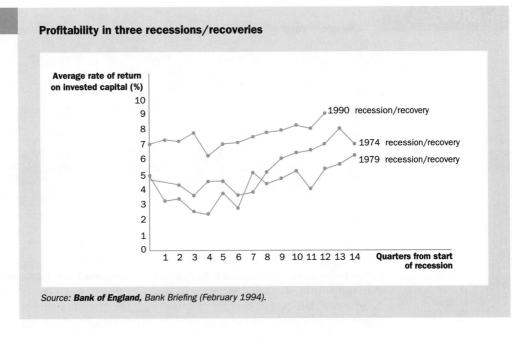

Source: **Bank of England,** Bank Briefing (February 1994).

Investment and changes in consumer demand: the 'accelerator effect'

*The **accelerator effect** is the principle that the level of aggregate investment is a function of the rate of change of income and product demand.*

Another factor which can influence investment prospects is the 'accelerator effect'.

This relates the level of planned investment to the rate of change of income and consumer demand for the output of businesses. To see how this works, consider an example of a firm producing aircraft seats which has for some years been experiencing a steady level of output and sales. Recently, however, these have risen substantially, and the growth of sales is expected to be maintained in the years ahead. How will the firm's investment requirement be affected?

We begin by making the following assumptions:

● The firm's investment capital has an average life of ten years;
● One-fifth of its capital stock comes up for replacement each year;
● It has a capital-output ratio of 2:1 – That is, it needs £2000 of investment capital to be able to deliver £1000 of output.

BOX 23.13

The accelerator effect

Year	Sales	Existing capital	Required capital	Replacement Inv.	Net Inv.	Total Inv.
1	100	200	200	40	0	40
2	110	200	220	40	20	60
3	120	220	240	40	20	60
4	130	240	260	40	20	60
5	130	260	260	40	0	40
6	120	260	240	0	0	0

In year 1, the size of the firm's capital stock is in equilibrium with 40 units of investment being undertaken to replace existing capital as it depreciates. In year 2, however, the 'acceleration' of sales generates an increased investment requirement of 60 units – 40 for capital replacement plus a further 20 net investment to bring the capital stock up to its required level. In years 3 and 4 further increased 'doses' of investment are again needed. However in years 5 and 6 the level of sales unexpectedly levels off and then declines. Note what happens – total investment collapses, first to 40 units and then to zero. The 'accelerator effect' thus relates the level of required investment for an individual firm, and the economy as a whole, to rates of change of output. This makes for unstable investment patterns following fluctuations in rates of change of output.

How does the accelerator theory of investment perform in practice? Research shows that often the accelerator theory has not been a good predictor of changes in investment levels! You will be able to work out for yourself the main reasons for this when you tackle Task 23.3.

TASK 23.3

In practice the accelerator does not drive investment so directly as Box 23.13 suggests, for firms will often seek to 'smooth' the potential accelerator effect by satisfying changes in demand with the minimum of changes in investment.

In terms of our aircraft seat supplier, above suggest **four** ways in which a firm might attempt to satisfy increases in demand **without** undertaking the full increases in capital employed suggested by the accelerator.

Investment and capital stock adjustment

In Task 23.4 you were asked to think of ways in which firms might be able, as it were, to 'squeeze' more output from a given capital stock. The notion that capital–output ratios are flexible in this way has given rise to an investment theory, the capital stock adjustment model, which states that investment levels are likely to be positively related to firms' level of output, and negatively related to their existing capital stock. So, for a given acceleration of output, the greater is the inherited capital stock, the less will be the level of investment required for replacing or adding to existing capacity. This suggests that at times of low economic activity with low levels of capacity usage, the link between demand and investment will be relatively weak. Higher investment in response to rising demand will tend to take place at times of high economic activity, when output is increasing sufficiently to stretch firms' production capacity. Research has shown the capital stock adjustment model to be quite effective in explaining investment levels.

Investment and debt levels

Firms' debt levels can also influence investment, as the extract in Box 23.14 makes clear.

BOX 23.14

Debt worries holding back investment

Britain's no-inflation recovery is being put at risk by weak business investment intentions, which are still struggling to recovery after the long recession, according to a financial economist of a leading financial group yesterday. William Simpson said that a strong rise in investment is necessary, to exploit advances in productivity and reduce long-term inflationary pressures. However investment is flagging because many businesses are still struggling to pay off debts they built up in the 1980s' boom. Also, according to William Simpson, many businesses are still finding it difficult to collect debts from each other. Only when this 'overhang' of debt is further reduced, will businesses be prepared to commit substantial funds for new investments.

*Source: Adapted from **press reports** (1994).*

Testing investment theories for the 1990s

In 1994 a Bank of England research survey on factors influencing investment found that:

- many firms were limiting investment because of uncertainty about demand (accelerator theory);
- nearly one-half of firms were limiting investment because of inadequate anticipated rates of return (profitability theory);
- in a number of sectors capital overcapacity was still limiting investment (Capital stock adjustment theory);
- investment intentions were often being constrained by concern about firms' financial position, especially in relation to high debt levels (debt factor).

Thus the research confirmed the predictive power of several of the theories we have examined. However the Bank's survey found that interest rates and changes in inflation were not significantly affecting investment:

- few firms were worried about the effect of rates of interest on the cost of financing investment
- many firms had not adjusted their investment strategies upwards to take account of lower inflation.

BOX 23.15

Japanese encourage change at Oxford Automotive Components

Component makers are the cinderellas of the motor industry, making up to 30 000 separate parts, employing 140 000 people and with exports worth £3 billion. Five of the top ten European car component suppliers are British, including Lucas, GKN and Pilkington. Many foreign businesses, such as Bosch, VW and Mercedes have set up in Britain to take advantage of low labour costs and the potential for high productivity. The underlying reason is that Japanese carmakers have helped turn UK suppliers into some of the most efficient in the world.

When Honda came to Britain, Oxford Automotive Components, a division of Unipart, sent them an application to supply plastic fuel tanks. Honda rejected it, with a 200-fault commentary. OAD reduced the fault level, sent back a new improved tank and eventually became sole supplier to Honda's new Swindon car plant.

When OAD got the Honda contract it faced great difficulty in introducing a modern production system into a factory steeped in traditional work practices. Encouraged by Honda, Japanese-style management was introduced. There were no bonuses, clocking-in checks or foremen. Small production teams carried out their own maintenance and quality control The result was that a failure rate of one tank in 100 went to one in every 400. OAD employees accepted new practices, along with 'staff status' giving them sickness pay, paternity leave and other benefits. Soon the Japanese-style management had rippled throughout Unipart, leading to big improvements in productivity.

*Source: Adapted from 'The Japanese Carmaker Invasion', **The Times** (September 1993).*

The quality of investment

We have focused in this chapter on the quantity of investment being undertaken by businesses in Britain. Numerous studies have shown that this is associated, via changes in efficiency, with the rate of economic growth. Sometimes it is argued that investment is not the cause but the result of economic growth. A high rate of economic growth means rapidly expanding production requirements, which could be seen as making it necessary for businesses to invest more in extra capital and capacity. The general view however is that investment is a necessary but not always a sufficient condition for economic growth. Improvements in efficiency and output will be related to the quantity of investment being undertaken – but will also depend on how effectively investment is put to use. One way of measuring this is through observed changes in capital–output ratios. The lower such a ratio, the more output is being obtained from a given quantity of invested capital and the less investment

is needed to generate a given increase in output capacity. How have capital – output ratios in the UK compared with other economies?

For much of the post-war period, capital–output ratios for the UK economy as a whole, and in manufacturing in particular were disappointingly high. In the 1970s, for instance, new investments in the United States were on average twice as efficient as corresponding British ones, in terms of labour and capital productivity! By the 1980s, however, the efficiency of British investments was starting to improve significantly. One reason for this was that two recent and severe recessions had 'knocked out' a lot of inefficient capacity of older vintage. Secondly, 'Thatcherite' supply-side policies probably contributed to improvements in efficiency. Thirdly, and very important, a surge of inward foreign investment helped greatly to 'pull up' UK business performance, as indicated in the extract in the Review below.

BOX 23.16	**How the Pas de Calais and Kent could benefit from the Channel Tunnel**

Belgian holidaymakers are certainly benefiting from the Channel Tunnel. The new Autoroute from Brussels, designed to improve access to the tunnel and Channel ferries, takes them for a weekend break past the terminal at Calais to the 'Opal Coast' south of Boulogne, and the Le Touquet summer playground. Since last year when the Autoroute opened, the number of Belgian holidaymakers in the Pas de Calais area has risen by 60 per cent. There are plans for a 'Project Napoleon' to provide more shops and eating places on the Boulogne waterfront, and talk there of extending the £16 million Nausicaa saltwater aquarium as visitor numbers climb past 6000 towards 8000 a year. Tourism can be developed quickly, requires few subsidies and absorbs unemployment faster than manufacturing. Much of the coastline is unspoilt and the farming country inland is attractive, and improved roads and rail links are making these areas more accessible to tourist visitors. Even Londoners are using the Shuttle to take more short breaks to France.

But so far the town of Calais itself hasn't got much from the Tunnel. Selling snacks to tourists as they board the shuttles or boats doesn't help the jobless of Calais very

BOX 23.16

much. One difficulty is that after being bombed in the Second World War, Calais was rebuilt with so little charm. So the day-trippers go elsewhere when they can. Calais councillors are doing their best to attract more spending from the flow of traffic around their town, but this is proving hard. Yet unemployment in Calais, which fell to 16 per cent during tunnel construction, is now close to 18 per cent. Unfortunately, older industries, such as paint-whiteners, chemicals, and talcum powder are the mainstays of its manufacturing. But there is cheap space available for industry in Calais, and Eurotunnel is aiming to invest £10 billion in developing La Cite de L'Europe, which will be a 250-acre complex of business park, shops, hotels and leisure facilities. It is also hoped that haulage and distribution companies will be drawn to the Calais. But so far such knock-on investment from the Tunnel has been modest.

Could Kent, on the English side of the Channel, also benefit more from the Tunnel? It could perhaps learn from the 'French Connection' which has shown the importance of infrastructure spending to service the Tunnel, and of education and training to support the skills needed for economic regeneration.

*Source: adapted from the **Times,** 25/7/94.*

REVIEW

After studying this chapter, what is your conclusion – was unnecessarily low investment in the early 1990s a threat to the UK economy? We noted the apparent failure of many British firms to increase investment in response to low inflation. We also noted that at this same time foreign businesses were 'queueing up' to invest here. So were British firms failing to appreciate and take up domestic investment opportunities? However, we should remember that investment levels in the UK now compared well with other advanced economies. Also, as we have seen, the quality of investment had improved. Could it be that the high investment hurdles which businesses were employing, and being so criticised for, simply reflected their improved business performance? Where this generates a large number of promising investment projects, imposing high rate-of-return hurdles is the best means of selecting the very best! As so often in economic affairs, the answers to important questions become clearer only with the outcome of events. For the present, a reasonable end-of-term report on British investment in the early 1990s might be, 'Considerable improvement in performance to date, but a bit over-cautious on inflation. Keep trying, quite a lot still to do'.

REVIEW TASK

How foreign investment can strengthen Britain's economy

The UK economy is now one of the most international in the western world. Why has foreign investment been so much higher in the UK than elsewhere? Over recent decades, the USA and Japan have directed around 40 per cent of their direct overseas investment into the UK – by 1992, Japanese manufacturing companies employed a total of 65,000 workers there. German investors were also active in the UK. Almost 1,000 German companies employed a total of more than 100,000 people there, half of them in manufacturing. Why so much foreign investment? It was encouraged when economic deregulation encouraged freer movement of capital, and by favourable economic growth. Also businesses outside the EC build plants inside the Community to sidestep import

REVIEW TASK

barriers. Again, the high cost of technology encouraged international companies to spread development costs. This explains the international flavour of successful UK industrial companies such as Pilkington or GKN, which have not been slow to acquire overseas rivals and gain access to new markets.

In an intensely competitive environment, companies are increasingly prepared to sell off failing businesses interests. This provides investment opportunities both for foreign businesses in Britain and for British ones abroad. This is how Italy's Fiat built up its European truck market position by buying in to the Ford plant in Berkshire.
According to a CBI study, when the UK hosts top-quality foreign businesses it learns about best practice in manufacturing methods, quality standards and product development. Hence the way UK car components makers have raised quality standards to meet the demands of Japanese clients. And German engineering groups are increasingly integrating into the UK scene.

Adapted from press reports August 1993

1   Why has foreign investment been so much higher in Britain than elsewhere?
2   What do foreigners own, and will their presence prove a strength, or a weakness, in the UK of the late 1990s?
3   How might inward investment be spurred by deregulation?

QUESTIONS

Multiple choice

Question 1 is based on the diagram below.

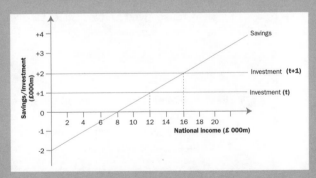

1   **If the diagram represents a closed economy with no government sector, the change in national income equilibrium resulting from the increase in investment from (t) to (t + 1) suggests that the investment multiplier is**

A   4.00
B   2.00
C   1.33
D   0.75
E   0.25

(ULEAC, 1994)

2 **What would cause the value of the accelerator to increase?**
A   a reduction in the tax rates
B   an increase in the capital–output ratio
C   an increase in the saving ratio
D   an increase in the marginal propensity to consume.

(WJEC, 1994)

3 **Investment is said to be interest elastic when**
A   a fall in interest rates leads to an increased volume of investment
B   a fall in interest rates leads to an increased value of investment
C   a change in interest rates leads to a greater proportionate change in the value of investment
D   a change in interest rates leads to a smaller proportionate change in the value of investment
E   a change in interest rates leads to a similar proportionate change in the value of investment.

(ULEAC, 1994)

4 **The accelerator principle states that**
A   the rate of interest determines the rate of investment
B   the capital/output ratio is altered by changes in demand
C   the rate of change in demand for consumer goods has a more than proportionate effect on the rate of investment
D   the rate of change in investment affects the rate of change in output
E   an increase in induced investment will lead to a more than proportionate increase in autonomous investment.

(ULEAC, 1994)

5 **The marginal efficiency of capital will increase if there is a rise in**
1   the price of capital goods
2   the marginal productivity of capital
3   business confidence about the future of the economy.

A   1 only
B   1 and 2
C   2 and 3
D   1,2 and 3

(IB, 1994)

Data response

Study the tables below carefully, then answer each of the questions which follow.

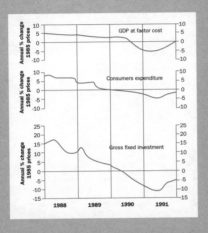

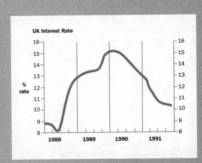

a   Describe the trends in consumption, investment and GDP between 1988 and 1991.

b   i   What does the data suggest about the relationship between GDP and investment?

   ii   Explain whether this relationship is the one which might be expected in economic theory.

c   Did the fall in interest rates during 1990 have the effect upon consumption and investment which might have been expected? Give reasons for your answer.

d   Explain two possible reasons why the Government might have increased interest rates so sharply during 1988 and 1989.

(WJEC)

4.24

FOCUS

UK inflation, 1945-95

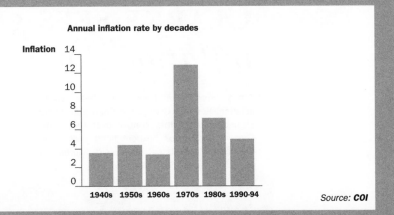

Annual inflation rate by decades

Source: *COI*

Inflation CONTINUES TO SURPRISE

Recent inflation data has continued to surprise. Earlier this year we concluded there was good reason for believing that low inflation could be sustained in the medium term. However economic conditions are now reawakening new inflation fears.

*Source: **Adapted from Lloyds Bank Economical Bulletin** (December 1994).*

Surging INPUT PRICES INCREASE INFLATION FEARS

New government figures showed a rise in prices charged by manufacturers for finished goods and paid for raw materials, raising fears over inflation. At the moment manufacturers are absorbing higher costs but there are fresh worries that those operating close to full capacity will soon be passing these costs on to customers. Building costs are set to rise up to 10%, stainless steel prices have risen for the 22nd consecutive month, and plastics prices are going through the roof.

*Source: Adapted from **The Times** (26 July 1994 and 13 December 1994).*

CLARKE SEES *growth up, inflation down*

The government has lowered its predictions for inflation. Kenneth Clarke, the Chancellor of the Exchequer, says that control over the money supply and price expectations are both favourable. The latest economic figures are quite the best combination of circumstances pointing to sustainable growth with low inflation which he can remember for a long time.

Source: Adapted from ***The Times*** *(10 June 1994).*

World OF FALLING PRICES

There are reasons for arguing that inflation world-wide will continue falling so that by the end of the 1990s it will to all extents and purposes have disappeared – perhaps to be replaced by minus inflation. If this seems absurd, remember that prices in the UK were roughly the same in 1930 as they were in 1650. We could be starting a century of falling prices.

*Source: Adapted from **Independent**, (18 March 1994).*

Low inflation IS JUST A BLIP

Low inflation is just a blip, for there has been no fundamental improvement in Britain's inflation performance since the early 1980s. Once the old demand pressures return, inflation can be expected to rise again.

*Source: Adapted from **New Economy** –*
Labour Party Think Tank (1995).

Wage fears SPOIL INFLATION HOPES

The CBI has renewed its warnings about increasing cost pressures on inflation, particularly from rising wage settlements, which are running at a higher level than abroad. Pay awards in manufacturing are running at 3.4%, well up on last year's 2.3%, and are being masked only by improving productivity. Government ministers however insist that there is no evidence of rising wage settlements.

*Source: Based on **press reports***
(28 December 1994)

Preview

In this chapter we will investigate the following key areas:

- methods of measuring inflation;
- the equation of exchange;
- the monetary 'transmission mechanism';
- the monetary theory of inflation;
- Keynesian theories of inflation;
- expectations and inflation.

Inflation is often defined as a continual and persistently rising general price level. In recent decades inflation has been one of Britain's most pressing economic issues. Economists are far from agreeing on the causes of inflation, and this is reflected in the differing views expressed in Focus 4.24 on Britain's inflation prospects. You can see that some commentators thought that inflation was well and truly beaten. Others believed there was a real risk of higher inflation. Three main theories

have been developed to try to explain inflation and these underlie the arguments in Focus 4.24:

- monetary inflation due to excessive expansion in the supply of money;
- demand inflation due to excessive expansion of aggregate demand in relation to aggregate supply;
- cost inflation due to upward cost pressure on the general price level, independently of the level of aggregate demand.

Demand inflation – inflation resulting from an excessive expansion of aggregate demand in relation to aggregate supply;

Cost inflation – upward pressure on the general price level, independently of the level of aggregate demand, due to increasing costs

Measuring inflation

Retail price indexes

*The **Retail Prices Index** (RPI) is the basic 'headline' rate of inflation, based on the observed retail prices of a basket of goods and services, and published monthly by the Central Statistical Office.*

However before we examine possible causes of inflation it is useful to look at how it is measured. When we say that the general price level has 'risen by 5%', what do we mean? We obviously don't mean that the price of every single good and service has risen by exactly that much. What we mean is that prices on average have risen that much. A retail price index is a convenient way of measuring this. Index numbers deal with percentage changes and in a price

index the number 100 is used as the base or starting point for measuring price changes, first for individual goods and services over a given period, and then for combining these in an overall index for the general price level.

One leading set of inflation indexes measure changes in the retail prices of a 'representative' basket of consumer goods and services, as explained in Box 24.1.

BOX 24.1

RPI, RPIX, and RPIY

The 'headline' rate of inflation is the rate of change of the Retail Prices Index (RPI). This is based on the observed prices of a basket of goods and services, and is published each month by the Central Statistical Office. Two other important measures are obtained by taking items out of the basket.

- RPIX is the RPI excluding mortgage interest payments. This is the measure for which the Government has set a 1-4% inflation target.
- RPIY is RPIX excluding indirect and local authority taxes.

Source: **Bank of England Bank Briefing** (November 1994).

RPIX is the RPI excluding mortgage interest payments.

RPIY is the RPIX excluding indirect and local authority taxes.

*The **GDP deflator** is a measure of changes in the prices of all goods and services produced over a given period (not just a sample), derived from converting GDP at current prices, to GDP at constant factor prices.*

Index of input prices – an index which measures changes in the prices of the materials, fuel and other inputs used by manufacturers.

Index of output prices – an index which measures changes in the prices of manufacturing products 'at the factory gate', before they move on to the retail stage for final sale.

The GDP deflator

A more basic measure of inflation is provided by the GDP deflator.

In contrast to the retail price indexes, which measure a sample of price changes the GDP deflator measures changes in the prices of all goods and services over a given period. It does this by using national income account data, to convert current-price GDP over a given period, to GDP at constant factor prices. The GDP deflator is more comprehesive in scope, and in principle more accurate, than the retail price indexes, though these have the advantage of being quick and easy to compile on a monthly basis. In practice, movements in the two sets of indexes described do not diverge very much.

Indexes of input and output prices

Businesses and governments are also interested in changes in manufacturing input and output prices for these often provide a guide to future movements of prices at the retail level. An index of input prices measures changes in the prices of the materials, fuel and other inputs, many of which are imported, used by manufacturers. An index of output prices measures changes in the prices of manufacturing products 'at the factory gate', before they move on to the retail stage for final sale.

BOX 24.2

Removing indirect taxes from the RPI

Why invent another measure?

The Government's target range for inflation is defined in terms of the RPI excluding mortgage interest payments (RPIX). With such a specific objective, the performance of policy-makers is easy to monitor, since RPIX is published monthly along with the headline rate. So why construct a further measure?

The main purpose is to distinguish between those changes in inflation that are the result of either a temporary movement or a step adjustment to the price level, and those that reflect a change to the underlying inflation rate.

Government itself is a major source of one-off disturbances to the price level. In 1991, the increase in the standard rate of VAT had an immediate effect on many of the prices included in the RPI, and resulted in a step change in prices. Last year's transition from the Community Charge to the Council Tax produced a similar step change, as the average household bill dropped by around 9%. The forthcoming broadening of the VAT base will cause a further step increase. The so-called 'double indexation' effect of excise duties resulting from last year's move to a unified Autumn Budget will cause two step changes within the year (once-a-year indexation has no effect on twelve–month inflation rates).

These step changes may affect measures of inflation in the short run in a way which runs in the opposite direction to their medium-term effects. So removing the transitory, direct price effects of fiscal and monetary policy should provide a guide to underlying inflationary pressure.

What does RPIY measure?

As the November Inflation Report described, RPIY measures inflation excluding all local authority and indirect taxes (VAT and duties), in addition to mortgage interest payments. About 60% of the RPI basket currently attracts VAT. Excise duties are also levied on items such as alcohol, tobacco and petrol – which represent around 15% of the basket; together with VAT, these duties can account for more than half of the retail price.

Because RPIY removes that part of the final price which the retailer passes on to the government in the form of tax and duties, it can be thought of as an index of the prices faced by final suppliers. These prices sometimes move quite differently from those faced by consumers. When indirect taxes are raised, for example, retailers may decide not to pass on the whole increase. Final consumers may then face a smaller-than-expected price rise, while final suppliers accept a price fall.

BOX 24.2

How is RPIY calculated?

Although RPIY is a simple concept, calculating is not straightforward. Identifying and removing excise duties and VAT from the component price series should, strictly, be done at a level of disaggregation which reveals the range of variation in duties and VAT status. RPIY is calculated using a more aggregated approach, but the same basic procedures, for identifying and removing taxes from component prices and for reweighting the adjusted series within the new index are applied.

Conventionally, duties are fixed in cash terms. This means that the published price indices must first be expressed as cash prices, by applying a base-period price. The cash value of duties can then be deducted, and a new price index computed. The effect of the calculation can be striking. In January 1990, a litre of 4-star petrol sold at around 41p, of which 26p was duty and VAT. Four years later, the price had risen to about 56p – a 36% increase. But if indirect taxes are excluded, the supply price rose by only 10%.

Reweighting the adjusted price series is a key part of calculating RPIY. The petrol example shows that removing the indirect tax component can have a big effect on the cash price. In calculating RPIY, we have adjusted the weights of the component series to reflect these changed cash values. Items such as petrol have a much-reduced weight, while for items such as food – where only a small proportion is subject to VAT – the new weights are larger than in the standard RPI basket.

The chart compares RPIX and RPIY inflation since 1979.

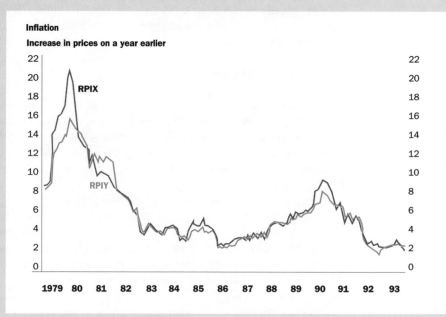

*Source: **Bank of England Inflation Review** (February 1994).*

TASK 24.1

1 What is the main purpose of constructing a separate RPIY index?
2 Why would it be preferable to subtract indirect taxes from prices at a 'disaggregated level' (i.e. for separate goods and services)?
3 Why should RPIY inflation have been much lower than RPIX inflation around 1980?

BOX 24.3

RPI, RPIX, and RPIY, 1992–94

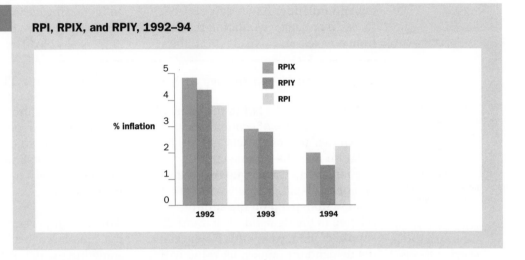

BOX 24.4

Is 3 per cent inflation 'really' zero inflation?

The inflation indexes we met above are not designed to take account of changes in the quality of goods and services produced and sold. If over a given year the UK price of a Fiat Tipo goes up from £8000 to £8200, this is entered into an inflation index, along with price changes of other goods and services, as a 2.5% price increase. But what if the Tipo at the end of the period is a much improved product, with, say, improved braking and road holding, so that Tipo drivers reckon the car is now actually better value for money? Isn't there a sense in which the 'real' price of a Tipo car may have fallen?

The quality of many goods and services purchased over the years in the UK has probably improved significantly – think of personal computers, mountain bikes and supermarket wines, for instance. Some economists reckon such quality improvements amount to 1–2% improved value. Secondly, inflation indexes, by missing out on supermarket 'special offers', car boot sales, charity shops, etc. could be overstating inflation by around another 2%. So 3 per cent inflation might 'really' be zero inflation. And 3 per cent inflation turns out to be near the centre of the UK government's inflation target range!

Three theories of inflation

Now that we have looked at the costs and measurement of inflation it is time to examine the three leading theories which economists have developed to explain inflation. As we saw above these are: monetary inflation resulting from an excessive expansion in the supply of money; demand inflation resulting from an excessive expansion of aggregate demand in relation to aggregate supply; and cost inflation due to increasing costs independently of the level of aggregate demand.

1 The monetarist theory of inflation: the Quantity Theory of Money

Monetary inflation –
inflation resulting from an
excessive expansion in the
supply of money;

*The **quantity theory of***
***money** is the assertion*
that, in terms of the
equation of exchange,
there is a direct, one-way
relationship between
changes in the supply
of money, M, and
resulting changes in the
price level, P.

Since inflation is a fall in the value of money, the group of economists who are known as monetarists assert that inflation must be a 'monetary' phenomenon. They argue that the value of money, like that of any other good or asset, will depend on the supply relative to the demand for it. So if the supply of money expands faster than the demand for money, its value will fall – there will be a rise in the general price level. We can look at this idea through the equation of exchange (also known as the Fisher equation) which relates the stock of money to the general price level.

The version of the equation which we shall be using is:

$$MV = PY$$

where for a given period: M is the stock of money being held by economic agents; V is the 'income velocity of circulation', which is the average number of times a unit of money is used in purchasing goods and services; P is the average price of each good or service produced; Y is real income – that is, the total volume of goods and services produced.

Since MV measures total expenditure on output over a period and PY measures the value of output being produced, by definition total expenditure MV must equal total receipts PY.

Now it is important to understand that the equation of exchange is a truism, something which is true at all times by definition. It explains nothing, but it is useful for exploring how M, P, V and T might relate to one another. Monetarists believe, on the basis of their analysis and research, that Y and V tend to be constant. Hence any changes in M will lead to corresponding changes in P – 'P will vary as M'.

This direct, one-way relationship between changes in money and resulting changes in the price level, is called the Quantity Theory of Money

According to this theory, then, if M is expanding at (say) 15 per cent, P will also increase at that rate. A zero expansion of M would deliver zero inflation.

Why should Y be constant?

Why do monetarists believe that Y is constant? The equation of exchange gives no help: it is true by definition and will 'work' whether Y (and V) are constant or not.

The answer is that monetarists accept the predictions of the classical model of the economy which we examined in Chapter 22. You will recall that this asserts that an increase in aggregate demand may lead to short-term expansion in national output, but in the long term national output Y will always return its 'natural rate'. In terms of the equation of exchange, changes in total expenditure PT will have no effect on the long-term level of national output Y.

Why should V be constant?

Monetarists also believe that V will tend to be constant. This amounts to saying that that there will be a stable demand for money on the part of economic agents, in that they will seek to hold a stable proportion of their assets in the form of money.

You can explore the framework for this in Box 24.6.

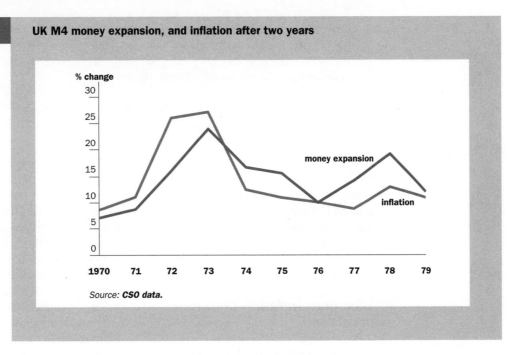

BOX 24.5   **UK M4 money expansion, and inflation after two years**

Source: CSO data.

BOX 24.6

The monetary 'transmission mechanism'

Consider the case of an increase in the money supply. In the first instance, this will create an imbalance between the demand and supply of money. Economic agents will therefore seek to 'unload' unrequired excess money balances. Some balances will be used to purchase financial assets, some to purchase goods and services.

The first operation – purchasing financial assets – will drive up the price of assets, and reduce their market yield, which means a reduction in the rate of interest. Given some inertia in the setting of nominal wages and prices, the lower level of nominal interest rates will, in the short run, imply a lower level of real interest rates. This will increase real aggregate demand in two main ways. First, the lower rate of interest, by reducing the opportunity cost of holding money, will lead to a switch of spending from the future to the present, as saving becomes less attractive. Second, lower real interest rates will increase asset prices and hence wealth. Both effects will, indirectly, increase consumer spending and private investment and hence the demand to hold money.

The second operation – purchasing goods and services – will lead to a direct short-term expansion in the output of goods and services, and a related increase in the demand to hold money. The two operations will continue until the extra demand for money balances the initial increase in its supply. Evidence suggests the time needed for the adjustment is variable but, for the UK, of the order of 18 months.

*Source: **Bank of England Quarterly Bulletin** (August 1994).*

Box 24.6 shows how the demand for money is positively related to the level of output and prices, and negatively related to the rate of interest. Monetarists believe these two factors will tend to cancel out, leaving a stable demand to hold money, and hence a stable value for V.

Why does inflation tend to accelerate?

One common feature of inflation is that it often tends to accelerate. If people hold adaptive expectations (see Chapter 21) actual inflation will feed off expected inflation, with this year's general price level consisting of an expansion-of-monetary demand effect plus an expected change in prices. This is likely to occur when a government undertakes an expansion of the money supply in an attempt to reduce unemployment below its natural level. In the short term the economy expands with an improvement in employment. In the longer term, however, employment falls back to its natural rate, but at a higher price level. If the government tries again to reduce unemployment below its natural level will need to expand the money supply by more than on its first attempt. This is because as well as reducing unemployment it must now also accommodate a higher expected level of inflation. In order to keep unemployment below its natural rate, the government would have to accept an accelerating rate of inflation.
Look at Box 24.7.

BOX 24.7

'Holding a tiger by the tail'

According to Friedrich Hayek, a government which finds itself in the money expanding position described above is 'holding a tiger by the tail'. Sooner or late it will have to 'let go' and reduce the expansion of money, if it is to resist accelerating inflation. The outcome will then be a severe recession. The longer the delay, the worse this recession will be.

2 Two Keynesian theories of inflation

Exogenous determination of money is the view that the supply of money is determined by the monetary authority, outside and independently of the economic system

Endogenous determination of money is the view that the supply of money is determined inside the economic system, by the level of economic activity and demand for money.

The Keynesian inflation model is similar to that used by monetarists. The analysis, however, is different. Keynesian economists argue that Y and V in the equation of exchange are not constant. Therefore there won't necessarily be a direct link between changes in the money supply M and changes in the price level P, in other words changes in the price level could be due to non-monetary factors. First, in the Keynesian macroeconomic model there is no 'natural' level of output and so Y cannot be assumed constant. Secondly, in the the monetary 'transmission mechanism' described in Box 24.6 the demand effect for goods and services is believed by Keynesians to be relatively weak. Hence it is the indirect rate of interest effect on the demand for goods and services which dominates. This means that the demand to hold money, and its velocity of circulation, will not be stable in the way monetarists predict. Keynesians argue this is supported by data (see Chapter 4.25) which make clear the instability in the velocity of circulation for two measures of money in the UK.

Keynesians also disagree with monetarists about the causation of any link between M and P. It is true that an expansion of money is frequently observed to accompany increases in prices – but which is causing which?

Monetarists see the causation as running from M to P: more money causes higher prices. Keynesians believe the causation runs the other way, that a higher level of aggregate demand can generate an expanding money supply. (Monetarists believe the quantity of money to be independently, 'exogenously' determined, Keynesians believe it 'endogenously' determined.)

According to Keynesians, a higher level of economic activity will increase the demand for money balances. This will cause an increased flow of notes and coins (M0), via the Bank of England and the banks, to economic agents. It will also encourage the creation of more bank deposits (the main component of M4). So an increase in the demand for money can increase its own supply. However, even if the supply of money was not allowed to increase in this way, the unsatisfied money demand would, as explained above, lead to higher interest rates and an increase in its velocity of circulation. To satisfy the extra demand for it, the existing supply of money would have to 'work harder' and circulate more rapidly!

3 The Keynesian theory of demand inflation

In the Keynesian macroeconomic model equilibrium in the national economy is determined by both aggregate supply and aggregate demand. A sustained expansion in aggregate demand would eventually encounter increasingly inelastic conditions of aggregate supply. As a result there would take place an increase in the general price level. Facing difficulty in obtaining sufficient labour to meet rising product demand would compete for labour and bid up wage rates, thus increasing costs and exerting further upward pressure on prices. Moreover, higher wages would become a source of income for renewed expansion of aggregate demand. Hence a self-sustaining wage-price spiral could develop, the whole process being 'fuelled' by an expanding money supply or, failing this, an increase in its velocity of circulation.

Keynesians thus see demand inflation as an outcome of excessive expansion of aggregate demand in relation to aggregate supply. In principle this could be caused by any of its four components: household consumption, business investment, net exports or government spending on goods and services (see Chapter 27). Sometimes it might be over-expansionary government spending which would be primarily responsible. However, in the UK in the late 1980s sharp rises in consumption and investment were also important sources of inflationary pressure. In the mid-1990s, there were even fears that a rapid rise of exports could be generating an inflationary expansion of aggregate demand.

4 The Keynesian theory of cost-push inflation

The onset of 'stagflation' in the 1970s – rising inflation and falling employment – dealt a heavy blow to the Keynesian theory of demand inflation. In other words, at this time increases in the price level seemed to be occurring independently of the level of aggregate demand. Some Keynesians therefore abandoned the demand theory of inflation in favour of a 'cost' explanation, which we shall now consider. Cost-push inflation is said to occur when, independently of the level of aggregate demand, increasing costs of production become a source of upward pressure on the general price level. Since in the UK labour costs account for about two-thirds of total costs, attention has focused on wage increases as a source of inflationary pressure. Another potential source could be rising import prices.

Cost-push inflation can be linked to the concept of the target real wage, which asserts that worker groups in their wage bargaining aim for a given real wage increase each year. If the growth of the economy is insufficient to sustain this, worker groups are likely to aim for higher settlements and wage increases will tend to outstrip output, resulting in upward pressure on costs and prices. Since wage costs are part of final prices, it is natural to interpret rising wage settlements as a source of cost inflation. On the other hand, trade unions point out that rising wage settlements are often a response to rising prices, which may have been caused by demand inflation. The term wage-price spiral is often used to describe the way in which wages and prices may apparently 'chase' each other.

A falling exchange rate and cost inflation

Cost inflation could also result from rising import prices associated with a falling exchange rate of a country's currency, as for example occurred in the UK in early 1970s, when sterling was on a 'floating' exchange rate. First, a fall in the exchange rate would increase the unit cost of imports and lead to a rise in the general price level and cost of living. This would trigger new wage claims as employees sought to maintain their target real wage. If granted, these would work their way into further price increases, which would have the effect of reducing the competitiveness of the country's products and weakening its export–import balance. The result could be renewed depreciation of the currency and a further rise in the cost of living, leading to a further escalation of wage claims and so on. A dangerous 'hyperinflation' spiral might quickly develop – a situation that was approached in the UK in 1973, when against a backdrop of rising oil prices following an OPEC 'hike', sterling depreciated 18 per cent, and wage inflation briefly reached 30 per cent.

The four Tasks which follow will help you consolidate your understanding of a number of aspects of inflation.

TASK 24.2

Import prices and UK inflation

Overseas inflation will affect UK inflation only to the extent that it feeds through to the prices of tradable goods... In the short term import prices can affect UK inflation in two ways. First, higher import prices increase the cost of UK firms, since imports account for around 35% of manufacturers' costs. Second, imports of consumer goods have a direct impact on the RPIX, by increasing the costs of retailers... How much of the increased costs of manufacturers and retailers is passed on to purchasers depends on the level and elasticity of demand. Raw material prices now have less effect on UK inflation than they did in the 1970s and 1980s. In 1973, non-oil raw materials represented 17% of UK imports; in 1990, the figure was nearer 9%.

*Source: **Bank of England Inflation Report** (February 1994).*

1 Under what circumstances of elasticity of demand might overseas inflation have a large impact on UK prices?
2 Why might non-oil raw materials have fallen from to 17% of UK imports in 1973 to some 9% in 1990?
3 Why was the food price inflation index expected to fall further in the coming months?
4 Why had prices for food fallen relative to those of other goods and services?

BOX 24.8

Food prices and the RPI

The recent fall in RPIY inflation has been partly brought about by reductions in food prices. Food price inflation – as measured by the twelve-month change in the food component of the RPI – has fallen from 3.0% at the time of the last Report to less than 1% in December. Movements of this size are not unusual – food price inflation rose by nearly three percentage points between January and July last year. But they normally reflect movements in the prices of a comparatively small number of items, such as fresh produce, whose supply is seasonal. As Chart A shows, most of the fall since September has been the result of price reductions in the larger non-seasonal food category, which began last summer and intensified in the autumn.

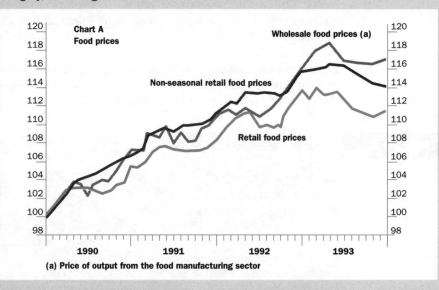

Chart A
Food prices
Wholesale food prices (a)
Non-seasonal retail food prices
Retail food prices

(a) Price of output from the food manufacturing sector

Why have food prices fallen?

Non-seasonal food price reductions of this size and duration are unusual. In recent years, non-seasonal prices have usually been reviewed in the winter and spring, and then held broadly stable through the summer and autumn. The increases in the first half of last year fitted this pattern. Because many agricultural support prices were raised sharply around the start of 1993 following currency re-alignments, however, it seemed possible that retail food prices would rise faster. Why did this not happen?

Competition in the food-retailing industry has intensified sharply with the onset of important structural changes. The market leaders have continued to invest in new superstores, offering a wide product range away from traditional town centre sites. At the same time, a new group of discount food stores – many with European or US parent companies – have entered the market, offering a limited range of high volume, basic food products on low margins. The price promotions started last autumn by the leading supermarkets made large price reductions on a similar narrow range of own-label products in a direct response to this move.

BOX 24.8

What does this mean for inflation?

The competition for market share means that the lower prices are likely to continue. As yet, discount stores occupy a relatively small share of the retail food market. But they are expanding, and are being joined by similar ventures parented by existing medium-sized supermarket chains. The pressures on the market leaders are reflected in the performance over the past year of their shares, compared with the FT-SE-A All-Share index (see Chart B).

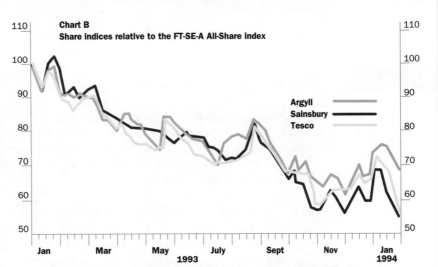

(a) In measuring how the individual share prices performed relative to the FT-SE-A All-Share index, allowance has been made for the normal relationship between the return on each individual share and the return on the index, as measured by each share's ß, estimates of which were provided by the London Business School.

Because the supermarket promotions have concentrated on own-label products, their impact has probably not yet been fully reflected in the inflation measures.
Producers of branded products are reconsidering their price structure in the light of the increased competition, and it is unlikely that the competitive changes are yet complete. In addition, it takes time for changing patterns of expenditure – such as the growing use of discount stores and the expansion of own-label sales – to be fully reflected in the official statistics.

The contribution to inflation from non-seasonal food prices is therefore likely to be low for some time. The price reductions seen so far will hold measured inflation down until they drop out of the twelve-month calculation later this year. The pressure that they have generated means that the price reviews occurring now and over the next few months are more likely to be biased towards further restraint. If that is so, food price inflation may fall further in the coming months.

*Source: **Bank of England Inflation Review** (February 1994).*

TASK 24.3

The Cambridge economist and the Paris landlady

The French franc experienced numerous devaluations in the period after the Second War. One of these occurred when a Cambridge economist was attending a conference in Paris. On leaving his hotel he was surprised to discover that his bill had been increased by 20 per cent. On protesting, the Cambridge economist was told – 'Monsieur, devaluations always lead to inflation –surely you know that!'

Does this (true) incident illustrate passive, adaptive or rational inflation expectations? Explain your answer.

TASK 24.4

Which inflation model does the Bank of England use?

Inflation is a fall in the price of money in terms of goods. In the long run, the supply of goods is determined by the supply of labour and capital and their productivity. Changes in the relative price between money and goods have short-term effects on output, but do not directly alter the long-run productive potential of the economy. They reflect changes in the demand for and supply of money...

But in the short run, the demand for and supply of both money and goods are apt to fluctuate as a result of shocks... These shocks take time to work through the economy, but just how long is uncertain. So the relationship between money, activity and inflation is, at least in the short run, diffficult to predict. Nevertheless, an analysis of monetary developments is essential to an understanding of the long-run path of inflation.

*Source: **Bank of England Inflation Report** (February 1994).*

1 According to the extract, does the Bank of England employ a monetarist or Keynesian model of inflation?

2 Why might an analysis of monetary developments be essential to an understanding of the long-run path of inflation?

Can increases in the quantity of money 'validate' inflation?

Monetary validation is increases in the money supply which have the effect of accommoding, or encouraging, inflation.

*The **target real wage** is the assertion that worker groups in their wage bargaining aim for a given real wage.*

Consider the case of cost inflation deriving from, say, an upward 'hike' in OPEC oil prices. The target real wage theory predicts that workers will demand wage increases to compensate for rising prices.

But suppose the supply of money is held fixed and its velocity of circulation is stable. This implies that employers as a whole would be unable to finance the level of wage settlements being demanded. Some groups of workers would then be in danger of 'pricing themselves' out of jobs, and might be prepared to accept wage cuts to price themselves back into employment. In this way, the inflationary thrust of rising costs would be eliminated.

In 1973 and 1979 the UK, like many other countries, was twice affected by 'hikes' in OPEC oil prices. Fearing higher unemployment if wage settlements did not prove flexible, governments of the day were prepared to increase the money supply, so that employers could afford to support employment at higher wage levels. This was likely also to maintain inflationary expectations and a high level of wage settlements and price increases. Hence the potential inflationary pressure of the OPEC oil price shock became validated by a goverment decision to increase the money supply. Look at Boxes 24.9 and 24.10.

BOX 24.9

'Higher wages don't cause inflation'

Higher wages do not cause inflation – so long as they are not validated by monetary expansion. But if economic agents expect monetary policy to accommodate higher levels of wages and prices, this itself can lead to increased wage settlements.

*Source: **Adapted from Bank of England Inflation Report** (May 1994).*

BOX 24.10

Inflation theories through the ages

One of the first-documented episodes of inflation occurred in ancient Rome. Between the middle of the second century AD and the end of the third, the price of wheat rose 200-fold. The inflation that this reflected was caused by the debasement of the metal currency; a succession of Emperors assumed that their personal credibility would be sufficient to maintain the value of coins even if they were reduced in size. Ordinary citizens simply joined in the practice of cutting the edges off the coins.

Following various efforts to maintain the value of the British currency in relation to the price of gold, in 1717 its value was fixed explicitly by the astronomer Sir Isaac Newton. The equivalence was maintained until 1931, except for brief periods at around the time of the Napoleonic wars and during and after the First World War. In the period of the Gold Standard, the predominant view of what determined the price level was based on the 'quantity theory' – the idea that a change in the money supply would eventually cause prices to rise in the same proportion.

W. S. Jevons was one of the first people to develop the concept of a price index. His work was stimulated by the fall in the value of gold, following the Australian and Californian discoveries of 1849. Jevons argued that it was crucial to 'discriminate permanent from temporary fluctuations of prices'. He also hypothesised that 'commercial tides' might be a reflection of the periodic fluctuations in sunspot activity observed by astronomers in the 19th century – but his observations on the importance of distinguishing absolute and relative price changes have proved the more robust.

The depression of the 1930s saw the main focus of economics switch towards output and employment, and away from money and prices; this was epitomised in Keynes' General Theory with its concept of unemployment equilibrium. With the re-emergence of inflation in the 1940s, however, came the Keynesian notion of an 'inflationary gap': inflation was seen as the product of an excess of desired demand over productive potential. Productive potential set a ceiling beyond which output could not rise; any excess *ex ante* demand would simply translate into inflationary pressure. This approach proved inadequate, however, to explain the coexistence of inflation and unemployment.

In 1958, A. W. Phillips fitted a curve through a scatter diagram of the rate of change of money wages plotted against the level of unemployment over the period 1861–1957. The curve suggested an inverse relationship between the two variables: the lower the level of unemployment, the faster the rise in wages. Moreover, there was a rate of unemployment greater than zero at which wage inflation was zero and the level of (frictional) unemployment was matched by the number of vacancies. As M. Blaug put it: 'the old hope of simultaneous achievement of stable prices and full employment had to give way to the notion of a trade-off between price stability and full employment'. The trade-off mentality was born.

BOX 24.10

The statistical relationship captured by the Phillips curve began to break down in the mid-1960s when inflation persisted despite a continuous rise in unemployment – the Phillips curve seemed to be shifting outwards. The main theoretical response to this phenomenon was the expectations-augmented Phillips curve; inflation was taken to be a function of unemployment and expected inflation. In M. Friedman's explanation of this theory, there was a 'natural' rate of unemployment (determined by institutional factors) at which the Phillips curve was vertical. Any attempt by government to stimulate the economy and reduce unemployment could have an impact only for as long as employees' inflation expectations remained below actual inflation. Over time, inflation expectations would adjust and unemployment would move back to its natural rate. The theory raised the question of how expectations are formed. In the extreme case, where expectations are assumed to be 'rational', it implied that there was no trade-off between inflation and unemployment even in the short tun, and that an economy remained permanently on its vertical long-run Phillips curve.

More recent work on inflation has focused on the credibility of the monetary authorities in their pursuit of anti-inflationary policies. Building on the idea that only unexpected inflation can affect growth, because expected inflation will be built into agents' decision-making processes, Kydland and Prescott developed the concept of 'time-inconsistency'. According to them, policy surprises cannot occur systematically, since agents will begin to anticipate the government's behaviour and build this into their expectations – with the result that growth will be unchanged but inflation will be higher. The way around this for the authorities was to be able somehow to offer a credible commitment not to spring policy surprises. The body of economic work developing this approach has been widely used to support the case for central bank independence.

Source: **Bank of England Bulletin** (May 1994).

TASK 24.5

1 How might debasement of Roman coinage have led to inflation?

2 Why should the concept of an 'inflationary gap' prove inadequate to explain the coexistence of unemployment and inflation?

3 What form of expectations is implied by the analysis in the extract's final paragraph?

REVIEW

In this chapter we have looked at the monetarist and Keynesian explanations of inflation. We saw that the monetarist theory of inflation, or quantity theory of money, asserts that, in terms of the equation of exchange, there is a direct, one-way relationship between changes in the supply of money, **M**, and resulting changes in the price level, **P**. Hence inflation is everywhere and at all times a monetary phenomenon. Unlike monetarists, Keynesians believe that the money supply is endogenously determined, so that changes in the quantity of money are an outcome and indicator of inflation pressures, not the underlying cause. Demand inflation can result from an excessive expansion of aggregate demand encountering increasingly inelastic conditions of aggregate supply. Cost-push inflation occurs when, independently of the level of aggregate demand, increasing costs of production become a source of upward pressure on the general price level. In practice, all three inflationary processes are apt to become inter-related. Hence the difficulties for anti-inflationary policy – which we examine in Chapter 25.

REVIEW TASK

TASK 1

Consider a situation where a rapid expansion of aggregate demand threatens inflationary pressure, as was the case in the UK in the late 1980s, when household consumption and business investment both grew rapidly.

1 Assume the supply of money is held fixed, and that its velocity of circulation is stable. Assuming first adaptive and then rational expectations, use aggregate demand and supply analysis to show how, following a surge in aggregate demand, the level of real output in an economy might return to its original level.

2 Given an acommodating increase in the supply of money, how might demand inflation pressure become 'validated'?

TASK 2

In the 1970s the Irish Republic experienced a long bank strike, which had the effect of 'freezing' and making inaccessible much of the supply of narrow and broad money.

Using the analysis of this chapter, what predictions would you make on the likely impact of the strike on the level of prices and national output in Ireland?

QUESTION

Multiple choice
'Cost-push' inflation may be caused by

1 increased prices of imported raw materials used in industry
2 the effects of devaluation
3 wage increases unrelated to rises in productivity

A 1 and 2 are correct
B 2 and 3 are correct
C 1 only is correct
D 1,2 and 3 are correct

(ULEAC, 1994)

FOCUS

Inflation policy

If you want price stability you have to do what is necessary to achieve it. It is no good...shrinking from the rise in interest rates which is necessary to bring it about. I do often wake up in the night fearing [price stability] might all be thrown away. If inflation isn't held now it could explode later as it did in the 1980s.

*Source: **Eddie George, Governor of the Bank of England,** (May 1995).*

I am not raising interest rates. I do endeavour to be my own man – I take my own decisions.

*Source: **Kenneth Clarke, Chancellor of the Exchequer,** (May 1995).*

A business spokesman said higher interest rates not only threaten the recovery of output, but also indirectly increase the pressure for price rises. Most businesses believe there is no threat of inflation in the foreseeable future, and no need to increase either taxes or interest rates in the medium term.

Monetary policy is operating 'without an anchor'. Where do we now look for indicators of inflationary pressure – M0 and M4, house prices, the exchange rate, unemployment figures, the Divisia index?

The Bank of England's analysis is dangerously wrong-headed, and it can no longer be trusted on inflation policy. There is no reliable correlation between how low inflation falls at the bottom of this economic cycle and how high it rises at the next peak. Why is the Bank of England so keen on high interest rates? Trying to crush so-called inflationary expectations now, won't curb inflation in a few years time. The way to do this is through discretionary, not rule-based interest rates policy.

*Source: **Paraphrased from press reports** (1994–5).*

Preview

In this chapter we shall investigate the following key areas:
- objectives, intermediate targets and instruments;
- costs imposed by inflation;
- measures of money;
- monetarist inflation policy;
- the framework of monetarist policy;
- Keynesian inflation policy;
- UK inflation policy since 1979.

Inflation is generally defined in terms of a continual and persistently rising general price level. We saw in Chapter 24 that according to 'monetarists', inflation is a monetary phenomenon resulting from an excessive expansion in the supply of money. Keynesians however believe inflation can result from an excessive expansion of aggregate demand in relation to aggregate supply (demand inflation), and from upward cost pressure on the general price level, independently of the level of aggregate demand (cost inflation)

The extracts in Focus 4.25, which relate to inflation policy, reflect these differing views on the cause of inflation. Monetarists believe the way to defeat inflation is by controlling the money supply, particularly through higher interest rates, which have the effect of reducing the quantity of money in use. As you can see, the extracts in Focus 4.25 are critical of monetary policy, which has mainly been used by successive Conservative Governments since 1979. Keynesians see excessive money expansion merely as an indicator of inflation pressure. One way to attempt to defeat inflation is by 'fine-tuning' the state of spending in the economy through fiscal policy – that is, by changing the levels of government spending and taxation. Another might be through a prices and incomes policy.

Can inflation pressure be accurately forecast? What does it mean to say that monetary policy is operating 'without an anchor?' Are the side-effects of monetary policy too high? Would fiscal policy be more effective? What is the difference between discretionary- and rule-based policy? Is there any way inflation can be defeated? In this chapter we shall be discussing these and other issues in the context of UK experience.

Objectives, intermediate targets and instruments

Defeating inflation is an objective (goal) of policy. (Other important policy objectives are full employment, high economic growth and a sound balance of payments, and in Chapter 27 we shall be seeing whether it is possible to reconcile these objectives – to attain them all at the same time.) How does a government attempt to defeat inflation? It uses policy instruments, such as changes in the rate of interest described in Focus 4.25. Sometimes an instrument operates though an intermediate target. For example, a rise in interest rates (instrument) by the Bank of England might be intended to reduce the growth of money supply (intermediate target), and hence the rate of inflation (objective). One of the features of economic policy is that in some circumstances targets and instruments may 'change places'. For instance, sterling's exchange rate is normally a policy instrument. However in the late 1980s it became for a time an intermediate target (see below). Again what some economists see as an intermediate target, others may see as an indicator. Thus monetarists perceive changes in the money supply as an important intermediate target, which causes changes in inflation. Keynesians regard changes in the money supply as an indicator, reflecting inflation pressure but not causing it.

Does inflation matter?

Economists have devoted a lot of time and effort, especially in the period since 1945, to trying to understand and defeat inflation – so it's a fair bet that inflation does matter! Inflation in fact imposes a number of serious costs, even when it is anticipated by economic agents.

Menu costs

When there is inflation, shops have to alter their price tags and modify their checkout programs. Similarly, restaurants have to change menus to take account of rising prices. At a time of very high inflation – hyperinflation – such changes, which involve a lot of time and effort, may be required every day, or even more often. In the 1923 German inflation prices rose so rapidly that people were being paid several times a day, and sprinted to the shops while they could still afford to buy!

Shoe-leather costs

Inflation tends to reduce the real value of narrow-money cash holdings, since interest is not usually paid on these.

The higher the level of inflation, the greater becomes the opportunity cost of cash holdings, and the greater the incentive for economic agents to economise on these by making more frequent visits to the bank, in order to transfer funds between accounts. Also, in times of inflation economic agents will be less clear about changes in relative prices, and will need to spend more time and effort·'shopping around'.

Loss of efficiency

The uncertain effects of inflation make it harder for businesses to plan production and investment.

Loss of competitiveness

Other things being equal, a relatively high inflation rate in one country reduces the competitiveness of its products, compared with those of other countries.

Redistributional costs

Unanticipated inflation also imposes costs.

Unanticipated inflation can arbitrarily redistribute income and wealth in a number of ways. Employees who fail to achieve wage settlements in line with inflation will undergo a reduction in real income. So will pensioners on fixed pensions, which fail to take account of prospective inflation. If nominal interest rates fail to take account of inflation, real rates will fall and debtors will gain at the expense of creditors. Wealth holders will experience both favourable and adverse effects, depending on the form of wealth held – see Chapter 23. (When inflation is anticipated economic agents can take advantage of indexing schemes, which are designed to protect real income by taking inflation into account in wage settlements, pension contracts, and so on.)

Subjective costs

The inflation costs described above impose considerable psychological costs, in terms of uncertainty, stress and so on. High rates of inflation often make people feel worse off, even when real income is not in fact reduced. However reducing inflation – deflation – can also cause difficulties, as Box 25.1 makes clear.

BOX 25.1

'Zero is just another number'

Why go for zero inflation – why not be content with a low rate of inflation? The sharp falls in inflation required can do harm as well as good.

In the first place, 3% inflation may according to some economists 'really' be zero inflation – in the sense that the inflation indexes do not take account of improvements in the quality of goods and services.

Secondly, aiming for zero inflation makes it difficult to reduce the real value of debt burdens, such as many households and businesses carried over from the boom of the 1980s.

Thirdly, a zero inflation environment puts businesses under extreme pressure to reduce costs by any means. This can lead to a sense of insecurity for employees, particularly part-time and self-employed.

Fourthly, pressure to cut costs can erode the productive base of the economy, as businesses 'cherry-pick' their best units and markets, and shed the rest. United States experience suggests also that indiscriminate cost-cutting can make businesses less competitive, for when resources are stretched, there are fewer funds for innovation, product and process quality suffer, and jobs are lost.

TASK 25.1

1 Should governments attempt zero inflation – or should they merely aim for a low inflation rate?

2 Examine the arguments for and against inflation indexing, described above.

Can inflation be defeated? The monetarist approach

A 'monetarist' approach to inflation has dominated UK policies since the late 1970s. Monetarists argue that inflation, being a fall in the value of money, must essentially be a 'monetary' phenomenon. If over a period of time the supply of money expands faster than the demand for money, its value will fall – there will be a rise in the general price level. Monetarist inflation policy therefore focuses on controlling the expansion of the money supply. This involves:

M0 'narrow' money is a measure of money consisting mainly of notes and coins in circulation.

M4 (formerly M3) 'broad' money is a measure of money consisting of notes and coins in circulation plus bank deposits of various kinds.

- deciding which 'measure' of money supply to target;
- deciding which instruments can achieve control over that money supply.

Measures of money

'Money is as money does.' That is to say, money can be defined as any asset which performs the functions of money – notably to act as a medium of exchange. In practice there is a whole spectrum of assets which can do this. When targeting money supply, a distinction is often drawn between 'narrow' money and 'broad' money.

The first of these, M0, consists mainly of notes and coins in circulation. 'Broad' money has a number of measures – (formerly known as M3), M4 for instance, consists of notes and coins in circulation plus bank deposits of various kinds. The authorities have targeted these two measures because they believed they give a good indication of the behaviour of the quantity of money as a whole.

The framework of monetarist policy

*The **public sector borrowing requirement** (PSBR) is the amount a government needs to borrow, in order to finance a given budget deficit.*

According to monetarists, controlling the quantity of money is the only effective means of dealing with inflation. Reducing the expansion of the supply of money relative to its demand will lead to a short-term contraction expansion in the output of goods and services, followed by a long-term reduction in the growth of money wages and prices (see the transmission mechanism described in Chapter 24).

The framework in which monetary policy operates can be explored through the 'flow-of-funds' or 'money counterpart' equation. In a simplified form this states that:

Change in M4 'broad' money supply
= public sector borrowing requirement (PSBR) (1)

    minus change in non-bank private sector loans to the government (2)

    plus change in bank loans to non-bank private sector (3)

This equation looks complicated but actually is little more than common sense! Take the first counterpart item, the PSBR. When this is positive, by definition the government's expenditure exceeds its revenues. The effect of the PSBR is to generate extra money in the form of notes and coins and private sector deposits, as the government will be paying more funds into the banking system than it is drawing from it. Non-bank private sector loans to the government, however, reduce the amount of extra money which needs to be created to finance the PSBR. So, depending on their scale, such loans will offset part, or all, of the PSBR's money-creating effect. Conversely, bank loans to the non-bank private sector, by generating fresh deposits, in turn add to the change in money supply. With this framework in place let us study the mechanics of monetary policy.

The instruments of monetary policy

For monetarists, the aim of inflation policy is to control the expansion of the money supply by influencing the sum of the 'money counterparts' in the equation above. In the UK in the 1980s this was attempted through three main instruments:

Through interest rates

As a major lender and borrower on the financial markets, the Bank of England has a strong influence on long- and short-term rates of interest. Where necessary higher rates of interest are raised, with the dual aim of

encouraging loans to the government (item (2) in the money counterpart equation), and discouraging bank loans and deposit creation for the non-bank private sector (item (3)).

Through sales of 'debt'

The money counterpart equation shows that the higher the level of non-bank private sector loans to the government (sales of 'debt') , the less is the required expansion of the money supply. These loans take the form, in the main, of sales of government securities, known as 'debt'. On occasion the UK authorities have attempted to 'squeeze' the money supply by engaging in 'over-funding' – that is, selling more government securities than actually needed to cover a current PSBR.

By measures to reduce the PSBR
In the 1980s and mid-1990s the UK authorities sought, through increases in taxation, economies in government expenditure, and through privatisation to reduce the PSBR.

These three sets of operations should determine the sum of the three counterparts on the right-hand side of the equation, and hence growth of the supply of money on the left-hand side of the equation.

BOX 25.2

Do 'open-market operations' reduce the supply of money?

Open-market operations refers to sales and purchases of existing government securities, unrelated to funding a current PSBR, by the Bank of England. Some text books suggest that the supply of money can be reduced by such sales of government securities. When economic agents in the private sector purchase these securities, they pay for them with cheques drawn on banks. These in turn pay the Bank of England from their cash balances held there. These balances constitute part of the 'cash base' which supports banks' lending – deposit creation – to customers. A reduction in the cash base should therefore lead to a reduction in the level of deposits, which in turn form the main part of "broad' money. In practice, the Bank does not manipulate the money base in order to control the money supply, for open-market operations are used only to control short-term interest rates. In simple terms, the effect of open-market sales of securities is to put banks and other financial institutions under increased pressure to secure funds from the Bank of England. This it will always provide – but at a price (rate of interest) of its own influencing. Thus it is not correct that open-market operations directly reduce the supply of money.

TASK 25.2

Eddie George, Governor of the Bank of England, stated yesterday that the economy was still expanding at a rate above its long-term trend. Although retail sales and industrial output had slowed, most indicators were showing continuing inflationary pressure. He said that he was committed to raising interest rates in small steps to prevent inflation building up. Otherwise, 'savage' interest rate rises as seen in the past, would be required.

*Source: **Adapted from press reports** (1 February 1995).*

1 In what sense can the economy expand at a rate above its long-term trend?
2 What indicators can be used to monitor inflationary pressure?
3 How might raising interest rates restrain inflation?
4 Why might raising interest rates in small steps be preferable to 'savage' interest rate rises?
5 What undesirable side-effects might higher interest rates have?

Can inflation be defeated? Keynesian policies

We saw earlier that Keynesians have two theories of inflation. Demand inflation is the outcome of an excessive expansion of demand in relation to aggregate supply. Cost-push inflation is related to conditions of aggregate supply and occurs when, independently of the level of aggregate demand, increasing costs of production become a source of upward pressure on the general price level. Keynesian inflation policies can likewise be divided into two kinds, corresponding to the two causes of inflation.

Using demand management to attack demand inflation: fiscal policy

Fiscal or budgetary policy is changes in the level of government expenditure and taxation, aimed at controlling fluctuations in the level of aggregate demand.

The main element of demand management advocated by Keynesians is fiscal policy.

This consists in using changes in government spending and taxation to influence the level of aggregate demand in the economy. Government spending represents an addition to spending levels, taxation is a subtraction. In the context of demand inflation, fiscal policy would involve decreasing the level of government spending and/or raising the level of taxation. This would reduce the expansion of aggregate demand and therefore the amount of inflation. Anti-inflationary fiscal policy was used in the UK on a number of occasions between 1945 and 1970. In practice it was not a very effective method of regulating economic activity, and in the mid-1970s it was effectively abandoned.

Fiscal policy and the money supply effect

In the 1970s Milton Friedman raised a fundamental objection to fiscal policy when he focused on the relationship between fiscal policy and changes in the money supply. Consider a situation where, in order to reduce inflation, a tight fiscal policy of reduced government spending and higher taxation is introduced. This will lead to a reduced PSBR which, in terms of the 'money counterpart' equation, implies a reduction of the money supply. Fiscal policy is thus seen as an indirect form of monetary policy.

Why not then employ monetary policy directly, using fiscal policy and changes in the PSBR as supporting measures? Reflationary fiscal policy, cutting taxation and increasing government spending, tends to increase the PSBR and generate an expansion of the money supply. This can lead to increased inflationary pressure, as was the case in the early 1970s when Prime Minister Edward Heath and Chancellor Anthony Barber made a 'dash for growth' which quickly needed to be followed by severe anti-inflationary measures.

Using demand management to attack demand inflation: changes in interest rates

We saw above that changes in interest rates, through their effect on the quantity of money, are a central instrument of monetary policy. Unlike monetarists, Keynesians do not consider the relationship between interest rates and money as significant. However, in the Keynesian model the level of interest rates does have an indirect non-monetary effect on aggregate demand. A rise in the level of interest rates will first, by encouraging saving, reduce consumption, and secondly by increasing the cost of finance reduce investment. Increases in interest rates will, through 'a multiplier effect' (Chapter 23), reduce the pressure of

aggregate demand, and exert a downward effect on inflation. Such a policy was used at various times in the 1950s and 1960s. One difficulty was to estimate how sensitive aggregate demand would be to changes in interest rates. Another problem was how to 'synchronise' inflation policy with other objectives, such as full employment, high economic growth and a sound balance of payments (Chapter 27). Some commentators have argued that the Major Government's post-1992 'monetary' policy was really a form of discretionary fiscal policy (see below). Look at Box 25.3.

BOX 25.3	**Fiscal policy and monetary policy: ' discretion versus rules'**
A rules-based policy is the setting by the government of well-publicised policy rules, for instance money supply targets, in order to influence the long-term behaviour and expectations of economic agents.	Monetarists are critical of fiscal policy, which is 'discretionary'. Discretion means that the authorities retain the option to **vary policy** as conditions change, so that it can be 'fine-tuned', to take account of policy errors , shocks and so on. However the existence of time lags in the effects of policy makes it difficult to achieve successful fine-tuning. Taking measures in anticipation of future changes wouldn't help, since forecasting is not reliable – and in any case economic shocks by definition cannot be anticipated. At worst, attempts at fine-tuning could lead to **over-correction**, leading at times to **worse** inflation. Monetarists favour the use of well-publicised, long-term, anti-inflationary **rules** (for example for money supply) which it is made clear the authorities will at all times adhere to. The use of rules should help to reduce inflation **expectations**. Secondly, rules require less intervention in the economy than discretion, leaving firms and households with a freer environment in which to take decisions and plan ahead. Thirdly, rules provide a means of absorbing economic shocks which, over a period of time, may be expected to 'average out'.

Keynesian inflation policy: Prices and incomes policies

Supply shocks and cumulative cost inflation

Cost-push inflation occurs when, independently of the level of aggregate demand, increasing costs of production become a source of upward pressure on the general price level. These pressures may come from wage increases and from rising import prices. Analysis often focuses on the notion of the target real wage (remember Chapter 24), which asserts that worker groups in their wage bargaining aim for a given real wage increase each year. If the growth of the economy is insufficient to sustain this, wage increases will outstrip output and there will be cost inflation. Keynesians argue that this analysis explains well the two 'inflation bursts' in the UK around 1973 and 1979, when employees sought to protect real wages against the effects of increases in the prices of oil and other commodities.

A prices and incomes policy

A prices and incomes policy aims to relate the growth of incomes, particularly wages, to the growth of national output, so as to prevent excessive increases in costs and prices.

Keynesians argue that a prices and incomes policy has a valuable role to play in preventing or reducing cost inflation.

It takes the form usually of an agreement between government, employers and workers on a set of 'norms' for wage and price increases.

On its part the government agrees to support the level of employment by maintaining a high level of aggregate demand. This is conditional, however, on employers and workers observing their norms and restraining the level of prices and wage settlements.

Prices and incomes policies in practice

In the period from 1961 to 1979 prices and incomes policies were a virtually continuous element of inflation policy. However they ran into a number of difficulties, and were finally abandoned by the 1979 Thatcher Government. In the first place, it proved difficult to persuade all firms and employees to accept and then observe their norms. Demands for 'special treatment' were common – for instance, from employees in short supply in expanding industries, or firms faced with unavoidable cost increases. Secondly, it proved virtually impossible to supervise and enforce thousands of pay settlements and price changes. Thirdly, measures to restrain profit dividends ran into difficulties. Fourthly, by distorting relative wage, price and profit levels and interfering with the workings of market forces, the policies almost certainly harmed economic efficiency.

TASK 25.3

A Three times in our recent history a burst in inflation has destroyed a recovery and taken us back to deep recession. A fraudulent inflationary boom which 'feels good' would soon turn to 'feel very bad' as the bust followed the boom. Inflation breeds uncertainty, distorts business decisions and leads to a less efficient economy. The effects of inflation are insidious and affect us all.

B We have to ensure that increase in aggregate demand are translated into more growth, not more inflation. That means eliminating the skills shortages and bottlenecks that have blocked progress in the past.

Source: **Extracts based on Chancellor of the Exchequer's Mansion House speech** (June 1994).

Explain statements A and B, using appropriate aggregate supply and demand analysis.

Inflation policy since 1979

UK monetary policy in the early 1980s: the Medium Term Financial Strategy

*The **medium term financial strategy (MTFS)** was a policy of low and steady medium-term growth of the money supply, aimed at allowing a low level of inflation.*

In the main, governments since 1980 have eschewed the use of demand management and have concentrated on employing monetary policy to control inflation. In 1979 Mrs Thatcher's new Government introduced a monetary policy in the form of a rule-based Medium-Term Financial Strategy (MTFS)

Using the three monetary instruments described earlier, the MTFS aimed to control the medium-term expansion of money as an intermediate inflationary target. The money measure initially targeted was broad-money M3, corresponding to the current M4. Monetarists do not claim that the causal relationship between money and the

price level is exactly predictable: variable time-lags between changes in money growth and the reaction of the price level are expected. In the UK these lags have been estimated at around 18 months on average, but with extreme values of anything from 6 to 30 months The MTFS did not aim therefore at short-term 'fine-tuning' or 'tweaking' of the money supply, but at a low and steady medium-term growth of the money supply, which would on balance and over a period of time control inflation.

It was believed also that clear MTFS targets would reduce inflationary expectations and the level of price and wage settlements.

The failure of the 'new monetarism'

The 'new monetarism' of the early 1980s soon ran into difficulties. First, the PSBR proved hard to reduce, and remained above target. Secondly, M3 did not respond predictably to attempts to control it, and its expansion was often above target. In 1982 M3 targets were actually raised, instead of being lowered. The attempt to restrain money growth also led to very high levels of interest rates. Although inflation declined from the 18% recorded in 1980, it was still running at 6% in 1985.

Also, the M3 velocity of circulation proved unstable. A new narrow measure, M1 (consisting of notes and coins and bank sight deposits), and a new ultra-wide measure, PSL2 (M3 plus some building society deposits), were now introduced as additional targets. These also proved difficult to control, and were later replaced by cash base M0. None of these measures, however, proved satisfactory.

Inflexible inflationary expectations

The UK economy was soon experiencing the deepest recession since the 1930s. In the 18 months after mid-1979, UK manufacturing output fell nearly 20 per cent, and in 1982 unemployment reached 3 million, compared with only 1.2 million in 1979. In terms of the equation of exchange, attempts to reduce M were leading to reductions in real output Y, rather than the price level P. Unemployment remained high for some years, and there was no quick return to the 'natural' level of unemployment

predicted by monetarists. The natural level in fact may have increased, as large numbers of long-term unemployed became less capable of future work.

In 1985 monetary policy based on the MFFS was officially abandoned. It was replaced by new strategy for controlling inflation – using interest rates to influence sterling's exchange rate. This too, failed when sterling left the European Exchange Rate Mechanism (ERM) in 1992. Look at Boxes 25.4, 25.5 and 25.6.

BOX 25.4	**Why did inflation fall in the early 1980s?: a Keynesian explanation**

According to Keynesians the experience of the new monetary policy in the first half of the 1980s confirmed that the quantity of money cannot be reliably controlled. Inflation is caused by 'real' factors relating to the level of aggregate demand in relation to aggregate supply, and an effective inflation policy needs to address these real factors. The decline in inflation in the early 1980s, Keynesians argue, was in the main **due to the sharp contraction of aggregate demand** resulting from attempts to control money, reinforced by the associated rise in the sterling exchange rate. A second anti-inflationary factor was the decline in primary product input prices for much of the 1980s – oil prices, for instance, halved to $10 per barrel in 1986.

BOX 25.5	**Why did the new monetary policy go wrong?: 'Goodhart's Law'**

Goodhart's Law –
When you attempt to
control a target you
inevitably distort its use as
a policy instrument.

According to Keynesian economists changes in **M** are an indicator of possible inflation pressures, not a cause. Keynesians believe **M** to be 'endogenous', determined inside the economic system, by the level of aggregate demand and the need for money. An important corollary of this is known as Goodhart's Law: As soon as you seek to control money supply, the relationship between it and the level of economic activity will break down. Suppose, as for a time in the 1980s, the authorities target and try to restrict the growth of narrow money, M1. What happens? Economic agents will switch to using other more accessible forms of money, such as M4. If M4 then also becomes targeted, agents will switch again to obtain money – to M5, or even foreign and euro-currencies. According to Goodhart, who himself worked at the Bank of England on monetary policy, the quantity of money is like a balloon. In terms of the needs of an expanding economy, if you squeeze it here, it expands somewhere else. Squeeze it there as well – and it still finds a way of bulging out. The quantity of money is seen as endogenously determined by the level of economic activity, and when you attempt to control this target you distort its use as a policy instrument. Attempts to defeat inflation through monetary control are thus self-defeating.

BOX 25.6

What determines the velocity of circulation of M0?

M0 consists of notes and coin in circulation (over 99% of the total) and bankers' operational deposits held at the Bank of England. Its prime importance as an aggregate stems from the fact that it is through the supply of M0 that the authorities influence short-term interest rates (by setting the interest rate at which the Bank of England provides liquidity to the banking system). This means that the quantity of M0 is determined by the demand at prevailing interest rates.

Given that M0 is demand determined, explaining its behaviour is a matter of identifying the factors that influence its demand. These factors can be split into two categories: those linked to the value of transactions for which money is used (cash-financed transactions); and those linked to the stock of money required to undertake those transactions (the velocity of circulation of money).

Measures of cash-financed transactions

Conventionally, the stock of money is assumed to be related to the value of total expenditure in the economy. Although this may be appropriate for a broad aggregate like M4, in the case of M0 we know that the use of notes and coin is concentrated in transactions undertaken by consumers. In 1990, 66% of M0 was held by the personal sector; and other holdings (8% by companies, 19% by banks and 7% by the overseas and public sectors) were related largely to demand for cash by the personal sector (for example, till money held by banks). This suggests that the demand for M0 is most likely to be related to some measure of consumer transactions. It does not, however, indicate which measure should be used.

Charts 1 and 2 show estimates of the sources and uses of cash by the personal sector.

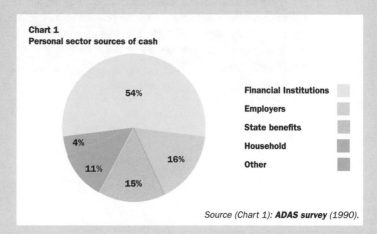

Chart 1
Personal sector sources of cash

- 54%
- 16%
- 15%
- 11%
- 4%

- Financial Institutions
- Employers
- State benefits
- Household
- Other

*Source (Chart 1): **ADAS survey** (1990).*

Chart 1 shows that the most important source of cash is withdrawals from financial institutions, which suggests that the demand for cash is determined by expenditure rather than income.

BOX 25.6

And Chart 2 shows that cash-financed expenditures, though concentrated in spontaneous retail transactions, are spread over a large range of transactions in non-durable goods. This implies that either retail sales or consumers' expenditure on non-durable goods may be reasonable measures of cash-financed spending. Statistical tests suggest that, of these, retail sales is the measure most closely related to M0.

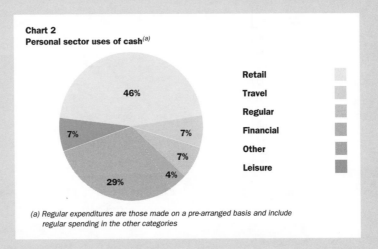

Chart 2
Personal sector uses of cash[a]

- Retail
- Travel
- Regular
- Financial
- Other
- Leisure

(a) Regular expenditures are those made on a pre-arranged basis and include regular spending in the other categories

The velocity of circulation

Having chosen an appropriate measure of cash-financed expenditure, the next step in explaining the behaviour of M0 is to consider the relationship between cash holdings and cash-financed expenditure: the velocity of circulation. As Chart 3 shows, the most notable feature of the velocity of circulation of M0 is its steady upward trend. In other words, the stock of money as a proportion of total retail sales has been falling over time. Chart 4 shows that this is not just a recent phenomenon.
Four factors lie behind this upward trend:

- as people's overall expenditure rises, the required money holdings per transaction may fall. This reflects the changing pattern of expenditure at different levels of income;
- the use of cash, even for retail sales, has tended to fall over time as the use of cheques and credit and debit cards has increased;
- new technology such as ATMs (Automated Teller Machines) may have reduced required cash holding for a given level of cash-financed expenditure; and
- a declining proportion of the working population is paid in cash.

But although these factors, which can all be described as forms of financial innovation, are clearly important, there is no satisfactory way of identifying their direct impact on money holdings or of predicting their future impact.

BOX 25.6

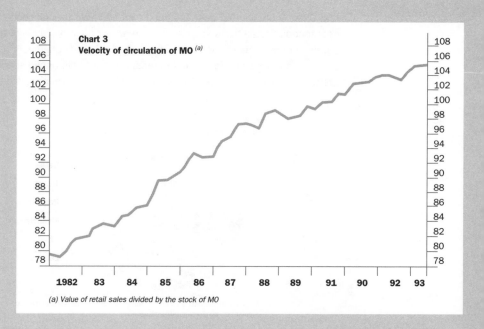

Chart 3
Velocity of circulation of MO [a]

(a) Value of retail sales divided by the stock of MO

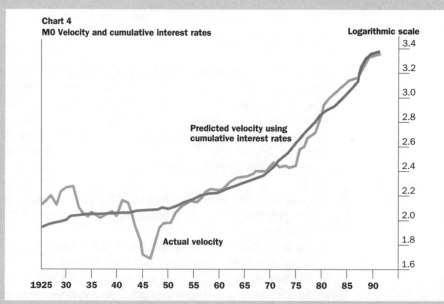

Chart 4
MO Velocity and cumulative interest rates

Logarithmic scale

Predicted velocity using cumulative interest rates

Actual velocity

Previous work has suggested that this trend towards lower money holdings can be identified by measuring the incentive to make innovations which affect the size of money holdings. Because cash bears no interest, high interest rates provide an incentive both to introduce and to exploit financial innovations that allow people to hold less cash. One result of this will be to increase both the demand for and supply of innovations (such as

BOX 25.6

ATMs); and because innovations are unlikely to be reversed, they may have a permanent effect on money holdings. Temporary changes in interest rates can, therefore, have permanent effects on the demand for M0. The cumulation of interest rates over time may provide a reasonable proxy for the process of innovation. Clearly this cannot capture all the factors that determine the incentive to innovate, but it has proved relatively successful in explaining the trend in M0 over a long period. For example, Chart 4 shows that between 1925 and 1992 cumulative interest rates seem to explain quite well the trend in M0 velocity (defined here in terms of GDP, because of data constraints).

In the short term, changes in interest rates can affect velocity relative to its long-run trend through the incentive they generate to economise on money holdings for a given level of financial innovation. This effect may be particularly important at present, when the velocity of circulation is rising less quickly after a period of falling interest rates. But gauging the extent to which this fall arises from recent changes in interest rates is difficult, because estimates of the short-run effect of interest rates on the demand for M0 vary widely. Chart 5 presents different estimates of the effect of a one percentage point reduction in short-term interest rates on the rate of growth of M0 using three different M0 equations: the Treasury equation; the current Bank quarterly M0 equation; and an earlier equation estimated by the Bank in 1989. These estimates show similar medium-term effects but very different short-term effects, and illustrate how difficult it is to predict M0 velocity shortly after a change in interest rates.

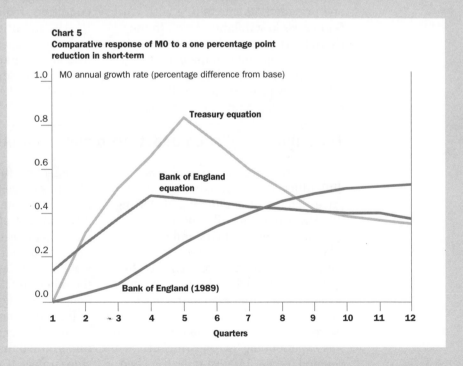

Chart 5
Comparative response of M0 to a one percentage point reduction in short-term

Source: Bank of England Quarterly Bulletin (May 1995).

INVESTIGATING ECONOMICS

TASK 25.4

1 Why has the M0 velocity of circulation been falling over time?
2 Why does the importance of cash withdrawals from financial institutions suggest that the demand for cash is expenditure-determined, rather than income-determined?

UK inflation policy by 'remote control': following the German mark after 1986

By 1986 a new way of attacking inflation was being tried – inflation policy by 'remote control'. West Germany had a long history of low inflation: why not 'import' this to the UK by tying the pound to the German mark? A controlled rate of exchange between the two currencies should lead to inflation in the UK converging on the German rate. High UK inflation would reduce the competitiveness for UK products, leading to job and production losses. Economic agents in the UK would therefore accept wage and price settlements in line with West Germany's low inflation level. In the shorter term, movements in the sterling-mark exchange rate on the market would provide an indicator of inflationary pressure in the UK, replacing the money supply targets

which had now been abandoned. High UK inflation relative to that in West Germany would lead to falling UK competitiveness and a rising balance of imports over exports, causing a fall in the value of the pound against the mark. To control the exchange rate, the UK authorities would raise interest rates, bringing about a tightening of UK monetary conditions and a reduction of inflation. The quicker economic agents adapted to the new regime, the faster would be inflation convergence, and the less the tightening of monetary conditions required. From 1986 to 1990, the UK authorities accordingly adopted a policy of 'shadowing the mark' on the exchange markets. In October 1990 this was formalised, when the pound entered the ERM at a central rate of £1 = DM2.95.

The failure of inflation policy by 'remote control'

The new inflation strategy soon ran into difficulties. Early on, rising world oil prices led to a strengthening of sterling (the UK being a net oil exporter), against the German mark and most other ERM currencies. The UK authorities were therefore required to undertake a reduction in interest rates to stabilise sterling against the mark. Unfortunately this was at a time when, as we indicated above, the UK economy was experiencing 'overheating' of demand. Lower interest rates thus had

the effect of stimulating the expansion of domestic demand, and increasing the inflationary pressure! The government now found itself in the uncomfortable position of needing to move the interest rate instrument in one direction to stabilise sterling against the mark, and the other direction to control domestic demand. Using tighter fiscal policy to reduce inflation was ruled out, not least because higher taxes would have undermined the government's supply-side strategy (Chapter 27). On a political level, these difficulties led to tension between Chancellor Nigel Lawson and Prime Minister Margaret Thatcher, who had never been convinced about the merits of shadowing the German mark. Eventually Mr. Lawson resigned.

The new policy came to an end very suddenly. In September 1994, sterling 'fell out of' the ERM. You can read about this in Chapter 30, where we see,

amongst other things, how the very high interest rates which had finally been required to support the sterling – mark rate now had the effect of intensifying the collapse of domestic demand which led to the 1992-4 recession. UK monetary policy had now lost a second monetary 'anchor', following the earlier failure of the money-supply targets. Inflation policy by 'remote control' was at an end.

TASK 25.5

Tying sterling to the mark was intended to make inflation in the UK converge on the German low inflation rate:

1 Why has Germany traditionally been a low-inflation economy?
2 Why should tying sterling to the mark not lead German inflation to converge upwards on a high UK low inflation rate?

Inflation in the mid-1990s: inflation policy without an anchor?

During the recession of 1992-3 inflation fell to low levels. However, as the material in Focus 4.25 makes clear, fears of renewed inflation were appearing by 1994. First, there were worries that the eventual sterling depreciation of 7%, following its exit from the ERM, would add to inflationary pressure. This could happen through the expansionary effect on aggregate demand of increased exports and import substitution, and higher import costs. Secondly, the level of PSBR (which we saw earlier contributes to monetary expansion) remained high. The government therefore introduced several interest rate increases to restrain potential inflationary pressure.

But how could inflationary pressure be assessed, now that both monetary 'anchors' had been lost? Given the absence of any policy rules, John Major's Government could be seen as turning back towards Keynesian-style demand management, which had fallen out of favour in the 1970s and been rejected by Conservative Governments in the 1980s. Without a formal medium-term monetary target, there cannot be any 'rule' to drive monetary policy – its use becomes discretionary and dependent on a range of ad hoc month-to-month inflation indicators.

Discretion-based policy is policy which is designed to be variable, to take account of errors and difficulties in operating policy, economic shocks, and so on.

Could the 'Divisia' M4 money measure be a suitable 'anchor'?

After the loss of the ERM monetary anchor, the search was on for new indicators of inflation pressure. The government stated that it would take into account a range of indicators: unemployment and employment figures, price indices, house prices, and so on. One of these was the Bank of England's new Divisia measure of monetary growth. We saw above that one of the difficulties with the use of money-supply targets in the 1980s was their unreliability. The 'Divisia' M4 measure of money-supply expansion seeks to overcome this by identifying and weighting the various elements of M4 according to how much they are used for transactions (spending) purposes, as opposed to saving and other functions. The higher their transactions component the more likely it is that these will be used to finance expenditure. A 'high-powered' transactions-weighted M4 measure might provide an improved indicator of the expansion of 'spendable' money, hopefully providing an eventual policy intermediate target or 'anchor'. At the time of writing the Bank is optimistic that Divisia M4 is proving a stable measure of monetary growth and inflation pressure.

BOX 25.7

Recent changes in M4 velocity of circulation

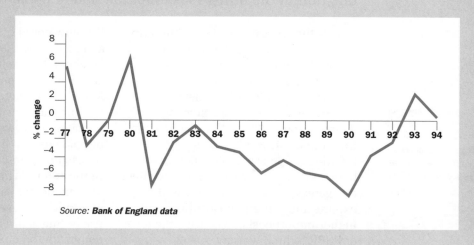

Source: **Bank of England data**

BOX 25.8	**Inflation strategies: a comparison between countries**

In the mid-1990s inflation strategies varied between countries. As the table below makes clear, some authorities were using instruments in relation to rule-based intermediate targets, particularly for money supply. Others were using instruments in direct relation to inflation indicators, often in a discretionary fashion.

USA	Central bank intermediate target	1–5% for M2, 0–4% for M3, 3–7% for bank credit
Germany	Central bank intermediate target	4–6% for M3
UK	Indicator	1–4% on RPIX
Sweden	Indicator	1–3% on RPIX
France	Central bank intermediate target plus indicator	2% on RPIX, 5% for M3
Japan	No target or indicator	

Constraints in monetary policy

*An **exchange rate** is the rate at which one currency exchanges for another.*

Since the rate of interest is the 'price' of money, it is evident that the authorities cannot control both the quantity of money and the rate of interest. At the start of the 1980s, for instance, attempts to control the expansion of money led to very high rates of interest – which could have undesirable side-effects. In the late 1980s, when there was a policy of tying sterling to the German mark, such constraints of policy became even more evident.

Consider a situation where the Bank of England was to restrain a rising pound against the German mark. It could do so by purchasing marks with sterling on the foreign exchange market. However the pounds thus sold must come from somewhere, and the operation would require an expansion of the narrow money supply, with an associated fall in the level of interest rates. Alternatively, keeping down the pound-mark exchange rate could be viewed as a policy of using lower rates of interest, to induce an outflow of funds from the UK, reducing the demand for sterling and hence its exchange rate. It is clear that the variables of monetary policy – money supply, rates of interest and the exchange rate – are inter-related. Focusing on one of these variables may mean forgoing control of the others.

REVIEW

UK experience since the 1970s suggests that inflation is a 'syndrome': a harmful condition which can be provoked by a number of causes. If inflation was always due to just one factor – say, rising costs – it would be easier to understand and control. The record of failure to control inflation in 1971-3, 1979 and 1988-9 underlines how difficult it can be to pinpoint a particular source of inflationary pressure.

Controlling inflation involves unpleasant short-term costs and therefore requires considerable **political will.** The political cycle of general elections tempts every government in the run-up to an election to over-expand the economy for short-term political gain, at the cost later of increased inflation.

But had the inflation tide perhaps changed in the mid-1990s? Was inflation in the UK at last being defeated, or at least contained at a low level? There were reasons for believing so. First, the supply-side performance of the economy had improved. Second, intense global competition was putting severe pressure on businesses in many countries to control wage and price levels. Third, in the UK all political parties seemed agreed on the need to control the expansion of money as a condition for defeating inflation. Finally, inflation expectations on the part of consumers, employees and producers were at an historically low level. Perhaps some of the optimistic predictions in Focus 4.25 would prove correct!

REVIEW TASK

In the first part of 1994 'core' inflation as measured by the RPIY index, fell below 2%, which is at the bottom of the government's inflation target range. Low inflation is likely to be maintained, but there are three main risks which could increase it.

● Rates of money growth – both narrow and broad – have been increasing. If this were to continue in the months ahead, the implications for inflation would be more disturbing.

● Inflation expectations have risen and are no longer coming down into line with the government's inflation target. Higher expectations affect the behaviour of economic agents and markets, and can make it more difficult to achieve the combination of low inflation and output expansion.

● Average wage earnings are accelerating, perhaps in response to expectations, and pay developments will need to be monitored closely. Higher wages do not cause inflation – so long as they are not validated by monetary expansion. But if monetary policy is expected to accommodate higher levels of wages and prices, this itself can lead to increased wage settlements. A belief in low inflation must be supported by firm monetary policy.

*Source: Adapted from **Bank of England Inflation Report** (May 1994).*

1 Why might inflation expectations have risen out of line with the government's inflation target?

2 Why might accommodating monetary policy lead to increased wage settlements?

3 How might higher expectations, through the behaviour of economic agents and markets, make it more difficult to achieve the combination of low inflation and output expansion?

Multiple choice

1 Which of the following statements would not be supported by a Monetarist?

   A. An increase in government spending reduces the public sector borrowing requirement
   B. A reduction in public sector borrowing reduces the money supply
   C. A reduction in the money supply reduces prices
   D. A reduction in prices increases employment.

(IB, 1995)

2 Other things being equal, control of demand inflation will be made easier in an economy if there is an increase in

   1 exports
   2 productivity
   3 saving.

(ULEAC, 1994)

3 A government wishing to reduce the rate of inflation by using monetary policy is most likely to

   A raise taxes to reduce consumer spending
   B raise interest rates to reduce consumer spending
   C encourage an upward movement in the exchange rate
   D reduce taxes to raise real incomes
   E increase public sector borrowing to prevent tax rises.

(ULEAC, 1994)

4 If the Bank of England wanted to encourage credit creation it would be most likely to

   A buy securities on the open market
   B sell securities on the open market
   C raise interest rates
   D increase Special Deposits
   E fund short-term debt.

(ULEAC, 1994)

Data response

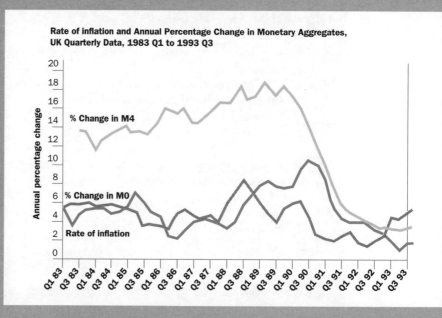

Rate of inflation and Annual Percentage Change in Monetary Aggregates, UK Quarterly Data, 1983 Q1 to 1993 Q3

a   Explain what is meant by the monetary aggregates M0 and M4.

b   Why is it considered necessary to have several measures of monetary aggregate?

c   i   How has the monetary aggregate M4 changed over the period depicted by the graph?

   ii   Give one reason that might explain why the trend in the growth of M4 is not the same as the trend in the growth of the money supply. Explain your answer with reference to both M0 and M4.

d   Does the graph give evidence to support the expected relationship between the rate of inflation and the rate of growth of the money supply? Explain your answer with reference to both M0 and M4.

(University of Cambridge Local Examinations, specimen paper, A/S level, November 1995)

26 Can the unemployment problem be solved?

UK unemployment

We used to think that you could increase employment by cutting taxes and boosting government spending. I have to tell you, in all candour, that option no longer exists: and that insofar as it ever did exist, it only worked by injecting bigger doses of inflation into the economy followed by higher levels of unemployment as the next step.

James Callaghan, Labour Prime Minister (1976).

No government can guarantee full employment.

Margaret Thatcher, Conservative Prime Minister (1985).

A properly working labour market is the key to more jobs.

Nigel Lawson, Conservative Chancellor of the Exchequer (1988).

According to employer surveys, employment is falling, according to household surveys it is rising.

Press report (1994).

Long-term unemployment is a drag anchor on the economy.

Howard Davies, CBI Director-General (1994).

A welfare-to-work programme is needed to tackle the problem of long-term unemployment.

Tony Blair, Labour Opposition Leader (1994).

Labour market flexibility will not produce low unemployment on its own: economic growth is also required. It's not the government that creates jobs – it's businesses producing goods and services that people want to buy.

Michael Portillo, Conservative Employment Minister (1995).

Flexibility labour market policies do not seem to have raised the level of employment over the business cycle.

Bill Callaghan, TUC chief economist (1995).

Preview

In this chapter we shall investigate the following key areas:

- measuring unemployment;
- the costs of unemployment;
- theories of unemployment;
- the role of labour market failure;
- the concept of 'natural unemployment';
- remedies for unemployment.

The unemployment problem

From 1945 to the mid-1960s the number of unemployed in the UK was rarely above 750 000. Yet in 1973 unemployment passed 1 million, and in the two recessions in the early 1980s and 1990s it reached 3 million: 12 per cent of the country's labour force. Even in the economic recovery of the mid-1990s, the number of jobless was over 2 million. As the extract in Focus 4.26 suggests, economists and politicians have not always agreed on the cause of this problem. Up to the 1970s insufficient aggregate demand was believed to be the main cause of unemployment, and expansionary demand management (often through fiscal policy) the appropriate policy for it. Then in 1976 came a celebrated speech in which the Labour Prime Minister, James Callaghan, – the quote in Focus 4.26 is from it – turned ideas on unemployment upside down, saying 'you can't spend your way out of unemployment'. Instead of lack of aggregate demand, inefficient labour markets were coming to be seen as the root cause of unemployment. So the solution must be to make labour markets more flexible and responsive to changes in economic conditions. Yet at the end of the late 1980s after several years of such policies, and with a now very high level of aggregate demand, UK unemployment was still 1.6 million: two to three times its normal pre-1970s' level. The search for job creation now came to focus on improved labour markets, combined with higher long-run economic growth.

BOX 26.1

Unemployment in 1995: an international comparison

Country	Unemployment (%) February 1995
Spain	23.9
Poland	16.5
France	12.6
Italy	11.8
Belgium	10.2
UK	8.5
Germany	8.2
USA	5.4
Switzerland	4.5
Czech Republic	3.2
Japan	2.8

Source: *Economic Trends* (1995).

Measuring unemployment

*In the UK, the government counts as **unemployed** those who are registered as such and claiming benefit.*

Unemployment is a stock concept; that is, it is measured at a point in time. The unemployment rate, in principle, is calculated by dividing the size of the population of working age into the number of people without a job and seeking work, then multiplying by 100 to obtain a percentage.

In practice, however, the measurement of unemployment is fraught with difficulties. For example, how do we know how many people are seeking work? Would more or less people be seeking work if current wage levels were different? Should people who are without a job and are physically incapable of work be counted as unemployed? Are housewives, or househusbands to be counted as unemployed, even if they deliberately choose not to make themselves available to the labour market because they regard family matters as having a higher priority?

Unemployment rates can be calculated by measuring the number of people claiming unemployment benefit. An obvious criticism of this method is that simply by reducing entitlements to benefit, a government can create an apparent reduction in the rate of unemployment. The current British method of calculating unemployment has been criticised for being less accurate than the standards used internationally by bodies such as the International Labour Organisation (ILO).

The ILO recommends the approach taken by countries such as the USA and Japan, where a sample survey is taken in order to identify the employed and unemployed. Such surveys take time, and the results might have to be published several months apart; and as with any sample survey the representativeness of the chosen sample is very important; but generally this method is more respected by statisticians than the British way. During the 1980s and early 1990s, with unemployment around 2.5 million, a rate of nearly 6%, the Conservative government in the UK changed the basis on which it calculated unemployment over twenty times. Curiously, each change reduced the amount of measured unemployment. For example, in 1988 young people were excluded from the unemployment register on the grounds that training schemes were available for all, and so nobody under the age of 18 could be unemployed. At the same time, obstacles to the entitlement to benefit have allegedly discouraged thousands of potential workers from even bothering to claim, thus causing a certain amount of 'hidden' unemployment. It has also been alleged that unemployment figures have been 'massaged' by putting pressure on the long-term unemployed to go onto a temporary training scheme of some sort, or to take a low-paid job for which they are grossly over-qualified.

There has been some cynicism over British government statistics, and one commentator has stated that the government would not be beneath announcing 'Good news for hay fever sufferers' if it altered the basis on which it calculated the pollen count! (On the other hand, the Organisation for Economic Co-operation and Development (OECD) has published unemployment figures for the UK based on monthly surveys and come up with figures which are only slightly higher than official UK unemployment estimates.

BOX 26.2

UK total and long-term unemployment (million), April 1990–95

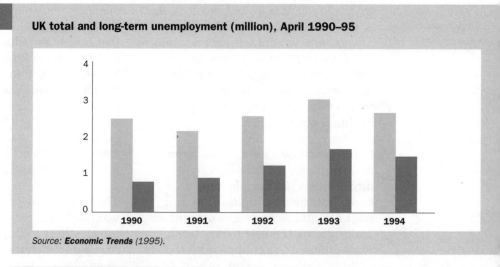

Source: *Economic Trends* (1995).

The costs of unemployment

Most of us are clear in our own minds that unemployment imposes costs. Some of these fall on the unemployed themselves. Thus there is a financial cost, in the difference between income in employment, and the unemployment and social benefits which replace it. However, people lose more than income when they become jobless: they also may lose the personal satisfaction which a job often gives. According to the business theorist A. H. Maslow, the workplace can satisfy a hierarchy of important personal needs. At a social level, you can gain a sense of belonging, experience friendships, and take part in social activities. Your job can also be a source of self-esteem, providing opportunities for responsibility, recognition, achievement and status. It can also confer benefits in terms of personal development, and the display of talent, flair and creativity. (Of course a job can also be a source of stress and frustration.) Losing this job satisfaction can help lead to strained relations with family and friends, and even crime and vandalism.

Unemployment also imposes costs on society. It not only leads to a direct loss of national output, but also generates indirect economic losses. First, the government suffers a loss of direct and tax indirect revenue, due to the reduced income and expenditure of the unemployed. Second, businesses forgo the profits which they might have been made had there been higher employment and output.

Unemployment may however be associated with the following possible benefits. First, short-term 'frictional' unemployment 'between jobs' (see below) may indicate that a labour force is mobile and responsive to changing patterns of demand and supply. Secondly, someone voluntarily leaving their present job in search of a new one may rate improved job prospects above any temporary reduction in income. Thirdly, some unemployed people might prefer the utility of extra leisure to the disutility of work effort. Finally, among some 'supply-side' economists it is possible to detect a strand of thought which seems to suggest that in order to maintain inflation at low levels, it might be necessary to deliberately maintain a 'pool' of unemployed people, so that wage claims are moderated by the threat of unemployment.

Theories and types of unemployment

'Disequilibrium' unemployment

'Disequilibrium' unemployment is said to exist when, for some reason, the real wage for labour is above the level which would clear the market, so that the market supply of labour exceeds the demand for it.

If the price of labour is above the market equilibrium, there may be an 'excess supply'.

It may be that an 'excess' labour supply rapidly leads to a fall in the real wage, so that the labour market 'clears' and achieves equilibrium. However if the real wage is 'sticky' and very slow to adjust, there could be a long period of excess labour supply, and hence disequilibrium unemployment. Disequilibrium unemployment could be seen as a form of labour market failure, where there is a lack of 'flexibility' in the labour market (see Chapter 9).

Classical unemployment

An excessive real wage level could occur in three main types of situation. One of these is when institutional factors lead to an excessive real wage. Thus trade unions and professional organisations may exploit their power over labour supply to secure a real wage which is above the market-clearing level. Secondly, employers may offer a real wage which is deliberately designed to be above the market-clearing level! Why should this be? It

can be a way of 'creaming off' high quality members of the work-force and, by creating a pool of reserve would-be employees, keeping existing employees on their toes. Thirdly, government-enforced minimum wages and social benefit arrangements may lead to an 'employment trap' which has the effect of creating an excess labour supply. Unemployment resulting from institutional factors is known as 'classical unemployment'

Cyclical unemployment

A second way in which an excessive real wage level may occur is as a result of a downturn in the business cycle. A recession develops, and aggregate labour demand therefore declines. If the real wage level now remains 'stuck' classical unemployment will occur. However even if the real wage did fall, the resultant reduction in wage incomes might lead to a further decline in household spending, and a further leftward shift of aggregate labour demand, so the real wage level would still be too high! To achieve labour market equilibrium, a further fall in the wage level would now be required, leading to a further decline in wage incomes and household spending, and so on. Excess labour supply of this type is known as 'cyclical unemployment'.

'Foreign competition' unemployment

When the USA, Canada and Mexico signed the North American Free Trade Agreement (NAFTA), there were fears in the USA that factories would re-locate to Mexico to take advantage of the substantially lower wage costs there. Some of these fears have proved to be well founded. In Britain, a once world renowned textile industry has suffered from cheap imports from less developed countries.

The above are examples of unemployment caused by foreign competition; however, this type of problem does not only arise out of competition with low-wage economies. Unemployment in Britain's motor and electronics industries has been caused by a failure to invest in new technology at sufficient levels to compete with other developed countries such as Japan.

'Mismatch' unemployment

*There are a number of ways in which **mismatch unemployment** might occur, known as frictional or 'search' unemployment, seasonal unemployment and structural unemployment respectively.*

We have seen how an excessive real wage might lead to three types of disequilibrium unemployment – classical unemployment, cyclical unemployment and 'foreign competition' unemployment. However unemployment can occur when the general level of real wages is 'right' and aggregate labour supply equals labour demand. Even if the number of job vacancies equals the number of people unemployed in the economy as a whole, it may still be the case in a particular labour market, say bricklaying or steel-making, that there is a labour supply excess, representing a 'mismatch' between labour supply and demand. Frictional unemployment occurs when people are between jobs, and in any society a certain amount of frictional unemployment is probably inevitable. The amount can be reduced by improving the information services which publicise the existence of vacancies ('Job-Centres' and the like), and by taking steps to increase the mobility of labour, so that the unemployed can move more easily to where the work is, or can re-train in order to acquire new skills.

Seasonal unemployment

Seasonal unemployment, as the name suggests, occurs in industries where there are peaks and troughs in activity throughout the seasons of the year.

Structural unemployment

Structural unemployment occurs in industries which are in long-term decline due to changes in market conditions. The coal industry, for example, has suffered from a long-term change in public tastes, away from open-hearth fires and in favour of gas-fired central heating, together with technological changes such as the rise of nuclear and gas-fired electricity generating stations.

A special kind of structural unemployment is known as regional unemployment, and this occurs when long-term decline in certain industries, such as steel, coal, shipbuilding and textiles, affect certain regions of the country more drastically than others. It is sometimes said that in Britain there is a 'North–South divide', with regions to the north and west of a line drawn from the Bristol Channel to the Wash having higher unemployment, lower incomes, and other social and economic problems which are much worse than the southern and eastern regions. Government regional policy generally attempts to move work to where the workers live (a 'pull' policy) rather than encouraging workers to move to where the work is (a 'push' policy). Generally, this makes economic sense, because it benefits the more prosperous areas by reducing congestion and pressure on their social amenities such as housing, hospitals and schools, when the infrastructure in the less prosperous areas is under-utilised. Industry can be attracted to 'assisted areas' by both 'carrot' and 'stick' policies; that is, they can be enticed by incentives, and forced to go by refusal to permit development in the more prosperous areas. EU assistance to areas suffering from regional unemployment is now an important part of the economic scene. On the whole European regional assistance is aimed at improving infrastructure such as roads, whereas traditional British policy tended to try to compensate industrialists for the poor communications in places such as Wales and the north of England. The EU philosophy is that money should be directed at improving these aspects of infrastructure so that further inducements to industrialists become less necessary.

What is the 'natural rate' of unemployment?

In Chapter 21 we examined the idea that there may be a 'natural rate' of unemployment. You will remember that we were looking at what happens to national output when an increase takes place in High Street spending – consumption. In the short run an increased demand for goods and services will lead to a fall in the output stocks of firms. It will also have the effect of bidding up the prices of goods and services, leading to a rise in firms' profits. These two effects will encourage firms to expand output, and hire more workers. They will therefore bid up wage rates but, in order to protect their profits, are likely to do so by less than the increase in prices. In the long run, workers may have 'passive' expectations – they have a 'money illusion' that prices are stable when in fact they are not. They therefore (wrongly) interpret their rise in money wages as an improvement in their real wage and remain on the labour market. Producers go on earning higher real profits and so the improvement in output and unemployment become permanent.

Voluntary unemployment is the idea that unemployment is caused by people refusing to take low paid jobs.

But we saw that there might also be the converse case in which employees have 'adaptive' expectations about the future price level, and correctly foresee a rise in general prices. They will then require increases in their money wage to offset the inflation which they anticipate. Real profits and real wages will fall to their original level, and output will revert to what it was before the increase in aggregate demand took place, with unemployment therefore also returning to its original 'natural rate'. Many economists believe there is likely to be such a natural rate of unemployment, without necessarily agreeing with the supply siders' ideas of 'voluntary unemployment'.

Anti-unemployment policy

Reducing unemployment through expansionary demand management

We saw above that disequilibrium unemployment might result from a deficiency of aggregate demand. This suggests a possible unemployment remedy, namely for the government to undertake an expansion of aggregate demand, so as to stimulate national output and hence employment. As we shall see in Chapter 27, such 'demand management' might be aimed for through a combination of expansionary fiscal policy and interest rate reductions. But would such a policy deliver a lasting gain in employment? We come back yet again to the issue of expectations. Chapter 21 showed that the outcome depends on which model we select to make sense of the way the economy works. Keynesians predict that in an economy where economic agents hold passive expectations, and which is operating well below its production capacity, aggregate supply will be highly elastic. So the risk of inflation resulting from expansionary demand management will be slight, and there could be lasting gain in employment. [Some Keynesians recommend using prices and incomes policies to further reduce any inflationary tendencies (see Chapter 25).] Classical economists, however, would disagree with this analysis, arguing that because of adaptive expectations, expanding demand will merely deliver a short-term improvement in output and employment. In the longer run, as costs catch up with prices, both will revert to their natural rate. The New Classical economists are even more pessimistic. They assert that using expansionary fiscal policy and interest rate reduction to reduce unemployment will be a complete waste of time. Given rational expectations, economic agents will realise instantly that any improvement in real wages or profits associated with increased aggregate demand will be illusory. Costs and prices will immediately adjust upwards, and so output and employment will remain at the natural level. There will be no improvement in employment, not even in the short run. At the present time, there is no general agreement among economists as to which of these three models best describes the workings of the real economy. Therefore the role of expansionary demand management in employment policy will remain open to debate.

Reducing unemployment through labour market reform

Government policies aimed at creating a more 'flexible' workforce have been discussed in Sections 2 and 3.

It should not be assumed that only non-Keynesian economists advocated 'supply-side' solutions to the problems of unemployment. While Keynesians concentrate on the demand-side in the short run, they also recognise the value of supply-side policies in the long run. However, instead of focusing on such aspects as anti-union legislation and 'flexible' wages, they are more likely to focus on the importance of education and training in increasing competitiveness and hence creating employment opportunities in the future. Look at Box 26.3.

REVIEW

In this chapter we have investigated the meaning of unemployment, theories of unemployment, and possible cures for unemployment.

BOX 26.3

Nice training scheme, shame there's no job afterwards

Businessmen and the Treasury are asking whether Training and Enterprise Councils give value for money, says Philip Basett.

'If you look at the amount of money Britain has spent on training over the past 20 years, then I think it's perfectly right to question whether we have got value for that money.' Such questioning of the consensus of the value to Britain's economy of the industrial training – restated by the Prime Minister yesterday at the end of the G7 summit in Naples – is uncomfortable.

It is all the more so when it comes from Sir Geoffrey Holland, former permanent secretary at both the Employment and Education Departments, and probably Britain's foremost government specialist on the issue. And it is acutely so when Sir Geoffrey suggests most government officials would, if pushed, be in great difficulty in trying to mount an adequate defence. To the 700 industrialists and business leaders gathering in Birmingham today for the annual conference of the Training and Enterprise Councils (TECs), the private sector-led bodies that run UK training, publicly, at least, the answer is clear...

As ministers prepare themselves for what they hope will be a further drop in Britain's unemployment figures tomorrow, John Major was unequivocal about the value of training. 'Look at unemployment across the world,' he said at the end of the G7 summit. 'People with skills are more likely to get employment. People without skills are less likely.' Such views are far from lost on a group of youngsters on the first day of a residential youth training programme in the unlikely setting of a farm in the North Yorkshire moors national park. All are from the hard-hit industrial conurbation of Teeside 40 miles away. Peat Rigg farm is a life away from the decaying industrial base of Middlesbrough, where male unemployment in parts is as high as 90 per cent.

BOX 26.3

The youngsters face an intensive week of preparation for work, which includes learning to turn up on time as well as training on computers, and resourcefulness-training such as canoeing, camping out and building bridges over moorland streams. The programme looks tough to youngsters just out of school, but worthwhile. 'Most of the schemes I've been to have just been sitting about doing nothing at all, just waiting for someone to turn up,' said Norman Johnston, 17, and already a scheme veteran. 'This is the best scheme I've seen.' Stacey Inskip, 16, agreed. 'This has got more to offer.' But no one among the dozen or so young people sitting in the farm's dining room disagreed when Jimmy Joyce, 16, said he did not see much prospect of a job back on Teeside when they went home.

How much training will help them is central to the unstated gamble of Britain's system of industrial training. To compete internationally, the theory goes, Britain must be a high-skill, high-value-added economy. To achieve that, UK skills levels must be pulled up to those of competitors like Germany and Japan. The Government's solution, lifted in the 1980s from the US, is the TECs.

Michael Heseltine, President of the Board of Trade, who sees TECs as a vital component of his Business Link scheme to provide one-stop help for British business, is clear about the support TECs enjoy from business. He said: 'There is a great enthusiasm in industry for the TEC movement.' Sceptics point to the turn-over of TEC directors as local private sector business leaders become overwhelmed by the numbing bureaucracy with which TECs are burdened as more evidence of industrial dissatisfaction, while even a supporter of an employer-led training policy such as Howard Davies, of the CBI, suggests the current system may not best be designed to aid the long-term unemployed: 'A more flexible labour market may need a more flexible training policy.'

[TECs chief] Mr Howell is zealous about the difference training makes: 'The most important thing is that if you look at the countries which have done well against those who have not, it's education and training which makes the difference.' Such words will strike a chord with the Michael Heseltines of this world, but Mr Howell's officials privately acknowledge that in the St Hilda's area across the road from the TEC's HQ, just to put that as your address on a job application all but guarantees rejection. That encapsulates what some feel is the problem at the heart of Britain's training system – using employers to address the supply deficiency of trained labour, insufficient attention is being given to stimulating the demand for training among them.

In a forthcoming study on Britain's skills gap and economic activity, Ken Mayhew, a labour economist, from Pembroke college, Oxford, and Ewart Keep, his colleague, will argue that training is as much a demand as a supply problem. Their report suggests training in Britain tends to be confined to big firms, and that most companies, as small firms, do not train. Not only that, they neither want to, nor see the need to: they are supplying markets which need only low-cost, low-skill, low value-added products. That is where their living comes from, and they do not need training to make such a living. In the unlikely event of them needing someone who is trained, they simply offer a bit more money to poach someone from somewhere else.

BOX 26.3

Training protagonists, such as those who will flood today's TEC conference in Birmingham, may well view with despair what they would see as such industrial short-sightedness. But however ill-advised it might be, the reality may well be more in line with what the study will say – that the training gap in Britain is as much the fault of employers and their product market strategies as their actual or potential employees and their supply of skills.

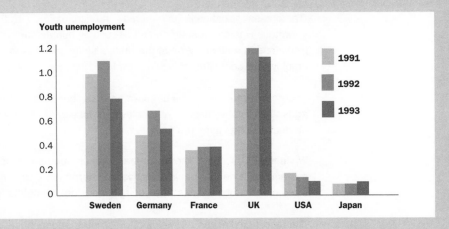

Source: **The Times** (Tuesday 12 July 1994).

BOX 26.4

'Joblessness is worst since '30s', says ILO
By Robert Taylor, Employment Editor

30 per cent of the world's workforce – some 820 million people – are unemployed or underemployed, the highest figure since the Great Depression of the 1930s, according to the International Labour Organisation in its first annual employment report, published today.

'The present situation is both morally and economically irrational. It is creating an enormous waste of resources and deepening human suffering,' says Mr Michael Hansenne, director-general of the United Nations agency in an introduction. A full employment commitment would provide a 'common vision to inspire action'.

'A defeatist attitude on full employment risks becoming a self-serving prophecy', he adds. 'The relative neglect of employment issues as opposed to inflation and industrial productivity) has gone too far.'

While the ILO accepts 'the maintenance of an open and efficient global economic system' must be the 'basic objective' of international action and argues strongly against trade protection, it insists 'the social dimension' cannot be ignored.

The report challenges the views of other international bodies such as the Organisation for Economic Cooperation and Development, the International Monetary Fund and the World Bank. The ILO secretariat believes they downplay the gravity of the global unemployment crisis. It will be debated at the world social development summit in Copenhagen next month.

Its arguments reflect the views of a number of academic labour economists and of Mr Robert Reich, the US labour secretary, the European Commission's social affairs directorate and the international trade union movement. The report endorses trade liberalisation and the world trade deal reached under the General Agreement on Tariffs and Trade, international cooperation to stabilise financial markets and government investment promotion policies. It calls for the adoption of 'more open export-oriented economic policies that will guide production and trade towards activities in line with a country's comparative advantage'. The 'artificial promotion or protection of activities which have no hope of becoming internationally competitive' should be avoided.

But it rejects 'pure laissez-faire policies' as well as 'the failed policies of classical import substitution'. The report backs government-based adjustment programmes which allow sufficient time for adaptation to change and minimise social unrest. It also favours cuts in non-wage labour costs such as payroll taxes and social security benefits, particularly for low paid workers as well as incentives to encourage the long-term jobless back to work.

It also argues that labour market rigidities in western Europe are not the main reason why its unemployment rates are higher then those in the more deregulated US. High unemployment in industrialised countries is blamed on 'a persistent inadequacy of

BOX 26.4

economic activity for 20 years' due to 'the lack of coordination' and the 'deflationary bias of European economic policies'. It agrees 'excessive' pay rises contributed to rising European unemployment between the first oil shock of 1973–1974 and the mid-1980s but this 'no longer appears to be true'.

'It cannot be said the level of wages continues to be a significant problem and indeed their reduction would only have a meagre impact on unemployment. . . . Wages across countries only marginally adjust to changes in unemployment and not in a way that would clear the market.'

It also says 'at best the evidence is unclear' that decentralised pay bargaining provides greater flexibility in real wage adjustment. In the UK, it says, 'real wages have risen faster than productivity growth and aggregate employment has not increased, in spite of the decline in union density and decentralisation of pay bargaining. . . . The fact that three of the world's most successful economies – the US, Japan and Germany – all have vastly different levels and coverage of bargaining and union density undermines the case for the superiority of decentralised systems,' it says.

Most evidence on the imposition of a national minimum wage has an 'insignificant' impact on aggregate employment levels in industrialised economies. It questions whether high unemployment benefit paid out in western Europe for long periods has much impact on the jobless numbers. The report favours 'appropriate labour market regulation', arguing employment security measures 'increase the propensity of firms to train and the willingness of workers to invest in upgrading their skills'.

'Rules that protect the income and employment security of workers can increase productive efficiency by creating incentives for competition to occur more through product market innovation and market strategy.'

Source: **Financial Times** (22 February 1995).

REVIEW TASK

Read the articles in Box 26.3 and Box 26.4 and then answer the following questions:
1 To what extent is unemployment an international problem rather than a purely national one?
2 What kinds of international action might be successful in reducing global unemployment?

Multiple choice

1 **If a government believes that large-scale unemployment is caused by demand deficiency it may seek to increase employment by**

1   reducing welfare payments to the unemployed

2   raising interest rates to reduce price and wage inflation

3   increasing government spending on capital projects and final consumption.

(ULEAC, 1995)

2 **Which of the following might reduce the 'natural' rate of unemployment? An increase in**

1   the government budget deficit

2   the money supply

3   retraining programmes.

A   1

B   1 and 2

C   2 and 3

D   1,2 and 3

(ULEAC, 1995)

3 **The natural rate of unemployment is the actual unemployment rate**

A   if there is no unemployment benefit

B   after adjustment for seasonal variations

C   when the labour market is in equilibrium

D   when the rate of inflation is falling

E   when frictional and structural elements are excluded.

(ULEAC, 1995)

.27 How can the economy be stabilised?

FOCUS

Stabilising the economy

Is a plan to raise taxes sharply when the economy is just recovering, only to give all the money back when it is at full capacity, anything other than mad?

*Source: **Financial Times** (3 April 1995).*

Business cycles have usually lasted ten years or more, and we are now, in 1995, in the middle period of the present business cycle. This should last three to four years at the present rate of economic expansion. The final inflationary overheating phase is a long way off. There is no need to tighten the instruments of macroeconomic policy.

*Source: Adapted from **press reports** (May 1995).*

There are signs that rapid output expansion is leading to overheating of the economy as capacity constraints are being hit – capacity utilisation in manufacturing is already at its highest level for six years.

*Source: Adapted from **Bank of England Bank Briefing** (May 1995).*

Preview

In this chapter we shall investigate the following key areas:

- the causes of macroeconomic fluctuations, including the business cycle;
- using automatic and discretionary fiscal policy to achieve macroeconomic stability;
- inter-relationships of policy objectives and Tinbergen's policy rule;
- macroeconomic stabilisation policy since 1960;
- the role of economic indicators;
- the Laffer curve and fiscal policy as supply-side policy;
- the significance of the government's 'public sector borrowing requirement' (PSBR).

The role of stabilisation policy

Stabilisation policy is the use of various instruments to achieve simultaneously the four main objectives of macro-economic policy – price stability, good economic growth, a sound balance of payments and a low level of unemployment.

The extracts in Focus 4.27 point to two important economic concepts. One is the regular fluctuation in economic activity known as the business cycle. The other is macroeconomic stabilisation policy which aims at controlling economic fluctuations. What complicates this quest is that governments often aim for stabilisation in the context of four main policy objectives: price stability (controlling inflation), good economic growth, a sound balance of payments and a low level of unemployment. These objectives are all clearly desirable, but suppose it turns out that in making progress on one objective – say, reducing unemployment – ground is lost in achieving another – say, a sound of payments? Or suppose trying to reduce inflation often leads to higher unemployment? In other words, how far is it possible to achieve all of the objectives of macroeconomic policy simultaneously, in an economy which is unstable in terms of levels of economic activity? This is what stabilisation policy is about.

Why are economies unstable?

*The **business cycle** is the tendency for periodic fluctuations in the level of economic activity.*

One reason why economies tend to be unstable is that they will from time to time be subject to random and unexpected changes in aggregate demand or supply, known as economic shocks. In the 1970s two successive 'hikes' in OPEC oil prices caused considerable disturbance to the economies of energy-importing countries. Another example, affecting all of Europe, was the economic unification of communist east Germany with capitalist west Germany after 1989.

Secondly, most developed economies are prone to regular fluctuations in economic activity known as the business (or trade) cycle. Typically a business cycle consists of four phases:

- The bottom of the cycle is the slump or depression. Economic activity in terms of output, employment and incomes will be at a low level, as too will business and consumer confidence. There will be little inflationary pressure and the general price level may actually be falling.
- In the recovery phase of the cycle an upswing of economic activity takes place. Output, income and employment will expand, and some upward pressure on prices may develop.
- The third and peak phase is one of boom. Confidence, and business and consumer expenditure will be riding high. Unemployment will now be low, and inflationary demand and cost pressures mounting. A high level of imports may be leading to balance of payments difficulties.
- In the final phase, a recession leads to a decline in economic activity and the prospect of a new slump.

BOX 27.1

The business cycle

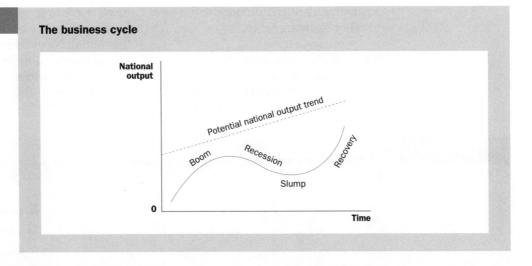

TASK 27.1

What major economic shocks, apart from the economic reunification of Germany, have affected the UK and other major economies in the last decade?

An explanation of the business cycle

e multiplier–accelerator model is the theory which ribes the business cycle to the interaction of the multiplier effect and accelerator principle.

Why do business cycles occur?
A leading explanation is that of the multiplier-accelerator model.

We saw in Chapter 24 how the multiplier process relates changes in the equilibrium level of national income to changes in aggregate demand. The accelerator principle, on the other hand, relates changes in investment to changes in the level of national income. Both the multiplier and the accelerator, then, are connected with the level of national income. It is suggested that the two processes may inter-react in such a way as to 'throw' economic activity into a cyclical pattern.

Consider the recovery upswing of the cycle. Rising income and output levels are likely to be fed by rising investment, the effect being enhanced through the multiplier. However rising incomes will

in turn, through the accelerator, 'feed back' to stimulate investment – which generates a renewed multiplier, and so on. At the peak of the boom, however it becomes difficult to sustain investment levels. For one thing, as successive investment projects get 'used up', investment rates of return may be falling. For another, constraints on labour and capital availability are likely to act as a brake both on investment and continued output expansion. Investment then starts to fall, and a 'backward multiplier' leads to a contraction of output and incomes. The accelerator now picks this up and translates it into reduced investment – which leads to a fresh 'backward multiplier'. Hence the fall in economic activity – like the rise before it – becomes self-sustaining. Eventually, after a period of recession or depression, new investment opportunities appear. Income expansion, rising confidence and a new recovery upswing set in.

In the multiplier–accelerator model, then, fluctuations in investment play the major part in the cyclical process: the role of household consumption is more stable and passive. What we have presented is only a simplified version o the model. Nevertheless it appears to provide a plausible explanation for observed fluctuations in economic activity. Look at Box 27.2.

BOX 27.2

Anatomy of a recession: percentage changes in UK aggregate demand, 1988–94

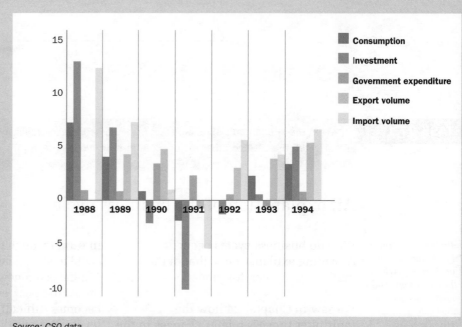

Source: CSO data.

BOX 27.3

Is there an economic super-cycle?

Economists often tend to ignore the analysis of long-term economic cycles, even though these could be just as important as the shorter 'Keynesian' cycles which figure in most textbooks. Two influential economists – Nicolai Kondratieff of Russia, and Michal Kalecki of Poland – sought to explain how long-term cycles **might occur.** Kondratieff saw evidence for a cycle of up to 60 years, with the 1930s depression being the **bottom, the 1950s and 1960s the boom peak and the 1990s a likely new period of depression.** However a 45-year cycle would interpret the economic and financial crises of the 1970s and 1980s as a repeat of similar conditions in the 1920s and 1930s. But why should such economic super cycles occur? One possibility could be very long-term fluctuations in construction and related industries. Kalecki saw an explanation in terms of unemployment and the class struggle. In the 1930s, heavy unemployment resulted in zero inflation behaviour and expectations on the part of economic agents. In the '50s and '60s full employment policies led to the re-emergence of the class struggle, with aggressive wage bargaining leading to new inflationary conditions. This conflict reached its climax in the stagflation of the '70s. The resulting abandonment of high employment in the '80s and '90s led to a new period of low- or zero inflation. One day, the struggle may renew, with a new period of inflation. How long does this 'dialectic' take? The answer could be, about 50 years.

*Source: adapted from **press reports 1993**.*

TASK 27.2

1   Why might long-wave cycle hypotheses be dismissed as science fiction?
2   How did Michal Kalecki predict 1970s-type stagflation?

The mechanics of fiscal policy

For much of the period from 1945 to 1980 the main policy instrument selected in the UK for stabilising the macro-economy was fiscal policy.

In this context government spending represents an injection (addition) into aggregate demand whereas taxation represents a leakage (subtraction) from it. A policy for increasing economic activity would aim to expand aggregate demand by raising the level of government spending and/or decreasing the level of taxation. Conversely, a policy for reducing the level of economic activity would aim to contract aggregate demand by decreasing the level of government spending and/or raising the level of taxation. It follows that expansionary fiscal policy will tend to generate budget deficits and an increasing PSBR, while contractionary fiscal policy will lead towards budget surpluses and a reduced PSBR.

Some of the main categories of UK government spending on goods and services are health, education and defence. The two categories of taxes are taxes on income ('direct taxes') and taxes on expenditure ('indirect taxes'). Examples of direct taxes are: personal income tax, national insurance contributions on employers and employees, corporation tax on business profits and capital gains tax on the disposal of assets. Indirect taxes include value added tax (VAT), and excise duties levied on petrol, etc.

Fiscal policy is divided into automatic and discretionary policy. The former depends on the fact that the size of the government budget deficit or surplus will to some extent vary automatically according to the state of the business cycle. In a boom, many tax revenues will tend to increase with rising earnings and expenditure. Some elements of government spending will, however, fall – unemployment benefit and social security assistance, for example. The combined effect of these two processes will be to act as a brake on the expansion of aggregate demand and economic activity. In a recession the opposite effect will tend to occur, helping to reduce the decline in economic activity. Elements of government expenditure and taxes which fluctuate automatically in this way are known as automatic stabilisers, and they have the effect of smoothing out business cycle fluctuations.

Discretionary fiscal policy involves a conscious decision, expressed in the government's annual budget, to alter the level of government expenditure and rates of taxation.

BOX 27.4	UK taxation and expenditure, 1995

Taxes on income (£ billion, 1995)

Income tax	63.1
Corporation tax	19.3
Capital gains tax	0.9
Inheritance tax	1.4
Stamp duties	1.8
Petroleum revenue tax	0.7
Total	87.2

Taxes on expenditure (£ billion, 1995)

Value added tax	41.8
Petrol tax	14.3
Tobacco tax	7.4
Alcoholic drinks tax	5.5
Betting tax	1.2
Customs duties	2.1
Total	72.3

Government expenditure (£ billion, 1994–95)

Law and order	16.2
Defence	24.3
Education	31.8
Health	36.8
Social security	90.3
Debt interest	18.1
Transport	5.1
Total	222.6

Source: *HMSO data*

Fiscal policy: exploiting the Keynesian multiplier

We have seen that in the Keynesian model a change in aggregate demand – consumption or investment – will generate a final income effect which exceeds the original change in aggregate demand. To understand how fiscal policy can exploit this we first need to extend the analysis we undertook in Chapters 21 and 23 to a four-sector model consisting of households, businesses, government and foreign trade sectors. In such a model, aggregate demand will consist of four components : consumption (C), businesses investment (I), government expenditure (G) and the balance of export expenditure over import payments (X-M). Imports are subtracted because part of consumption, business investment and government expenditure is on imports and therefore does not generate any domestic income. Hence:

$$AD = C + I + G + (X-M)$$

Consider now Box 27.5.

BOX 27.5

The 45°-graph

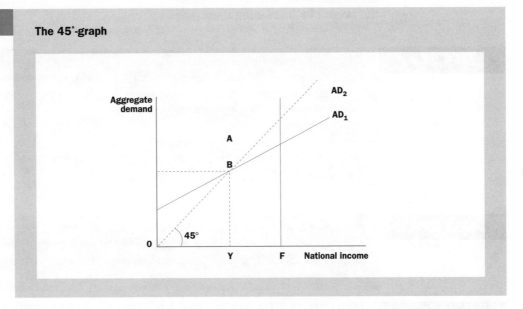

We see that the equilibrium level of national income is OY. However this falls short of the level OF which would correspond to full employment of resources. The economy is thus in a state of underemployment – in terms of the businesses cycle, it is experiencing a recession or depression. Clearly, if aggregate demand had been AB higher in the graph, at AD_2, the resulting level of national income would have been such as to deliver full employment.

This deficiency of aggregate demand is known as a deflationary gap. The aim of expansionary fiscal policy would be to 'lift' aggregate demand to the level AD_2 to close the gap. The authorities could seek to achieve this by using tax reductions, to encourage higher consumption and business investment. They could also raise aggregate demand directly by increasing government expenditure: an increase in expenditure on rail modernisation, for instance, would raise incomes initially, through the pay of workers and the receipts of suppliers and contractors, and indirectly as this income got re-spent, generating fresh income, and so on. It should be noted that tax changes would generally have a smaller multiplier effect than direct increases in government expenditure. The reason is that part of any tax reduction will tend to be offset by compensating spending changes. For instance, a household faced with lower income tax, rather than increasing its consumption expenditure as the authorities intended, might choose to 'absorb' part or all of the tax cut by increasing its savings.

In Box 27.5 it can be seen that a relatively small increase AB in aggregate demand would, through the multiplier process, generate a large, multiple expansion YF of income (the ratio YF/AB in fact measures the multiplier coefficient). In effect then fiscal policy might use the multiplier as an economic lever. Unfortunately, in practice the multiplier is weakened by a number of expenditure leakages in the shape of saving, taxation and imports. So instead of coming out at 4 or 5, as in textbook models, in practice it is nearer to unity.

TASK 27.3	The Keynesian model we have been using assumes constant prices and wage levels over a broad range of national output, and it follows that employment will then vary in line with income over this range. Consequently the process we have been examining also constitutes an employment multiplier.
	According to the classical macro-model, the value of the employment multiplier is likely to be less than unity in the short run, and zero in the long run. How would you account for this prediction?

TASK 27.4	Construct a '45-degree graph' in which there is an inflationary gap at the initial level of aggregate demand. Show how contractionary fiscal policy might be used to reduce aggregate demand and close this gap. Explain the 'backward' multiplier process which might result.

TASK 27.5	Would a high value for the multiplier make fiscal policy easier, or more difficult?

Problems of fiscal policy

Although the theory of fiscal policy looks clear-cut, practice has thrown up a number of problems. First, economic indicators are often unreliable, and estimating actual and desired levels of economic activity difficult. Secondly, it is often hard to predict the extent of time lags between the execution of fiscal policy and its final effect. Thirdly, as Milton Friedman showed, there is a close relationship between the use of fiscal policy and changes in the money supply. Consider an expansionary fiscal policy which aims at increasing real output and employment. This will lead towards an increased PSBR. and an expansion of the money supply (Chapter 24). According to monetarist economists the outcome will be a higher general price level, which would undermine the underlying aim of expanding real output. Friedman argues that fiscal policy is thus fatally flawed as a policy instrument.

Inter-relationships of policy objectives

To understand now how fiscal policy might affect macro-stabilisation, consider the situation illustrated in Box 27.6. Initially, national income is in equilibrium at OY_1 where aggregate demand AD_1 is equal to aggregate supply AS. This falls, however, well short of the income level OY_2, which is assumed to correspond to the desired level of employment. The schedule X represents the level of exports, which is horizontal and exogenously determined, being independent of the level of national income. The upward-sloping schedule M represents the level of imports, which is endogenously determined: the higher the level of income, the more is likely to be imported by households and businesses. At OY_1 there is a surplus AB of exports over imports.

The effect of expansionary fiscal policy on employment and the balance of payments

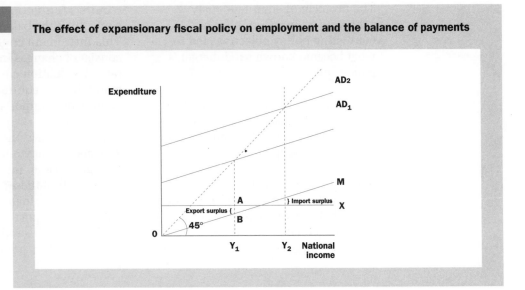

A 'stop–go' cycle is the tendency for politically influenced changes in aggregate demand to generate fluctuations in the level of economic activity.

Suppose the government now undertakes expansionary fiscal policy, aimed at achieving higher employment. Fiscal policy is used to increase aggregate demand to AD₂, and equilibrium national income rises to OY₂. Box 27.6 shows, however, that the increase in income will generate extra imports, the level of exports remaining unchanged. The outcome is an import surplus, compared with the previous export surplus. The greater the propensity to import, the larger this swing to import surplus will tend to be. In other words, any improvement in employment would be attained at the expense of a worsening balance of payments. Reducing aggregate demand would improve the balance of payments – but employment would then fall back again.

There is thus a 'trade-off' between the policy objectives. We can have high employment, or we can have a sound balance of payments – but not both.

This type of conflict was at the heart of the 'stop–go' cycle in the UK's post-war economy.

During an expansionary 'go' phase (for instance, the mid-1960s) aggregate demand would be allowed to expand, resulting in an expansion of output and employment. However, a combination of higher inflation and rapidly rising imports would lead to a 'crisis'. Measures to reduce aggregate demand would then be put in place, and the cycle's 'stop' phase (late 1960s) would set in. In due course (early 1970s) rising unemployment would lead the government – of whichever political party – to initiate new expansionary 'go' policies. And so on. Now if all of the policy objectives could somehow be achieved together, the economy would have an opportunity to expand smoothly, without the 'stutters' of the stop-go cycle. In this chapter we shall be examining to what extent this has proved possible.

Tinbergen's policy rule

The problem of simultaneously achieving a number of possibly conflicting policy objectives led to what became known as Tinbergen's policy rule.

This states that successful macro-economic stabilisation requires at least as many separate instruments of policy as there are independent objectives.

Suppose a government has two objectives – say, high employment and a strong balance of payments. It might opt for expansionary fiscal policy to improve employment, but would then require a further instrument for controlling the balance of payments. This instrument could, for instance, consist of changes in the exchange rate: devaluation could be used to maintain the required balance of exports over imports.

In the real world there are, however, four main policy objectives. Are there enough separate instruments of policy to serve all of these? Instruments which have been employed at various times in the UK in the post-war period include: fiscal policy, discretionary and rule-based monetary policy, exchange-rate policy, prices and incomes policy and supply-side policy. So there are at least five types of policy instrument available to serve four policy objectives – Tinbergen's policy condition could in principle be satisfied. Which set of instruments then might be assigned to the policy objectives? One way of approaching this, is to study the UK experience of stabilisation policy in recent periods.

Stabilisation policy in the 1960s

In the main, one central policy instrument – fiscal policy – was used for much of the 1960s in the UK to aim at the four policy objectives. As the analysis in Box 27.6 indicates, it is not surprising (in retrospect) that the outcome was unsuccessful and that the decade was one of 'stop–go'. In 1967 a second policy instrument – devaluation of sterling's exchange rate – was introduced to improve exports and curb rising import levels. By 1970 the UK economy, although 'firing on only two instruments', was in fact performing reasonably well in terms of the four policy objectives.

Stabilisation policy in the 1970s

The 1970s saw a number of policy instruments in play. Early on, expansionary fiscal and monetary policies were employed to stimulate the expansion of output and employment (the 'dash for growth') . Then a falling sterling exchange rate was added, to try to stabilise the balance of payments. Finally, a fourth instrument – prices and incomes policy – was increasingly directed at controlling inflation. So Tinbergen's policy condition was being satisfied: four policy objectives, four policy instruments. However the outcome was far from successful. The decade was one of 'stagflation', with low economic growth, and inflation and unemployment both on a rising trend.

Stabilisation policy in the 1980s

Why was stabilisation policy so unsuccessful in the 1970s? Some economists put this down to bad luck. There were a number of 'economic shocks' – notably two OPEC oil price increases – which had an adverse effect on costs, prices, employment and import levels, making it difficult to stabilise the economy. If these shocks had not occurred, stabilisation policy might have been much more successful. Other economists argue that the real problem was that two of the stabilisation instruments in use – fiscal policy and prices and incomes policy – were quite simply ineffective. A successful stabilisation-mix 'à la Tinbergen' would require four independent and effective instruments.

In the early 1980s Mrs. Thatcher's new government rejected fiscal and prices and incomes policies. Instead, rule-based monetary policy was introduced to control inflation, and a number of supply-side policies directed to achieving high levels of growth and employment.

Supply-side policies are policies such as labour market reform, privatisation, de-regulation and tax reform which aim to deliver long-term improvements in aggregate supply and economic efficiency.

The level of economic growth turned out quite well but inflation and unemployment remained high. Later, rule-based monetary policy was abandoned (see Chapter 25).

In the later 1980s the government opted for a mix of supply-side policies for growth and employment, combined with discretionary monetary policy for controlling demand and inflation. A high exchange rate, based on 'shadowing' the German mark, was introduced, not to regulate the import–export balance, but to exert downward pressure on inflation. However the end of the 1980s saw the UK experiencing a combination of high inflation, high unemployment and a large balance of payments deficit. The economy had returned to the bad old days of 'stop–go': inflationary boom to be followed soon by a severe recession. So stabilisation policy had again failed! Look at Box 27.7.

The conduct of economic policy: the view of a former Chancellor

In the extract which follows, a former Chancellor of the Exchequer, Nigel (now Lord) Lawson, explains in a 1994 lecture why the business cycle will always 'be there', and seeks to show the dangers of an over-concentration on stabilisation policy. In his view, attempting to 'fine tune' the economy may well result in an increased severity of the cycle.

BOX 27.7

The conduct of economic policy

There can be little doubt that the question at the centre of the economic debate in this country at the present time is whether the substantial, but sadly necessary, tax increases due to come into force in a fortnight's time will kill – or at least severely maim – the recovery from the recession and, if so, what the Government should do about it. This is essentially a special case of the continuing obsession with the short-term progress of the economy, in which each new statistic that is published – many of which will subsequently be revised, in any case – is hailed as cause either for reassurance that the recovery is 'on course', or for concern that it is not.

It is hard to imagine a more futile focus of attention than this. In the first place, there is overwhelming practical evidence that economies – certainly, free economies – move in cycles. There are rival explanations of why this should be so, and rival theories of what – if anything – can be done about it. But the evidence of an – albeit irregular – cyclical pattern is painfully evident.

For Keynes, who was a close observer of, and active participant in, the financial markets, and whose thinking was greatly coloured by this, the cycle was essentially a matter of mood swings, from optimism to pessimism and back again *ad infinitum* – although this was made to sound rather more scientific by being described in the *General Theory* as fluctuations in the marginal efficiency of capital. The 'marginal efficiency of capital', however, was defined in terms of the expected return on new investment: and what fluctuated, Keynes explained, was expectations.

Thus, to quote from the *General Theory*, in terms which describe with uncanny accuracy what occurred in the United Kingdom in the late 1980s:

BOX 27.7

'A boom is a situation in which overoptimism triumphs over a rate of interest which, in a cooler light, would be seen to be excessive.'

Sooner or later this overoptimism is shattered as it comes up against cold reality, leading to what Keynes describes as 'disillusion', leading to 'a contrary "error of pessimism" '. It was the problem of correcting this that particularly exercised him: It is not so easy to revive the marginal efficiency of capital, determined, as it is, by the uncontrollable and disobedient psychology of the business world. It is the return of confidence, to speak in ordinary language, which is so insusceptible of control in an economy of individualistic capitalism.

Hence the need, as he saw it, for the government to step in with a programme of public works.

The Keynesians subsequently refined and complicated their master's analysis – to no great advantage. The essence remained a cycle which occurred as a result of the wayward behaviour of the private sector; and which, they claimed, could be stabilised not by monetary policy (that had been tried and tested during the pre-Keynesian era; but as Keynes had argued in the passages quoted above, did not work) but by an active countercyclical fiscal policy. Unfortunately, in the half century and more since the publication of the *General Theory*, the active use of fiscal policy has been demonstrated to be no more effective in eliminating the economic cycle then Keynes considered monetary policy to be. What it has done, however, is to leave many countries with a higher level of public spending, public deficits and public debt than they are comfortable with.

This failure inevitably opened the door to the post-Keynesian monetarist thesis. This essentially held that, so far from monetary policy being ineffective in suppressing the cycle, it was the ill-judged active use of monetary policy that largely caused the cycle. All governments needed to do was to maintain a consistent, steady, non-inflationary growth of the money supply – easier said than done – and the cycle would cease to be a problem.

There are insights in both these approaches; but at the end of the day both of them, I believe, have done more harm than good – and indeed continue to do so.

Keynes' emphasis on mood swings from excessive optimism to unwarranted pessimism I find wholly convincing. One channel through which this can affect the economy, which has been important in a number of countries – including the United Kingdom – in recent years, is the credit cycle. The UK economy may be particularly prone to a pronounced credit cycle, as a result of our unusual pattern of housing tenure, with very little private rented accommodation and thus disproportionate emphasis on credit-financed homeownership; and the cycle was certainly further amplified in the 1980s by the once-for-all effects of financial deregulation.

But the essential phenomenon is a general one, by no means confined to this country. To put it at its simplest, when people are feeling confident they are likely to increase

BOX 27.7

their borrowings and spend more than they earn. But sooner or later, they will inevitably reach a point at which they feel (or their bank manager points out to them) that their indebtedness has gone as far as – if not further than – is prudent, and they will rein back. If this ebb and flow is an individual phenomenon, then nothing follows from this; but as soon as it becomes a herd phenomenon, as it frequently does, then a cycle is born.

I find it wholly unconvincing to believe that the credit cycle (to take this one example: there are of course others) is caused simply by mistakes in monetary policy. Of course, such mistakes can exacerbate the cycle; but the cycle could be there without them. There is no way in which the monetary authorities can fine-tune bank lending, any more than they can fine-tune expectations. Friedman's famous observation that monetary policy works with long and variable lags is highly relevant in this context. Nor of course is there any way the authorities can predict the point at which the credit cycle is likely to turn of its own accord – although turn it inevitably will.

The harm that both these approaches to the business cycle do is twofold. First, the one thing they have in common is, I believe, profoundly mistaken. Both of them – and even more the two of them cumulatively – reinforce in the public mind what might be termed the myth of the straight line.

Keynesian economics has been popularly understood to say that macroeconomic stabilisation policy – in this case, fiscal policy – can prevent the discomforts of boom and recession, and ensure that the economy grows in a steady and sustainable straight line. So much so, in fact, that even fluctuations that last only a few months are seen as aberrations that call for explanation, rather than an inescapable feature of the real world. And monetarist economics too has been popularly understood to proclaim that it is within the power of the authorities – in this case, by avoiding monetary error – to ensure steady, sustainable, non-inflationary straight-line growth.

Surely by now we have enough experience in country after country throughout the world to know that this simply isn't true. For all practical purposes, the cycle is endemic. That is not to say that governments can or should do nothing at all about it. The maintenance of financial discipline at all times should not only keep inflation low – an important end in itself – but also make far less likely the emergence of an explosive boom. How financial discipline is best maintained will vary from time to time and is in any case closer to an art than a science.

*Source: **Bank of England Quarterly Bulletin** (May 1994).*

TASK 27.6

1 Why might focusing on short-term policy analysis be 'futile'?
2 In what circumstances might it be important, but difficult, to try to revive the marginal efficiency [profitability] of investment?
3 Why is the business cycle probably 'endemic'?

TASK 27.7

What mix of stabilisation instruments was used by John Major's government in the first half of the 1990s? How effective were they?

TASK 27.8

The New Cambridge Policy Group of economists has proposed a stabilisation strategy based on the use of the following set of instruments – import controls, fiscal policy, prices and incomes policy, exchange rate. Which instruments do you consider would be assigned to each of the four policy objectives? How effective do you think a New Cambridge Policy Group stabilisation strategy would be?

Using economic indicators

In order to undertake successful stabilisation policy, it is necessary for the authorities to be able to assess the state of economic activity and the business cycle. This involves using data known as economic indicators.

Economic indicators are data which provides a guide to the level and direction of economic activity.

For the UK:
- A longer leading indicator predicts levels of economic activity from 7 to 17 months ahead. It incorporates data on company cash flows, the state of business optimism, house-building starts and share-price levels.
- A shorter leading indicator predicts levels of economic activity up to 6 months ahead and incorporates data on levels of household borrowing, new car registrations and new business orders.
- A coincident indicator attempts to reflect the current state of economic activity. It incorporates data on current prices output and retail sales, together with estimates of current levels of business capacity utilisation.

- A lagging indicator points to the state of recent economic activity, and incorporates data on employment and unemployment, and investment in manufacturing plant and machinery.

Unfortunately, economic indicators are often unreliable, so estimating actual and desired levels of economic activity can be extremely difficult. Typically, there will be no consistent picture emerging from these various indicators. In fact at the turning point of a business cycle – peak or trough – some indicators may be pointing to upward activity, others to downward. We now know, for example, that the UK economy in 1988 was experiencing severe over-heating in terms of demand expansion. However according to the Chancellor, Nigel Lawson, most of the indicators were failing to pick this up. When he did realise the true state of the economy, it was, he has argued, too late to control demand. Trying to stabilise the economy has been likened to driving a car which has an inaccurate speedometer, and erratic brakes and accelerator!

Fiscal policy as supply-side policy

Supply-side policies aim at long-term improvements in economic efficiency, independently of the level of economic activity, and are not therefore directly related to stabilisation policy. However, one supply-side policy – tax reform – also inter-reacts with fiscal policy and can therefore usefully be examined in this chapter. How did supply-side economics start? We saw in Chapter 24 how many economists came to believe that expanding aggregate demand to stimulate growth and unemployment would defeat itself by inevitably leading to accelerating inflation. They therefore focused analysis on seeking improvements in aggregate supply for obtaining better economic performance. The four main supply-side policies adopted in the UK – and increasingly in many other countries – were: labour market reform; privatisation; de-regulation; and tax reform. The first three of these were considered in earlier chapters. In the section which follows we focus on the relationship between tax reform and fiscal policy. Look at Box 27.8, in which Ronald Fajerfjäll argues that macroeconomics is in danger of losing touch with the 'real world' of microeconomics. How far do you agree with him?

BOX 27.8

Economists who are out of touch
Ronald Fagerfjäll

Think of the five leading economists in your country. How familiar are they with the companies that run the major part of the economy? Can any one really understand a company balance sheet? Name more than a few of the leading European entrepreneurs? Of course not, you might answer, because you know that they are so-called macro-economists.

Macro-economists parted with companies and markets at the beginning of the century and became advisers on a higher governmental level. They discuss things such as national growth, employment, budget deficits, inflation and current balance with governments without having to bother too much about the corporate world. Company economists are called micro-economists or business and administration specialists. There is even a Nobel prize mainly for the type of economist that avoids companies. To a company writer it all seems a bit strange. How can you understand the economy without understanding companies?

In the economy the real competition is not between nations, but between enterprises and entrepreneurs. Nothing new about that, it just went out of the expert focus for a while.

Governments can redistribute results from the company sector and build the environment for competitive enterprising, sometimes with excellent results, such as in Singapore. But when they try to be more 'hands on' the result is often unimpressive. British governments, for example, invented 'stop and go' economic policies and Swedish governments fine-tuned them. That both countries lost their leading positions in Europe is not coincidence.

BOX 27.8

In Italy the heroes behind the economic miracle are small and medium-sized companies in the northern part of the country that managed to reach the top despite confused – not to say corrupt – governments.

I read OECD reports on European countries. They often tell the same business cycle story, because countries are frequently closely linked through companies. Half of a smaller country's economy is typically called 'foreign trade', but there is very little foreign about it because a large part of the movement of goods and services over borders takes place within companies. Some borders in Europe hardly exist in the real company world.

Another macro-economic confusion is about service trade and the emerging service sector. The macro-economic numbers give a tilted picture of this phenomena. Some decades ago industrial companies supplied service as part of sales and kept all kinds of specialists within the organisations, from catering to advertising. There were few independent vendors selling services to companies and we had a small service sector in macro-economic terms. Today companies tend to buy these services from outside sources. That has created part of the visible 'service growth'.

But the biggest service change is invisible and happening within the old manufacturing companies because there are fewer blue-collar workers and more white-collar experts running production. Virtually every company is becoming a service company.

A third problem of macro-economics concerns company size. Some small companies are dependent on one or two corporations that buy products, whereas some small subsidiaries are independent. There are large corporations, organised like federations, where small business units deal with anyone they like, and there are giant companies with integrated production and strict controls. To classify them into size categories is difficult and the result would show a different pattern from the one we know through conventional economic statistics.

Many of our economic problems stem from the way we interpret statistics. Economists and politicians have to learn more about companies and how they work.

A company-oriented economist has to keep track of pluralistic and changing pictures. Models help, but can never replace detailed knowledge about the patterns and players that enter the picture daily.

*Source: **The European** (13 January 1995).*

TASK 27.9

1 Why is it misleading to speak of the 'foreign trade sector' of an economy?
2 How might the emergence of 'service companies' undermine the
   macroeconomic model?

Tax reform and supply-side improvements

The 'tax wedge' is the effect of high marginal tax rates in creating a gap between the earned and disposable income which may act as a disincentive to work and effort.

A high level of direct taxation at the margin may act as a 'wedge' between the earned income of employees and their disposable income, net of tax.

One effect of this can be to create a disincentive on further effort: why should a person 'losing', say, 60 per cent tax at the margin, bother to go for overtime or promotion? Secondly, the tax wedge can contribute to an 'employment trap', when people are deterred from seeking employment by increased tax and loss of social benefits which may amount to 100% or more of prospective earnings. Thirdly, a tax wedge could encourage higher pay demands, as employees seek to recoup taxed income. Fourthly, a tax wedge could encourage tax evasion and activity in the black economy. Lastly, by reducing the effective rate of investment return, the tax wedge could damage investment prospects.

In addition, tax distortion can have the unintended effect of damaging economic efficiency. For instance, preferential tax relief on house-loans and insurance policies might discourage households from investing in business. The economy's financial and housing sectors would thus over-expand at the expense of the business sector.

A supply-side programme of tax reductions and harmonisation might therefore provide substantial improvements in economic efficiency and aggregate supply. In the UK the period after 1980 saw substantial tax reform, not in respect of the level of direct taxation (which changed little) but in removal of distortion and reductions of marginal rates. The lower and top income tax rates were reduced to 20, 25 and 40 per cent respectively, compared with the two 33 and 83 per cent bands of 1979.

There is however a 'downside' to such tax reform. Unless accompanied by appropriate reductions in government expenditure (which are also an element of supply-side policies), tax reductions will stimulate aggregate demand and tend to increase the PSBR. Supply-side directed tax reform might therefore in the short term set off inflationary conditions.

Tax cuts and the level of tax revenues

In the long term there is a better chance that tax reform would be self-sustaining. Likely improvements in aggregate supply would increase the size of the economy's tax base and the potential for tax revenues. Also, it is possible that a reduction in tax rates could directly increase tax revenues! The analysis goes like this. Consider tax changes in terms of the 'cost' of leisure. Reducing the rate of tax will increase the opportunity cost of leisure: an extra hour's leisure costs more in terms of income forgone. The substitution effect between work and leisure will now 'tell' people to work more. The income effect of reduced tax could however go either way. People might regard leisure as a normal good and use higher income to buy more of it – work less. Or they might regard leisure as an inferior good and work more. The overall outcome on work amounts will depend on the combined effect of these substitution and income effects. Advocates of tax reduction believe the substitution effect predominates, in some circumstances to such an extent that outcome could be an increase in tax revenues.

This idea is illustrated in the Laffer curve shown in Box 27.9.

At high tax levels above OT in Box 27.9 the work level is so discouraged that tax revenues actually fall. Reducing taxes would then lead to increased revenues. Attempts to quantify these effects has proved difficult. The sweeping tax reductions undertaken in California in the 1980s delivered disappointing tax yields: many people preferred increased leisure to work. In the UK the evidence is mixed: tax cuts have probably encouraged the supply of work from employed married women and high income earners, but not from male employees on average incomes.

*The **Laffer curve** is a* *curve which claims to describe the relationship between tax rates and the level of associated tax revenues.*

BOX 27.9

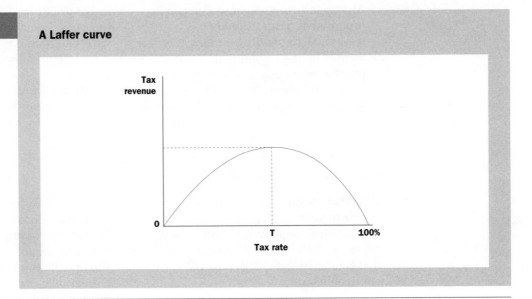

A Laffer curve

What is a 'good' tax?

Before we examine what might constitute a 'good' tax, we need to distinguish between progressive, proportional and regressive taxation. A progressive tax takes an increasing proportion on income or capital as either increases. An example is UK income tax, where the effect of granting allowances at the bottom of the scale, combined with a special high rate on large incomes, is to make the whole system progressive.

A proportional tax takes the same proportion at all income or asset levels.

A regressive tax takes a declining proportion of income or capital as either increases: for example the licence fees for television and cars.

The effects of taxation

- Taxation reduces the level of disposable income. This is true not only of taxes on income, where the effect is obvious and direct, but also of taxes on expenditure where the effect is to reduce purchasers' income through increased prices on goods and services, and/or to reduce businesses' profits to the extent that they absorb a tax without putting up prices. Taxation is also likely to lead to a redistribution of income, especially in the case where progressive taxation is directed at reducing the inequality of incomes. An expenditure tax, however, can be progressive, proportional or regressive, depending on how it is levied. Taxing a good which was purchased mainly by the very rich – 'grand cru' claret, for instance – would have a progressive effect. But a similar tax on a good bought mainly by poorer people might be very

regressive. Studies have shown that the overall outcome of the UK's expenditure tax system is probably on balance regressive.
- Taxation tends to reduce the ability save. This is clearly true of direct taxes, but it may not be true of expenditure taxes, whose effect through higher prices may be to det consumption and encourage saving
- Taxation may affect prices. A direct tax like income tax has no direct effect on prices but indirectly, by reducing disposable income and aggregate demand, it may lead to lower prices than would otherwise the case. Expenditure taxes, howeve will tend to increase prices, the extent depending on the elasticity conditions of the goods being taxed
- Taxation may affect levels of effort and enterprise. You read about this earlier in this chapter.

Principles of taxation

Now that we have studied the main effects of taxes, we can examine the principles of a 'good' tax, starting with Adam Smith's canons of taxation, first set out in the 1770s, but still applicable today.

- A good tax is convenient. Under the UK's Pay As You Earn (PAYE) scheme tax is deducted automatically at source by employers so as to render the payment of income tax as trouble-free as possible for the tax-payer. However a system of income tax self-assessment, along the lines in

the United States, where tax payers estimate their own individual tax liability is coming into use in the U Self-assessment would greatly redu the level of the Inland Revenue's collection costs – which brings us t our next principle.

- A good tax is cost-effective. Most major UK taxes meet this criterion, with estimated collection costs at around 1 per cent of tax revenues.
- A good tax is certain. Tax laws should allow tax-payers to be able t work out their liabilities and allowances without uncertainty or too much difficulty.

- A good tax is fair or equitable, meaning that it should be levied according to ability to pay.

Two present-day canons which economists have added to those above are:

- A good tax minimises the disincentive effect on levels of effort and enterprise (see above).
- A good tax will be compatible with other tax regimes – in the case of the UK, notably those in the EU.

What is a good tax?: UK taxation reform 1985–95

Janet Bush says that a report by the Institute for Fiscal Studies proves the Tories' tax policy has made the rich richer and the poor poorer. Look at Box 27.10.

BOX 27.10

Winners and losers in the Tories' tax reforms

Progressive and regressive are not words that set the world alight, but their meaning is really quite dramatic in the context of the Conservative Government's tax reforms. Make the assumption that a tax system should be weighted so that the poorer members of society pay proportionately less and the rich proportionately more and what these words actually mean is 'fair' and 'unfair'.

The importance of the contribution to the tax debate made yesterday by the politically independent Institute for Fiscal Studies is that it proves that the Conservatives' tax policy has made the rich richer and the poor poorer. This is what many of us had rather assumed, but here it is in black and white, another unmistakable embarrassment for the Government.

Those who have done the worst under Tory management of the economy are unemployed people with children, although the IFS is swift to point out that the Lamont and Clarke Budgets of 1993 mean that virtually everybody will be worse off, with middle-class voters the biggest losers.

Chris Giles, co-author with Paul Johnson, sums up one key finding of the report. 'Cutting income tax rates and shifting the burden on to other taxes, especially indirect taxes, increases the gap between those on high and low incomes. This makes the UK tax system much less progressive.' That means much less fair.

High income households gained substantially from reductions in income tax rates that outweighed increases in indirect taxes. In contrast, poorer households gained little or nothing from cuts in headline rates and will be hit proportionately harder by the imposition, for example, of VAT on fuel. Worst hit have been unemployed couples with children, more than three quarters of whom are worse off, followed by single parent families, nearly two-thirds of whom are worse off.

BOX 27.10

Impact of tax changes, 1985–95

Decile	% losing	% gaining	Average gain/loss (£ per week)	Average gain/loss (% of net income)
1	66	7	-3.0	-2.9
2	44	13	-1.4	-1.4
3	47	23	-1.8	-1.5
4	43	40	-1.1	-0.8
5	37	50	0.7	0.4
6	33	57	1.6	0.7
7	29	64	3.1	1.2
8	25	69	4.4	1.5
9	23	72	6.3	1.8
10	20	76	31.3	5.8
All	37	47	4.10	1.70

Decile 1 contains the 10% of households with the lowest income, decile 10 the 10% with the highest incomes

Proportions of income taken in personal tax

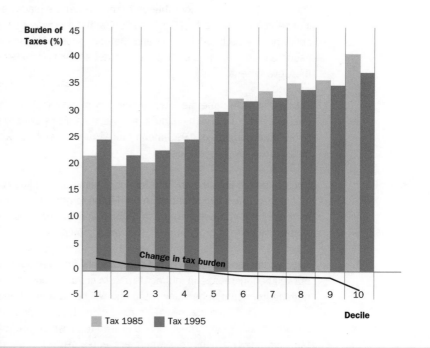

Source: **The Institute for Fiscal Studies**

BOX 27.10

It is a sobering thought for observers of the more abandoned rhetoric of the Conservative right wing that it has often been those groups of society that have been least well served by economic policy that are now being targeted for criticism and, in some cases, punitive treatment. The IFS also finds that those earners who have children are much more likely to lose out than those who do not have children, an important finding in the context of Conservative claims to be the party that promotes family values.

The IFS – almost exclusively – has the technical know-how and tax database to give a truly accurate picture of how changes in tax policy affect the different stratas of society. The institute is able to break down the effects on different types of household and on different income levels and includes both direct and indirect taxes.

One big disappointment with the report is that the institute has chosen only to survey tax changes between 1985 and 1995. Part of the reason cited for this is that this constitutes a neat ten-year comparison. Another rationale is that it was in 1986 that the major Conservative tax-cutting programme began. But there were extremely significant tax changes before 1985 from the Conservative Budget in 1979. In that year, British taxpayers were offered a mixed bag, with cuts in the basic and top rates of tax offset by a very large rise in VAT when the two-tier rate of 8 per cent and 12.5 per cent were replaced with a single 15 per cent rate. The next year saw National Insurance rates raised and the reduced 25 per cent rate band abolished.

In the famously harsh Budget of 1981, employees' national Insurance rates went up again and personal allowances were frozen in cash terms, the largest single-year tax rise in Britain's post-war history. National Insurance contributions were raised again in 1982 and 1983, but this action was offset by a resumed rise in personal allowances in real terms. The 1984 and 1985 Budgets were roughly neutral, and then the tax-cutting bonanza of the late 1980s began.

The IFS says it has not worked out whether tax policy in the early 1980s left the bulk of the population better or worse off, but privately acknowledges that the net effect on taxpayers, except for the rich, was probably negative.

This would certainly back up the findings of the survey by *The Times* in this space on January 13, which took the whole period of Tory Government from 1979 to 1995. *The Times* found that the average family will pay far more in direct taxes – income tax and National Insurance – once the full effects of the Lamont and Clarke Budgets come into effect – than they would have done under the last Labour Government in 1978–79. Even a wealthy family with earnings four times the national average – or £78,000 – will give up more of its income to the tax man than it would have done under the last year of Labour.

After more than a week of pressure from the Labour Party, the Treasury was forced to release figures broadly confirming *The Times* analysis. Although the Government gamely argued that it did not matter that most households were paying a higher proportion of their income in tax because they had seen thumping increases in their earnings under

BOX 27.10

Conservative stewardship, it remains an incontrovertible fact that the tax take as a proportion of the whole economy will rise to 38.5 per cent in the fiscal year 1998–99, more than in any year of Labour Government.

The methodology of the IFS analysis is to take important tax rates and levels as they were in 1985 and as they will be in 1995. Figures are in real 1993 prices and all 1985 values have been uprated by inflation between December 1985 and September 1993. In other words, it applies both the 1985 and 1995 tax regime to the same population. The IFS shows that the overall effect has been to reduce the direct burden of taxes on the personal sector by about £5.2 billion annually at current prices. This implies an average gain to households of about £4 a week. However, Mr Giles said that this was not a particularly meaningful figure (based on a fairly crude calculation) and was not that the IFS wanted attention concentrated on.

What the institute is at pains to emphasise is the extremely uneven way tax changes have affected people. The top table shows that, even in the 1985–95 period, the bottom 40 per cent of the population are worse off, with the middle classes marginally better off, and the very richest seeing a huge 5.8 per cent gain as a percentage of their income. The bottom table confirms this pattern, with the downward slope of the black line describing a regressive tax system.

A true picture of the increasing inequality of the British economy must include this analysis, but also a picture of what has happened with earnings. Since 1979, the poorest fifth of the population have seen their real incomes decline by 3 per cent while the real incomes of the top fifth have risen by up to 50 per cent. The poorer in Britain have faced a double whammy: proportionately small increases in their wages and proportionately higher taxes.

Kenneth Clark has had to admit that the vast bulk of British people face a higher tax burden now than they did under Denis Healey, the last Labour Chancellor. Now he will have to acknowledge that his party has rewarded the rich and penalised the poor. The emperor is running out of clothes.

Source: *The Times* (9 February 1994).

BOX 27.11

What is a 'sustainable' budget?

We shall see later in this chapter that the size of the PSBR is considered important because a large PSBR could lead to difficulties in a number of directions: for instance, excessive expansion of money supply, and 'crowding out' the private sector. In particular, a period of high PSBRs – growing national debt – could lead to difficulties, if a situation developed where the interest payment requirement 'exploded' to a level which could not be sustained out of tax yields. This in turn raises the question, how large a budget deficit – or sequence of budget deficits – would be 'sustainable' in terms of preventing an explosion of debt – and interest payment requirements? It turns out that the ratio of national debt to national income needs to be contained, if a debt explosion is to be avoided. Luckily, because of the way debt tends to compound itself, a small improvement in this year's PSBR makes it cumulatively easier to achieve successive improvement in the PSBR in future years. For instance, the ratio of national debt to national income for the UK in 1994 was about 50 per cent. Back in 1981 the UK government of the day had attacked the PSBR through steep tax increases, amounting to 2 per cent of GDP. It has been calculated that if this 2 per cent tax increase had not taken place, and if tax levels and other key economic variables in subsequent years had remained unchanged, the higher debt-path after 1981 would have led to a national debt to national income ratio for the UK in 1994 not of 50 per cent but of 100 per cent! This illustrates how important it is for a government to aim for sustainable budgets. While many countries saw large increases in government debt burdens between 1979 and 1994, the UK and Norway both achieved significant improvements.

*Adapted from **press reports**, 1994*

TASK 27.10

1 What is meant by the 'sustainability' of budgets?
2 How might debt interest become a 'Frankenstein monster' with a life of its own?
3 What do the UK and Norway have as a common advantage in reducing levels of government debt?

Why is the PSBR considered so important?

The Public Sector Borrowing Requirement (PSBR) is defined as the excess of the total expenditure of the public sector over its annual total receipts. The public sector consists of central government, local government and state-owned businesses. In practice, the PSBR is dominated by changes in central government receipts and expenditure. When the government's taxation revenue and other receipts exceed its expenditure, there will be a budget surplus and an opportunity for debt repayment: a public sector debt repayment (PSDR) situation. In simple terms, a UK government faced with a PSBR will borrow, at interest, by issuing IOUs. Short-term government IOUs, for periods mainly up to 3 months, are known as Treasury bills. Long-term government IOUs are known as government stocks. The higher the budget deficit, the more of these IOUs will need to be issued. Box 27.12 shows that the scale of IOU issues required reached an annual rate of nearly £50 billion in 1994. So does it matter if there is a large PSBR? There are several reasons why the size of the PSBR could matter.

BOX 27.12

UK PSBR, 1987–94

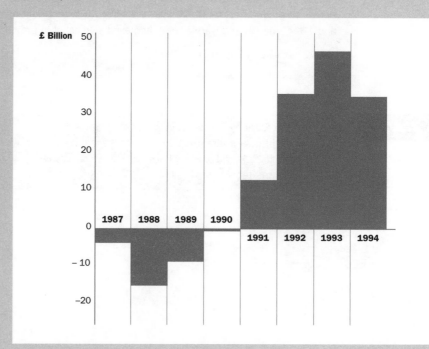

Source: *Barclay's Economic Review.*

State of the business cycle

Analysis earlier in this chapter suggests that the behaviour of the PSBR could be an important indicator of the state of the business cycle. We saw that the size of the government budget deficit or surplus will to some extent vary automatically according to the state of the business cycle. In a boom, some tax revenues will tend to increase with rising earnings and expenditure. Government spending, however, will tend to fall, due to lower payments for unemployment benefit and social security assistance, for example. Therefore the PSBR will tend to fall, perhaps to be replaced with a PSDR. In a recession the opposite effect will tend to occur. It is true, as we saw, that these effects will be modified by the use of fiscal policy to stabilise business cycle fluctuations. Nevertheless, unanticipated changes in the PSBR/PSDR can be an important pointer to the way the economy is behaving. In 1990, for instance, a PSDR of £2 billion for 1991 was being forecast. In the early months of 1991, it became clear that something was 'wrong'. Tax revenues were being overtaken by government spending and the anticipated PSDR was becoming replaced by a PSBR, which would amount to £14 billion. The reason? An unexpectedly severe economic downturn, signalling a long-lasting and severe recession.

Expansion of the money supply

In Chapter 25 we noted the connection between the state of PSBR and the expansion of the country's money supply. We found that monetary policy can be explored through a 'flow-of-funds' or 'money counterpart' equation which states that:

Change in M4 'broad' money supply = public sector borrowing requirement (PSBR) (1)
minus change in non-bank private sector loans to the government (2)
plus change in bank loans to non-bank private sector (3).

This equation shows that the effect of the PSBR is to generate extra money in the form of notes and coins and private sector deposits, as the government pays more funds into the banking system than it is drawing from it. Bank lending to the non-bank private sector, by generating fresh deposits, adds to the PSBR effect on the money supply. Non-bank private sector lending to the government, however, reduces the amount of extra money which needs to be created to finance the PSBR.

Crowding-out the private sector

A high PSBR might 'crowd-out' the private sector. We have seen that a government faced with a PSBR will borrow, at interest, by issuing IOUs. As the PSBR increases, so also will the rate of interest required to persuade economic agents to buy these IOUs. However, we saw in Chapter 24 that higher interest rates will tend to inhibit private sector investment. So an increased PSBR resulting from, say, higher expenditure on military aircraft might, through its effect on interest rates, 'crowd-out' civil aircraft manufacturing projects. (Higher government expenditure financed through increased taxation on the private sector might also lead to crowding-out.) Such a transfer of resources from the trading private sector to the non-trading public sector might lead to de-industrialisation and low economic growth, and to balance of payments difficulties (Chapter 29). This idea was investigated in 1978 by two economists, Bacon and Eltis, who came to the view that a degree of crowding-out had indeed occurred in the UK.

National debt difficulties

A period of high PSBR could lead to increased national debt difficulties. By 'national debt' we mean the total amount of government debt outstanding at a given time. In a sense today's national debt is the sum total of all past PSBRs and PSDRs. In the case of the UK, only a small fraction of this debt is owed abroad. When the national debt is very large, annual interest on it can become a heavy claim on tax revenues: in the UK in the early 1990s, for instance, annual national debt interest ran at about £20 billion. In theory, if a very high national debt was financed at high interest rates, a situation could develop where the interest rate requirement 'exploded' to a level which could not be sustained out of tax yields and GDP growth.

Worsening balance of payments

A high PSBR might threaten the balance of payments. A high PSBR, through its upward effect on interest rates, is likely to attract capital from abroad. This will lead to a higher exchange rate, resulting in fewer competitive exports compared with imports and possibly a worsening balance of payments. You can read about this in Chapter 29. Finally, look at Box 27.13.

BOX 27.13

The PSBR and high employment
Full employment is the only real route to low taxes
Graham Sergeant

Debate on the bulk of economic, industrial and social security policy now rests on one simple question: do you think full employment is attainable?

The next general election might even be fought, indirectly, on this issue.
Until recently, few dared challenge the nostrum that mass unemployment is a bad thing and, therefore, governments should aim to get rid of it. Only the means, and the definition of sustainable full employment, were at issue. Some economists touted the concept of a practical limit, the non-accelerating inflation rate of unemployment (NAIRU). It turned out pretty high. NAIRU was meant to excuse a high base level of unemployment in the 1980s: it never fell below 1.6 million. But the corollary was always that policy should focus on the supply side of the economy to get NAIRU down – if not to the 250,000 of a generation ago, then perhaps to half a million. Supply-side policies did not work, any more than throwing money at industry to keep jobs did in the 1970s. Gradually, Government policy has quietly and half-heartedly adapted to the assumption that unemployment is here to stay, even when lip service is still paid to job creation and full employment.

A few are brave enough to come out of the closet. Michael Portillo, on becoming Employment Secretary, argued that full employment was no more than an aspiration. Tim Melville-Ross, on becoming director-general of the Institute of Directors, suggested it was only achievable in inefficient command economies and that industry needed a pool of unemployed to be flexible and competitive. Behind the few are the many, not brave enough to be honest.

If you take this view, then it is a waste of taxpayers' money for the DTI to pay foreign firms to build factories in jobless areas, or to spend large sums in export promotion and advice. Some of Mr Portillo's inherited programmes would also fail a zero-budgeting test.

The state's job would be to provide a stable economic background through monetary policy, to control inflation and allow the economy to keep growing without needless recessionary shocks. Government should balance its budget, to avoid high long-term interest rates that crowd business projects out. It should keep the tax burden low, to avoid stifling enterprise, and maintain free markets, in labour as well as trade, to allow competition to make the economy efficient.

The rest is up to the private sector. Only business folk can determine the sustainable rate of growth. As studies from both the CBI and the Bank of England have shown, they are so chary of investing, demand such high returns and have such little faith in economic stability, that growth rates will remain low. If private sector activity then leaves permanent mass unemployment, as its low growth expectations imply, government must operate its own spending, tax and monetary policies to match. The Bank of England sees little reason to expect a long-term growth rate much above the 1.75 per cent suggested by some formal studies. Judging from international experience, this might

BOX 27.13

crudely comprise about 1.25 per cent from technical and market improvements, about 0.5 per cent from Britain's subdued rate of investment in new capital but nothing from increased labour resources. Smoothing out booms and slumps, and counting the number of people employed and how long each labours, total hours worked have been on a downtrend for the past 30 years. Making policy on such gloomy assumptions tends to be self-fulfilling, but sounds realistic.

If measured unemployment is to stay above 1.5 million, and semi-employment and associated poverty remain permanent, then it is hard to get taxes down. Since, say, the National Health Service will continue to absorb at least its existing proportion of national income, other programmes must be cut if even income taxes are to come down. If welfare demands are to remain high, the social security budget must itself be kept under control: by cutting the amount of national income spent on universal benefits such as pensions and child benefit; by paring benefit rates, by converting long-term unemployment benefit and much invalidity benefit into much lower income support. This strategy is not, however, as realistic as it sounds. The Government has been pursuing it surreptitiously for a dozen years, but has still ended with higher public spending and, on Treasury projections, a higher tax burden. In the mid-1960s, general government spending ran at less than 38 per cent of gross domestic product. Even at the height of the late-1980s boom, with the North Sea bounty, it ran at 39 per cent. Last year, it was 45 per cent and after all the planned spending cuts and economic recovery, the Treasury still projects 41 per cent public spending in 1998–99. Two prime ministers, five Chancellors and even more Chief Secretaries have tried hard to get public spending down. They have waged war on waste, shed the burden of state industry, cut defence, slashed student grants, economised on pensions. But they have failed.

The reason is clear. The cuckoo in the nest was always eating up more. There has been an inexorable rise in what statisticians call cyclical social security spending, but which has now become permanent poverty relief. From 3.25 per cent of GDP in 1979–80, it climbed to 4.5 per cent at the height of the following boom in 1989–90. From about 5.7 per cent at the bottom of the 1981–82 recession, it has climbed to 6.4 per cent. That realistic counsel of despair is therefore unrealistic. The only way to get the tax burden down permanently is to cut unemployment and poverty. Even low inflation, balanced budgets and free markets will not of themselves allow the tax burden to be cut. Old-style state spending does not work. If the private sector is not sustaining enough jobs that can finance a family, then business should be offered different signals, so that market forces deliver the right result. If tax cuts, and probably living standards, depend on that policy focus, the debate should be about what signals will be most effective at least start-up cost to the public purse. The party differences will be just as great but the prospect more hopeful: to cut taxes by ending mass unemployment.

*Source: **The Times** (8 August 1994).*

TASK 27.11

1 What was the probable NAIRU level in the 1980s?
2 Why have successive governments failed to reduce the level of taxation?
3 How does successful tax reduction depend on governments giving the private sector the 'right' signals?

REVIEW

In this chapter we looked at why economies tend to be unstable, and how far it might be possible to stabilise an economy in terms of low inflation, good economic growth, a sound balance of payments and low unemployment. This raised the question of which set of policy instruments might best be assigned to meet the policy objectives. Our survey of UK stabilisation policy from the 1960s suggested that no mix of instruments has yet proved successful. What of the future? At the time of writing, the economic manifestos of the Conservative and Labour political parties look broadly similar, with scepticism about the effectiveness of three of the instruments which have been used in the past: fiscal policy, prices and incomes policy, and rule-based monetary policy. If these are ruled out, a future government might be left with the following 'menu'.

● Supply-side policies for improving growth and employment;
● Changes in the exchange rate for achieving a sound balance of payments;
● Discretionary monetary policy for controlling the level of demand and inflation.

Could this perhaps be the shape of UK stabilisation policy in the future?

REVIEW TASK

Inflation looking higher

RPIX inflation is looking high for the next 12 months, and close to the top of the government's 1%–4% target range. Although M0 and M4 money expansion is within target, we believe there is still a high inflation risk. Output growth is still very strong and above long-run trend in sectors dependent on foreign demand, but much slower in industries dependent mainly on domestic demand.

Tightening labour market

The state of the labour market suggests employment will rise further, boosting incomes, and this is likely to outweigh the squeeze on disposable income, and consumption, resulting from tighter fiscal policy in the last two years. The capacity–output gap will continue to close and the labour market tighten. However the rate of wage settlements should be modest. Investment is growing only slowly, but as capacity bottlenecks emerge it will probably rise. Other manufacturing costs are also rising, with profitability probably being squeezed. As a result output price inflation may well rise.

Declining exchange rate

Sterling's exchange rate has continued to decline, leading to a temporary pick-up in import inflation. The balance of payments on current account is in surplus, helped by a fall in the visible deficit and a strong invisible surplus. Prospects for demand growth in the UK's major trading partners are good.

*Source: Adapted from **Bank of England Bank Briefing** (May 1995).*

1   What stage of the business cycle does the data above suggest?
2   What influences seem to be leading to higher inflation?
3   Given a tight labour market, what factors might be making for a relatively modest rate of wage settlements?
4   What mix of instruments would you recommend for stabilising the UK economy in the period ahead?

QUESTIONS

Multiple choice

1 In the UK the National Debt is most likely to increase by £100m in the event of
A   an increase in investment of £100m by Ford of America in the UK
B   a net outflow of £100m of property income
C   a balance of payments deficit of £100m
D   a Public Sector Borrowing Requirement of £100m
E   a net outflow of £100m from savings banks.

(ULEAC, 1995)

2 An increase in government expenditure either **'crowds out'** or **'does not crowd out'** private expenditure.
An increase in money supply is either **'the main cause'** or **'one possible cause'** of inflation.
Which one of the following options most accurately reflects the Monetarist and Keynesian views of the effects of an increase in government expenditure and an increase in the money supply?

	Effect of increased government expenditure on private expenditure		Effect of increased money supply on inflation	
	Monetarist view	*Keynesian view*	*Monetarist view*	*Keynesian view*
A	Crowds out	Does not crowd out	The main cause	One possible cause
B	Does not crowd out	Crowds out	The main cause	One possible cause
C	Crowds out	Does not crowd out	One possible cause	The main cause
D	Does not crowd out	Crowds out	One possible cause	The main cause

(IB, 1995)

QUESTIONS

The first diagram shows an economy's schedules of leakages and injections. Its trade balance schedule is shown in the second diagram.

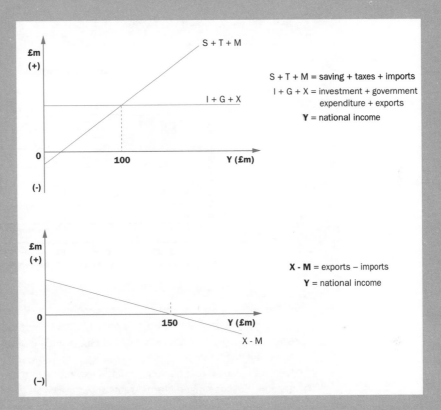

S + T + M = saving + taxes + imports

I + G + X = investment + government expenditure + exports

Y = national income

X - M = exports − imports

Y = national income

If the full employment level of national income is £125m, what is the situation of the economy?

A   excess demand and a trade deficit

B   excess demand and a trade surplus

C   unemployment and a trade deficit

D   unemployment and a trade surplus.

(WJEC, 1994)

Data response

1 Study the diagrams and text below

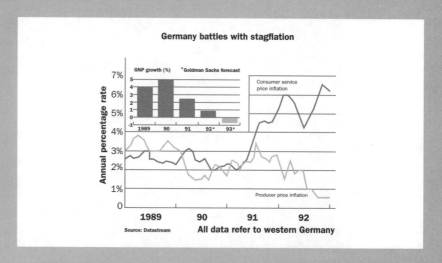

Germany battles with stagflation

Source: Datastream

All data refer to western Germany

As the plight of German industry has deepened, the Bundesbank has come under increasing pressure from within Germany to lower German interest rates and thus reverse the D-Mark appreciation of the last year. The diagrams explain the Bundesbank's dilemma. Easing monetary policy now, and allowing the D-Mark to depreciate, would fuel domestic inflationary pressures by pushing up producer price inflation. But the longer interest rates must stay high to bring the domestic inflationary pressures under control, the deeper the industrial recession. All of which explains why the Bundesbank has been so keen for the federal government to bring public spending under control; and why last week's three per cent pay increase for German public sector workers, announced on the same day that German headline interest rates fell, was much the more important economic use for Europe.

*Source: Adapted from an article by Edward Balls, **Financial Times** (London) (8 February 1993).*

a i What is meant by the phrase 'D-Mark appreciation'?
   ii Why would an easing of monetary policy allow the D-Mark to depreciate?
b   What evidence is there in the diagrams that 'the plight of German industry has deepened'?
c i Briefly explain what is meant by the term 'stagflation'.
   ii When did the German economy begin to experience stagflation? How can you tell?
d   The passage states that the Bundesbank is 'keen for the federal government to bring public spending under control'. Explain why this might be necessary.

e   Explain how high interest rates might
    i   reduce 'domestic inflationary pressures'
    ii   deepen the 'industrial recession'.
f   The passage states that a relatively low pay increase for German public
    sector workers is 'important economic news' for the rest of Europe. Suggest
    why it might be
    i   good news
    ii   bad news.
    Justify your answers.

(IB, 1994)

2   *Study the extract below*
**The Japanese government approves a plan of economic recovery valued at nearly
8 billion pesetas**

1   The Japanese government, in an unprecedented financial effort, yesterday
    approved a package of measures valued at $87000 million (7.9 billion
    pesetas), intended to stimulate the country's economy, which is affected by one
    of its worst crises. The measures have been proposed by the experts of the
    Liberal Party, in power since 1955, and form part of the most significant
    government assistance measures in post-war times.

2   Financial analysts emphasise that the government project, which includes a
    budgetary expansion of $24000 million in public works, fiscal investment
    incentives, and facilities for the recovery of the financial system, will not give
    results until at least a year after their application. Yoshiro Mori, president of the
    Liberal Party Political Research Council, declared in a press conference that the
    government was also thinking of introducing measures to promote imports to
    reduce its balance of payments surplus. "It is necessary to take these steps to
    achieve this objective," he said.

3   In line with the optimistic estimates of some experts, the multi-million package
    destined for the construction of public schools, one of the principal motors of
    the plan, can provoke an increase of one point in the **Gross Domestic Product**
    (GDP), which actually is increasing at a rate of 2%.

4   The size of the approved financial injection surpasses the calculations made
    weeks ago in the cabinet. The seriousness of the crisis, possibly the worst
    since World War II, has called for boldness in finding ways and means for an
    extraordinarily generous payment.

5   The Bank of Japan, meanwhile, can proceed to a new reduction in the official
    rate of interest in order to cheapen the price of money.

*Source: Adapted from an article by Juan Jesús Aznárez in **El Pais** (Madrid) 29 August 1992.*

QUESTIONS

a   Explain the meaning of the following terms in bold in the extract:
   i   Economic recovery (in the title)
   ii   Gross Domestic Product (paragraph 3)
   iii Injection (paragraph 4)

b   Paragraphs 1 and 4 refer to an economic crisis in Japan. What sort of crisis does this appear to be?

c   Paragraph 2 mentions 'fiscal' and 'financial' measures as ways of stimulating the economy.
   (i) Describe the main differences between these two types of policy.
   (ii) Briefly explain how each measure can help stimulate the economy.

d   Paragraph 2 mentions 'public works', and paragraph 3 suggests that building schools can increase GDP. Use your knowledge of Keynesian economic theory to explain how extra spending on public works can increase GDP.

e   In paragraph 2 it is mentioned that the Japanese government wishes to promote imports in order to *reduce* its balance of payments *surplus*.
   (i) Describe *two* ways in which a government might promote imports.
   (ii) Explain why a government might wish to reduce a balance of payments surplus.

(IB, 1994)

3 The data below include an adaptation of an article published in *The Economist* on 3 October 1992.
Study the data carefully then answer each of the questions which follow.

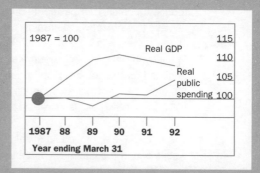

The bond market for Government securities is rediscovering an old British horror: the Government's Public Sector Borrowing Requirement (PSBR) is running at 6% of Gross Domestic Product (GDP). This is a reversal of the Public Sector Debt Repayment (PSDR) of 3% of GDP in 1989–90.

Since the Prime Minister has often said that he would like lower taxes, he is bound to disappoint the markets and the taxpayer – unless he and his ministers get a grip on public expenditure.

What matters most is how the total for the Government spending is divided. The Government must curb what really drives the spending total – social security payments such as pensions and unemployment benefit. These account for a third of all Government expenditure, with little regard for incentives to save and work. Boldness in cutting these payments would let the government increase public investment. The public sector has a vital role to play in expanding and improving Britain's roads and other infrastructure. That kind of spending will encourage private-sector investment by British and foreign companies.

Adapted from **The Economist** *(3 October 1991)*

a   Compare the trends in public spending and GDP between 1987 and 1992.
b   Explain the causes of the change in the Government's borrowing requirement between 1989 and 1992.
c   Briefly explain the economic arguments for and against cutting social security payments.
d   How far do you agree with the view that public sector spending on infrastructure 'will encourage private-sector investment by British and foreign companies'?

(WJEC, 1994)

4 Study the extract and graph below
Europe alone in Recession

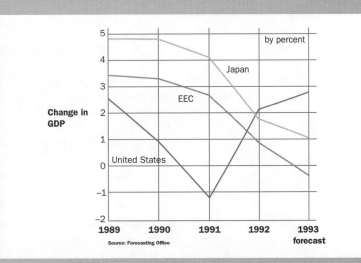

Source: Forecasting Office

(1) The English-speaking developed countries, the United States, the United Kingdom, Canada, Australia, New Zealand, which all went through a true **recession** at the beginning of the 1990s have now all returned to a positive trend of growth. A recovery has still been held back by excess debt remaining from the previous decade, but it appears to be strong enough to continue

through 1993. An annual average growth rate of about 3% is still foreseen for the United States in 1993.

(2) After a long period of relative stagnation, vibrations have been felt in Japan since the beginning of the year. Economic activity should make progress during the course of 1993, supported by a series of plans for stimulation.

(3) Many developing countries are experiencing a period of very favourable growth, even if others continue to go backwards. The IMF has recently judged the average 1992 growth rate of developing countries as a whole to be 6.1%, a rhythm which has been unknown for more than ten years. It is, therefore, principally in Europe, both Eastern and Western, where the present difficulties are concentrated.

(4) In Germany, a worsened economic climate can be found. Industrial production has fallen a further 3.7% between the fourth quarter of 1992 and the first quarter of 1993. Investment in equipment and consumption of consumer durables are continuing to fall.

(5) The recession hit France late, in the autumn of 1992. It has continued since then: despite having relatively high revenue, firms as well as households have been holding back their spending. As for foreign trade, it has suffered from the poor recovery in the rest of Europe, cancelling the competitive advantage of French exporters.

(6) In fact, it really is the European economy as a whole which is stuck in recession. The main cause of this is the excessive level of interest rates, which is particularly damaging in a situation where both households and firms consider themselves too heavily in debt, and because this has resulted in overvaluation of the European currencies.

(7) To prevent the recession from becoming too severe, the conditions are clear: short-term German interest rates must continue to fall until they are cancelled in real terms, and the dollar and the yen must rise relative to the European currencies.

a   What is meant by the term 'recession' (paragraph 1)? According to the graph, during which year(s) did the United States experience a recession?

b   Refer to the graph and find the data for the growth of Japanese GDP. If you developed an index and set Japan's GDP as the base year, what would be the level of its GDP in 1991? State your answer as a whole number.

c   Paragraph 1 indicates that debt within a country can hold back economic recovery. Briefly explain this relationship.

QUESTIONS

d Paragraph 7 suggests that a rise in the value of the dollar and the yen would prevent a European recession from becoming too severe. Briefly explain why this would be so.

e Paragraph 6 states that high interest rates result in an overvalued currency. Explain this briefly, using a supply and demand diagram for a currency market.

f Using an aggregate demand and aggregate supply diagram, explain the effects of falling investment and falling household consumption on an economy. Refer to paragraph 4.

(IB, 1995)

5

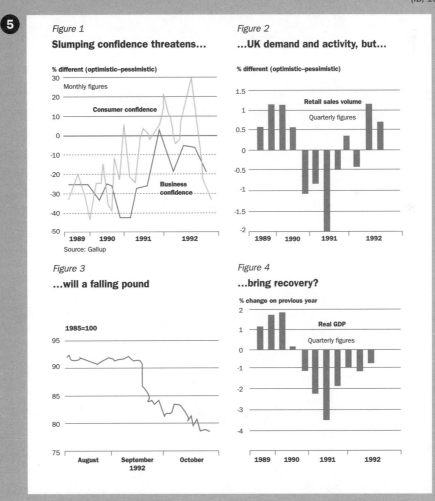

Figure 1

Slumping confidence threatens...

Figure 2

...UK demand and activity, but...

Figure 3

...will a falling pound

Figure 4

...bring recovery?

*Figure 1 shows the percentage difference between respondents who were optimistic and those who were pessimistic. If those who are pessimistic exceed those who are optimistic in any one month, then the % difference will be in the negative portion of the vertical axis.

*Source: P. Norman, 'Still fumbling for first gear', **Financial Times** (31 October 1991).*

a   With reference to the data, what evidence is there to support the view that the UK economy was in recession in the early 1990s?

b   With reference to Figures 1 and 4, analyse the relationship between consumer and business confidence and economic activity in the UK.

c   Figure 3 shows an index of the sterling foreign exchange rate.
   i   Examine how a falling pound could generate economic recovery.
   ii What might be the disadvantages of a falling pound for the UK economy?

d   Outline the factors which are likely to affect:
   i   consumer confidence;
   ii business confidence.

(ULEAC, 1995)

Section 5
International Issues

A traditional English breakfast

The Seaview Hotel, Blackpool

SPECIAL TODAY

TRADITIONAL ENGLISH BREAKFAST

Grapefruit
(grown in South Africa)
|

Cornflakes
(made from corn or maize grown in the USA)
|

Egg & bacon
(eggs from a farm 100 miles away, bacon from Denmark)
|

Toast & marmalade
(toast made from locally baked bread,
marmalade made from oranges from Seville, Spain)
|

Tea or Coffee
(tea from a plantation in Sri Lanka,
coffee from beans grown in Brazil)

Preview

In this chapter we shall investigate the following key areas:

- the theory of comparative advantage;
- free trade and its implications;
- customs unions and free trade areas;
- the GATT and international trade organisations.

Why does the UK trade?

Focus 5.28 demonstrates how dependent we are on international trade with the various components of the breakfast travelling approximately 15,000 miles to reach the table in Blackpool. There is nothing more British than a cup of tea, a product grown in Asia and the Far East. The UK is about the fifth largest trading nation in the world and exports more per person than the Japanese.

For some products the case for trade seems pretty clear-cut. If we wish to consume products such as coffee, cocoa, cotton and copper which we cannot grow because of our climate or produce because of a total lack of resources, we have to buy them from overseas producers. In return we may be able to sell those countries products which they cannot produce but would like to consume. Trade occurs, and the countries are better off due to the fact that they can now consume a wider range of products.

If the UK produces cars and Zambia produces copper then with a given quantity of resources (or unit of resources) their production may be as shown in Box 28.1.

BOX 28.1

Simple trade

	UK (units)	Zambia (units)
Before trade		
Cars	50	0
Copper	0	80
Total production	**50**	**80**
After trade		
Cars	25	25
Copper	40	40

As a result of trade, each country exchanges half of its production with the other country and so is able to consume both products.

For simplicity we are making certain assumptions about the conditions in which trade is taking place:

● there are only two countries,
● there are only two products,
● both countries would like to consume both products.

Another situation could be that both countries are capable of producing both products but with different levels of efficiency. But before progressing with this example, we will need to add some further assumptions:

● the products produced by the two countries are of exactly the same quality (the products are homogeneous);

● there are no transport costs between countries;
● there are no problems regarding foreign exchange;
● there are no economies of scale to be gained nor do countries experience diminishing returns as they increase output;
● there is perfect mobility of factors between different kinds of production;
● there are no barriers to trade.

These assumptions might appear to make any example of limited use in understanding the real world, but this matter will be considered later.

In the case of the UK and Portugal, both countries might be able to produce wine and cars but the UK is the more efficient country in the production of cars and Portugal the more efficient country in the production of wine. An example is shown in Box 28.2.

BOX 28.2		

The basis of trade

	Cars (units)	Wine (units)
Before trade		
UK	50	10
Portugal	20	70
Total production	70	80
After specialisation		
UK	100	0
Portugal	0	140
Total production	100	140
After trade		
UK	50	70
Portugal	50	70

Absolute advantage is a situation in which one nation can produce a given output at a lower resource cost than its trading competitors.

In this case, using 1 unit of resources, the UK can produce 50 units of cars compared to Portugal's 20. The UK is more efficient at car production and, we would say, has the absolute advantage in car production.

Using one unit of resources, Portugal can produce 70 units of wine compared to the UK's 10. Portugal has the absolute advantage in the production of wine.

Each country will gain if it specialises on producing the product in which it

has absolute advantage. This makes good economic sense because it will maximise the output from a given quantity of resources. So now the UK will use its two units of resources to produce cars rather than trying to produce wine. Portugal will use its two units of resources to specialise in wine production.

Now the two countries can trade and, we assume that each country exchange half of its production, will both be better off. Again it is clear that both *he law of comparative advantage* *states that a country which is more efficient at producing all products will still be able to gain from trade if it specialises in producing those products in which it relatively most efficient. Less efficient producers gain from trade if they specialise in producing those products in which they are comparatively least inefficient.*

countries will benefit from trade taking place if both specialise in producing the product in which they have an absolute advantage.

A third situation may arise when one of the countries is most efficient at producing both products. Why should the more efficient country bother to engage in trade; why should it not produce all of the goods it requires itself?

This problem was originally addressed by David Ricardo writing in 1817. He developed the law of comparative advantage to explain what might happen.

An example is illustrated in Box 28.3. It shows the output of cars and shoes from the UK and Portugal.

BOX 28.3

The law of comparative advantage: 1

	UK (units)	Portugal (units)
Before trade		
Cars	50	20
Shoes	100	80
Total production	150	100

Comparative advantage is a situation where one country may be more efficient than another in producing a number of products but relatively it will be more efficient in some than in others.

In this case the UK has the absolute advantage in the production of both products. Ricardo said that in this situation trade would still benefit both countries but that we now had to look at the comparative efficiency of each country. With 1 unit of resources the UK can produce 2.5 times as many cars as Portugal but in the production of shoes, the UK can only produce 25% more shoes. The UK is more efficient in the production of both products but is comparatively more efficient in the production of cars (it has comparative advantage in the production of cars).

Portugal is less efficient in the production of both products but it is comparatively least inefficient in the production of shoes.

Ricardo argued that both countries will gain from trade if the country which is more efficient in both products specialises in the production of that product in which it is comparatively most efficient. The country which is less efficient in both should specialise in the production of that product in which it is comparatively least inefficient. Therefore, in Box 28.3 the UK should specialise in the production of cars and Portugal should specialise in the production of shoes. The result of this specialisation is shown in Box 28.4.

BOX 28.4

The law of comparative advantage: 2

	UK (units)	Portugal (units)
Before trade		
Cars	100	0
Shoes	0	160
Total production	100	160
After trade		
Cars	50	50
Shoes	80	80

Looking at the example, the question is whether both countries have, in fact, gained from trade? To consider this we need to look at the opportunity costs of producing both of the products in each of the countries.

If the UK stops producing cars and turns that unit of resources over to the production of shoes, it will produce 100 units of shoes. In other words, the opportunity cost of producing 50 units of cars is 100 units of shoes or the opportunity cost of 1 unit of cars is 2 units of shoes.

If Portugal stops producing cars and turns its resources over to the production of shoes, it will produce 80 units of shoes. In other words, the opportunity cost of 20 units of cars is 80 units of shoes or the opportunity cost of 1 unit of cars is 4 units of shoes.

Now if the UK can produce 1 unit of cars, sell it to another country and obtain more than 2 units of shoes in return it would be better off than if it tried to produce the shoes itself.

If Portugal can produce shoes, sell less than 4 units of shoes to another count in return for 1 unit of cars, it will be better off than if it tried to produce the cars itself.

So if 1 unit of cars can be exchanged f somewhere between 2 units of shoes and 4 units of shoes, both countries w be happy because they will have benefited from trade taking place. The rate at which one country's goods are exchanged for another's is known as t terms of trade so, in this case, if the terms of trade are 1 unit of cars for 3 units of shoes both countries would gain from trade.

*The **terms of trade** describe the rate at which the goods of one country exchange for the goods of another.*

Ricardo appears to have proved that trade will always operate to the benefit of countries, the only exception being where there is no comparative advantage, i.e. the more efficient country is equally as efficient at producing both products. Work out what the trade outcome would be from the examples given in Task 28.1.

TASK 28.1

Comparative cost examples

In each of the following examples state which countries have absolute advantage in which products and whether there is a basis for trade to take place. Calculate what the limits to the terms of trade might be.

(a)	Country A (units)	Country B (units)
Good X	200	100
Good Y	20	50

(b)	Country A (units)	Country B (units)
Good X	200	100
Good Y	50	20

(c)	Country A (units)	Country B (units)
Good X	100	120
Good Y	50	100

Criticisms of the law of comparative advantage

We now need to revisit the assumptions that were made at the start of this section. The assumptions about only two countries and only two products obviously do not hold in the real world. The introduction of more countries will make the calculations of comparative cost more complex but should not negate the conclusions of the theory. The strength of the demand for the various products will not match each other exactly, and this strength will influence the terms of trade established.

In practice, the quality of goods produced by different countries will vary, indeed, firms will try to ensure that their products are different from imported products to make imports a less perfect substitute for home produced products. However, in the markets for commodities (raw materials) and foodstuffs it is possible to ensure that products produced are of similar quality by the introduction of a grading system.

There are transport costs in moving products from one country to another and this will offset, to some extent, differences in comparative advantage. Australia might have advantages in the production of some goods but the high transport cost may mean that the UK still does not buy the product. (In recent years transport costs have fallen to reduce this problem.)

Foreign exchange problems are more difficult. In the last 20 years currencies have basically floated, meaning that their value has changed according to the forces of supply and demand. A country could have had a comparative advantage in the production of a certain product but this could have been eroded by currency movements. The uncertainty associated with this would also discourage countries shifting from one supplier to another. This would lead to a reduction in the level of trade taking place.

As countries increase the production of goods they are able to achieve economies of scale which lower their costs still further. This should lead to increased cost differences and the potential for more benefits from trade. But there is a major difficulty for countries in that factors of production are not perfectly mobile. As it becomes clear that another country has a comparative advantage in the production of a particular product, the resources employed in that industry should shift into other industries. This may happen quite slowly and during the transition period resources may remain unemployed.

The assumption that there is no protection of domestic industries does not reflect reality. For a variety of reasons countries do protect their industries and it is organisations such as the General Agreement on Tariffs and Trade (GATT) which have been negotiating to reduce the level of tariffs.

Trade is an extremely complex process. Countries do not stop producing a product when they see a new, cheaper competitor arriving on the scene. They fight to preserve their own position knowing that a change in exchange rate could lead to a readjustment of costs and a change in comparative advantage. Countries do not like to allow themselves to become dependent on overseas suppliers, particularly if the product has some strategic value. Hence governments are often keen to see the defence equipment industry survive as well as agriculture. Look at Box 28.5.

BOX 28.5

The motor bike revival

Triumph FOR MOTORCYCLES OVER CARS

Joanna Walters

MOTORCYCLES – particularly British bikes – are again a hot mode of transport, with volumes racing ahead while car sales are stuck in reverse.

The Retail Motor Industry Federation says that motorcycle sales in the UK soared by 21.5 per cent in April and have grown by 7 per cent to 16,000 so far this year.

Sales of new cars fell by 2.3 per cent last month to 139,000 compared with April 1994. While fleet sales held firm, demand from private motorists slumped by seven per cent.

The two-wheeled revival is being driven by better training for novice riders, who now have easier access to a full motorcycle licence and hence the more powerful machines, and by the re-emergence of European-built models, industry observers believe.

The Japanese still dominate the UK market but have lost share to British, German and Italian bikes, and the status-symbol US Harley-Davidson. Triumph, of Hinckley, Leicestershire, has kick-started the comatose British motorcycle industry in the Nineties.

Annual production now exceeds 10,000 bikes, with the bulk for export, and Triumph tripled its share of the British market from 2 per cent in 1992 to 6 per cent of last year's 45,000 UK motorcycle sales.

Industry sources say Triumph, BMW of Germany, Italy's Ducati and Harley-Davidson collectively took 23 per cent of the market

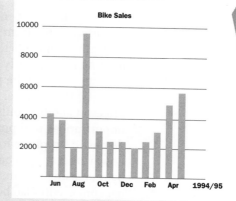

Bike Sales

last year while the four dominant Japanese makers took 68 per cent. Honda was the leader with 28 per cent, followed by Yamaha, Kawasaki and Suzuki.

In 1992 the three European leaders and Harley-Davidson enjoyed only 8 per cent of the British market and the Japanese 82 per cent.

Kevin Kelly, of the RMI's Motorcycle Retailers Association, said: 'Last year the market was up 5 per cent and it is up 6 this year. Triumph is leading a European resurgence based on price and quality.' Kelly says motorcycling's image is improving as training and testing rules tighten.

*Source: **Observer** (21 May 1995).*

TASK 28.2

How does a knowledge of comparative cost theory help us to understand what has happened in the motorcycle industry in recent years?

There is also a question about the fairness of trade. One country may be able to produce goods more cheaply than another but that cost advantage may be due to the employment of child labour or a hidden subsidy from the government. There is a danger that once a foreign producer gains a monopoly of the supply of a product, it will then begin to push up price with very little that the buying country can do. So the theory may remain sound but implementing free trade in practice is more difficult.

The gains from trade

We have already seen one of the most important gains from trade: that specialisation leads to resources being used more efficiently. Output rises helping to tackle the problem of scarcity. With greater efficiency, the prices of goods should fall and falling import prices will put pressure on domestic suppliers to lower their prices. Lower prices will benefit the consumer by increasing real incomes but the consumer will also benefit from the wider choice of goods available and the improvement in quality.

Free trade should be of benefit to producers. Firms will have access to larger markets which will enable them to produce on a larger scale. This will bring economies of scale, lower costs, improve competitiveness and increase profitability. Expansion of firms should bring with it economic growth and rising living standards for the country which should assist in the fight to keep unemployment down.

Despite these advantages, many countries have chosen to protect their industries. There can be some economic justification for this but if all countries adopt the policy there will follow a massive decline in trade which will threaten jobs and living standards across the world. Some experience of this was gained during the 1930s when growing protectionism led the world into the Great Depression.

The case for protection

Free trade generally is of greater benefit to the strong rather than the weak. Well-established firms can move into new markets selling goods at relatively low prices because of their scale of production. The danger here is that they can snuff out any competition from domestic firms before those firms have really become mature enough to compete on equal terms. In this case it could be justified to protect an industry during its early stages of development so that it has a chance to show that some comparative advantage exists. These 'infant industries' could be protected but only for a short period. There could be a case for the protection of the British film industry which seems to be an infant industry compared with Hollywood. Box 28.6 presents some of the arguments.

BOX 28.6

Protecting the film industry

MOVIES NEED *tax breaks*, SAY MPS

The British film industry will be able to compete for business only when it adopts the Irish solution of tax breaks, a committee of MPs said yesterday.

"Owing to competition from abroad, where a number of tax incentives are available, we are losing work we could get if we had comparable incentives," said Gerald Kaufman, chairman of the National Heritage Committee, which produced the report on the British film industry.

Investment in Ireland, where tax breaks of up to 30 per cent are available, rose from £1 million in 1992 to £100 million last year, One notable coup was to persuade Mel Gibson to move much of the production of his £40 million movie 'Braveheart' from Scotland last year.

Mr Kaufman said his group's aim was to turn Britain into more than a Hollywood production facility. "We have a huge history of making some of the best films ever. The whole point is to encourage British people to put money into making British films."

*Source: **Guardian** (5 April 1995).*

TASK 28.3

What method of protection is mentioned in the article?
Should the British film industry receive any protection?

The dynamics of the world economy mean that at any one time some industries will be in decline. If those industries were responsible for a significant amount of employment in a country, their decline could cause problems of regional unemployment. It is justified for a country to protect a contracting industry to slow down the rate of decline so that time is given for people to find jobs elsewhere in the economy.

Some countries experience imbalance in their trade with the rest of the world. If they are importing too many goods, countries may correct a temporary problem by placing tariffs on imports. This would be appropriate where there is an identifiable specific problem but not if there was a more fundamental loss of competitiveness.

Dumping is a problem which concerns countries. It is the selling of products on overseas markets at prices below those prevailing on domestic markets. The danger here is that the dumping of products could cause prices to drop drastically. This could be good news for consumers in the short run but, in the long run, domestic producers could be forced out of business leaving a clear run for the foreign suppliers in the future. Producers may be off-loading product on foreign markets to keep prices up in their home markets. Therefore the effects of dumping are undesirable and, if it can be detected, some protection against its effects is justified.

Some arguments are offered in support of protection which might not stand up to economic scrutiny. Protection is certainly used to promote political objectives and did appear to be effective in achieving a just outcome in South Africa. Economic sanctions can be used to achieve political ends.

Protecting industry as a retaliation for protection introduced by other countries is questionable. It was used by the USA when it felt that the EU was using hidden subsidies to lower the price of steel exported to the USA but this is difficult. If countries protect an industry for valid reasons, others retaliating simply prevent the original objective from being achieved while reducing the welfare of consumers.

Protecting industry against 'unfair' competition is also questionable. Countries often will claim that competition is unfair when, in fact a country may just be using its comparative advantage to lower costs. This argument is used against some of the low wage economies and the difficult issue is to decide whether wages are low due to the abundance of labour as a factor of production or whether exploitation is present. If the latter is the case, protection may not be the answer to the problem. Box 28.7 raises some of the issues here.

BOX 28.7

FAIR TRADE?

Some people in America and Europe want the further opening of markets to developing countries to be made conditional on those countries accepting minimum labour standards. Imported goods which use child labour, slave labour or prison labour, or which deny workers the right to form trade unions and bargain collectively, they argue, should be banned. Their motive is to improve the lot of the poor workers in the third world. The developing countries suspect, however, that it is really a pretext for protectionism; an attempt by the rich countries to deny them the benefit of their comparative advantage in cheap labour.

The argument for linking trade more broadly to labour standards comes from two sides. First there are those who argue that poor working conditions amount to an unfair trade advantage. Industrialised countries cannot compete against sweat shop labour. If such competition is allowed, it will increase the pressure on employers to trim workers' rights in the rich countries. The second argument is that there are some basic human rights which it is the duty of the rich countries to foster even if they have to do this by the use of sanctions.

Trade sanctions may be introduced with the best of intentions but their effectiveness is debatable. If they have the effect of driving children out of employment, the alternative could well be begging, prostitution or starvation. If imports from countries using such practices are banned, this keeps those countries poorer for longer.

There is a more fundamental objection to attempts to link trade privileges to labour standards. The argument that lower standards are giving developing countries an unfair advantage strikes at the whole rationale for trade. The playing field of international trade will never be level; nor should it be. Competition between firms in different countries can never be 'fair' in the same way as competition between firms in the same country. Countries have different endowments of resources and different tastes and priorities. The benefits of international trade come from allowing countries to exploit their comparative advantage, not from requiring them to be identical. And much of the developing countries, comparative advantage lies, in one way or another, in their cheap labour. Asking for all countries to adopt similar standards is the same as asking for all comparative advantages

BOX 28.7

to be eliminated before trade begins. As one economist put it. 'It is like Finland arguing that Ecuador has an unfair advantage in growing bananas because it has more sun.'

A better course of action might be for the rich countries to give greater aid to improve primary education to reduce child labour and encouraging more trade should boost living standards and do more to reduce poor working conditions.

Source: Adapted from **The Economist** *(1 October 1994).*

TASK 28.4

What are the arguments for and against the developed countries protecting their industries against unfair competition from the developing countries?

Methods of protection

Countries have used a range of techniques to protect home markets:

Tariffs are taxes imposed on imported goods. The objective is to raise the prices of imported goods so that home producers are better able to compete. They are especially useful if the demand for the imports is elastic for then a rise in price will cause a more than proportionate decrease in demand. They are a particularly visible means of protectionism and have formed the focus for much of the discussion at the GATT negotiations.

Quotas place a limit on the quantity of goods imported. They might appear to have no effect on price but, in fact, they do. The importer, knowing that supplies will be limited, may well increase prices or may choose to import higher priced goods with higher profit margins. This will then enable home producers to raise their prices as well. Quotas are more likely to be used against products for which the demand is relatively inelastic.

Subsidies may be used to protect domestic suppliers or be used to make it easier for firms to penetrate foreign markets. The USA complained about the EU's use of subsidies to support the steel industry and there is debate about the level of subsidy given to industries at the time of privatisation.

Voluntary export restraint (VER) is a method used where countries might be persuaded that limiting their own exports to a country could be preferable to stronger action from the importing country. For many years the UK had an arrangement with the Japanese car manufacturers to limit their exports to the UK to 11% of the market, and this kind of limit might well have influenced the decisions of Nissan and Toyota to set up production plants in the UK.

Import deposits involve the government making it financially more difficult for firms to import goods. Any importing firms could be required to deposit a proportion of the value of the order with the government before they could go ahead with the deal. This would act as a discouragement to importers and could affect the profitability of handling imports.

Foreign exchange controls could be used to prevent citizens getting access to the quantity of foreign currency they might need to purchase foreign goods. Again this would make importing more difficult.

Non-tariff barriers have increasingly been used to replace the more visible forms of trade restriction. Insisting that all imported products conform to particular standards, specified forms of labelling, pollution levels or noise levels have all been used to cut foreign competition. The cultural attitudes of some countries are negative towards imported products and this has created tension between the USA and Japan, with the USA feeling that the Japanese have not done enough to open up their market. The UK decision to retain driving on the left hand side of the road could be considered as a non-tariff barrier and some motor manufacturers believe that in the long term this will eventually change.

The response to protectionism

In a world of protectionism, how should countries respond? Would it be sensible for a country to be such a strong supporter of free trade that it says that, whatever protectionist policies other countries may pursue, its borders will be open for free access by any country?

This is unlikely since those other countries could well exploit the openness of those borders. The most preferred policy might be free trade but in the absence of free trade, what should be the second best policy?

The shoe industry: should it be protected?

Shoe industry ON ITS UPPERS

BY PAUL ROGERS

THE TOWN of Keighley, Yorkshire reeled when Peter Black Holdings recently announced it was closing its shoe factory. The town's second largest employer plans to make 285 people redundant, almost half its local workforce.

"We have gone down fighting," claimed joint chairman Gordon Black. "We left no stone unturned in trying to save production of footwear in Keighley." The company blamed its distress on the usual culprit – cheap imports – but others think more complex changes are afoot.

Peter Black is not alone. A spate of closures and receiverships has rocked Britain's already down-at-heel footwear industry recently.

Somerset-based C&J Clark, one of the sector's largest firms, this month closed its children's shoe plant in Radstock, Avon, with 360 job losses. In Stalybridge, Manchester, Futura shoes is in voluntary receivership, So is Chatterbox Shoes, makers of down-market footwear in Blaby, Leicestershire. It will close in May, with 95 job losses.

They also pointed to inexpensive foreign imports as the source of their woes. Countries such as Indonesia, Italy, Spain, China and Portugal have grabbed a steadily growing share of the UK market for decades. But industry observers say this time the imports are not at fault.

BOX 28.8

Britain's footwear industry is finally going through a badly needed rationalisation. Cost-efficient producers such as Lotus, the core division of conglomerate FII Group, are doing well. Many have growing export sales and a steady share of Britain's admittedly shrinking domestic market. Those less well equipped to face the future are falling by the wayside.

Futura is typical of the companies feeling the pinch most severely. Martin Holt, the slipper-maker's managing director, said his company was unable to arrange financing this year. But Malcolm Shierson of receiver Grant Thornton said the company's problems ran deeper. "What we're seeing is the collapse of companies that have old, outdated equipment," he said. "The equipment Futura uses still works, but it's well past its sell-by date." The company is for sale.

The shake-up has been expected for at least two years. In 1993 three bidders tried to scoop up C&J Clark. Alan Bowkett, chairman of Berisford International, one of the failed bidders, argued then that the industry was ripe for consolidation.

What would have happened if Berisford had succeeded with its £184m bid is moot.

The debate now is about Clark's future as a shoe-maker. The plants closure emphasises its increasing reliance on outside suppliers for stock.

Britain's shoe, boot and slipper-makers have been in decline for so long that few people notice when another firm slides under. In the 1960s the industry employed 116,000, according to the Leicester and County Footwear Manufacturers' Association. Today it has 35,000. During that period foreign imports rose from 18 per cent to 62 per cent by value.

Recently the situation has changed. By 1993 import volumes had returned to their 1989 level, around 177 million pairs. British exports over the past five years have grown from 25 million to 31 million pairs. But total sales in the UK fell from a peak of 310 million in 1990 to 260 million pairs as recession-battered consumers held on to their old leather.

It is no coincidence, argues Paul Baines of Charterhouse Bank. "You only get shake-outs when there are financial pressures. It's not a bad thing for the industry to become leaner. It will leave it better placed to fight off imports."

Source: **Independent on Sunday** (26 February 1995).

TASK 28.5

What has caused the decline of the British shoe industry?
Should the industry receive protection? If so, in what way?

Free trade areas and customs unions

Many countries have tried to get the benefits of free trade in a protectionist world. They have formed free trade areas or customs unions with other countries with similar interests. The EU has grown to include 15 member countries and, with a further three countries, form the European Economic Area (EEA). The USA, Canada and Mexico have formed the North American Free Trade Association (NAFTA) and the Asia-Pacific Economic Co-operation forum (APEC) is working towards free trade in an area stretching from New York to Bangkok and Chile to China. Increasingly, the world seems to be forming into the powerful trading blocs illustrated in Box 28.9.

BOX 28.9

The importance of the trading blocs, 1993

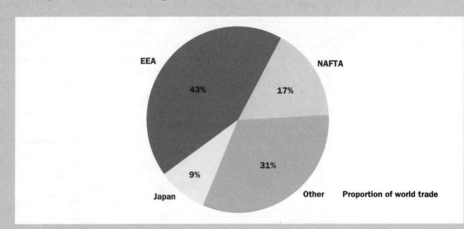

Free trading areas and customs unions

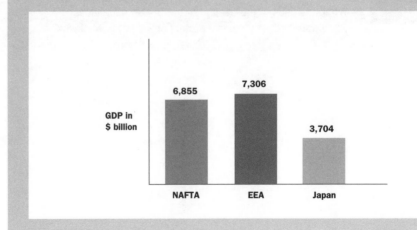

*A **free trade area** is a group of countries which abolish trade barriers between members but retain their own independent policy towards trade with other countries, e.g. NAFTA.*

*A **customs union** is a free trade area but where, in addition, the members adopt a common policy towards other countries, e.g. the EU.*

***Trade creation** when countries become members of customs unions there will be an increased amount of trade between member states as the gains from trade develop.*

***Trade diversion** is the formation of a customs union may deny countries access to cheaper products which could have been bought from countries outside the customs union. The result will be less trade with countries outside the union.*

A free trade area is where countries remove trade barriers between member countries but retain their own policy towards imports from outside the free trade area. A customs union takes this a stage further with all members adopting the same approach towards countries outside the union. The EU is an example of a customs union with all members adopting the same common external tariff on goods entering the union.

The major advantage of a customs union is that the members should be able to benefit from the gains from trade that will result from the abolition of trade barriers within the union. There should result an increase in specialisation and efficiency, lower prices and more choice. The gains will be that much greater if the member countries previously had a high level of protectionism and the formation of the union causes tariffs to tumble. The increase in trade between member states is known as trade creation but it is likely that trade with countries outside the union will decrease.

This may well mean that cheaper supplies of goods from outside the union will be denied to the union's consumers. This has been an important effect of membership of the EU. Access

to cheaper world supplies of, especially, many agricultural products has kept prices higher than they would otherwise have been. The reduction of trade with third party countries is known as trade diversion.

The overall effect of membership of a union is dependent on the balance of these two forces.

The effects of UK membership of the EU will be covered in Chapter 30 but NAFTA looks to be an interesting example of a free trade area. It is an example of two rich countries joining with a middle income country and it is expected that there will be some transfer of jobs to the lower waged Mexican economy. There should also be some technology transfer as US firms shift production south. The increased demand for the labour of Mexico should have the effect of raising wages and the inward investment should assist the development process. However, there is a fear that the low value, low skill, high polluting forms of production will move into Mexico with firms exploiting the more relaxed environmental controls. Also, there is no certainty that the newly created income will be distributed more evenly amongst Mexico's population so that there may remain widespread poverty.

The General Agreement on Tariffs and Trade (GATT)

***General Agreement on Tariffs and Trade (GATT)** is an organisation with the objective of lowering trade barriers throughout the world.*

The GATT was set up following the 1944 world trade conference held at the Mount Washington Hotel, Bretton Woods, New Hampshire, USA. There have been eight rounds of negotiation with the latest, the Uruguay round, being completed at the end of 1994. The final deal, which ran to 22,500 pages, produced $744 billion in tariff

cuts and should, by the year 2005, produce benefits to world trade worth $500 billion. It was signed by 115 nations, itself a major achievement.

As a result of the GATT agreement, 95% of goods traded will be subject to a maximum tariff which can be used, known as a tariff binding. Monitoring the performance of countries in meeting the GATT requirements will be the job of the World Trade Organisation (WTO) which began work on January 1 1995.

A General Agreement on Trade in Services (GATS) was also concluded which should have the effect of opening up markets to companies providing services. This should be of greatest benefit to the USA and Europe since this is where most of the service companies are based.

GATT established new rules for the control of intellectual property rights to give greater protection to creative work. Many companies have suffered from cheap copies being made without any permission being sought or given.

Agriculture has been a major area of protection and possibly costs consumers around $400 billion per year.

The EU has been one of the biggest protectors of agriculture but the agreement should lead to the reduction of tariffs on agricultural products by 36% over the next six years. The multi-fibre agreement, which effectively kept out competition from low cost textile manufacturing countries, is also due to be phased out over a 10 year period.

This agreement took eight years to hammer out so it is not surprising to see that countries are forming links with a relatively smaller number of trading partners where the negotiation process may be far simpler. Multinational companies still remain a major threat since they can move capital around the world, take advantage of different laws applied in different countries and can ensure that their profits are earned in low tax areas. Monitoring their activities will be an important activity of the WTO.

REVIEW

Trade is an important motor of the world economy. It provides a way out for the developing countries and a way of securing further prosperity for the developed world. Comparative cost theory provides the economic justification for the pursuit of free trade but fair trade is more elusive. Many countries have attempted to gain the benefits of free trade by setting up free trade areas or customs unions but a more general reduction in the level of protectionism has been achieved through the successful completion of the GATT negotiations. Trade is not fair and it is likely that even the outcome of GATT will mainly benefit the rich.

REVIEW TASK

Read the following extract about multinational companies:

1 What do you understand by a multinational (transnational) firm?
2 Comment on the role of multinationals in world trade.

United Nations reveals how multi-national groups dominate global economy

ELITE COMPANIES RULE *world of trade*

Larry Elliott – Economics Correspondent

THE increasing domination of the world economy by a small number of multi-national companies was highlighted today when a new study by the United Nations found that trans-national corporations (TNCs) account for one third of global output.

According to the World Investment Report from the United Nations Conference on Trade and Development, (Unctad) the workplace is being shaped by TNCs, with trade unions and national governments largely impotent to prevent the biggest companies setting their own agenda in terms of jobs, industrial relations and training.

The report found that the sales from trans-national corporations were worth $4,800 billion – bigger than total international trade – and formed "the productive core of the globalising world economy".

The report noted that workers employed by foreign multi-nationals tended to enjoy better wages, conditions of work and social security benefits than those working for domestic firms.

And despite fears that the concentration of economic muscle in a small number of companies would lead to longer dole queues, Unctad said the immediate impact of TNCs on current levels of unemployment was small.

But it added that the longer term consequences for the labour market through stimulating economic growth and improving international competitiveness could not be underestimated. "Because of this, questions regarding the social responsibilities of TNCs demand increasing attention, as do the critical issues of redefining policies and approaches confronting national governments and trade unions.

"The fact is that labour markets and industrial relations are beginning to emerge slowly from their national confines and to adapt to a world economy that, in other respects, is more integrated than at any time in its history, and is becoming more so."

Unctad's research revealed that the global network of TNCs is comprised of 37,000 parent firms, which control 200,000 foreign affiliates, not including numerous non-equity links. Two-thirds of the parent firms – 26,000 – are from 14 wealthy developed countries, an increase of 19,000 since the end of the 1960s, when economies tended to be far less open to overseas competition.

Even within the world of TNCs, there is an elite group. The 100 largest multi-nationals held $3,400 billion in assets by the end of 1992, of which about 40 per cent were assets located outside of their home countries. In addition, the top 100 – which includes 11 UK firms – control about one-third of the world stock of foreign direct investment.

The report added that the scope for still greater expansion of TNCs had been enhanced by the signing of the Uruguay Round of Gatt trade talks, the North American Free Trade Agreement and by other regional and bilateral trade treaties. One third of all world trade is already intra-firm.

In the early years of the current decade, the flow of foreign direct investment (FDI) from TNCs slowed up, but Unctad said this was the result of the global recession and not the start of a trend. FDI fell from a peak of $232 billion in 1990 to $171 billion in 1992, before recovering to $195 billion last year.

The US was both the biggest source and the biggest recipient of FDI, with American-based companies investing a record $50 billion in 1993. Britain moved up from fifth to second in the list of FDI outflows, while Japanese corporate retrenchment has seen Japan slip from first in 1980s to fifth.

Forty per cent of FDI in 1993 went to developing countries, but Unctad said the bald figures disguised the fact that the lion's share was concentrated in 10 to 15 countries in Asia and Latin America.

China alone accounted for $26 billion in 1993 but a third of the developing countries in the world – mostly in Africa – have been shunned by foreign investors.

Source: Guardian (31 August 1994).

Multiple choice

1 **If the terms of trade of a country have improved, then its**
A   currency has depreciated.
B   balance of payments has worsened.
C   gold and foreign currency reserves have risen.
D   exports have become more expensive in relation to imports

(IB November 1994).

2 Two countries have the following opportunity cost ratios for wheat and cloth.

	Wheat (units)	Cloth (units)
COUNTRY A	2	1
COUNTRY B	5	1

If the terms of trade are such that 2.5 units of wheat exchange for 1 unit of cloth, then economic theory predicts that
A   there is no advantage in trade between the two countries
B   country B should specialise in cloth
C   neither country has an absolute advantage in producing wheat
D   both countries will benefit from specialisation and trade.

(AEB, November 1994).

3 **Answer this question with reference to the following:**
A   1,2 and 3 are correct
B   1 and 2 only are correct
C   2 and 3 only are correct
D   1 only is correct

The establishment of a common internal market by the EU is likely to result in
1   increased mobility of factors
2   less international specialisation
3   less harmonisation of tax between countries.

(AEB, November 1994).

4 **Which of the following factors would tend to prevent international specialisation?**
A   Countries having different factor endowments
B   Goods having different opportunity costs of production
C   Some countries being able to produce more goods and services than other countries
D   Some countries having no mobility of factors between industries.

(AIB, Higher, May 1995).

5 The growth of regional trading blocks might lead to increased efficiency in the allocation of resources in the short run because they

A increase the scope for economies of scale

B encourage trade diversion

C lead to increased government revenue

D reduce unnecessary competition.   *(IB, Higher, May 1995).*

6 Smith, Jones and Brown are shipwrecked on a desert island. The only occupations open to them are fishing, hunting and collecting fruit. If they specialise in only one activity, their possible weekly output is as follows:

Output per week (units of food)			
	Fishing	*Hunting*	*Fruit collecting*
Smith	20	20	20
Jones	60	40	20
Brown	30	20	30

Which of the following statements is (are) correct?

1 Jones has a comparative advantage in the production of fish over Smith

2 Jones has an absolute advantage in the production of fish

3 Brown will collect fruit.

A 1,2 and 3 are correct

B 1 and 2 only are correct

C 2 and 3 only are correct

D 1 only is correct   *(ULEAC, January 1995).*

7

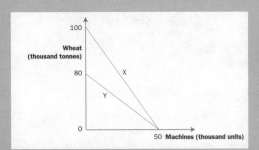

In the above diagram X represents the production possibility frontier of Country X and Y represents the production possibility frontier of Country Y. Assuming mutually beneficial terms of trading between X and Y, which of the following statements is true?

A Y will import wheat and export machines

B Y will export wheat and import machines

C Y will import both wheat and machines

D No trade can take place between X and Y because Y has no comparative advantage over X

E Y will import wheat but has nothing to export to X which X wishes to have.

               (ULEAC, January 1995).

FOCUS

The Investigator: THE 'TRADE FIGURES'

Export and import worries

Although domestic demand is still slack, Britain's visible trade deficit with non-EC countries widened last month, mainly due to a sharp jump in imports. Earlier this year imports were fairly subdued and exports were buoyant. But recently the start of a weak UK economic recovery has pulled in fresh imports on an alarming scale. Britain's exports to non-EC countries, a number of which are enjoying boom conditions, and which account for about one-third of Britain's exports, are also disappointing. It is also worrying that trade with non-EC countries, who are mostly showing good economic growth, is deteriorating. Over-all trade data for July showed Britain's current account deficit jumping to £1.5 billion from £1.2 billion in June, with sales of new cars overseas dropping sharply. These figures suggest that British exports, particularly to European markets, are running up against falling demand, which is blunting the competitive advantage brought about by sterling's devaluation out of the ERM. At the same time, Britain's consumers are spending heavily on imported goods. The import–export situation is disturbing many economists.

Pound threatens record low

Political feuding inside Mr. Major's government combined with worries about renewed inflation and surging imports, to send sterling plunging yesterday. Financial analysts forecast the pound could soon fall below its all-time low against the German mark, and that upward pressures on interest rates will increase.

Preview

In this chapter we shall investigate the following key areas:

- the nature of the balance of payments accounts;
- causes of balance of payments difficulties;
- automatic and policy adjustment of the balance of payments;
- exchange rate systems;
- balance of payments flow-of-funds analysis;
- recent UK balance of payments experience.

Introduction

As the extracts in Focus 5.29 show, balance of payments data in the form of 'trade figures' is frequently a focus of media attention. The material in Focus 5.29 is typical in the sense that a trade deficit is seen as economically undesirable. Before we test this proposition we need to be quite clear however about what a trade deficit actually is. It refers to a situation in which a country's payments for imports of physical goods exceed receipts from its exports of physical goods. However, 'visible' trade is only part of the story. Countries also import and export services of various kinds, and the UK, for instance, frequently earns a surplus on such 'invisible' items. Examples of invisibles are sea transport, civil aviation, tourism and travel, and financial services. Combining the visible and invisible balances gives us the balance of payments on current account. This balance will fluctuate from month to month but its state over the medium term – say, over the course of the business cycle – will tell us to what extent a country is 'paying its way' with the rest of the world. Look at Box 29.1.

BOX 29.1

UK, visible, invisible and current accounts, 1983–93

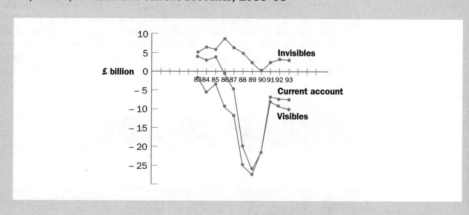

Trade deficit is a situation where payments for visible imports exceed receipts from visible exports.

As Box 29.1 makes clear, in the period from the mid-1980s the UK had a chronic (persistent) current account deficit. It was not paying its way with the rest of the world and was running into foreign debt on a substantial scale.

Initially, the UK had a valuable 'nest egg' of net foreign assets, but Box 29.2 shows that by the early 1990s these were in danger of becoming negative, and there would then be no 'cushion' left to support further trade deficits.

BOX 29.2

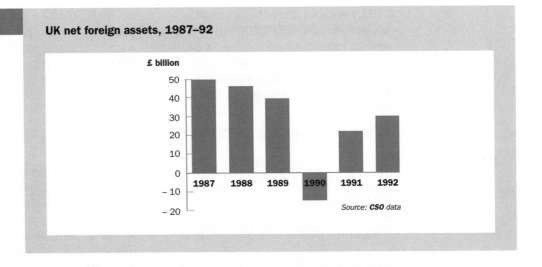

UK net foreign assets, 1987–92

£ billion

Source: *CSO* data

The danger of a balance of payments deficit

balance of payments is a summary of a country's financial transactions with the rest of the world.

A balance of payments crisis is an unstable situation where a country's balance of payments deficit provokes a collapse in the demand for its currency, leading to a harmful combination of higher interest rates and falling exchange rate.

Autonomous capital movements are international money movements not related to the financing of trade, but undertaken on their own accord.

Accommodating capital movements are international money movements related to the financing of trade.

A balance of payments deficit can become dangerous if levels of foreign debt become excessive, in a sense we shall now examine.

Consider the position in 1993, when the UK current account deficit was around £10,000 million. Since the UK was 'over-importing' by this amount, in simple terms foreigners would find themselves accumulating £10,000 million of sterling 'IOUs'. As long as foreigners viewed their new assets as attractive, and were prepared to go on holding them, the position would remain stable. But suppose (due, say, to worries about the rising level of UK foreign debt) the flow of foreigners prepared to go on lending to the UK by holding sterling IOUs were to dry up. Mass selling of these IOUs could cause the exchange rate of sterling to fall sharply. One effect of this would be to make the financing of UK imports more difficult and expensive. Another would be to put upward pressure on interest rates and prices. If these tendencies got out of control, a balance of payments crisis could develop.

In point of fact, financing the UK's deficit in the period under consideration did not prove difficult. In the first place, favourable UK economic conditions made sterling-denominated assets generally attractive, so there was no shortage of potential sterling holders. (Money drawn into a country, often on a short-term basis, to finance an import surplus is known as accommodating capital.) Secondly, there were at times considerable inflows of autonomous capital into the UK; that is, foreign money being invested here 'of its own accord' for the long-term return it could obtain: for example, Japanese investments in the UK car industry. However, in most years the net tendency of UK autonomous capital flows was in fact strongly outward – much more of this investment was leaving the UK than was entering it. For example in

1993, over and above the current account deficit of £10 000 million, there was an estimated net long-term capital outflow of £53 000 million. Hence the UK's 'overall' deficit, and financing requirement was a huge £63 000 million! So could the UK could continue to run up foreign debt on su a scale, without running into a crisis' We begin by examining the underlyin factors behind this situation.

Why was there a persistent UK balance of payments defici

There are a number of possible reasons why the UK's balance of payments might be in deficit.

The state of the business cycle

Rapidly rising income in a period of boom will tend to 'pull in' imports and 'pull back' domestic output, which might otherwise have been exported. (A recession will have the opposite effect of reducing imports but encouraging exports.) Also, high inflation at the end of a boom reduces the international competitiveness of a country's products, and low inflation in a recession improves competitiveness. 'Over-heating' of the UK's domestic economy in the late 1980s certainly helped lead to a large payments deficit. However, in the following recession a considerable deficit remained. This suggests other reasons for the payments deficit.

The size and efficiency of the UK's manufacturing base

There was a contraction in the UK's manufacturing base – de-industrialisation – in the 1980s, and this undoubtedly contributed to the decline in net manufacturing exports. There was evidence too that many UK businesse had become 'locked' into old-fashion products, with poor export potential. Happily, the 1990s saw a degree of 're-industrialisation' as UK manufacturing expanded and became more efficient and competitive. By 19 the UK was becoming a net exporter a number of products, for instance cars and TVs, where earlier it had bee heavily import-dependent.

A decline in UK net exports of services

Net exports of services have usually made a large contribution to the UK's foreign balance. These might have bee expected to grow as the services secto of the economy expanded in the 1980 In fact, there was a sharp fall in net invisible exports in the late 1980s followed by some recovery in the 199

BOX 29.3

UK invisibles, 1993

Exports of services:	£ billion, 1993
General government	0.4
Sea transport	3.8
Civil aviation	5.1
Travel	9.1
Financial	18.2
Total	**36.6**

Imports of services:	£ billion, 1993
General government	2.3
Sea transport	4.3
Civil aviation	5.5
Travel	12.2
Financial	7.2
Total	**31.5**

*Source: **COI**, **Pink Book** (1994)*

A fall in net UK oil exports

UK oil production peaked in the mid-1980s and had fallen significantly by 1990. In the mid-1990s, however, there were indications of a second 'oil boom' as more UK oil reserves became accessible to modern low-cost technologies.

An 'overvalued' pound could have damaged UK exports

*An **overvalued currency** is a currency with an excessive exchange rate which damages the competitiveness of that country's products.*

Other things being equal, a rise in the exchange rate will make a country's products more expensive and less competitive. A persistent import surplus such as that experienced by the UK might indicate that a country's currency was seriously overvalued.

In Box 29.4 you can read how an overvalued pound may have damaged the UK's economy. (Note that the nominal exchange rate measures at a given time the value of one currency in terms of another – for example, £1 equals 9 French francs. A real exchange rate takes account also of changes in price levels between countries. So if the £ rose from 9 to 12 francs, and the UK's price level also happened to fall compared with France's, the increase in sterling's real exchange rate in terms of francs would exceed that in its nominal rate.)

BOX 29.4

Changes in sterling's real exchange rate, 1976–93

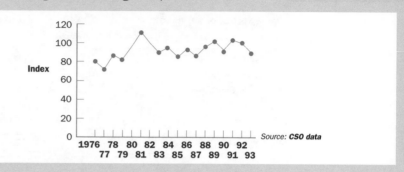

Source: **CSO data**

TASK 29.1

Box 29.4 above shows that the real exchange rate since 1979 has on average been 18 per cent higher than it was in earlier decades. Such a prolonged period of adverse industrial competitiveness should, according to the textbooks, have had several effects on the economy, all of them favouring consumption over production.

First, it should have shrunk the manufacturing sector (which depends heavily on trade with the rest of the world) relative to the services sector. This has indeed happened. The share of manufacturing in GDP has fallen from 29 per cent in the mid-1970s to 23 per cent now.

Second, consumption should have benefited relative to investment and net exports. Sure enough, it has. The share of consumption in GDP has risen by about four percentage points over the same period.

Third, the balance of payments should have worsened markedly. Again, the textbooks have triumphed. The trade balance, as everyone now knows, is running at its worst level since the Second World War, adjusted for the stage of the economic cycle.

Fourth, unemployment should have risen, at least for a transitional period. No one needs reminding that the jobless total has indeed more than doubled – with the 'transition' so far lasting almost 15 years. Finally, all of this should have reduced the rate of inflation. And it has – by much more than anyone thought likely a decade ago.

The high real exchange rate policy, which has been the distinguishing feature of Treasury strategy since the Conservatives came to power, has therefore delivered its main objective – low inflation – at the expense of an apparently permanent shift in the structure of the economy towards excess consumption and away from manufacturing, investment, exports and employment.

(Source: Adapted from **Gavyn Davies, Independent** (19 March 1993).

1 How might a high sterling exchange rate help reduce the general level of prices?
2 Why might governments in the 1980s have been reluctant to take measures to reduce the exchange rate of the pound?
3 Why should a high exchange rate shrink the manufacturing sector relative to the services sector?

1992: sterling devaluation and the UK balance of payments

Devaluation is a reduction of a currency's exchange rate.

The sterling devaluation in September 1992, when sterling left the ERM (see Section 5), provided an opportunity to test the idea that it had previously been overvalued, for restored competitiveness for UK products should then have boosted UK exports and import substitution. In the extract in Box 29.5 you can study how some typical British businesses reacted to the 1992 devaluation.

BOX 29.5

The 1992 devaluation

With a large current account deficit, it is vital that manufacturers take full advantage of their current export potential and sterling's devaluation.

With domestic prices apparently battened down for the time being, there is a marvellous incentive to charge into export markets and rebuild profits that way – indeed, export margins have risen dramatically. Throughout the recession, there has been little choice for those firms bent on survival but to look overseas for demand and, what is cheering, is that many companies seem determined to go for maximum growth in export market rather than raising export price margins.

Avon Rubber makes anything rubber from inflateable dinghies to a vast array of items for the car industry. With plants in France and the US, 60 per cent of its production is bought by customers outside the UK. Helped substantially by devaluation, Avon says the company is much more interested in launching an attack on the European auto components market than raising margins.

On the import price side of the equation, there are tentative signs that the impact of sterling's devaluation may not turn out to be quite as severe as in the past because overseas economies are under ever more intense competitive pressure and are experiencing painful economic slowdown.

PAL International makes headwear and hygiene products for the drug and food industries and exports 50 per cent of output. Richard Brucciani, PAL chairman and head of the CBI's smaller firms council, believes devaluation will help increase export of chefs' hats to France by 15 per cent. What is interesting about his experience since devaluation is the behaviour of his suppliers of imported raw materials. He buys paper and non-woven materials from Sweden and France. Sweden has also devalued so prices are no higher, but France has not. But PAL's French supplier matched Swedish prices to keep the business. Mr. Brucciani said: 'there is a lot of evidence that foreign suppliers are prepared to squeeze margins to get orders.'

BOX 29.5

Something similar has been seen at **Courtaulds Textiles**, where Martin Taylor, chairman and executive, has been surprised to see that the costs of imported raw materials like dyestuffs have not risen by the 20 per cent they had expected. With a number of large customers, such as Italy and Spain, also devaluing their currencies, importers may have no choice but to keep prices competitive or lose business.

*Source: Adapted from **Janet Bush, The Times** (March 8 1993).*

TASK 29.2

1 The article indicates that following devaluation, UK import prices might have risen much less than anticipated. What does this suggest about elasticities of demand and supply for Britain's imports?

2 Are increased export levels the key to a better trade balance – or more import substitution?

3 Do you think the evidence in the extract supports the view that sterling was overvalued before 1992?

It is sometimes argued that a low sterling exchange rate might beneficially encourage an inward flow of capital as foreign firms set up in the UK.
Explain how this might come about.

Was the UK economy 'financially imbalanced'?

We examined above five possible factors behind the UK's balance of payments deficit. Some economists have argued that a financial imbalance in the UK economy may have been at the root of the UK's balance of payments difficulties. The analysis focuses on the relationship between the financial balances of the public, private and foreign trade secto which together comprise the UK economy. Since one sector's income is another's expenditure, these three balances must by definition add up to zero. You can see in Box 29.6 and 29.7 how the state of these might lead to balance of payments difficulties.

BOX 29.6

UK financial balances, by sector, 1980–93

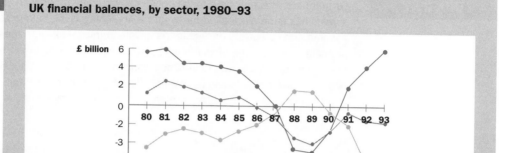

BOX 29.7

Is the financial balance of Britain's economy wrong?

It is clear from Box 29.6 that it is perfectly normal for the private sector (households and businesses) to run a financial surplus, while the public sector runs a deficit. The trade position is determined by relative sizes of these two imbalances. If the private surplus is larger than the public deficit, then the trade account is in surplus and vice versa.

There are two aspects of the present situation that are out of the ordinary. First, the private sector is running a particularly large financial surplus, in excess of 6 per cent of GDP. Although there have been surpluses of this size in the past, this has only occurred when inflation was running at double-digit rates from 1975-81. In those years, rapid inflation was eroding the real value of private savings, and this induced companies and individuals to attempt to replenish their savings by running large financial surpluses. Why is this? Almost certainly, it is because the private sector has been curtailing expenditure to pay off debt...

On all past performance, the economy is unlikely to recover unless the private sector's surplus begins to decline. In fact, it is reasonable to suppose that it might one day decline from the present 6 per cent of GDP to about 2 per cent, which is where it stood on average in the low-inflation period before 1973. If the whole of this decline were to be reflected in an improvement in the public-sector deficit, with none of it leaking into the trade deficit, then the public deficit would automatically improve from 8 per cent of GDP to about 4 per cent. But even that would still not be enough to produce an acceptable out-turn for the government accounts over the medium term.

BOX 29.7

Furthermore, this may be a touch optimistic. In the past, a decline in the private-sector surplus has generally leaked partly into a worsening in the balance of payments. Assume that half of the decline in the private surplus leaks into the balance of payments, with the remainder being reflected in a narrowing of the public deficit. Under these circumstances, the trade deficit would rise from 2 per cent of GDP to 4 per cent, and the public deficit would narrow only from 8 per cent of GDP to 6 per cent – an entirely unacceptable out-turn for both the trade and budget deficits.

Source: Adapted from **Gavyn Davies, Independent** *(5 June 1993).*

TASK 29.3

1　Why, if the UK's two internal sectors are in overall deficit, should their excess spending spill over into a corresponding current account deficit?

2　What effect would a recovery of private sector – that is, households and businesses – spending be likely to have on the balance of payments?

3　What policies might help bring the UK's two internal sectors into total surplus, and so promote a strong balance of payments?

How is balance of payments adjustment achieved?

The process of converting a weak balance of payments into a strong one is known as balance of payments adjustment. This can occur in two ways: automatically through natural forces, and secondly through policy measures. We now examine each of these in turn.

'Automatic' balance of payments adjustment

The idea we are looking at here is that a payments deficit will generate forces which feed back to eliminate that deficit.

● Adjustment could take place through changes between the price levels of non-foreign traded goods (e.g. haircuts) and foreign traded goods (e.g. cars). When the price of traded goods is low relative to that of non-traded goods, domestic demand for traded goods will tend to exceed the supply of traded goods, leading to a gap which gets filled by imports. In theory the excess demand for traded goods would increase their relative price, while the excess supply of non-traded goods would to reduce their price. This process would lead towards price equalisation and an import-export balance.

● A 'flow-of-funds' adjustment might occur. We saw above that when there is a current account deficit, the economy as a whole – government and private sectors – must have an equal and corresponding financial deficit with the rest of the world. Now recent UK governments have been committed to balancing their budget over the business cycle as a whole. Also it is true that the UK private sector is not likely to allow itself to accumulate debt indefinitely. Hence, it is argued, the UK economy as a whole must eventually move towards a state of internal financial balance, and any external deficit will thus be self-rectifying. A variation on this 'flow-of-funds' adjustment theme sees the UK's current account deficit as an outcome of the attractiveness of its economy to foreign investment.

The more capital comes in from abroad, the more the current account – which is the accounting counterpart of capital flows – must move into deficit. Either way, balance of payments deficits are seen as 'taking care of themselves'. This analysis was taken very seriously by Nigel Lawson when UK Chancellor of the Exchequer in the late 1980s.

TASK 29.4   What snags might the two equilibrating mechanisms just described encounter in practice?

Balance of payments adjustment through policy

The main policies available improving the balance of payments are:

- Import restrictions
  Tariffs, quotas, subsidies, exchange controls and VERs can certainly curb import levels. However, they have a number of undesirable side effects, including restricting consumer choice, encouraging inefficiency and retaliation, and violating international agreements. Therefore import restrictions have not figured in recent UK balance of payments policy.

- Deflationary expenditure-reduction
  Reducing the growth of aggregate demand in the economy – for instance, through higher interest rates or a more restrictive fiscal policy (Chapter 27) – will benefit a country's balance of payments in two ways. First, a reduction in inflation will bring prices more into line with those in other countries, and so help restore the competitiveness of its

products. Second, a contraction in the growth of money incomes means that people and businesses will have less available to spend on imports (remember that the UK has a high propensity to import). Exports may rise, as businesses switch sales from domestic to foreign markets.

- Expenditure-switching: reducing the exchange rate
  A country facing a persistent import surplus might choose, or be forced, to devalue its currency – reduce its exchange rate in terms of other currencies. Devaluation will make a country's exports cheaper and more competitive, and its imports dearer and less competitive. This will encourage expenditure-switching from imports to exports. Provided the demand for both imports and exports is sufficiently elastic an improvement will take place in the value of exports relative to imports.

However the process of import and export adjustment following devaluation will require time. In the immediate stages after a devaluation, the volume of exports may be unchanged, with no benefit to export value in terms of foreign currency. Equally, import volumes may remain high, and since their price in terms of home currency will have risen, the value of imports could rise appreciably.

So the surplus of imports over exports could temporarily increase. Only when export and import volumes have had time to fully react to devaluation – perhaps a year or two later – will the value of exports be able to exceed that of imports. This is known as the J-curve effect. (On a time graph, the initial downward move to increased deficit followed later by a rise towards surplus resembles a letter J.) Look at Box 29.8.

BOX 29.8

The J-curve effect

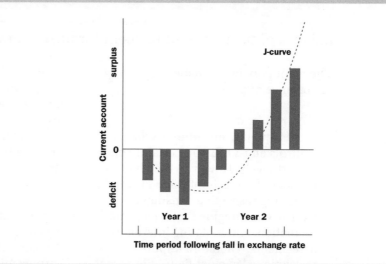

Types of exchange rate systems

Floating exchange rates

The foreign exchange market – the network of buyers and sellers in foreign currencies – is necessary because different countries use different currencies. A UK firm importing, say, mountain bikes from the USA will need to obtain dollars to pay for them, since the American supplier cannot use sterling to pay its wages and other costs. Even if it did accept sterling, it would still need later to convert it into US dollars. Conversely a US importer of a UK product would probably need to buy sterling to pay its British supplier. Assume that the banks and other agencies on the foreign exchange market find themselves doing a similar amount of currency business in both directions: sterling-into-dollars and dollars-into-sterling. The foreign exchange value – exchange rate – of sterling against the US dollar would now remain stable. But suppose UK exports to the USA were to boom. The demand for sterling would now overtake the demand for dollars, and the exchange rate of sterling against the US dollar would rise or appreciate. Conversely a rise in UK imports would lead to a fall in sterling's exchange rate, which would depreciate. In theory, appreciation or depreciation would continue until an equilibrium exchange rate was established, where the foreign exchange demand and supply of the currency were in balance.

It is claimed that a free market in foreign exchange dealings – a system of floating exchange rates – would function as an automatic adjustment mechanism for a country's import-export balance. How would this happen? Take the case of a rise in UK imports. By leading to a depreciation of sterling, this would improve the competitiveness of UK products. For instance, a fall in sterling from $2.00 to $1.50 would, other things remaining equal, reduce the American price of a £50,000 British yacht from $100,000 to $75,000. Conversely, a sterling depreciation would increase the sterling price of American mountain bikes. Given a sufficient degree of responsiveness – elasticity – in the demand for exports and imports, sterling depreciation would permit the establishment of a new import-export balance.

But suppose a country's import and export demand was totally inelastic to price changes following a depreciation in its exchange rate. Import and export volumes would then remain unchanged, with no benefit. In fact the import-export imbalance would worsen, since imports would now be dearer in terms of exports.

It turns out that exchange rate stability can be achieved provided that the sum of the elasticity of demand for a country's imports plus the elasticity of demand for its imports, is greater than unity – the Marshall-Lerner condition.

For a country like the UK, which imports from a wide variety of sources and supplies a range of products facing world-wide competition, import and export demand elasticities turn out to be quite high (case studies have indicated UK export elasticities as high as 4.5 to 6.0).

Problems of floating exchange rates

How effectively have floating exchange rates been, in practice? We can get a clue to the answer from the fact that many countries opted for floating exchange rates in the 1930s and again in the 1970s – but each time they abandoned them in favour of managed exchange rates, where countries intervene to fix or otherwise influence their currency's exchange rate. Evidently, such countries were not convinced about the benefit of a floating exchange rate!

- Erratic exchange rates
  In practice floating exchange rates have often fluctuated quite wildly. Sometimes this has been due to economic shocks affecting import-export patterns and hence foreign exchange conditions. Sometimes it has been due to the way in which unanticipated changes in interest rates and other factors have led to currency speculation (see below). Wildly fluctuating exchange rates increase the risks faced by businesses and investors, and are bad for trade and investment.

- Foreign exchange speculation
  Currency speculation occurs when economic agents buy or sell foreign currencies, not for financing trade, but with the intention of re-buying or selling later at a profit. There are at least three groups who are known to be able and willing to move speculative funds quickly and on a large scale: multinational companies, banks managing clients' (or their own) capital, and the central banks of

certain countries. When for some reason a currency begins to depreciate, speculators may decide to sell it now, in order to buy it back cheaper later at a profit. In so doing, they will accentuate the fall in the exchange rate. 'Leads-and-lags' speculation may also occur, as exporters delay sales and importers accelerate purchases. Conversely, an appreciating currency might attract speculative purchases, and so strengthen further. The danger is that a spiral of cumulative speculation could occur as more and more 'weak' currencies become sold and 'strong' ones bought. You can read more about an important episode of sterling speculation – it took place in 1992 – in Chapter 30.

- 'False' floating exchange rates
  A third problem of floating systems arises when a country decides to covertly manipulate a floating exchange rate. In a period of recession its central bank might be directed to secretly sell its currency on the foreign exchange market, with the aim of reducing its exchange rate in order to boost exports, import substitution and employment. In a boom, the temptation would be to push up the currency's exchange rate to try to reduce inflationary pressures. Such actions would undermine the logic of floating exchange rates, which is that the exchange value of a currency should be determined at a viable level by the forces of supply and demand.

Arbitrage

Textbooks usually analyse exchange rates in terms of a two-currency model. But how do thousands of exchange rates in the real world get 'kept in line' at consistent rates? For example, suppose the pound is worth 2 dollars and also 10 Danish crowns – what keeps the dollar–crown rate at a consistent cross-rate of $1 = DKR 5.00? The answer is 'arbitrage'. If the actual dollar-crown rate was 'out of line' at say $1=DKR4.00, it would pay a broker to carry out the following arbitrage operation. First, he uses a capital of £100 to purchase DKR 1000. Next, he uses the DKR 1000 to buy $250. Finally he converts this into £125, making a profit of £25 on the operation. As a result of brokers rushing to buy pounds with crowns, the rate of crowns against pounds would appreciate, until an orderly pattern of cross-exchange rates quickly became established.

Currency 'hedging'

We said above that wildly fluctuating exchange rates increase the risks faced by businesses and investors. It is, however, possible for these to in a sense 'insure' themselves against unwanted changes in exchange rates. An example will make clear how this can be done. Take the case of an American who has bought as an investment £10,000 of UK interest-bearing three-month bills with dollars being at a rate of £1 = $2.50. If sterling were to depreciate, this would involve him in a loss when later he converted back to dollars. He would then protect his position by carrying out the following 'hedge'. First he sells pounds to a broker for delivery in three months' time at an existing 'forward' rate of say $1 = $2.47. (Supply and demand on the forward market are not likely to be the same as on the present 'spot' market, so exchange rates may differ between the two.) Three months later, if sterling has not in fact depreciated he merely loses $.03 per £, when he has to buy sterling 'spot' to honour the forward contract he made at the start. If sterling has in fact depreciated, say to $2.10, he will make a loss on his sterling investment of $4,000. But against this he will now make a hedging profit of $3,700 when he now buys cheap spot sterling at $2.10 to honour his original $2.47 forward contract. In effect he has insured himself against a sterling depreciation at a cost of 3 US cents per pound sterling.

The purchasing power parity theory of exchange rates

This theory states that the exchange rate of one currency against another will settle at a level where the domestic purchasing power of the first currency in terms of goods and services is equal to that of the second currency in its country. Suppose £1.00 = DKR 10.00, but 1 pound happens to buy more in the UK than 10 crowns do in Denmark. Agents would then buy up 'cheap' British products and sell them 'dear' in Denmark. Increased purchases of sterling and sales of Danish crowns would lead to an appreciation of sterling which equalised the domestic purchasing power of the two currencies.

Tourists often discover that the domestic purchasing power of different currencies is in fact not the same – why is this?

'Managed' exchange rates

Given the drawbacks of floating exchange rates, many countries have from time to time opted for a regime of 'managed' exchange rates, where central banks intervene on the foreign exchange markets to stabilise exchange rates. Suppose sterling were to threaten to depreciate at a rate which caused the sort of problems described earlier. Under a managed exchange rate, the Bank of England would be directed to intervene on the foreign exchange markets to support sterling's value, buying sterling with foreign currency from its own reserves (or funds obtained from other central banks). Conversely, sales of sterling could be undertaken, with the aim of preventing an unwanted appreciation. In this way sterling could be fixed or 'pegged' at, or around, a desired parity level. There have been a number of such managed exchange rate regimes, notably the IMF scheme which, in its full mode, operated from 1947 to the early 1970s. Unfortunately, managed exchange rates do have drawbacks:

- Selecting a viable exchange rate for a period of time when economic shocks and other factors may greatly change a country's balance of payments conditions, can be difficult – some economists would say impossible.

- Managed exchange rates tend to attract 'one-way' speculation, and dealing with this can be extremely difficult (see Chapter 30)

- Ensuring cooperation between countries' central banks, in terms of compatible exchange rate management and domestic policies, can be a problem.

The best known recent managed exchange rate system has been the European Exchange Rate Mechanism (ERM), which you can study in depth in Chapter 30.

Could UK imports be on a falling trend?

In the mid-1990s there was some good balance of payments news – UK imports appeared to be on a falling trend. Why was this? On the supply side, improving productivity in British manufacturing and services, combined with a low level of wage settlements and the sterling devaluation of September 1992, had helped competitiveness. On the demand side, consumer caution was holding back demand for consumer durables, many of which are imported. Finally, the trend to more old and fewer young people in the population might be aligning consumption towards services, which have a low import content, and away from manufactured products, which have a higher import content.

BOX 29.9

Why do the Japanese import so little?

Japan is known as a high-exporting, high-saving economy. But increasingly Western businesses and governments are asking the Japanese to export and save less – and to direct more spending at Western imports. Otherwise, how can a country like the USA, which has still-rising annual trade deficit with Japan of around $50 billion, find a way to a more balanced payments relationship with it? Japanese spokesmen argue that the position is the outcome of the superior competitiveness of Japanese products. Americans and others often point to a range of alleged Japanese NTB (non-tariff barrier) import restrictions: for instance, changing pollution standards, and complex customs procedures, which have the effect of excluding or delaying the import of foreign products. Why else, they ask, do US industries such as telecommunications and medical equipment, which are world-leaders and highly successful exporters, find it so hard to sell in Japan? Yet bilateral trade negotiations between the two countries have failed to make much progress. On their side the Japanese point to market factors which lead to low import levels: for instance, language barriers and a fierce domestic competition which leads to standards of design, reliability and service which non-Japanese businesses often cannot match.

Yet UK exports to Japan have been doing rather well. Fortnum and Mason food delicacies, Burberry raincoats, Laura Ashley fabrics have successfully penetrated to Japan's high streets. And UK power generation equipment and pharmaceutical products are doing well in Japan, too. In fact, Nissan (UK) have even been re-exporting their cars back to Japan – complete with the Union Jack on! Could other countries do as well – or is this due to special UK factors, such as the devaluation of sterling when it left the ERM? The explanation for Japan's low propensity to import is likely to be in dispute for some time to come.

*Source: Adapted from **UK Press Reports** (1995).*

TASK 29.6

1 Why might US firms with proven success in world markets have failed to penetrate Japan's markets?

2 Why have UK exports to Japan been rising quite rapidly?

BOX 29.10 **Recent current account trends**

Current account imbalances in the major economies have changed quite sharply in the past few years – as the table shows.

This box analyses the recent trends. But in view of the volatility of currencies in the first part of this year, the box focuses mainly on the role of exchange rates and competitiveness.

Current account balances
As a percentage of GDP

	1992	1993	1994(a)
Canada	-3.9	-4.3	-3.3
France	0.3	0.8	0.7
Germany	-1.2	-1.2	-1.9
Italy	-2.3	1.1	1.4
Japan	3.2	3.1	2.8
Spain	-3.0	-0.5	-0.9
Sweden	-3.5	-2.1	0.4
United Kingdom	-1.6	-1.9	–
United States	-1.1	-1.6	-2.3

(a) First three quarters for France, Italy and Spain

Changes in US, Japanese and German real exchange rates, measured using nominal effective rates adjusted for relative changes in consumer prices, are shown in the chart below. The most significant recent change has been for Japan, where the real exchange rate appreciated by around 30% in the two years to March. Germany's real exchange rate rose by less and the US real rate has fallen, but only gently. The relative stability of the dollar's real exchange rate, despite the currency's weakness against the Deutsche Mark and the yen, reflects both its appreciation against the Canadian dollar and a higher rate of consumer price inflation than in some of its major competitors, particularly Canada and Japan (which account for 55% of the weight in the US effective exchange rate).

Within Europe, some countries' real exchange rates fell sharply after the ERM crisis in 1992, as the chart shows.

In the 2$\frac{1}{2}$ years after September 1992, Italian, Spanish and Swedish rates fell by at least 20%. Sterling's real exchange rate fell by around 10% over the same period, while French and German real exchange rates appreciated. These changes in competitiveness have contributed to changes in current account balances, and within Europe those countries whose real exchange rates fell most have experienced the greatest improvement in the last few years. Between 1992 and 1994, for instance, Italian and Swedish current accounts improved by around 4% of GDP, compared with 2% in Spain and around 1% in the United Kingdom.

BOX 29.10

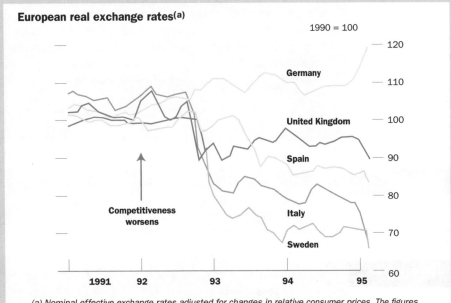

European real exchange rates(a)

1990 = 100

Germany

United Kingdom

Spain

Italy

Sweden

Competitiveness
worsens

1991   92   93   94   95

120
110
100
90
80
70
60

(a) Nominal effective exchange rates adjusted for changes in relative consumer prices. The figures used for March are derived from changes in the nominal effective exchange rate only.

Germany's current account deficit rose in 1994, largely because of a sharp fall in its balance on interest, profits and dividends, which may have reflected its currency appreciation. In France, the current account moved into surplus in 1992 and, by the third quarter of last year, this was around 0.8% of GDP. This partly reflected the weakness of French demand relative to its major competitors, but also an improvement in the terms of trade following the franc's appreciation.

The US current account deficit rose from 2% of GDP in the first quarter of 1994 to 2.6% by the fourth. The rise was mainly the result of a rising visible trade deficit stemming largely from the strength of US relative demand. US domestic demand rose by 4% in 1994, compared with 2% – -2% in the rest of the G7; US import volumes rose strongly, by 13%. Export volumes also rose – partly in response to improved competitiveness – but by less than import volumes. If domestic demand grows by less in the United States than in its competitors this year, the US current account deficit may stop rising. But the dollar's appreciation against the Canadian dollar and Mexican peso over the last year may partly offset the effects of any changes in relative demand.

Japan's current account surplus fell by 10% in yen terms last year. The yen's strength over the last few years has affected trade volumes. But the fall in the surplus to date has been less than after the currency's sharp appreciation between 1985 and 1987. A rise in Japanese relative demand would reinforce the effects of the rising real exchange rate.

BOX 29.10

In recent years, Canada has had the largest current account deficit in the G7: over the last ten years or so, it has averaged more than 3% a year. Its visible balance has, however, been in surplus for most of the last 20 years (and this is likely to be reinforced by recent improvements in competitiveness). The main counterpart to its current account deficit has been a high public sector deficit and consequently there has been a large net outflow of interest, profits and dividends, reflecting the high level of foreign-held debt.

Source: ***Bank of England Quarterly Bulletin*** *(May 1995)*

TASK 29.7

1 Why is Canada's strong visible account surplus a poor guide to its overall balance of payments position?
2 How might the strength of the yen affect Japanese trade volumes?

REVIEW

We have seen in this chapter that there is a sense in which the balance of payments certainly **does** matter. A country with a persistent deficit can easily end up with dangerously high levels of foreign debt, the erosion of net foreign assets, and a balance of payments crisis. Secondly, a persistent payments deficit can act as a block on economic expansion. An economy with a robust balance of payments can easily absorb the increase in imports which takes place in the boom phase of the economic cycle. But if there is a weak underlying balance of payments, all too often it becomes necessary for the authorities to put the brakes on expansion prematurely, when there is still unused supply capacity available. Only when imports have been restrained by recession is it felt safe to undertake renewed expansion. This damaging 'stop–go' scenario was a common feature in the UK in the 1970s and 1980s .

However, we have seen that what is also important is **how** a balance of payments deficit is dealt with. There exist automatic adjustment mechanisms, and so there is a sense in which the balance of payments 'doesn't matter' – because it would (eventually) take care of itself. Unfortunately these mechanisms may be slow to achieve their effect. Therefore adjustment policy may be called for. This can take the form of expenditure-reduction or expenditure-switching. In the case of the UK, an opportunity for expenditure-switching occurred in 1992 when sterling left the ERM and was devalued. But, as Chapter 5.30 shows, this happened by accident, not design.

REVIEW TASK

UK balance of payments summary, 1993[a]

Current account [b]	£ million	Transactions in UK assets and liabilities[b]	£ million
Visible exports	121 414	Net investment overseas by UK residents:	
Visible imports	– 134 623	Direct[c]	– 7 790
Visibles balance	– 13 209	Portfolio	– 45 594
		Total	– 53 384
Invisibles balance	2 898	Other capital transactions	62 399
		Addition to reserves[d]	– 702
Current balance	–	Net transactions in assets and liabilities	8 313
		Balancing item	1 998
		Total	**10 311**

Source: *COI, Pink Book, 1994*

Notes:

a Receipts from the rest of the world are referred to as credits while payments to the rest of the world are referred to as debits.

b The data consist of two sections: the current account and transactions in assets and liabilities. The current account mainly records transactions in goods and services. Transactions in assets and liabilities mainly records flows of capital.

c Capital outflows are given a negative sign in the account, capital inflows are given a positive sign. Direct investments are investments in real assets such as plant and machinery. Portfolio investments consist of the international sale and purchase of financial instruments such as company shares or government bonds. Other, short-term, capital flows arise mainly because of transactions in the balance of payments current account.

d Changes in the foreign exchange reserves reflect operations undertaken by the Bank of England to influence the exchange rate of sterling. A fall in the reserves would indicate that the Bank was using reserves to purchase and support sterling on the foreign exchange market. In the accounts this would appear as a credit item.

e The balancing item records the net total of data errors and omissions. If all the items in the accounts were dead accurate the balancing item would be zero.

Tasks:

1 Calculate (a) the visibles balance and (b) the current balance.

2 Was sterling's exchange rate probably experiencing upward or downward pressure in 1993?

3 Assuming for simplicity that current account, and direct and portfolio transactions, are autonomous, and all other transactions are accommodating, calculate the total net 'autonomous currency flow'. Comment on your finding in relation to the likely stability of the UK's balance of payments situation in 1993.

4 Comment on the statement that, since the accounts overall must 'balance', there can be no such thing as a balance of payments problem.

Multiple choice

1 **A government may seek to improve the current account balance of payments by introducing either expenditure-reducing or expenditure-switching policies. Which of the following is an expenditure-reducing policy?**

A   a government subsidy on home produced products

B   a rise in income tax

C   devaluation of the currency

D   the imposition of a tariff.

(WJEC, 1995)

2

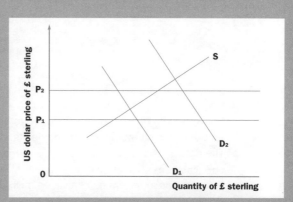

The British monetary authorities are committed to maintaining the exchange rate of £ sterling against the US dollar between P_1 and P_2 on the diagram.
What might they do if demand changes from D_1 to D_2?

A   impose controls on UK investment overseas

B   increase interest rates

C   sell dollars out of foreign exchange reserves

D   sell pounds on the foreign exchange markets.

(WJEC, 1995)

3 **A country with a freely floating exchange rate joins a fixed exchange rate system, at a rate above the existing parity. Which of the following is/are likely to be reduced?**

1   Interest rates

2   Holdings of official reserves

3   The current account balance

A   1

B   1 and 2

C   2 and 3

D   1, 2 and 3.

(IB, 1995)

QUESTIONS

4 The following price elasticities of demand for exports and imports are for four countries A, B, C and D. If each country's exchange rate depreciates by the same percentage, and if all other things remain equal, which has the best chance for an improvement in its Balance of Payments?

	Exports	Imports
A	0.8	1.3
B	2.6	1.7
C	1.9	0.8
D	0.3	0.2

(IB, 1995)

5 All other things remaining equal, which of the following is/are likely to halt or reduce an inflow of speculative money into Country A?

1 a fall in Country A's interest rates
2 an appreciation of Country A's currency
3 a growing Balance of Payments surplus in Country A

A 1
B 2 and 3
C 2 and 3
D 1, 2 and 3

(IB, 1995)

6 Assuming full freedom of action, if the UK government wanted to prevent the exchange rate of sterling from falling, it might consider

1 raising interest rates
2 instructing the Bank of England to buy sterling on the foreign exchange markets
3 placing quantitative restrictions on imports.

A 1
B 2 and 3
C 2 and 3
D 1, 2 and 3

(ULEAC, 1995)

5.30 What is the UK's position in Europe?

Monetary union

On balance our members are in favour of monetary union.

Confederation of British Industry (1994).

On balance our members are against monetary union.

Institute of Directors (1994).

There are potential economic advantages in monetary union... But there are also potential economic risks... It would be an enormous step.

*Eddie George, Governor of the **Bank of England** (1994).*

You can't convince people using propaganda. You have to tell the truth openly about monetary union – the advantages and the historical necessity as well as the risks involved

*Hans Tietmeyer, **German Bundesbank** President (1994).*

For the businessman, it is very simple... If Britain is not a member, I am afraid we would be very embarrassed.

*Chan Bae, managing director, **Samsung Electronics UK** (1994).*

Reproduced by kind permission of the European Commission.

FOCUS

If the effect was to make the UK less competitive, we would be at an obvious disadvantage.

Ian Gibson, managing director, **Nissan UK** *(1994).*

The problem is that we are in uncharted territory here.

Vauxhall UK *(1994).*

In my view, a single currency cannot be made to work in Europe in the foreseeable future... a number of countries, including Spain, Portugal, Greece, Italy and Belgium, will be unable to join a monetary union for several years – perhaps decades.

Tim Melville-Ross, Director-General of the **Institute of Directors** *(1994).*

A single currency wouldn't work... I believe it is time we consigned this particular idea to the mounting scrapheap of Euro-rubbish.

Teresa Gorman, **MP** *(1994).*

Preview

In this chapter we shall investigate the following key areas:

- customs unions and common markets;
- the 1993 European Single Market;
- the significance of the Maastricht Treaty;
- the Common Agricultural Policy (CAP);
- Maastricht's Social Chapter;
- European monetary union and the single currency;
- the disintegration of the Exchange Rate Mechanism (ERM);
- 'widening' the Community versus 'deepening' it.

European monetary union: final stage for European economic integration?

Since it was set up in 1958 Europe's economic community, now known as the European Union, has undergone continual economic integration – the bringing together of the economies of its member states. In 1986 its president, Jacques Delors, proposed further integration in the shape of 'economic and monetary union'. Economic union means achieving a full common or 'single' market. Economic union is economic integration in the form of a 'single market' with harmonised policies. Monetary union means the adoption of a single currency and monetary policy, proposals for which were set out in the 1993 Maastricht Treaty. Progress towards the single market was quite rapid, but as the extracts in Focus 5.30 show, moving towards monetary union would prove difficult and controversial. It is easier to understand the significance of monetary union, if we first study how economic union was arrived at. We start with the origins of the community.

The economic community out of which today's European Union evolved was set up as a customs union, plus some elements of a common market.

A customs union is a trading area with no internal tariffs, and a common tariff against non-members. A common market is a trading area which has no internal barriers to trade, and which also has free movement of goods, people and capital.

Originally the common market had six 'founder members' – Belgium, Holland, Luxembourg, Italy, France and West Germany – but today membership embraces 15 countries, including the UK which joined in 1973. In a customs union a group of countries abolish tariffs among themselves, and apply a common tariff against non-members. A common market is formed when a group of countries not only abolish tariffs and all other mutual barriers to trade, but also eliminate restrictions between themselves on the free movement of goods, people and capital. A further feature of the Community has been harmonisation of member countries' economic policies, for example in agricultural and social policies.

BOX 30.1

The meaning of Maastricht

Under the terms of the **Maastricht Treaty**, which became effective in 1993, the European Community was absorbed into the **European Union** marking a new stage towards 'creating an ever-closer union among the peoples of Europe'. New harmonised 'single market' policies were to be negotiated in many areas including industry, communications, health, education and social policy (the 'Social Chapter'). Majority voting in the Community's Council or 'cabinet' was to be extended and the European Parliament's powers increased. Probably the most important element of Maastricht was the objective of **monetary union**, to be complementary to economic union and achieved in three stages by 1997 or at the latest 1999.

Economic benefits of a common market

One reason for setting up the economic community was political: to promote cooperation and interdependence between its members to such an extent that European wars become a thing of the past. However the community also aimed for economic benefits. First, there would be benefits of factor mobility. Increased mobility of factors of production should lead to improvements in total output, as factors of production – enterprise, labour and capital – became free to move from low to high productivity uses and areas.

Secondly, an enlarged product market would be likely to generate trade creation through increased specialisation. First there would be static trade gains. In a small national market even very successful firms ma⟨y⟩ be unable fully to exploit economies ⟨of⟩ scale and product development. A larger market encourages this and als⟨o⟩ competition which increases pressur⟨e⟩ for greater efficiency and innovation. This in turn may attract foreign investment seeking to exploit new opportunities. Secondly dynamic tra⟨de⟩ gains could be expected as different areas in the community came to specialise in products in which they held comparative advantage. Look at Box 30.2.

BOX 30.2

Exploiting comparative advantage in Europe

General view of the buildings occupied by the European Parliament during its sessions in Strasbourg

Reproduced by kind permission of the European Commission.

In an age of easy and rapid international technology transfer how can Europe, with its high wages and other cost levels, compete with other parts of the world? Economists point to areas of comparative advantage where Europe has points of excellence, and opportunities for high value-added production, which it would be difficult to match elsewhere. In manufacturing, European advantage is quite strong generally in upper-middle technology, oil, pharmaceuticals and services. Individual areas of Europe have strong specialisms too: Italy for design and quality clothing, Germany for precision engineering, dental and medical equipment, France for telecommunications, perfume and toiletries, the UK for high-performance cars, pop music, and financial services, Spain and Portugal for tourism, and so on. European economic integration, culminating in economic and monetary union should, through the operation of market forces and increased competition, further encourage such specialisation.

Euro-brands

ARE 'all-in' EUROPEAN FOOD BRANDS THE SHAPE OF THE FUTURE?

Germans like ice-cream which is freed of all unnecessary additives, Italians are fond of creamy traditional ice-cream, the British tend to go for sweet, flavoured varieties. In the same way, British ales are a long way from the lagers of Continental Europe. Yet the firms which produce these and other food brands are always looking for economies of scale and research – which suggests the possible benefits of mass-producing 'all-in' European food brands. So could consumers end up faced with 'European' brands only? Already Coca-Cola is a top buy in the UK, Germany and France. And Procter and Gamble's Ariel soap powder sells well in these countries. Many businesses have been merging, so that now just two companies, Nestlé and Unilever,

produce one-quarter of the top 100 European food brands. At the same time, businesses have been centralising their production in a small number of European centres. And all this is reinforced by intense market research and marketing.

But how far can a grocery band be 'stretched' to meet tastes as far afield as Finland and Greece? And is it significant that harmonisation of taste in the nutritional supplement market – vitamin tablets, garlic pills and the like – has been very slow? Could there be a backlash from consumers looking for more local variety? Michael Perry, chairman of Anglo-Dutch Unilever admits that the quest for 'all-in' European food brands could give rise to 'possibilities for horrendous error'.

EUROPE'S BIGGEST GROCERS

Postn	Parent co.	Sales ($m)	Brands in Top 100	Main brand names in Top 100
1	Unilever	5,675	14	Langnese (ice cream), Iglo (frozen foods), Persil, Algida (ice cream), Flora, Omo, Skip, Rama (margarine), Becel (margarine), PG Tips, Birds Eye
2	Coca-Cola	5,080	3	Coca-Cola, Fanta, Sprite
3	Nestlé	4,465	11	Nescafé, Chambouráy, Findus, Nestlé, Perrier, Bärenmarke (condensed milk), Maggi (sauces and soups), Kit Kat, Nesquik
4	Procter & Gamble	4,290	6	Ariel, Pampers, Dash, Lenor, Daz, Vizir
5	BSN	3,930	6	Danone (yogurt, fromage frais, desserts), Lu (biscuits), Evian, Panzani Noodles
6	Philip Morris	2,555	5	Jacobs Coffee, Milka, Kraft Philadelphia Cheese, Kraft cheese, Gevalia coffee
7	Mars	2,480	6	Whiskas, Pedigree/Pal, Kit E Kat, Sheba, Mars Bar
8	Ferrero	1,900	6	Nutella (chocolate spread), Ferrero Kinder (cakes, chocolate), Mon Cheri, Ferrero Rocher
9	Barilla	1,280	2	Barilla pasta, Mulino Blanco biscuit
10	CPC	1,080	3	Knorr (dry soups, sauces, stock cubes)

Source: Nielsen/Checkout magazine
Adapted from press reports, (1993).

Seeking economic union: the 1993 European 'Single Market'

In 1986 economic union of the Community was proposed, to develop it into a full common or 'single' market. The programme was to be completed by 1993. Up to that time the common market was incomplete, for there were still many national barriers on trade and factor mobility between members. The main barriers identified were:

- Customs and administrative formalities;
- Closed government contracting;
- Differing technical and commercial standards between member countries;

- Differing levels of indirect taxes between member countries;
- Non-recognition of equivalent professional qualifications between member countries.

The programme for abolishing all such barriers was set out in the Single European Market (SEM) Act of 1986. By 1993 many of these barriers had been removed, with an estimated efficiency gain of up to 6% of members' GNP.

| BOX 30.4 | **Benefits of a single market** |

VITAMIN COSTS ARE *bitter pill* TO FOLLOW

Marcus Gibson reports that a single market in nutritional supplements could cut prices by half

The cost of vitamins, minerals and supplements around Europe could be halved if the mass of differing national regulations was replaced by a single system, say German pharmaceutical giant Merck. Ernst Mauer, managing director of Merck's pharmacy healthcare division, believes that if one product could be distributed across the whole of Europe there would be a 40 per cent saving in production costs and a ten per cent saving in marketing and advertising costs.

Europeans devour a huge amount of nutritional supplements across Europe, even though most doctors insist that a balanced diet is sufficient and that only the very young, the elderly and pregnant mothers may need additional vitamins and minerals.

Some recent US studies suggest that certain betakeratin and anti-oxidant vitamins (C and E) can reduce heart disease and other illnesses but the results have not been universally accepted.

For a manufacturer such as Merck, with 20,000 products, the plethora of contrasting vitamins, minerals and supplements (VMS) regulations within Europe involves immense duplication of production, marketing and sales activities.

'If a multivitamin selling one million units in a single EU country could achieve five million unit sales across Europe,' said Maurer, 'it could easily be produced for up to 60 per cent less, certainly at half price.'

The maze of specific requirements for nutritional supplements and daily intake of vitamins and minerals in different countries have dogged vitamin makers such as Merck and the largest producer, Switzerland's Roche.

BOX 30.4

Contrasting regulations mean that manufacturers must sell vitamins with different dosages and preparations in as many as 20 countries. Small production batches add greatly to total costs.

Before selling can begin, local experts in each country must verify vitamin samples, undertake multiple registration, and present separate analysis and product-stability data guaranteed for at least two years to national health bodies.

Gilbert Mertens, Merck's spokesman, said: 'How can vitamin needs change just because you cross a border? How can Germans or Portuguese have such different requirements? Why should consumers be denied the opportunity of buying favourite products in another country?'

Differing product formulae entail different packaging, even where there are no health claims, if it is not considered a medicine, which leads to another major problem: differences in sales regulations covering VMS products. This costs several hundred thousand dollars per country.

VMS sales are subject to radically different sales regimes. Some countries classify vitamins as medicines to be sold through prescription in pharmacies, others consider them as food supplements and available for sale almost anywhere.

Over-the-counter sales predominate in Britain, the Dutch permit supermarkets to sell them and the Swedes allow vitamins via mail order, but these are often banned in the rest of Europe. In Portugal vitamin purchases are reimbursed by the social security system.

The sale of minerals encounters similar problems. 'Selenium can be sold in Germany only if it is derived from yeast, but not from chemicals', said Mertens. Kellogg's cereal makers must put iron into products in France owing to national regulations. Not so in Germany. Under national regulations, dosages of vitamin C, the biggest-selling sector product in Europe, vary from between 45mg in Italy to 75mg in Germany.

To complicate matters further, measurements differ too, from body weight of the recipient to minimum and maximum daily dosage. In addition, the permitted dosage of vitamin A varies from 2,333mg in Italy to 10,000mg in Austria.

The market for VMS products in Europe, worth $5.81 billion ($8.8bn), is considerable. The health conscious Germans consume 26.3 per cent of Europe's total intake and it forms one of the top five best-selling pharmaceutical product categories.

An important segment is the curiously large minerals and supplements market – mostly ginkgo biloba, garlic, and various immune-stimulant products. It is thought sales in this area reach $750 million annually. Magnesium tops the minerals list, worth $250m each year. About $20 million units of minerals are sold outside pharmacies.

In France, Italy and Spain, VMS is not among the top five categories, but maintain markets valued at $1.23bn, $520m and $480m respectively. Belgium, however, is slightly larger than Spain's market with $490m, with Merck's Omnibionta and Roche's Redexon leading.

The British market, conversely, remains highly competitive at $750m, or 12.9 per cent of the European total. Many markets are stagnating. Italy's total of 6.5m unit sales have changed little since 1987. France also, is in decline – from a total of 125m units in 1987 to 90m last year.

Sales outside pharmacies, from independent chains and health food shops, have hit prices, and US-style promotion techniques, such as discounts and free trial products, have increased competition.

In the Netherlands, 400 50mg tablets of vitamin C can cost less than $5. No economies of scale are possible and, Maurer claims, there is little time to develop export markets, handicapping Europe's VMS share in world markets.

He says that new products are not being funded because pan-European profits are required to meet development costs.

Dr Hubertus Cranz, of the industry body European Proprietary Medicines Manufacturer's Association (AESGP) in Brussels, said that there was little hope of greater uniformity in VMS regulations. First, there was no pressure from governments. Second, the AESGP could find no encouragement from the European Commission.

'There are no initiatives forthcoming towards harmonisation,' he said.

Source: *The European* (6–12 January 1995).

TASK 30.1

1 Why do you think consumers are sometimes denied the chance to buy favourite products of another country?
2 Why does the pattern of demand for nutritional supplements vary so much across national borders?

TASK 30.2

Europe: a single market: or merely linked markets?

Following the setting up of the Single Market in 1993, a greater concentration of specialisation in particular countries was expected. Investment flows and trading patterns did change but many manufacturing businesses decided not to service the Single Market from one location. Many businesses found that in order to overcome nationalist sentiment, and to be able to react to differing national tastes and demand, they still needed a local presence to access continental markets. A scatter of plants around the community would also insulate them against foreign exchange risks. Ford, and the Japanese motor manufacturers, continued to build engines in one country, construct gearboxes in another and assemble them into cars in a third. However some continental businesses were slow to adapt in this way, and became vulnerable in the new environment. This gave UK businesses an opportunity to absorb a number of competitors and broaden their European operations.

Source: *Adapted from* **Press Reports** (1995).

1 Why should industrialists doubt their ability to supply the single market from a single location?
2 What factors would make for differences in national taste and demand?

TASK 30.3

Provisions for a single European market came into force from 1993 – but how long would they take to 'bite'? Read the extract below and answer the questions which follow it (note: the European Commission is the Community's 'civil service' which in practice has very wide powers for implementing policy) –

The Single Market – is it working for cars?

In the early 1990s, car prices in the European Union varied by up to 40 per cent, with cars in the UK being the most expensive. Even after the devaluation of the pound after its exit from the European Exchange Rate British cars remained relatively dear. One reason was that 'red tape' – bureaucratic regulations by manufacturers, dealers and governments – hindered car-buyers from 'shopping around' for car bargains in other countries. This was especially true of Portugal, Ireland and the UK, where exclusive dealerships made it easier for dealers to keep up prices. In Italy and Greece the main difficulty was customs delays of up to four months, which led to car-buyers being forced to use black markets. EU rules on competition stated that price differences for the same car in different EU markets should not exceed 12 per cent and that car-buyers must be free to import from outside their own country. Yet as late as 1993, a three-door Opel Corsa would cost, before tax, 50 per cent more in the UK than in Belgium.

The European Commission warned car firms that exclusive dealerships could be at risk, unless they published European-wide price lists and made it easier for individual buyers to import cars from other countries. The Commission also warned manufacturers not to penalise dealers for selling to cross-border customers. Unfortunately car firms were able to resist these reforms, saying that, due to the mass differences in European taxes and specifications, it was impossible to quote single European prices. So there still wasn't a workable European single market for cars.

Source: *Adapted from **Press Reports** (1993).*

1 Why might car prices in the UK be so much higher than in Belgium?
2 Why should car manufacturers want to penalise car dealers for selling to cross-border customers?
3 How, and why, did the car industry defy the EC's new single market provisions?

Harmful trade effects: the CAP and 'trade diversion'

Unfortunately, a customs union can also generate harmful effects. These take place when its common external tariff encourages the transfer of production from low cost areas outside the union, to high cost ones inside the union. This is known as trade diversion. In the case of Europe's agriculture, trade diversion undoubtedly takes place on a massive scale. This is due to the Common Agricultural Policy (CAP) which has led over a long period of time to the substitution of dear European foodstuffs for cheaper foreign.

The Common Agricultural Policy (CAP) is an EU agricultural protection scheme based on guaranteed minimum product prices, variable import duties and centralised absorption and disposal of excess supplies.

The main aims of the CAP have been:

- To increase agricultural production;
- To ensure a fair level of income for farmers;
- To stabilise agricultural markets;
- To provide food for consumers at reasonable prices;
- To encourage agricultural specialisation in the Community.

It is clear that some of these aims – for instance, for farm income and consumer prices – were potentially in conflict. This becomes clearer when we briefly examine the protection mechanisms used to support the CAP's aims, namely:

- Guaranteed minimum product prices set each year for Community farmers;
- Variable import duties on farm products entering the Community;
- Absorption and disposal of excess supplies through CAP intervention purchases, combined with their storage, destruction or subsidised sale outside the Community.

In practice the CAP produced some benefits for Community farmers, but at the cost of high prices for consumers and expensive financial support, running at up to $30 billion per year. To reduce stocks of unsold farm output, it would be necessary to reduce support prices, so as to discourage production and encourage consumption. Attempts to reduce farm support had some success but also provoked ugly protests from farmers in some continental countries. Much of the thrust for CAP reform has come from the GATT and from the UK inside Community, but there has been resistance from countries with large, high-cost farming such as Spain and France.

The GATT (General Agreement on Tariffs and Trade) seeks through international agreement to free trade from import restrictions.

BOX 30.5

The CAP and subsidy corruption

The CAP has generated financial support of up to £30 billion per year. The extract below, by Francois d'Aubert, and that in Box 30.6, both highlight the risks of corruption when large sums of money are being handled by EU officials.

THE SILENCE OF THE *subsidies*

Tobacco cultivation, as opposed to cigarette manufacture, was a sector which received more subsidies from the EC – based on the number of recipients (170,000 growers) and the area under cultivation (200,000 hectares) than any other.

On average, tobacco subsidies were 35 times greater than for wheat and supported tens of thousands of poor families in Italy's Mezzogiorno – the economically depressed south – as well as in Greece. As such, it was politically untouchable.

The everyday organisation of the tobacco market, already known for its operational irregularities, had adopted some curious methods.

The first went as follows: the head of the European Agricultural Guidance and Guarantee Fund's (Eaggf) tobacco division allowed a cartel of four major Italian and Greek processors to bid and win contracts for thousands of tonnes of surplus intervention tobacco stocks which the Community, as in other sectors, sought to dispose of.

The lists of those bidding for the contracts were supplemented at the last minute by occasional latecomers. With this system, the cartel obtained tobacco at the lowest possible price, defrauding the Eaggf of millions of ecus.

A second series of embezzlements related to aid for tobacco production. For a grower to receive a subsidy, tobacco had to have been grown in his locality at least once during the previous five years.

This rule was not applied fairly: in Greece, in 1989, 30 per cent of Virginia-type tobacco came from areas not eligible for subsidies.

Observers also recall a sudden craze among Italian growers – in their fund declarations – for an unsaleable variety of black tobacco called Badischer Geudertheimer over another equally mediocre variety called Forscheimer Havana, just when the subsidy for the former exceeded the other by Ecu0.625 per kilo.

The switch from one variety to another usually corresponded to a simple name change to enable growers to pocket further aid.

The same applied to other common frauds such as fictitious leaf deliveries to processing companies, contracts with undated and unsigned crop declarations, wrong tobacco varieties so as to tap the highest subsidies, frauds concerning acceptable humidity levels, aid spent on tobacco originating from Yugoslavia and Turkey, and so on.

These practices were commonplace in southern Italian towns such as Benevento and Lecce.

The third type of swindle involved refunds. In August 1988, a Greek operator reported that leaf tobacco ineligible for refunds was being shipped from Greece and Italy to Bulgaria at the rate of 20,000 tonnes per annum under the heading 'baled tobacco'.

This description was extremely suspect because the time between tobacco picking by growers and its export was obviously too short for any processing to have occurred. Yet the Commission failed to react.

Consequently, growers exceeded authorised quotas for each variety; the production of low-quality tobaccos escalated; larger and larger Italian and Greek surpluses accrued; and irregular exports triggered a massive rise in Commission budgets and attendant repercussions.

BOX 30.5

The organisation of the tobacco market was eventually reformed in 1992 with the elimination of refunds and subsidies, a reduction in varieties from 34 to eight and stricter controls.

But the most curious aspect of this affair remains the law of silence imposed by the Commission on a scandal involving a high-ranking Italian official.

Furthermore, the findings of the inquiry into the management of Eaggf's tobacco division have never been published. Even the Court of Auditors has failed to obtain a copy of the report.

The Commission maintains that the inquiry, which began in 1988, is still going on. A court auditor was finally given permission in April 1993 by the Commission to read (but not to copy) 'a report containing information arousing suspicions of fraud'.

This examination revealed nothing to confirm any steps had been taken by the Commission or a member state to bring the alleged guilty parties to justice.

The court also asked the Commission for a copy of a contract signed by a company linked to a retired Commission official and who actually led the enquiry in question, but this was also unsuccessful. The Commission is instead imposing 'Euromerta' on past misappropriations in the tobacco division.

In settlement, it will simply ask Italy and Greece to pay back Ffr400m, a pittance when offset against the frauds committed between 1987 and 1990.

This scandal reveals an enormous problem involving administrative and financial organisations and – while one should not generalise – the infiltration of corruption into the Brussels mechanism.

Source: The European (6 January 1995).

TASK 30.4

The bigger the subsidy, the greater the corruption.

Discuss in relation to the extract above; add to your answer when you have read Box 30.6.

BOX 30.6　　**Euro-fraud**

War ON FRAUD TO SAVE BILLIONS FROM EU

Rory Watson BRUSSELS

A new strategy to crack down on fraud – which is believed to cost the European Union up to $7.9 billion a year – will be unveiled next week.

Member states have put increasing pressure on the European Commission to put its house in order. They believe this will defuse criticism left over from the bitter debate on the Maastricht treaty and will convince the Commission's critics of the merits of enlarging the Union and expanding its powers.

The new campaign, to be announced by European Anti-Fraud Commissioner Peter Schmidhuber on 24 March, seeks to plug financial loopholes which have appeared since most internal EU frontiers in effect disappeared – as well as agricultural fraud, which has become almost traditional. The move comes as the EU gears up to spend more than $520 billion of taxpayers' money over the next six years.

'Fraud is now a high political priority', a senior Commission official explained. 'Our aim is to devise a system so tight that anyone tempted to indulge in fraud will know the risks are very great. We have to show we can command the situation.'

The strategy will include:
- Establishing a blacklist of companies or individuals found breaking EU rules and barring them from future contracts.
- Extending anti-fraud activities to all European Commission departments.
- Reviewing EU legislation to block legal loopholes.
- Strengthening co-operation between Union and national authorities, including police and Customs.
- Focusing investigations on patterns of fraud, rather than on individual cases.
- Concentrating on possible new frauds involving the EU's regional and social funds, money laundering and sophisticated financial crimes.

A few departments, such as agriculture, have their own small teams of investigators.

Last year the dozen officials involved uncovered more than a score of farm frauds costing the EU budget $452 million. These included paying $203 million for storing non-existent durum wheat in Italy, and earlier this month Rome received a bill for $37 million for the cost of olive oil storage fraud.

But this figure is tiny when compared with the ten per cent of the EU's annual $79.03 billion budget which members of the European Parliament believe is lost through administrative blunders and deliberate theft – equivalent to almost $23 for every man, woman and child in the Union.

*Source: **The European** (18 March 1994).*

TASK 30.5

What are the elements of the EU's new anti-fraud strategy? How successful do you consider it will be?

TASK 30.6

Maastricht's Social Chapter: would it damage economic performance?

The Maastricht Treaty granted the European Commission additional authority to pursue social measures in the form of a Social Chapter committing member states (except for the UK, which secured an op-out), the promotion of employment, improved living and working conditions, proper social protection, dialogue between management and labour, the development of human resources with a view to lasting high employment and the combating of exclusion'.

The Social Chapter was a continuation of an existing movement towards labour market regulation. It aimed to ensure that workers, as well as businesses and consumers, would secure the benefits of the single market. Measures would include: more social security benefits to cover the effects of short-term unemployment, moves to limit working hours, increased worker participation in management, more worker access to company information, equal pay for women, and increased parental leave rights. The Social Chapter was criticised, notably by the British government, on two grounds:

● Its enforcement would lead to more bureaucracy at the European Commission in Brussels;

● It would damage economic performance by raising Europe's employment costs and making its labour market less flexible compared with those of the United States, Japan and the newly industrialised countries.

In what ways might a Social Chapter improve economic efficiency in Europe?

Monetary union in Europe

The Community really was much closer to becoming a full common market after 1993. However, each national area still had its own currency. In a sense, therefore, the 'single' market still contained elements of a number of national sub-markets, separated by various currency trading costs. It was suggested that a single currency was now required to complete the single market. Calculations showed that eliminating exchange rate fluctuations and foreign exchange transaction costs would deliver gains in terms of increased competition, efficiency and economies of scale, estimated at up to 10.5% of community GNP: £450 billion. There would also be a number of other benefits (see below). Proposals for a single currency and monetary union were set out in the Community's Maastricht Treaty, which became effective in 1993. The main features would be:

- Permanent and irreversible locking of member currency exchange rates, followed by the adoption of a single currency, which would float against other world currencies;
- A unified monetary (interest-rate) policy, with price stability as its ultimate goal, to be pursued by a single monetary authority in the form of a European central bank;
- Binding procedures to restrain member countries from operating large fiscal deficits (these might undermine the unified monetary policy).

The single currency is the EU currency to be issued by the European central bank, replacing national currencies which would cease to be legal tender.

The European central bank is the central bank created to take responsibility for the single currency and for monetary union policy.

Monetary union would take place in three stages.

- Stage one had in fact already been established before Maastricht, in the form of the European Monetary System (EMS). The main feature of the EMS was its system of pegged but adjustable member currency exchange rates, known as the Exchange Rate Mechanism (ERM). The ERM was seen as a first stage or stepping stone to eventual monetary union. Unfortunately this first stage was 'shot away' in a series of

currency crises after 1992.
- In stage two of monetary union, from 1 January 1994, a European Monetary Institute (EMI) would be created as a prototype single monetary authority; member countries would steer their economies towards increasing economic convergence – the attainment of similar levels of costs and prices – and member currency exchange rates in the ERM would be pegged ever closer together. (In point of fact, with the break-up of the ERM exchange rates actually unpegged.)

The European Monetary Institute (EMI) is the prototype single monetary authority set up as forerunner to the European central bank.

- On the first day of stage three, 1 January 1997 or 1999, member currency exchange rates would be permanently locked and a single currency would be 'rapidly' issued by the European central bank, with national currencies ceasing to be legal tender. The EMI would convert into a single monetary authority, the European central bank. National central banks, now made independent, would cooperate with the European central bank on a harmonised monetary policy.

Economic advantages and risks of European monetary union

European monetary union is such a complex subject that a full treatment would require a book in itself! For the purpose of this chapter we present here in summary form the main potential economic advantages and risks of European monetary union.

Main advantages of monetary union:

- The elimination of exchange rate fluctuations and risks would enhance trade and specialisation among participant countries. It is estimated that total GNP would be boosted by 5% to 10%: between £200 billion and £400 billion;

- The use of a single currency, eliminating foreign exchange transaction costs, would lower production costs by up to 0.5% of Europe's GNP: £20 billion per year;

- By enhancing the single market, monetary union would encourage secure further specialisation and economies of scale;

- Firms would no longer have to publish different-currency price lists for national markets, and book-keeping, accounting and other operations would be made far easier;

- Monetary union would put member countries under pressure to match low German inflation levels;

- Reduced inflation and trade risks would lead to lower real interest rates, encouraging investment and innovation within and from outside the monetary union.

Main risks of monetary union:

- It would involve loss of national control over exchange-rate, monetary and to some extent fiscal policy;

- Areas with inflexible labour markets, and with inadequate convergence, might when exposed to price- or cost-raising shocks be vulnerable to stagnation and unemployment. Supporting such areas, either out of large transfers of tax revenues, or by assisting massive labour migration, could be expensive and difficult;

- Many Continental countries will one day be faced with rapidly ageing populations, leading to a need for large tax increases to finance pensions commitments. The UK, with less of an ageing population, and many private self-financing pension schemes, might unfairly find itself shouldering part of this burden;

- In the UK, unlike other countries in Europe, most long-term business and household borrowing is on a variable interest basis. Changes in interest rate policy undertaken by the European Bank would hit the UK much harder than elsewhere, where such borrowing is mainly at fixed interest;

- Since the UK exports more to North America than most of the other countries, determining a single-currency exchange rate against the dollar appropriate for both the UK and others would be difficult;

- Large changes in world oil prices, were they to occur, would tend to benefit the UK, an oil-exporter, compared with other EU members. Determining an interest rate policy appropriate for both the UK and the other members would be virtually impossible;

- The costs of introducing a single currency would be substantial. In 1971, when British currency was decimalised, it took Barclays Bank two years to distribute the three new coins. Introducing the complete range of European single-currency notes and coins would be even harder. One bank identified 35,000 computer programs that would need to be changed with conversion costs put at £500 million!

Obstacles to European monetary union

The timetable for monetary union set out in Maastricht quickly ran into three obstacles: the disintegration of the ERM, pressure for Maastricht opt-outs and inadequate economic convergence.

1 The 'break-up' of the Exchange Rate Mechanism

The Exchange Rate Mechanism (ERM), first set up in 1979, was the principal feature of the European Monetary System (EMS) and it came to constitute an essential stepping stone to monetary union.

The European Monetary System (EMS) is a system set up in 1979 whose principal feature was the introduction of the European Exchange Rate Mechanism.

Any study of monetary union must therefore focus on the experience of the ERM. The ERM was a system of pegged exchange rates between member currencies. Pegged exchange rates, designed to be stable, encourage trade between countries, with its related benefits. In the ERM each member currency had an official central exchange rate against the EMS's unit of account, known as the European currency unit (ecu). To assist the mechanics of pegging, each member currency was allowed a fluctuation margin of 2.25% against this central rate. A currency which threatened to 'break out' of its pegged range would be

required to be stabilised. In the case of weakening currency, support measures could include higher interest rates in it country, together with purchases of the currency out of the foreign exchange reserves of member central banks and the EMS. A persistent currency weakness might indicate a need for deflationary action to bring its domestic costs into line with other members. Failing these support measures, the ESM member in question would need t seek a re-pegging of its currency at a lower central exchange rate (devaluation) against the ecu and other member currencies. In the case of an over-strong currency, an upward revaluation of its ecu peg might be necessary. The UK was not initially an ERM member, but in 1987 it adopted an 'informal' ERM policy by tying sterling against the strongest ERM currency, the German mark. In October 1990 the UK became a full ERM member.

As stable exchange rates became established in the ERM this would constitute a natural first stage to eventual locking as a single currency. In stage two of monetary union, from 1 January 1994, exchange rates in the ERM were planned to move ever closer together, in preparation for locking in stage three. A successful ERM would promise well for a successful single currency.

The ERM achieved considerable exchange rate stability in the 1980s, but in the 1990s it ran into difficulties. The first crisis came in 1992 when the pound (and the Italian lira) 'fell out of' the ERM. The difficulties of the pound in the ERM were connected with two factors: its possible over-valuation on entry in the ERM, and the effect of high German interest rates on ERM currencies.

- The ERM entry rate of sterling
The actual rate at which to enter a
currency into a fixed exchange rate
system involves a complicated
judgement. If the rate turns out to be
'too high' the country's products will
lose in competitiveness. Shortly
before its 1990 ERM membership, the
pound fell to an exchange rate of
2.71 against the German mark – a
rate which the markets judged would
be competitive against the main
continental currencies. It was widely
argued therefore that the actual entry
rate of sterling, corresponding to 2.95
German marks, was too high. If so,
higher UK rates of interest might
come to be required to attract foreign
funds to support the pound.

- High interest rates in unified
Germany. One way for the German
government to fund the state side of
massive infrastructure rebuilding
required in the east of the country,
following unification, would have
been out of tax increases. Instead it
opted for a politically 'soft' policy of
borrowing the necessary funds. Also,
by selecting a very favourable
conversion rate of 'east' marks into
'west' marks, the German
government made possible a rapid
expansion of domestic demand.
These two decisions were to lead to
inflationary pressures and rising
German interest rates at a time when
other ERM members, including
Britain, were in recession and
looking to lower interest rates
needed to promote recovery.

Would the UK have the political will to
support sterling against the mark by
matching Germany's rising interest
rates? Many observers doubted this, and
by the summer of 1992 speculative
selling of sterling was occurring.
Although UK interest rates were put up,
speculation against sterling became so
intense that in spite of considerable
foreign exchange support from other
EMS members, it finally fell through its
ERM floor. The British government
could have repegged sterling lower
inside the ERM, but decided instead to
let it 'float' outside. The Italian lira also
came under pressure and, like the
pound, left the ERM. Some other
weakened currencies were devalued
within the ERM.

In 1993 it was the turn of the French
franc to come under pressure, which
led to its effective devaluation against
the mark and remaining ERM core
currencies. To prevent further crises it
was now decided to allow ERM
currencies to fluctuate within a much
wider margin of 15%. In spite of this, a
further currency crisis in 1995 forced
the Spanish and Portuguese currencies
into further devaluations within
the ERM.

Hence by the mid-1990s the ERM as a
system of stable and potentially
convergent exchange rates had ceased
to exist, and an important part of the
route to European monetary union had
in effect been blown away. This left two
options for the run-up to monetary
union. Either a 'tight' ERM would need
to be somehow reconstituted, or a direct
transition from floating to locked
exchange rates undertaken. Neither
would be easy.

2 Maastricht opt-outs

Monetary union could impose costs as well as benefits. One of these was political: the loss of national control over exchange rate, monetary and to a lesser extent fiscal policy. Some, as we saw earlier, were economic. Two EU members – the UK and Denmark – negotiated Maastricht clauses allowing them should they wish to opt-out temporarily or permanently from participation in monetary union.

3 Inadequate economic convergence

A necessary condition for successful monetary union is economic convergence: that is, the attainment of similar levels of costs and prices in member countries. If this does not happen, and some countries experience higher costs and prices than others, economic difficulties can occur. Outside of monetary union, high-cost countries can protect employment by devaluing their currencies to restore competitiveness. Inside a monetary union, with a single currency, this option is unavailable. Therefore it was necessary for participants in monetary union to move towards economic convergence. The Maastricht Treaty laid down five convergence conditions which a majority – eight – of the EU countries must attain for monetary union to be able to go ahead. These were:

- An inflation rate of not more than 1.5% above the average of the three EU countries with lowest inflation;

- Long-term interest rates within 2% of of the average of the three EU countries with the lowest interest rates;

- An exchange rate which must have stayed inside its normal ERM band;

- A government budget deficit of less than 3% of its GNP;

- A national debt not greater than 60% of its GNP.

BOX 30.7

Contenders for the single currency

	Gross Debt % of GDP			Budget Deficit % of GDP			Inflation (%)			Long-Term Interest Rates (%)			Overall
	94	95	Pass/ Fail	94	95	Pass/ Fail	94	95	Pass/ Fail	94	95	Pass/ Fail	Pass/ Fail
Inner Core													
Germany	51	59	✓	5.6	3.6	✗	3.0	2.3	✓	6.9	6.9	✓	✗
Netherlands	81	82	✗	3.8	3.6	✗	1.9	1.9	✓	7.0	6.9	✓	✗
Austria	58	60	✓	4.2	5.0	✗	3.1	2.6	✓	6.8	7.0	✓	✗
Luxembourg	9	10	✓	1.3	1.6	✓	2.3	3.0	✓	-	-		✓
Outer Core													
France	50	52	✓	5.5	4.7	✗	1.7	1.8	✓	7.5	6.8	✓	✗
Belgium	146	145	✗	5.8	4.7	✗	2.4	2.5	✓	7.8	7.2	✓	✗
Denmark	82	83	✗	4.2	3.0	✓	1.8	2.4	✓	7.9	7.7	✓	✗
Special Case													
Ireland	92	87	✗	2.3	2.0	✓	2.5	2.5	✓	8.1	7.5	✓	✗
UK	53	55	✓	4.8	2.5	✓	2.4	2.9	✓	8.2	7.4	✓	✓
Periphery													
Italy	122	125	✗	10.6	9.4	✗	3.9	3.6	✗	10.6	10.9	✗	✗
Finland	80	80	✗	4.6	5.1	✗	1.7	2.1	✓	9.0	8.6	✓	✗
Sweden	94	103	✗	11.2	10.2	✗	2.0	2.4	✓	8.4	10.0	✗	✗
Portugal	81	82	✗	7.1	6.6	✗	4.6	4.3	✗	10.8	10.5	✗	✗
Spain	64	68	✗	7.0	6.5	✗	4.6	4.4	✗	9.8	10.5	✗	✗
Greece	118	119	✗	13.1	11.6	✗	11.1	9.9	✗	18.9	19.5	✗	✗

Pass and fail are based on 1995 estimates

*Source: HSBC Markets, Barclays Bank, **European Commission**.*

BOX 30.7

Maastricht economic convergence criteria. Countries must comply with the following:

- Fiscal discipline: governments' financial positions must be sustainable; the annual budget deficit must be no more than three per cent of gross domestic product (GDP); outstanding government debt must be no more than 60 per cent of GDP.

- Price stability: annual inflation rate must not be more than 1.5 per cent above the average rate in the three countries with the lowest rate of inflation.

- Interest rates: to indicate the durability of a member state's convergence, long-term interest rates must be no more than two per cent above the average rate on 10-year government bonds in the three countries with the lowest inflation.

- Exchange rate: must have been stable within the exchange rate mechanism during the preceding two years (ie no devaluation). For a start date of 1 January, 1997, all pass except Finland, Greece and Sweden, which have yet to join the ERM.

*Source: **The European** (27 January 1995).*

Following the disintegration of the ERM the exchange rate condition for progress on monetary union was in disarray. Putting this aside, however, in 1995 only six or seven countries looked likely to achieve the other qualifications by 1997: the UK, the Netherlands, Germany, Luxembourg, Ireland, Austria and possibly France. Four more, Portugal, Spain, Finland and Denmark might meet the criteria, while the chances for Belgium, Italy, Sweden and Greece were remote. So at best only a 'core' of EU members were likely to be able to participate in monetary union in its early stages (assuming enough members qualified for it to start at all).

The remainder could join later when they had achieved convergence.

The Maastricht convergence conditions were essentially financial in nature, being geared to conditions promoting low inflation. The UK suggested an additional criterion: participating countries should have flexible labour markets which could react quickly to, and absorb, economic shocks. Applicant countries with highly regulated and inflexible labour markets, and prone to high unemployment would, it was argued, be poor candidates for monetary union.

TASK 30.7

'The ERM has meant that Germany's main export to France and other member countries has been not machine tools or cars, but unemployment. Under European monetary union this would be even more true.' Critically examine this statement.

TASK 30.8

The United States, which has a GNP and population similar to those of the EU, is often cited as a case of highly successful monetary union. Why then has there been continuing, and at times controversial, debate about the viability of monetary union in Europe?

How would the single currency be introduced: Big Bang, double Big Bang or no Bang?

Under the terms of Maastricht, the locking of currencies in the monetary union must be followed 'rapidly' by a switch to the use of the single currency (to be issued by the European central bank). But how rapid is 'rapid'? Under the Big Bang scheme, there would be a one-off introduction to the single currency, carried out over a four-day bank holiday. Since this would put banks, businesses and households under a lot of pressure, many observers advocated a phased Double Big Bang introduction. After currency-locking, national currencies would continue to circulate over a change-over period of 6 months, giving time for systems to be adapted to a single currency. (One drawback would be that banks would

then need to operate dual- or multiple-currency accounts and records.) A third possibility would be for the new currency to operate indefinitely alongside national currencies as a parallel or common currency. Economic agents would choose individually when to 'convert' to this. If they did so on a large scale, this would amount to a rapid validation of the single currency. If not, transition could (in the words of the Governor of the Bank of England) last 'for a generation'. The UK government favoured this evolutionary approach and tried to have it adopted as an official EU route to monetary union (the common currency would be known as the hard ecu).

What if the national currencies 'unlocked' in the introductory stage?

The Maastricht Treaty speaks of the 'irreversible' locking of currencies before the switch to the use of the single currency. But would this locking necessarily 'hold'? The experience of the ERM shows us how difficult it can be to fix exchange rates. Consider a situation during the changeover to the single currency where it was suspected (wrongly) that a monetary union member, say the UK, was considering

withdrawing from currency locking in order to be able to devalue its currency. Economic agents would then sell sterling, and the central banks and the European Central Bank would be required to use foreign exchange reserves and swaps to support it. At worst, a situation like the ERM crises of September 1992 and July 1993 could easily develop.

What would the single currency be called?

The unit of account of the EMS is known as the ecu. The French wouldn't mind calling the single currency this, as 'ecu' is also an old French word for 'crown'. The Germans, who are sensitive about losing their own prestige currency, would like the single currency to be called some sort of mark.

One way-out possibility would be for each member to use its own currency's name – the single currency would be called pounds in London, marks in Frankfurt, francs in Paris, and so on. You can probably see the problems this would cause! In the event it was decided that the single currency would be called the 'euro'.

BOX 30.8 **Could a European monetary union cope with economic shocks?**

European monetary union would aim at a zone of **monetary stability** – stable exchange rates and convergence of domestic prices. Now such a system needs to be able to adjust to the random unanticipated events which we call **economic shocks**. A difficulty arises if a shock impacts **unequally** on individual economies in such a zone – for instance, due to differences in the mix of products they consume or produce, or foreign markets in which they sell. Take the case of an unexpected increase in world oil prices. For energy-exporting member countries, such as the UK and Holland, this would imply a need for **higher real exchange rates** against world currencies, but for the other, energy-importing, members lower exchange rates. In theory this could be achieved by short-term relative changes in local wages and prices – downwards for energy-exporters and upwards for the others. It is doubtful whether in practice European economies possess such flexibility. Opponents of monetary union argue therefore that plans for union were flawed: the intended monetary zone would not have the capacity to absorb shocks.

This analysis relates to the concept of an **optimal currency area**, defined as an area within which all factors of production are perfectly mobile. An ideal world would consist of a number of such areas, each with its own currency. Random shocks would then be absorbed by changes in exchange rates between areas. However in practice optimal currency areas may be quite small. Due to language, cultural and other influences, labour is relatively immobile within Europe, which might thus prove to be severely **non-optimal** as a single currency area. Some economists believe the strongest benefits of economic and monetary union might develop within a 'golden triangle' linking London, Paris and Milan. In outer fringes areas like southern Italy, Portugal and Northern Ireland, major regional problems could occur.

Should monetary union be delayed: 'Widening' the Community instead of 'deepening' it?

The prospect of monetary union in the late 1990s, coming on top of the 1993 single market, would represent a considerable further degree of economic integration or 'deepening' of the Community's economic system. In the mid-1990s there was however mounting scepticism inside and outside the UK about the viability of full monetary union. In Germany for instance, although the government there had ratified the Maastricht Treaty, both the public and the Bundesbank were becoming weary of constant ERM crises, and anxious about replacing their own strong currency with a single European currency. Many Germans felt that plans for European monetary union might 'get in the way' of exploiting economic opportunities in Eastern Europe, where a number of countries now wished to join the Community. It might be preferable to widen the Community rather than deepen it. Enlarging the single market would cement political stability in Eastern Europe. This would also offer further economic benefits, in terms of increased opportunities for investment, specialisation and factor mobility, both for new and existing members.

According to the Maastricht Treaty 'Any European state may apply to become a member of the union… The conditions of admission… will be the subject of an agreement between the member state and the applicant state.'

By 1995, a number of countries, including Hungary, Poland, Slovakia and the Czech Republic, were pressing for early membership. However there was resistance inside the Community, notably from France and the smaller Mediterranean countries, to an early widening of membership. One difficulty was that the economies of the would-be entrants were quite poor, compared with existing members. The cost of admitting Greece and Portugal, also poor countries, in terms of subsidies and other support for their economies, had been very large. The support to which Hungary, Poland and the others could be entitled to might eat up an estimated two-thirds of the Community's total budget.

A second difficulty was that the east Europeans' economies tended to have comparative advantage in two areas – agriculture and heavy industry- where existing members' economies were already in substantial over-capacity, often with heavy local unemployment. The economies of the most recent entrants, Austria, Finland and Sweden, had been complementary to existing members' economies, rather than competitive.) Thirdly, admitting the east Europeans might lead to mass labour migration to the more prosperous west.

In 1992-4 the Community did sign free-trade pacts with Hungary, Poland, Slovakia, the Czech Republic, Romania and Bulgaria. However these pacts contained a number of protectionist clauses in 'sensitive areas' like iron and steel, and agriculture. Opposition to their full membership remained considerable. Look at Box 30.9.

BOX 30.9

The Czech Republic: a candidate for early and full EU membership?

In November 1994, Vaclav Klaus, Prime Minister of the Czech Republic, announced that his country would be applying for membership of the EU in 1996, and would hope to enter by 1999: later admission would be 'unacceptable'. How strong was the Czech Republic's claim for admission? In 1994 the Czech Republic was able to fulfil the convergence conditions for European monetary union better than any of the existing members of the EU, except for Luxembourg! The Czech Republic was running both government budget and balance of payments surpluses, and its long-term interest rates were lower than in Italy and Spain. Inflation, at 9 per cent, was high but this was still less than the inflation rate in Greece. Other economic indicators in the Czech Republic were also impressive. Following economic liberalisation and reform, unemployment there was down to 3 per cent and expected output growth was 4 per cent. Financially, the Czech Republic was now an established borrower on internationaly credit markets, with a better security rating than Greece, a full EU member. Could it be that the Czech Republic's economy was too strong for existing EU members to dare to admit it?

REVIEW

How much European economic integration should the UK go for?

Should the UK embrace the single currency and go for full European economic integration? In this chapter we have looked at the economic risks and advantages of monetary union. However monetary union might lead to European political union, in which a whole range of non-economic matters – law and order, defence, diplomacy, social policy – would end up under the central control of the EU. This was perceived as a danger in some quarters, and with both the main political parties in Britain being split on this issue, a national referendum might be required to test public opinion.

The approach of the UK government was therefore one of 'wait and see'. It had already committed itself to keeping sterling out of the ERM 'until after the next general election'. This would probably be in 1997 (after the European Inter-governmental Conference which is a meeting between EU members to examine progress on convergence and stage three of proposed monetary union. So the UK would be unable to meet the exchange rate convergence condition, and would officially be unable to join before 1999. Then, at a 1995 meeting, EU Finance ministers decided to delay the timetable for monetary union. Since it could take up to four years to produce all the single-currency coins and notes required, a single currency might not be introduced until well into the 21st century.

REVIEW TASK

1 31 July 1993: the day the ERM disintegrated

The Bank of France team realised the situation was hopeless immediately after an earlier meeting with the Bundesbank at lunchtime on Thursday 29 July. They now asked the French prime minister, Edouard M. Balladur, for permission to float the franc the next day. Balladur resisted this, apparently hoping that Germany's Helmut Kohl would

REVIEW TASK

instruct the Bundesbank to lower its interest rate. This would reduce the foreign exchange demand for marks and take pressure off the French franc. Balladur knew his plan had gone wrong at the next meeting, when Herr Tietmeyer of the Bundesbank greeted everyone with a 'bonjour'. When asked why he was not speaking German or English, he replied 'apparently we are all now required to speak French in the EMS'. In other words, the Germans were cross, and would refuse to reduce their interest rate.They requested an immediately widening of the ERM bands, to allow the franc and other weak currencies to float lower.

A Portuguese official suggested that instead of this, the countries with strong currencies might lock these and so move to immediate monetary union. A German official replied: 'I hope that proposal was intended as a joke.' The French now raised their back-up plan – Germany should temporarily take the mark out of the ERM! To the surprise of the French, Germany readily agreed – which probably meant that Germany no longer considered the ERM a credible system and did not mind being blamed for its collapse. So the French gave in and accepted Germany's original proposal – a widening of the ERM fluctuation margins. With time running out before the financial markets opened in Tokyo, a decision had to be reached quickly . Belgium now proposed a 15 per cent currency fluctuation margin. The Bundesbank agreed, and the meeting ended within minutes. In practical terms, the ERM had ceased to exist.

*Source: Adapted from **The Times** (12 August 1993).*

1 Why should the French prime minister, Balladur, resist proposals to float the French franc downwards?
2 Why would the Bundesbank be reluctant to reduce German interest rates?
3 Why would the French be surprised at the readiness of Germany to temporarily leave the ERM?
4 Why weren't the British involved in the discussions?

2 The politics of pegged exchange rates

France is paying a high price for the 'franc fort' (strong franc) policy which locked the French currency to the mark after 1987. The French believed that devaluation of the franc would undermine the ERM and damage the Maastricht timetable for monetary union. Out of pride, France refused Germany's offer, at the time of German unification, to up value the mark against the franc and other currencies. The effect was to increase European interest rates and intensify the recession. By resisting devaluation of the franc, France has damaged its foreign exchange reserves, its fragile banking system, and its manufacturing base.

*Source: Adapted from **The Times** (31 July 1993).*

1 Why might France 'out of pride' resist an up-valuing of the German mark?
2 How might a 'franc fort' (strong franc) policy damage France's economy?

INVESTIGATING ECONOMICS

Data response

The trade performance of four EC member states, 1973 – 91

The United Kingdom and Ireland joined the European Economic Community (EEC) in 1973; one of the main economic benefits of membership has been tariff-free access to a large market of consumers in some of the world's most developed economies. The table shows how their experience to 1991 compares with that of Germany and the Netherlands, which are two of the original countries who formed the EEC in 1957.

To benefit from trade, it is very important that countries remain competitive in relation to their trading partners. The table also shows how real unit labour costs, the actual cost of employing workers, has changed over the period from 1973 to 1991.

	UK		Ireland		Germany		Netherlands	
	1973	1991	1973	1991	1973	1991	1973	1991
Total Visible Exports as % GDP	23.7	24.0	38.0	65.0	22.0	34.4	47.4	58/2
of which Visible Exports, to rest of EC, as % of GDP	6.1	9.4	24.9	44.0	9.9	15.8	28.4	40.7
Total Visible Imports as % GDP	26.2	25.5	44.8	58.0	19.1	28.3	44.2	54.0
of which Visible Imports, to rest of EC, as % of GDP	7.6	10.9	30.7	35.6	8.6	13.7	24.1	30.3
Real unit labour costs (1980 = 100 for EC as a whole)	99,8	100.0	92.1	80.9	100.2	90.0	98.9	87.0

*Source: The European Economy, **Annual Economic Report**, 1990 – 91, EC Commission.*

a i   Which country had the most open economy in 1991? Explain your answer.
  ii   Which country had a deficit on its balance of trade in 1973 and 1991? Explain how you arrived at your answer.
b i   The four countries shown in the table are members of a customs union. How in theory would you expect their trading relationships to develop?
  ii   Discuss the evidence in the table to support this theory.
c i   Compare the change in unit labour costs between the UK and Ireland between 1973 and 1991.
  ii   State two reasons which might explain these changes.
d   Suppose a Japanese electronics manufacturer is looking to set up a European base in one of four countries. Comment upon the factors, as well as unit labour costs, which will be taken into account in the location decision.

(University of Cambridge Local Examinations, specimen paper, A/AS level, November 1995)

5.31 Are inequality and poverty a problem?

A snapshot of Britain

Poverty and inequality

- **Percentage below half average (mean) income, adjusted for household size, after housing costs.**

% of total population in poverty
% of children in poverty

Source: Households Below Average Income

- **Percentage of total disposable income, adjusted for household size**

Richest 20% (right scale)
Poorest 20% (left scale)

Source: IPPR

- **Change in income, 1979-1991/92, adjusted for household size, after housing costs.**

Poorest tenth
Richest tenth

Source: Households Below Average Income

- **Poverty and life expectancy, selected European countries, 1975 – 85**

% change relative poverty
Increase in life expectancy, years

UK Ireland Denmark W. Germany Belgium Greece France

Source: Wilkinson: Health, Redistribution and Growth

Source: Guardian (25 October 1994)

● **Unemployment**

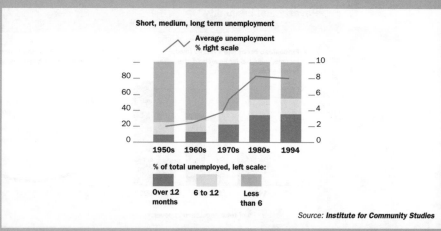

Short, medium, long term unemployment

Average unemployment
% right scale

% of total unemployed, left scale:

Over 12 months | 6 to 12 | Less than 6

Source: *Institute for Community Studies*

Source: *Guardian* (25 October 1994)

● **Wage costs**

Manufacturing labour costs, $ per hour

W Germany
Netherlands
Japan
US
France
Italy
UK
Spain
Taiwan
S.Korea
Poland
Thailand

Source: *John Wybrew*

Source: *Guardian* (25 October 1994)

Use the appropriate graphs to comment on the:
a   degree of poverty in Britain in the early 1990s compared to the late 1970s and 1980s.
b   change in total income and relative shares of income for different income groups since 1979
c   causes of poverty in Britain in the 1990s.

Preview

In this chapter, we shall investigate the following key areas:

- different perspectives on wealth and income distribution;
- the difference between income and wealth;
- the difference between poverty and inequality;
- how poverty and inequality can be measured;
- recent trends in income and wealth distribution;
- reasons for wealth inequalities;
- whether inequality is really necessary.

This section also draws upon the analysis developed in Chapter 2.9 on the reasons for differences in incomes.

The issue of distribution: an introduction

The question of the way in which society's resources are distributed has long been of major concern to economists, directly affecting as it does the level of social welfare. Changes in the size and distribution of the national output not only raise important questions of efficiency, but also involve basic issues of equity or fairness.

However, what is 'equitable' is a matter of considerable debate amongst economists of different political persuasions. Those on the political right, i.e. proponents of the unfettered free market, would argue that justice automatically arises from the interaction of demand and supply and the existence of competitive markets: in such a scenario, each factor receives what it is worth in terms of the value of its marginal output contributed to the productive process (Chapter 9). Thus disparities in income and wealth would

be justified by reference to such factors as greater levels of innate or acquired skills which enable some factors to be more productive than others and to thus command greater remuneration. Differences in wealth and income distribution would therefore be viewed as inevitable and also desirable in that they provide the necessary inducements for individuals to study, train, supply their factor services, set up new businesses, etc., and thus allow the smooth operation of the price system.

Economists on the political left would not however view this matter in quite the same light. A basic belief of socialism is that income should be distributed on the basis of human need; as all people objectively need such things as food, clothing and shelter, an unequal distribution which deprives many of 'effective demand' for these essentials of life cannot be justified.

Such a view would imply various restrictions by the government on the operation of 'free' markets so as to ensure greater equality and equity.

Marxists would take the above argument a stage further by arguing that equity can only be achieved when capitalism as an economic system is replaced by socialism; for Marxists capitalism is characterised by class conflict and exploitation – capitalists own the means of production and employ workers who have only their labour power to sell. Inequality is endemic to the system as capitalists pay wages which are less than the value of output produced, and extract what is known as 'surplus value' in order to accumulate more and more capital – the driving force of capitalist production.

Two important differences identified

The difference between income and wealth

Wealth is the value of an accumulated stock of assets existing at a particular point in time.

Income is a flow, usually in money form, arising over a period of time from the possession of wealth, be it in financial, physical or human form.

From the point of view of the individual, both wealth and income are measures of the ability to buy goods and services, ie purchasing power, but with a significant difference: wealth reflects the extent of purchasing power at a particular point in time, while income represents the change in purchasing power over some period of time.

Put another way, we can say that an individual's wealth is the monetary value of his or her accumulated stock of assets at any given moment in time; for example, a person may possess financial wealth in the form of shares and cash in a building society account; physical wealth in the form of land, property and consumer durables; and human wealth or capital which may be an inherent attribute, e.g. the natural skills of Pele, the great Brazilian footballer, or an attribute acquired through past education or training, e.g. the skills of the brain surgeon. All three categories of wealth are capable of generating income over a period of time.

Income, on the other hand, which can accrue in the form of wages, rent interest and profit, is a flow, usually of money, arising from the possession of wealth, be it in financial, physical or human form; for example an individual's bank account may yield interest, land may yield rent, and personal skills required by the labour market may earn wages/salaries.

Our distinction between income and wealth has so far focused on the level the individual, but the distinction can also be applied at the national level: a country's wealth is the sum of all the residents' wealth, and includes the national capital stock, which is that part of the country's stock of resources which could be used to produce goods and services; it includes the country's capital goods and raw materials as well as state owned social capital such as schools, hospitals, bridges and roads; the national income, on the other hand, is the aggregate flow of additional wealth over some period of time, in the form of output of goods and services, that arises from the productive use of the national capital stock.

The difference between poverty and inequality

Poverty is a situation facing those people whose material needs are least satisfied and who are at the bottom end of the income distribution.

Inequality is the disparity between individuals in terms of wealth and income.

Both poverty and inequality can be judged in terms of statistical data on wealth and income. However, as concepts they are not identical: inequality is concerned with the disparities between individuals in terms of the income they earn and/or the wealth they possess; poverty is a situation facing those people whose material needs are least satisfied, i.e. those who are at the bottom end of the income distribution, and the study of poverty involves attempts to define and measure it, and to estimate the extent to which it exists.

We next consider how both poverty and inequality can be measured.

How can poverty be measured?

Look at Box 31.1

BOX 31.1

Poverty: the dragon Beveridge failed to slay

Beveridge's report in 1942 led the way to a social security system and National Health Service which were to have slain the `five dragons' of want, idleness, ignorance, disease and squalor; but today's children show the unacceptable face of poverty in Tory Britain five decades later.

Beveridge's proposals were based on definitions of an acceptable standard of living rather than a bare subsistence level. Today, however, in 1994, the government does not even accept a `poverty line', nor is it prepared to disclose the standard of living its jobseeker's allowance and income support are aimed at.

The Child Poverty Action Group identifies the UK as showing the greatest rise in poverty in the EU between 1980 and 1985, and claims that, in 1989, 12 millions of the UK's citizens lived in a state of poverty.

*Source: Adapted from **Observer** (23 October 1994).*

Although most of us possess an intuitive grasp of what poverty is, even if we have not experienced it personally, the precise nature of poverty is not always easy to define, with the extent of its existence being a matter of some controversy between economists of differing political persuasions; it is not uncommon, for example, for right wing economists and politicians to claim that there are no poor people in the UK today, a view that is hotly disputed by most others further to the left.

Most certainly there is an enormous difference between those classified as poor in the developing nations, who may lack such basic necessities of life as food, clothing and shelter, and those defined as poor in a relatively more prosperous nation such as the UK, who may well possess such things as a refrigerator, television or even a car. So which group of economists is correct? To a certain extent the answer to this question depends on how we define poverty – the term may be defined in two main ways: in an absolute and a relative sense.

Absolute poverty

Absolute poverty occurs where households or individuals receive a level of income which is insufficient to provide for the basic necessities of life.

This is sometimes also referred to as subsistence poverty, and is usually defined in terms of some minimum level of income necessary for bare subsistence. Such a definition was used by Rowntree in his major study of poverty at the turn of the century in which he concluded that poverty was having an income which was insufficient to provide for such items as food, housing and clothing, which represent the minimum necessary requirements for survival.

This type of definition involves the identification of a poverty line in terms of the basic necessities of life, the main problem being that it is extremely difficult, and necessarily somewhat arbitrary, trying to establish what these minimum requirements should be, bearing in mind differences between individuals and changing circumstances over time.

When those on the political right claim that 'poverty no longer exists in the UK' they are clearly referring to absolute poverty. However, the large numbers of people sleeping rough on the streets of the country's cities, the number of old people who die prematurely because they cannot afford to adequately heat their homes and the greater incidence ill-health/shorter life expectancy amongst the lower income groups, all suggest that absolute poverty is very much with us in the UK of the 1990s.

Relative poverty

In contrast to the absolute definition of poverty, the relative definition does not seek to establish some fixed minimum standard of living; rather, it makes value judgements about what would represent an acceptable standard of living according to the conventions of a particular society at a certain point in time, and would consequently classify as 'poor' all those who were unable to attain this acceptable standard by their inability to participate in the customary activities of the society. Thus, according to this definition, a person living in the UK today, who did not have hot running water in their house, was unable to have one holiday per year or who did not possess a refrigerator,

might be classified as poor, even though that person might be many times better off in absolute terms than the majority of the inhabitants of a country such as Nepal.

Such an approach to the definition of poverty has to allow for the fact that what is considered to be a reasonable standard of living will vary markedly, not only from one period of time to another, but also from one country to another. The process of economic and political change inherent in all societies would therefore necessitate frequent revisions of what constitutes 'relative poverty'.

How can inequality be measured?

There are a variety of ways in which inequality may be measured, which depict the different standpoints from which the problem may be viewed.

The functional distribution of income

This measures the distribution of income between the factors of production, i.e. labour, capital and land, and it indicates the relative shares in the national income accruing in the form of wages, profit, rent and interest, and their rate of change over time.

This indicator of income distribution has provided a further source of

controversy between those at different ends of the political spectrum, with socialists viewing the relative shares going to labour and capital as the outcome of the inevitable distributional struggle between two antagonistic classes, i.e. capitalists and workers; and those on the right viewing the outcome in terms of the inherent justice provided by the interaction of market forces.

The relative shares are indicated in Box 31.2 although the headings given do not correspond exactly with the definitions of factor incomes as usually provided by economists.

BOX 31.2

Shares in total domestic income, 1971–81, 1983–93

Percentage

	Average 1971–1981	1983	1984	1985	1986	1987	1988	1989	1990	1991	1992	1993
FACTOR INCOMES												
Before providing for stock appreciation												
Income from self-employment	9.4	9.3	9.8	9.8	10.6	11.0	11.6	12.1	12.6	11.8	11.5	11.2
Gross trading profits of industrial and commercial companies	15.4	17.1	18.5	19.2	16.8	18.0	18.3	17.8	16.4	15.1	14.6	15.8
Gross trading profits of financial companies	-1.6	-2.2	-3.1	-2.7	-2.5	-1.9	-2.6	-3.0	-3.1	-3.3	-3.0	-2.4
Gross trading surplus of public corporations	3.3	3.8	3.0	2.3	2.5	1.9	1.9	1.5	0.8	0.4	0.5	0.6
Gross trading surplus of general government enterprises	0.2	–	–	0.1	–	–	–	–	–	–	–	0.1
Rent	6.5	7.1	7.0	7.0	7.2	7.2	7.3	7.5	8.0	9.0	9.5	9.6
Non-trading capital consumption	0.9	0.9	0.9	0.9	0.9	0.9	0.9	0.9	0.9	0.9	0.8	0.7
Gross profits and other income	34.2	36.0	36.1	36.6	35.7	37.1	37.3	36.8	35.6	33.8	33.9	35.6
Income from employment	65.8	64.0	63.9	63.4	64.3	62.9	62.7	63.2	64.4	66.2	66.1	64.4
Total domestic income at factor cost	100.0	100.0	100.0	100.0	100.0	100.0	100.0	100.0	100.0	100.0	100.0	100.0

*Source: CSO, **National Income Blue Book.***

TASK 31.1

a What was the most important source of income in the UK in 1993?

b Identify the factors which may cause changes in the relative shares of total income.

Also included in this measure of inequality would be the distribution of income between specific types of factors, e.g. the disparities in earnings between particular occupational groups of labour such as college principals and road-sweepers. Possible reasons for such differences were discussed in Chapter 9.

The distribution of income according to recipient

Such distribution statistics could take the form of representing income differences as between:

- regions; e.g. the South East as compared to the South West of Britain;

- men and women;

- household composition

Again, we discussed the reasons for income differences in these cases in Chapter 9.

The size distribution of income

The size distribution of income typically portrays the percentage of total income received by each quintile group; e.g. the share gained by the top 20% of income earners compared with other quintile groups, such as the bottom 20%. This is illustrated in Box 31.3.

BOX 31.3

Percentage shares of post-tax income by quintile groups of households, UK, 1979–91

Quintile group	1979	1981	1983	1985	1987	1989	1991
Bottom 20%	9.5	9.0	8.9	8.6	7.6	6.9	6.3
2nd 20%	13	13	13	13	12	11	10
3rd 20%	18	17	17	17	16	16	15
4th 20%	23	22	22	23	22	23	23
Top 20%	37	39	39	39	43	43	45
All households	100	100	100	100	100	100	100

Source: Adapted from *Economic Trends* (1994).

*The **size distribution of income/wealth** is a measure of income/wealth distribution, expressed in terms of percentage shares accruing to each quintile group.*

*The **Lorenz curve** is a graphical representation of the degree of equality/inequality in the size distribution of income.*

During the 1970s (not shown by the data), the distribution of income became slightly more equal. However, during the 1980s and early 1990s, this trend was dramatically reversed, with the share of total income of the bottom 20% of people, i.e. the very poorest, falling from 9.5% to 6%, whilst the top 20%, i.e. the very richest, increased their

share from 37% to 43%. In short, the size distribution of income became very much more unequal over the period in question.

The degree of equality or inequality in the size distribution of income can be statistically measured using a device known as the Lorenz Curve. Such a curve is illustrated in Box 31.4.

BOX 31.4

A Lorenz curve

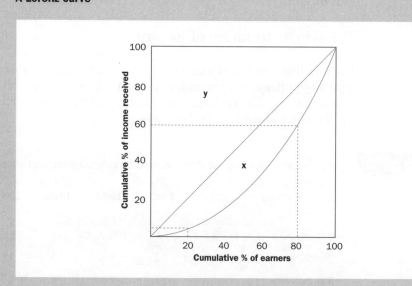

In Box 31.4, the curved line represents a Lorenz curve, which plots the cumulative percentage of income recipients, ranked from poorest to richest, against the cumulative percentage of total income. Along the straight-line diagonal, there is an equal distribution of income, such that the poorest 10% of the population would receive 10% of total income, the poorest 20% would receive 20% of total income and so on. If the actual relationship between the two variables were to follow a path similar to the curved line, then this would be indicative of an unequal distribution of income. For instance, you can see from the broken lines on the graph that, in this particular instance, the bottom 20% of income earners command 5% of total income, while the richest 20% obtain 40% of total income.

*The **Gini coefficient** is a measure of the degree of inequality in a given distribution of income, expressed in percentage terms: 100% represents perfect inequality and 0 perfect equality.*

The ratio between the areas x and y on the graph is known as the Gini coefficient. Thus

$$G = x/y$$

where G is the Gini coefficient; x is the area between the Lorenz curve and the diagonal; y is the area above the diagonal.

If there is a completely equal distribution of income, then G = 0 and the Lorenz curve is a diagonal. The distribution of income becomes more unequal as G increases and gets closer to 1, and this could occur, for example, if more people received nothing, as the lower end of the Lorenz curve would move rightwards along the horizontal axis. As 100% of the population must receive 100% of total income, the top right hand end of the Lorenz curve must touch the top right hand end of the diagonal. However, if the top quintile groups obtain a higher proportion of income, the Lorenz curve will bulge further to the right in its upper regions before it reaches the top right hand corner. In the hypothetical extreme where one person earned all the income and everyone else obtained nothing, the area below the Lorenz curve would disappear and G would be very near to 1. Thus G will lie between 0 and 1, and the greater it is, the more the inequality.

From 1979 to 1990, the post-tax Gini coefficient in the UK increased from 0.29 to 0.40, indicating the growing inequality during this period of time.

The size distribution of wealth

The size distribution of wealth in the UK from 1976 to 1991 is shown in Box 31.5.

Both the size distribution of income and the size distribution of wealth are unequal, but comparing Box 31.5 with Box 31.3, it can be seen that the distribution of wealth is very much more unequal than the distribution of income. In 1991, for instance, the wealthiest 50% of the population owned 92% of the nation's wealth, leaving just 8% for the least wealthy 50% of the population, a statistic that has remained roughly constant since 1976. In fact, over the 15 year period shown by the data, there has been remarkably little distributional change in any of the five categories shown, indicating a consolidation of fundamental wealth disparities into UK society.

BOX 31.5	The size distribution of wealth, UK, 1976–91. United Kingdom: percentages and £ billion			
Marketable wealth	**1976**	**1981**	**1986**	**1991**
Percentage of wealth owned by:				
Most wealthy 1%	21	18	18	18
Most wealthy 5%	38	36	36	37
Most wealthy 10%	50	50	50	50
Most wealthy 25%	71	73	73	71
Most wealthy 50%	92	92	90	92
Total marketable wealth (£ billion)	280	565	955	1694

Source: *Social Trends* (1994).

Why is wealth so unevenly distributed in the UK?

There are several reasons for the extremely unequal distribution of wealth:

● Perhaps the most important reason is that much wealth in the UK has been inherited; i.e. it has been passed on from one generation to the next, and traditionally, even under Labour Governments, there has been very little effective taxation of wealth.

Although a number of taxes on inherited wealth have been in existence over the years, e.g. estate or death duty, capital transfer tax and now the inheritance tax, apart from being granted extremely generous allowances to lessen tax liability, the rich have proved themselves to be very adept at finding loopholes to avoid payment of such taxes.

Typically, revenue from capital taxation has amounted to a very small proportion of total government tax revenue, usually under 2%.

● Wealth begets wealth: the ownership of significant wealth in the form of such assets as land/property, deposit accounts and shares, in turn generates large incomes in the form of rent, interest and dividends, respectively. If this income is not all spent, which it is unlikely to be, it will accumulate as further wealth.

● The rich are able to save a far greater proportion of their income than the poor; i.e. they have a larger average propensity (inclination) to save, and hence the already wealthy are able to accumulate ever greater amounts of wealth. In contrast, the poor have a high average propensity to consume – most, if not all, of their income is spent on the necessities of life, and

therefore the scope for wealth accumulation is very limited.

● In times of inflation, wealth owners benefit from rising asset prices, so that as the price of land, property, gold etc. increase, the value of wealth holdings automatically rise. In contrast, for the poor, who may be unable to increase their incomes in line with inflation, rising prices may mean a fall in real income.

● For a few people, significant wealth accumulation may be the result of good fortune, e.g. National Lottery winners, entrepreneurial expertise (such as the case of Alan Sugar building up the Amstrad company from scratch), or 'sleaze', (such as the bosses of the privatised utilities awarding themselves astronomical pay increases and receiving large share holding options).

Is inequality necessary?

BOX 31.6

Two views on inequality

'If I have a cake and there are ten persons among whom I wish to divide it, then if I give exactly a tenth to each, this will not, at any rate automatically, call for justification; whereas if I depart from this principle of equal division I am expected to produce a special reason'.

*Sir Isaiah Berlin (quoted in A. Atkinson, **Unequal Shares,** Penguin 1972).*

"We believe that everyone has the right to be unequal".

Margaret Thatcher, *Blackpool Conservative Party Conference, October 1975.*

Since their election to power in 1979, successive Conservative Governments, following the belief of Margaret Thatcher that the 'tall should be allowed to grow taller', have pursued policies to make the distribution of income markedly more unequal.

Predictably, this has been heralded by some as an essential ingredient in the government's 'economic miracle', whilst being bitterly opposed by other So what are the arguments on both sides of the divide?

Arguments in support of inequality

- Differences in wages, just like differences in prices, are essential for the smooth operation of a dynamic price system, as they facilitate the process of resource allocation – successful, expanding sectors of the economy will offer higher wages, so as to bid labour away from those less successful parts of the economy where demand and profits are falling. This process was explained more fully in Chapter 12, and you might find it useful to look back to this section now.

- Differences in income provide the necessary incentives for people to supply their factor services and to try to better themselves in life. Without such differentials nobody would be prepared to spend years studying or training to obtain the necessary qualifications to undertake highly skilled occupations, nobody would wish to undertake the more dangerous or unpleasant jobs, the

incentive to work harder would be lost and few would be prepared to seek promotion and assume greater responsibilities.

- An unequal distribution of income i necessary to ensure economic efficiency and a faster growth rate – by making the rich richer, the size o the national cake will grow and the benefits therefrom will 'trickle dowr to the less well-off. As a general rule the rich save a larger proportion of their income than the poor, and thus the greater the disparity in income distribution, the greater the volume of savings that is likely to be generated; the supply of loanable funds that savings represent, permit higher level of investment in productive assets to take place, and thus the achievement of greater future rates of economic growth. Conversely, therefore, greater equali would lead to less saving and less economic growth.

Arguments against inequality

There are a number of grounds on which the arguments for inequality may be rebutted:

● In terms of the smooth operation of a price system, an unequal distribution of income leads to some consumers being very much more sovereign than others in terms of their consumer 'voting power' (see Chapter 12). This may cause a misallocation of society's scarce resources: the poor, who lack effective demand in the market place, would have insufficient 'consumer votes', and the resulting pattern of resource allocation would reflect the wants of the rich rather than the real needs of the poor.

● A more egalitarian society would not present major problems in terms of the supply of factor services to particular occupations, as people are not motivated solely by monetary rewards; for example, people would be prepared to undergo lengthy education/training in the knowledge that they would obtain more satisfying work than could be acquired without qualifications; people would work hard to gain promotion and take on extra responsibilities because many enjoy the 'buzz' of power; conversely, those who were not prepared to study or take on positions of responsibility would presumably be willing to work in the less fulfilling occupations.

TASK 31.2

Class survey and discussion

Imagine the following situation: all wages for different occupations are roughly equal; students in your class are presented with a choice – either they can enter the labour market immediately, working for the rest of their lives in relatively unskilled jobs such as refuse collection and road sweeping, or they can complete their 'A' levels, proceed to university, study for several years and then acquire a more skilled job, such as a doctor or a surveyor; in either case the wage offered would be roughly the same.

1 Find out how many in your class would choose each option.
2 Discuss the reasons for the choices made by your class.
3 Can any general conclusions be drawn from your class findings?

- There is little empirical evidence to support the claim that economic performance will be enhanced by the promotion of inequality. The World Development Report 1991, issued by the World Bank, concluded that there is no evidence that saving is positively related to income inequality or that income inequality leads to higher growth. If anything, it seems that income inequality is associated with slower growth. Economies such as the USA, for instance, experienced considerably slower productivity growth in the 1980s than did countries such as Sweden and Japan where income distribution is more equal.

The American economist J.K. Galbraith has wryly noted that the idea that economic efficiency necessitates greater inequality is a very 'convenient theory', requiring as it does making the rich richer, e.g. through tax cuts, and making the poor poorer, e.g. through benefit cuts.

There are a number of specific reasons why a more egalitarian income distribution would not necessarily adversely affect the level of savings, investment and economic growth; e.g.

- in most industrial societies the bulk of saving is undertaken by the state and firms rather than by individuals so a fall in personal saving could be offset by state encouragement of greater institutional saving or higher taxation;

- a redistribution from rich to poor might reduce the savings of the rich but might be countered by greater savings on behalf of those whose incomes had risen; however, even if the level of personal savings fell, investment and economic growth might be stimulated through the greater levels of consumption of the relatively poor who have a high marginal propensity to consume.

- Greater inequality plunges ever greater numbers of people into poverty, causing not only a variety of human costs, but also an increase in economic inefficiency in terms of wasting human talent and systematically squandering economic potential. The manifestation of this is in the form of, for example, high unemployment, deregulated labour markets, growth of low wage, low productivity employment and a lack of investment in the nation's capital stock.

REVIEW

In this chapter, we have investigated the degree of inequality and poverty that exist in the UK today, and have also examined different perspectives on the issue. So, are inequality and poverty a problem? As we have seen in the case of other important issues in Economics, economists at different ends of the political spectrum would provide very different answers to this question.

REVIEW TASK

NUMBER *of poor doubles*

DSS survey confirms record rise since '79

Tory policies have more than doubled the number of poor people since 1979, official statistics revealed yesterday.

A Department of Social Security survey showed that 25 per cent of the population had incomes of less than half the average income in 1993, compared to 9 per cent in 1979.

The Households Below Average Income report exposes often-repeated government claims that all sections of society are better off.

It showed that real income has declined for people in the lowest-earning 10 per cent of the population.

Undeterred by the facts, Social Security Secretary Peter Lilley said that 'increased prosperity was shared by all family types and economic status groups.

`The results show how government policies have continued to increase the prosperity of the population as a whole, illustrating the substantial increase in the well-being of the most vulnerable groups, such as pensioners,' he said.

The report says that in recent years there have been structural changes in society which have affected the figures.

'The key changes which have affected those in the lower income groups have been increases in unemployed families and increases in the number of self-employed families, combined with an increased risk of their being on low income.

'Income share results are particularly affected by the increasing number of households reporting very low incomes – which may not accurately reflect their living standards.

'Income share results also reflect large increases in incomes at the top of the income distribution scale.'

The number of unemployed families in the lowest-income group rose from 16 per cent of all families in 1979 to 31 per cent in 1993, reflecting the general increase in joblessness.

Single parents remain over-represented in the poorest group, comprising 7 per cent of the group in 1979, but 12 per cent in 1993.

The self-employed, who made up 10 per cent of the bottom group in 1979, made up 17 per cent in 1993.

*Source: **Morning Star** (3 June 1995).*

Using the above article and other data in this chapter, evaluate the claim of the Social Security Secretary that since 1979 'increased prosperity was shared by all family types and economic status groups and that government policies have continued to increase the prosperity of the population as a whole, illustrating the substantial increase in the well being of the most vulnerable groups, such as pensioners'.

32 What can governments do about inequality?

Distribution OF INCOME TOP OF AGENDA FOR REFORM

The big problem is to find a solution to rising inequality. In societies that have increasingly relied on markets to determine wages, and where markets favour inequality, the problem is to find policies that will redistribute income without destroying market efficiencies.

What sorts of policies? Policies that strengthen the market forces that operate against inequality – that create ladders of opportunity for the less advantaged to gain skills and education and that help new businesses. Policies that strengthen the prime market institution that operates against inequality – trade unions – and that strengthen the hand of shareholders in determining the pay of executives. Policies that provide a decent safety net for those who, despite their own effort, are poorly rewarded by markets – earnings tax credits, benefits, minimum wages, social benefits, and safety nets that make sure we are all housed and fed and clothed.

The radical reforms that will solve today's problems and tomorrow's problems will be quite different than those of the past 15 years. It's not the economy – the marketeers have fixed that up, more or less, it's the distribution of income.

Richard B. Freeman is a professor of economics at Harvard University on sabbatical at the London School of Economics.

*Source: **Guardian** (30 January 1995).*

Preview

In this chapter, we shall investigate how governments attempt to deal with inequality, and the effectiveness of the various policy instruments available; this includes a discussion of the following key areas:

- general approaches;
- taxation policy;
- cash benefits;
- benefits in kind;
- negative income tax;
- minimum wage legislation;
- anti-discrimination laws.

General approaches

In general terms, a particular government's approach to inequality will depend to a large extent on where it stands along the political spectrum.

The political right

Recent Conservative Governments, for example, whose underpinning philosophy is that of the political right, have never recognised inequality as a particular problem, and have in fact actively pursued policies such as tax cuts for the rich and deregulation of labour markets, which have had the effect of making the distribution of income very much more unequal. Indeed, the political right would espouse the arguments for inequality outlined in Chapter 31. In their view, direct measures to help the poor and to lessen income disparities, such as cash benefits, should be strictly 'targeted' at the 'genuine' poor to provide a minimum safety net. Any other lessening of inequality should arise as a by-product of the successful implementation of supply-side policies; otherwise equity would only be achieved at the expense of efficiency: for example, better trained workers are likely to be more occupationally and geographically mobile, and therefore better able to help themselves acquire higher paid jobs; suitably deregulated/privatised product and labour markets will, it is argued, promote greater economic efficiency, greater growth and benefit all, including the poor.

The political left

There are several different shades of opinion on the political left, but most would be at variance with the above, except perhaps for the need for greater education and training. Marxists, for example, as previously pointed out, would view inequality as an inevitable and inherent feature of capitalism, which could only be eliminated through the transition of society to socialism. Others on the political left, basing their analysis within the confines of the market system, would argue for specific measures to help the poor, e.g. a higher level of child allowances, as well as greater government intervention in the operation of the economy, for instance in the form of nationalisation of the 'commanding heights' or minimum wage legislation.

Specific measures

The specific policy options available to lessen inequality may be categorised into two broad types :

- Fiscal methods – these would include taxation, cash benefits, benefits in kind and negative income tax.

- Market regulation – this would include minimum wage legislation and legislation banning discriminatory practices in the labour market.

We shall consider all of these various policy options in turn:

Taxation

As we have seen, the level and pattern of taxation is important because it affects both efficiency (economic performance) and equity (the distribution of income).

A government wishing to create a more equal society would shift the burden of taxation to direct, progressive taxes and away from indirect, regressive taxes, and redistribute income through the cash benefit system. A government seeking to make society more unequal

would pursue an opposite course of action – i.e. decrease direct taxes, increase indirect taxes and reduce benefits. One of the justifications of the latter course of action is that high direct taxes have serious disincentive effects on both the willingness to supply labour and work effort.

The data in Task 32.1 will allow you to explore some of these issues.

TASK 32.1

Revenue raised from the different categories of taxation as a percentage of total income raised by taxation and social security contributions, UK, 1976–92

	1976 (%)	1981 (%)	1986 (%)	1992 (%)
Direct taxes on households	39	30	28	30
Direct taxes on corporate incomes	5	9	11	6.8
Indirect taxes	36	43	43	41
Social security contributions	19	17	18	17.9

Treasury SCORES OWN GOAL ON TAX CUTS

By Christopher Huhne,
Economics Editor

A study commissioned by the Treasury at a cost of nearly £500,000 has found no evidence for the Chancellor's view that large incentive effects, beneficial to the economy, will flow from income tax cuts.

The research which must count as an expensive own goal, was begun in 1979 to examine evidence for the Thatcherites' conviction that tax cuts are crucial to improving the supply side of the economy.

The research was supervised by Professor C. V. ('Chuck') Brown of Stirling University, an authority in the field. It relied on an expensive and thorough collection of special survey data by the Office of Population Censuses and Surveys, looking into the behaviour and work habits of 3,300 households.

The survey confirms one common finding of previous work: that tax cuts tend to make virtually no difference to the amount people across the highest band of average incomes want to work. The reason is that the extra incentive to work more, because of lower taxes, is offset by the temptation to work less because income has risen and leisure is preferred.

However, the study goes beyond this conclusion by finding that the institutional arrangements of most workers mean that they are simply unable to work longer hours even if tax cuts were to persuade them to do so.

The Brown research finds that 79 per cent of employees could not do any more work in their main job even if they wanted to. Thus tax cuts simply could not have any substantial effect on the supply of labour – on work effort or length of hours.

*Source: **Guardian** (15 December 1986).*

Lawson's 1988 tax-cutting bonanza helped the rich disproportionately, and was accompanied by the claim: 'Excessive rates of income tax destroy enterprise, encourage avoidance and drive talent to more hospitable shores overseas. As a result, far from raising additional revenue, over time, they actually raise less.'

In a new study*, the tax experts Professors CV Brown and CT Sandford say: 'We have found no evidence that the very substantial reduction in the higher rates of income tax announced in the 1988 Budget has encouraged work or reduced emigration. It follows that there will be no revenue gain from more work or less emigration...

'The combination of evidence about lack of disincentive effects from higher rates of income tax combined with lack of disincentive effects from the basic rate of tax means that there is little evidence to support an important and long-standing element in the Government's economic strategy.'

Taxes & Incentives, Institute for Public Policy Research

*Source: **Observer** (17 March 1991).*

a Describe the main changes in the pattern of taxation which took place between 1976 and 1992.

b Use the table of figures and the articles provided to discuss the likely effects of the changes described in part a on:
  (i) the distribution of household incomes;
  (ii) the incentive to effort and enterprise.

Cash benefits: income subsidies/social security

Universal benefits are benefits paid to certain categories of people, irrespective of their income and wealth.

Means-tested benefits are benefits paid to claimants which are related to income and/or savings.

Most would agree that the social security system reduces both poverty and inequality. There is much less of a consensus as regards the most appropriate level and type of cash benefit, and the possible effects on efficiency of such payments. There are two main types of cash benefit:

● Universal or categorical benefits
These are paid to certain categories of people irrespective of their income and wealth; for example, child benefit is paid to all people with children, and state pensions are paid to all those over a certain age.

● Means-tested benefits
The payment of means-tested benefits, in contrast to universal benefits, is strictly related to the income and, in some cases, the savings of the claimant. Receipt of such benefits is therefore dependent upon making a special application, and on applicants allowing the authorities to test their means.

There are two categories of means-tested benefit – those that are paid for specific purposes, e.g., housing benefit grants, and grants and loans from the Social Fund to meet particular needs of those on income support; and those which provide general support, such as income support, which is payable to those working below a specified number of hours per week, and family credit, which can be claimed by people working in excess of the limit to claim income support, but who are on low income and are supporting a child.

Universal or means-tested benefits?

Those on the political right would tend to favour means-tested benefits. They would argue that such benefits can be selectively targeted at those most in need, and are therefore more efficient and cheaper than universal benefits which are paid to all people in a certain category, irrespective of whether they are rich or poor.

Socialists and those towards the political left, on the other hand, favour universal benefits. They would argue that universalism is more efficient than selectivism, because the payment of benefits to all people in a particular category is administratively simple (no means tests are necessary), involves lower administration costs and has take-up rates which are often close to 100%. To the claim that they are wasteful because they are paid to rich and poor alike, a socialist might argue that the rich should be made to contribute more in the first place in the form of a steeply progressive tax system.

Moreover, in practice, the use of means-tested benefits, as a device for making the distribution of income more equal, has suffered from a number of defects:

● as peoples' means must be assessed before they can receive benefits,

administration tends to be complex and costly;

● the take-up of means-tested benefits tends to be low, and people eligible for such benefits often do not apply, perhaps because of:
– the complexity and difficulty of form filling required
– a lack of awareness of the benefits available;
– expectations of low or zero entitlement;
– the perceived stigma involved.

Box 32.1 illustrates this problem well.

BOX 32.1

2.6 MILLION *miss out on benefits*

Over 2.6 million people have missed out on a share of £2,730 million worth of means-tested benefits, official figures showed yesterday.

The figures are for 1992 – the year Social Security Secretary Peter Lilley launched his offensive on so-called scroungers and pledged a tough crackdown on claimants.

The latest Department of Social Security figures show that one in three of the 480,000 people entitled to Family Credit – a top-up for low-paid workers – claimed it.

They left £200 million unclaimed.

Up to 1.57 million entitled to income support

did not claim any, leaving up to £1,920 million unclaimed.

And up to 600,000 people did not collect housing benefit worth up to £610 million.

The figures take no account of people entitled to benefits who are living in bed and breakfast accommodation, residential care or nursing homes.

Means-tested benefits have a notoriously low take-up level, compared to universal benefits, which are cheaper and easier to administer.

*Source: **Morning Star** (21 January 1995).*

*The **poverty trap** is the phenomenon whereby those on low incomes in work find themselves keeping very little of any extra income earned, because of the loss of entitlement to state means-tested benefits and the liability to pay additional tax.*

*The **unemployment trap** is the phenomenon whereby those on low incomes who are out of work find themselves trapped into unemployment as they are likely to be better off living on welfare payments.*

The use of means-tested benefits, together with a progressive income tax system, may create serious disincentive effects for those on low incomes in work, and thus give rise to efficiency costs; this is because of the existence of a poverty or earnings trap.

This arises as a result of the overlap between the point at which eligibility to pay income tax starts, known as the tax threshold, and the point at which means-tested benefits are no longer paid, known as the means-tested benefits ceiling; a small increase in income might take a worker into this zone of overlap, with the result that each extra pound earned is not only subject to income tax and national insurance for the first time, but also that part or all of the worker's right to receive selective benefits is removed. People on low incomes often find themselves trapped into poverty as any small increase in income subjects them to an extremely high marginal rate of tax (often much higher than the very rich would ever pay) and imposes severe disincentive effects in terms of work and effort.

Means-tested benefits may also give rise to the related problem of the unemployment trap. This affects people on low incomes who are out of work; for such people there may be little or no incentive to obtain paid employment as they are likely to be better off living on welfare payments. This is because the only employment available for such people is likely to be poorly paid, and the need to pay income tax and national insurance, coupled with the possible loss of some or all of their right to claim means-tested benefits, may actually make them worse off in work than out of work.

An overview of social security payments

The political left and centre

For those on the political left and centre, the system of social security payments, especially those of a universal type, together with a progressive tax system, represent an indispensable part of the government's armoury to alleviate poverty and to make society more equitable and equal; the basis of competition and the free market, by their very nature, is that some win and some lose; and as the market does not in itself possess a 'heart', the losers, who in practice are likely to be many, would, in the absence of suitable government support, become ever more impoverished.

The political right

Against this view, those on the political right tend to inherently view all welfare support with distrust. They emphasise a number of disincentive/distortive effects; for example, Patrick Mimford from the University of Liverpool, has argued that those on unemployment benefit are more willing to trade off money for leisure than those in employment; i.e. that they may be happy to remain unemployed, provided the level of benefit is high enough. It was this type of reasoning that persuaded the Conservative Government in 1994 to replace unemployment benefit with the 'job-seekers' allowance', which is only payable for the first 6 months of unemployment.

An even more extreme argument was put forward in the 1980s by the American economist, Charles Murray, who suggested that the provision of social security creates a 'culture of dependency' and that 'welfare provision causes poverty' as it is responsible for creating 'an underclass' of people with no incentive to work. Others have suggested a long-term correlation between social security payments and the level of savings: high social security payments, it is argued, reduce an individual's incentive to save as they reduce future uncertainty; and it has been suggested that the universal provision of state pensions has led to a disincentive to supply labour in terms of a widespread withdrawal of older workers from the labour force.

So, how effective are social security payments in making society more equal? Well, as with most key issues in Economics, the answer to this question depends to a large extent on the political standpoint from which you start!

Benefits in kind

Benefits in kind may be in the form of price subsidies on particular goods or services, e.g. housing and travel, or the provision of goods which are free at the point of contact, e.g. merit goods such as health and education. The most important types of benefit in kind are given in the table in Box 32.2, which shows how income is redistributed through taxes, cash benefits and benefits in kind.

As regards the specific redistributional effects of price subsidies, most economists would probably agree that equity objectives are best achieved through cash transfers to low income households rather than by charging subsidised or non-market prices for goods and services. Whilst subsidies do reduce market prices (depending on the extent of the subsidy), and thus increase real incomes, the benefits of subsidies are somewhat indiscriminate and unpredictable as they are not related to ability to pay, and thus high income as well as low income households gain. Cash subsidies on the other hand, particularly if they are means-tested, may be directly related to the personal financial circumstances of the claimants. In addition, price subsidies must obviously be paid for out of general taxation, which may in part be levied on the poor themselves.

Health care and education are the most important 'free' goods provided by the state, and we examined the arguments for and against such provision in Section 3.

Box 32.2 distinguishes between original, gross, disposable, post-tax and final income:

- original income refers to total household income before taxes have been deducted or benefits added;
- gross income is original income plus cash benefits;
- disposable income is gross income minus direct taxes;
- post-tax income is disposable income minus indirect taxes;
- final income is post-tax income plus the value of benefits in kind.

BOX 32.2

Redistribution of income through taxes and benefits, UK, 1991

£ per year

	Quintile groups of households ranked by equivalised disposable income					
	Bottom fifth	Next fifth	Middle fifth	Next fifth	Top fifth	All house holds
Average per household (£ per year)						
Earnings of main earner	1,000	3,870	8.880	13,400	23,990	10,230
Earnings of others in the household	90	610	2,440	5,060	7,640	3,170
Occupational pensions, annuities	200	570	990	1,190	1,550	900
Investment income	180	420	740	1,170	3,630	1,230
Other income	100	180	250	290	400	240
Total original income	1,570	5,650	13,310	21,100	37,220	15,770
plus Benefits in cash						
Contributory	1,920	1,990	1,350	840	560	1,330
Non-contributory	1,970	1,530	970	530	330	1,060
Gross income	5,460	9,170	15,630	22,470	38,110	18,170
less Income tax and NIC	200	780	2,140	3,830	7,660	2,920
less Community charge (gross)	540	580	660	680	660	620
Disposable income	4,730	7,820	12,830	17,960	29,790	14,620
less indirect taxes	1,320	1,870	2,920	3,690	4,470	2,860
Post-tax income	3,410	5,940	9,900	14,270	25,320	11,770
plus Benefits in kind						
Education	1,090	900	1,190	890	560	920
National Health Service	1,480	1,410	1,280	1,120	940	1,250
Housing subsidy	140	120	50	30	10	70
Travel subsidies	50	50	50	60	90	60
School meals and welfare milk	70	30	20	10	10	30
Final income	6,230	8,450	12,500	16,380	26,910	14,090

Source: *Social Trends* (1994).

TASK 32.2

a Compare the distribution of original income with the distribution of final income in 1991.

b Account for the inequalities in the distribution of original income.

c Discuss the relative importance of taxation, cash benefits and benefits in kind as devices for reducing income inequalities.

Negative income tax

Negative income tax is an income maintenance scheme in which those with an income below some break-even level receive payments in relation to the level of income.

The idea of a negative income tax (NIT) arose because of concerns over the complexities and disincentive effects of the social security system and its tendency to overlap with the tax system, which causes the problem of poverty trap. A NIT or tax credit system would merge the existing income tax and benefits structures.

NIT is an income maintenance schem in which a single tax threshold would be established. Anyone earning an income above this level would pay positive income tax, whereas anyone earning an income below this level would be eligible to receive payments from the Inland Revenue, i.e. would receive a negative income tax. Such payments would replace other cash benefits. This is illustrated in Box 32.3

BOX 32.3

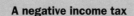
A negative income tax

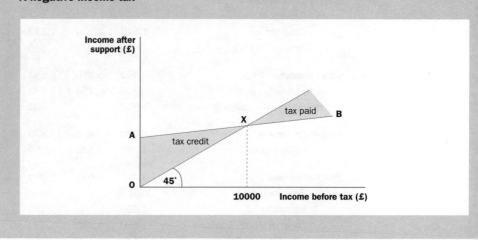

In Box 32.3, income before tax is shown on the horizontal axis, income after tax on the vertical axis, and the 45-degree line locates all the points where the two are equal. The line AB indicates the relationship between income before and after tax. The point of intersection of these two lines, point X, represents a break-even income, in this particular example, of £10,000. For different levels of income, the shaded area above X shows positive tax paid, and the shaded area below X shows negative tax received (i.e. tax credits paid by the government).

So how effective would such a system be in reducing poverty and redistributing income? As you would no doubt expect, there are both potential advantages and disadvantages of the scheme.

Possible advantages include the following points:

● A NIT would be administratively more simple to operate than the present two-tier system of taxation and social security, as only one agency, the Inland Revenue would be involved. Substantial savings on administration costs might also therefore be made.

● By merging the social security system with the tax system, the problem of the poverty and unemployment traps would be eliminated, as there would not be a particular level of income at which social security payments are withdrawn, as is the case under the present system. A NIT might thus have less of a disincentive effect on the supply of labour.

● As all households in the country would be required to complete a tax return for purposes of positive or negative assessment, the scheme would not suffer from the problem of low take-up, the reasons for which (previously outlined in this chapter) would be removed.

● A NIT scheme would involve greater selective targeting of benefits at the most needy, and might thus have a large redistributive effect.

Possible disadvantages include the following points:

● The introduction of a NIT scheme would represent a movement away from the principle of universalism and towards greater selectivity – the principle of means-testing would be reinforced, with the job of welfare assessment falling upon civil servants employed by the Inland Revenue.

● Special payments for particular categories of people in special need might still have to be paid, e.g. to the long-term sick or disabled.

● The conflict between equity and efficiency might still remain and problems would arise in setting suitable tax rates and threshold levels; e.g., if the threshold was set too high, many people on relatively high incomes who could afford to pay tax would actually receive payments from the government – disincentives to work might be lessened, but only by sacrificing equity. A similar effect on equity might be experienced if tax rates were set too low, as those in most need might not be adequately provided for in terms of the level of negative tax that they would be eligible to receive; raising the level of taxation, on the other hand, to provide more for the poor might have disincentive effects on work effort and the willingness to supply labour at all.

Minimum wage legislation

BOX 32.4	**New evidence fuels debate on minimum wage**

New government statistics reveal that approximately one in six full-time manual workers earns less than £3.75 an hour, before tax and deductions, and that almost half the 5.9 million part-time workers are being paid less than £4.15 an hour with more than half a million earning less than £3 an hour. These low pay figures disguise regional variations, so that in Yorkshire, for example, more than 50 per cent of the part-time workforce earn less than £4 an hour.

These figures will add considerable weight to the Labour Party's intention to introduce a statutory minimum wage, and also indicate how substantial would be the effect of setting the minimum at half the middle range of male hourly pay, preferably £4.05.

Source: Adapted from **Guardian** *(28 December 1994).*

A minimum wage is one which is fixed by the government or one of its agencies, and is the lowest amount which may legally be paid to a worker for a standard period of time at work.

Unlike most other industrial countries, the UK does not currently have a statutory minimum wage, although up until 1993 a system of wages councils did exist. These were first established as far back as 1909 by Winston Churchill on behalf of the ruling Liberal Government, and were set up to prevent workers being exploited in various poorly unionised occupations. The councils were legally empowered to fix minimum hourly rates of pay for the industries that they represented. They were abolished in 1993 by the Conservative Government as part of its deregulatory programme to 'allow markets to work more efficiently', which in practice has meant even lower wages for many of those already at or below the poverty line. Since 1992 the Labour party has actively committed itself to implementing a national minimum statutory wage if and when it comes to power.

As a weapon for combating poverty and inequality, the minimum wage represents a form of legislative fixing of factor prices, and as to be expected, it has its advocates and opponents. We shall begin our examination of the various standpoints by considering the case against a national minimum wage.

Arguments against a minimum wage:

- The general case against a minimum wage would be made by those on the political right on the grounds that government interference with the operation of the price system is, in itself, an undesirable thing. They would argue that prices and wages are best left to find their own levels through the interaction of demand and supply, and that labour will be allocated to its most efficient uses if free market forces prevail – government intervention will always cause market distortions and a loss of economic efficiency. Moreover, workers who feel that their wages are unreasonably low in a particular line of employment are not forced to remain there; they are free to change their jobs to obtain higher remuneration elsewhere.

- The anti-minimum wage case is discussed in Chapter 2.9.
  It is argued that an excess supply of labour, i.e. unemployment, may result as a consequence of the imposition of a minimum wage fixed above the equilibrium wage.
  Any increased unemployment due to a minimum wage would depend on the extent to which the employer can pass the increased costs on to the consumer in the form of higher prices. This in turn would depend on the elasticity of demand for labour – an elastic demand would lead to a relatively large increase in the numbers being made unemployed, whilst an inelastic demand would involve a relatively small change in employment numbers.
  In addition, it is argued that the people likely to be most affected by any increase in unemployment would be the young and the unskilled who, if not dispelled from the labour market, may find extreme difficulty in entering it at the fixed minimum wage.

- The establishment of a minimum wage would encourage increased mechanisation, which might further increase unemployment; firms faced with higher labour costs might seek to implement labour saving devices and where possible substitute capital for labour.

- A minimum wage would raise business costs. The more inelastic the demand for the final product, the more firms would be tempted to pass the additional cost on to consumers in the form of higher prices in order to protect their profit margins, and this would obviously increase inflationary pressures in the economy. The rise in prices might then make UK firms' exports less competitive in overseas markets, as well as preventing improvements in real income for consumers of the goods whose prices have risen.

- In order to keep their costs low and to maintain profit margins, firms might be tempted to circumvent the minimum wage legislation by employing more workers on a part-time, casual basis. This would be possible if the legislation only applied to employees working a certain number of hours per week. Alternatively, more unscrupulous firms might employ workers through the unofficial, black economy in which neither income tax, national insurance nor the minimum wage would be paid.

- Greater levels of pay for those at the bottom end of the income scale would induce higher-paid workers to seek an increase in wages in order to restore traditional pay differentials. This would exacerbate inflationary pressures as well as making it more difficult to recruit skilled workers.

Arguments in favour of a minimum wage:

- The basis of the case for a national statutory minimum wage is that all workers have a fundamental right to receive an income which would guarantee acceptable minimum living standards.

- The free market argument that nobody forces workers to remain in low wage occupations, and that all those aggrieved by their level of pay are free to 'get on their bikes' to seek more remunerative employment elsewhere, overlooks the problems that most people face in trying to change jobs; aside from the difficulty of finding any work in times of mass unemployment (currently about 2.5 million), many people tend to be occupationally and geographically immobile.

In those occupations where the lowest wages prevail (sometimes referred to as the 'sweated trades'), e.g. hotels and catering and the 'rag trade', the payment of very low incomes is not so much a reflection of the free interplay of market forces, but more a reflection of exploitation: of the fact that trade union organisation is very difficult in such industries where workers are rarely all 'under one roof' and may even be working from home.

Some economists on the political left would view the payment of low wages to workers in terms of an expropriation of surplus value. This point is well illustrated in Box 32.5 which contains an extract from a newspaper produced in the USA.

BOX 32.5

Expropriation of surplus value

Manufacturing workers
PRODUCE $114,100 EACH PER YEAR
– AND KEEP $385 A WEEK

The following figures for 1991, the most recent available, are taken from the Census of Manufactures issued by the U.S. Census Bureau:

U.S. workers in 20 manufacturing industries produced, on average, $114,100 per worker per year, at a rate of $56.70 per hour. In a 40-hour week, therefore, each worker added $2,268 to the value of the product.

Yet, the average gross wage for the same set of workers came to $460 for a 40-hour week. Estimating deductions for a married man with two children leaves a 'take home' of $385 – and that is for workers in better-paying manufacturing jobs. The total tax burden of $75 is a small fraction of the total $1,883 deducted from the worker's product each week.

Of course, there are classifications of work where the value of production is not the same in relation to wages as this example. But whether we are considering youngsters flipping hamburgers for minimum wage at the local drive-in, or an auto worker on a highly automated production line, the net effect is that worker-consumers cannot buy back the products of their own labour.

Paycheck stub	
Manufacturing Value Produced Per Worker Per Week (1991)	**$2,268**
Weekly Take-Home Pay Per Worker in Manufacturing	**$385**
Total Deductions Per Worker Per Week	**$1,883**

(includes money for company's retained profits, stockholder dividends, interest payments, rents, insurance premiums, executive salaries, legal fees, sales, advertising, all taxes)

Source: ***New Unionist*** *(November 1994).*

● Related to the previous point is the argument that workers in the UK, a country that is a full member of the EU, should have the same rights as their European counterparts: if, as part of the provisions of the Social Chapter, workers in other EU countries can enjoy the benefits of minimum wage levels as well as a variety of other rights at work, why should workers in the UK not be entitled to the same?

● Raising the level of pay of the very poorest workers might generate a number of positive economic advantages: as the poor tend to have a high marginal propensity to consume, a higher level of demand in the economy would be created which might stimulate investment and economic growth and also reduce the current very high levels of unemployment; also the government would enjoy a 'double-edged' benefit in terms of a reduced demand for welfare payments and greater tax and National Insurance revenues from the higher wages being earned.

- The case against is flawed on a number of grounds:
- as a minimum wage would apply to all workers, the relative competitiveness of firms within the economy should not be greatly affected;
- the adverse effects of higher wage costs on employment and prices may be greatly mitigated by productivity gains; forced to pay higher wages, firms may be induced to become more efficient by increasing their investment in plant and machinery and new technology; the resulting rise in labour productivity would make job losses and price increases unnecessary; empirical evidence from a number of EU countries where a minimum wage exists suggests that the above process will often be the case.

In summary, we have demonstrated that the question of a national minimum wage is another issue over which economists and politicians are sharply divided – the effects are by no means clear-cut. Low wages are patently a major cause of poverty and inequality, and some action is needed on this front. However, the minimum wage could never eliminate these two problems on its own as poverty and inequality are also caused by unemployment – as the unemployed receive no wage they would derive no benefit from a minimum wage; hence the need for complementary fiscal support.

Anti-discrimination laws

Gender, ethnic and social discrimination in the labour market can be a major factor in explaining income differences. Therefore, one way of reducing income inequalities is for the government to pass legislation, such as the Equal Pay Act of 1970 or the Sex Discrimination Act of 1975, which ban discriminatory practices.

Discrimination may involve the problem of dual labour markets with women and people from ethnic minority groups being forced to work in segregated, low wage markets where they are unable to contribute to society in accordance with their full potential. Thus a successful banning of discrimination in the labour market would allow certain groups of people to switch to occupations where the value of their marginal product would be greater: total output, welfare and wage levels in the jobs from which they moved would all rise, whilst income inequality would fall.

The difficulty in practice, however, of anti-discrimination laws is that they are easily circumvented by employers; whilst a person may know with some certainty that a job opportunity or promotion has been denied on the grounds of race or sex, it is another matter entirely to prove this to be the case in a court of law.

TASK 32.3

Class debate

This house believes that the current degree of inequality which exists in the UK today is neither morally nor economically justifiable, and that an upper and lower limit on earnings ought to be imposed.

Elect a chairperson (possibly your teacher), two main speakers to support the motion and two to oppose it. Remember that the essence of a good debate is that everyone, main speakers and speakers from the 'floor of the house' i.e. the rest of the class, should be well prepared!

BOX 32.6

The Rowntree Report, 1995

A report by the Joseph Rowntree Foundation, a charity renowned for its social research, has painted a chilling picture of a divided Britain, and has revealed a dramatic increase in the gulf between rich and poor – possibly the first time, since the Middle Ages, that the trend towards greater equality has been reversed. The report disproves the idea that inequality promotes growth and shatters the Conservative claim that all benefit as wealth trickles down from the richest to the poor. These are the facts established:

- Since the late 1990s the poor have trebled in number, having previously been in decline.

- The poorest 30% derived no benefit from the economic growth of the 1980s, with the incomes of the poorest 5% falling by 17%. The richest 5% of the population, on the other hand, received about 30% of the rise in national income during this period.

- Since 1978, the average wage has risen by 35% in real terms, but the lowest paid have had no wage increase once inflation is taken into account.

- Whilst 18% of the white population is in the poorest one-fifth of the population, more than one-third of non-whites are.

- Since 1975 the number of homes with no earners has risen from 3% to 11%, and the number of households with two working adults has risen from 51% to 60%.

- In 1994, 75% of unemployed couples were still unemployed a year later, as compared with 41% in 1979. The length of time that a non-earning household can expect to stay that way has risen from 18 to 54 months.

In this chapter, we have investigated a wide range of issues in relation to the distribution of income and wealth. We have attempted to demonstrate that considerable differences of opinion exist between economists regarding the extent to which distributional issues are seen as problematic, and the appropriate measures that a government might pursue. What cannot be disputed, however, is the fact that the UK has become a very much more unequal society since the early 1980s, and that the effect of this in human, social and economic terms has been profound.

Why AN UNEQUAL BRITAIN IS PAYING THE PRICE FOR 'EFFICIENCY' FALLACY

DEBATE

Andrew Glyn and David Miliband

Inequality in Britain today is shocking, and growing. But is it necessary? For 15 years, the Government has given an unequivocal answer: we have been told that incentives are a spur to economic efficiency, and inequalities their unfortunate price.

In accordance with this theory, top tax rates have been cut, Wages Councils abolished, and markets deregulated. Sure enough, the gap between rich and poor has widened dramatically since 1979. The top 1 per cent of income earners received 93 times as much per head in tax cuts between 1979 and 1992 as the bottom 50 per cent. The gap between the highest and lowest paid has increased to a level last seen in 1886. And the number of children living in households where income is less than half the average has increased from 10 per cent in 1979 to 31 per cent today.

Even the Government have had to accept that the wilder claims of 'trickle down' theory are wrong. By making the rich richer, government does not make the poor richer, too. Since 1979, the real income of the bottom 10 per cent of the population has fallen by 14 per cent.

But the assertion that inequality is an inescapable product of successful market economies remains central to the economic and political hegemony of the Right. And the Left is uncertain whether the price of greater equality will be lower growth.

The problem is that while the medicine of inequality has been applied, the disease of economic underperformance has got worse. Growth under the Tories since 1979 has been lower than that achieved under Labour in the 1970s (1.6 per cent compared to 1.9 per cent). And Britain is not alone. Across the industrialised countries as a whole, there is no macroeconomic evidence – from longitudinal data within nations or cross-national comparison between countries – to support the case that greater equality is detrimental to efficiency.

If anything, the opposite is the case: the fastest growing economies in the 1980s were also the more equal societies. We all pay for inequality – in higher taxes, poor health, and high crime. From education to inheritance, from cradle to grave, inequality is a burden we cannot afford.

The work of labour and health economists, educationalists and criminologists, and social policy and taxation experts collected together in our new book* shows that inequality on current levels is an economic disaster.

Take the examples of health, education and the labour market. It is now commonly accepted, even on the Right, that ill-health is expensive, because of the rising cost of treatment and the opportunity cost of lost production, and that it is inversely correlated with wealth. The poor are more ill more often than their richer peers. But what is not appreciated is that good health is influenced by relative and not just absolute standards of living, and that differences in income distribution are the most important explanation of differences in average life-span between countries.

Richard Wilkinson's work shows that the UK's slippage in terms of income distribution over the last 20 years correlates with its slippage in terms of mortality rates. Were our income distribution to correlate with our continental neighbours, we could expect to see a two-year improvement in average life-span. This would not only come from older people living longer, the widening of UK income distribution in the 1980s correlates with a rise in death rates for men and women aged 15 to 44.

In education, ours is an early selection low achievement system. In France, by contrast, which a decade ago suffered problems similar to our own, the government is set to meet its target of getting 80 per cent of school leavers to baccalaureat (university entrance) standard by the year 2000. More does not mean worse.

Not only is our system geared to the needs of a minority, it is not meritocratic. Children of unskilled manual workers currently in the labour force are one tenth as likely to have been to university as those of professional parents, and eight times as likely to have achieved no qualifications whatsoever. This is an economic drain we can ill afford. In the labour market, the Government and its supporters use crude models of supply and demand to show that an increase in the price of labour reduces demand for it. In fact, the labour market is dogged by endemic market failure. New research shows that employers at the bottom end of the labour market underpay their employees by around 15 per cent of their productive value. This generates a double inefficiency: fewer workers are willing to work and incentives for increased productivity are reduced because workers receive so little of the proceeds.

Of course, many who oppose redistribution of income or opportunity do so because they do not wish to pay for it. But efficiency arguments have been central to the case against egalitarian policies and these arguments are often spurious, and need to be exposed as such.

*Andrew Glyn and David Miliband (eds): *Paying for Inequality: The Economic Cost of Social Injustice*, Rivers Oram Press/Institute for Public Policy Research.

Source: Guardian (25 April 1994).

Real median income: by quintile group

United Kingdom   Indices (1979 bottom fifth=100)

	Quintile groups of individuals					
	Bottom fifth	Next fifth	Middle fifth	Next fifth	Top fifth	Average of all individuals
Net income after housing costs						
1979	100	138	177	226	312	197
1981	96	135	174	225	323	196
1987	99	143	200	267	406	236
1988–1989	100	153	217	289	438	255
1990–1991	97	155	222	304	467	267

*Source: **Social Trends** (1994).*

a (i) Use the median income table to assess the extent to which all income groups experienced an increase in their living standards over the period in question.

   (ii) What other evidence might help in assessing changes in living standards?

b Use your knowledge of economics and the article on income inequality to discuss the possible effects on the UK economy resulting from the pattern of income distribution indicated by the above table.

Multiple choice

1 **Which of the following factors is most likely to explain why there is income inequality within many Less Developed Countries (LDCs)?**
   A a lack of productive resources
   B the concentrated ownership of land and capital
   C insufficient aid from developed countries
   D trade restrictions on exports

(IB, November 1994)

2 **Within a country, absolute poverty is usually measured by estimating for the country concerned the amount of money.**
   A earned by the poorest 20% of the population.
   B spent on goods and services by an average family.
   C donated as food aid to starving people.
   D needed to buy a minimum level of subsistence.

(IB, May 1995)

3 **The term 'poverty trap' is used to describe a situation when those on low incomes**
   A do not claim all the state benefits to which they are entitled
   B have insufficient liquidity to meet their current consumption
   C receive insufficient state benefits to mitigate the worst effects of poverty
   D are faced with a very high effective marginal tax rate.

(AEB, June 1991)

4 **Which of the following will NOT tend to produce greater equality in the distribution of income?**
   An increase in
   A personal income tax rates
   B old age pensions
   C supplementary benefits
   D value added tax
   E corporation tax.

(ULEAC, January 1994)

Essays

1 a Explain why there are inequalities in the present distribution of income and wealth in the United Kingdom.

     b Assess whether the government should introduce policies which are designed to make the distribution of income more equal.

(AEB, June 1993)

2 a Distinguish between income and wealth.

     b Discuss the possible economic effects of policies aimed at significantly reducing inequalities in income and wealth.

(AEB, November 1991)

3 a How can the existence of relative poverty in the United Kingdom be explained?

     b Evaluate the various policies the government could adopt to help the poor.

(AEB, November 1994)

4 a Explain the factors which may give rise to an unequal distribution of
     i income;
    ii wealth
     b Evaluate the different approaches which a government today might adopt to reduce the degree of inequality within society.

(AEB, June A/S level, 1993)

5 **Since 1979, the distribution of income in the UK has become more unequal.**
     a Explain how fiscal policy might be used to reverse this trend.
     b Assess the costs and benefits of a fiscal policy which aims to make the distribution of income more equal.

(AEB, Specimen paper)

Case Study: THE MINIMUM WAGE DEBATE

ITEM A

The Minimum Wage Debate

After more than a decade, minimum wage legislation has returned to the UK political agenda. This renewed interest reflects a growing awareness of increased wage inequalities during the 1980s, and may also reflect the prospect of closer European ties after 1992. The political debate on minimum wage legislation has been heightened by the Labour party's proposal for a national minimum wage (NMW), in the run up to the general election.   5

The Labour party proposal is for an NMW at the level of 50% of male median earnings; the equivalent of approximately £3.40 per hour in 1991–92. The earnings of men rather than both sexes would be taken as this would help to close the gender gap in pay.

The NMW proposal is the subject of great controversy. Its supporters argue that it would   10
provide a safety net that would help the poor substantially and help to prevent the exploitation of workers. Its critics regard an NMW as an obstacle to the operation of the labour market that would cause increased unemployment (particularly among the low paid) and inflation. These views were put recently by the Employment Minister, Michael Howard, who referred to the NMW proposal as an 'absurd policy . . . of staggering   15
economic illiteracy' (*The Times, 5 September 1991*). The Low Pay Unit claims that low pay is a major cause of poverty, and this claim seems to be upheld by the 1990 'New Earnings Survey' which reports that 9.5 million adult workers (approximately 45% of the UK workforce) were earning below the Low Pay Unit's definition of low pay, which is two thirds of male median earnings. Of these 5.5 million were in full time employment, and   20
two-thirds were female.

With 1992 upon us, the situation in the UK (and Ireland) in relation to legislation contrasts sharply with that in other European states. France, Luxembourg, the Netherlands, Portugal and Spain have statutory minimum wages across the board. In Belgium and Greece general minimum wages are fixed by national agreement. In   25
Denmark, Italy and Germany legally binding minimum wages are set by industry-level collective agreements which cover almost the entire workforce. ITEM B shows a comparison of minimum wages in EC countries.

But what of the benefit of the policy? It is clear that the direct benefits are felt by those whose wages increase (and who keep their job), but how do these benefits add up in   30
terms of the overall impact on poverty?

The answer to this question depends on identifying who are the low paid and, in particular, what is the relationship between low pay and poverty. It may seem obvious that low pay is a major cause of poverty, but more careful thought reveals some doubt. We have already seen that considerable numbers of the low paid are part-time workers;   35 of the remainder, many are either married women or young people living at home with their families. Many of those who are low paid live in households that are not poor. Research by the Institute for Fiscal Studies attempts to identify the gainers from an NMW of £3.50 per hour. The results are summarised in ITEM D. On the horizontal axis we have groups of households arranged by income; group 1 is the poorest 10%, group 2 the next poorest 10% and so on up to the richest 10% in group 10. On the vertical axis is the annual average gain to a household from the £3.50 NMW. We can see that the poorest group benefits by only around £30, while the middle income households gain by as much as £300.

It seems that the relationship between low pay and poverty is not so strong after all, and that the benefits of an NMW go largely to the non-poor sections of the population.

ITEM B

European Minimum Wage Rates

(Denmark and Germany operate different minimums for different trades)

UK — Labour's proposed minimum — based on £3.40 per hour
Netherlands
Portugal
Spain
Luxembourg
Germany (up to £720)
Denmark (up to £970)
Belgium

0   100   200   300   400   500   600   700   800

£ sterling equivalent monthly wage adjusted to remove the effects of different costs of living in each country.

*Source: from **Economic Update** (1992)*

ITEM C

Percentage shares of household income (UK)

	Quintile groups of households				
	Bottom fifth	**Next fifth**	**Middle fifth**	**Next fifth**	**Top fifth**
Original income					
1977	4	10	18	26	43
1988	2	7	16	25	50
Disposable income					
1977	10	14	18	23	36
1988	8	11	16	23	42

Note: due to rounding the figures may not add exactly to 100
Source: CSO, Social Trends 1992

*Source: **The Economy in Focus** (1992/93)*

QUESTIONS

ITEM D

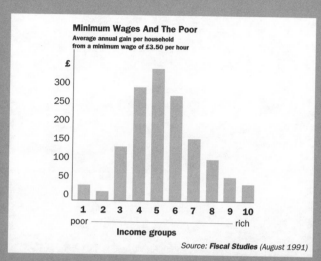

Minimum Wages And The Poor
Average annual gain per household
from a minimum wage of £3.50 per hour

Source: **Fiscal Studies** (August 1991)

Source: **Economic Review** (1992).

A (i) Using economic theory, draw a labelled diagram to illustrate the effects of implementing a national minimum wage (NMW) in a low wage industry.

(ii) Explain the economic justification for Michael Howard's view that the NMW proposal is an 'absurd policy . . . of staggering economic illiteracy' (ITEM A lines 15-16).

B How might using the earnings of men to determine the NMW 'help to close the gender gap in pay'? (ITEM A lines 8-9).

C Discuss the possible impact of a NMW on the level of national income.

D Using the data in ITEM B, discuss the impact on UK competitiveness of introducing an NMW.

E Examine ITEM C showing percentage shares of household income.

(i) Briefly describe the changes in the distribution of disposable income which have occurred.

(ii) Evaluate two alternative policies to the NMW which are available to a government wishing to reduce inequalities in disposable income.

(Adapted from AEB, Wessex Project, June 1994)

.33 How does economic development affect living standards?

Global poverty

PUBLIC ENEMY *number one*

The offences include shortening life and causing starvation, disability, mental illness, suicide, family break-up and substance abuse. The guilty party, as named today in the 1995 World Health Organisation report, is poverty. Chris Mihill pursues the global criminal.

The world's biggest killer, the greatest cause of ill-health and suffering across the globe, is listed almost at the end of the International Classification of Diseases, the giant tome which records all ailments known to medical science. It is given the code Z59.5. It doesn't stand for cancer, heart disease, HIV or even malnutrition. It stands for extreme poverty.

Poverty is the main reason why babies are not vaccinated, why clean water and sanitation are not provided, why treatment is unavailable and why mothers die in childbirth. It is the underlying cause of reduced life expectancy, handicap, disability and starvation. It is a major contributor to mental illness, stress, suicide, family disintegration and substance abuse.

The words come not from some leftwing pressure group or Third World agency. They are the opening statements of the 1995 annual report of the World Health Organisation, which is published today. WHO, not usually noted for ringing denunciations of health inequalities, states: 'Every year in the developing world 12.2 million children under five die, most of them from causes which could be prevented for just a few US cents per child. They die largely because of indifference but most of all they die because they are poor.'

The report is entitled *Bridging the Gaps*. But in a relentless catalogue of facts and figures it shows how in many areas the health gaps are not closing but widening – between rich and poor, between North and South, between men and women, between employed and unemployed, between young and old.

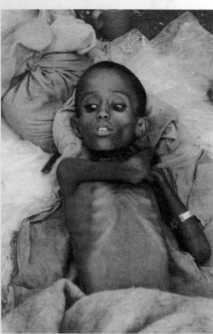

© UN photo 164609/John Isaac.

In the time taken to read this sentence, somewhere a baby has died in its mother's arms. It will not stem that mother's grief to know that eight out of 10 children in the world have been vaccinated against the five major killer diseases of childhood, or that since 1980 infant mortality has fallen by 25 per cent, while overall life expectancy has increased by four years, to about 65.

Beneath the heartening facts about decreased mortality and increasing life expectancy, and many other health advances, lie unacceptable disparities in health. In WHO's words: 'For most people in the world today every step of life from infancy to old age is

taken under the twin shadows of poverty and inequity and under the double burden of suffering and disease. For many the prospects of longer life may seem more like a punishment than a gift.'

The true obscenity highlighted by the report is that millions of deaths could be avoided for a few pence – yet the world chooses not to give the money. By the end of this century, we could be living in a world without polio, without new cases of leprosy, without deaths from neonatal tetanus and measles. Other old scourges could be greatly reduced. But today the money that some developing countries have to spend per person on health over an entire year is just US$4 – less than the small change carried by most people in industrialised countries.

A person in the least developed countries of the world has a life expectancy of 43 years; in the most developed the life expectancy is 78. That inequity alone should stir the conscience of the world – but in some of the poorest countries the picture is getting worse. In five countries – Cîte d'Ivoire, Central African Republic, Congo, Uganda and Zambia – life expectancy at birth is expected to decrease by the year 2000, whereas everywhere else it is increasing. In the richest countries life expectancy will reach 79 years. In some of the

poorest it will fall to 42. By 2000, at least 45 countries will have life expectancy at birth of under 60.

The number of children under five who died in 1993 – more than 12.2 million – equals the populations of Norway and Sweden combined. If developing countries enjoyed the same standard of living as the developed, more than 90 per cent of those deaths could have been avoided.

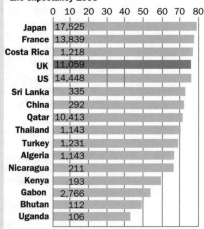

Life expectancy 1993

Country	Value
Japan	17,525
France	13,839
Costa Rica	1,218
UK	11,059
US	14,448
Sri Lanka	335
China	292
Qatar	10,413
Thailand	1,143
Turkey	1,231
Algeria	1,143
Nicaragua	211
Kenya	193
Gabon	2,766
Bhutan	112
Uganda	106

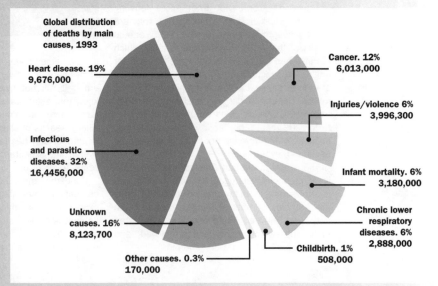

Global distribution of deaths by main causes, 1993

Heart disease. 19% 9,676,000

Infectious and parasitic diseases. 32% 16,4456,000

Unknown causes. 16% 8,123,700

Other causes. 0.3% 170,000

Cancer. 12% 6,013,000

Injuries/violence 6% 3,996,300

Infant mortality. 6% 3,180,000

Chronic lower respiratory diseases. 6% 2,888,000

Childbirth. 1% 508,000

Source: *Guardian* (2 May 1995).

What is economic development? Is it the same thing as growth? What are the differences between More Developed Countries (MDCs) and Less Developed Countries (LDCs)? What are the special problems of LDCs and how can they be overcome?

Preview

In this chapter we shall investigate the following key areas:
- Measures of economic and human development;
- Strategies for development.

Students and teachers wishing to study some of the issues in more detail should refer to a companion Macmillan book, *Economic Development, Growth and Welfare*, by Charles Smith, in the Economics Today series.

BOX 33.1

The HDI and some other indicators, selected countries, 1992

Country	HDI	GNP pc (US $)	Rank on HDI	Rank on GNP pc	Rank out of 160 countries HDI	Rank out of 160 countries GNP pc	Adult literacy rate 1990 (%)	Average annual inflation rate 1980-90 (%)	Life expectancy at birth 1990 (years)
Japan	0.981	25 430	1	1	2	3	99.0	1.5	78.6
UK	0.962	16 100	2	3	10	21	99.0	5.8	75.7
Germany	0.955	22 320	3	2	12	10	99.0	2.7	75.2
Rep. of Korea	0.871	5 400	4	6	34	39	96.3	5.1	70.1
Singapore	0.848	11 160	5	4	40	25	88.0	1.7	74.0
Brazil	0.739	2 680	6	7	59	54	81.1	284.3	65.6
Saudi Arabia	0.687	7.050	7	5	67	33	62.4	-4.2	64.5
Thailand	0.685	1 420	8	8	69	79	93.0	3.4	66.1
Sri Lanka	0.651	470	9	10	76	120	88.4	11.1	70.9
China	0.612	370	10	11	79	130	73.3	5.8	70.1
Cameroon	0.313	960	11	9	118	88	54.1	5.6	53.7
Tanzania	0.268	110	12	14	126	158	65.0	25.8	54.0
Uganda	0.192	220	13	13	133	141	48.3	107.0	52.0
Sierra Leone	0.062	240	14	12	159	145	20.7	56.1	42.0

Source: **UNDP, Human Development Report** (1992).

Economic growth and development

Development differs from growth in that it focuses attention on the distribution and composition of national output, not just its size.

Economic growth takes place when there is an increase in either the national income of a country (actual growth) or in the country's productive capacity (potential growth). Economic growth does not necessarily lead to an increase in living standards. The concept of a country's standard of living is a vague one, but it is generally linked to people's command over goods and services. Since an increase in national income is likely to increase spending power, then there is likely to be a link between economic growth and higher living standards. However, if 'Karenia' has twice the GNP of 'Alisonia', it does not necessarily follow that the average citizen of Karenia has twice the standard of living of the average citizen of Alisonia. Allowances have to be made for differences in the size of the population, the distribution of incomes within the population, the cost of living in each country, the level of taxes within each country, and the provision of public goods and social services. As well as focusing on the quantity of goods and services available, it is also necessary to attempt to measure the quality of life in each country, and this involves investigating such things as pollution levels, stress, and other externalities.

Economic and human development

Human development is a measure of living standards taking account of income, education and health.

Economic development can be regarded as a process of growth and change aimed at raising people's living standards. It involves growth in total and average income, and is accompanied by fundamental changes in the structure of an economy. These changes in structure usually involve industrialisation, greater participation in international trade, and the development of financial institutions and other services. Each year the World Bank publishes a World Development Report, which charts development progress and puts countries in order of rank according to their economic success, based on GNP per head and its rate of change. Within this ranking it is possible to place a fairly arbitrary dividing line, and at 1994 prices economists following a 'World Bank' view of development would generally accept that LDCs are countries with less than $5000 GNP per head, and MDCs are those with more.

It would be possible to adopt the above definition of development, and conclude that development is taking place in spite of the fact that a country suffers from, say racial discrimination, violent dictatorship, a state of war, chronic pollution, or massive inequalities between rich and poor people. Because this is hardly a satisfactory conclusion, the United Nations Development Programme (UNDP) is developing a new Human Development Index (HDI) which is published each year in the Human Development Report (HDR).

The UNDP defines human development as a 'process of enlarging people's choices', and three types of 'choice' are regarded as being particularly important:

- Access to resources (purchasing power, which is calculated from GNP and cost of living figures);

- A long and healthy life (as reflected by life expectancy statistics);

- Education (measured by the adult literacy rate).

Figures for each of these measures are 'weighted' and combined to give a number between 0 and 1, and the closer to 1 the higher the level of 'Human Development'.

As time goes on, the UNDP intends to refine the way in which in calculates the HDI. It would be possible to find some way of including measures of such things as infant mortality, income distribution, military spending compared to health and educational spending, unemployment and, controversially, political freedoms and human rights. Other economists, such as Professor David Pearce of London University, are working on measures of 'sustainable development', which focus on such things as pollution levels and use of non-renewable resources. It is possible that no single index can convey the full implications of human development, and it might be more meaningful to keep the HDI relatively simple, while publishing as much supplementary information as possible.

In Box 33.1, the differences in rankings based on GNP compared with rankings on HDI show the value of including as many indicators as possible. In some countries, GNP lags behind HDI, while in others the reverse is true. Countries with a high level of GNP can plummet down the HDI rankings if their literacy rates are low (indicating a lack of access to education for the mass of the population); similarly countries with low GNP per head can move up the HDI rankings if their cost of living is low, or if they give high priority to spending on health as opposed to, say, military spending. Look at Box 33.2

INVESTIGATING ECONOMICS

BOX 33.2

Main HDI rankings, 1993

Overall top-ranked countries	Top developing nations
1. Japan	1. Barbados
2. Canada	2. Hong Kong
3. Norway	3. Cyprus
4. Switzerland	4. Uruguay
5. Sweden	5. Trinidad and Tobago
6. United States	6. Bahamas
7. Australia	7. S Korea
8. France	8. Chile
9. Netherlands	9. Costa Rica
10. Britain	10. Singapore
11. Iceland	11. Brunei
12. Germany	12. Argentina
13. Denmark	13. Venezuela
14. Finland	14. Dominica
15. Austria	15. Kuwait
16. Belgium	16. Mexico
17. New Zealand	17. Qatar
18. Luxembourg	18. Mauritius
19. Israel	19. Malaysia
	20. Bahrain
	21. Grenada
	22. Antigua and Barbuda

Source: **UNDP, Human Development Report** (19

The 1993 HDR argued that it is possible to regard the USA as three countries instead of one. The black population shares so few of the benefits of US society that it ranks 30 places behind the white population on the HDI. The Hispanic population would be 35 places behind, putting it lower than some of the Latin American countries such as Chile.

This indicates one of the strengths of the HDI, which is that it can be used to indicate the quality of life of different groups in society, such as ethnic minorities, or women as opposed to men. A problem is that the HDI is subjective. The weighting of purchasing power, life expectancy and literacy are arbitrary, and can come up with some surprises, such as the suggestion that Argentina is more successful than Singapore. On the other hand, the HDI has the merit of reminding us that development is a process which can be identified in any country, not just the LDCs, and it is possible for countries to 'de-develop' as well as develop. While the USA and UK have increased their GNPs in recent years, it is arguable that greater income inequalities and the creation of a poor 'underclass' threaten to cancel out any gains in terms of human welfare.

Strategies for development

Primary production

Primary production involves the extraction of raw materials, agriculture and fishing. Some LDCs might have a comparative advantage in certain primary products, such as copper, oil, tea or cocoa. There are problems with this strategy. First, the terms of trade of many primary products have been moving against the primary producers (particularly in the case of non-oil products). This means that the world price of tea, for example, rises much more slowly than the world price of everything else. So a country dependent upon tea exports for development has to produce more and more tea in order to be able to buy the same amount of everything else. Secondly, primary product prices tend to fluctuate unpredictably; a few years ago, for example, the world price of tin collapsed totally. This is because of low elasticities combined with unpredictable shifts in demand and/or supply. Thirdly, the prices of many basic commodities are established on speculative markets, where dealers trade not in actual goods but in 'futures' or 'options'. In effect, a string of middlemen make decisions about the prices and quantities of theoretical outputs, while the local producers in the LDCs are left with real goods at a fraction of the world price.

On the other hand, LDCs whose products experience favourable terms of trade on the world market, can use earnings as a basis for quite rapid development, as the Arab oil states showed so spectacularly in the 1970s. Whether the 'economic' development that the oil boom generated was accompanied by 'human development' in the sense discussed above is very much open to question. The MDCs are perhaps lucky that, say, the iron-ore producing countries of the world did not adopt the price-raising tactics of the Organisation of Petroleum Exporting Countries (OPEC). In the mid-1990s, many commentators have identified water as a precious resource which will give those countries able to collect, store and perhaps export it a significant advantage in the twenty-first century.

Investment

In order to encourage development, countries must invest in both physical and human capital.

Physical investment (accumulating a country's stock of machines, buildings, roads, railways, etc.), may take place in two ways. One is capital widening, where extra capital is combined with an increased amount of labour, so that the ratio of capital to labour remains more or less the same. Another is capital deepening, where investment leads to an increase in the amount of capital per worker. This is often linked to innovation, which includes improved management techniques, the adoption of new technology, or the use of resources which have previously not been exploited. Capital deepening can be expected to yield faster and more dramatic results than capital widening, because of its gains in labour productivity; however, rapid increases in population sizes make it very difficult to achieve for many LDCs.

Human investment refers to education, training, and such things as public health programmes. It has been calculated that the rates of return on human investment, although sometimes difficult to measure, can be just as high as the more obvious returns on capital investment. In the educational field, for example, one of the most effective investments an LDC can make, with high rates of return in terms of future development, is the building and staffing of primary schools. This is especially true in countries whose cultures allow girls to participate fully in education. Since women play such an important part in the 'socialisation'

of families, educating girls is one of the most cost-effective ways of promoting development. And the education and training that is needed not merely in matters of basic literacy, such as reading, writing and using numbers; nor indeed in technical matters such as the use of new technology; social education is just as important. For instance, in the LDCs where rapid population growth is one of the main barriers to future development, it is essential that both boys and girls should be made fully aware of contraceptive techniques; and when HIV infections in LDCs are set to massively outnumber those in MDCs health education raising awareness of AIDS and a whole host of health and nutritional matters is absolutely essential.

Food production

In the poorest LDCs, increased food production is a top priority, so investment and technological change often need to be geared towards improving agricultural techniques. Only when a population is adequately fed is it appropriate to move away from concentration on primary production and to diversify an economy into the secondary (manufacturing and construction) and tertiary (service) sectors.

It should not be assumed that simply boosting food production will automatically solve food-related problems and lead to economic development. Food is sometimes regarded as a 'cash crop' which generates foreign currency earnings, rather than as a means of directly sustaining the local population. In Ghana, half the children are

malnourished, and half the farming land is used to grow chocolate bars. In Kenya, large tracts of land are artificially irrigated to produce beans for European supermarkets and roses for Mother's Day, while nearby settlements are without clean drinking water.

Some countries have severe problems with food distribution, as opposed to food production. Professor B.G. Kumar has argued that while some famines are explained by populations growing too large for the available food supply, or some natural disaster leading to sudden shortages, as has happened in recent years in Ethiopia, it is also possible to find instances of famines where potential food supplies were more than adequate. In Bengal, for example, people have starved to death in front

Children receiving food at a relief centre in Korem, Ethiopia.

© UN photo 164609/John Isaac.

of full granaries, lacking the means with which to purchase the grain; the main problem is therefore one of income inequality: 'for whom?' rather than 'what?' or 'how?' to produce.

Citizens of LDCs suffer not just from relative poverty (income levels below an established average), but also from absolute poverty (an inability to purchase even the most basic necessities of life. At 1992 prices, the World Bank's 'poverty line' is put at an income of $370 (approximately £200) per year. While most citizens of MDCs would find it totally unimaginable to even try to live for a year on the money it takes to buy a mountain bike, we find that even if some of the more ambitious targets for development are achieved, there are likely to be over 800 million people in the world living below this level in the year 2000 and beyond.

Meanwhile, in the MDCs, some of the systems in use to protect agricultural incomes, such as the Common Agricultural Policy (CAP) of the EU create a tremendous wastage of surplus food, which can only rarely be usefully shipped to the LDCs, and further compounds the problems of the LDCs by creating barriers to their exports. Consumers in the MDCs therefore pay higher food prices, and also higher taxes, because it is deemed necessary to transfer part of their incomes to farmers. Meanwhile the earnings of producers in the LDCs are depressed while, in effect, food exports from the LDCs are kept out of the MDCs because they are too cheap! From an economist's point of view, this hardly appears to be a case of 'making the best use of resources'.

Industrial and technological change

Industrialisation in the longer-established MDCs such as the UK was linked to the growth of particular groups of industries, such as textiles, coal, and iron and steel. However, 'development', as opposed to 'growth' involves spill-over effects on other sectors as well. So, along with the 'industrial revolution' in Britain, there was an agricultural revolution, a transport revolution, and in many ways a social and political revolution involving massive increases in food production, the rapid building of railways and other forms of communication, and changes in political and social structures in order to house, feed, educate and govern a rapidly expanding and more urbanised population, together with a new social infrastructure that included schools, houses, hospitals, water supplies and sewers.

It is sometimes assumed that in order to develop, all that today's LDCs need to do is to copy what happened to countries like the UK, USA and Germany in the late nineteenth century. However, is it possible or desirable for all countries of the world to become industrial exporters? The modern world is unlikely to be able to bear the social costs, including the levels of pollution and resource-depletion, that this would cause. Many economists therefore advocate the use of 'appropriate' technology, which can be defined in a general way as the technology yielding the greatest rate of return, particularly when the wider social costs and benefits of the use of technology are accounted for. It is sometimes suggested that small-scale operation is more compatible with the existing social and economic structures in LDCs, and is more suitable than

The Singapore Banking Centre

Reproduced by kind permission of the Singapore Tourist Promotion Boar

large-scale production for rural areas. Thus the debate about appropriate technology often becomes entwined with a debate about the scale of production; it is also often assumed that economic development will inevitably lead to a growth in capital-intensive methods of production and a reduction in labour-intensive methods; the World Bank is often accused of supporting investment programmes which displace local communities, so that cheap labour and unemployment become spin-offs of so-called 'development'. Look at Box 33.3.

BOX 33.3

The INVESTIGATOR

The Durable Car Company

The Morris Minor motor car was in production in Oxford, England throughout the 1950s and 1960s. there are still 250 000 of these cars in use around the world including 800 000 in the UK. In the city of Bath the Morris Minor Centre is a Mecca for aficionados of the Morris Minor. Here, they can find spare parts, get their cars repaired, or purchase a replacement car. The centre is owned by Mr Charles Ware. Over the years Mr Ware purchased sets of Morris Minor design blueprints and machine tools from the Rover Group, and in 1991 he formed a partnership with Mr Dhanapala Samarasekara to build a Morris Minor factory in Sri Lanka. This cost £100 000 to set up, which is a tiny amount in car manufacturing terms. The Durable Car Company was deliberately geared towards labour-intensive production techniques.

Mr Samarasekara stated that the Morris Minor was an ideal car for Sri Lanka because of its reliability, and its 'low-level technology'. There were no expensive and difficult-to-service gadgets such as electronic ignition. If the car needed repair in any part of Sri Lanka, then traditional skills could be used: a broken fan belt, for instance, could be temporarily replaced with a piece of rope. The project had the backing of the Sri Lankan government, who supported its use of local resources. Mr Ware stated that in the factory 95 per cent of operations would use only a minimal amount of electricity. 'We are investing in people,' he said, 'not in machinery.'

Here is an example of the importance to LDCs of both entrepreneurship and appropriate technology.

*Source: **The Investigator.***

The success of the group of countries known as the 'Asian Tigers' (including Singapore and Hong Kong) are a useful reminder that the capital-/labour-intensive dichotomy is often a false one; the electronics and information technology industries, for example are in fact knowledge- and skills-intensive. Whereas 20 years ago these industries were dominated by huge corporations such as IBM, today there is room for relatively small firms to produce and sell products such as computer software; indeed, firms such as Microsoft which a few years ago were minnows are themselves now large-scale enterprises, which can expect competition in the future from unpredicted sources, not necessarily in the MDCs. The nature of the new technology is that it is much more divisible than before. Whereas in years gone by only large firms could afford to invest in computers, today it is quite feasible for a farmers' co-operative in Chile to use a personal computer to control irrigation flows, or for a corner shop in Cairo to use a PC to keep stock records. Provided education and training systems are in place, it is not inevitable that LDCs need be restricted to simple technologies. However, simpler technologies often produce simpler products suitable for low-income users; complex technologies may produce complicated products which are often beyond the reach of local consumers. Even in MDCs, car drivers often find that they cannot repair the simplest faults themselves, because they involve the replacement of banks of micro-chips; some no doubt would prefer the simpler technology referred to in Box 33.3. In the LDCs, the ability to maintain machines without becoming slaves to the output of multinational enterprises is a small step on the road to 'empowerment' of local people. Appropriate technology therefore results in appropriate products.

International relationships

It is sometimes asked: what is the key to development: trade or aid? We are living in an increasingly interdependent world. The successful economies of the world are open economies, actively involved in international trade. The former planned economies regard trade liberalisation, or the removal of trade barriers, as an important part of their transition into market economies. LDCs with an outward-looking, export-orientated economic strategy have generally had more rapid development through the multiplier effects of export-led growth than those with an inward-looking policy of import substitution, aiming at self-sufficiency. Just compare the experience of Singapore, Hong Kong, South Korea and Taiwan with that of the former Soviet Union. Among business people there is increasing interest in the vast potential of China, as it gradually moves from a closed to an open economy.

International trading relationships are increasingly being negotiated through international institutions, such as GATT (see Chapter 29).

The word 'aid' is something of a misnomer, because gifts, grants, food deliveries and emergency relief account for only a fraction of the total of world aid. The majority of what is generally referred to as world 'aid' is in fact in the form of loans at below-market rates of interest. This aid can be 'official', in which case it is channelled through governments or international agencies, or 'unofficial', in which case it is administered by a non-governmental body such as a charity. Much of the aid is 'tied', which means that it is conditional upon some sort of trading arrangement between the donor and recipient country. Look at Box 33.4.

BOX 33.4

Per capita aid receipts (US $), 1989

Country	Aid receipts per capita	GNP per capita
Israel	282.07	8650
Jordan	108.95	1500
Gambia, The	102.63	200
Senegal	78.85	650
Zambia	63.73	290
Egypt	29.91	660
Nepal	22.05	180
Ethiopia	21.05	120
Syrian Arab Republic	16.34	1680
Bangladesh	14.62	170
Pakistan	13.32	350
Myanmar	11.22	_[a]
Indonesia	9.34	440
India	2.58	340
China	1.84	330
Nigeria	1.09	290

[a] GNP per capita estimated at less than $500.

Source: **Organisation for Economic Cooperation and Development and World Bank data.**.

Box 33.4 reveals one of the main problems associated with aid. Most aid is 'bilateral' aid (from one country to another), as opposed to multilateral aid, where groups of donor countries assist groups of recipient countries through agencies. Most of this aid follows historical or political ties. Thus Israel tops the list, due to its links with the USA, and the result is that 40% of aid flows to countries containing only 20% of the world's poor. Even multilateral aid has its problems. The World Bank's so-called 'structural adjustment' loans have been criticised because they tend to be used to finance large-scale projects, such as hydro-electric dams, which displace rather than assist local people, and they are also conditional upon countries adopting economic policies which cause unemployment and reduce social security provision. Cheap labour is thus an unwritten side-effect.

BOX 33.5

Money flows to LDCs from IMF and World Bank, 1982-9

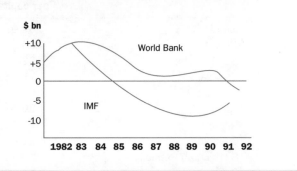

$ bn

World Bank

IMF

Source: **UNDP, Human Development Report** (1992).

Box 33.5 indicates that in recent years, more money flows annually from the LDCs to the MDCs rather than in the direction we might expect. This is a result of the debt crisis, when western banks lent money to countries mainly in Latin America, but also in Africa and Asia, while taking insufficient regard of the purposes to which this money was put. In many cases, instead of being invested in industries whose output could provide the revenues to repay the loans, much of the money was spent on military goods. The resulting debt crisis causes problems not just for the LDCs involved, but also for the world as a whole. There is, for example, much concern about the effects of land degradation in the tropical rain forests; and this problem can be linked to the debt crisis, as LDCs are induced to liquidate these assets, thus using natural resources for quick profits in a way which is unsustainable in the long run, adding to global warming and reducing bio-diversity.

On the whole, the amount of aid flowing from MDCs to LDCs for purely economic purposes has been too small to have made much impact. Aid directed at military and political purposes has probably had far greater impact on everyday lives, for example in countries unfortunate enough to hav played host to military 'advisers' from the USA or the old USSR. The LDCs, however, still regard aid as an importan feature of their economies, and are ver sensitive to attempts to interfere with i as witnessed in the problems between the UK and Malaysia surrounding the Pergau Dam affair in the early 1990s.

In the late 1970s an independent commission chaired by a former Chancellor of West Germany, Willy Brandt, recommended that the amount of aid given each year should be increased to 0.7% of the MDCs. Very few MDCs have come anywhere near this target, and MDCs as a whole spend six times as much per year on alcohol and tobacco than they do on aid. LDCs are currently earning from their export 10 times as much as they receive from aid; this ratio has doubled over the last 20 years, giving a clear answer to the question of 'trade or aid'. The future of economic development lies in trade not aid.

Government and markets

In earlier sections of this book we have focused on the issue of 'planning' versus 'markets', and have discussed what it is that markets can and cannot achieve, and the rationale for government intervention.

Some economists have a profound faith in the ability of either markets or governments to work their 'magic'; but outside the world of the ivory-tower, economics is not merely a set of mathematical relationships. Economic issues are inextricably linked to questions concerning the type of society in which we wish to live. Thus it is not a question of 'either' governments 'or' markets, it is a question of balance between the two. Jenny Wales has stated in *Investigating Social Issues* (a volume in the Macmillan *Economics Today* series) that the comparison should be between an imperfect market and an imperfect government, not a choice between two ideal alternatives. Among the LDCs which have developed most rapidly in recent years we can detect at least some idea of 'partnership' between the enterprise economy and the state. In Singapore, for instance, the doyen of free markets, there is definite recognition of the fact that their phenomenal growth rate simply would not work without state investment in education, transport and housing. It could further be argued that among the MDCs showing stagnation or decline over the last 20 years, there has been too much reliance on either 'market forces' or 'state intervention'; too many privatisation decisions based on political dogma, and too little attention paid to finding pragmatically the most socially and economically efficient balance for the mixed economy.

Sustainable development

Sustainable development is development which ensures that what is consumed can be replaced, and where the true costs of using resources are borne by the consumer.

Is the one-third of humanity living in China a vast potential market, offering an opportunity to the business world? Or is it a threat to the survival of the world's ecosystem? Should the MDCs export the consumerism which they have enjoyed themselves, or is the possibility of every Chinese family owning an atmosphere-polluting motor car too terrible to contemplate? Pollution, land degradation, deforestation, global warming, and depletion of the ozone layer are all barriers not only to economic development, but to human development in the broadest sense.

Economics, as we said at the beginning of this book, is to do with making the best use of resources. As a student of economics, you are in an excellent position to contribute to debate on some of the most crucial issues facing this planet. The true cost of using resources will have to be built into prices, by governments and markets working in partnership. And this partnership will not work if it is restricted to national levels, nor even in international trading blocs. We hope that you, as a young economist, will be able to take a global view of issues, and that your knowledge of economics will enable you to use a range of fairly simple theories, concepts and principles to help you investigate some very complex issues.

REVIEW

In this chapter we have introduced some of the issues central to the branch of economics known as development economics. The issues are closely related to concepts studied elsewhere in this book, including market theory, externalities, market failure and international trade.

REVIEW TASK

Recent trends in foreign direct investment for the developing world

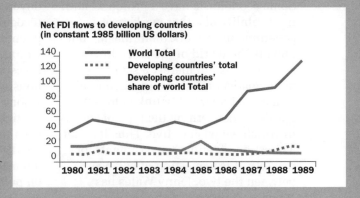

Net FDI flows to developing countries
(in constant 1985 billion US dollars)

- World Total
- Developing countries' total
- Developing countries' share of world Total

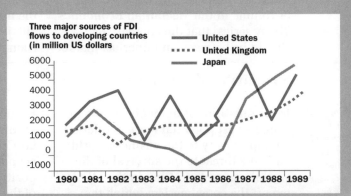

Three major sources of FDI flows to developing countries
(in million US dollars

- United States
- United Kingdom
- Japan

1 During the second half of the 1980s, the volume of foreign direct investment (FDI) grew from approximately $47 billion in 1985 to $132 billion in 1989. Flows to developing countries also increased during this period; however, they grew at a much lower rate then the flows to developed countries. As a result, the developing countries' share of global FDI flows fell from about 24% to 13% over the same period. Moreover, about two thirds of the flows to developing countries were concentrated in East Asia (primarily China, Malaysia and Thailand) and Latin America (mainly Brazil, Argentina, Mexico and Columbia).

2 The trends that are portrayed in the data point to several underlying forces that are at work in the world economy:

● International investment, in particular direct investment, has been growing more rapidly than the world investment, implying an increase in the integration of the world economy through finance and ownership.

● There are parallels between rapid growth in foreign investment now, and the rapid growth of international trade over the last several decades. The rapid growth of world trade was led first by trade amongst developed countries. Later, developing countries joined in as the structure of the world economy changed and many of the developing economies abandoned policies with an anti-trade bias. In a similar fashion, during the 1980s, the increase in international direct investment was led by investment among developed countries.

● The decade of the 1980s saw a marked shift in the attitudes of developing countries toward foreign investment. Many developing countries began actively seeking private sources of capital, particularly foreign investment, by redefining their development strategies, liberalising their economies, and implementing a range of new policies.

3 The issue now facing developing countries is whether they can increase their share of growing world FDI flows, and thus participate more fully in the internationalisation of production that is now occurring.

*Source: Adapted from an article in **Finance and Development** (IMF, Washington DC) (March 1992).*

a   What is meant by the phrase 'Foreign Direct Investment'?

The article suggests that there is a difference between international investment and world investment. What is the difference?

b   Explain what is meant by each of the following phrases, using an example in each case:
(i) 'integration of the world economy'
(ii) 'policies with an anti-trade bias'
(iii) 'liberalising their economies'.

c   Point 1 states that FDI flows to less developed countries were concentrated in certain regions and countries. Suggest why this concentration took place.

d   i   Why, according to economic theory, is the level of investment important to an economy?
ii   Suggest why most FDI flows go from developed countries to other developed countries.
iii What would be the main costs and benefits for less developed countries if they received a larger share of FDI?

(IB, 1995).

Essays

1 What government policies can encourage rapid and sustainable economic development? Is development possible without government intervention?

(IB, 1995)

2 As an economist, how would you tackle the task of comparing the welfare of a citizen of a country like India with that of a citizen of a country like the United States? What would be the main problems involved?

(IB, 1995)

Investigations

Here are some suggested lines of enquiry for students
undertaking coursework assignments, and we hope that this
selection of topics will in turn help to inspire teachers and
students to think of further possibilities. We strongly believe
that even if you are following a course which does not
require you to submit a formal assignment for assessment,
you would still benefit from adopting an 'investigative'
approach, as this is the most effective and interesting way
of studying Economics.

Investigating... CRIME

Economics is not solely concerned with technical matters such as interest rates and marginal utility. A branch of Economics which deserves more attention than it sometimes gets in schools and colleges is the whole area of Social Economics. Ten years ago, social scientists were able to predict that crime was likely to increase, because a study of social trends indicated that most crime was committed by young people, and a 'bulge' was expected in the relevant age group. In October 1995, the Home Secretary claimed that government policies had been successful in reducing crime; his critics argued that most of the change could again be attributed to changes in the age profile of the population.

Economists could contribute to the debate by, for instance, studying correlations between unemployment rates and crime rates, together with analysing unemployment rates among different age groups.

In April 1994, the *Guardian* newspaper, together with *The New York Times*, *Asahi Shimbun* (Japan), and *Der Spiegel* (Germany) conducted a social attitudes opinion poll among a balanced cross-section of the electorates of their four countries. When asked: 'What is the most serious problem facing the world?' 23 per cent of British respondents said

'war'. Pollution, poverty and famine were the next most popular answers. In the USA, 'crime' was the top answer, followed by 'war'. In Japan and Germany, respondents mentioned ethnic strife, pollution, the economy, and famine, but crime did not figure in their top six answers at all. Perhaps these responses reflect the world-view people pick up from their surroundings and the mass media. In the US, for example, 'true life' crime shows are accused of creating a fear of crime out of all proportion to the actual risks of being directly affected by it, and the same is beginning to be said about British programmes such as *Crimewatch UK*.

Economists and philosophers have studied criminal behaviour for centuries. Recently, a Nobel prize for Economics went to the American economist Gary Becker, who has attempted to show that economic principles, including ideas such as 'trade-offs' and 'rational choices' can be used to analyse aspects of some complex issues such as crime and punishment. Another possibility is to regard crime as a type of 'market failure', and criminal activity as a type of externality. A factory pollutes a river, a blaring radio disturbs people on a crowded beach, a thief steals a credit card. These activities have something in common: they create a negative externality, or external cost, where someone engages in an activity while someone else suffers the consequences.

Some interesting questions that could be investigated include:

Is it possible to discuss criminal behaviour using the concepts of demand theory? Do criminals 'trade off' the illicit gains against the risks of being caught? Do criminals react to increases in punishment levels in the same way as consumers react to price increases by buying fewer goods? If 'prison works' is there any evidence that other things being equal, harsher sentencing reduces crime? What is the elasticity of the response of criminals to an increase in the level of punishment?

It is a well known economic principle that money has a 'time value'. A dishonest £100,000 in ten years' time might be preferable to an honest £1000 now. So a criminal might prefer to rob a bank rather than do an honest job, if he or she believes that the money can be stashed away for ten years. By how much would the term of years need to be increased to provide a real deterrent? As an economist you cannot, of course, interview known criminals to get the answers; so we are not suggesting that you should take questionnaires around to Parkhurst Prison. However, you could investigate such matters by interviewing 'ordinary' young people; as we said earlier, most crime is committed by this age group; and it would not be surprising to find that

much crime is committed by basically honest people: it is opportunistic rather than pre-planned. You could therefore begin by asking fairly innocuous questions, such as whether people would go out of their way to pay for a bus ticket if the conductor appeared to be passing them by; and then you could design some further questions incorporating an incline in the gravity of the crime, comparing responses to the harshness of the likely punishment. Remember that for 'honest' people the formal punishment (fines, etc.) are often less of a deterrent than the informal punishment (such as the shame of being named in the local newspaper). Also bear in mind that Economics usually assumes rational behaviour; the family and friends that you interview will be rational people (we hope) and so your findings might not apply to the Hannibal Lecters of this world.

As well as investigating the causes of crime, another line of enquiry could be to look at its effects. Some reports suggest that 90% of British companies have been hit at some time by thieves, and company managers fear crime more than they fear economic recession. Many householders know the costs of crime at first hand, having lost their lawnmowers from unlocked garden sheds, or having their cars ruined by 'aggravated car theft'. By investigating the costs of crime in your own neighbourhood, you could make a reasonable estimate of the cost of crime to the population of the UK as a whole.

Investigating... DEMOGRAPHIC CHANGE

The pie-chart shows the cost of social provision and the slice that it takes out of government expenditure. Because of demographic trends (changes in the size and structure, especially the age structure, of the population) no future British government can afford to ignore the problems of financing expenditure on such things as health, unemployment benefit and pensions.

premiums paid by customers which are then 'pooled' into a fund, from which the fortunate many who never suffer a loss compensate the unfortunate few who do. Statisticians known as actuaries calculate the probabilities of certain events happening, and ensure that the fund is maintained at a sufficient size to allow for future eventualities.

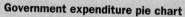

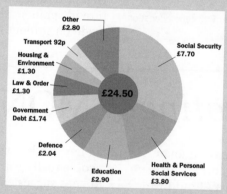

This is how the £24.50 the government spends on your behalf each day is shared out.
Source: UK National Accounts (1995)

Although most employers, and their employees pay, every week or month something called 'National Insurance Contributions', there is no national social fund. NICs are, in effect, another type of income tax, and instead of being a 'funded' scheme, Britain's national insurance scheme is a 'current' scheme, whereby today's taxpayers support today's recipients. The money received in benefits is known by economists as a 'transfer payment', because it is compulsorily transferred by the government from one section of society to another.

Britain has a scheme for 'social insurance' which provides protection against financial problems caused by sickness, unemployment and old age. One of the basics of commercial insurance schemes is the idea of a 'pool'. Insurance companies collect

Due to higher living standards people are living longer, and in the future it will become very difficult for the working population to produce enough income, and be persuaded to pay enough tax, to meet social security commitments at their present levels. In the 1980s, the Conservative government encouraged private pension firms to try to fill part of this gap.

There is much scope here for useful investigative work.
Look at the block diagram in Box i.2

BOX i.2

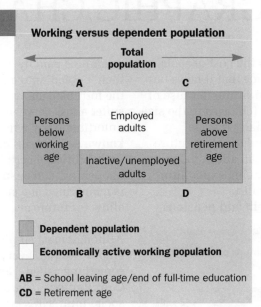

Working versus dependent population

Total population

A   C

Persons below working age

Employed adults

Persons above retirement age

Inactive/unemployed adults

B   D

Dependent population

Economically active working population

AB = School leaving age/end of full-time education
CD = Retirement age

How is the balance between working population and dependent population likely to change in the next 30 years? How will this affect government expenditure? What are the costs and benefits of replacing this government commitment with schemes from the private sector? Britain is accused of lagging behind other countries in the number of students it persuades to stay in Higher Education after the age of 18 What are the economic consequences of this? How would an increase in Higher Education numbers affect the balance between working and dependent populations? How would it affect government finances? How should students be financed in the future; should they and their parents pay for Higher Education? Should the state provide grants? Should more reliance be made on student loans?

Investigating... MONEY

What is money? Why have human beings invented those curious tokens we call 'notes and coins'? Could we conceivably live without them? Suppose we were visited by a traveller from Mars, who had never seen money before, and wanted to know what it was for?

The economist Keynes called the demand for money 'liquidity preference' and this phrase reminds us of something important: people do not want money as an end in itself. People who want money because they like to hoard notes and coins are known as misers, and present a rather sad spectacle. People hold money because it is liquid (can easily be exchanged) and it is the goods and services which

money can be exchanged for what people really want, not money itself. Keynes suggested that people hold money, or prefer liquidity, for three reasons, or motives.

The transactions motive involves holding money for everyday purchases. The amount of money held at any particular time for everyday transactions depends on such things as prices, incomes, and the frequency with which wages are paid. The precautionary motive involves holding money in case of unexpected things which might happen; a burst water pipe, a car puncture. Keynes argued that once everyday transactions and precautions have been allowed for, people still have some money left. He argued that this money was held for a speculative motive. Depending on rates of return, this money might be invested in 'bonds', or it might be kept as cash. Keynes argued that if an individual expects the price of bonds to fall, he or she will switch from bonds to money. Therefore the desire to hold money is related to expectations about the change in price of other assets. It is also possible, in times of inflation, that people would prefer to hold goods rather than money; for example to buy a car now instead of in six months' time when its price might have risen. This might be called a deflationary motive for holding money.

Which is the most important reason for holding money?

You could devise a questionnaire containing examples of transactions, precautions, speculations, etc., and see whether people are aware of reasons for holding money. Some economists claim that Keynes over-emphasised the importance of the speculative motive. Can you find evidence for this?

What is the importance of different forms of money, such as notes, coins, cheques and credit cards?

It has been estimated that by value, roughly 10% of transactions in Britain take the form of notes and coins, while 90% are in the form of cheques, plastic, etc. Conduct a survey among family and friends to find out how often they use notes, coins, cheques, etc., and the relative value of the different forms of transaction. A reasonable hypothesis would be that while notes and coins are used more often, they tend to be used for relatively small value transactions, whereas cheques and plastic money are used less often, but account for larger values. Do your findings support this hypothesis?

Investigating... BANKS

Any government which wishes to control the money supply must also control the banks. During the 1980s, 'monetarist' attempts to tackle inflation through monetary targets failed, and other techniques had to be used largely because, at the same time, the banking system was 'de-regulated', or freed from government controls. But (outside of Scotland) banks are no longer permitted to print their own bank notes, so how can they influence the money supply?

Many students have opportunities to undergo a period of work experience, and if you are able to take advantage of one of these schemes by working at a bank, then this might give you an opportunity for an investigation into the influence of banks on the money supply, and on the local and national economy.

If you are in a position to observe transactions taking place across the bank counter, then you are likely to notice an important fact: the value of money being deposited far exceeds the amount of cash (notes and coins) being withdrawn. As observed in the investigation on money, cash transactions are a relatively small proportion of total transactions. Suppose the ratio is in the region of

10%. Economists refer to this as a 'Liquidity Ratio', and it means that for every £100 deposited, only £10 is likely to be demanded in the form of cash. The rest will be transferred using cheques and plastic cards, and these transactions do not involve any 'real' money changing hands; they simply involve computers adjusting the balances held on record in people's accounts. This liquidity ratio enables banks to be profitable, because it enables them to lend money to borrowers at a rate of interest. The lower the liquidity ratio, the greater the ability of banks to lend, and to increase the supply of money.

BOX i.3

Bank credit multiplier

Assume: *Liquidity ratio of 10% operated by all banks;
*Initial deposit of £1000.

	Assets		**Liabilities**		
			Cash		*Loans*
Bank A	1000	=	100	+	900
Bank B	900	=	90	+	810
Bank C	810	=	81	+	729
Bank D	729	=	72.9	+	656.1
	Etc.		Etc.		Etc.
Totals	**10,000**	**=**	**1,000**	**+**	**9,000**

While each individual bank lends less than the cash it receives, the bank system as a whole lends more than it has in cash. An initial deposit of £1,000 has created liabilities of £10,000 of which £1,000 are cash deposits and £9,000 are loans. These are matched by £1,000 of liquid assets (cash) and £9,000 of 'promises to repay' (contracts to repay loans, which are less liquid).

Note that most banks can reduce their liquidity ratios (LRs) because they have other assets in reserve, such as government bonds, stocks and shares, and buildings, which could be 'liquidated' in emergency.

The relationship between the LR and the bank credit multiplier is as follows:-

$$BCM = \frac{1}{LR}$$

so if the LR is 10%, or $\frac{1}{10}$, then BCM = 10. This means that a deposit of £1 can create liabilities of £10, of which £9 are loans, and £1 is cash.

Question
Investigate how an increase/decrease in the LR will decrease/increase the BCM and hence affect the money supply. Calculate the effects of an LR of (a) 5% (b) 20%. Why might an LR of 0% be profitable but imprudent?

Use library facilities to find a newspaper on CD ROM. Find out as much as you can about a bank failure, such as that of the Bank of Credit and Commerce International (BCCI) or the problems of Barings Bank. In what way is the idea of a prudent 'Liquidity Ratio' relevant to these cases?

Are you a bank customer? Write to your bank to see if you can discover the 'Liquidity Ratio' which it uses. And the best of luck!

Competition between banks has increased in recent years, largely due to the trend for certain Building Societies to end their 'mutual' status and turn themselves into limited companies.

What is 'mutuality'? What are the advantages and disadvantages of turning a mutual society into a company?

How much competition is there between banks in your town, and in which ways to banks compete? Can they compete in terms of 'prices'? Is the banking market becoming less 'oligopolistic'? If so, what consequences would economic theory predict? Is there any evidence of the benefits of increased competition between banking institutions in your town?

Investigating... THE FINANCE OF INDUSTRY

What sources of funds are available for firms? They might raise capital for investment purposes from retained profits (plough-back); by borrowing from banks in the form of loans (longer-term borrowing for specific projects) or overdrafts (short-term borrowing to cover temporary difficulties; by selling shares (on the Stock Exchange, in the case of Public Limited Companies) or by other means such as leasing (renting equipment). Would large firms raise finance differently from small and medium size firms? What factors affect the investment decisions of firms? There are several possibilities.

- **Interest rates**
  Economic theory predicts that as interest rates rise, so the level of investment falls. Suppose a haulage company is considering buying a truck for £30,000. If interest rates are high, then the opportunity cost of investing in a truck is high, because the money might be more profitably invested elsewhere.

- **Consumer demand**
  The greater the demand for goods and services, the greater the demand for investment goods which are used to produce them.

- **The price of investment (capital) goods**
  If the purchase price of plant and equipment rises faster than the prices

at which output can be sold, then investment is discouraged.

- ### Expectations, or 'business confidence'
  As well as reacting to changes in consumer demand, firms try to predict future demand, and their confidence in the future can affect their decisions to invest at the present time. Business confidence can be affected by such things as growing markets, economic expansion or recession; political stability; government incentives; taxes; labour relations;

- ### Innovation, enterprise and technology
  A country is more likely to experience long-term growth, and therefore firms are more likely to invest, if its people are willing to develop skills through education and training, adopt enterprising attitudes and, when necessary, forgo present consumption in order to invest and so enjoy higher consumption levels in the future.

Which of these factors are the most significant? Economics textbooks tend to concentrate on the role of interest rates. You can identify ways in which interest rates might affect each of the sources of capital mentioned above. However, many studies suggest that the demand for funds for investment purposes is interest-inelastic, and that the general state of 'business confidence' is a more important factor. During the 1980s, for example, when the Conservative government relied heavily on high interest rates to discourage spending as an anti-inflation measure, the Confederation of British Industry argued that high interest rates were actually inflationary, as they increased the cost of industry by making it more expensive for firms to do something which they had to do anyway, that is to invest for the future.

You could investigate these possibilities, by using a case study of a firm which has made an investment in a factory or retail development in your local area; or you could survey several firms using a questionnaire. You could ask respondents to list the factors affecting a recent investment decision in order of priority, analyse the results, and discuss the extent to which your findings might reflect the experience of British industry as a whole.

Investigating... TRANSPORT

What are the determinants of demand for train travel?

The demand for train travel is a derived demand, that is it is consumed as a means of achieving something else, such as going to work or shopping. A person must spend both time and money in order to travel; it is possible to regard the 'generalised cost' (GC) of a train journey to a consumer as a sum of 'disutilities'; and it can be assumed that customers (a) try to minimise the disutilities of train travel, and (b) try to maximise the net benefit (utility) they receive from the journey. Generalised cost depends on a number of factors, and these can be expressed as follows

$$GC = f\{p, ps, a, w, r, c\}$$

which means that GC is a function of (depends upon):

p, the price of the railway journey;

ps, the price of substitutes, such as a bus journey (an opportunity cost);

a, access time, or the time it takes to travel to a railway station;

w, waiting time at the station (which in turn depends on the frequency of trains);

r, running time (the duration of the journey);

c, comfort factors (the standard of service on the train, degree of overcrowding, buffet facilities, etc.)

The demand for train travel is also likely to depend on the incomes of travellers, the influence of advertising, and other factors.

There is plenty of scope for investigative work in trying to assess the relative importance of these factors; and it might also be possible to do some practical work with elasticity concepts. Why is price elasticity of demand important to a railway operation wishing to increase its total revenue? How will the price elasticity of early-morning commuters differ from that of afternoon shoppers? How will this influence the firm's pricing policies for peak-time and off-peak travel? How important is the frequency of trains? If the frequency is increased, so that waiting time at the station is reduced, will this have an effect on demand? Is there such a thing as 'frequency elasticity' and how might it be measured?

Investigating...
COSTS AND BENEFITS

In Section 3 we discuss the uses of Cost Benefit Analysis (CBA) for decision-makers. A small scale CBA project can be a useful form of investigation for a student of Economics.

For example, in the spring of 1995, a 'Carer's Bill' was brought before parliament, with the intention of providing help for people who have to stay at home to care for sick or elderly relatives. It was proposed to allow these carers to have a holiday for a couple of weeks a year by providing a paid carer to take their place. Of course, this would cost money, but the supporters of the bill claimed that by providing a service that would otherwise have to be undertaken by the state, carers saved the taxpayer £30 billion per year.

Using reasonable assumptions, it would be possible to investigate whether this figure is an accurate one. Your starting point would be to ask: how many people in your area are being cared for

by relatives? You should be able to obtain this information from your social services department, or voluntary agencies in your area. Assume that these people have to have one person with them around the clock. What is the average wage for professional care workers likely to be? How would you find this out? Is it likely to be near or below the average manual weekly wage? Use the figure you come up with to estimate the nominal cost of care being provided locally. Then extrapolate (i.e. increase the figures for your local population by a suitable amount to reflect the population of the country as a whole) and you might well find that £30 billion is a conservative figure; especially if you consider the opportunity costs to the country. People acting as carers might well be able to earn significantly higher sums than the carer's average wage, if they were able to follow the careers for which they were trained rather than having to adopt the carer's role.

i

Investigating...
MULTIPLIER EFFECTS

It is sometimes thought that since investigations are likely to involve local research and fieldwork, then microeconomic topics are more suitable than macroeconomic ones. However, it is possible to investigate macroeconomic issues at a local level. International trade, for example, can be investigated by a study of imported goods available in local shops and supermarkets. Similarly, multiplier effects can be studied locally.

When a new investment project, such as a new factory or retail park is announced, the press will often claim that jobs will be created both 'directly and indirectly'. Direct employment includes temporary work during the construction phase, and permanent posts at the new facility. Indirect employment refers to 'spin-off' effects on the local economy. For example, a new factory will bring benefits to local suppliers, sub-contractors, and even schools, the local housing market, etc. In economic terms, there is a local multiplier effect. Often these figures are suspiciously high, and there is the possibility that they are exaggerated by the promoters of a scheme. When a certain town in South Wales was chosen as the site of a new privatised prison, newspaper reports (presumably based on government press releases) stated that over 1000 jobs would be created. Given a prison population of 1000, a ratio of 1 staff member for every prisoner would seem rather unrealistic, and so the figure must have included both direct employment and estimated indirect employment.

There are two broad methods of investigating local multiplier effects.

One is to assume that value of the local multiplier is roughly the same as the national multiplier, in the region of 1.5, and estimate the income and job creating possibilities of a new investment project. You will need to make reasonable assumptions; you could assume, for example that a job is created whenever an injection creates an annual income equal to the national average wage. This is a crude and general assumption, but perfectly reasonable as a starting point.

The second line of enquiry is to use published figures for the value of an investment project and its expected creation of jobs, and use these to work out the value of the multiplier effect that is being claimed. You can then consider whether this coefficient is a realistic one.

Investigating...
CURRENT EVENTS

One of the main reasons for studying Economics is that it enables you to follow current events with a critical awareness. You should find that as you progress through the subject you become better equipped to read newspaper reports, or follow TV and radio news, with a trained eye or ear. Many economics teachers encourage students to bring newspaper cuttings to class, and to make brief presentations explaining why the news item is relevant to the economic principles they have been studying.

Take these two press cuttings for example.

BOX i.4

SEEKING *salvation* IN SERVICES

The departure lounge at Alicante airport has a bewigged string quartet playing Mozart and the Beatles. It has a Burger King, an English pub and entertainers to keep the children happy. What it does not have are any planes leaving the ground.

It is a reminder of why going on holiday is therapeutic: not because of the opportunity to be treated like cattle on a package flight, but because it brings home just how efficient parts of Britain are compared to the rest of the world.

For example, there may be no fast rail link to the Channel Tunnel, but the purpose-built terminal at Waterloo knocks spots off the make-do-and mend at Gare du Nord.

No question, Britain's service sector works. It is innovative, cheap and, in today's ghastly jargon, customer-driven.

But is it the key to future prosperity? Does it really matter that Britain in the words of one leading economist, has a "comparative advantage in bullshit", with talent attracted to disciplines that require the gift of the gab – PR, law, journalism, auctioneering – rather than manufacturing?

It probably does. For as a start, world trade in manufactures is four times the size of trade in services, so a country that doesn't make things has to be fantastically good in other areas to compensate. Second, Britain's international position is not that wonderful. Largely due to the extinction of its merchant shipping fleet and the increase in overseas travel, the surplus on services last year was unchanged in current prices from 1979. As the graph shows, Britain's share of world trade in services has been steadily declining since 1960.

Once school of though argues that the preoccupation with manufacturing is a form of inverted snobbery which, in essence, fails to appreciate that the world has changed and that the lucrative markets will be in services. "If it does turn out that we are relatively [more] efficient in world terms at providing services than at producing goods, then our national interest lies in a surplus on services and a deficit on goods", the then Chancellor, Nigel Lawson, told a select committee on overseas trade a year ago.

This view was dismissed by Arnold

BOX i.4

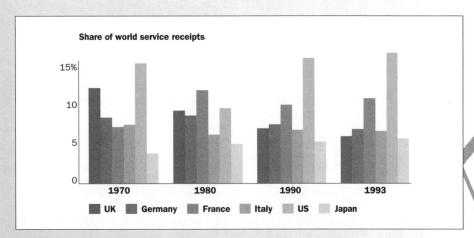

Share of world service receipts

Weinstock, the chairman of GEC, who told the same committee that he wondered what the service sector would actually be servicing if there was no manufacturing base. "We will supply the changing of the guard. We will supply the Beefeaters around the Tower of London. We will become a curiosity. I do not think that is what Britain is about; I think that is rubbish".

A decade later, the received wisdom is that Lord Weinstock was over-gloomy and that prospects are rosy for both manufacturing and services. Devaluation, the supply-side improvements in the 1980s, the impact of inward investment, or a combination of all three, have transformed the outlook for trade, resulting in the current account no longer acting as a constraint on growth.

But suppose for a moment that nothing much has changed. Instead, assume that the effects of devaluation have now washed through the system, that the value of exports from foreign-owned plants is largely offset by the high import quotient of the goods sold, and that the hard evidence of the 1980s reforms is still proving elusive.

In those circumstances, the odds would be on the current account widening, particularly in the event that consumer spending were let off the leash. The UK tends to have a higher propensity to suck in more imports when times are good than other countries. The potentially

disastrous consequences of pumping up consumption ahead of the next election in pursuit of cheap votes are well known to both the Bank of England and the Treasury. Their view is that another circuit on the boom-bust roller coaster would be one too many.

The potential problems have been laid out in a paper by three Cambridge academics, Andy Cosh, Alan Hughes and Rob Rowthorn, for the commission on Public Policy and British Business, established by the Institute for Public Policy Research.

So what could go wrong? Not much, providing world trade grows rapidly over the next 10 years, by around 7.5 per cent a year. If that happened, Britain would be able to continue expanding at its long-run postwar trend of around 2.5 per cent without a worsening current account position.

But 7.5 per cent world trade growth is quite an assumption, representing almost a doubling of the performance in the 1980s, even allowing for the promised benefits of the Uruguay round that is pushing it. Instead, the Cambridge paper assumes a more modest, but almost certainly more realistic, 5.5 per cent annual growth in world trade.

From this starting point, the paper adumbrates three paths for the economy, a base projection, a Super-Serv scenario focused on the expansion of Britain's traditional

BOX i.4

strength in non-manufactured tradable goods such as financial services, telecommunications and TV, and a Fast-Man option predicted on a larger and more internationally-competitive manufacturing sector.

Under the base scenario, the gradual tendency of imports to grow more rapidly than exports gradually reasserts itself as the impact of devaluation wears off. With growth of 2.5 per cent a year, manufactured exports would grow by 64 per cent by 2003; the problem is that imports would grow by 71 per cent.

Although financial and miscellaneous services do well in this scenario – exports up 51 per cent against imports growing by just 20 per cent – it is not enough to counteract the decline in the manufacturing balance combined with the growing deficit on interest, profits and dividends (IPD), one of the three components of the invisible trade balance.

IPD, which wiped out the visible deficit with a record £10 billion surplus in 1994, is expected to take a turn for the worse as a result of the growing burden of borrowing to finance current account deficits already stretching back a decade. The conclusion of the base scenario is that Britain is stuck on a low-growth path, with unemployment remaining at around 2 million.

The Super-Serv scenario illustrates what it would take for the service sector to compensate for the decline of manufacturing. The assumption here is that the trend in manufacturing remains the same as in the base projection, but the volume of financial and miscellaneous services exports doubles.

If this happened, Cosh, Hughes and Rowthorn estimate that the current account would be just back in the black by 2003, and unemployment would be back to 1 million.

All it would take for this to happen would be for London to absorb "all of the current international financial activity of New York or Tokyo – in addition to the increase already envisaged under the base scenario". The other parts of the tradable service sector – telecommunications, films and television, consultancy, royalties and other miscellaneous services – would also need to show similar growth.

By the year 2003, total British exports of F&M services would exceed those of the US and would be double those of Japan. Per head of population, Britain would export five times more F&M services than the US and four times more than Japan.

This might be pushing things – certainly Cosh, Hughes and Rowthorn think so. They conclude, taking into account that UK trade in manufactures at £230 million last year was more than eight times the £27 billion trade in financial and miscellaneous services, that "improvements on this scale are quite inconceivable".

Finally, then, there is Fast-Man. The assumption here is that there is an attempt to build up the manufacturing base, with capital investment rising by around 50 per cent from £12 billion to £18 billion a year (or from 2 per cent to 3 per cent of GDP).

This expansion allows manufacturing exports to rise by 14 per cent more than under the base projection, while import substitution means that imports are down by 4 per cent. After 20 years in the red, the manufacturing account returns to small surplus in 2003, and the overall current account is safely in the black because of the surplus on services.

How likely is this? Last week's figures show that manufacturing investment is at long last beginning to show signs of picking up. The Government's view is that it can best leave things to the private sector to respond positively to the new low-inflation environment.

On this basis, investment allowances or spending on the infrastructure are a waste of money. As opposed, of course, to cutting personal taxation, which has a miraculously beneficial economic impact. In Alicante.

The received wisdom is that prospects are rosy for both manufacturing and services. Devaluation, the supply-side improvements in the 1980s, the impact of inward investment, or a combination of all three, have transformed the outlook for trade.

*Source: **Guardian** 28 August 1995*

BOX i.5

LIFE AND DEATH COSTS *in the real world economy*

When Eddie George, the Governor of the Bank of England, sweeps over to the Treasury in his air-conditioned Jaguar next week, he is unlikely to be thinking about the pollution which has recently been choking London. But if Mr George still wants to wring a interest rate out of the Chancellor at their monthly monetary policy meeting, perhaps he should.

New research shows that building the cost of pollution and the use of natural resources into economic modelling changes the UK picture significantly, suggesting higher interest rates may be required to ensure sustainable growth.

How it this conclusion reached? There are three stages. The first is simple – placing a value on the cost of lost natural assets, such as coal and gas.

The second bit, working out the economic cost of pollution, is much more controversial. For a start, the maths is fiendishly difficult. Take the additional costs to the health service of respiratory diseases caused by airborne pollutants.

The National Asthma Campaign said last week the cost of asthma to the National Health Service was about £450 million a year, while if indirect costs such as time off work were included, the cost was closer to £1 billion. Of course, not all of this is related to pollution.

This is just one of hundreds of economic factors considered by Kirk Hamilton, a senior research associate at University College London, who has attempted to estimate the effects of air pollution on the economy.

Other effects in Mr Hamilton's model are similarly straightforward in concept. An example is the effect of acid rain on buildings. Research shows that acid rain damages mortar and steel, unlike brick and slate. The distribution of materials used in Birmingham is assumed to be representative of the whole, extrapolated out to the country, and then matched with levels of emissions. The same is done for other pollutants on other "receptors". Some of the end results are that the building-related cost of sulphur dioxide is £310 a tonne, while each tonne of nitrous oxide impacts on forests to the tune of £787. But the most damaging pollutant for humans is "particulate matter" – dust and dirt less than 10 microns (0.001mm) in size which pour out of car exhausts and power stations. These carry health costs of £6,667 a tonne, and some experts think even this may be an underestimate.

Other costs are more difficult to quantify. Take the price of death. Or more accurately, the value of life. Mr Hamilton reckons a life, described slightly chillingly as the "Value of a Statistical Life, or VSL," is about £2 million. Arriving at a VSL is understandably tricky. One way of getting a number is to ask people how much they would pay to reduce the chances of being killed. The example given by Mr Hamilton is a person prepared to pay £1,000 to reduce risk of dying by 1/1000. Multiplying one by the other produces a VSL of £1 million. Another approach is to look at "danger money" paid to people with hazardous jobs. Combining analyses using both yields the £2 million figure.

This number-crunching may seem callous but, as Mr Hamilton points out, governments are more ready to listen to hard numbers than bleeding hearts.

Taking all potential effects together, the total cost, in terms of percentage of GDP, of different air pollutants fell from 2.6 per cent in

1980 to 1.5 per cent in 1990, as emissions fell by 23 per cent.

Once these first two stages are complete, Mr Hamilton calculates what he calls a genuine savings level for the UK economy. This is done by taking the gross savings rate, less depreciation costs to give net savings – so far staying in line with orthodox economics – and then subtracting both the cost of resource depletion and of pollution damage.

Throughout the 1980s, the UK had a gross savings rate of 15–20 per cent and a net rate of 5–10 per cent. But Hamilton's "genuine" rate was in negative figures, varying between -1.6 per cent and -3.1 per cent until 1987, when the fall in the value of oil reduced the rate of resource depletion. His conclusion is that for most of the 1980s inadequate steps were taken to offset asset loss.

In other words, adding environmental costs to the saving and spending balance shows the UK has been "dissaving" for a large period of the decade – development was unsustainable.

The implication is that more needs to be done to encourage saving and dampen consumption. The most obvious policy response is to put up interest rates, although additional incentives to forgo consumption in favour of future pensions could also help, Mr Hamilton says.

However if Mr George did present a green-tinged case for dearer borrowing, Mr Clarke would find it pretty hard to sell to fear-struck backbenchers – especially as much of the current research is as much a matter of faith as measurement. But as Mr Hamilton says: "This certainly isn't about easy choices".

*Source: **Guardian** 28 August 1995*

They were both found in the same newspaper on the same day. And someone who has been studying Economics is likely to get much more out of them than a non-economist.

An excellent exercise for a student of Economics is to keep a 'Portfolio' of press cuttings, along with commentaries. These commentaries should show LINKAGES between economic principles that are studied in the classroom and the news item in question, and INSIGHTS, or special perspectives that an economist is able to bring to bear on the topic. At least one major examining board is proposing to use this type of Portfolio as a basis for school-assessed coursework.

News item number 1 is related to British industrial performance, and UK competitiveness. In 1850, the UK had 41% of world trade in manufactures; this fell to 14% by 1960, 9% in 1970, and 6% in 1991. In the late nineteenth century, Prince Albert warned that British technology was falling behind that of competing countries, especially Germany, and Prime Minister Gladstone initiated an enquiry into the British education system to see whether changes could improve industrial performance. In 1945 the UK had the third highest GDP per head among industrialised nations; but by the 1990s she was fourteenth and falling, to be challenged by some of the so-called 'poor' countries of Europe, such as

Spain and Italy. UK growth rates have been lower than general western European rates for over 100 years, and countries like Singapore are now growing faster, albeit from a lower starting point. These statistics trace a path of decline through the economic league tables. Does manufacturing matter? How can UK competitiveness be improved? This article discusses some of the issues.

News item number 2 is related to our discussion of externalities in Section 3. Why be an economist as opposed to an accountant? News items such as this provide an answer. As time goes on,

governments, citizens, and ultimately industries, are going to have to take account of much wider concepts than narrow accounting costs and returns. As we point out in Chapter 33, economic development both in more developed and less developed countries is going to have to be sustainable development. The true costs of producing and consuming are going to have to be built into prices as scarce resources are shared among perhaps 10 billion people. Economics, as we said at the start of this book, is about the 'best use of resources', and so what subject could be more relevant to the future of this planet?

Signing off

We wish you well in your studies of Economics, and hope that once you have acquired the habit of 'INVESTIGATING ECONOMICS' you will find its techniques and world view useful not only as a passport to higher education or into a job, but as an essential part of your mental toolkit as an aware citizen, throughout your life.

– The Authors.

INDEX

All entries in blue are defined in the text.